Fodor's

SCOTLAND

WELCOME TO SCOTLAND

Scotland packs spectacular landscapes, as well as rich history and tradition, into a small country. From the Lowlands to the Highlands, its lush woodlands, windswept moors, and deep lochs may take your breath away. Impressive castles, whisky distilleries, and golf courses entice, and cities such as Edinburgh and Glasgow tweak tradition with cutting-edge festivals and vibrant cultural scenes. Scotland's iconic products and customs—from tartans to bagpipes—may travel the globe, but there's nothing like experiencing them firsthand.

TOP REASONS TO GO

★ **Castles:** Stirling, Glamis, Floors, and others tell tales of a complex, turbulent past.

★ **Cool Cities:** Edinburgh's International Festival and Fringe; Glasgow's nightlife.

★ **Islands:** Skye's misty mountains, Islay's seabirds, Orkney's prehistoric remains.

★ **Whisky:** Distillery tours and tastings refine an appreciation for the national drink.

★ **Landscapes:** Crystal-clear lochs and rivers, wooded hills, wide-open moors.

★ **Golf:** The great names here include St. Andrews, Gleneagles, and Western Gailes.

13 ULTIMATE EXPERIENCES

Scotland offers terrific experiences that should be on every traveler's list. Here are Fodor's top picks for a memorable trip.

1 Prehistoric Monuments

Around Scotland, haunting structures like the Calanais Standing Stones (pictured) on the Isle of Lewis provide an intriguing glimpse into the past. Sights are scattered across the landscape, but Orkney claims a large concentration. *(Ch. 8, 10, 11)*

2 Seaside Towns

The country's jagged coastline and many islands create scenic settings for towns such as Tobermory on the Isle of Mull, with its colorfully painted houses. *(Ch. 8)*

3 Isle of Skye

With the misty Cuillin Mountains and rocky shores, Skye has few rivals among the country's islands for sheer loveliness. Links to Bonnie Prince Charlie add further allure. *(Ch. 10)*

4 Glencoe

The wild beauty of Glencoe's craggy peaks and deep valley provided the background for a tragic massacre in 1692. Today the area is popular for outdoor activities. *(Ch. 9)*

5 Whisky Tours

From Speyside to Islay (pictured), whisky distilleries offer tours and tastings of Scotland's signature drink. Their often-spectacular settings are an added bonus. *(Ch. 4, 6–11)*

6 Loch Lomond and the Trossachs

Its clear water, plus access to Edinburgh and Glasgow, make Loch Lomond a coveted retreat. The Trossachs' lakes and hills are the essence of the Highlands. *(Ch. 6)*

7 Glasgow

An urban renaissance has brought great shopping and nightlife to complement the city's rich architectural heritage and museums like the Kelvingrove (pictured). *(Ch. 3)*

8 Edinburgh

Scotland's capital charms with its Royal Mile and Old Town, and events such as the Edinburgh International Festival and the Fringe keep areas like the Grassmarket lively. *(Ch. 2)*

9 Castles

Whether in ruins or full of treasure, castles dating from the medieval period to Victorian times are among Scotland's glories. Dunnottar (pictured) overlooks the North Sea. *(Ch. 2–11)*

10 Seafood

From salmon to oysters, the superb fish and seafood from rivers, lakes, and the sea are treats to savor. Delicately smoked fish is a specialty, served hot or cold. *(Ch. 2–11)*

11 Border Abbeys

The towering ruins of the region's great medieval abbeys, such as red-sandstone Melrose (pictured), retain echoes of their past grandeur and recall Scottish history. *(Ch. 4)*

12 Jacobite Steam Train

The famous trip from Fort William to the coast at Mallaig offers spectacular views of mountains and lochs as well as a ride over the 21 arches of the Glenfinnan Viaduct. *(Ch. 9)*

13 Golf

The home of golf, Scotland claims some of the world's most challenging holes but has courses for all levels, many in beautiful settings by lakes, hills, or the ocean. *(Ch. 2–10)*

CONTENTS

CONTENTS

ABOUT THIS GUIDE

Fodor's Recommendations

Everything in this guide is worth doing—we don't cover what isn't—but exceptional sights, hotels, and restaurants are recognized with additional accolades. Fodor'sChoice★ indicates our top recommendations. Care to nominate a new place? Visit Fodors.com/contact-us.

Trip Costs

We list prices wherever possible to help you budget well. Hotel and restaurant price categories from $ to $$$$ are noted alongside each recommendation. For hotels, we include the lowest cost of a standard double room in high season. For restaurants, we cite the average price of a main course at dinner or, if dinner isn't served, at lunch. For attractions, we always list adult admission fees; discounts are usually available for children, students, and senior citizens.

Hotels

Our local writers vet every hotel to recommend the best overnights in each price category, from budget to expensive. Unless otherwise specified, you can expect private bath, phone, and TV in your room. For expanded hotel reviews, facilities, and deals, visit Fodors.com.

Top Picks	Hotels &
★ Fodor'sChoice	Restaurants
	⊞ Hotel
Listings	⬒ Number of
✉ Address	rooms
✉ Branch address	⑂Ⅰ Meal plans
☎ Telephone	✕ Restaurant
📠 Fax	⚘ Reservations
⊕ Website	🏛 Dress code
✉ E-mail	⊟ No credit cards
🗎 Admission fee	⑂ Price
⊙ Open/closed	
times	**Other**
Ⓜ Subway	⇨ See also
⇶ Directions or	☞ Take note
Map coordinates	⚘ Golf facilities

Restaurants

Unless we state otherwise, restaurants are open for lunch and dinner daily. We mention dress code only when there's a specific requirement and reservations only when they're essential or not accepted.

Credit Cards

The hotels and restaurants in this guide typically accept credit cards. If not, we'll say so.

EUGENE FODOR

Hungarian-born Eugene Fodor (1905–91) began his travel career as an interpreter on a French cruise ship. The experience inspired him to write *On the Continent* (1936), the first guidebook to receive annual updates and discuss a country's way of life as well as its sights. Fodor later joined the U.S. Army and worked for the OSS in World War II. After the war, he kept up his intelligence work while expanding his guidebook series. During the Cold War, many guides were written by fellow agents who understood the value of insider information. Today's guides continue Fodor's legacy by providing travelers with timely coverage, insider tips, and cultural context.

EXPERIENCE
SCOTLAND

SCOTLAND TODAY

It may have just 5.3 million people, but today Scotland has some big ideas about where it's headed socially, culturally, and economically. International sporting events, the lively (but ultimately defeated) 2014 referendum on whether to become an independent nation, and even First Minister Nicola Sturgeon's state visits to the United States and elsewhere continue to focus worldwide attention on Scotland.

Travel in the 21st Century

The experience of traveling in Scotland has changed markedly for the better in recent years, with wholesale improvements in standards of hospitality and food especially.

Today hotels and restaurants charge prices similar to those in the rest of the United Kingdom. On the other hand, most of Scotland's biggest and best museums and galleries are free. Walk through well-tended gardens, along bustling waterfronts, and in beautifully renovated neighborhoods—a good day out can show you everything but cost nothing at all.

In 2018 Scotland will present its Year of Young People, putting center stage the country's youth through a packed program of collaborative events. Future themed years celebrate natural beauty and Scots imagination: 2020 is the Year of Scotland's Coasts and Waters, and 2022 will present a Year of Scotland's Stories.

Independence and Brexit

Dominating Scotland's public life in recent years has been the relationship of Scotland with the U.K. Parliament, and the increasingly troubled state of this 300-year-old union. Through devolution, Scotland elected its first parliament in 300 years in 1999. In 2014, the independence referendum saw 55% vote against Scotland becoming an independent country.

But that vote by no means resolved the matter, especially given the unpopularity in Scotland of the 2016 U.K. vote to leave the EU, or Brexit, when only 38% of Scots voted to leave and 62% to remain. With the prospect that leaving the single-market EU might lead to further economic turmoil across the United Kingdom, First Minister of Scotland Nicola Sturgeon has called for a second independence referendum, due to a significant material change. Sturgeon's SNP (Scottish Nationalist Party) reset the timetable for triggering "IndyRef 2" for when the outcome of Brexit negotiations plays out in the autumn of 2018.

Besides the prospect of being dragged out of the EU against the wishes of its people, why are many Scots dissatisfied with the U.K. government? In a time of budget woes, the Westminster government has been slashing public services. Many of these cuts deeply offend the Scots, who are committed to free education and free health care from the publicly owned National Health Service.

Culture

The arts continue to thrive, a sign of Scotland's creative energy. Edinburgh's arts festivals grow bigger every year, attracting visitors from around the globe. The National Theatre of Scotland has been such a resounding success that productions have made their way to Broadway. Glasgow is renowned for contemporary arts: Glasgow artists often win the Turner Prize, Britain's most prestigious art honor.

In a sign of vitality, culture is not confined only to the large cities. Far to the north, Shetland (already drawing audiences with its folk festivals) has built Mareel, a remarkable live-music venue and cinema. Dundee is the United Kingdom's sole

1

UNESCO City of Design (Detroit represents the United States) and will be the location of the first outpost of London's Victoria and Albert Museum, due to open in 2018. Perth's renewal will center on the transformation of Perth City Hall into a museum and gallery.

In 2013 a new mural was unveiled in Glasgow's subway system that employs the words of Scottish novelist Alasdair Gray: "Work as if you live in the early days of a better nation." Undoubtedly the artists of Scotland have taken him to heart.

Land

It's a disturbing fact that just 500 people own half the land in Scotland, many of them wealthy foreigners who have become absentee landlords. Experts say that giving residents a say on what happens to the land they live on is crucial if communities are going to thrive. New models of community ownership and management are being hard won, particularly in the Western Isles. There have been some community buyouts in which farming communities get the government's help to purchase the land where they live and work.

Still, the depopulation of rural Scotland continues. The popularity of holiday homes has meant that some villages are fully inhabited for only a few weeks each summer. Those who want to live here permanently find that low wages, a high cost of living, and a lack of affordable housing mean that they are priced out of a home surrounded by such beauty.

Wind Power

Urged by the government to help the country meet its ambitious targets for renewable energy, Scottish landowners began leasing land to the corporations behind wind farms. Scotland now has many large-scale commercial wind farms—including Europe's largest—and hundreds of smaller ones, many in community ownership. This has sparked vociferous debate. The pro-wind lobby argues in favor of emission-free energy that's better for the environment than coal or nuclear plants, while the anti-wind camp decries the environmental damage to ancient peat bogs and bird populations.

Turbines are now being built offshore, which is another cause for dispute. Donald Trump, who ignored environmental activists while building his sprawling golf estate, has had a very public fallout with government officials over the "ugly" planned offshore turbine plant that will be visible from his golf course. Trump continues to withhold the multimillion dollar investment he promised at the outset.

Scotland, Finally Winning

When it comes to sports, the Scots have reveled in their traditional role as the underdog. But Olympic gold medal–winning cyclist Chris Hoy and tennis Grand Slam winner Andy Murray have shown that this narrative needs rewriting.

As well as regularly hosting major golf tournaments—the Ryder Cup at Gleneagles in 2014 and Open Golf at St. Andrews (2015), Royal Troon (2017), and Carnoustie (2018)—Scotland has proved itself of late as a worthy and welcoming venue for multisport international events. After the success of the Glasgow Commonwealth Games in 2014, and with a Football World Cup 2018 Qualifying Group involving a clash with the auld enemy England, pride in Scottish sports is growing.

WHAT'S WHERE

1 Edinburgh and the Lothians. Scotland's captivating capital is the country's most popular city, famous for its high-perched castle, Old Town and 18th-century New Town, ultramodern Parliament building, and Georgian and Victorian architecture. Among the city's highlights are superb museums, including the National Museum of Scotland, and the most celebrated arts festival in the world, the International Festival. If Edinburgh's crowds are too much, escape to the Lothians and visit coastal towns, beaches, ancient chapels, and castles.

2 Glasgow. The country's largest city has evolved from prosperous Victorian hub to depressed urban center to thriving modern city with a strong artistic, architectural, and culinary reputation. Museums and galleries such as the Kelvingrove and Gallery of Modern Art (GoMA) are here, along with the Arts and Crafts architecture of Charles Rennie Mackintosh and iconic institutions such as Glasgow University. Glasgow is also the place to shop in Scotland.

3 The Borders and the Southwest. Scotland's southern gateway from England, the Borders, with its moors and gentle hills and river valleys, is rustic but historically rich. It's known for being the home of Sir Walter Scott and has impressive stately homes such as Floors Castle and ruined abbeys including Melrose. The Southwest, or Dumfries and Galloway region, is perfect for scenic drives, castles, and hiking.

4 Fife and Angus. The "kingdom" of Fife is considered the sunniest and driest part of Scotland, with sandy beaches, fishing villages, and stone cottages. St. Andrews has its world-famous golf courses, but this university town is worth a stop even for nongolfers. To the north in Angus are Glamis Castle, the legendary setting of Shakespeare's *Macbeth*, as well as the city of Dundee with its increasing cultural attractions, not least of which are the new V&A Museum of Design and a rejuvenated waterfront.

5 The Central Highlands. Convenient to both Edinburgh and Glasgow, this area encompasses some of Scotland's most beautiful terrain, with rugged, dark landscapes broken up by lochs and fields. Not to be missed are Loch Lomond and the Trossachs, Scotland's first national park. Perth and Stirling are the main metropolitan hubs and worth a stop; Stirling Castle has epic views that stretch from coast to coast.

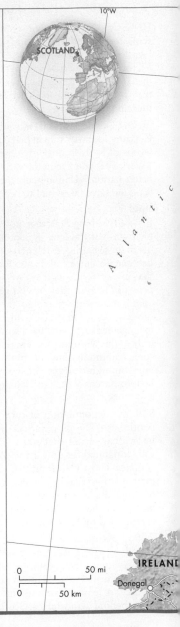

10°W

SCOTLAND

Atlantic

0   50 mi

0   50 km

IRELAND

Donegal

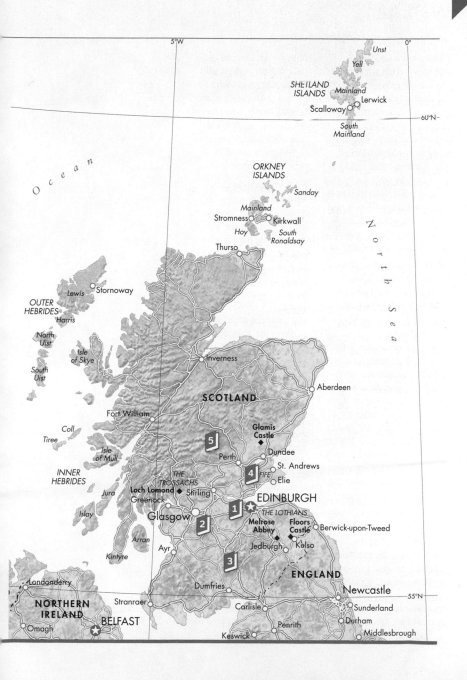

WHAT'S WHERE

6 Aberdeen and the Northeast. Malt-whisky buffs can use the prosperous port city of Aberdeen, known for its silvery granite buildings, as a base for exploring the region's distilleries, including those on the Malt Whisky Trail. Aberdeen also makes a good starting point for touring Royal Deeside, with its purple moors and piney hills as well as the notably rich selection of castles built over many centuries, including Balmoral.

7 Argyll and the Isles. Remote and picturesque, this less visited region of the southwestern coastline has excellent gardens, religious sites, and distilleries. To experience the region in full, catch a ferry from adorable Oban to Mull and the southern isles. If you like whisky, a trip to Islay is a must; if it's mountains you're after, try Jura; if a Christian site strikes a chord, head to Iona. The Isle of Arran is the place to see Scotland's diversity shrunk down to a more intimate size.

8 Around the Great Glen. An awe-inspiring valley laced with rivers and streams defines this part of the country. A top spot for hikers, this Highland glen is ringed by tall mountains, including Ben Nevis, Britain's tallest mountain. Rugged Cairngorms National Park lies to the east

of this area. Glencoe and Culloden are historic sites not to miss; those who believe in Nessie, Scotland's famous monster, can follow the throngs to Loch Ness. Inverness, the capital of the Highlands, is useful as a base for exploring.

9 The Northern Highlands and the Western Isles. This rugged land is home to the lore of clans, big moody skies, and wild rolling moors. It's also the place to see one of Scotland's most picturesque castles, Eilean Donan, which you pass on the way to the beautiful, popular Isle of Skye. The stark, remote Outer Hebrides, or Western Isles, offer ruined forts and chapels. This is where you go for real peace and quiet.

10 Orkney and Shetland Islands. Remote and austere, these isles at the northern tip of Scotland require tenacity to reach but have an abundance of intriguing prehistoric sites, including standing circles, *brochs* (circular towers), and tombs, as well as wild, open landscapes. A Scandinavian heritage gives them a unique flavor. The Shetland Isles, with their barren moors and vertical cliffs, are well known for bird-watching and diving opportunities.

10°W

SCOTLAND

Atlantic

IRELAND

Donegal

0 _____ 50 mi

0 _____ 50 km

1

O c e a n

Unst

Yell

SHETLAND ISLANDS *Mainland*
Scalloway ○ ○ Lerwick

60°N

South Mainland

ORKNEY ISLANDS

Sanday

10

Mainland
Stromness ○ ○ Kirkwall
Hoy *South Ronaldsay*

Thurso ○

N o r t h   S e a

OUTER HEBRIDES

Lewis ○ Stornoway

9

Harris

North Uist

Isle of Skye

Inverness ○ ● Culloden

Eilean Donan Castle ◆

● Loch Ness

South Uist

8

6

Aberdeen ○

Fort William ○

Cairngorms National Park ●

Balmoral Castle ●

Coll

● Ben Nevis

Tiree

Iona ◆

Glencoe ●

Isle of Mull

Oban ○

Perth ○

Dundee ○

SCOTLAND

St. Andrews ○

INNER HEBRIDES

ARGYLL

Elie ○

Jura

Stirling ○

EDINBURGH ⊛

Islay

7

Greenock ○

Glasgow ○

Kelso ○

Berwick-upon-Tweed ○

Arran

Jedburgh ○

Kintyre

Ayr ○

○ Londonderry

Dumfries ○

ENGLAND

NORTHERN IRELAND

Stranraer ○

Carlisle ○

Newcastle ○

55°N

Sunderland ○

○ Omagh

BELFAST ⊛

Penrith ○

Durham ○

Keswick ○

Middlesbrough ○

5°W

0°

NEED TO KNOW

AT A GLANCE
Capital: Edinburgh

Population: 5,404,700

Currency: British pound

Money: ATMs common, credit cards widely accepted

Language: English

Country Code: 44

Emergencies: 999

Driving: On the left

Electricity: 230V/50 cycles; plugs have three rectangular blades

Time: Five hours ahead of New York

Documents: Up to six months with valid passport

Mobile Phones: GSM (900 and 1800 bands), UMTS (900 and 2100 bands)

Major Mobile Companies: O2, EE, Vodaphone

WEBSITES
VisitScotland:
⊕ www.visitscotland.com

Scotland.com:
⊕ www.scotland.com

People Make Glasgow:
⊕ www.peoplemakeglasgow.com

GETTING AROUND

✈ **Air Travel:** Edinburgh and Glasgow airports are the largest; Aberdeen and Glasgow Prestwick also get international traffic.

🚌 **Bus Travel:** Scotland's bus (short-haul) and coach (long-distance) network is extensive. Bus service is comprehensive in cities, less so in country districts. Express service links main cities and towns.

🚗 **Car Travel:** If you stick mostly to the cities, you will not need a car. For countryside jaunts, a car will make journeys faster and easier.

🚆 **Train Travel:** The extensive train service within Scotland is generally run by Abellio ScotRail.

PLAN YOUR BUDGET

	HOTEL ROOM	MEAL	ATTRACTIONS
Low Budget	£70	£20	National Museum of Scotland, free
Mid Budget	£140	£50	Edinburgh Castle, £17
High Budget	£250	£90	Opera ticket, £75

WAYS TO SAVE
Hit the local pub. Most of Scotland's local pubs serve hearty meals at reasonable prices.

Go private. Countless private apartments are available for rent for short stays in Scotland, usually offering cheaper rates than hotels as well as a full kitchen.

Explorer Pass No. 1. Scottish Citylink's three-, five-, and eight-day Explorer Passes offer great savings on bus travel throughout the country.

Explorer Pass No. 2. Historic Scotland also offers an Explorer Pass good for three or seven days of free entry to nearly 80 top historic sights including Edinburgh and Stirling castles.

Hassle Factor	Low. Several direct flights are available from North America, and many connections are possible through larger airports in England.
3 days	Explore historic Edinburgh, then take a side trip to lochside Linlithgow Palace, birthplace of Mary, Queen of Scots.
1 week	Spend a few days in Edinburgh, then head north to the golf mecca of St. Andrews. Continue up to Loch Ness and Inverness, the gateway to the Highlands. Head back south to end your trip with two days in Glasgow.
2 weeks	Spend three days in Edinburgh, then head north to St. Andrews and Inverness and continue into the Highlands with stops at Eilean Donan Castle and the Isle of Skye. Head south again and stop at Loch Lomond before ending with a few days in Glasgow.

WHEN TO GO

High Season: Peak tourist season runs from mid-May through mid-September. Crowds at main attractions can be heavy, and prices are at their highest. Summer days are very long, and temperatures can linger in the 60s, 70s, or 80s, with dry spells lasting a week or two.

Low Season: November to March marks the low season for travel. Winter sees lots of rain, some snow, and icy winds, not to mention the short days. City museums stay open year-round, but some tourist sites such as castles and historic houses close from November to Easter.

Value Season: You can get some excellent deals in spring (April to mid-May) and fall (mid-September to October); weather is cool and often rainy, but crowds are not as intense.

BIG EVENTS

January: One of the world's largest Celtic festivals is Glasgow's half-month Celtic Connections. ⊕ www.celtic-connections.com

May–September: Towns all over Scotland celebrate the Highland Games, an ancient festival including music, dance, and (most important) athletic events.

August: Edinburgh Festival Fringe is the world's largest annual arts fest, with more than 3,000 shows from some 50 countries filling the Scottish capital. ⊕ www.edfringe.com

December–January: Scotland's festive version of New Year's Eve, called Hogmanay, lasts several days.

READ THIS

■ **The Prime of Miss Jean Brodie,** Muriel Spark. An unconventional teacher in 1930s Edinburgh.

■ **Waverley,** Sir Walter Scott. The Jacobite uprising of 1745.

■ **Sunset Song,** Lewis Grassic Gibbon. Scottish life in the early 20th century.

WATCH THIS

■ **Braveheart.** William Wallace leads a Scottish uprising against England in the 14th century.

■ **The 39 Steps.** Hitchcock's Scottish thriller is one of his finest.

■ **Trainspotting and T2 Trainspotting.** A look at drug-addicted Scottish youths in the 1980s and their latest misadventures.

EAT THIS

■ **Haggis**: minced offal of sheep, pig, or cow mixed with suet

■ **Scotch pie**: small, double-crusted meat pie

■ **Stovies**: stew of meat (usually beef) and vegetables

■ **Cullen skink**: thick smoked-haddock soup

■ **Clootie dumpling**: rich dessert with dried fruit

■ **Cranachan**: dessert of fresh raspberries and whipped cream, often with whisky

FILM LOCATIONS THROUGHOUT SCOTLAND

Scotland's dramatic scenery and the character of its people have left impressions on viewers since the birth of the moving image. Today, visitors not only seek out the locations seen in blockbuster series such as *Outlander*, *Game of Thrones*, and James Bond films, but also classic and cult movie scenes: from *Local Hero* and *Wicker Man* to *Shallow Grave* and *Trainspotting*. Here is a selection of some standout film locations:

Edinburgh and the Lothians

Edinburgh and the Lothians' handsome architecture is the backdrop for many productions. In the 1969 adaptation of Muriel Spark's novel *The Prime of Miss Jean Brodie*, Oscar winner Maggie Smith leads her 1930s schoolgirls around Edinburgh Academy on Henderson Row, Greyfriars Churchyard, and the Vennel (Grassmarket), retreating to Cramond. In *Trainspotting's* (1994) opening sequence Renton and pals flee the police down Princes Street and steps toward Calton Street Bridge. *T2*, the 2017 sequel, revisits this iconic chase scene and also includes Commercial Street, Leith, Arthur's Seat, Scottish Parliament, Royal Circus, and Stockbridge. The feel-good musical *Sunshine on Leith* (2013), based on the Proclaimers' rousing tunes, plays out in Old Town and on the Port of Leith's cobblestone streets. Auld Reekie's magical skyline and atmosphere is captured in the charming animation *The Illusionist* (2010).

Outlander (2014) season one and two feature Hopetoun House, Blackness Castle and Linlithgow Palace. For a map of Outlander locations, see ⊕ *www.visitscotland.com/see-do/attractions/tv-film/outlander*.

Glasgow

Glasgow's street grid makes it a good stand-in for U.S. cities including Philadelphia in zombie flick *World War Z* (2013) starring Brad Pitt; while Blythswood Hill resembles San Francisco in *Cloud Atlas* (2012). The grand City Chambers stand in for: Belle Époque New York mansions in *House of Mirth* (2000); the Vatican in *Heavenly Pursuits* (1986); and the Kremlin in *An Englishman Abroad* (1983). Hutcheson's Hall on Ingram Street appears in *The Wife* (2017), starring Glenn Close. *Mission Impossible's* (2000) railway chase finale is a blur of East Ayrshire countryside and Bollochmyle Viaduct. Brooding landscapes make the Borders & the Southwest ripe for intrigue, murder, and mystery. Hermitage Castle's role in 16th-century regal plotting appears in *Mary Queen of Scots* (1971), starring Vanessa Redgrave and Glenda Jackson; a lavish retelling began shooting in 2017. Chilling cult B-feature *The Wicker Man* centers on a pagan Scottish isle, with many creepy scenes filmed around Newton Stewart, including St. Ninian's Cave, Castle Kennedy, and Logan Botanic Gardens.

Fife and Angus

Many visitors to Fife and Angus hum Vangelis's *Chariots of Fire* (1984) synthesizer sound track, reenacting the slow-motion sprint along St. Andrews West Beach. The Royal and Ancient club and Fife's coastal links also appear in *Tommy's Honour* (2017), telling the story of Old and Young Tom Morris's relationship and golfing history.

Central Highlands

Doune Castle in the Central Highlands is synonymous with *Monty Python and the Holy Grail* (1975), the first Winterfell in *Game of Thrones* (2011), and then

1

Castle Leoch for *Outlander*. The Falls of Dochart appear in the *39 Steps* (1959) and *Casino Royale* (1967).

Aberdeen and the Northeast
Fans of the much-loved *Local Hero* (1983) with Burt Lancaster and Peter Reigert make a pilgrimage to Aberdeen and the Northeast harbor village Pennan's red telephone box and nearby Banff's Ship Inn. For the fictional west-coast village of Furness's beach and Ben's Shack go west to Camusdarach, Morar. Royal Deeside and Balmoral Estate are at the heart of *The Queen* (2009), *The Crown* (2016), and *Mrs. Brown* (1997).

Argyll and the Isles
Duart Castle in Argyll and the Isles has staged real-life kidnap attempts and celluloid dramas including *I Know Where I'm Going* (1945) and *Entrapment* (1999). Mull's Treshnish Peninsula and Oban feature in the spy thriller the *Eye of the Needle* (1981), starring Donald Sutherland.

Inverness and Around the Great Glen
Glen Nevis is clan central in *Braveheart* (1995), while *Rob Roy* (1995) rampages around Glen Coe, Rannoch Moor, Lochs Morar, and Leven, and Eilean Donan Castle. The lochside castle also stars in *Master of Ballatrae* (1953) with Errol Flynn, *Highlander* (1986) with Sean Connery, and *The World is Not Enough* (1999) as MI6 HQ Scotland. Another Bond movie, *Skyfall* (2012), has a spectacular A82 driving scene. Billie Wilder's *The Private Life of Sherlock Holmes* (1971) introduces Urquhart Castle for some Loch Ness monster encounters. Glenfinnan Viaduct has become synonymous with the *Harry Potter* films; Claichaig Gully, Glencoe, Steall falls in Glen Nevis and Loch Eilt also appear.

Northern Highlands and Western Isles
Skye's Cuillin mountain outcrops are now so popular with jet-setting fans of *Outlander*, *Macbeth* (2015), *Prometheus* (2012), *Skyfall* (2012), and *Stardust* (2007) that they are best visited in low season. Animation adventure *Brave* (2012) enchants children with its hyper-realistic depictions of Calanais Standing Stones, Glen Affric, and Dunnotar Castle. Dunrobin Castle impersonates a French chateau in Stanley Kubrick's adaptation of William Makepeace Thackeray's novel *Barry Lyndon* (1975). *Whisky Galore* (1949) was filmed on Barra while the 2016 remake barrels around the mainland (see ⊕ *www.visitscotland.com/blog/films/whisky-galore*).

Orkney and Shetland Islands
The essence of Scotland's far-flung isles and the evacuation of St. Kilda inspired *The Edge of the World* (1937), filmed on Foula in the Orkney and Shetland Islands. Pioneering filmmakers Jenny Gilbertson and Margaret Tait were stirred by the landscapes and communities on these archipelagos, directing *The Rugged Island* (1934) and *Blue Black Permanent* (1992), respectively. Four seasons of crime drama *Shetland* (2013–) showcase the windswept Nordic scenery, including extinct volcano Eshaness.

Film Tours
Open Roads Scotland. Open Roads offers James Bond, *Harry Potter*, and *Outlander*–themed tours. ☎ *0141 /634–8444* ⊕ *openroadscotland.com*.

Mary's Meanders. Mary's has themed tours including *Outlander* film locations. ⊕ *www.marysmeanders.co.uk/outlander-tours/* 🖃 *From £80.*

FLAVORS OF SCOTLAND

Superb Fish and Seafood

Some of the most coveted fish and seafood in the world lives in the rivers and lakes, as well as off the coasts, of Scotland. Don't miss the wild salmon, trout, haddock, mackerel, herring (often served as cold-smoked kippers), langoustines, scallops, mussels, oysters, and crabs.

Smoked fish is the national specialty—so much so that the process of both hot and cold smoking has developed to a fine art. Scots eat smoked fish for breakfast and lunch, and as an appetizer with their evening meal. The fish is often brushed with cracked pepper and a squeeze of lemon, and accompanied by thin slices of hearty bread or oat crackers. Places like Arbroath as well as the isles of North Uist and Skye have won international praise for locally smoked haddock, salmon, and trout, which are synonymous with delicacy.

Other seafood to try includes the traditional fish-and-chips, *the* Scottish favorite not to be overlooked. The fish is either cod or haddock, battered and deep-fried until it's crispy and golden. Another classic preparation is *Cullen skink,* a creamy fish stew thick with smoked haddock, potatoes, and onions. It's perfect on cold winter nights as a tasty hot appetizer. For a special treat, grilled, sautéed, or baked langoustines offer the ultimate seafood indulgence, succulent and tasty.

Tempting Baked Goods and Sweets

The Scots love their cakes, biscuits, breads, and pies. There's always something sweet and most likely crumbly to indulge in, whether after a meal or with a nice cup of tea. Bakeries are the perfect places to sample fresh goodies.

Some of the local favorites range from conventional butter-based shortbreads, empire biscuits (two shortbread cookies with jam in between, glazed in white icing and topped with a bright red cherry), whisky cake, mince pies (small pies filled with brandy, stewed dried fruits, and nuts), and scones. Treacle tarts, gingerbread, butterscotch apple pie, and oatcakes (more a savory cracker than a sweet cake) with local cheese are also popular as late-morning or early-afternoon temptations.

Not to be missed are the many treats named after their place of origin: Balmoral tartlets (filled with cake crumbs, butter, cherries, and citrus peel), Abernethy biscuits (cookies with extra sugar and caraway seeds), Islay loaves (sweet bread with raisins, walnuts, and brown sugar), and Dundee cake (full of cherries, raisins, sherry, and spices). Home bakers are much celebrated, and the catering tents at Highland games are worth seeking out to sample a community's finest.

Scots confectioners created 20th-century sweeties with iconic packaging popular to this day. Pairing well with a pot of tea are Tunnock's of Lanarkshire's Caramel Wafer biscuits and marshmallowy chocolate-coated Teacake. Lee's of Coatbridge launched the Macaroon bar in 1931, still available alongside other fondant favorites: Raspberry Coconut Ice and Jaffa Orange. Edinburgh Rock, made with sugar and cream of tartar, is formed into crumbly, soft sticks. A few traditional or retro sweet shops remain, with jars filled with colorful boiled sweets, rhubarb and custards, violet creams, and even Irn Bru humbugs (orange soda-flavored hard candy). Across the country in local shops is the ubiquitous and often homemade Tablet, a crumbly confection of butter, condensed milk, and sugar.

Traditional Scottish Fare

Food in Scotland is steeped in history, and a rich story lies behind many traditional dishes. Once the food of peasants, haggis—a mixture of sheep's heart, lungs, and liver cooked with onions, oats, and spices, and then boiled in a sheep's stomach—has made a big comeback in more formal Scottish restaurants. If the dish's ingredients turn you off, there's often an equally flavorful vegetarian option. You'll find "neeps and tatties" alongside haggis; the three are inseparable. Neeps are yellow turnips, potatoes are the tatties, and both are boiled and then mashed.

Black pudding is another present-day delicacy (and former peasant food) that you can find just about everywhere, from breakfast table to the local fish-and-chips shop to formal dining establishment. It's made from cooked sheep's or goat's blood that congeals and is mixed with such ingredients as oats, barley, potato, bread, and meat. Black pudding can be grilled or deep-fried. The Scottish prefer it for breakfast with fried eggs, bacon, beans, square sausages, toast, and potato scones. These fried, triangular-shape scones have the consistency of a dense pancake and are an intimate part of the Scottish breakfast, aptly called a fry-up because—apart from the beans and toast—everything else on the plate is fried. Another popular breakfast dish is porridge with salt. Sweet porridge doesn't go down well in Scotland.

Whiskies and Real Ales

"Uisge beatha," translated from Scottish Gaelic, means "water of life," and in Scotland it most certainly is. Whisky helps weave together the country's essence, capturing the aromas of earth, water, and air in a single sip.

Whiskies differ greatly between single malts and blends. This has to do with the ingredients, specialized distillation processes, and type of oak cask. Whisky is made predominantly from malted barley that, in the case of blended whiskies, can be combined with grains and cereals like wheat or corn. Malts or single malts can come only from malted barley.

The five main whisky regions in Scotland produce distinctive tastes, though there are variations even within a region: the Lowlands (lighter in taste), Speyside (sweet, with flower scents), the Highlands (fragrant, smooth, and smoky), Campbeltown (full-bodied and slightly salty), and Islay (strong peat flavor). Do sample these unique flavors; distillery tours are a good place to begin.

Real ales—naturally matured, cask-conditioned beer made from traditional ingredients—have arrived in the United Kingdom. These ales are not, at present, as popular as whisky, but are quickly making their mark on the Scottish beverage scene. Good brews to try include Arran Blonde (Arran Brewery), Dark Island (Orkney Brewery), White Wife (Valhalla Brewery, Shetland), Deuchars IPA (Caledonian Brewery), and Skye Red (Skye Brewery).

PLAYING GOLF IN SCOTLAND

There are some 550 golf courses in Scotland and only 5.3 million residents, so the country has probably the highest ratio of courses to people anywhere in the world. If you're visiting Scotland, you'll probably want to play the "famous names" sometime in your career.

So by all means play the championship courses such as the Old Course at St. Andrews, but remember they *are* championship courses. You may enjoy the game itself much more at a less challenging course. Remember, too, that everyone else wants to play the big names, so booking can be a problem at peak times in summer. Reserving three to four months ahead is not too far for the famous courses, although it's possible to get a time up to a month (or even a week) in advance if you are relaxed about your timing. If you're staying in a hotel attached to a course, get the concierge to book a tee time for you.

Happily, golf has always had a peculiar classlessness in Scotland. It's a game for everyone, and for centuries Scottish towns and cities have maintained courses for the enjoyment of their citizens. Admittedly, a few clubs have always been noted for their exclusive air, and some newer golf courses are losing touch with the game's inclusive origins, but these are exceptions to the tradition of recreation for all. Golf here is usually a democratic game, played by ordinary folk as well as the wealthy.

Tips About Playing

Golf courses are everywhere in Scotland. Most courses welcome visitors with a minimum of formalities, and some at a surprisingly low cost. Other courses are very expensive, but a lot of great golf can be played for between about £30 to £100 a round. Online booking at many courses has made arranging a golf tour easier, too.

Be aware of the topography of a course. Scotland is where the distinction between "links" and "parkland" courses was first made. Links courses are by the sea and are subject to the attendant sea breezes—some quite bracing—and mists, which can make them trickier to play. The natural topography of sand dunes and long, coarse grasses can add to the challenge. A parkland course is in a wooded area and its terrain is more obviously landscaped. A "moorland" course is found in an upland area.

Here are three pieces of advice, particularly for North Americans: (1) in Scotland the game is usually played fairly quickly, so don't dawdle if others are waiting; (2) caddy carts are hand-pulled carts for your clubs and driven golf carts are rarely available; and (3) when they say "rough," they really mean "rough."

Unless specified otherwise, hours are generally sunrise to sundown, which in June can be as late as 10 pm. Note that some courses advertise the SSS, "standard scratch score," instead of par (which may be different). This is the score a scratch golfer could achieve under perfect conditions. Rental clubs, balls, and other gear are generally available from clubhouses, except at the most basic municipal courses. Don't get caught by the dress codes enforced at many establishments: in general, untailored shorts, round-neck shirts, jeans, and sneakers are frowned upon.

The prestigious courses may ask for evidence of your golf skills by way of a handicap certificate; check in advance and carry this with you.

Costs and Courses

Many courses lower their rates before and after peak season—at the end of September, for example. It's worth asking about this. ■TIP→ Some areas offer regional golf passes that save you money. Check with the local tourist board.

For a complete list of courses, contact local tourist offices or VisitScotland's official and comprehensive golf website, ⊕ *golf. visitscotland.com*. It has information about the country's golf courses, special golf trails, regional passes, special events, and tour operators, as well as on conveniently located accommodations. U.K. Golf Guide (⊕ *www.uk-golfguide.com*) has user-generated reviews. *For information about regional courses, also see individual chapters; see Tours in Travel Smart Scotland for some golf tour operators.*

Best Bets Around Scotland

If your idea of heaven is teeing off on a windswept links, then Scotland is for you. Dramatic courses, many of them set on sandy dunes alongside the ocean, are just one of the types you'll encounter. Highland courses that take you through the heather and moorland courses surrounded by craggy mountains have their own challenges.

Boat of Garten Golf Club, Inverness-shire. With the Cairn Gorm Mountain as a backdrop, this beautiful course has rugged terrain that requires even seasoned players to bring their A game. As an added bonus, a steam railway runs alongside the course.

Carnoustie Golf Links, Angus. Challenging golfers for nearly 500 years, Carnoustie is on many golfers' must-do list. The iconic Championship Course has tested many of the world's top players, while the Burnside and Buddon courses attract budding Players and Watsons.

Castle Stuart Golf Links, Inverness-shire. A more recent addition to Scotland's world-class courses offers cliff-top hazards, sprawling bunkers, and rolling fairways overlooking the Moray Firth.

Cruden Bay Golf Club, Aberdeenshire. This challenging and enjoyable links course was built by the Great North of Scotland Railway Company in 1894. Its remote location beside a set of towering dunes makes it irresistible.

Dunbar Golf Club, East Lothian. This classic and challenging links course has dramatic weather and scenery, with a backdrop of the Firth of Forth, Bass Rock, and a lighthouse.

Gleneagles, Perthshire. Host of the 2014 Ryder Cup championship, Gleneagles has three 18-hole courses that challenge the pros and a 9-hole course that provides a more laid-back game. It's also home to the PGA National Golf Academy.

Machrihanish Golf Club, Argyll. A dramatic location on the Mull of Kintyre and some exciting match play make these links well worth a journey.

Royal Dornoch Golf Club, Sutherland. Extending across a coastal shelf, Royal Dornoch has fast greens, pristine beaches, and mountain views. In spring yellow gorse sets the green hills ablaze.

St. Andrews Links, Fife. To approach the iconic 18th hole in the place where the game was invented remains the holy grail of golfers worldwide.

Western Gailes Golf Club, near Glasgow. This splendid links course is a final qualifying course for the British Open. Sculpted by Mother Nature, it's the country's finest natural links course.

GREAT ITINERARIES

HIGHLIGHTS OF SCOTLAND IN 10 DAYS

Scotland isn't large, but its most famous cities and most iconic landscapes take time to explore. This itinerary packs in many national icons: Edinburgh's enormous charm and Glasgow's excellent museums; a castle or two; lochs, mountains, and an island. It's a busy pace, but you'll still be able to fit in a whisky distillery visit and even a round of golf. You can do parts of this trip by public transportation, but beyond the cities, a car allows more flexibility.

Days 1 and 2: Edinburgh

The capital of Scotland is loaded with iconic sights in its Old Town and New Town. Visit **Edinburgh Castle** and the **National Gallery of Scotland,** and take tours of the **National Museum of Scotland** and the modern **Scottish Parliament** building. Walk along Old Town's **Royal Mile** and New Town's **George Street** for some fresh air and retail therapy. Later on, seek out a traditional pub with live music.

Logistics: Fly into Edinburgh Airport if you're flying via London. If you're flying directly into Glasgow from overseas, make your way from Glasgow Airport to Queen Street station via taxi or bus. It takes an hour to travel from Glasgow to Edinburgh by car or bus, about 45 minutes to an hour by train. Explore on foot or by public transportation.

Day 3: Stirling to St. Andrews

Rent a car in Edinburgh and drive to the historic city of **Stirling.** Spend the day visiting **Stirling Castle** and the **National Wallace Monument.** If you're eager to tour a distillery, make time for a stop at the **Famous Grouse Experience** at the Glenturret Distillery in **Crieff.** For your overnight stay,

drive to the seaside town of St. Andrews, famous for golf.

Logistics: It's 35 miles or a one-hour drive to Stirling from Edinburgh, and 50 miles and 90 minutes from Stirling to St. Andrews. You can easily take a train or bus to these destinations.

Day 4: St. Andrews to Aviemore

Spend the morning exploring **St. Andrews,** known for its castle and the country's oldest university as well as its golf courses. If you've booked well in advance, play a round of golf. After lunch, drive to **Aviemore.** Along the way, stretch your legs at one of Scotland's notable sights, **Blair Castle** (just off the A9 and 10 miles north of **Pitlochry**). Head to Aviemore, gateway to the Cairngorm Mountains and Britain's largest national park, for two nights. The town is a center for outdoor activities and has many choices for accommodations, dining, and shopping, but you can also consider the more attractive surrounding villages and towns such as **Kingussie** for your stay.

Logistics: It's 120 miles from St. Andrews to Aviemore via the A9, a drive that will take 2½ hours. You can also take a train or bus.

Day 5: The Cairngorms

For anyone who enjoys outdoor pursuits or dramatic scenery, the arctic plateau of the Cairngorms is a must. Hiking, biking, and climbing are options (Glenmore Lodge is a renowned outdoor-sports center), but so is visiting attractions such as the **Cairngorm Reindeer Centre** and **Highland Folk Museum.**

Day 6: The Isle of Skye

Leave Aviemore early and head to Inverness, which has a busy center suited for a wander. **Inverness Castle** and the **Inverness Museum and Art Gallery** are worth seeing. The drive southwest to Skye is peaceful, full of raw

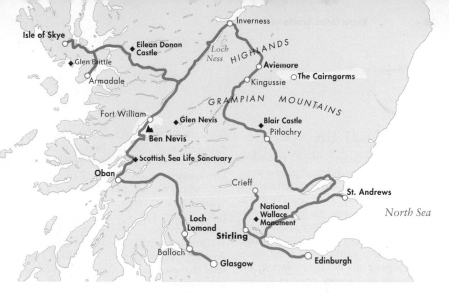

landscapes and big, open horizons. Stop at **Eilean Donan Castle** on the way. Set on an island among three lochs, the castle is the stuff postcards are made of from the outside, although the interiors are comically underwhelming. Explore Skye: **Glen Brittle** is the perfect place to enjoy mountain scenery including the crystal-clear **Fairy Pools** at the foot of the Black Cuillins; and **Armadale** is a good place to go crafts shopping. End up in Portree for dinner and the night.

Logistics: It's 30 miles (a 40-minute drive) via the A9 from Aviemore to Inverness, and then it's 80 miles (a two-hour drive) from Inverness to Skye. Public transportation is possible but connections take time, so a car is best.

Day 7: Oban via Ben Nevis

Leave Skye no later than 9 am and head for **Fort William**. The town isn't worth stopping for, but the view of Britain's highest mountain, the 4,406-foot Ben Nevis, is. If time permits, take a hike in **Glen Nevis**. Continue on to **Oban**, a traditional Scottish resort town on the water, to overnight. Outside Oban, stop by the **Scottish Sea Life Sanctuary**. At night, feast on fish-and-chips in a local pub.

Logistics: It's nearly 100 miles from Skye to Oban; the drive is 3½ hours without stopping. Public transportation is challenging.

Days 8 and 9: Loch Lomond and Glasgow

Enjoy a waterfront stroll in Oban. Mid-morning, set off for **Glasgow** via **Loch Lomond**. Stop in **Balloch** on the loch for fresh oysters and a walk along the bonnie banks. Arrive in Glasgow in time for dinner; take in a play or concert, or just relax in a pub on the first of your two nights in this rejuvenated city. Spend the next day visiting the sights: **Kelvingrove Art Gallery and Museum,** Charles Rennie Mackintosh's iconic buildings, and the **Riverside Museum** are a few highlights.

Logistics: It's 127 miles (a three-hour drive) from Oban to Glasgow via Balloch. Traveling by train is a possibility, but you won't be able to go via Balloch. Return your rental car in Glasgow.

Day 10: Glasgow and Home

On your final day, stow your suitcases at your hotel and hit Buchanan and Sauchiehall streets for some of Britain's best shopping. Clothes, whisky, and tartan items are good things to look for.

Logistics: It's less than 10 miles (15 minutes) by taxi to Glasgow's international airport in Paisley but more than 30 miles (40 minutes) to the international airport in Prestwick.

EAST COAST HIGHLIGHTS

Scotland's east coast is often overlooked for the more famed drama of the west, yet has gorgeous scenery, attractions, and some advantages, not least that it is sunnier and has fewer midges in the summer months. This itinerary packs in the urban pleasures of Edinburgh, Dundee, and Aberdeen; varied rural and coastal jaunts around the fishing villages of the East Neuk of Fife and around Cullen; Old Course golf and the singular university town St. Andrews; plus Great Glen majesty in Inverness and along the shores of Loch Ness. There's both historic and cutting-edge architecture—from Royal Deeside and Balmoral castles to Dundee's revamped waterfront centred around the new V&A Museum of Design. Wash it all down with Speyside's finest whisky at a distillery tour.

Day 1: Edinburgh

Get acquainted with the splendors of Scotland's capital, which is full of iconic sights. You won't be able to see everything in a day, but you can get a taste that will bring you back for more. Walk along Old Town's Royal Mile and explore the medieval streets and solid-stone architecture. Then head to the spacious Georgian New Town, taking in its Palladian architecture and eclectic shopping.

Logistics: Edinburgh's public transport allows freedom to explore the city and indulge in a drink or two.

Day 2: Edinburgh to Elie

Spend the morning exploring Edinburgh further, visiting the **Museum of Scotland** and galleries, perhaps walking part of the **Water of Leith** at **Stockbridge.** Pick up your rental car and head north along the A90 to the Forth crossing. Stop awhile to admire **Forth Bridge** at South Queensferry, a cantilevered railroad bridge that is a magnificent feat of Victorian engineering. Drive eastward on the A921 to explore the fishing villages and beaches of Fife's villages of East Neuk. **Elie** has a wonderful mile-long sandy beach; **Pittenweem's** community now thrives on homespun arts and the vestiges of a working harbor; **Anstruther** has a waterfront, **Scottish Fisheries Museum,** and quality fish-and-chips temptations; and **Crail** retains architectural allure.

Logistics: A rental car is essential for exploring the villages of East Neuk, which are not served by a train line. An alternative is to take a train to Leuchars for St. Andrews, and then use local buses.

Day 3: St Andrews to Dundee

Drive along the A917 to **St. Andrews** to sample its **Old Course,** golf course history, and cathedral ruins. Spend the morning here exploring the atmospheric **University of St. Andrews** quadrangles and museums, **St. Andrews Cathedral,** and beaches before heading over the River Tay to **Dundee,** Scotland's third-largest city. The resurgent city by the Tay River has a wealth of museums and cultural attractions. Explore its burgeoning waterfront attractions, including Captain Scott's **RRS *Discovery*** ship, **McManus Galleries, Dundee Contemporary Arts** center, and the emerging **V&A Museum of Design** outpost and waterfront regeneration centered on Slessor Gardens. Wander the leafy West End near the university, take in some theater at the **Dundee Repertory Theatre,** visit a local pub on the Perth Road, and then enjoy a meal in one of the city's many eateries.

Logistics: Today's itinerary can be done by public transport: rail and bus links

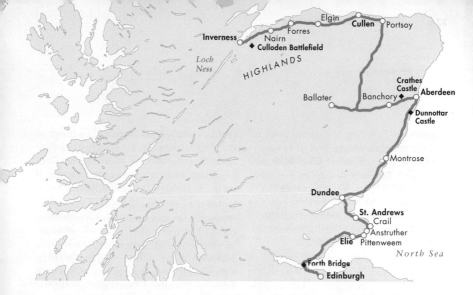

are excellent between St. Andrews and Dundee. The 15-mile journey takes just 25 minutes by car.

Day 4: Dundee to Aberdeen

Head north out of Dundee, on the A92 then A930, towards the suburbs of Broughty Ferry and Monifieth. Families might like to visit one of their fine sandy beaches and seek midmorning refreshments or an ice cream. Rejoin the A92 and proceed to **Montrose.** Linger to spot the abundant birdlife of the **Montrose Basin Local Nature Reserve.** Turn off again at Stonehaven and follow signs to **Dunnottar Castle** to clamber over some of Scotland's finest cliff-top ruins. Return to the A90 and spend some time looking around **Aberdeen** city center, seeking out its fine granite architecture, including **Marischal College** and **St. Nicholas Kirk.** In the evening head down to the old market area, the Green, to sample the city's famed craft beer and excellent seafood.

Logistics: A car is preferable for visiting Dunnottar Castle en route, but this 65-mile section can also easily be done using the regular East Coast rail services.

Day 5: Aberdeen to Cullen

Don't miss a walk around the cobbled lanes of **Old Aberdeen,** taking in the university quads and St. Machar's Cathedral's fine stained glass. Take the A93 southwest to Royal Deeside to enjoy the fresh mountain air at Victorian holiday towns **Banchory** and **Ballater.** Then take the A97 northwards towards Huntly and head to the coastal wonders and sandy beaches at **Portsoy** or **Cullen** for invigorating walks and ice cream. In the evening, sample the local fish-and-chips, or try a bowl of Cullen skink (creamy smoked-haddock soup).

Logistics: A car is essential for taking in all the attractions en route. This 60-mile section takes around 90 minutes without substantial breaks. Otherwise, plan ahead to catch the two-hour No. 35 bus from the Aberdeen bus station. The nearest train station is in Keith, 12 miles from Cullen, from where the infrequent No. 309 Deveron-run bus can be taken to Cullen.

Day 6: Cullen to Inverness

Rejoin the A98 to **Elgin,** stopping to visit the impressive cathedral ruins and the working monastery **Pluscarden Abbey.** At **Forres** there's the opportunity to head back to the coast at Findhorn to visit the enlightening **Findhorn Ecovillage** and a wonderful bay. Farther west on the A198, **Nairn** has historic attractions including spooky **Cawdor Castle** and a challenging golf course.

Alternatives: Explore distilleries both on and off the **Malt Whisky Trail** in Speyside. **Balvenie Distillery, Glenlivet, Glenfiddich,** and **Glen Grant Distillery & Garden** are good choices; check hours and tour times before heading out. The Moray Firth is home to dolphins, whales, and birds, which can be spotted on boat trips from harbors including Findhorn and Inverness.

Logistics: The direct route from Cullen to Inverness is 60 miles by car, not including detours. Via public transit, a bus to Elgin then a train to Inverness takes around three hours.

Days 7 and 8: Inverness

Spend the day in and around the Highland capital, **Inverness,** starting with a visit to the **Cathedral** and **Inverness Museum and Art Gallery** if the weather is poor. Don't visit too many sights or your day may become a forced march. An option for a day trip is to visit **Loch Ness,** though it's not one of Scotland's bonniest lochs; still, perhaps you'll spot Nessie. It's a 20-minute drive from Inverness. Just east of Inverness is Culloden Moor, where Bonnie Prince Charlie's forces were destroyed by the Duke of Cumberland's army.

Logistics: A car is best for this exploring the mountain scenery around Inverness. Rent one in Inverness or sign up for an organized tour; public transportation is not a viable option. Castles are often closed in winter; check in advance. Return south to Edinburgh on the A9 for some spectacular mountain scenery. It's a 160-mile, three-hour car ride, but, weather permitting, this photogenic route demands lots of lingering. By train it's a four-hour journey. *For scenic stop-off ideas en route consult Days 4 through 6 of the Highlights of Scotland itinerary.*

IF YOU LIKE

Castles

Whether a jumble of stones or a fully intact fortress, whether in private ownership or under the care of a preservation group, Scotland's castles powerfully demonstrate the country's lavish past and its once-uneasy relationship with its southern neighbor.

Caerlaverock. This triangular 13th-century fortress with red-sandstone walls in Dumfries was a last bastion in the 17th-century struggle for religious reform.

Castle Trail. Along Royal Deeside, west of Aberdeen, the Castle Trail has an eclectic group of castles all within a 100-mile radius. There's stirring Drum, stately Crathes, baronial Balmoral, memorabilia-packed Braemar, Corgarff, Kildrummy, and windswept Dunnottar.

Edinburgh Castle. This royal palace dominates the capital's history and skyline.

Eilean Donan. A ruin on the edge of three lochs in the Western Highlands, this is the most photogenic of Scottish castles and inspiration for the castle in the animated movie *Brave.*

Floors Castle. On the Duke of Roxburghe's estate outside Kelso, this castle has grand turrets, pinnacles, and cupolas.

Glamis Castle. Northeast of Dundee, Glamis Castle connects Britain's royalty from Macbeth to the late Queen Mother.

Hermitage Castle. This dark and foreboding place south of Hawick, near the English border, is where Mary, Queen of Scots, traveled to visit her lover, the Earl of Bothwell.

Stirling Castle. Beautifully restored Stirling Castle is the childhood home of Mary, Queen of Scots, and one of the finest Renaissance palaces in the United Kingdom.

Mountains and Lochs

For the snowcapped mountains and glassy lochs (lakes) for which Scotland is famous, you have to leave the south and the cities behind you—though some Lowland lakes are beautiful. Wherever you go in Scotland, nature is at your fingertips.

Ben Nevis. Looming over Fort William is dramatic Ben Nevis. No matter when you visit, you'll probably see snow on the summit.

Cairngorms National Park. The Great Glen is home to half of Scotland's highest peaks, many of them in Cairngorms National Park. This is an excellent place for hiking, skiing, and reindeer sightings.

Glen Torridon. East of Shieldaig in the Northern Highlands, Glen Torridon has the country's finest mountain scenery.

Loch Achray. This pretty loch is where you set out for the climb to Ben An, a sheer-faced mountain with fabulous views of the Trossachs.

Loch Katrine. In the heart of the Trossachs, this lake in the Central Highlands was the setting of Walter Scott's narrative poem *The Lady of the Lake.* In summer you can take the steamer SS *Sir Walter Scott.*

Loch Leven. Located in Fife, this loch is famed for its birdlife. It was also where Mary, Queen of Scots, signed the deed of abdication in her island prison.

Loch Lomond. Among Scotland's most famous lakes, Loch Lomond's shimmering shores, beautiful vistas, and plethora of water-sport options are 20 minutes from Glasgow.

Loch Maree. One of Scotland's most scenic lakes, Loch Maree is framed by Scots pines and Slioch Mountain in the Northern Highlands.

Museums

Scotland's rich history and the varied passions of its people provide a wealth of material and artifacts that fill museums and galleries across the land, from metropolitan art collections to small themed collections, many of them free.

Kelvingrove Art Gallery and Museum. Perennially popular, this grand Victorian palace in Glasgow houses Botticelli and Monet canvases to interactive Scottish history exhibits.

McManus Galleries. Dundee's major civic collection encompasses fine and contemporary art and Dundonian life and history, and hosts world-class visiting exhibits.

National Museum of Scotland. In Edinburgh, the renovated Victorian grand hall and 10 new galleries trace the nation's history from geologic deep time to contemporary life, with new spaces dedicated to fashion, design, science, and technology.

Riverside Museum. Scotland's Museum of Transport and Travel, set within a striking Zaha Hadid–designed structure alongside Glasgow's River Clyde and the handsome Tall Ship at Riverside, displays a dizzying array of vehicles.

Robert Burns Birthplace Museum. This interactive museum in Alloway explores the passions and poems of the much-loved poet and complex "man o' pairts."

Scottish Fisheries Museum. Buildings facing Anstruther Harbor in Fife house an absorbing collection of exhibits that illustrate the life of Scottish fisherfolk.

Shetland Museum. A suitably sail-like tower greets visitors to Lerwick's Hay's Dock and this wonderful museum, which tells many a salty and piquant tale of Shetland's way of life down the centuries.

V&A Museum of Design. Opening in 2018, Dundee's striking Kengo Kuma–designed waterfront museum is Scotland's first museum dedicated to the world of design, celebrating international and Scottish creativity.

Fabulous Festivals

With a culture that dates back hundreds of years, there's always something to celebrate in Scotland. No matter where you are, you can probably find a festival to suit you.

Celtic Connections. During the last two weeks of January, musicians from all over the world gather in Glasgow to play Celtic-inspired music.

Edinburgh Fringe. Running at the same time as the Edinburgh International Festival, this is a less formal, rowdier celebration of comedy, theater, and even kids' shows.

Edinburgh International Book Festival. Some of the world's most famous authors head to this annual festival, along with an audience that knows and loves literature.

Edinburgh International Festival. The most spectacular and famous event on Scotland's cultural calendar, August's festival has everything from traditional music to modern dance to cutting-edge theater.

Edinburgh Military Tattoo. Three weeks every August you can listen to the sound of pipe and drum while fireworks explode overhead.

Hogmanay. The world's biggest New Year's celebration takes place over several days in Edinburgh.

Pride Glasgow During August, Glasgow hosts Scotland's largest LGBTI festival.

St. Magnus Festival. Held in Orkney in June, this classical festival draws musicians from all over the world.

Up Helly Aa. This festival comes to a spectacular end with the torching of a replica of a Viking ship. It takes place in Lerwick, Shetland, on the last Tuesday of January.

Whisky Tours

Whisky tours are a great way to appreciate the varied flavors of Scotland's signature drink. Many distilleries are in lovely settings, and tours explore the craft that transforms malted barley, water, and yeast. In-depth tours and special tastings are available at some places, but it's best to check ahead and reserve if needed. Here's a sampling of distilleries around the country.

Edradour. This small distillery near Pitlochry makes a fine single malt and offers an informative and fun tour.

Glenfiddich. An entertaining visitor center enhances the tour of this Dufftown distillery; it also has an art gallery.

Glenlivet. Tours at the first licensed distillery in the Highlands include not only whisky making but also the fascinating story of the founder.

Highland Park. If you make it north to Orkney, visit Scotland's northernmost distillery and try its smoky but sweet malt.

Lagavulin. Among Islay's whiskies, this one has the strongest iodine scent; the distillery offers a number of special tours.

Laphroaig. Its distinctively peaty, iodine-and-seaweed flavor has earned this Islay whisky many devoted followers.

Macallan. There's a choice of two tours at this distillery in the northeast that matures its whisky in sherry and bourbon casks.

Talisker. The single malt from the Isle of Skye's only distillery has a peaty aroma; tours are popular.

Island Havens

A remote, windswept world of white-sand beaches, forgotten castles, and crisp, clear rivers awaits you in the Scottish isles. Out of the hundreds of isles, only a handful are actually inhabited, and here ancient culture and tradition remain alive and well. Each island has its own distinct fingerprint; getting to some might be awkward and costly, but the time and expense are worth your while.

Arran. With activities ranging from golf to hiking, this island has everything you'll find on the mainland but on a smaller, more intimate scale.

Bute. One of the more affordable and accessible islands, Bute draws celebrities to its estates for lavish weddings and Glaswegians to its rocky shores for summer holidays.

Iona. This spiritual and spectacular island was the burial place of Scottish kings until the 11th century.

Islay. Near the Kintyre Peninsula, this island is where you go to watch rare birds, purchase woolen goods, and sample the smoothest malt whiskies.

Northern Isles. Orkney and Shetland, two remote island groups collectively known as the Northern Isles, have a colorful Scandinavian heritage. Both have notable prehistoric artifacts and rollicking festivals. The green pastures of Orkney are an hour from the mainland, and wind-flattened Shetland will suit those who want a more remote feel.

Skye. With hazy mountains, hidden beaches, and shady glens, the Isle of Skye is unsurpassed for sheer beauty. It also has a good selection of hotels, B&Bs, and restaurants.

Hiking

People who have hiked in Scotland often return to explore the country's memorable rural landscapes of loch-dotted glens and forested hills. From Edinburgh's Arthur's Seat to Ben Nevis, Britain's tallest peak, the country holds unsurpassed hiking possibilities, no matter what your ambitions. Keep in mind that weather conditions can and do change rapidly in the Scottish hills, even at low altitude. The best time for hiking is from May to September.

Fife Coastal Path. This seaside trail is 117 miles long but can be done in chunks. It skirts along golden beaches, rocky inlets, and picturesque fishing villages.

Glen Nevis. Home of the magnificent peak of Ben Nevis, Glen Nevis has a number of moderate hikes with footpaths leading past waterfalls, ruined crofts, and forested gorges. There are also some more challenging climbs.

The Grampians. In the northeastern part of the country, this mountain range offers walks through some of the country's most varied terrain. The 8-mile route around Loch Muick, which passes Glas-allt Shiel, Queen Victoria's holiday home, is beautiful in any weather.

Southern Upland Way. The famous 212-mile coast-to-coast journey from Portpatrick to Cockburnspath is an undertaking, but it can be tackled in sections.

Trossachs National Park. In the Central Highlands, this vast area includes everything from quiet country strolls to ambitious climbs up craggy cliffs.

West Highland Way. From Milngavie to Fort William, this well-marked and well-trodden 96-mile trek follows a series of old coaching roads.

Megalithic Monuments

Scattered throughout the Scottish landscape are prehistoric standing stones, stone circles, tombs, and even stone houses that provide a tantalizing glimpse into the country's remarkable past and people. If you're interested in ancient remains, leave the mainland and head for the isles, where many of the most impressive and important sites are found.

Calanais Standing Stones. On the Isle of Lewis in the Outer Hebrides, this ancient site is reminiscent of Stonehenge. The impressive stones are believed to have been used for astronomical observations.

Jarlshof. A Bronze Age settlement dating from 2500 BC, Shetland's Jarlshof has been called the most remarkable archaeological site in the British Isles.

Machrie Moor Stone Circles. On the Isle of Arran these granite boulders and reddish-sandstone circles have a startling setting in the middle of an isolated moor.

Maeshowe. An enormous burial mound on Orkney, Maeshowe is renowned for its imposing burial chamber.

Mousa Broch. Accessible by boat on Shetland's South Mainland, this beautifully preserved fortified Iron Age stone tower is now a bird sanctuary.

Ring of Brodgar. Between Loch Harray and Loch Stenness on Orkney sits this magnificent circle made up of 36 Neolithic stones.

Skara Brae. Orkney's Neolithic village, first occupied around 3000 BC, was buried beneath the sand until its discovery in 1850. The houses are joined by covered passages, and with stone beds, fireplaces, and cupboards are intriguing remnants from the distant past.

EDINBURGH AND THE LOTHIANS

Updated by
Joseph Reaney

Edinburgh is a city so beautiful it breaks the heart again and again, as Alexander McCall Smith once wrote. One of the world's stateliest cities and proudest capitals, it is—like Rome—built on seven hills, making it a striking backdrop for the ancient pageant of history. In a skyline of sheer drama, Edinburgh Castle looks out over the city, frowning down on Princes Street's glamour and glitz. But despite its rich past, the city's famous festivals, excellent museums and galleries, as well as the modernist Scottish Parliament, are reminders that Edinburgh has its feet firmly in the 21st century.

Nearly everywhere in Edinburgh (the *burgh* is always pronounced *burra* in Scotland) there are spectacular buildings, whose Doric, Ionic, and Corinthian pillars add touches of neoclassical grandeur to the largely Presbyterian backdrop. Large gardens are a strong feature of central Edinburgh, while Arthur's Seat, a craggy peak of bright green-and-yellow furze, rears up behind the spires of the Old Town. Even as Edinburgh moves through the 21st century, its tall guardian castle remains the focal point of the city and its venerable history.

Modern Edinburgh has become a cultural capital, staging the Edinburgh International Festival and the Festival Fringe in every possible venue each August. The stunning National Museum of Scotland complements the city's wealth of galleries and artsy hangouts. Add Edinburgh's growing reputation for food and nightlife and you have one of the world's most beguiling cities.

Today, Edinburgh is the second-most-important financial center in the United Kingdom, and is widely renowned for its exceptional (and ever-expanding) dining and nightlife scenes—some of the reasons it regularly ranks near the top of quality-of-life surveys.

Take time to explore the city's streets—peopled by the spirits of Mary, Queen of Scots, Sir Walter Scott, and Robert Louis Stevenson—and enjoy candlelit restaurants or a folk ceilidh (pronounced *kay-lee*, a traditional Gaelic dance with music). But remember: you haven't earned your porridge until you've climbed Arthur's Seat. Should you wander around a corner, say, on George Street, you might see not an endless cityscape, but blue sea and a patchwork of fields. This is the county of Fife, beyond the inlet of the North Sea called the Firth of Forth—a reminder, like the mountains to the northwest that can be glimpsed from Edinburgh's highest points, that the rest of Scotland lies within easy reach.

TOP REASONS TO GO

Kaleidoscope of culture: Edinburgh covers it all, from floor-stomping *ceilidhs* to avant-garde modern dance, from traditional painting and sculpture to cutting-edge installations, from folksy fiddlers to the latest rock bands. The city's calendar of cultural festivals, including the remarkable Edinburgh Festival Fringe—the world's largest arts festival by a mile—is truly outstanding.

The Royal Mile: History plays out before your eyes in this centuries-old capital along the Royal Mile. Edinburgh Castle and the Palace of Holyroodhouse were the locations for some of the most important struggles between Scotland and England.

Timeless architecture: From the Old Town's labyrinthine medieval streets to the neoclassical orderliness of the New Town to imaginative modern developments like the Scottish Parliament, the architecture of Auld Reekie spans the ages.

Food, glorious food: Edinburgh has an ever-expanding restaurant scene that attracts celebrity chefs serving up dishes from around the world. Perhaps the most exotic, however, is genuine Scottish cuisine, with its classic dishes like *Cullen skink* and haggis with neeps and tatties.

Handcrafted treasures: Scotland has a strong tradition of distinctive furniture makers, silversmiths, and artists. Look to the "villages" of Edinburgh—such as Stockbridge and Leith—for exclusive designer clothing, edgy knitwear, and other high-end items.

ORIENTATION AND PLANNING

GETTING ORIENTED

For all its steep roads and hidden alleyways, Edinburgh is not a difficult place to navigate. Most newcomers gravitate to two areas, the Old Town and the New Town. The former funnels down from the castle on either side of the High Street, better known as the Royal Mile. Princes Street Gardens and Waverly station separate the oldest part of the city from the stately New Town, known for its neoclassical architecture and verdant gardens. To the north, the city sweeps down to the Firth of Forth. It is here you will find the port of Leith with its trendy pubs and fine-dining restaurants. The southern and western neighborhoods are mainly residential, but are home to a few attractions such as Edinburgh Zoo.

Old Town. The focal point of Edinburgh for centuries, the Old Town is a picturesque jumble of medieval tenements. Here are prime attractions such as Edinburgh Castle and the newer symbol of power, the Scottish Parliament. Amid the historic buildings you will find everything from buzzing bars and nightclubs to ghostly alleyways and vaults.

New Town. Built in the 18th and 19th centuries to prevent the wealthier residents of overcrowded Old Town from decamping to London, the neoclassical sweep of the New Town is a masterpiece of city planning. Significant sights include the National Gallery of Scotland and Calton

Hill, which offers some of the best views of the city from its summit. The city's main shopping thoroughfares, Princes Street and George Street, are also found here.

Haymarket. West of the Old Town and south of the West End is Haymarket, a district with its own down-to-earth character and well-worn charm. It's close to Edinburgh's second train station.

West End. Edinburgh's commercial center has boutiques aplenty as well as the Edinburgh Zoo.

Southside. Mostly residential, the Southside makes a good base for budget-conscious travelers. It's where most of the students live.

Leith. On the southern shore of the Firth of Forth, Edinburgh's port of Leith is where you'll find the now-retired Royal Yacht *Britannia,* along with some of the city's smartest restaurants and bars.

Side Trips: West Lothian and the Forth Valley, Midlothian and East Lothian. Known collectively as the Lothians, the areas of green countryside and seafront villages around Edinburgh are replete with historic houses, castles, towns, and museums. They are quick and easy to reach by car, bus, or train, making them welcome day-trip escapes from the summer festival crush.

PLANNING

WHEN TO GO

Scotland's reliably variable weather means that you could visit at the height of summer and be forced to wear a scarf. Conversely, conditions can be balmy in early spring and late autumn. You may choose to avoid the crowds (and hotel price hikes) of July and August, but you'd also miss some of the greatest festivals on Earth. May, June, and September are probably the most hassle-free months in which to visit, while still offering hope of good weather. Short days and grim conditions make winter less appealing, though there are few better New Year's Eve celebrations than Edinburgh's Hogmanay.

FESTIVALS

Beltane Fire Festival. Held every year on April 30th, this flame-filled Calton Hill extravaganza is inspired by an Iron Age Celtic festival, which was held to celebrate the return of summer. Expect drumbeat processions, bonfires, and fireworks, as costumed fire dancers reveal the fates of the May Queen and the Green Man. ⊠ *Calton Hill, Calton* ⊕ *www. beltane.org.*

FAMILY
Fodor'sChoice
★

Edinburgh Festival Fringe. During the world's largest arts festival in August, most of the city center becomes one huge performance area, with fire eaters, sword swallowers, unicyclists, jugglers, string quartets, jazz groups, stand-up comedians, and magicians all thronging into High Street and Princes Street. Every available performance space—church halls, community centers, parks, sports fields, putting greens, and nightclubs—is utilized for every kind of event, with something for all tastes. There are even family-friendly shows. Many events are free; others start at a few pounds and rise to £15 or £20. There's so much happening in the three weeks of the festival that it's possible to arrange your own

CLOSE UP

Festivals in Edinburgh

Walking around Edinburgh in late July, you'll likely feel the first vibrations of the earthquake that is festival time, which shakes the city throughout August and into September. You may hear reference to an "Edinburgh Festival," but this is really an umbrella term for five separate festivals all taking place around the same time. For an overview, check out ⊕ *www. edinburghfestivals.co.uk.*

The best-known and oldest of the city's festivals is the **Edinburgh International Festival,** founded in 1947 when Europe was recovering from World War II. In recent years the festival has drawn as many as 400,000 people to Edinburgh, with more than 100 acts by world-renowned music, opera, theater, and dance performers filling all the major venues in the city.

If the Edinburgh International Festival is the parent of British art festivals, then the **Edinburgh Festival Fringe** is its unruly child. The Festival Fringe started in 1947 at the same time as the International Festival, when eight companies that were not invited to

perform in the latter decided to attend anyway. It's now the largest festival of its kind in the world. Its events range from the truly brilliant to the downright awful; you could experience tomorrow's comedy, music, or dance megastar for free, or you could hand over your hard-earned cash to sit through an absolute car crash of a production. The risk is all part of the fun.

Edinburgh festival time can fill almost any artistic need. Besides the International Festival and Festival Fringe, look for the **Edinburgh Art Festival,** the **International Book Festival,** and the **Military Tattoo.**

Don't worry if you are visiting the city at another time; there's always something interesting happening. Other big festivals throughout the year include the **Edinburgh International Science Festival** (Easter), the **Children's Festival** (May to June), the **Film Festival** (June to July), the **Jazz & Blues Festival** (July), the **Storytelling Festival** (October), and, of course, **Edinburgh's Hogmanay** (New Year's Eve).

entertainment program from early morning to midnight. ■TIP→ Be **aware that hotels get booked up months in advance during the Fringe and bargains are virtually impossible to come by, so plan your trip as far in advance as possible.** ⊠ *Edinburgh Festival Fringe Office, 180 High St., Old Town* ☎ *0131/226–0026* ⊕ *www.edfringe.com.*

FAMILY **Edinburgh International Book Festival.** This two-week-long event held every August pulls together a heady mix of authors from around the world, from Nobel laureates to best-selling fiction writers, and gets them talking about their work in a magnificent tent village. There are more than 750 events in total, with the workshops for would-be writers and children proving hugely popular. ⊠ *Edinburgh International Book Festival Admin Office, Charlotte Sq. Gardens, New Town* ☎ *0131/718–5666* ⊕ *www.edbookfest.co.uk.*

FAMILY **Edinburgh International Festival.** Running throughout August, this flagship traditional arts festival attracts international performers and audiences to a celebration of music, dance, theater, opera, and art. Programs, tickets, and reservations are available from the Hub, set within the impressive Victorian-Gothic Tolbooth Kirk. Tickets for the festival go on sale in April, and the big events sell out within the month. However, you'll still be able to purchase tickets for some events during the festival; prices range from around £4 to £60. ⊠ *The Hub, Castlehill, Old Town* ☎ *0131/473–2015* ⊕ *www.eif.co.uk.*

Edinburgh International Film Festival. One of Europe's foremost film festivals, promoting the best of global independent cinema since 1947, this event takes place from mid-June to early July each year. It's a great place for a first screening of a new film—movies from *Billy Elliot* to *Little Miss Sunshine* to the *Hurt Locker* have premiered here. ⊠ *Edinburgh Film Festival Office, 88 Lothian Rd., West End* ☎ *0131/228–4051* ⊕ *www.edfilmfest.org.uk.*

FAMILY **Edinburgh International Science Festival.** Held around Easter each year, the Edinburgh International Science Festival is one of Europe's largest, and aims to make science accessible, interesting, and fun for kids (and adults) through an extensive program of innovative exhibitions, workshops, performances, and screenings. ⊠ *The Hub, Castlehill, Edinburgh* ☎ *0131/553–0320* ⊕ *www.sciencefestival.co.uk.*

Edinburgh Jazz & Blues Festival. Held over a week in late July, the Edinburgh Jazz & Blues Festival attracts world-renowned musicians playing everything from blues-rock to soul music, and brings local enthusiasts out of their living rooms and into the pubs, clubs, and Spiegeltents (pop-up performance spaces) around the city. ⊠ *Edinburgh Jazz and Blues Festival, 89 Giles St., Leith* ☎ *0131/467–5200* ⊕ *www.edinburghjazz-festival.com.*

Fodor's Choice **Edinburgh's Hogmanay.** Nowadays, most capital cities put on decent
★ New Year's celebrations, but Edinburgh's three-day-long Hogmanay festivities are on a whole other level. There's a reason this city is famous around the world as the best place to see in the New Year. Yes, it's winter and yes, it's chilly, but joining a crowd of 80,000 people in a monster street party, complete with big-name rock concerts, torchlight processions, ceilidh dancing, and incredible fireworks, is something you won't forget in a hurry. The headline city center events are ticketed (and can be pricey), but there are free parties happening all over the city. ⊠ *Princes St., Old Town* ⊕ *www.edinburghshogmanay.com* 💷 *£25.*

The Royal Edinburgh Military Tattoo. It may not be art, but The Tattoo (as it's commonly known) is at the very heart of Scottish cultural life. Taking place, like many of the city's festivals, during August, this celebration of martial music features international military bands, gymnastics, and stunt motorcycle teams on the castle esplanade. Each year, 22,000 seats are made available, yet it's always a sellout, so book your place early. If you are lucky enough to get tickets, dress warmly for evening shows and always bring a raincoat; the show goes on in all weathers. ⊠ *Royal Edinburgh Military Tattoo Office, 32 Market St., Old Town* ☎ *0131/225–1188* ⊕ *www.edintattoo.co.uk.*

2

PLANNING YOUR TIME

One of Edinburgh's greatest virtues is its compact size, which means that it is possible to pack a fair bit into even the briefest of visits. The two main areas of interest are the Old Town and the New Town, where you'll find Edinburgh Castle, the Scottish Parliament, Princes Street Gardens, and the National Gallery of Scotland. You can cover the major attractions in one day, but to give the major sights their due, you should allow at least two. You can also choose between the Palace of Holyroodhouse and the important museums of Edinburgh, or explore the Royal Botanic Garden and Holyrood Park. Head down to leafy, villagelike Stockbridge, then immerse yourself in the greenery along the Water of Leith, visiting the Gallery of Modern Art along the way.

Getting out of town is also an option for longer stays. Hop on a bus out to Midlothian to see the magnificent Rosslyn Chapel (it's of interest to more than just *The Da Vinci Code* fans), and visit Crichton Castle, parts of which date back to the 14th century. Consider spending another half day traveling out to South Queensferry to admire the three Forth bridges (including the iconic red railway bridge); then visit palatial Hopetoun House, with its wealth of portraits and fine furniture.

■TIP→ Some attractions have special hours during August, due to the large influx of festivalgoers. If you want to see something special, check the hours ahead of time.

GETTING HERE AND AROUND

AIR TRAVEL

Airlines serving Edinburgh, Scotland's busiest airport, include Air France, Aer Lingus, American, British Airways, Delta, easyJet, flybe, Iberia, Jet2, KLM, Lufthansa, Ryanair, and Virgin Atlantic.

American and United both fly direct to Edinburgh from New York's JFK airport. United also flies direct from Newark. Otherwise, your airline is likely to require a change somewhere in Europe. You could also fly into Glasgow Airport, 50 miles away, or the smaller Glasgow Prestwick, another 30 miles south, but these will add around an hour and a half to your journey.

AIRPORT   Edinburgh Airport is 7 miles west of the city center. Flights bound for Edinburgh depart virtually every hour from London's Gatwick, Heathrow, and City airports.

Airport Information Edinburgh Airport. ⊠ *Glasgow Rd., Ingliston* ☎ *0844/448–8833* ⊕ *www.edinburghairport.com.*

TRANSFERS   There are no rail links to the city center, so the most efficient way to do
FROM   the journey on public transport is by tram; the service runs every 8 to 12
EDINBURGH   minutes and takes about half an hour. Tickets cost £5.50. By bus or car
AIRPORT   you can usually make it to Edinburgh in a half hour, unless you hit the morning (7:30 to 9) or evening (4 to 6) rush hours. Lothian Buses runs an Airlink express service to Waverley railway station via Haymarket that usually takes around half an hour, depending on traffic. Buses run every 10 minutes (every 30 minutes throughout the night); tickets cost £4.50 one way or £7.50 round-trip and are available from the booth beside the bus. Local buses also run between Edinburgh Airport and the

city center every 15 minutes or so from 9 to 5, and roughly every hour during off-peak hours; they are far cheaper—just £1.50 one way—but can take twice as long.

You can arrange for a chauffeur-driven limousine to meet your flight at Edinburgh Airport through Transvercia Chaffeur Drive, Little's, or W L Sleigh Ltd., for upwards of £50.

Taxis are readily available outside the terminal. The trip takes 20 to 30 minutes to the city center, 15 minutes longer during rush hour. The fare is roughly £25. Note that airport taxis picking up fares from the terminal are any color, not the typical black cabs.

Airport Transfer Contacts Little's. ⊠ *1282 Paisley Rd. W, Glasgow* ☎ *0141/883–2111* ⊕ *www.littles.co.uk.* **Transvercia Chaffeur Drive.** ⊠ *The Harland Bldg., Unit 6, Suite 19, Pilrig Heights, Leith* ☎ *0131/555–0459* ⊕ *www. transvercia.co.uk.* **W L Sleigh.** ⊠ *Unit 11A West Craigs, Turnhouse Rd., Edinburgh* ☎ *0131/339–9607* ⊕ *sleigh.co.uk.*

BUS TRAVEL

National Express provides a coach service to and from London and other major towns and cities. The main terminal, Edinburgh Bus Station, is a short walk north of Waverley station, immediately east of St. Andrew Square. Long-distance coaches must be booked in advance online, by phone, or at the terminal. Edinburgh is approximately eight hours by bus from London.

Lothian Buses provides most of the services between Edinburgh and the Lothians and conducts day tours around and beyond the city. First runs additional buses out of Edinburgh into the surrounding area. Megabus offers dirt-cheap fares to selected cities across Scotland.

Bus Contacts First. ☎ *0871/200–2233* ⊕ *www.firstgroup.com.* **Lothian Buses.** ☎ *0131/554–4494* ⊕ *www.lothianbuses.com.* **Megabus.** ☎ *0900/160–0900* ⊕ *www.megabus.com.* **National Express.** ☎ *0871/781–8181* ⊕ *www.nationalexpress.co.uk.*

TRAVEL
WITHIN
EDINBURGH

Lothian Buses is the main operator within Edinburgh. You can buy tickets from the driver on the bus, though you will need the exact fare. Alternatively, you can buy tickets in advance at a Lothian Buses store or on your phone through the *Lothian Buses M-Tickets* app. It's £1.60 for a single ticket or £4 for a *DAYticket,* which allows unlimited one-day travel on the city's buses. A single NIGHTticket costs £3, or you can get unlimited travel from 6 pm to 4:30 am with a DAY&NIGHT ticket (£3.50). The Ridacard (for which you'll need a photo) is valid on all buses for seven days (Sunday through Saturday night) and costs £17; the four-week Rider costs £51. ■TIP➔ **Buses can be packed on Friday and Saturday nights, so you may want to consider a taxi.**

Information Lothian Buses. ⊠ *31 Waverley Bridge, Old Town* ☎ *0131/554–4494* ⊕ *www.lothianbuses.com.*

CAR TRAVEL

It's not necessary to have a car in Edinburgh as the city is quite walkable and well linked by an efficient bus system. Driving in Edinburgh has its quirks and pitfalls—particularly at the height of festival season.

POLITICAL POWER IN SCOTLAND

Three centuries after the Union of Parliaments with England in 1707, Edinburgh is once again the seat of a Scottish Parliament. A modern Parliament building, designed by Spanish architect Enric Miralles, stands adjacent to the Palace of Holyroodhouse, at the foot of the Royal Mile.

Some first-time visitors to Scotland may be surprised that the country still has a capital city at all, perhaps believing the seat of government was drained of its resources and power after the union with England—but far from it. The Union of Parliaments brought with it a set of political partnerships—such as separate legal, ecclesiastical, and educational systems—that Edinburgh assimilated and integrated with its own institutions.

In a hard-fought 2014 referendum, Scottish voters rejected full separation from the United Kingdom.

However, the ensuing debate led to even further powers being transferred from London to Edinburgh, and Scotland now has significantly more control over its own affairs than at any time since 1707. The 129 Members of the Scottish Parliament (MSPs), of whom almost half are women, have extensive powers in Scotland over education, health, housing, transportation, economic development, the environment and more. Foreign policy, defense, and economic policy remain under the jurisdiction of the U.K. government in London.

Following Brexit (the British departure from the European Union), First Minister of Scotland Nicola Sturgeon has formally requested a second referendum on Scottish independence, proposed for late 2018 or early 2019. However, at the time of this writing, it is unknown whether this will be approved by the U.K. government.

2

Metered parking in the city center is scarce and expensive, and the local traffic wardens are a feisty, alert bunch. Note that illegally parked cars are routinely towed away, and getting your car back will be expensive. After 6 pm the parking situation improves considerably, and you may manage to find a space quite near your hotel, even downtown. If you park on a yellow line or in a resident's parking bay, be prepared to move your car by 8 the following morning, when the rush hour gets under way. Parking lots are clearly signposted; overnight parking is expensive and not always permitted.

TAXI TRAVEL

Taxi stands can be found throughout the city, mostly in the New Town. The following are the most convenient: the west end of Princes Street; South St. David Street and North St. Andrew Street (both just off St. Andrew Square); Waverley Mall; Waterloo Place; and Lauriston Place. Alternatively, hail any taxi displaying an illuminated "for hire" sign.

TRAIN TRAVEL

Edinburgh's main train hub, Waverley station, is downtown, below Waverley Bridge and around the corner from the unmistakable spire of the Scott Monument. Travel time from Edinburgh to London by train is as little as 4½ hours for the fastest service.

Edinburgh's other main station is Haymarket, about four minutes (by rail) west of Waverley. Most Glasgow and other western and northern services stop here.

Train Contacts National Rail Enquiries. ☎ *08457/484950* ⊕ *www.nationalrail. co.uk.* **ScotRail.** ☎ *0344/811–0141* ⊕ *www.scotrail.co.uk.*

TRAM TRAVEL

Absent since 1956, trams returned to the streets of Edinburgh in 2014. The 8½-mile stretch of track runs between Edinburgh Airport in the west to York Place in the east. Useful stops for travelers include Haymarket, Princes Street, and St. Andrew Square (for Waverley station). Tickets are £1.60 for a single journey in the "City Zone" (which is every stop excluding the airport), or £5.50 to get to or from the airport. Day tickets, allowing unlimited travel, cost £4 in the City Zone and £9 including the airport.

Tram Contact Edinburgh Trams. ☎ *0131/555–6363* ⊕ *www.edinburghtrams. co.uk.*

TOURS

ORIENTATION TOURS

One good way to get oriented in Edinburgh is to take a bus tour. If you want to get to know the area around Edinburgh, Rabbie's Trail Burners leads small groups on several different excursions.

Edinburgh Bus Tours. Explore every corner of Edinburgh with this company's range of bus tours. The most popular are the Edinburgh Tour, which mainly covers Old Town sights including Edinburgh Castle, the Royal Mile, and the Palace of Holyroodhouse; and the Majestic Tour, which explores the New Town and farther corners of the city, including the Royal Yacht *Britannia* at Leith and the Royal Botanic Garden. Buses depart from Waverley Bridge, with each tour lasting an hour. ■TIP➔ **If you plan more than one bus tour during a weekend, buy a money-saving Grand 48 ticket.** ⊠ *Waverley Bridge, New Town* ☎ *0131/220–0770* ⊕ *www.edinburghtour.com* ⊠ *From £15.*

Rabbie's Trail Burners. Venture farther afield from Edinburgh on day trips run by this cheerful company. Its minibuses will take you a surprisingly long way and back in a day, with sights including Loch Ness, St. Andrews, Rosslyn Chapel, and Loch Lomond National Park. Groups are kept to a guaranteed maximum of 16, giving these a less impersonal feel than some of the big enterprises. ■TIP➔ **Book online for a discount.** ⊠ *207 High St., Edinburgh* ☎ *0131/226–3133* ⊕ *www.rabbies. com* ⊠ *From £28.*

PERSONAL GUIDES

Scottish Tourist Guides. This organization can supply guides (in 19 languages) who are fully qualified and will meet clients at any point of entry into the United Kingdom or Scotland. Guides can also tailor tours to your interests. ☎ *01786/451953* ⊕ *www.stga.co.uk* ⊠ *From £140.*

WALKING TOURS

The Cadies and Witchery Tours. Spooky tours tracing Edinburgh's ghouls, gore, and mysteries commence outside the Witchery Restaurant. The Cadies and Witchery Tours, a member of the Scottish Tourist Guides

Association, has built a reputation for combining entertainment and historical accuracy in its lively and enthusiastic Murder and Mystery and (in summer only) Ghosts and Gore tours. Both take you through the narrow Old Town alleyways and closes, with costumed guides and other theatrical characters popping up along the route. ✉ *The Witchery, 352 Castlehill, Old Town* ☎ *0131/225–6745* ⊕ *www.witcherytours. com* ✉ *From £10.*

The Edinburgh Literary Pub Tour. Professional actors invoke local literary characters while taking you around some of the city's most hallowed watering holes on these lively and informative tours. The experience is led by "Clart and McBrain"—one a bohemian, the other an intellectual—who regale you with tales of the literary past of Edinburgh's Old and New Towns. The experience is so witty and fun that you might just forget you're learning something along the way. Tours run daily from May to September, Thursday to Sunday in April and October, Friday and Sunday from January to March, and Friday only in November and December. Tours meet outside the Beehive Inn. ✉ *The Beehive Inn, 18–20 Grassmarket, Edinburgh* ☎ *0800/169–7410* ⊕ *www.edinburghliterarypubtour.co.uk* ✉ *£14.*

VISITOR INFORMATION

The VisitScotland Edinburgh iCentre, located next to Waverley station (follow the signs in the station), offers an accommodation-booking service, along with regular tourist information services. There's also a VisitScotland Edinburgh Airport iCentre, for any questions you have upon arrival in the city.

Visitor Information VisitScotland Edinburgh Airport iCentre. ✉ *East Terminal, Edinburgh International Airport, Edinburgh* ☎ *0131/473-3690* ⊕ *www. visitscotland.com.*

EXPLORING EDINBURGH

Edinburgh's Old Town, which bears a great symbolic weight as the "heart of Scotland's capital," is a boon for lovers of atmosphere and history. In contrast, if you appreciate the unique architectural heritage of the city's Enlightenment, then the New Town's for you. If you belong to both categories, don't worry—the Old and New Towns are only yards apart. Princes Street runs east–west along the north edge of the Princes Street Gardens. Explore the main thoroughfares, but don't forget to get lost among the tiny *wynds* and *closes*: old medieval alleys that connect the winding streets.

Like most cities, Edinburgh incorporates small communities within its boundaries, and many of these are as rewarding to explore as Old Town and New Town. Dean Village, for instance, even though it's close to the New Town, has a character all its own. Duddingston, just southeast of Arthur's Seat, has all the feel of a country village. Then there's Corstorphine, to the west of the city center, famous for being the site of Murrayfield, Scotland's international rugby stadium. Edinburgh's port, Leith, sits on the shore of the Firth of Forth, and throbs with smart bars and restaurants.

OLD TOWN

East of Edinburgh Castle, the historic castle esplanade becomes the street known as the Royal Mile, leading from the castle down through Old Town to the Palace of Holyroodhouse. The Mile, as it's called, is actually made up of one thoroughfare that bears, in consecutive sequence, different names—Castlehill, Lawnmarket, Parliament Square, High Street, and Canongate. This thoroughfare, and the streets and passages that wind off it on both sides, really *were* Edinburgh until the 18th century saw expansions to the south and north. Everybody lived here: the richer folk on the lower floors of houses; the less well-to-do families on the middle floors; and the poor highest up.

Time and progress (of a sort) have swept away some of the narrow closes and tall tenements of the Old Town, but enough survive for you to be able to imagine the original profile of Scotland's capital. There are many guided tours of the area, or you can simply stroll around at your leisure. The latter is often a better choice in summer, when tourists pack the area and large guided groups have trouble making their way through the crowds.

TOP ATTRACTIONS

Arthur's Seat. The high point of 640-acre Holyrood Park is this famously spectacular viewpoint. You'll have seen it before—countless photos have been snapped from this very spot. The "seat" in question is actually the 822-foot-high plateau of a small mountain. A ruined church—the 15th-century Chapel of St. Anthony—adds to its impossible picturesqueness. There are various starting points for the walk, but one of the most pleasant begins at the Scottish Parliament building. Cross the road from Parliament, skirt around the parking lot, cross a second road, and join the gently rising path to the left (rather than the steeper fork to the right). At a moderate pace, this climb takes around 45 minutes up and 30 minutes down, and is easy so long as you're reasonably fit. Even if you aren't, there are plenty of places to stop for a rest and to admire the views along the way. A faster—though less beautiful—way to reach the summit is to drive to the small parking area at Dunsapie Loch, on Queen's Road, then follow the footpath up the hill; this walk takes about 20 minutes. ⊠ *Queen's Dr., Old Town.*

Craigmillar Castle. This handsome medieval ruin, only 3 miles south of the city center, is the archetypal Scottish fortress: forbidding, powerful, and laden with atmosphere. It is best known for its association with Mary, Queen of Scots, as, during a stay here in 1563, her courtiers (successfully) hatched a plot to murder her troublesome husband, Henry Stuart. Rumors that Mary was involved were never substantiated, though they contributed to her ultimate downfall. Today Craigmillar is one of the most impressive ruined castles in Scotland. The 15th-century tower and courtyard are in excellent condition, including a well-preserved great hall. Climb the tower for a superb view across the city. Look out for the unusually ornate defensive arrow slits, shaped like inverted keyholes. ⊠ *Craigmillar Castle Rd., South Side* ☎ *0131/661–4445* ⊕ *www. historicenvironment.scot* ⊠ *£6* ⊗ *Closed Thurs. and Fri. in Oct.–Apr.*

FAMILY **Dynamic Earth.** Using state-of-the-art technology, the 11 theme galleries at this interactive science museum educate and entertain as they explore the wonders of the planet, from polar regions to tropical rain forests. Geological history, from the big bang to the unknown future, is also examined, all topped off with a 360-degree-dome movie-theater experience. Book tickets online for a 10% discount. ⊠ *112–116 Holyrood Rd., Old Town* ☎ *0131/550–7800* ⊕ *www.dynamicearth.co.uk* ☞ *£15 at door; £13.50 online* ⊙ *Closed Mon. and Tues. in Nov.–Mar.*

FAMILY
Fodor'sChoice
★

Edinburgh Castle. The crowning glory of the Scottish capital, Edinburgh Castle is popular not only for its pivotal role in Scottish history, but also because of the spectacular views from its battlements: on a clear day the vistas stretch all the way to the "kingdom" of Fife. You need at least three hours to see everything it has to offer (especially if you're a military history buff), though if you're in a rush, its main highlights can be squeezed into an hour and a half.

You enter across the **Esplanade,** the huge forecourt built in the 18th century as a parade ground. The area comes alive with color and music each August when it's used for the Military Tattoo, a festival of magnificently outfitted marching bands and regiments. Head over the drawbridge and through the gatehouse, past the guards, and you'll find the rough stone walls of the **Half-Moon Battery,** where the one-o'clock gun is fired every day in an impressively anachronistic ceremony; these curving ramparts give Edinburgh Castle its distinctive silhouette. Climb up through a second gateway and you come to the oldest surviving building in the complex, the tiny 11th-century **St. Margaret's Chapel,** named in honor of Saxon queen Margaret (1046–93), who persuaded her husband, King Malcolm III (circa 1031–93), to move his court from Dunfermline to Edinburgh. The story goes that Edinburgh's environs—the Lothians—were occupied by Anglian settlers with whom the queen felt more at home, as opposed to the Celts who surrounded Dunfermline. The **Crown Room,** a must-see, contains the "Honours of Scotland"—the crown, scepter, and sword that once graced the Scottish monarch—as well as the **Stone of Scone,** upon which Scottish monarchs once sat to be crowned. In the section now called **Queen Mary's Apartments,** Mary, Queen of Scots, gave birth to James VI of Scotland. The **Great Hall,** which held Scottish Parliament meetings until 1840, displays arms and armor under an impressive vaulted, beamed ceiling.

Military features of interest include the **Scottish National War Memorial,** the **Scottish United Services Museum,** and the famous 15th-century Belgian-made cannon Mons Meg. This enormous piece of artillery has been silent since 1682, when it exploded while firing a salute for the Duke of York; it now stands in an ancient hall behind the Half-Moon Battery. Contrary to what you may hear from locals, it's not Mons Meg but the battery's gun that goes off with a bang every weekday at 1 pm, frightening visitors and reminding Edinburghers to check their watches.

■ **TIP→** Avoid the queues by buying tickets online, which you can pick up from one of the automated collection points at the entrance. ⊠ *Castle Esplanade and Castlehill, Old Town* ☎ *0131/225–9846 Edinburgh Castle, 0131/225–9846* ⊕ *www.edinburghcastle.gov.uk* ☞ *£17.*

Edinburgh's Castle Fit for a King

Archaeological investigations have established that the rock on which Edinburgh Castle stands was inhabited as far back as 1,000 BC, in the latter part of the Bronze Age. There have been fortifications here since the mysterious tribal Picts first used it as a stronghold in the 3rd and 4th centuries AD. Anglian invaders from northern England dislodged the Picts in AD 452, and for the next 1,300 years the site saw countless battles and skirmishes.

In the castle you'll hear the story of how Randolph, Earl of Moray and nephew of freedom fighter Robert the Bruce, scaled the heights one dark night in 1313, surprised the English guard, and recaptured the castle for the Scots. During this battle he destroyed every one of the castle's buildings except for St. Margaret's Chapel, dating from around 1076, so that successive Stewart kings had to rebuild the castle bit by bit.

The castle has been held over time by Scots and Englishmen, Catholics and Protestants, soldiers and royalty. In the 16th century Mary, Queen of Scots, gave birth here to the future James VI of Scotland (1566–1625), who was also to rule England as James I. In 1573 it was the last fortress to support Mary's claim as the rightful Catholic queen of Britain, causing the castle to be virtually destroyed by English artillery fire.

✕ **Redcoat Café.** Enjoy lunch or afternoon tea with panoramic views of the city at the Redcoat Café. Cakes, sandwiches, soups, and drinks are all available at reasonable prices. **Known for:** seasonal dishes; spectacular views. ⊠ *Edinburgh Castle, Castlehill, Old Town* ☎ *0131/225–9746* ⊕ *www.edinburghcastle.gov.uk.*

High Kirk of St. Giles (*St Giles' Cathedral*). St. Giles, which lies about one-third of the way along the Royal Mile from Edinburgh Castle, is one of the city's principal churches. However, don't expect a rival to Paris's Notre Dame or London's Westminster Abbey; it's more like a large parish church than a great European cathedral. There has been a church here since AD 854, although most of the present structure dates from either 1120 or 1829, when the church was restored.

The tower, with its stone crown 161 feet above the ground, was completed between 1495 and 1500. Inside the church stands a life-size statue of the Scot whose spirit still dominates the place—the great religious reformer and preacher John Knox. But the most elaborate feature is the **Chapel of the Order of the Thistle,** built onto the southeast corner of the church in 1911 for the exclusive use of Scotland's only chivalric order, the Most Ancient and Noble Order of the Thistle. It bears the belligerent national motto "nemo me impune lacessit" ("No one provokes me with impunity"). Look out for the carved wooden angel playing bagpipes. ⊠ *High St., Old Town* ☎ *0131/225–9442* ⊕ *www.stgilescathedral.org.uk* ⊠ *Free; suggested donation £3; photography permit £2.*

High Street. The High Street (one of the five streets that make up the Royal Mile) is home to an array of impressive buildings and sights, including some hidden historic relics. Near Parliament Square, look on the west side for a **heart** mosaic set in cobbles. This marks the site of the vanished Old Tolbooth, the center of city life from the 15th century until the building's demolition in 1817. The ancient municipal building was used as a prison and a site of public execution, so you may witness a local spitting on the heart as he walks by—for good luck.

Just outside Parliament House lies the **Mercat Cross** (*mercat* means "market"), a great landmark of Old Town life. It was an old mercantile center, where royal proclamations were—and are still—read. Most of the present cross is comparatively modern, dating from the time of William Gladstone (1809–98), the great Victorian prime minister and rival of Benjamin Disraeli (1804–81). Across High Street from the High Kirk of St. Giles stands the **City Chambers,** now the seat of local government. Built by John Fergus, who adapted a design of John Adam in 1753, the chambers were originally known as the Royal Exchange and intended to be where merchants and lawyers could conduct business. Note how the building drops 11 stories to Cockburn Street on its north side.

A *tron* is a weigh beam used in public weigh houses, and the **Tron Kirk** was named after a salt tron that used to stand nearby. The *kirk* (church) itself was built after 1633, when St. Giles's became an Episcopal cathedral for a brief time. In 1693, a minister here delivered an often-quoted prayer: "Lord, hae mercy on a' [all] fools and idiots, and particularly on the Magistrates of Edinburgh." ⊠ *Between Lawnmarket and Canongate, Old Town.*

Fodor's Choice
★

Kirk of the Greyfriars. Greyfriars Church, built on the site of a medieval monastery, was where the National Covenant was signed in 1638. The covenant, which declared the Presbyterian Church in Scotland independent of the monarch, plunged Scotland into decades of civil war— informative panels here tell the full story.

However, the real attraction here is the sprawling, hillside graveyard, surely one of the most evocative in Europe. Its old, tottering tombstones mark the graves of some of Scotland's most respected heroes and despised villains. Some of the larger tombs are arranged in avenues; a few are closed off, but others you can wander. It's a hugely atmospheric place to explore, especially at twilight. Look out for two rare surviving *mortsafes*: iron cages erected around graves in the early 1800s to prevent the theft of corpses for sale to medical schools. Nearby, at the corner of George IV Bridge and Candlemaker Row, stands one of Scotland's most photographed sites: the statue of Greyfriars Bobby, a Skye terrier who supposedly spent 14 years guarding the grave of his departed owner. ⊠ *Greyfriars Pl., Old Town* ☎ *0131/225–1900* ⊕ *www.greyfriarskirk.com* ⊠ *Free.*

FAMILY
Fodor's Choice
★

National Museum of Scotland. This museum traces the country's fascinating story from the oldest fossils to the most recent popular culture, making it a must-see for first-time visitors to Scotland. Two of the most famous treasures are the Lewis Chessmen, 11 intricately carved 12th-century ivory chess pieces found on one of Scotland's Western Isles, and Dolly the sheep, the world's first cloned mammal and biggest ovine celebrity. A dramatic, cryptlike entrance gives way to the light-filled, birdcage wonders of the Victorian grand hall and the upper

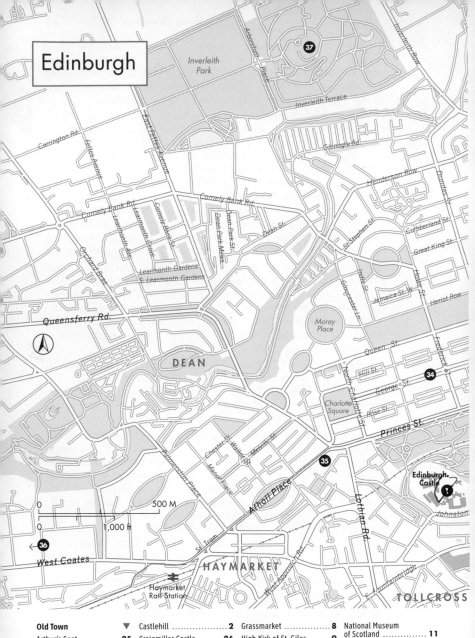

Edinburgh

Inverleith Park

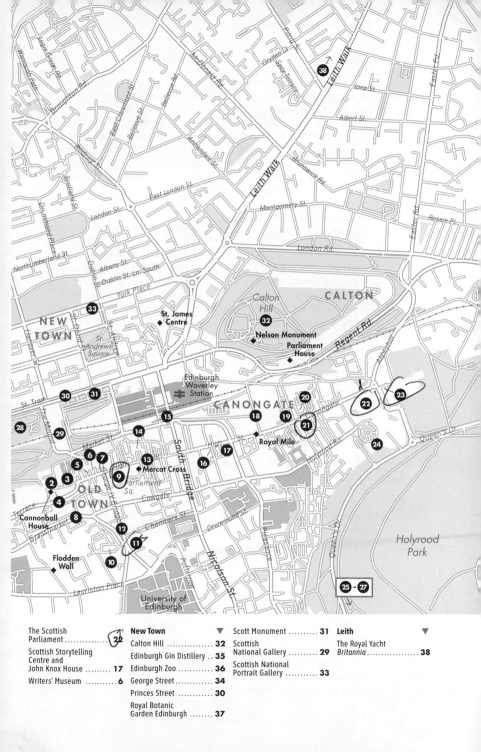

THE BUILDING OF EDINBURGH

Towering over the city, Edinburgh Castle was actually built over the plug of an ancient volcano. Many millennia ago, an eastward-grinding glacier encountered the tough basalt core of the volcano and swept around it, scouring steep cliffs and leaving a trail of matter. This material formed a ramp gently leading down from the rocky summit. On this *crag* and *tail* would grow the city of Edinburgh and its castle.

CASTLE, WALLED TOWN, AND HOLYROODHOUSE

By the 12th century, Edinburgh had become a walled town, still perched on the hill. Its shape was becoming clearer: like a fish with its head at the castle, its backbone running down the ridge, and its ribs leading briefly off on either side. The backbone gradually became the continuous thoroughfare now known as the Royal Mile, and the ribs became the closes (alleyways), some still surviving, that were the scene of many historic incidents.

By the early 15th century, Edinburgh had become the undisputed capital of Scotland. The bitter defeat of Scotland at Flodden in 1513, when Scotland aligned itself with France against England, caused a new defensive city wall to be built. Though the castle escaped destruction, the city was burned by the English Earl of Hertford under orders from King Henry VIII (1491–1547). This was during a time known as the "Rough Wooing," when Henry was trying to coerce the Scots into allowing the young Mary, Queen of Scots (1542–87), to marry his son Edward. The plan failed and Mary married Francis, the Dauphin of France.

By 1561, when Mary returned from France already widowed, the guesthouse of the Abbey of Holyrood had grown to become the Palace of Holyroodhouse, replacing Edinburgh Castle as the main royal residence. Her legacy to the city included the destruction of most of the earliest buildings of Edinburgh Castle.

ENLIGHTENMENT AND THE CITY

In the trying decades after the union with England in 1707, many influential Scots, both in Edinburgh and elsewhere, went through an identity crisis. Out of the 18th-century difficulties, however, grew the Scottish Enlightenment, during which educated Scots made great strides in medicine, economics, and science.

Changes came to the cityscape too. By the mid-18th century, it had become the custom for wealthy Scottish landowners to spend the winter in the Old Town of Edinburgh, in town houses huddled between the high Castle Rock and the Royal Palace below. Cross-fertilized in coffeehouses and taverns, intellectual notions flourished among a people determined to remain Scottish despite their Parliament being dissolved. One result was a campaign to expand and beautify the city, to give it a look worthy of its future nickname, the Athens of the North. Thus, the New Town of Edinburgh was built, with broad streets and gracious buildings creating a harmony that even today's throbbing traffic cannot obscure.

galleries. Other exhibition highlights include the hanging hippo and sea creatures of the Wildlife Panorama, beautiful Viking brooches, Pictish stones, and Queen Mary's *clarsach* (harp). Take the elevator to the lovely rooftop terrace for spectacular views of Edinburgh Castle and the city below. ✉ *Chambers St., Old Town* ☎ *0300/123–6789* ⊕ *www. nms.ac.uk* ⌨ *Free.*

Fodor's Choice **Palace of Holyroodhouse.** Onetime haunt of Mary, Queen of Scots, with
★ a long history of gruesome murder, destructive fire, and power-hungry personalities, the Palace of Holyroodhouse is now Queen Elizabeth's official residence in Scotland. A doughty, impressive palace standing at the foot of the Royal Mile, it's built around a graceful, lawned central court at the end of Canongate. And when royals are not in residence, you can take a tour. There's plenty to see here, so make sure you have at least two hours to tour the palace, gardens, and the ruins of the 12th-century abbey; pick up the free audio guide for the full experience.

Many monarchs, including Charles II, Queen Victoria, and George V, have left their mark on the rooms here, but it's Mary, Queen of Scots, whose spirit looms largest. Perhaps the most memorable room is the chamber in which David Rizzio (1533–66), secretary to Mary, met a nasty end in 1566, stabbed more than 50 times by the henchmen of her second husband, Lord Darnley. Darnley himself was murdered the next year, clearing the way for the queen's marriage to her lover, the Earl of Bothwell.

The **King James Tower** is the oldest surviving section of the palace, containing Mary's rooms on the second floor, and Lord Darnley's rooms below. Though much has been altered, there are fine fireplaces, paneling, tapestries, and 18th- and 19th-century furnishings throughout. At the south end of the palace front, you'll find the **Royal Dining Room,** and along the south side is the **Throne Room,** now used for social and ceremonial occasions.

At the back of the palace is the **King's Bedchamber.** The 150-foot-long **Great Picture Gallery,** on the north side, displays the portraits of 110 Scottish monarchs. These were commissioned by Charles II, who was eager to demonstrate his Scottish ancestry—but most of the people depicted are entirely fictional, and the likenesses of several others were invented and simply given the names of real people. The **Queen's Gallery,** in a former church and school at the entrance to the palace, holds rotating exhibits from the Royal Collection. There is a separate admission charge.

Holyroodhouse has its origins in an Augustinian monastery founded by David I (1084–1153) in 1128. In the 15th and 16th centuries, Scottish royalty, preferring the comforts of the abbey to drafty Edinburgh Castle, settled into Holyroodhouse, expanding the buildings until the palace eclipsed the monastery. However, you can still walk around some evocative abbey ruins.

After the Union of the Crowns in 1603, when the Scottish royal court packed its bags and decamped to England, the building began to fall into disrepair. It was Charles II (1630–85) who rebuilt Holyrood in the architectural style of Louis XIV (1638–1715), and this is the style you see today. Queen Victoria (1819–1901) and her grandson King George V (1865–1936) renewed interest in the palace, and the buildings were refurbished and again made suitable for royal residence. ⊠ *Canongate, Old Town* ☎ *0131/123–7306* ⊕ *www.royalcollection.org.uk* ⬚ *£12.50; £17.50 includes Queen's Gallery; £21.50 includes garden history tour.*

FAMILY **The Real Mary King's Close.** Buried beneath the City Chambers, this narrow, cobbled close, or lane, provides a glimpse into a very different Edinburgh. It was once a busy open-air thoroughfare with hundreds of residents and a lively market, but in 1753 it was sealed off when the Royal Exchange (now the City Chambers) was built on top. Today, costumed guides take you around the claustrophobic remains of the shops and houses, describing life here for the residents from plague and quarantine to rivers of sewage, as well as the odd murder mystery and ghost story. But for all the (somewhat over-the-top) theatricality, the real highlights here are historical; the sealed-in street is a truly fascinating insight into 17th-century Edinburgh. ⊠ *2 Warriston's Cl., Old Town* ☎ *0131/225–0672* ⊕ *www.realmarykingsclose.com* ⬚ *£14.75.*

The Scottish Parliament. Scotland's now-iconic Parliament building is starkly modernist, with irregular curves and angles that mirror the twisting shapes of the surrounding landscape. Stylistically, it is about as far removed from Westminster as can be. Originally conceived by the late Catalan architect Enric Miralles, and completed by his widow, Benedetta Tagliabue, the structure's artistry is most apparent when you step inside, where the gentle slopes, forest's worth of oak, polished concrete and granite, and walls of glass create an understated magnificence. Take a free guided tour to see the main hall and debating chamber, a committee room, and other areas of the building, or choose a specialist subject for your tour, from history to literature to art. All tour reservations must be made online. Call well in advance to get a free ticket to view Parliament in action. ⊠ *Horse Wynd, Old Town* ☎ *0131/348–5000* ⊕ *www.scottish.parliament.uk* ⊙ *Closed Sun.*

Fodor'sChoice **Scottish Storytelling Centre and John Knox House.** The stripped-down, low-
★ fi, traditional art of storytelling has had something of a resurgence in Britain over the last decade or so, and there are few places better than this to experience a master storyteller in full flow. Housed in a modern building that manages to blend seamlessly with the historic structures on either side, the center hosts a year-round program of storytelling, theater, music, and literary events. A café serves lunch, tea, and home-baked cakes.

The center's storytellers also hold tours of John Knox House next door. It isn't certain that the religious reformer ever lived here, but there's evidence he died here in 1572. Mementos of his life are on view inside, and the distinctive dwelling gives you a glimpse of what Old Town life was like in the 16th century—projecting upper floors were once commonplace along the Royal Mile. ⊠ *43-45 High St., Old Town* ☎ *0131/556–9579* ⊕ *www.tracscotland.org/scottish-storytelling-centre* ⬚ *Storytelling Centre: free; John Knox House: £5* ⊙ *Closed Sun. in Sept.–June.*

A GOOD WALK IN THE OLD TOWN

A perfect place to start your stroll through the Old Town is Edinburgh Castle. After exploring its extensive complex of buildings and admiring the view from the battlements, set off down the first part of the Royal Mile. The Camera Obscura's Outlook Tower affords more splendid views of the city. The six-story tenement known as Gladstone's Land, a survivor of 16th-century domestic life, is on the left as you head east. Near Gladstone's Land, down another close, stands the Writers' Museum, in a fine example of 17th-century urban architecture called Lady Stair's House. Farther down on the right are the Tolbooth Kirk (a *tolbooth* was a town hall or prison, and *kirk* means "church") and Upper Bow.

Turn right down George IV Bridge to reach the historic Grassmarket, where parts of the old city walls still stand. Turn left up Candlemaker Row and you can see the Kirk of the Greyfriars, and the little statue of faithful Greyfriars Bobby. On Chambers Street, at the foot of George IV Bridge, are the impressive galleries of the National Museum of Scotland.

Returning to the junction of George IV Bridge with the Royal Mile, turn right (east) down High Street to visit the old Parliament House; the High Kirk of St. Giles; the Mercat Cross; and the elegant City Chambers. Beneath the chambers is the eerie Real Mary King's Close, a lane that was closed off in the 17th century when the bubonic plague struck the city.

Walk farther down the Mile, past the Scottish Storytelling Centre, John Knox House, and the Museum of Childhood, until you see a distinctive clock jutting out overhead: this is Canongate Tolbooth. The Canongate Kirk awaits next door, while the Museum of Edinburgh stands opposite. This walk draws to a close, as it started, on a high note, at the spectacular Palace of Holyroodhouse.

TIMING

This Old Town walk can be completed in an hour if you're content to see everything from the outside, or can fill a whole weekend if you want to head inside each attraction—plan your time accordingly.

WORTH NOTING

FAMILY **Camera Obscura and World of Illusions.** View Edinburgh like a Victorian at the city's 19th-century camera obscura. Head up Outlook Tower for the headline attraction—an optical instrument that affords live bird's-eye views of the city, illuminated onto a concave table. It's been wowing visitors since 1853, and yet it retains a magical quality that can captivate even the most cynical smartphone-toting teen. After you've seen the camera obscura and enjoyed the rooftop views, head down to explore five more floors of interactive optical illusions. They are guaranteed to keep the kids entertained and educated for an hour or two. ⊠ *549 Castlehill, Old Town* ☎ *0131/226–3709* ⊕ *www.camera-obscura.co.uk* 🖃 *£15.*

Canongate. This section of the Royal Mile takes its name from the canons who once ran the abbey at Holyrood. Canongate—in Scots, *gate* means "street"—was originally an independent town, or *burgh*, another Scottish term used to refer to a community with trading rights granted by the monarch. In this area you'll find **Canongate Kirk** and its graveyard, **Canongate Tolbooth,** as well as the **Museum of Edinburgh.** ⊠ *Royal Mile, between High St. and Abbey Strand, Old Town.*

Canongate Kirk. This unadorned Church of Scotland building, built in 1688, is best known for its graveyard. It is the final resting place of some notable Scots, including economist Adam Smith (1723–90), author of *The Wealth of Nations* (1776), Dugald Stewart (1753–1828), the leading European philosopher of his time, and the undervalued Scottish poet Robert Fergusson (1750–74). The fact Fergusson's grave is even marked is due to the far more famous Robert Burns (1759–96), who commissioned an architect—called, incidentally, Robert Burn—to design a marker. Burn also designed the Nelson Monument on Calton Hill, visible from the graveyard.

Against the eastern wall of the graveyard is a bronze sculpture of the head of Mrs. Agnes McLehose, the "Clarinda" in the passionate letters sent to and from Robert Burns. The curiously literary affair ended when Burns left Edinburgh in 1788 to take up a farm tenancy and to marry Jean Armour. ⊠ *153 Canongate, Old Town* ☎ *0131/556–3515* ⊕ *canongatekirk.org.uk* ⊘ *Closed Oct.–Apr.*

Canongate Tolbooth and People's Story Museum. Nearly every city and town in Scotland once had a tolbooth. Originally a customhouse, where tolls were gathered, it soon came to mean town hall and later prison, as there were detention cells in the cellar. The building where Canongate's town council once met now has a museum, the **People's Story Museum,** which focuses on the lives of everyday folk from the 18th century to today. Exhibits describe how Canongate once bustled with the activities of the tradespeople needed to supply life's essentials. There are also displays on the politics, health care, and leisure time (such as it was) in days of yore. Other exhibits leap forward in time to show, for example, a typical 1940s kitchen. ⊠ *163 Canongate, Old Town* ☎ *0131/529–4057* ⊕ *www.edinburghmuseums.org.uk* ⊘ *Closed Mon. and Tues.*

Castlehill. This street, the upper portion of the Royal Mile, was where alleged witches were brought in the 16th century to be burned at the stake; a bronze plaque recalls this history. The cannonball embedded in the west gable of Castlehill's **Cannonball House** was, according to legend, fired from the castle during the Jacobite Rebellion of 1745, led by Bonnie Prince Charlie (1720–88)—though the truth is probably that it was installed there deliberately in 1681 as a height marker for Edinburgh's first piped water-supply system. Atop the Gothic **Tolbooth Kirk,** built in 1844 for the General Assembly of the Church of Scotland, stands the tallest spire in the city, at 240 feet. The church now houses the cheery Edinburgh Festival offices and a pleasant café known as **The Hub.**

The **Upper Bow,** running from Lawnmarket to Victoria Street, was once the main route westward from the town and castle. Before Victoria Street was built in the late 19th century, the Upper Bow led down into a narrow dark thoroughfare coursing between a canyon of tenements. All traffic struggled up and down this steep slope from the Grassmarket, which joins West Bow at its lower end. ⊠ *East of Esplanade and west of Lawnmarket, Old Town.*

**OFF THE
BEATEN
PATH**

Duddingston Village. Tucked behind Arthur's Seat, and about a 45-minute walk through Holyrood Park from the foot of the Royal Mile, lies this small community, which still has the feel of a country village. **The Duddingston Kirk** has a Norman doorway and a watchtower that was built to keep body snatchers out of the graveyard. The church and adjoining garden overlook **Duddingston Loch,** popular with bird-watchers. Pathways meander down to lochside **Thomson's Tower,** an octagonal tower built by William Playfair in 1825 as a curling clubhouse. Recently restored, it's home to a small museum. Moments away is Edinburgh's oldest hostelry, the **Sheep Heid Inn,** which serves a wide selection of beers and hearty food. For £12.50 an hour during the day, you can have a go on the oldest skittle (bowling) alley in Scotland—once frequented, it's said, by Mary, Queen of Scots. ⊠ *Duddingston Low Rd., Duddingston.*

Fruitmarket Gallery. This contemporary gallery behind Waverley station showcases cutting-edge art, mostly from Europe and the United States, including world-renowned artists like Louise Bourgeois, Eva Hesse, and Dieter Roth. Turner Prize–winning artist Martin Creed was also commissioned by the gallery to create a piece of public art nearby—walk up or down the Scotsman Steps to see his colorful marble creation. ■**TIP→ Free, hour-long tasting tours happen every Saturday at 2.** ⊠ *45 Market St., Old Town* ☎ *0131/225–2383* ⊕ *www.fruitmarket.co.uk.*

George IV Bridge. Here's a curiosity—a bridge that most of its users don't ever realize is a bridge. With buildings closely packed on both sides, George IV Bridge can feel to many like a regular Edinburgh street, but for those forewarned, the truth is plain to see. At the corner of the bridge stands one of the most photographed sculptures in Scotland, *Greyfriars Bobby.* This statue pays tribute to the legendarily loyal Skye terrier who kept vigil beside his master's grave for 14 years after he died in 1858. The 1961 Walt Disney film *Greyfriars Bobby* tells a version of the heartrending tale. ⊠ *Bank St. and Lawnmarket, Old Town.*

Gladstone's Land. This narrow, six-story tenement, situated next to the Assembly Hall, is one of the oldest buildings on the Royal Mile. It's a survivor from the early 17th century, and now stands as a re-creation of the living conditions of the time. Rooms are decorated in authentic period furnishings, and the sense of how cramped life must have been, even for the moderately successful, is deftly portrayed. Typical Scottish architectural features are evident on two floors, including an arcaded ground floor (even in the city center, livestock sometimes inhabited the ground floor) and some magnificent painted ceilings. Look out for the lovely spinet in the drawing room; the ingeniously designed instrument, resembling a space-saving piano, plucks strings rather than strikes them, producing a resonantly baroque sound. ⊠ *477B Lawnmarket, Old Town* ☎ *0131/226–5856* ⊕ *www.nts.org.uk/property/gladstones-land* ⊠ *£7.*

Grassmarket. For centuries an agricultural marketplace, Grassmarket now is the site of numerous shops, bars, and restaurants, making it a hive of activity at night. Sections of the Old Town wall can be traced on the north side by a series of steps that ascend from Grassmarket to

GRASSMARKET GALLOWS

Grassmarket's history is long and gory. The **cobbled cross** at the east end marks the site of the town gallows. Among those hanged here were many 17th-century Covenanters, members of the Church of Scotland who rose up against Charles I's efforts to enforce Anglican or "English" ideologies on the Scottish people. Judges were known to issue the death sentence for these religious reformers with the words, "Let them glorify God in the Grassmarket." Two Grassmarket pubs have names that reference the hangings; The Last Drop and Maggie Dickson's. The latter references a woman who was hanged and proclaimed dead, but when traveling for her burial, sprang back to life. She lived for another 40 years with the nickname Half Hangit Maggie.

Johnston Terrace. The best-preserved section of the wall can be found by crossing to the south side and climbing the steps of the lane called the Vennel. Here the 16th-century **Flodden Wall** comes in from the east and turns south at Telfer's Wall, a 17th-century extension.

From the northeast corner of the Grassmarket, **Victoria Street,** a 19th-century addition to the Old Town, leads to the George IV Bridge. Shops here sell antiques, designer clothing, and souvenirs. ⊠ *Grassmarket, Edinburgh* ⊕ *www.greatergrassmarket.co.uk.*

Lawnmarket. A corruption of "land market," Lawnmarket is the second of the streets that make up the Royal Mile. It was formerly the site of the produce market for the city, with a once-a-week special sale of wool and linen. Now it's home to **Gladstone's Land** and the **Writers' Museum.** At various times, the Lawnmarket Courts housed James Boswell, David Hume, and Robert Burns, while in the 1770s this area was home to the infamous Deacon Brodie, pillar of society by day and a murdering gang leader by night. Robert Louis Stevenson (1850–94) may well have used Brodie as the inspiration for his novella *Strange Case of Dr. Jekyll and Mr. Hyde.* ⊠ *Between Castlehill and High St., Old Town.*

FAMILY **Museum of Childhood.** Even adults tend to enjoy this cheerfully noisy museum—a cacophony of childhood memorabilia, vintage toys, antique dolls, and fairground games. The museum claims to have been the first in the world devoted solely to the history of childhood. ⊠ *42 High St., Old Town* ☎ *0131/529–4142* ⊕ *www.edinburghmuseums.org.uk* ⊘ *Closed Tues. and Wed.*

Museum of Edinburgh. A must-see if you're interested in the details of Old Town life, this bright yellow, 16th-century building is home to a fascinating museum of local history. It houses some of the most important artifacts in Scottish history—including the National Covenant, a document signed by Scotland's Presbyterian leadership in defiance of a reformed liturgy imposed by King Charles I of England that ignited decades of civil war—alongside Scottish pottery, silver, and glassware, as well as curios like Greyfriars Bobby's dog collar. ⊠ *142 Canongate, Old Town* ☎ *0131/529–4143* ⊕ *www.edinburghmuseums.org.uk* ⊘ *Closed Tues. and Wed.*

Princes Street Gardens. These beautifully manicured gardens, a.
overlooked by Edinburgh Castle, are just a few steps and yet a w.
world away from bustling Princes Street. The 38-acre park, divide
into the East and West Gardens, was first laid out in the 1760s, on
marshland created by the draining of a (long-since-vanished) loch. It
has a host of attractions, including a functioning floral clock on the
corner of Princes Street and The Mound, the Ross Fountain, a series of
memorials, a children's play park, and a café. The gardens often host
free concerts, and have a central role in the city's famed Hogmanay
festivities. ⊠ *Princes St., Old Town.*

Scotch Whisky Experience. Transforming malted barley and spring water
into one of Scotland's most important exports—that's the subject of
this popular Royal Mile attraction. An imaginative approach to the
subject has guests riding in low-speed barrel cars and exploring Scotland's diverse whisky regions and their distinct flavors. Sniff the various aromas and decide whether you like fruity, sweet, or smoky, and
afterward experts will help you select your perfect dram. Your guide
will then take you into a vault containing the world's largest collection
of Scotch whiskies. Opt for one of the premium tours (from £26 to
£70) for extras ranging from additional tastings to a Scottish dining
experience. ⊠ *354 Castlehill, Old Town* ☎ *0131/220–0441* ⊕ *www.
scotchwhiskyexperience.co.uk* ☜ *From £15.*

Writers' Museum. Situated down a narrow close off Lawnmarket is the
1662 Lady Stair's House, a fine example of 17th-century urban architecture. Inside, the Writers' Museum evokes Scotland's literary past with
such exhibits as the letters, possessions, and original manuscripts of Sir
Walter Scott, Robert Burns, and Robert Louis Stevenson. ⊠ *Lady Stair's
Close, Old Town* ☎ *0131/529–4901* ⊕ *www.edinburghmuseums.org.
uk* ☉ *Closed Mon. and Tues.*

NEW TOWN

It was not until the Scottish Enlightenment, a civilizing time of expansion in the 1700s, that the city's elite decided to break away from the
Royal Mile's craggy slope and narrow closes to create a new neighborhood below the castle. This was to become the New Town, with elegant
squares, classical facades, wide streets, and harmonious proportions.
Clearly, change had to come. At the dawn of the 18th century, Edinburgh's unsanitary conditions—primarily a result of overcrowded living
quarters—were becoming notorious. The well-known Scottish fiddle
tune "The Flooers (flowers) of Edinburgh" was only one of many ironic
references to the capital's unpleasant environment.

To help remedy this sorry state of affairs, in 1767 James Drummond, the
city's lord provost (the Scottish term for mayor), urged the town council
to hold a competition to design a new district for Edinburgh. The winner
was an unknown young architect named James Craig (1744–95). His
plan called for a grid of three main east–west streets, balanced at either
end by two grand squares. These streets survive today, though some of the
buildings that line them have been altered by later development. Princes
Street is the southernmost, with Queen Street to the north and George

et as the axis, punctuated by St. Andrew and Charlotte squares. A
at the map will reveal a geometric symmetry unusual in Britain. Even
Princes Street Gardens are balanced by the Queen Street Gardens,
e north. Princes Street was conceived as an exclusive residential
ss, with an open vista facing the castle. It has since been altered by
demands of business and shopping, but the vista remains.

The New Town was expanded several times after Craig's death and
now covers an area about three times larger than Craig envisioned.
Indeed, some of the most elegant facades came later and can be found
by strolling north of the Queen Street Gardens.

TOP ATTRACTIONS

Fodor's Choice
★
Edinburgh Gin Distillery. Whisky may be Scotland's most famous spirit,
but gin also has a long and storied history here—and it's making a
comeback. Edinburgh Gin is a small distillery and visitor center just off
Princes Street, offering tours and tastings that give a fascinating insight
into craft gin production. Two copper stills, Flora and Caledonia, produce a variety of gins, from the navy-strength Cannonball Gin to the
coastal botanical-infused Seaside Gin. Take a discovery tour (£10) or
a connoisseur tour (£25), then head into the Heads and Tales bar to
sample a good selection of Scottish gins and gin cocktails. ⊠ *1a Rutland
Pl., West End* ☎ *0131/656–2810* ⊕ *www.edinburghgin.com* ⊡ *£10.*

Fodor's Choice
★
Scottish National Gallery. Opened to the public in 1859, the Scottish
National Gallery presents a wide selection of paintings from the Renaissance to the postimpressionist period within a grand neoclassical building. Most famous are the Old Master paintings bequeathed by the Duke
of Sutherland, including Titian's *Three Ages of Man.* Many masters are
here: works by Velázquez, El Greco, Rembrandt, Goya, Poussin, Turner,
Degas, Monet, and Van Gogh, among others, complement a fine collection of Scottish art, including Sir Henry Raeburn's *Reverend Robert
Walker Skating on Duddingston Loch* and other works by Ramsay,
Raeburn, and Wilkie. The gallery also has an information center, gift
shop, and the excellent Scottish Cafe and Restaurant.

You can also hop on a free bus (£1 donation requested) from here to
the Scottish National Gallery of Modern Art, which has paintings and
sculptures by Pablo Picasso, Georges Braque, Henri Matisse, and André
Derain, among others. ⊠ *The Mound, New Town* ☎ *0131/624–6200*
⊕ *www.nationalgalleries.org.*

Scott Monument. What appears to be a Gothic cathedral spire that's been
chopped off and planted on Princes Street is in fact Scotland's tribute to
one of its most famous sons, Sir Walter Scott. Built in 1844 and soaring
to 200 feet, it remains the largest monument to a writer anywhere in the
world. Climb the 287 steps to the top for a stunning view of the city and
the hills and coast beyond. ⊠ *Princes St., New Town* ☎ *0131/529–4068*
⊕ *www.edinburghmuseums.org.uk* ⊡ *£5; cash only.*

**OFF THE
BEATEN
PATH**
Royal Botanic Garden Edinburgh. Explore Britain's largest rhododendron
and azalea gardens at this beautiful 70-acre botanical garden. Founded
in 1670 as a physic garden, it now has a range of natural highlights such
as soaring palms in the glass-domed Temperate House and the steamy
Tropical Palm House, an extensive Chinese garden, and a pretty rock

Ancestor Hunting

Are you a Cameron or a Campbell, a Mackenzie or a Macdonald? If so, you may be one of the more than 25 million people of Scottish descent around the world. It was the Highland clearances of the 18th and 19th centuries, in which tenant farmers were driven from their homes and replaced with sheep, that started the mass emigration to North America and Australia. Before or during a trip, you can do a little genealogical research or pursue your family tree more seriously.

VisitScotland (⊕ *www.visitscotland. com/about/ancestry*) has information about clans and surnames, books, and family-history societies. At the Register House, the ScotlandsPeople Centre (⊕ *www.scotlandspeople.gov.uk*) is the place to dip into the past or conduct in-depth genealogical research.

Willing to pay for help? Companies such as Scottish Ancestral Trail (⊕ *www.scottish-ancestral-trail. co.uk*) do the research and plan a trip around your family history. Throughout Scotland, you can check bookstores for information and visit clan museums and societies.

2

garden and stream. There's a visitor center with exhibits on biodiversity, a fabulous gift shop selling plants, books, and gifts, and two cafeterias. There's also the handsome 18th-century Inverleith House, which hosts art exhibitions. Guided walks of the gardens cost £7 and take place daily from April to October, or you can book a private tour including afternoon tea (£45 for two) at any time. It takes 20 minutes to walk to the garden from Princes Street, or you can take a bus. ⊠ *Arboretum Pl., Inverleith* ☎ *0131/248–2909* ⊕ *www.rbge.org.uk* ⊠ *Free; Glasshouses £6.50.*

Scottish National Portrait Gallery. Set within a magnificent red-sandstone Gothic building from 1889, this gallery is an Edinburgh must-see. Conceived as a gift to the people of Scotland, it divides into five broad themes, from Reformation to Modernity, with special galleries for photography and contemporary art—all centered around the stunning Great Hall. It also plays host to regular temporary exhibitions, including the annual BP Portrait Award. ⊠ *1 Queen St., New Town* ☎ *0131/624–6200* ⊕ *www.nationalgalleries.org.*

WORTH NOTING

Calton Hill. Robert Louis Stevenson's favorite view of his beloved city was from the top of this hill, and it's easy to see why. Located in the heart of the city, Calton Hill offers stunning vistas of the Old and New towns and out to the Firth of Forth, making it a popular setting for picnicking and watching festival fireworks. Great views aside, the hill is also home to a number of impressive monuments. The most notable is the so-called **National Monument,** also known as "Scotland's Disgrace," which was commissioned in 1822 and intended to mimic Athens's Parthenon. However, after 12 columns the money ran out, leaving the facade as a monument to high aspirations and poor fundraising. Nearby, the 100-foot-high **Nelson Monument,** completed in 1815 in honor of Britain's greatest naval hero, is topped with a "time ball" that is dropped at 1 pm every day. Other monuments include the circular Corinthian **Burns Monument** and **Dugald Stewart Monument,** named for the Scottish philosopher.

The hill is also home to the **City Observatory,** divided into the domed Playfair House and the old Gothic Tower. ⊠ *Bounded by Leith St. to the west and Regent Rd. to the south, New Town* ☎ *0131/529–7061* ⊕ *www.edinburgh.gov.uk* ✉ *Nelson Monument £5* ⊙ *Nelson Monument closed Sun. in Oct.–Mar.*

OFF THE BEATEN PATH

Edinburgh Zoo. Home to star attractions Tian Tian and Yang Gaung, the United Kingdom's only two giant pandas, Edinburgh's Zoo hosts more than 1,000 animals over 80 acres. Don't miss the famous Penguin Parade, which takes place every afternoon (as long as the penguins are willing), or the ever-popular Koala Territory, where you can get up close to the zoo's four koalas—including Yoonarah, born in 2014, the first-ever British-born koala. Discounted tickets are available online. ■**TIP➔ Free 15-minute panda-viewing sessions must be booked in advance.** ⊠ *134 Corstorphine Rd., Corstorphine* ☎ *0131/334–9171* ⊕ *www.edinburghzoo.org.uk* ✉ *£19.*

George Street. With its high-end shops, upmarket bistros, and five-star hotels, all with handsome Georgian frontages, George Street is a more pleasant, less crowded thoroughfare for strolling than Princes Street. It also has a couple of points of interest. First, there's the **statue of King George IV,** at the intersection of George and Hanover streets, which recalls the visit of George IV to Scotland in 1822; he was the first British monarch to do so since King Charles II, in the 17th century. Next, the **Assembly Rooms,** between Hanover and Frederick streets, are where Sir Walter Scott officially acknowledged having written the Waverley novels (the author had hitherto been a mystery, albeit a badly kept one). ⊠ *Between Charlotte Sq. and St. Andrew Sq., New Town.*

Princes Street. The south side of this dominant New Town street is occupied by the well-kept Princes Street Gardens, which act as a wide green moat to the castle on its rock. The north side is now one long sequence of chain stores with mostly unappealing modern fronts, with one or two exceptions: most notably the handsome Victorian facade that is home to Jenners department store. ⊠ *Waterloo Pl. to Lothian Rd., New Town.*

HAYMARKET

West of the Old Town and south of the West End is Haymarket, a district with its own down-to-earth character and well-worn charm. It offers varied shopping and dining options that become more upmarket as you head toward the West End and Leith.

WEST END

Handsome Georgian town houses give this neighborhood a dignified feel. People head here for the small boutiques and cafés, as well as the wide range of cultural venues.

2

CLOSE UP
Leith, Edinburgh's Seaport

Situated on the south shore of the Firth of Forth, Leith was a separate town until it merged with the city in 1920. After World War II and up until the 1980s, the declining seaport became known as an impoverished corner of Edinburgh, but in recent years, it has been completely revitalized with the restoration of commercial buildings and the construction of new luxury housing, hipster cafés, and trendy restaurants. All the docks have been redeveloped, looked over variously by a shopping mall and a government building.

In earlier times, Leith was the stage for many historic happenings. In 1560, Mary of Guise—mother of Mary, Queen of Scots—ruled Scotland from Leith; her daughter landed in Leith the following year to embark on her infamous reign. A century later, Cromwell led his troops to Leith to root out Scottish royalists. And in 1744, Leith became the so-called "home of golf," as official rules to the game were devised on Leith Links, a lovely park that remains to this day.

SOUTH SIDE

This residential district offers a peek at the comings and goings of regular Edinburghers. Cost-conscious visitors can find lots of affordable restaurants and budget B&Bs here.

LEITH

Just north of the city is Edinburgh's port, a place brimming with seafaring history and undergoing a slow revival after years of postwar neglect. It may not be as pristine as much of modern-day Edinburgh, but there are plenty of cobbled streets, dockside buildings, and bobbing boats to capture your imagination. Here along the lowest reaches of the Water of Leith (the river that flows through town), you'll find an ever-growing array of modish shops, pubs, and restaurants. Leith's major attraction is the Royal Yacht *Britannia*, moored outside the huge Ocean Terminal shopping mall. You can reach Leith from the center by walking down Leith Walk from the east end of Princes Street (20 to 30 minutes)—or, better yet, walk along the beautiful Water of Leith (a great way to forget you're in a capital city). Alternatively, take Lothian Bus 22.

FAMILY **The Royal Yacht *Britannia*.** Moored on the waterfront at Leith is the Royal Yacht *Britannia*—launched in Scotland in 1953, retired in 1997, and now returned to her home country. A favorite of Queen Elizabeth II (she is reported to have shed a tear at its decommissioning ceremony), it is now open for the public to explore, from the royal apartments on the upper floors to the more functional engine room, bridge, galleys, and captain's cabin. The visitor center, based within the hulking, on-shore Ocean Terminal shopping mall, has a variety of fascinating exhibits and photographs relating to the yacht's history. ⊠ *Ocean Dr., Leith* ☎ *0131/555–5566* ⊕ *www.royalyachtbritannia.co.uk* ⊠ *£15.50.*

WHERE TO EAT

Edinburgh's eclectic restaurant scene has attracted a brigade of well-known chefs, including the award-winning trio of Martin Wishart, Tom Kitchin, and Paul Kitching. They and dozens of others have abandoned the tried-and-true recipes for more adventurous cuisine. Of course, you can always find traditional fare, which usually means the Scottish-French style that harks back to the historical "Auld Alliance" of the 13th century. The Scottish element is the preference for fresh and local foodstuffs; the French supply the sauces. In Edinburgh, you can sample anything from Malaysian *rendang* (a thick, coconut-milk stew) to Kurdish kebabs, while the long-established French, Italian, Chinese, Pakistani, and Indian communities ensure that the majority of the globe's most treasured cuisines are well represented. *Use the coordinate (✥ B2) at the end of each listing to locate a site on the corresponding map.*

PRICES AND HOURS

It's possible to eat well in Edinburgh without spending a fortune. Multicourse prix-fixe options are common, and almost always less expensive than ordering à la carte. Even at restaurants in the highest price category, you can easily spend less than £35 per person. People tend to eat later in Scotland than in England—around 8 pm on average—and then drink on in leisurely Scottish fashion.

	WHAT IT COSTS IN POUNDS			
	$	**$$**	**$$$**	**$$$$**
Restaurants	under £15	£15–£19	£20–£25	over £25

Restaurant prices are the average cost of a main course at dinner or, if dinner is not served, at lunch.

OLD TOWN

The most historic part of the city houses some of its grander restaurants (though, interestingly, none of its current Michelin stars). It is also home to some of Edinburgh's oldest and most atmospheric pubs, which serve good, informal meals.

$ INTERNATIONAL 🍴 **Checkpoint.** Originally run as a pop-up during the Festival Fringe, this supercool café-bar became a permanent part of the Edinburgh dining scene in 2015. The coffee is sensational, but the comfort food is just as much of a draw. **Known for:** excellent coffee; delicious light lunches; hip hangout in the evening. [$] *Average main: £6* ✉ *3 Bristo Pl., Old Town* ☎ *0131/225–9352* 🌐 *www.checkpointedinburgh.com* ✥ F5.

$$ ITALIAN Fodor's Choice ★ 🍴 **Contini Cannonball.** The name refers to one of the most delightful quirks of Edinburgh's Old Town—the cannonball embedded in the wall outside, said to have been fired at the castle while Bonnie Prince Charlie was in residence (not true, but a good story). The atmosphere in this three-story restaurant and whisky bar is casual and relaxed, despite the gorgeous art deco dining room with views of the castle esplanade. **Known for:** scrumptious Italian-Scottish cuisine; great views

of the castle; bread-crumbed haggis cannonballs. [$] *Average main: £15* ✉ *356 Castlehill, Old Town* ☎ *0131/225–1550* 🌐 *www.contini.com/contini-cannonball* ⊕ E5.

$ VEGETARIAN 🍴 **David Bann.** This hip eatery, situated just off the Royal Mile, serves exclusively vegetarian and vegan favorites, and its inventive dishes and modern interior make it a popular place with young locals. The menu changes constantly, but the invariably creative, flavorful dishes often leave carnivores forgetting they're eating vegetarian. **Known for:** superb vegetarian and vegan cuisine; very affordable. [$] *Average main: £13* ✉ *56–58 St. Mary's St., Old Town* ☎ *0131/556–5888* 🌐 *www.davidbann.com* ⊕ G4.

$$ MIDDLE EASTERN 🍴 **Hanam's.** Kurdish food may not be as well known as other Middle Eastern cuisines, but dishes like *bayengaan surocrau* (marinated slow-roasted eggplant) and lamb *tashreeb* (a flavorful casserole) are worth checking out. Hanam's proudly cooks up Kurdish cuisine, but also serves more familiar Middle Eastern fare, from shish kebabs to falafel. **Known for:** traditional Kurdish cooking; BYOB; hookah on heated terrace. [$] *Average main: £15* ✉ *3 Johnston Terr., Old Town* ☎ *0131/225–1329* 🌐 *www.hanams.com* ⊕ E5.

$ BRITISH 🍴 **Howies.** The Victoria Street branch of this bistro chain is a good choice for contemporary Scottish fare, with lots of fresh local produce. Alongside the daily specials and quality Scottish steaks and salmon, there are some nicely inventive vegetarian options. **Known for:** quality Scottish menu; good value set-price lunch. [$] *Average main: £8* ✉ *10–14 Victoria St., Old Town* ☎ *0131/225–1721* 🌐 *www.howies.uk.com* ⊕ E5, F3.

$$$ FRENCH 🍴 **La Garrigue.** Edinburgh is blessed with several excellent French bistros, and this is one of the best. Although the modern decor evokes Paris, the food has the rustic flavor of the southern Languedoc region. **Known for:** rustic French cuisine; attentive service. [$] *Average main: £21* ✉ *31 Jeffrey St., Old Town* ☎ *0131/557–3032* 🌐 *www.lagarrigue.co.uk* ⊕ G4.

$$ BISTRO 🍴 **La Petite Mort.** This exceptionally fine bistro treats its seasonal, regional Scottish flavors with Continental reverence, and the crowds that pack the place to the rafters every night are testament to its success. With its superb flavors, its extensive wine list, and its wallet-friendly prices, we'll forgive them the indulgence of the name: La Petite Mort is French for, let's say... climax. **Known for:** beautiful velouté sauces; inventive cocktails; charming environs. [$] *Average main: £16* ✉ *32 Valleyfield St., Old Town* ☎ *0131/229–3693* 🌐 *www.lapetitemortedinburgh.co.uk* ⊕ D6.

$ CAFÉ Fodor's Choice ★ 🍴 **Lovecrumbs.** A bakery-café with an inordinately sweet tooth, Lovecrumbs joyously, deliciously, and unashamedly focuses on what *really* matters in life: cake. It serves wonderful cakes of all kinds, from pistachio and chocolate to heavenly peanut-butter brownies to mouthwatering tarts. **Known for:** extraordinary cakes galore; junk-shop-esque interior decor; hit-or-miss service. [$] *Average main: £4* ✉ *155 W. Port, Old Town* ☎ *0131/629–0626* 🌐 *www.lovecrumbs.co.uk* ⊕ D5.

$$ MODERN BRITISH 🍴 **Michael Neave Kitchen and Whisky Bar.** Young chef Michael Neave delivers exceptional cuisine at affordable prices in his restaurant just off the Royal Mile. With a mission to "explore the best of Scotland's larder," quality Scottish produce is the star here. **Known for:** superb Scottish cuisine; inventive sauces; great value fixed-price menus. [$] *Average main:*

£18 ✉ *21 Old Fishmarket Cl., Old Town* ☎ *0131/226–4747* 🌐 *www.michaelneave.co.uk* ⏲ *Closed Sun. and Mon.* ✥ F4.

$ BRITISH Fodor's Choice ★ 🍴 **Oink.** For a quick, cheap bite while wandering the Royal Mile, you can't beat Oink—possibly the best hog roast (pulled pork) in Edinburgh. Located at the bottom of the Royal Mile (there are two other outlets, but this one is the best), it was founded by two farmers in 2008, and their high-quality, hand-reared pork has proved a huge hit ever since. **Known for:** unbelievable pulled pork; extra crackling on request; great value lunch. [$] *Average main: £5* ✉ *82 Canongate, Old Town* ☎ *07584/637416* 🌐 *www.oinkhogroast.co.uk* ✥ H4.

$$$ SEAFOOD 🍴 **Ondine.** This fabulous seafood restaurant just off the Royal Mile has been making waves since 2009 with its expertly prepared dishes from sustainable fishing sources. A wall of windows shines bountiful amounts of sunlight on an attractive monochromatic dining room and an art deco oyster bar. **Known for:** spectacular seafood; lavish decor; snappy service. [$] *Average main: £25* ✉ *2 George IV Bridge, Old Town* ☎ *0131/226–1888* 🌐 *www.ondinerestaurant.co.uk* ⏲ *Closed Sun.* ✥ F5.

$ BRITISH Fodor's Choice ★ 🍴 **Timberyard.** There are few restaurants that feel so wonderfully, well, *Edinburgh* as this one. The freshest seasonal ingredients, mostly sourced from small local producers, go into creating delicious, inventive fare. **Known for:** exciting dishes; hip interior; pricey multicourse menus. [$] *Average main: £13* ✉ *10 Lady Lawson St., Old Town* ☎ *0131/221–1222* 🌐 *www.timberyard.co* ⏲ *Closed Sun. and Mon.* ✥ D5.

$$$ MODERN BRITISH Fodor's Choice ★ 🍴 **Wedgwood the Restaurant.** Rejecting the idea that fine dining should be a stuffy affair, owners Paul Wedgwood and Lisa Channon opened this Royal Mile gem in 2007. Local produce and some unusual foraged fronds enliven the taste buds, as Scottish and Asian influences are creatively fused together throughout the menu, including desserts. **Known for:** unfussy fine dining; Asian-influenced menu; unintrusive service. [$] *Average main: £20* ✉ *267 Canongate, Old Town* ☎ *0131/558–8737* 🌐 *www.wedgwoodtherestaurant.co.uk* ✥ G4.

NEW TOWN

The New Town, with its striking street plan, ambitious architecture, and professional crowd, has restaurants where you can get everything from a quick snack to a more formal dinner.

$$ ITALIAN 🍴 **Contini George Street.** Set within a grand former banking hall on George Street, this superb restaurant serves inspired Italian food and wine in a relaxing, airy setting. Refurbished in 2017, and now complete with grand Corinthian columns, an open marble-topped bar, intricate wall hangings, and soft gray banquettes, it offers light but satisfying Italian favorites divided into *primi, secondi,* and *formaggi*. **Known for:** lovely, light Italian cuisine; grand but relaxing setting; free Italian lessons in the bathrooms. [$] *Average main: £18* ✉ *103 George St., New Town* ☎ *0131/225–1550* 🌐 *www.contini.com/contini-george-street* ✥ D4.

$$ THAI Fodor's Choice ★ 🍴 **Dusit.** Tucked down narrow Thistle Street, Dusit doesn't register on most travelers' radars, but it has been a local favorite since 2002. An authentic, contemporary Thai restaurant run by Bangkok-born Pom, the menu here delights with deliciously creamy curries, spicy stir-fries, and fragrant seafood specialties, all of which use a mix of fresh local

produce and imported Thai vegetables. **Known for:** award-winning Thai food; locals' haunt; expensive mains. Ⓢ *Average main: £16* ✉ *49a Thistle St., New Town* ☎ *0131/220–6846* ⊕ *www.dusit.co.uk* ✛ E3.

$$$$
MODERN BRITISH

✗ **Forth Floor Restaurant at Harvey Nichols.** Harvey Nichols has become synonymous with chic shopping, and the department store's Forth Floor restaurant, located on the fourth floor, is no slouch when it comes to style. With views of the Forth of Firth (see what they did there?), the restaurant's decor is minimalist without being too severe, and the fixed-price menus make excellent use of local and seasonal produce. **Known for:** good food with a view; fashionable decor; great afternoon tea. Ⓢ *Average main: £26* ✉ *Harvey Nichols, 30–34 St. Andrew Sq., New Town* ☎ *0131/524 8350* ⊕ *www.harveynichols.com* ☾ *No dinner Sun. and Mon.* Ⓜ *St. Andrew Sq.* ✛ F3.

$$$
BRASSERIE
FAMILY
Fodor's Choice
★

✗ **Galvin Brasserie de Luxe.** This Parisian-style brasserie combines handsome surroundings with first-class cuisine from London brothers Chris and Jeff Galvin. Dapper waiters glide around the cavernous dining area with its central bar, while the menu marries classic French dishes alongside Scottish staples, so you should expect everything from steak tartare and duck terrine to smoked salmon and peppery haggis. **Known for:** delicious French-Scottish cuisine; superb service; a family favorite. Ⓢ *Average main: £22* ✉ *Waldorf Astoria Edinburgh—The Caledonian, Rutland St., New Town* ☎ *0131/222–8988* ⊕ *www.galvinbrasseriede-luxe.com* ✛ D4.

$$$
BISTRO
Fodor's Choice
★

✗ **The Honours.** Run by Edinburgh restaurant grandee Martin Wishart, the Honours is a more relaxed (though almost as pricey) alternative to his eponymous flagship in Leith. Inside its gorgeous black-and-white, art deco interior, diners can enjoy a range of excellent Scottish seafood dishes; but those in the know order the meat, with extraordinary rare-breed sirloin and fillet steaks as well as more unusual cuts like hanger steak and ox cheek. **Known for:** incredible meat dishes; beautiful Art Deco decor. Ⓢ *Average main: £24* ✉ *58a North Castle St., New Town* ☎ *0131/220–2513* ⊕ *www.thehonours.co.uk* ☾ *Closed Sun. and Mon.* Ⓜ *Princes St.* ✛ D4.

$
FRENCH
Fodor's Choice
★

✗ **L'Escargot Bleu.** When it comes to quality at a good value, this pretty little French bistro, situated on one of Edinburgh's trendiest streets, is almost impossible to beat. You're warmly welcomed into an upmarket but casual space of stripped wooden floors and period French posters, then shown a menu that seems to have a typo: £12.90 for a two-course lunch, or £14.90 for dinner of fine French cuisine as authentic as a withering stare on the Champs-Élysées. **Known for:** authentic French fare; hard-to-believe low prices; friendly service. Ⓢ *Average main: £13* ✉ *56 Broughton St., New Town* ☎ *0131/557–1600* ⊕ *www.lescargotbleu.co.uk* ☾ *Closed Sun.* ✛ F2.

$$$$
BRITISH

✗ **Number One.** Clublike but unstuffy, this outstanding basement restaurant, set within the Edwardian splendor of the Balmoral Hotel, is made for intimate dining. The food is extraordinary, with a menu that highlights the best of Scottish seafood and meat in inventive fashion, but the prices make this a place for serious special occasions; the regular three-course prix-fixe is £80 per person, while the 10-course tasting menu is £120, drinks not included. **Known for:** wonderfully intimate

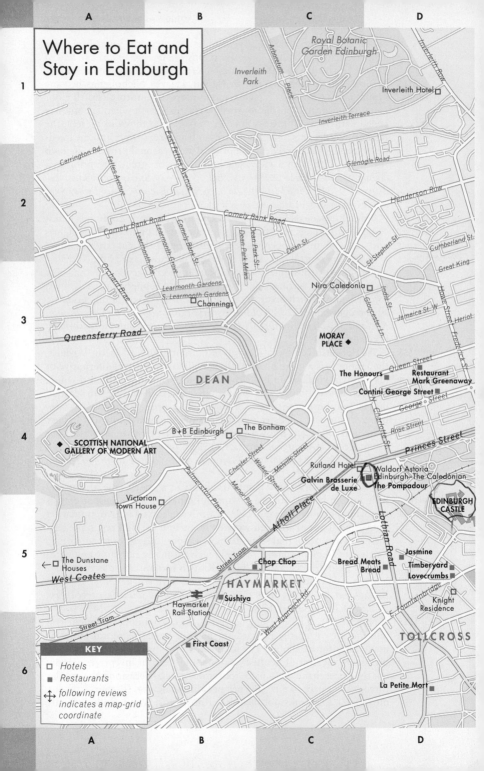

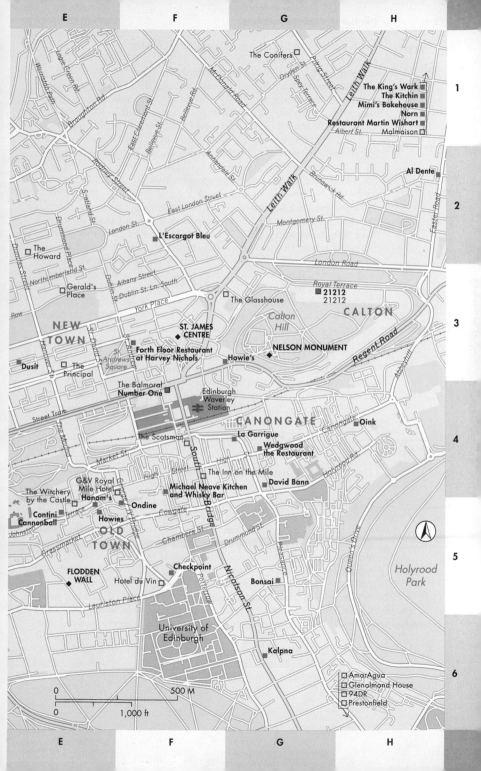

setting; inventive dishes; very expensive. [$] *Average main: £80* ✉ *Balmoral Hotel, 1 Princes St., New Town* ☎ *0131/557–6727* 🌐 *www.roccofortehotels.com* 🕒 *No lunch* [M] *Princes St.* ✣ F4.

$$$$ FRENCH FUSION
🍴 **The Pompadour.** Sophisticated surroundings and sumptuous cuisine make this restaurant, originally opened in 1925, one of Edinburgh's best spots for fine dining. London chef–restaurateur brothers Jeff and Chris Galvin impart their expertise in the classic French-inspired cuisine and impressive wine list. **Known for:** beautiful dining room; subtly sumptuous flavors; gorgeous presentation. [$] *Average main: £65* ✉ *Waldorf Astoria Edinburgh–The Caledonian, Princes St., New Town* ☎ *0131/222–8975* 🌐 *www.thepompadourbygalvin.com* 🕒 *Closed Sun. and Mon. No lunch Tues.–Fri.* ✣ C4.

$$$$ MODERN BRITISH
🍴 **Restaurant Mark Greenaway.** Fine dining with a real sense of fun is what makes Restaurant Mark Greenaway stand out from the crowd. Inventive dishes and serving styles populate the menu at this cozy but high-end eatery, from an amuse bouche served in a cardboard egg box to a broth that's boiled in a beaker at your table. **Known for:** fun and inventive food; attentive service; occasional style over substance. [$] *Average main: £28* ✉ *69 N. Castle St., New Town* ☎ *0131/226–1155* 🌐 *www.markgreenaway.com* 🕒 *Closed Sun. and Mon.* ✣ D3.

$$$$ MODERN FRENCH
Fodor's Choice ★
🍴 **21212.** Paul Kitching is one of Britain's most innovative chefs, and the theatrical dining experience at 21212 delivers surprises galore. Set within a Georgian town house, the Michelin-starred restaurant is sumptuously appointed; the Belle Époque decor and quirky crockery make this a perfect destination for couples (who should ask for a romantic alcove window table). **Known for:** contemporary Franco-Anglo-Scottish cuisine; romantic; friendly and informed staff. [$] *Average main: £85* ✉ *3 Royal Terr., New Town* ☎ *0131/523–1030* 🌐 *www.21212restaurant.co.uk* 🕒 *Closed Sun. and Mon.* ✣ G3.

HAYMARKET

This area has many restaurants that tend to be more affordable than those in the center of town.

$$ INTERNATIONAL
🍴 **First Coast.** This laid-back bistro, just a few minutes from Haymarket station, has a loyal following—and for good reason. Its multicultural menu has everything from Thai mango salads to Brazilian seafood stews to Korean rice cakes, as well as an unusually good selection of vegetarian options. **Known for:** great international fare; big on flavor; relaxing interior. [$] *Average main: £15* ✉ *99–101 Dalry Rd., Haymarket* ☎ *0131/313–4404* 🌐 *www.first-coast.co.uk* 🕒 *Closed Sun.* ✣ B6.

$ JAPANESE
Fodor's Choice ★
🍴 **Sushiya.** It may look underwhelming from the outside, but step inside for amazing, atmospheric, and authentic Japanese dining. It's a tiny place, with just 22 seats facing an open counter, but the array of sushi and sashimi assembled by the resident chef is magical. **Known for:** delicious sushi and sashimi; very affordable lunch. [$] *Average main: £9* ✉ *19 Dalry Rd., Haymarket* ☎ *0131/313–3222* 🌐 *www.sushiya.co.uk* 🕒 *Closed Sun. and Mon.* ✣ B5.

WEST END

Even after business hours, the city's commercial center is a good place to find a variety of international restaurants.

$ 🍴 **Bread Meats Bread.** This family-run burger joint, first opened in Glasgow in 2012 and expanded to Edinburgh in 2016, has already gained a nationwide reputation for its over-the-top add-ons like bone-marrow butter, kimchi, 'Nduja (spicy salami spread), and pomegranate molasses. Take a seat inside the chic, reclaimed-wood interior and choose from a menu packed with amped-up burgers, as well as chicken, veggie, and halal options. **Known for:** Lothian Wolf burger; some of the best burgers in United Kingdom; large portions; smart, modern interior. [$] *Average main: £13* ✉ *92 Lothian Rd., West End* ☎ *0131/225–3000* 🌐 *www.breadmeatsbread.com* ✥ D5.

BURGER
Fodor's Choice ★

$ 🍴 **Jasmine.** Fresh seafood and meat matched with just the right spices is the main attraction of this small, friendly Cantonese restaurant. The standout dishes here include steamed whole sea bass with ginger and spring onions and crispy almond chicken with orange sauce. **Known for:** delicious Cantonese cuisine; friendly service; a little cramped. [$] *Average main: £14* ✉ *32–34 Grindlay St., West End* ☎ *0131/229–5757* 🌐 *www.jasminechinese.co.uk* ✥ D5.

CHINESE
FAMILY

SOUTH SIDE

The presence of university professors and students means eateries that are both affordable and interesting.

$ 🍴 **Bonsai.** The owners of Bonsai regularly visit Tokyo to research the casual dining scene, and their expertise is setting a high standard for Japanese cuisine in Edinburgh. The succulent *gyoza* (steamed dumplings) are pliant and tasty, while the wide variety of noodle, teriyaki, and sushi dishes balance sweet and sour deliciously. **Known for:** authentic sushi; dragon gaijin-zushi (inside-out roll). [$] *Average main: £8* ✉ *46 W. Richmond St., South Side* ☎ *0131/668–3847* 🌐 *www.bonsaibarbistro.co.uk* ✥ G5.

JAPANESE

$ 🍴 **Kalpna.** Amid an ordinary row of shops, the facade of this vegetarian Indian restaurant may be unremarkable, but the food is exceptional, and a great value, too. You'll find south- and west-Indian specialties, including *dam aloo kashmiri (*a medium-spicy potato dish with a sauce made from honey, pistachios, and almonds) and *bangan achari* (super-spicy marinated eggplants). **Known for:** authentic veggie Indian fare; lively interior with exotic mosaics; great value. [$] *Average main: £9* ✉ *2–3 St. Patrick Sq., South Side* ☎ *0131/667–9890* 🌐 *www.kalpnarestaurant.com* ⏲ *No lunch Sun.* ✥ G6.

INDIANINDIAN
Fodor's Choice ★

LEITH

Seafood lovers are drawn to the old port of Leith to sample the freshest seafood amid the authentic seafaring setting. Some of Scotland's most renowned chefs have made Leith—and more specifically, The Shore, its upmarket waterfront—their home.

$$ BRITISH 🍴 **The King's Wark.** This gastropub at The Shore in Leith combines a beautiful historic setting with great quality food and a wide selection of Scottish gins. At lunchtime, the dark-wood bar does a roaring trade in simple fare such as gourmet burgers, fish cakes, and haggis (traditional or vegetarian), but in the evening, the kitchen ups the ante with a chalkboard menu of locally caught seafood specialties, from hake to monkfish. **Known for:** affordable quality cuisine; atmospheric setting. [$] *Average main: £16* ✉ *The Shore, 36 The Shore, Leith* ☎ *0131/554–9260* 🌐 *kingswark.co.uk/* ✣ H1.

$$$$ FRENCH 🍴 **The Kitchin.** A perennially popular high-end dining option, Tom Kitchin's Michelin-starred venture packs in the crowds. Kitchin, who trained in France, runs a tight ship, and his passion for using seasonal and locally sourced produce to his own creative ends shows no sign of waning. **Known for:** nose-to-tail philosophy; lovely setting; affordable prix-fixe lunch. [$] *Average main: £33* ✉ *78 Commercial Quay, Leith* ☎ *0131/555–1755* 🌐 *thekitchin.com* 🕑 *Closed Sun. and Mon.* ✣ H1.

$ BAKERY FAMILY Fodor's Choice ★ 🍴 **Mimi's Bakehouse - Leith.** Despite its large interior with acres of seating, this bakery-café still regularly has lines out the door. The reason is simple: it does the best cakes in Edinburgh, using everything from Oreos to Reese's Pieces to strawberries and cream. **Known for:** delicious and creative cakes; to-die-for breakfasts; fun and cheeky decor. [$] *Average main: £10* ✉ *63 The Shore, Leith* ☎ *0131/555–5908* 🌐 *www.mimisbakehouse.com* 🕑 *No dinner* ✣ H1.

$$$$ SCANDINAVIAN Fodor's Choice ★ 🍴 **Norn.** Opened in summer 2016, Norn is a relative newcomer to Leith's upmarket dining scene, but the signs are it's here to stay. Owner and chef Scott Smith serves up seasonal, Scandinavian-inspired fare with rare Scottish island ingredients, from beremeal (an ancient form of barley) bread to black potato. **Known for:** sublime and sustainable cuisine; unusual ingredients and tastes; four-course £40 prix fixe is a steal. [$] *Average main: £40* ✉ *50–54 Henderson St., Leith* ☎ *0131/629–2525* 🌐 *www.nornrestaurant.com* 🕑 *Closed Sun. and Mon.* ✣ H1.

$$$$ FRENCH Fodor's Choice ★ 🍴 **Restaurant Martin Wishart.** Leith's premier dining experience, this high-end restaurant combines imaginative cuisine, luxuriously understated decor, and a lovely waterfront location. Renowned Michelin-starred chef Martin Wishart woos diners with his inspired menu of artistically presented, French-influenced dishes. **Known for:** impeccable cuisine; exceptional and flexible service; beautiful location; weekend reservations essential. [$] *Average main: £85* ✉ *54 The Shore, Leith* ☎ *0131/553–3557* 🌐 *www.restaurantmartinwishart.co.uk* 🕑 *Closed Sun. and Mon.* ✣ H1.

WHERE TO STAY

From stylish boutique hotels to homey B&Bs, Edinburgh has a world-class array of accommodation options to suit every taste. Its status as one of Britain's most attractive and fascinating cities ensures a steady influx of visitors, but the wealth of overnight options means there's no need to compromise on where you stay. Grand old hotels are rightly renowned for their regal bearing and old-world charm, but if your tastes are a little more contemporary, the city's burgeoning contingent of chic-design hotels offers an equally alluring alternative a tighter budget, the town's B&Bs are the most likely cho previously found B&Bs to be restrictive, keep in mind th trusting people—many proprietors provide front-door key few impose curfews.

Rooms are harder to find in August and September, when the Edinburgh International Festival and the Festival Fringe take place, so reserve at least three months in advance. B&Bs may prove trickier to find in the winter months (with the exception of Christmas and New Year), as this is when many proprietors choose to close up shop and go on vacation themselves.

PRICES

To save money and see how local residents live, stay in a B&B in one of the areas away from the city center, such as Pilrig to the north, Murrayfield to the west, or Sciennes to the south. Public buses can whisk you to the city center in 10 to 15 minutes. *Hotel reviews have been shortened. For full information, visit Fodors.com. Use the coordinate (✛ B2) at the end of each listing to locate a site on the corresponding map.*

WHAT IT COSTS IN POUNDS			
$	**$$**	**$$$**	**$$$$**
Hotels under £100	£100–£160	£161–£220	Over £220

Hotel prices are the lowest cost of a standard double room in high season, including 20% V.A.T.

OLD TOWN

The narrow *pends* (alleys), cobbled streets, and steep hills of the Old Town remind you that this is a city with many layers of history. From medieval to modernist, these hotels all are within a stone's throw of the action.

$$$$
HOTEL
Fodor'sChoice
★
🏨 **G&V Royal Mile Hotel.** The bright primary colors, striking stenciled wallpapers, and bold, eclectic furnishings inside this übertrendy design hotel contrast with the Gothic surroundings of the Royal Mile—and yet, somehow, it works. **Pros:** perfect location in the heart of the city; bold and fashionable decor; inventive cocktails. **Cons:** decor is a little Austin Powers in places. $ *Rooms from: £260* ✉ *1 George IV Bridge, Old Town* ☎ *0131/220–6666* ⊕ *gvroyalmilehotel.com* 🛏 *136 rooms* ❤️ *Breakfast* ✛ F4.

$$$
HOTEL
Fodor'sChoice
★
🏨 **Hotel du Vin.** Leave it to one of the United Kingdom's most forward-thinking hotel chains to convert a Victorian-era asylum into this understated luxury property, which combines a real sense of history with contemporary decor and trappings. **Pros:** unique and historic building; trendy design; lively on-site dining and drinking. **Cons:** quarter-mile walk to nearest parking; neighborhood can be noisy. $ *Rooms from: £195* ✉ *11 Bristo Pl., Old Town* ☎ *0131/285–1479* ⊕ *www.hotelduvin. com* 🛏 *47 rooms* ❤️ *Breakfast* ✛ F5.

$$$ **B&B/INN** 🏨 **The Inn on the Mile.** This chic and welcoming boutique inn could hardly be more central—some rooms even overlook the Royal Mile. **Pros:** views of the Royal Mile; lovely staff; great design. **Cons:** lots of steps and no elevator; sometimes noisy; nearest parking at a public lot (three-minute walk). [$] *Rooms from: £195* ✉ *82 High St., Old Town* ☎ *0131/556–9940* 🌐 *www.theinnonthemile.co.uk* 🛏 *9 rooms* 🍴 *Breakfast* ✣ F4.

$$$$ **HOTEL** 🏨 **The Scotsman.** This magnificent turn-of-the-20th-century building, with its grand marble staircase and its fascinating history—it was once the headquarters of the *Scotsman* newspaper—now houses this modern luxury hotel. **Pros:** gorgeous surroundings; personalized service. **Cons:** no air-conditioning; spa can be noisy; could do with some renovation. [$] *Rooms from: £270* ✉ *20 N. Bridge, Old Town* ☎ *0131/556–5565* 🌐 *scotsmanhotel.co.uk* 🛏 *69 rooms* 🍴 *Breakfast* ✣ F4.

$$$$ **HOTEL** 🏨 **The Witchery by the Castle.** This lavishly theatrical lodging promises a night to remember. **Pros:** Gothic drama and intriguing antiques; a truly romantic retreat; sumptuous dining. **Cons:** can be noisy at night; decor not for everybody; pricey. [$] *Rooms from: £345* ✉ *352 Castlehill, Old Town* ☎ *0131/225–5613* 🌐 *www.thewitchery.com* 🛏 *9 suites* 🍴 *Breakfast* ✣ E5.

NEW TOWN

Calton Hill, which offers some of the best views of the city from its summit, is just one of the reasons to base yourself in the New Town, filled with gorgeous 18th- and 19th-century architecture.

$$$$ **HOTEL** **Fodor's Choice** ★ 🏨 **The Balmoral.** The attention to detail in the elegant rooms—colors were picked to echo the country's heathers and moors—and the sheer Edwardian splendor of this grand, former railroad hotel, make staying at the Balmoral a special introduction to Edinburgh. **Pros:** big and beautiful Edwardian building; top-hatted doorman; top-notch spa. **Cons:** small pool; spa books up fast. [$] *Rooms from: £325* ✉ *1 Princes St., New Town* ☎ *0131/556–2414* 🌐 *www.roccofortehotels.com* 🛏 *188 rooms* 🍴 *Breakfast* ✣ F4.

$$$ **HOTEL** 🏨 **The Glasshouse.** Glass walls extend from the 19th-century facade of a former church, foreshadowing the daring, modern interior of one of the city's original boutique hotels. **Pros:** near all the attractions; very modern and stylish; good dining in the brasseries. **Cons:** a little sterile for some; noise from the street sometimes a problem. [$] *Rooms from: £195* ✉ *2 Greenside La., New Town* ☎ *0131/525–8200* 🌐 *www.theglasshousehotel.co.uk* 🛏 *98 rooms* 🍴 *Breakfast* ✣ F3.

$$$ **HOTEL** 🏨 **The Howard.** This intimate New Town boutique hotel is set within a classic Georgian town house, elegantly proportioned and superbly outfitted, and has the decor, service, and views to match its five-star status. **Pros:** small but grand building; friendly staff; very special afternoon tea. **Cons:** decor a little tired; noisy neighborhood. [$] *Rooms from: £205* ✉ *34 Great King St., New Town* ☎ *0131/557–3500* 🌐 *www.thehoward.com* 🛏 *19 rooms* 🍴 *Breakfast* ✣ E2.

$ **B&B/INN** 🏨 **Inverleith Hotel.** Across from the Royal Botanic Gardens, this renovated Victorian town house has cozy, well-lit rooms with velour bedspreads, dark-wood furniture, and pale-gold curtains—at an incredible value. **Pros:** quiet surroundings; knowledgeable staff; cheap parking nearby (free on weekends). **Cons:** some rooms are small; uphill walk to the city center. [$] *Rooms from: £80* ✉ *5 Inverleith Terr., New Town* ☎ *0131/556–2745* 🌐 *www.inverleithhotel.co.uk* 🛏 *15 rooms* 🍴 *Breakfast* ⊕ D1.

$$$$ HOTEL 🏨 **Nira Caledonia.** A modern and worldly boutique hotel on the edge of the New Town, Nira Caledonia defiantly casts aside old Edinburgh luxury in favor of contemporary comfort and style. **Pros:** refreshingly modern luxury; individually designed rooms; comfy king beds. **Cons:** a little out of the center. [$] *Rooms from: £270* ✉ *6–10 Gloucester Pl., Stockbridge* ☎ *0131/225–2720* 🌐 *www.niracaledonia.com* 🛏 *28 rooms* 🍴 *Some meals* ⊕ D3.

$$$$ HOTEL Fodor's Choice ★ 🏨 **The Principal.** Built in 1775 for Edinburgh's elite, this row of five Georgian town houses in the heart of the New Town now hosts a luxury hotel. **Pros:** excellent central location; stylish and comfortable rooms; fast Wi-Fi throughout. **Cons:** regular wedding parties in reception. [$] *Rooms from: £235* ✉ *19–21 George St., New Town* ☎ *0131/225–1251* 🌐 *www.phcompany.com/principal/edinburgh-george-street* 🛏 *240 rooms* 🍴 *Breakfast* ⊕ E3.

$$$$ HOTEL 🏨 **Waldorf Astoria Edinburgh—The Caledonian.** An imposing and ornate red sandstone building situated at the west end of Princes Street Gardens, "The Caley" has dramatic Victorian decor, beautifully restored interiors, and the best hotel dining in Edinburgh. **Pros:** impeccable service; not as pricey as some other grande dame hotels; outstanding restaurants. **Cons:** expensive parking (£20 per night); no wow factor for some. [$] *Rooms from: £245* ✉ *Princes St., New Town* ☎ *0131/222–8888* 🌐 *www.thecaledonian.waldorfastoria.com* 🛏 *241 rooms* 🍴 *Breakfast* ⊕ D4.

HAYMARKET

Close to one of Edinburgh's two main train stations, Haymarket—beyond the west end of Princes Street—can make a good base for exploring the city.

$$$$ HOTEL Fodor's Choice ★ 🏨 **The Dunstane Houses.** Set within two Victorian town houses that sit across the road from one another, this hotel is one of Edinburgh's most luxurious boutique options. **Pros:** beautifully appointed town-house buildings; excellent food and service; quiet, residential area. **Cons:** no elevator (and stairs to climb); a 20-minute walk to Princes Street. [$] *Rooms from: £235* ✉ *4 W. Coates and 5 Hampton Terr., Haymarket* ☎ *0131/337–6169* 🌐 *www.thedunstane.com* 🛏 *35 rooms* 🍴 *Breakfast* ⊕ A5.

$$ B&B/INN 🏨 **Victorian Town House.** This handsome B&B, situated in a quiet, leafy crescent but within walking distance of Princes Street, offers bright and spacious rooms with a quirky mix of Edwardian and modern furnishings. **Pros:** serene surroundings; gracious staff; beautiful Water of Leith at your doorstep. **Cons:** no parking nearby; a little way from the Old Town. [$] *Rooms from: £120* ✉ *14 Eglinton Terr., Haymarket* ☎ *0131/337–7088* 🌐 *www.thevictoriantownhouse.co.uk* 🛏 *3 rooms* 🍴 *Breakfast* ⊕ B5.

WEST END

With easy access to some of the city's trendiest shops and cafés, the West End has lodgings that take advantage of the neighborhood's handsome Georgian-style town houses.

$$ B&B/INN FAMILY **B+B Edinburgh.** Standing out along an elegant and tranquil West End terrace, this excellent B&B is the first Scottish outpost of supertrendy B+B Belgravia of London. **Pros:** fascinating building in tranquil area; superb views; newly refurbished rooms. **Cons:** no night porter; hint of previous institutional use. [$] *Rooms from: £135* ✉ *3 Rothesay Terr., West End* ☎ *0131/225–5084* 🌐 *www.bb-edinburgh.com* 🛏 *27 rooms* 🍴 *Breakfast* ✣ B4.

$$$ HOTEL **The Bonham.** There's a clubby atmosphere throughout this hotel, where the typical high-ceilinged town-house rooms have gorgeous late-19th-century architectural features mixed with boldly colored furnishings, vibrant fabrics, and contemporary Scottish art. **Pros:** thorough yet unobtrusive service; excellent restaurant; pleasant location. **Cons:** few common areas; needs upgrading in places. [$] *Rooms from: £175* ✉ *35 Drumsheugh Gardens, West End* ☎ *0131/226–6050* 🌐 *www.thebonham.com* 🛏 *49 rooms* 🍴 *Some meals* ✣ B4.

$$ HOTEL **Channings.** Five Edwardian terraced town houses make up this intimate, elegant hotel, with a clubby, oak-paneled lobby lounge and quiet guest rooms complete with well-chosen antiques and marble baths. **Pros:** near Stockbridge shops and eateries; inventive color schemes; good discounts available online. **Cons:** not all rooms equally nice; breakfast could be better. [$] *Rooms from: £125* ✉ *12–16 S. Learmonth Gardens, West End* ☎ *0131/315–2226* 🌐 *www.channings.co.uk* 🛏 *42 rooms* 🍴 *Breakfast* ✣ B3.

$$ HOTEL Fodor's Choice ★ **Rutland Hotel.** Nominated for several style awards, this chic boutique hotel at the west end of Princes Street offers 12 luxury guest rooms with flamboyant fabrics and classic furnishings, as well as nine stylish serviced apartments, a flexible option for a family or two couples traveling together. **Pros:** friendly staff; unpretentious; great bar and restaurant. **Cons:** decor too loud and busy for some. [$] *Rooms from: £150* ✉ *1–3 Rutland St., West End* ☎ *0131/229–3402* 🌐 *www.therutlandhotel.com* 🛏 *26 rooms* 🍴 *Breakfast* [M] *West End-Princes St.* ✣ D4.

SOUTH SIDE

The B&Bs and restaurants in this residential area offer good value.

$$ B&B/INN **AmarAgua.** Four-poster beds, a tranquil location, and bountiful breakfasts set this Victorian town-house B&B apart. **Pros:** quiet setting; snug rooms; wonderful and varied breakfasts. **Cons:** far from the city center; minimum two-night stay. [$] *Rooms from: £105* ✉ *10 Kilmaurs Terr., Newington* ☎ *0131/667–6775* 🌐 *www.amaragua.co.uk* ⏲ *Closed Jan.* 🛏 *5 rooms* 🍴 *Breakfast* ✣ H6.

$$ B&B/INN **Glenalmond House.** Elegantly furnished rooms, a friendly atmosphere, and a hearty breakfast are three big factors that make this town-house B&B a popular budget stay. **Pros:** knowledgeable owners; elegant furnishings; amazing sausages at breakfast. **Cons:** a 30-minute walk to the Royal Mile. [$] *Rooms from: £100* ✉ *25 Mayfield Gardens, South*

Side ☎ 0131/668–2392 🌐 *www.glenalmondhouse.com* 🛏 *9 rooms* 🍴 *Breakfast* ✥ H6.

$$ B&B/INN
🏨 **94DR.** Like the infectiously optimistic owners, Paul and John, 94DR reaches for the stars with its stylish decor and contemporary trappings, while maintaining a comfortable, homey feel. **Pros:** warm welcome; gay-friendly vibe; smashing breakfast; free bikes to help get into the center. **Cons:** 25-minute walk to the city center. [$] *Rooms from: £160* ✉ *94 Dalkeith Rd., South Side* ☎ *0131/662–9265* 🌐 *www.94dr.com* 🛏 *7 rooms* 🍴 *Breakfast* ✥ H6.

$$$$ HOTEL Fodor's Choice ★
🏨 **Prestonfield.** The Highland "coos" (cows), peacocks, and grouse wandering around this hotel's 20-acre grounds transport you to a whole new world; one that's only five minutes by car from the Royal Mile. **Pros:** baroque grandeur; comfortable beds; extensive grounds. **Cons:** underwhelming showers; brooding decor can look gloomy. [$] *Rooms from: £235* ✉ *Priestfield Rd., Prestonfield* ☎ *0131/225–7800* 🌐 *www.prestonfield.com* 🛏 *23 rooms* 🍴 *Some meals* ✥ H6.

LEITH

Staying in Leith means you'll be away from the main Old and New Town sights, but near to the Royal Yacht *Britannia* and some of the city's best dining options.

$$ B&B/INN
🏨 **The Conifers.** This small family-run guesthouse in a red sandstone town house offers simple, traditionally decorated rooms and warm hospitality. **Pros:** nice mix of old and new; many original fittings; hearty breakfasts. **Cons:** a long walk to the city center; one bathroom not en suite. [$] *Rooms from: £100* ✉ *56 Pilrig St., Leith* ☎ *0131/554–5162* 🌐 *www.conifersguesthouse.com* 🛏 *4 rooms* 🍴 *Breakfast* ✥ G1.

$$ HOTEL
🏨 **Malmaison.** Once a seamen's hostel, this French-inspired boutique hotel, which is part of a pioneering U.K.-wide chain, draws a refined clientele to its superchic shorefront rooms. A dramatic black-and-taupe color scheme prevails in the public areas, while the hip rooms are dominated by tartan designs and shades of heather, with bolder fabrics and brighter features in the suites. **Pros:** impressive building; elegant interiors; great waterfront location. **Cons:** price fluctuates wildly; bar sometimes rowdy at night; a long way from the center of town. [$] *Rooms from: £135* ✉ *1 Tower Pl., Leith* ☎ *0131/285–1478* 🌐 *www.malmaison-edinburgh.com* 🛏 *100 rooms* 🍴 *Breakfast* ✥ H1.

NIGHTLIFE AND PERFORMING ARTS

NIGHTLIFE

The nightlife scene in Edinburgh is vibrant—whatever you're looking for, you'll find it here. There are traditional pubs, chic modern bars, and cutting-edge clubs. Live music pours out of many watering holes on weekends, particularly folk, blues, and jazz, while well-known artists perform at some of the larger venues.

Edinburgh's 400-odd pubs are a study in themselves. In the eastern and northern districts of the city, you can find some grim, inhospitable-looking places that proclaim that drinking is no laughing matter. But throughout Edinburgh, many pubs have deliberately traded in their old spit-and-sawdust vibe for atmospheric revivals of the warm, oak-paneled, leather-chaired *howffs* (meeting places). Most pubs and bars are open weekdays, while on weekends they're open from about 11 am to midnight (some until 2 am on Saturday).

The List and *The Skinny* carry the most up-to-date details about cultural events. *The List* is available at newsstands throughout the city, while *The Skinny* is free and can be picked up at a number of pubs, clubs, and shops around town. The *Herald* and *The Scotsman* newspapers are good for reviews and notices of upcoming events throughout the city and beyond.

OLD TOWN
BARS AND PUBS
The Canons' Gait. In addition to a fine selection of local real ales and malts, The Canons' Gait has live jazz and blues performances, as well as edgy comedy shows in the cellar bar. ⊠ *232 Canongate, Old Town* ☎ *0131/556–4481* ⊕ *www.gait.bar.*

Fodor'sChoice ★ **The Holyrood 9A.** Billed as "great beers, great burgers," this wood-paneled hipster hangout has a fine array of craft beers on tap, as well as an impressive whisky collection. The gourmet burgers are worthy of their billing, too. ⊠ *9A Holyrood Rd., Old Town* ☎ *0131/556–5044* ⊕ *www.theholyrood.co.uk.*

The Last Drop. There's plenty of atmosphere (and plenty of tourists) amid the nooks and crannies at the Last Drop. The name has a grim double meaning, as it was once the site of public hangings. ⊠ *74–78 Grassmarket, Old Town* ☎ *0131/225–4851* ⊕ *www.nicholsonspubs.co.uk.*

The Three Sisters. This pub is a hive of activity during festival season, when the courtyard transforms into a beer garden with food stalls, and is packed wall-to-wall with revelers until the wee hours. Outside of the summer months, it remains a lively local favorite, and the best place to watch live sport in Edinburgh. ⊠ *139 Cowgate, Old Town* ☎ *0131/622–6802* ⊕ *www.thethreesistersbar.co.uk.*

Under the Stairs. As the name suggests, this shabby-chic cocktail barcum-bistro is secreted below street level. A cozy, low-ceilinged place, full of quirky furniture and hip art exhibits, Under the Stairs serves specialty, seasonal cocktails, as well as superb bar food, to a mostly young crowd. ⊠ *3A Merchant St., Old Town* ☎ *0131/466–8550* ⊕ *www.underthestairs.org.*

FOLK AND JAZZ CLUBS
You can still find folk and jazz musicians performing in pubs and clubs throughout the Old Town.

Fodor'sChoice ★ **The Jazz Bar.** This basement music venue delivers exactly what the name promises: jazz, in all its many weird and wonderful forms. Blues, funk, acoustic, electric—there's something new to discover every night of the week. There's usually a small cover charge (cash only), but this all goes to musicians, not the venue. ⊠ *1A Chambers St., Old Town* ☎ *0131/220–4298* ⊕ *www.thejazzbar.co.uk.*

The Royal Oak. With a piano in the corner, this cozy, friendly pub presents excellent live blues and folk music most nights—usually with no cover charge. ⌧ *1 Infirmary St., Old Town* ☎ *0131/557-2976* ⊕ *www.royal-oak-folk.com.*

Whistle Binkies Live Music Bar. This atmospheric North Bridge bar, accessible from Niddry Street (as it's *in* the bridge), presents rock, blues, and folk music every night of the week, with as many as six or seven acts on Saturday nights. ⌧ *4–6 South Bridge, Old Town* ☎ *0131/557-5114* ⊕ *whistlebinkies.com.*

NIGHTCLUBS

Cabaret Voltaire. The vaulted ceilings of this subterranean club reverberate with dance music most nights, with an ever-changing lineup of cutting-edge DJs on the decks. The club also hosts regular live gigs and, during the Fringe, stand-up comedy shows. ⌧ *36–38 Blair St., Old Town* ☎ *0131/247-4704* ⊕ *www.thecabaretvoltaire.com.*

NEW TOWN

BARS AND PUBS

The Basement. This funky, cheerful bar has something of the 1950s jet-setter vibe—which might explain its ethnically confused, happy-go-lucky mash-up of cocktails, Mexican food, and Hawaiian-shirted bar staff. ⌧ *10A–12A Broughton St., New Town* ☎ *0131/557-0097* ⊕ *www.basement-bar-edinburgh.co.uk.*

Bramble Bar. This easily walked-by basement bar on Queen Street—take the stairs down to a clothing-alteration shop and you'll see a small sign—is one of Edinburgh's great hidden gems. Expect superb cocktails, eclectic music (DJs spin most nights), young crowds, and lots of nooks and crannies. ⌧ *16A Queen St., New Town* ☎ *0131/226-6343* ⊕ *www.bramblebar.co.uk.*

Fodor'sChoice ★ **Café Royal Circle Bar.** Famed for its atmospheric Victorian interiors— think ornate stucco, etched mirrors, tiled murals, stained glass, and leather booths—the Café Royal Circle Bar has been drawing a cast of Edinburgh characters since it opened in 1863. Regulars and newcomers alike pack in for the drinks (a host of real ales and malt whiskies) and tasty bar food—everything from yummy sandwiches and small plates to elaborate seafood platters. ⌧ *19 W. Register St., New Town* ☎ *0131/556-1884* ⊕ *www.caferoyaledinburgh.co.uk.*

Cask and Barrel. A spacious, traditional pub on trendy Broughton Street, the Cask and Barrel serves hand-pulled ales from a horseshoe-shaped bar, ringed by a collection of brewery mirrors. ⌧ *115 Broughton St., New Town* ☎ *0131/556-3132.*

Guildford Arms. Like the Café Royal Circle Bar on the other corner of the same Victorian block, the Guildford Arms has a spectacular interior of intricate plasterwork, elaborate cornices, and wood paneling. The ornate ceiling alone is worth the visit. Stay for the range of excellent Scottish ales on tap. ⌧ *1 W. Register St., New Town* ☎ *0131/556-4312* ⊕ *www.guildfordarms.com.*

Hogmanay: Hello, New Year

In Scotland, New Year's Eve is called Hogmanay. Around Scotland, celebrations continue the next day with customs such as "first-footing"—visiting your neighbors with gifts that include whisky, all with the purpose of bringing good fortune. It's so important that January 2 as well as January 1 is a holiday in Scotland, while the rest of the United Kingdom trudges back to work.

WHAT TO EXPECT

Edinburgh's Hogmanay celebrations extend over several days, with music, dance, and theater performances taking place throughout the city. The lineup changes every year, but always includes a number of free events. Festivities featuring fire add a dramatic motif; buildings may open for rare night tours; a ceilidh has everyone dancing outdoors to traditional music; and family concerts and serious discussions during the day round out the agenda. At the

heart of Hogmanay, though, is the evening street party on New Year's Eve, with different music stages, food and drink (and people *do* drink), and the heart-lifting—despite the cold—sight of glowing fireworks over Edinburgh Castle. And it all ends with a communal renditions of "Auld Lang Syne." written by Scotland's own Robert Burns.

PLANNING BASICS

Besides the £25 you'll pay to get into the street party celebrations, expect to shell out extra for some related events; for example, the big-name concert in the Princes Street Gardens will run you £50 or more, while the torchlight procession on December 30 costs around £12. Book rooms as far ahead as possible. Obvious but essential is warmth: super-fluffy hats and the bundled-up look are de rigueur. Check out ⊕ *www.edinburghshogmanay.com* for full details, and have a happy Hogmanay!

FAMILY
Fodor'sChoice
★
Joseph Pearce's. One of six Swedish bars and restaurants in Edinburgh owned by the Boda group, Joseph Pearce's has a distinctly northern European feel, despite its solidly Edwardian origins. Scandi-themed cocktails are popular here, as are the meatballs, open sandwiches, and other Swedish dishes. There's a children's corner with toys to keep the little ones occupied, and a sunny outdoor space in summer. ⊠ *23 Elm Row, New Town* ☎ *0131/556–4140* ⊕ *www.bodabar.com/joseph-pearces.*

Fodor'sChoice
★
Juniper. Situated right opposite Waverley station, Juniper cultivates an air of glamorous fun, helped by its postcard-worthy views of the city and the castle. The wine list is good (if a little pricey), but it's the wildly imaginative cocktails that really make this place. A longstanding favorite is Strawberries and Steam, a strawberry-infused gin cocktail served in a teapot that's bubbling over with dry ice. You can soak up your drinks with nibbles from the modern Scottish "street food" menu. ⊠ *20 Princes St., New Town* ☎ *0131/652–7370* ⊕ *www.juniperedinburgh.co.uk.*

Kay's Bar. Housed in a former Georgian coach house, this diminutive but friendly spot serves 50 single-malt whiskies, a range of guest ales, and decent bottled beers. Check out the cute little wood-paneled library room, with its tiny fireplace and shelves full of books. ⊠ *39 Jamaica St., New Town* ☎ *0131/225-1858* ⊕ *www.kaysbar.co.uk.*

Starbar. Well worth seeking out, the tucked-away Starbar has a beer garden, table soccer, and—a rarity—a very good jukebox. It is also rumored to be haunted—get the owners to regale you with scary stories, including a specific clause in their lease that prevents them from removing a human skull from the building. ⊠ *1 Northumberland Pl., New Town* ☎ *0131/539-8070.*

Tonic. This stylish basement bar has bouncy stools, comfy sofas, and a long list of superb cocktails. There's relaxing music Monday to Thursday, acoustic acts Friday, and resident DJs on the weekend. ⊠ *34A N. Castle St., New Town* ☎ *0131/225-6431* ⊕ *www.bar-tonic.co.uk.*

GAY AND LESBIAN

There's an ever-expanding gay and lesbian scene in Edinburgh, and the city has many predominantly gay clubs, bars, and cafés. However, don't expect the scene to be quite as varied as in London, New York, or even Glasgow. *The List* and *The Skinny* have sections that focus on gay and lesbian venues.

CC Blooms. Modern and colorful, CC Blooms is a club spread over two levels, playing a mix of musical styles and with regular cabaret nights. Open nightly, it's been a mainstay on the gay scene since the early '90s, and can now count several other gay-friendly bars and clubs as neighbors. ⊠ *23–24 Greenside Pl., New Town* ☎ *0131/556–9331* ⊕ *www. ccbloomsedinburgh.com.*

Regent. Billing itself as "the best real ale gay pub in Edinburgh," this popular drinking hole is warm, homey, and welcoming—and it's dog-friendly too. As advertised, the real ales selection is great. ⊠ *2 Montrose Terr., Abbeyhill* ☎ *0131/661–8198* ⊕ *www.theregentbar.co.uk.*

NIGHTCLUBS

Liquid Room. Top indie bands and an eclectic mix of club nights (techno, hip-hop, and alternative, to name a few) have made the Liquid Room a favorite after-dark venue since 1997. ⊠ *9C Victoria St., New Town* ☎ *0131/225-2564* ⊕ *www.liquidroom.com.*

Opal Lounge. This casual but stylish nightspot with a glam VIP lounge was favored by Prince William when he was a student at St. Andrew's University. ⊠ *51A George St., New Town* ☎ *0131/226-2275* ⊕ *www. opallounge.co.uk.*

COMEDY CLUBS

The Stand. Laugh until your sides split at The Stand, a legendary basement comedy club that hosts both famous names and up-and-coming acts all throughout the year, though it's particularly popular during the Fringe. There's a free improv show every Sunday lunchtime. ⊠ *5 York Pl., East End* ☎ *0131/558-7272* ⊕ *www.thestand.co.uk.*

WEST END
BARS AND PUBS

Blue Blazer. This cozy and characterful bar has an extensive selection of real ales, malt whiskies, and rums, all of which are enjoyed by a friendly, diverse crowd. ⊠ *2 Spittal St., West End* ☎ *0131/229–5030.*

The Hanging Bat. A favorite with beer-loving locals, this stylish modern bar of reclaimed wood and exposed brickwork has an extensive, regularly changing selection of craft beers from across the United Kingdom on tap, from IPAs to saisons to porters. The food, cooked in the in-house smoker, is great, too (try the smoked pulled pork.) ⊠ *133 Lothian Rd., West End* ☎ *0131/229–0759* ⊕ *www.thehangingbat.com.*

Fodor'sChoice ★ **The Jolly Botanist.** Gin lovers are spoiled for choice at this self-proclaimed "liquor emporium." Take a seat amid the quirky period furnishings and flick through a menu of 72 gins from around the world, which can be enjoyed with your choice of tonic or as part of an inventive gin cocktail. There's also good bar food available. ⊠ *256–260 Morrison St., West End* ☎ *0131/228–5596* ⊕ *www.thejollybotanist.co.uk.*

CEILIDHS AND SCOTTISH EVENINGS

Edinburgh Ceilidh Club. One of Edinburgh's most popular ceilidhs, this traditional Scottish music and dance night is held each Tuesday at Summerhall. It's ideal for beginners, as a caller teaches the dance steps before the live band begins each song. The club also holds irregular nights at Assembly Roxy near South Bridge. ⊠ *Summerhall, Summerhall Pl., South Side* ☎ *0131/560–1580* ⊕ *www.edinburghceilidhclub.com/* ☒ *£6.*

SOUTH SIDE
BARS AND PUBS

Fodor'sChoice ★ **Andrew Usher and Co.** (*Ushers*). A small wooden door leads down a dimly lit staircase—not the most auspicious of entrances. But as you emerge into the chic basement bar, all wood panels and whitewashed brickwork and shiny taps, you can see what all the fuss is about. Ushers is a paradise for ale aficionados, with dozens of craft beers from all over the world on draft, as well as some superb home brews served straight from the barrel. What's more, the pub food is excellent. It's the perfect place to while away a wet afternoon. ⊠ *32b W. Nicolson St., South Side* ☎ *0131/662–1757* ⊕ *www.andrewushers.co.uk.*

Cloisters. Set within an old church parsonage, Cloisters now offers a very modern form of sanctuary: real ales, fine whisky, and good food at reasonable prices, with a total absence of music and game machines. ⊠ *26 Brougham St., Tollcross* ☎ *0131/221–9997* ⊕ *www.cloistersbar.com.*

Leslie's Bar. Retaining its original mahogany island bar, the late-Victorian-era Leslie's Bar is renowned for its gorgeous interior and for serving a range of traditional Scottish ales and malt whiskies. ⊠ *45–47 Ratcliffe Terr., South Side* ☎ *0131/667–7205* ⊕ *www.realalepubedinburgh.co.uk.*

LEITH
BARS AND PUBS

Fodor'sChoice ★ **King's Wark.** Set within a charming 15th-century building, the popular King's Wark is renowned for its superb yet sensibly priced food, from the legendary breakfasts to the lip-smacking Sunday roasts to the sublime Scottish cheese boards. The specials board here often features freshly caught seafood and traditional Scottish fare. In warm weather you can snag a table on the sidewalk. ⊠ *36 The Shore, Leith* ☎ *0131/554-9260* ⊕ *kingswark.co.uk.*

Malt & Hops. First opening its doors in 1749, Malt & Hops has a fine waterfront location and serves microbrewery cask ales—with a selection good enough to be endorsed by CAMRA (the Campaign for Real Ale). It also has a resident ghost. ⊠ *45 The Shore, Leith* ☎ *0131/555-0083* ⊕ *www.barcalisa.com.*

Fodor's Choice **Teuchter's Landing.** Tucked away down a side street near The Shore, ★ Teuchter's Landing is a perennially popular pub for its wide range of whiskies and beers, its excellent pub food (try the nachos with cheddar and haggis), and its pontoon for sunny days. It's also a great place for watching live sports. If you're feeling lucky, try the "Hoop of Destiny" game, for your chance to land a vintage dram for a fraction of its usual price. ⊠ *1c Dock Pl., Leith* ☎ *0131/554-7427* ⊕ *www.aroomin.co.uk/teuchters-landing-bar-edinburgh.*

PERFORMING ARTS

Think Edinburgh's arts scene consists of just the elegiac wail of a bagpipe and the twang of a fiddle? Think again. Edinburgh is one of the world's great performing-arts cities. The jewels in the crown are the famed Edinburgh Festival Fringe and Edinburgh International Festival, which attract the best in music, dance, theater, circus, stand-up comedy, poetry, painting, and sculpture from all over the globe in August. The *Scotsman* and *Herald,* Scotland's leading daily newspapers, carry listings and reviews in their arts pages every day, with special editions during the festival. Tickets are generally sold in advance; in some cases they're also available from certain designated travel agents or at the door, although concerts by national orchestras often sell out long before the day of the performance.

DANCE

Festival Theatre. Scottish Ballet and other dance productions (including off–West End musicals) appear here. ⊠ *13–29 Nicolson St., Old Town* ☎ *0131/529-6000* ⊕ *www.edtheatres.com/festival.*

The Lyceum. Visiting contemporary dance companies perform at the Lyceum, also known as the Royal Lyceum. ⊠ *Grindlay St., West End* ☎ *0131/248-4848* ⊕ *www.lyceum.org.uk.*

FILM

Cameo. Cameo has one large and two small auditoriums, both of which are extremely comfortable, showing a good mix of mainstream and arthouse films. There's also a bar serving snacks late into the evening. ⊠ *38 Home St., Tollcross* ☎ *0131/229-7828* ⊕ *www.picturehouses.com.*

Fodor's Choice **Filmhouse.** Widely considered to be among the best independent cinemas ★ in Britain, the excellent three-screen Filmhouse is the go-to venue for modern, foreign-language, offbeat, and any other less-commercial films. It also holds frequent live events and mini-festivals for the discerning cinephile, and is the main hub for the International Film Festival each summer. The café and bar here are open late on weekends. ⊠ *88 Lothian Rd., West End* ☎ *0131/228–2688* ⊕ *www.filmhousecinema.com.*

MUSIC

Edinburgh Playhouse. This venue leans toward popular artists, comedy acts, and musicals. ⊠ *18–22 Greenside Pl., East End* ☎ *0844/871–3014* ⊕ *atgtickets.com.*

Festival Theatre. This theater hosts regular concerts, as well as musical theater and Scottish Opera productions. ⊠ *13–29 Nicolson St., Old Town* ☎ *0131/529–6000* ⊕ *www.edtheatres.com.*

The Queen's Hall. This intimate venue hosts a range of music events, from indie and rock concerts to jazz and classical music recitals. ⊠ *85–89 Clerk St., Old Town* ☎ *0131/668–2019* ⊕ *www.thequeenshall.net.*

Usher Hall. Edinburgh's grandest concert venue, Usher Hall hosts a wide range of national and international performers, from Kraftwerk and Ryan Adams to the Royal Scottish National Orchestra. ⊠ *Lothian Rd., West End* ☎ *0131/228–1155* ⊕ *www.usherhall.co.uk.*

THEATER
MODERN

King's Theatre. Built in 1906 and adorned with vibrant murals by artist John Byrne, the art nouveau King's Theatre has a great program of contemporary dramatic works. ⊠ *2 Leven St., Tollcross* ☎ *0131/529–6000* ⊕ *www.edtheatres.com/kings.*

Traverse Theatre. With its specially designed space, the Traverse Theatre has developed a solid reputation for new, stimulating plays by Scottish dramatists, as well as innovative dance performances. ⊠ *10 Cambridge St., West End* ☎ *0131/228–1404* ⊕ *www.traverse.co.uk.*

TRADITIONAL

Church Hill Theatre. The intimate, 335-seat Church Hill Theatre, managed by the city council, hosts high-quality productions by local amateur dramatic societies. ⊠ *33 Morningside Rd., Morningside* ☎ *0131/220–4348* ⊕ *www.assemblyroomsedinburgh.co.uk.*

Edinburgh Playhouse. Big-ticket concerts and musicals, along with the occasional ballet and opera production, are staged at the popular Playhouse, with its enormous 3,000-seat auditorium. ⊠ *18-22 Greenside La., East End* ☎ *0844/871–3014* ⊕ *www.atgtickets.com.*

The Lyceum. Traditional plays and contemporary works, including previews or tours of London West End productions, are presented here. ⊠ *Grindlay St., West End* ☎ *0131/248–4848* ⊕ *www.lyceum.org.uk.*

SHOPPING

Despite its renown as a shopping street, **Princes Street** in the New Town may disappoint some visitors with its dull modern architecture, average chain stores, and fast-food outlets. One block north of Princes Street, **Rose Street** has many smaller specialty shops; part of the street is a pedestrian zone, so it's a pleasant place to browse. The shops on **George Street** in New Town tend to be fairly upscale. London names, such as Laura Ashley and Penhaligons, are prominent, though some of the older independent stores continue to do good business.

The streets crossing George Street—Hanover, Frederick, and Castle—are also worth exploring. **Dundas Street,** the northern extension of Hanover Street, beyond Queen Street Gardens, has several antiques shops. **Thistle Street,** originally George Street's "back lane," or service area, has several boutiques and more antiques shops.

As may be expected, many shops along the **Royal Mile** in Old Town sell what may be politely or euphemistically described as "touristware"—whiskies, tartans, and tweeds. Careful exploration, however, will reveal some worthwhile establishments, including shops that cater to highly specialized interests and hobbies. A street below the Royal Mile, East Market Street, close to the castle end of the Royal Mile, just off George IV Bridge, is **Victoria Street,** with specialty shops grouped in a small area. Follow the tiny West Bow to **Grassmarket** for more specialty stores.

Stafford and William Streets form a small, upscale shopping area in a Georgian setting. Walk to the west end of Princes Street and then along its continuation, Shandwick Place, then turn right onto Stafford Street. William Street crosses Stafford halfway down.

North of Princes Street, on the way to the Royal Botanic Garden Edinburgh, is **Stockbridge,** an oddball shopping area of some charm, particularly on St. Stephen Street. To get here, walk north down Frederick Street and Howe Street, away from Princes Street, then turn left onto North West Circus Place.

Edinburgh's newest (and hippest) shopping area is **The Arches,** which has a number of glass-fronted independent stores set within Victorian-era archways. You'll find it on East Market Street, to the east of Waverley train station and below the Royal Mile. And coming in 2020 is the refurbished **Edinburgh St. James,** a vast, state-of-the-art shopping complex being built between Princes Street and Leith Walk.

OLD TOWN

BOOKS, PAPER, MAPS, AND GAMES

Armchair Books. Just a two-minute walk from Grassmarket, Armchair Books is a chaotic but characterful bookshop heaving with secondhand and antiquarian books. ✉ *72–74 W. Port, Old Town* ☎ *0131/229–5927* ⊕ *www.armchairbooks.co.uk.*

Carson Clark Gallery. This gallery specializes in antique maps, sea charts, and prints. ✉ *34 Northumberland St., Old Town* ☎ *0131/556–4710* ⊕ *www.carsonclarkgallery.co.uk.*

Main Point Books. This bibliophile's haven is stacked high with obscure first editions and bargain tomes. It also hosts regular literary events. ✉ *77 Bread St., Old Town* ☎ *0131/228–4837* ⊕ *www.mainpointbooks. co.uk.*

CLOTHING BOUTIQUES

Bill Baber. One of the more imaginative Scottish knitwear designers, Bill Baber's creative and colorful pieces are a long way from the conservative pastel woolies sold at some of the large mill shops. ⊠ *66 Grassmarket, Old Town* ☎ *0131/225–3249* ⊕ *www.billbaber.com.*

Ragamuffin. First established on the Isle of Skye, Ragamuffin's Edinburgh outlet sells some of the funkiest, brightest, and most elegant knitwear produced anywhere in Scotland. ⊠ *278 Canongate, Old Town* ☎ *0131/557–6007* ⊕ *ragamuffinloves.blogspot.co.uk.*

JEWELRY

Clarksons. A family firm, Clarksons handcrafts a unique collection of jewelry, from Celtic to contemporary styles. The pieces here are made with silver, gold, platinum, and precious gems, with a particular emphasis on diamonds. ⊠ *87 West Bow, Old Town* ☎ *0131/225–8141* ⊕ *www.clarksonsedinburgh.co.uk.*

SCOTTISH SPECIALTIES

Fodor's Choice ★ **Cranachan & Crowdie.** This lovely gourmet shop on the Royal Mile is brimming with the finest Scottish food and drink, from crunchy oatcakes to melt-in-the-mouth shortbread. There's even a chocolate counter for those with a particularly sweet tooth. Staff are happy to put together hampers of food for any occasion—including an impromptu picnic back in your room. They also sell tweeds, handmade candles, and other gift-worthy knickknacks. ⊠ *263 Canongate, Old Town* ☎ *0131/556–7194* ⊕ *www.cranachanandcrowdie.com.*

Geoffrey (Tailor) Highland Crafts. This shop can clothe you in full Highland dress, with high-quality kilts made in its own workshops. ⊠ *57–59 High St., Old Town* ☎ *0131/557–0256* ⊕ *www.geoffreykilts.co.uk.*

NEW TOWN

ANTIQUES

Fodor's Choice ★ **Unicorn Antiques.** This Victorian basement is crammed with fascinating antiques, including artworks, ornaments, silverware, and other such curios. ⊠ *65 Dundas St., New Town* ☎ *0131/556–7176* ⊕ *www.unicornantiques.co.uk.*

CLOTHING BOUTIQUES

Elaine's Vintage Clothing. This wee boutique in trendy Stockbridge is crammed full of vintage threads for women and men. The finds span the 20th century, but most are from the '40s to the '70s. The friendly owner is happy to share her knowledge of the many elegant and quirky outfits on her rails. ⊠ *55 St. Stephen St., New Town* ☎ *0131/225–5783.*

DEPARTMENT STORES

Harvey Nichols. Affectionately (and almost universally) known as Harvey Nicks, this high-style British fashion chain has its Scottish outpost near Princes Street, carrying the store's chic, upscale style choices. ⊠ *30–34 St. Andrew Sq., New Town* ☎ *0131/524–8388* ⊕ *www.harveynichols.com.*

Fodor's Choice ★ **Jenners.** Jenners, a long-standing Edinburgh landmark that is now part of the U.K.-wide House of Fraser chain, specializes in traditional china and glassware, as well as Scottish tweeds and tartans—though you'll find everything else you'd expect from a large department store, too. Its famous food hall, run by Valvona & Crolla, stocks traditional culinary delights including shortbread, marmalade, and honey. ⌧ *48 Princes St., New Town* ☎ *0344/800–3725* ⊕ *www.houseoffraser.co.uk.*

2

John Lewis. John Lewis specializes in furnishings and household goods, but also stocks designer clothes. It's part of the Edinburgh St. James shopping complex, which is currently closed for extensive redevelopment (due to finish in 2020), but John Lewis remains open as usual with access from Leith Street. ⌧ *Edinburgh St. James, Leith St., New Town* ☎ *0131/556–9121* ⊕ *www.johnlewis.com/our-shops/edinburgh.*

Marks & Spencer. Fairly priced, stylish clothes and accessories are on offer at Marks & Spencer. You can also buy quality food and household goods. ⌧ *54 Princes St., New Town* ☎ *0131/225–2301* ⊕ *www.marksandspencer.com.*

HOME FURNISHINGS

Hannah Zakari. Quirky handmade pieces, including embroidered cushions, are a specialty at Hannah Zakari. Keep an eye out for unusual jewelry, artwork, and accessories, too. ⌧ *43 Candlemaker Row, New Town* ☎ *0131/226–5433* ⊕ *www.hannahzakari.co.uk.*

JEWELRY

Hamilton and Inches. Established in 1866, this jeweler is worth visiting not only for its gold and silver pieces, but also for its late-Georgian interior. Designed by David Bryce in 1834, it's all columns and elaborate plasterwork. ⌧ *87 George St., New Town* ☎ *0131/225–4898* ⊕ *www.hamiltonandinches.com.*

Joseph Bonnar. Tucked behind George Street, Joseph Bonnar stocks Scotland's largest collection of antique jewelry, including 19th-century agate jewels. ⌧ *72 Thistle St., New Town* ☎ *0131/226–2811* ⊕ *www.josephbonnar.com.*

Fodor's Choice ★ **Sheila Fleet.** As much art gallery as jewelry shop, designer Sheila Fleet's store in Stockbridge displays a variety of stunning jewelry inspired by her native Orkney, from wind and waves to Celtic spirals to island wildlife. ⌧ *18 St. Stephen St., Stockbridge* ☎ *0131/225–5939* ⊕ *www.sheilafleet.com.*

OUTDOOR SPORTS GEAR

Cotswold Outdoor. This specialist chain store sells outdoor clothing for all weather, as well as accessories, maps, guides, and more. The staff are invariably helpful and informed. ⌧ *72 Rose St., New Town* ☎ *0131/341–2063* ⊕ *www.cotswoldoutdoor.com.*

WEST END

CLOTHING BOUTIQUES

Concrete Wardrobe. For an eclectic mix of quirky knitwear and accessories, dive into Concrete Wardrobe. You can also find vintage furnishings and other crafty treats. ⊠ *50a Broughton St., West End* ☎ *0131/5587130* ⊕ *www.concretewardrobe.com.*

Herman Brown. This secondhand clothing store is where cashmere twinsets and classic luxe labels are sought and found. ⊠ *151 W. Port, West End* ☎ *0131/228–2589* ⊕ *www.hermanbrown.co.uk.*

SOUTH SIDE

ANTIQUES

Courtyard Antiques. This lovely shop, tucked down a tiny alleyway, stocks a mixture of high-quality antiques, toys, and militaria. ⊠ *108a Causewayside, Sciennes* ☎ *0131/662–9008* ⊕ *www.edinburghcourtyardantiques.co.uk.*

LEITH

ARCADES AND SHOPPING CENTERS

Ocean Terminal. As well as being home to Royal Yacht *Britannia,* this on-the-water mall also has an impressive range of big-name brand stores and independent craft shops, as well as bars, restaurants, and a cinema. ⊠ *Ocean Dr., Leith* ☎ *0131/555–8888* ⊕ *www.oceanterminal.com.*

OUTDOOR SPORTS GEAR

Tiso Edinburgh Outdoor Experience. This sizable store stocks outdoor clothing, boots, and jackets ideal for hiking in the Highlands. It also sells tents and camping accessories, for the truly hardy. There's a café inside, too. ⊠ *41 Commercial St., Leith* ☎ *0131/554–0804* ⊕ *www.tiso.com.*

SPORTS AND THE OUTDOORS

FOOTBALL

Like Glasgow, Edinburgh is mad for football (soccer in the United States), and there's an intense rivalry between the city's two professional teams.

Heart of Midlothian Football Club. Better known simply as "Hearts," the Heart of Midlothian Football Club plays in maroon and white and is based at Tynecastle. The club's crest is based on the Heart of Midlothian mosaic on the Royal Mile. ⊠ *Tynecastle Stadium, McLeod St., Edinburgh* ☎ *0333/043–1874* ⊕ *www.heartsfc.co.uk.*

Hibernian Football Club. Known as the Hibs, the green-and-white-bedecked Hibernian Club was founded in 1875—one year after Hearts—and plays its home matches at Easter Road Stadium in Leith. ⊠ *Easter Road Stadium, 12 Albion Pl., Leith* ☎ *0131/661–2159* ⊕ *www.hibernianfc.co.uk.*

GOLF

2

Edinburgh is widely considered to be the birthplace of modern golf, as its first official rules were developed at Leith Links. Naturally, there are a number of great courses in the city. For more information, the VisitScotland website has an extensive, searchable guide to Scottish courses.

Braid Hills. Known to locals and many others as Braids, this course is beautifully laid out over a rugged range of small hills in the southern suburbs of Edinburgh. The views in each direction—the Pentland Hills in the south; the city skyline and Firth of Forth to the north—are worth a visit in themselves. The city built this course at the turn of the 20th century after urban development forced golfers out of the city center. There's also a 9-hole "Wee Braids" course for beginners and younger players. Reservations are recommended for weekend play. ✉ *27 Braids Hill Approach, Edinburgh* ☎ *0131/447–6666* ⊕ *www.edinburghleisure.co.uk/venues/braid-hills-golf-course* ⊠ *Braids, £25 weekdays, £27 weekends; Princes, £14 weekdays, £16 weekends* ⚑ *Braids: 18 holes, 5865 yards, par 71; Wee Braids: 9 holes, 2232 yards, par 31.*

Bruntsfield Links. The British Seniors and several other championship tournaments are held at this prestigious Willie Park–designed course, 3 miles west of Edinburgh. The course meanders among 155 acres of mature parkland and has fine views over the Firth of Forth. A strict dress code applies. Bruntsfield takes its name from one of the oldest golf links in Scotland, in the center of Edinburgh, where the club used to play—all that remains there is a 9-hole pitch-and-putt course. ■ **TIP→ Full-day tickets are available for just £20 more than the cost of a single round.** ✉ *32 Barnton Ave., Davidson's Mains, Edinburgh* ☎ *0131/336–1479* ⊕ *www.bruntsfieldlinks.co.uk* ⊠ *£75 weekdays, £80 weekends* ⚑ *18 holes, 6437 yards, par 70* ⛳ *Reservations essential.*

Duddingston Golf Club. Founded in 1895, this excellent public parkland course is 2 miles east of the city. The first hole is located in an idyllic deer park (watch out for four-legged spectators). Braid Burn—a stream that flows across the southern part of Edinburgh—also runs through the course, creating a perilous hazard on many holes. Prices drop sharply in the winter months for those willing to risk strong winds and rain. ✉ *Duddingston Rd. W, Duddingston* ☎ *0131/661–7688* ⊕ *www.duddingstongolfclub.co.uk* ⊠ *£25 Mar., Apr., and Oct.; £55 May–Sept.; £19 Nov.–Feb.* ⚑ *18 holes, 6466 yards, par 72.*

Liberton. Built in 1920, this 82-acre public parkland course has narrow fairways and smallish greens. The 18-hole course has been well landscaped with trees and bunkers; many of the trees are still maturing, meaning that the pleasant character of the course is slowly developing over time. The club also has a treatment room, offering a wide range of holistic therapy treatments—including Reiki, Indian head massage, and deeply relaxing hot stone massages. Call ahead to book a session. ✉ *Kingston Grange, 297 Gilmerton Rd., Liberton* ☎ *0131/664–3009* ⊕ *www.libertongc.co.uk* ⊠ *£28 weekdays, £33 weekends* ⚑ *18 holes, 5344 yards, par 67.*

Royal Burgess Golfing Society. Edinburgh's other Victorian courses are newcomers when compared to Royal Burgess—it opened in 1735, making it one of the world's oldest golf clubs. Its members originally played on Bruntsfield Links; now they and their guests play on elegantly manicured parkland in the city's northwestern suburbs. It's a challenging course with fine, beautifully maintained greens. There's a fairly conservative dress code—no denim or T-shirts allowed, and you must wear a jacket and tie in the clubhouse. ⊠ *181 Whitehouse Rd., Barnton* ☎ *0131/339–2075* ⊕ *www.royalburgess.co.uk* ⊠ *£100* ↑ *18 holes, 6511 yards, par 71* ⚑ *Reservations essential.*

RUGBY

Fodor'sChoice **Murrayfield Stadium.** Home of the Scottish Rugby Union, Murrayfield
★ Stadium hosts rugby matches in early spring and fall, including internationals. Crowds of good-humored rugby fans from all over the world add greatly to the sense of excitement in the streets of Edinburgh. Stick around after the game as there's often live music, food, and drinks to enjoy in the stadium grounds. Outside of the rugby season, you can still see Murrayfield with a stadium tour; tickets are £10 for adults. ⊠ *Roseburn St., Murrayfield* ☎ *0131/346–5250* ⊕ *www.scottishrugby.org.*

SIDE TRIPS: WEST LOTHIAN AND THE FORTH VALLEY

If you stand on an Edinburgh eminence—the castle ramparts, Arthur's Seat, Calton Hill—you can plan a few Lothian excursions without even the aid of a map. The Lothians is the collective name given to the swath of countryside south of the Firth of Forth and surrounding Edinburgh. Many courtly and aristocratic families lived here, and the region still has the castles and mansions to prove it. And with the rich came deer parks, gardens in the French style, and Lothian's fame as a seed plot for Lowland gentility.

West Lothian comprises a good bit of Scotland's central belt. The River Forth snakes across a widening floodplain on its descent from the Highlands, and by the time it reaches the western extremities of Edinburgh, it has already passed below the mighty Forth bridges and become a broad estuary. Castles and historic houses sprout thickly on both sides of the Forth. You can explore a number of them, and the territory north of the River Forth, in a day or two, or you can just pick one excursion for a day trip from Edinburgh.

GETTING HERE AND AROUND
BUS TRAVEL
First Bus and Lothian Buses link most of this area. If you're planning to see more than one sight in the region by bus, it's worth planning an itinerary in advance.

CAR TRAVEL

The Queensferry Road, also known as the A90, is the main thoroughfare running through this region. After crossing the Forth Bridge, it joins the M90 heading north, with branches off to Culross (on the A985), Dunfermline (on the A823), and the Ochil Hills (on the A91).

TRAIN TRAVEL

Dalmeny (for South Queensferry), Linlithgow, and Dunfermline all have rail stations and can be reached from Edinburgh stations.

VISITOR INFORMATION

There is a VisitScotland iCentre in Dunfermline, open mid-June through August.

ESSENTIALS

Visitor Information VisitScotland. ⊠ *1 High St., Dunfermline* ☎ *01383/720999* ⊕ *www.visitscotland.com.*

SOUTH QUEENSFERRY

7 miles west of Edinburgh.

This pleasant little waterside community, a former ferry port, is completely dominated by the Forth Bridges, three dramatic structures of contrasting architecture (dating from the 19th, 20th, and 21st centuries) that span the Firth of Forth at this historic crossing point. It's near a number of historic and other sights.

GETTING HERE AND AROUND

The Queensferry Road, also known as the A90, is the main artery west from Edinburgh toward the Forth Bridge, Hopetoun House, the House of the Binns, and Blackness Castle.

EXPLORING

Dalmeny House. The first of the stately houses clustered on the western edge of Edinburgh, Dalmeny House is the home of the Earl and Countess of Rosebery. This 1815 Tudor Gothic mansion displays among its sumptuous interiors the best of the family's famous collection of 18th-century French furniture. Highlights include the library, the Napoléon Room, the Vincennes and Sevres porcelain collections, and the drawing room, with its tapestries and intricately wrought French furniture. Admission is by guided tour in June and July only. ⊠ *South Queensferry* ☎ *0131/331–1888* ⊕ *dalmeny.co.uk* ⊠ *£10* ☉ *Closed Thurs.–Sat., in June and July; closed Aug.–May.*

Forth Bridge. Opened in 1890, when it was hailed as the eighth wonder of the world, this iconic red cantilevered rail bridge is a UNESCO World Heritage Site. The extraordinary, 1½-mile-long crossing expands by another yard or so on a hot summer's day. The famous 19th-century bridge has since been joined by two neighbors; the 20th-century Forth Road Bridge (opened 1964) and the 21st-century Queensferry Crossing (opened 2017). ⊠ *South Queensferry.*

Hopetoun House. The palatial premises of Hopetoun House are among Scotland's grandest courtly seats, and are now home to the Marquesses of Linlithgow. The enormous property was started in 1699 to the

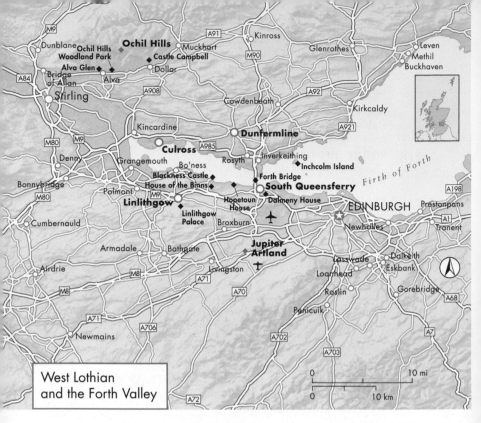

West Lothian
and the Forth Valley

original plans of Sir William Bruce, then enlarged between 1721 and 1754 by William Adam and his sons Robert and John. The house has decorative work of the highest order and a notable painting collection, plus all the trappings to keep you entertained: a nature trail, a restaurant in the former stables, a farm shop, and a museum. The estate also specializes in clay pigeon shooting; groups of six or more can book an expert-led introductory session, with prices starting at £45 per person. ⊠ *Lime Ave.* ☎ *0131/331–2451* ⊕ *www.hopetoun.co.uk* ✉ *£9.85; grounds only £4.65* ⊘ *Closed Oct.–mid-Apr.*

Fodor's Choice
★

Inchcolm Island. Accessible by boat tour from South Queensferry, Inchcolm Island is home to a beautifully preserved 12th-century abbey, a First World War fortress, green cliffs, sandy beaches, and an abundance of wildlife, from playful gray seals to brightly colored puffins. Prepare to be dive-bombed by seagulls if you visit during nesting season. The island is run by Historic Scotland, which levies an entry fee of £6, but boat tours (run by Maid of the Forth and Forth Boat Tours) include this in the price of their tickets. ⊠ *Inchcolm Island* ☎ *01383/823332* ⊕ *www.historicenvironment.scot* ✉ *£20 (boat tour and island entry).*

WHERE TO EAT

$$
MODERN BRITISH
✕ **The Boat House.** Scotland's natural larder is on display at this romantic restaurant on the banks of the Forth. Seafood is the star of the show, and chef Paul Steward is the man behind the imaginative yet unfussy recipes. **Known for:** delicious seafood; spectacular views from the patio. $ *Average main: £18* ⊠ *22 High St.* ☎ *0131/331–5429* ⊕ *www.theboathouse-sq.co.uk.*

JUPITER ARTLAND

10 miles west of Edinburgh.

For anyone drawn to interesting art and beautiful open spaces, a visit to this open-air collection of sculptures by world-renowned artists is a must.

GETTING HERE AND AROUND

To reach Jupiter Artland from Edinburgh, take the A71 southwest toward Kilmarnock. Just after Wilkieston, turn right onto the B7015. It's also easy to reach by bus: the X27 departs from Princes Street, while Bus 27 leaves from Dalry Road near Haymarket.

EXPLORING

Fodor's Choice
★
Jupiter Artland. The beautiful grounds of a Jacobean manor house have been transformed by an art-loving couple, Robert and Nicky Wilson, into an impressive sculpture park. With the aid of a map you can explore the magical landscapes and encounter works by renowned artists including Andy Goldsworthy, Anya Gallaccio, Jim Lambie, Nathan Coley, Ian Hamilton Finlay, and Anish Kapoor, among many others. A highlight is walking around Charles Jencks's *Cells of Life,* a series of shapely, grass-covered mounds. ⊠ *Bonnington House Steadings, Wilkieston, Edinburgh* ☎ *01506/889900* ⊕ *www.jupiterartland.org* ▣ *£8.50* ۞ *Closed Oct.–Apr. and Mon.–Wed. in May, June, and Sept.*

LINLITHGOW

12 miles west of Edinburgh.

Linlithgow is best known for its lochside palace, the impressive remnants of what was once the seat of the Stewart kings. But there are also two impressive fortifications nearby.

GETTING HERE AND AROUND

From Edinburgh, take the A90 westward, continuing onto the A904 and M9, to reach Linlithgow. You can also board a train to Linlithgow station, which is just a short walk from the palace.

EXPLORING

Blackness Castle. Standing like a grounded ship on the very edge of the Forth, this curious 15th-century structure has had a varied career as a strategic fortress, state prison, powder magazine, and youth hostel. The countryside is gently green and cultivated, and open views extend across the blue Forth to the distant ramparts of the Ochil Hills. ⊠ *Blackness, Linlithgow* ☎ *01506/834807* ⊕ *www.historicenvironment.scot* ▣ *£6* ۞ *Closed Thurs. and Fri. in Oct.–Mar.*

House of the Binns. The 17th-century general "Bloody" Tam Dalyell (c. 1599–1685) transformed a fortified stronghold into a gracious mansion, the House of the Binns. The name derives from *bynn,* the old Scottish word for hill. The present exterior dates from around 1810 and shows a remodeling into a kind of mock fort with crenellated battlements and turrets. Inside, see magnificent Elizabethan-style plaster ceilings. ⊠ *Off A904, Linlithgow* ☎ *01506/834255* ⊕ *www.nts.org.uk* 🎫 *£10.50* ⊙ *House closed Oct.–May and Sun.–Tues. Estate always open.*

Linlithgow Palace. On the edge of Linlithgow Loch stands the splendid ruin of Linlithgow Palace, the birthplace of Mary, Queen of Scots. Burned, perhaps accidentally, by Hanoverian troops during the last Jacobite rebellion in 1746, this impressive shell stands on a site of great antiquity, though an earlier fire in 1424 destroyed any hard evidence of medieval life here. The palace gatehouse was built in the early 16th century, and the central courtyard's elaborate fountain dates from around 1535. The halls and great rooms are cold, echoing stone husks now in the care of Historic Scotland. ⊠ *Kirkgate, Linlithgow* ☎ *01506/842896* ⊕ *www.historicenvironment.scot* 🎫 *£6.*

OCHIL HILLS

24 miles northwest of Edinburgh.

The scarp face of the Ochil Hills looms unmistakably. It's an old fault line that yields up hard volcanic rocks and contrasts with the quantities of softer coal immediately around the River Forth. The steep Ochils provided grazing land and water power for Scotland's second-largest textile area.

GETTING HERE AND AROUND
There are two ways to get here by car: take the A90 north of the Forth Bridge, or go via Stirling on the M9. The A91 passes Alva and the Ochil Hills.

EXPLORING
Alva Glen. There's a gorgeously green gorge at Alva Glen. Lovely walking paths follow the gushing Alva Burn and pass many abandoned woolen mills, though be prepared: some paths are steep. ⊠ *Brook St., Alva.*

Castle Campbell. With green woods below, bracken hills above, and a view that on a clear day stretches right across the Forth Valley to the tip of Tinto Hill near Lanark, Castle Campbell is the most atmospheric fortress within easy reach of Edinburgh. Formerly known as Castle Gloom, it stands out among Scottish castles for the sheer drama of its setting. The sturdy square of the tower house survives from the 15th century, when the site was fortified by the first Earl of Argyll. Other buildings and enclosures were subsequently added, but the sheer lack of space on this rocky eminence ensured that there couldn't be any drastic changes. In 1654, the castle was captured by Oliver Cromwell and garrisoned by the English. It's now cared for by Historic Scotland, and is part of the historic Clackmannanshire Tower Trail. To get here, follow a road off the A91 that slowly climbs up the east side of a wooded hill. ⊠ *Castle*

Rd., Dollar ☎ *01259/742408* ⊕ *www.historicenvironment.scot* ✉ *£6* ⊘ *Closed Thurs. and Fri. in Oct.–Mar.*

Ochil Hills Woodland Park. East of Alva is the Ochil Hills Woodland Park, which provides access to lovely Silver Glen, so called because the precious metal was mined here in the 18th century. ✉ *Off A91, Alva* ☎ *01259/213131* ⊕ *www.ochils.org.uk/ochils-woodland-park.*

CULROSS

17 miles northwest of Edinburgh.

The town is a fascinating open-air museum that gives you a feel for life in Scotland in the 17th and 18th centuries.

GETTING HERE AND AROUND

To get here by car, head north of the Forth Bridge on the A90, then westward on the A985. You can get here by bus (No. 8) from Dunfermline, which in turn is easily reached by train from Edinburgh.

EXPLORING

Fodor'sChoice
★

Culross. With its mercat cross, cobbled streets, tolbooth, and narrow wynds (alleys), seaside Culross is a picturesque little town. It's also a living museum of 17th-century Scottish life, with preserved historic properties open to the public. Culross once had a thriving industry and export trade in coal and salt (the coal was used in the salt-panning process), but as local coal became exhausted, the impetus of the Industrial Revolution passed Culross by, while other parts of the Forth Valley prospered. Culross became a backwater town, and the merchants' houses of the 17th and 18th centuries were never replaced by Victorian developments or modern architecture. In the 1930s, the National Trust for Scotland started to buy up the decaying properties with a view to preservation. Today, ordinary citizens live in many of these properties, but others—namely the palace, study, and town house—are available to explore. Town walking tours are also available for a small fee. ✉ *Culross Palace* ☎ *01383/880359* ⊕ *www.nts.org.uk* ✉ *Palace: £10.50; town tour: £3* ⊘ *Palace closed Nov.–mid-Apr.; Sun. in mid-Apr.–May, Sept., and Oct.; Tues. in June.*

DUNFERMLINE

16 miles northwest of Edinburgh.

Oft-overlooked Dunfermline was once the world center for the production of damask linen, but the town is better known today as the birthplace of millionaire industrialist and philanthropist Andrew Carnegie (1835–1919). Undoubtedly Dunfermline's most famous son, Carnegie endowed the town with a park, library, fitness center, and, naturally, a Carnegie Hall, still the focus of the town's culture and entertainment.

GETTING HERE AND AROUND

When you're driving, head north on the A90, turning off onto the A823 a few miles north the Forth Bridge. You can also reach the town by train from Edinburgh in about 35 minutes.

EXPLORING

Andrew Carnegie Birthplace Museum. Scottish-American industrialist and noted philanthropist Andrew Carnegie was born here in 1835. Don't be misled by the simple exterior of this 18th-century weaver's cottage— inside it opens into a larger hall, where documents, photographs, and artifacts relate his fascinating life story. The collection includes art from a wide range of periods, from medieval to 19th century to art deco, as well as displays on the genus of Jurassic dinosaur named after the great man—*Diplodocus carnegii.* ⊠ *Moodie St.* ☎ *01383/724302* ⊕ *www. carnegiebirthplace.com* 🎫 *Free* ☉ *Closed Dec.–Feb.*

Dunfermline Abbey and Palace. This impressive complex, the literal and metaphorical centerpiece of Dunfermline, was founded in the 11th century as a Benedictine abbey by Queen Margaret, the English wife of Scottish king Malcolm III. The present church is a mishmash of medieval and Norman work, and a decorative brass tomb here is the final resting place of Robert the Bruce (1274–1329). A palace was also part of the complex here, and was the birthplace of Charles I (1600–49); its ruins lie beside the abbey. Dunfermline was the seat of the royal court of Scotland until the end of the 11th century, and its central role in Scottish affairs is explored by means of display panels dotted around the drafty but hallowed buildings. ⊠ *St. Margaret St.* ☎ *01383/724586* ⊕ *www.historic-scotland.gov.uk/places* 🎫 *Free, but donations welcome* ☉ *Closed Nov.–Feb.*

SIDE TRIPS: MIDLOTHIAN AND EAST LOTHIAN

Stretching east to the sea and south to the Lowlands from Edinburgh, the regions of Midlothian and East Lothian, and their many attractions, are all within an hour's reach of Edinburgh.

Despite its countless tourist draws, including Scotland's finest stone carvings at Rosslyn Chapel, associations with Sir Walter Scott, outstanding castles, and miles of rolling countryside, Midlothian (the area immediately south of Edinburgh), remained off the beaten path for years. Fortunately, things are starting to change, as visitors look beyond the capital and the well-manicured charm of East Lothian to explore the pretty working towns and suburbs of Midlothian.

East Lothian, on the other hand, has been a draw for decades. An upmarket stockbroker belt, East Lothian's biggest draws are its golf courses of world rank, most notably Muirfield, plus a scattering of stately homes and interesting hotels. Its photogenic villages, active fishing harbors, dramatic cliff-side castles, and vistas of pastoral Lowland Scotland seem a world away from bustling Edinburgh—yet excellent transport links mean they're easy and quick to reach.

GETTING HERE AND AROUND

BUS TRAVEL

Buses from Edinburgh serve towns and villages throughout Midlothian and East Lothian. For details of all services, inquire at the Edinburgh Bus Station, immediately east of St. Andrew Square in Edinburgh.

CAR TRAVEL

A quick route to Rosslyn Chapel follows the A701, while the A7 heads toward Gorebridge and the National Mining Museum Scotland. The A1 passes Newhailes, Haddington, and Dunbar. Take the A198 to Gullane, North Berwick, and Tantallon Castle.

TRAIN TRAVEL

There is no train service in Midlothian. In East Lothian, there are tracks running east along the coast, with regular services to North Berwick and Dunbar.

NEWHAILES

5 miles east of Edinburgh.

With sumptuous interiors and relaxing grounds, this neo-Palladian villa a few miles east of Edinburgh hosted many luminaries of the Scottish Enlightenment.

GETTING HERE AND AROUND

To get here from Edinburgh, take the A1 east, then transfer to the A6095. You can also get here by Lothian Bus 30 or by train to Newcraighall station, a 20-minute walk from the villa.

EXPLORING

Newhailes. This fine late-17th-century house was designed by Scottish architect James Smith in 1686 as his own home. He later sold it to Lord Bellendon, and in 1707 it was bought by Sir David Dalrymple, first Baronet of Hailes, who improved and extended the house, adding one of the finest rococo interiors in Scotland. The library here played host to many famous figures from the Scottish Enlightenment, as well as inveterate Scot-basher Dr. Samuel Johnson, who dubbed the library "the most learned room in Europe." Most of the original interiors and furnishings remain intact, and there are beautiful walks around the landscaped grounds and through the surrounding woodland. ⊠ *Newhailes Rd., Musselburgh* ☎ *0131/653–5599* ⊕ *www.nts.org.uk* 🖾 *£12.50* ☺ *House closed Nov.–Mar; Tues. and Wed. in Apr.–June, Sept., and Oct. Grounds and estate open all year.*

ROSLIN

7 miles south of Edinburgh.

It may be best known for its extraordinary chapel, but Roslin itself is a pleasant place to while away some time. There are some lovely walks from the village along the North River Esk.

GETTING HERE AND AROUND

By car, take the A701 south from Edinburgh, turning off onto the B7006 just north of the town. Lothian Buses also shuttle passengers from Edinburgh: Bus 37 from North Bridge is the most direct way.

EXPLORING

Fodor'sChoice ★ **Rosslyn Chapel.** This chapel has always beckoned curious visitors intrigued by the various legends surrounding its magnificent carvings, but today it pulses with tourists as never before. Much of this can be attributed to Dan Brown's bestselling novel *The Da Vinci Code*, which featured the chapel heavily, claiming it has a secret sign that can lead you to the Holy Grail. Whether you're a fan of the book or not, this Episcopal chapel (services continue to be held here) remains an imperative stop on any traveler's itinerary. Originally conceived by Sir William Sinclair (circa 1404–80) and dedicated to St. Matthew in 1446, the chapel is outstanding for the quality and variety of the carving inside. Covering almost every square inch of stonework are human figures, animals, and plants. The meaning of these remains subject to many theories; some depict symbols from the medieval order of the Knights Templar and from Freemasonry. The chapel's design called for a cruciform structure, but only the choir and parts of the east transept walls were fully completed. Free talks about the building's history are held daily. ✉ *Chapel Loan* ☎ *0131/440–2159* 🌐 *www.rosslynchapel.com* 🎫 *£9.*

WHERE TO EAT

$ BRITISH 🍴 **The Original Rosslyn Inn.** This atmospheric inn, on the crossroads in the center of Roslin village, serves tasty, hearty pub grub, including fish-and-chips, burgers, and pies, plus good veggie options. The inn is very close to Rosslyn Chapel; walk past the car park for a few minutes and you'll see it on the other side of the main road. **Known for:** great steak-and-ale pie; convenient location. [$] *Average main: £9* ✉ *2–4 Main St., Roslin, Edinburgh* ☎ *0131/440–2384* 🌐 *www.theoriginalrosslyninn.co.uk.*

THE PENTLANDS

2 miles south of Edinburgh.

GETTING HERE AND AROUND

The easiest way to reach the Pentlands is by car—simply follow the A702 south. Bus101 from the town center also follows this route. Alternatively, you can cycle into the hills in under an hour.

EXPLORING

Fodor's Choice ★ **The Pentlands.** These unmistakable hills begin almost in the suburbs of Edinburgh, and they make for a very welcome escape from the city crowds. There are access points to the hills along the A702, but the best two are Snowsports Centre and Flotterstone. At each of these you can find a parking lot, a lovely pub, and quiet walking paths leading up into the hills. ✉ *Penicuik.*

WHERE TO EAT

$ BRITISH 🍴 **The Steading.** This pleasant pub, set within a converted farm building on the roadside of the A702, serves traditional. freshly prepared pub food, along with hearty snacks like sandwiches, baked potatoes, and nachos. It is right by the parking lot for the Snowsports Centre, from which several Pentlands walking trails begin. **Known for:** hearty pub grub; beautiful building; great location. [$] *Average main: £10* ✉ *118–120 Biggar Rd., Edinburgh* ☎ *0131/445–1128* 🌐 *www.thesteadingedinburgh.co.uk.*

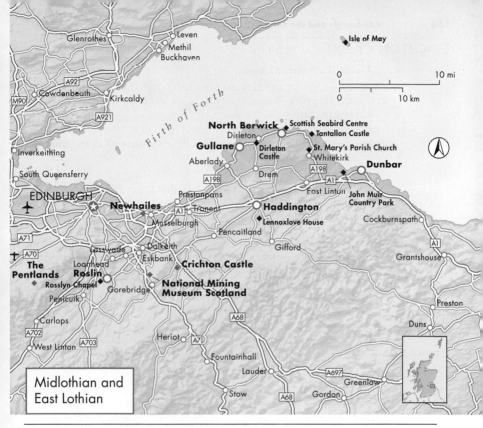

NATIONAL MINING MUSEUM SCOTLAND

9 miles southeast of Edinburgh.

The museum provides visitors with a sobering look into the lives of coal miners and the difficult conditions they endured down Scotland's mines.

GETTING HERE AND AROUND

To get here by car, head south on the A1 (turning into the A6106 and A7) to Newtongrange. You can also take Lothian Buses 29 or 33, or First Buses X95.

EXPLORING

National Mining Museum Scotland. In the former mining community of Newtongrange, the National Mining Museum Scotland provides a good introduction to the history of the country's mining industry. With the help of a guided tour and video exhibits, you can experience life deep below the ground. There are also interactive displays and "magic helmets" that bring the tour to life and relate the power that the mining company held over the lives of workers in Scotland's largest planned-mining village. This frighteningly autocratic system, in which the company owned the houses, shops, and even the pub, survived well into the 1930s. Tours are conducted by ex-miners. ⊠ *Lady Victoria Colliery, A7, Newtongrange* ☎ *0131/663–7519* ⊕ *www.nationalminingmuseum.com* 🎟 *£9.*

CRICHTON CASTLE

14 miles southeast of Edinburgh.

Sitting on a terrace overlooking a beautiful river valley, this 14th-century structure with diamond-faceted facade was home to the Crichtons, and later the earls of Bothwell.

GETTING HERE AND AROUND

Head south on the A1 and A68, then take the turnoff to the B6372 just before Pathhead.

EXPLORING

Crichton Castle. Standing amid rolling hills that are interrupted here and there by patches of woodland, Crichton was a Bothwell family castle. Mary, Queen of Scots, attended the wedding here of Bothwell's sister, Lady Janet Hepburn, to Mary's brother, Lord John Stewart. The curious arcaded range reveals diamond rustication on the courtyard stonework; this particular geometric pattern is unique in Scotland and is thought to have been inspired by the Renaissance styles in Europe, particularly Italy. The oldest part of the structure is the 14th-century keep (square tower). Note that there are no toilets at the castle. ✉ *B6367, Pathhead* ☎ *01875/320017* ⊕ *www.historic-scotland.gov.uk* ▨ *£5* ⊘ *Closed Oct.–Mar.*

DUNBAR

29 miles east of Edinburgh.

In the days before tour companies started offering package deals to the Mediterranean, Dunbar was a popular holiday beach resort. Now a bit faded, the town is still lovely for its spacious Georgian-style properties, characterized by the astragals, or fan-shape windows, above the doors; the symmetry of the house fronts; and the parapeted rooflines. Though not the popular seaside playground it once was, Dunbar has an attractive beach and a picturesque harbor. It's also one end of the John Muir Way, a cross-Scotland hiking trail.

GETTING HERE AND AROUND

From Edinburgh, head east on the A1 to get to Dunbar. You can also take a direct train from Waverley.

EXPLORING

John Muir Country Park. Set on the estuary of the River Tyne, winding down from the Moorfoot Hills, the John Muir Country Park encompasses varied coastal scenery: rocky shoreline, golden sands, and the mixed woodlands of Tyninghame, teeming with wildlife. Dunbar-born conservationist John Muir (1838–1914), whose family moved to the United States when he was a child, helped found Yosemite and Sequoia national parks in California. ✉ *Off A1087.*

SPORTS AND THE OUTDOORS

GOLF

Dunbar Golf Club. There's a lighthouse at the 9th hole of this seaside course, first laid out in 1856. It's a good choice for experiencing a typical east coast links, including the unique challenges presented by coastal winds. Within easy reach of Edinburgh, Dunbar Golf Club has stunning views of the Firth of Forth and Bass Rock. The club is currently undergoing an expansion which may see some changes to the course, as well as a new clubhouse and a hotel. Greens fees drop by nearly half in winter, when it's open midweek only. ⊠ *East Links, Golf House Rd.* ☎ *01368/862317* ⊕ *www.dunbargolfclub.com* ⊠ *£75 weekdays, £95 weekends* ⅄. *18 holes, 6597 yards, par 71* ⌕ *Reservations essential.*

HIKING

John Muir Way. Completed in 2014, this much-praised scenic hiking path stretches from Helensburgh, northwest of Glasgow, to Dunbar. The trail's terminus is outside John Muir's birthplace, on the town's High Street. The 130-mile coast-to-coast route passes through some spectacular scenery (especially at the Helensburgh end). It takes about a week to traverse completely, but the official website has maps covering all the various sections. ⊠ *The John Muir Way (East End), 125 High St.* ⊕ *www.johnmuirway.org.*

NORTH BERWICK

24 miles northeast of Edinburgh.

The pleasant little seaside resort of North Berwick manages to retain a small-town personality even when it's thronged with city visitors on warm summer days. Eating ice cream, the city folk stroll on the beach and in the narrow streets or gaze at the sailing craft in the small harbor. The town is near a number of castles and other sights.

GETTING HERE AND AROUND

Travel east on the A1 and A198, or take one of the regular trains from Edinburgh Waverley.

EXPLORING

Fodor'sChoice **Isle of May.** This small island in the middle of the Firth of Forth is home
★ to many interesting sights, from the ruins of a medieval priory to a Gothic lighthouse to a wartime signal station. But it's the seabirds that really bring in the visitors. The Isle of May is the largest puffin colony on the east coast of Britain, and is home to a quarter of a million birds nesting on the cliffs during late spring and early summer, as well as seals basking on the shore. To visit the island, you'll need to take a 12-seat RIB (rigid inflatable boat) across choppy waters, including a sail by Bass Rock—the world's largest colony of gannets. Tours start from the Scottish Seabird Centre and last four hours, including two hours on the island. ■ **TIP→ Book in advance online to avoid disappointment.** ⊠ *North Berwick* ⊕ *www.seabird.org* ⊠ *Tour: £46* ⊙ *Closed Oct.–Mar.*

FAMILY **Scottish Seabird Centre.** An observation deck, exhibits, and films at this excellent family-friendly attraction provide a captivating introduction to the world of the gannets and puffins that nest on the Firth of Forth islands. Live interactive cameras let you take an even closer look at the bird colonies and marine mammals. Kids will enjoy the "Flyway Tunnel," a 3-D multimedia exhibit that simulates walking through an underwater passage, learning all about local nesting birds and sea life along the way. There are plenty of family-focused activities, nature walks, and photography shows, as well as a great café and gift shop on-site. ✉ *The Harbour* ☎ *01620/890202* 🌐 *www.seabird.org* 🎟 *£8.95.*

St. Mary's Parish Church. The unmistakable St. Mary's Parish Church, with its beautiful red-sandstone Norman tower, stands in the village of Whitekirk, 3 miles south of Tantallon Castle. Occupied since the 6th century, the church was a place of pilgrimage in medieval times because of its healing well. Behind the kirk, in a field, is a tithe barn—the tithe is the portion of a farmer's produce that was given to the local church. Beside this stands a 16th-century tower house, once used to accommodate visiting pilgrims. In the 15th century, the church was visited by a young Italian nobleman, Aeneas Sylvius Piccolomini, after he was shipwrecked off the East Lothian coast; two decades later, Piccolomini became Pope Pius II. ✉ *A198, Whitekirk* 🎟 *Free.*

Tantallon Castle. Travel east along the flat fields from North Berwick, and the imposing silhouette of Tantallon Castle, a substantial, semiruined medieval fortress, comes dramatically into view. Standing on a headland with the sea on three sides, the red sandstone walls are being chipped away by time and sea spray, with the earliest surviving stonework dating from the late 14th century. The fortress was besieged in 1529 by the cannons of King James V, and again (more damagingly) during the civil war of 1651. Despite significant damage, much of the curtain wall of this former Douglas stronghold survives, and is now cared for by Historic Scotland. From the grounds, you can see Bass Rock out to sea, which looks gray during winter but bright white in summer. Look through the telescope here and you'll see why. ✉ *Off A198* ☎ *01620/892727* 🌐 *www.historicenvironment.scot* 🎟 *£6.*

WHERE TO EAT AND STAY

$ SEAFOOD Fodor's Choice ★

🍴 **The Lobster Shack.** North Berwick's most talked-about dining option isn't a traditional restaurant, or even a restaurant at all—it's a shack. That's testament to the sheer quality of the seafood served at this take-away stand, where freshly caught lobster (£16), sea bass, and haddock are cooked before your eyes and served in a box with double-dipped chips, ready to eat on a fold-up chair, a harbor wall, or while strolling along the beach. **Known for:** amazing lobster and chips; beautiful harborside location; good value. [$] *Average main: £9* ✉ *North Berwick Harbour* ☎ *07910/620480* 🌐 *www.lobstershack.co.uk* ⏲ *Closed Oct.–Mar.*

$$ B&B/INN

🏨 **The Glebe House.** This dignified 18th-century building was once a *manse* (minister's house), but is now a delightful and luxurious B&B. **Pros:** peaceful atmosphere; interesting antiques; sociable breakfast around a mahogany table. **Cons:** books up well in advance; too precious for some. [$] *Rooms from: £140* ✉ *Law Rd.* ☎ *01620/892608* 🌐 *www.glebehouse-nb.co.uk* 🛏 *4 rooms* 🍽 *Breakfast.*

GULLANE

20 miles northeast of Edinburgh.

Follow the coastline on either side of Gullane and you're faced with golf course after golf course. Fairways are laid out wherever there is available links space along this stretch of East Lothian, with Muirfield just one of the courses here replete with players clad in expensive golfing sweaters. Apart from golf, visitors can enjoy restful summer-evening strolls at Gullane's sandy beach.

GETTING HERE AND AROUND

From Edinburgh, drive east on the A1, then head north along the coast on the A198. There are also two regular direct buses from the capital, run by East Coast Buses: 124 and X5.

EXPLORING

Dirleton Castle. In the center of tiny Dirleton, 2 miles east of Gullane, sits the impressive-looking 12th-century Dirleton Castle. It's now a ruin, but its high outer wall is relatively complete, and the grounds behind the walls feature a 17th-century bowling green, set in the shade of yew trees and surrounded by a herbaceous flower border that blazes with color in high summer. The castle was occupied in 1298 by King Edward I of England as part of his campaign for the continued subjugation of the unruly Scots. ⊠ *Dirleton Rd. (A198)* ☎ *01620/850330* ⊕ *www. historicenvironment.scot* ⊠ *£6.*

GOLF

Gullane Golf Club. Often overshadowed by Muirfield, Gullane provides an equally authentic links experience, as well as a far more effusive welcome, than its slightly snooty neighbor along the road. The three championship courses here crisscross Gullane Hill, and all command outstanding views of the Firth of Forth. No. 1 is the toughest, but No. 2 and No. 3 offer up equally compelling sport, and for significantly lower green fees. Day tickets can also be purchased, and for No. 3 it's little more than the price of a single round. ⊠ *W. Links Rd.* ☎ *01620/842255* ⊕ *www.gullanegolfclub. com* ⊠ *No. 1: £120 weekdays, £150 weekends; No. 2: £57 weekdays, £62 weekends; No. 3: £37 weekdays, £43 weekends* ⅄. *No. 1 Course: 18 holes, 6583 yards, par 71; No. 2 Course: 18 holes, 6385 yards, par 71; No. 3 Course: 18 holes, 5259 yards, par 68* ⌂ *Reservations essential.*

Muirfield. Home of the Honourable Company of Edinburgh Golfers and the world's oldest golfing club, Muirfield has a pedigree that few other courses can match. Although this course overlooking the Firth of Forth is considered one of the world's most challenging, players also talk about it being "fair," which means it has no hidden bunkers or sand traps. The club has a well-deserved reputation for being stuffy (you will be refused entry to the restaurant if you aren't wearing a jacket and tie); and, while it finally agreed to begin accepting female members in 2017 after it looked set to lose hosting rights to The Open, its waiting list means there are unlikely to be any until at least 2020 (though women can play as guests). Visitors are allowed only on Tuesday and Thursday, and you must apply for a tee time well in advance. ⊠ *Duncur Rd.* ☎ *01620/842123* ⊕ *www.muirfield.org.uk* ⊠ *£235 Apr.–Oct., £110 Nov.–Mar.* ⅄. *18 holes, 7245 yards, par 71.*

HADDINGTON

18 miles east of Edinburgh.

One of the best-preserved medieval street plans in the country can be explored in Haddington. Among the many buildings of architectural and historical interest is the Town House, designed by William Adam in 1748 and enlarged in 1830. A wall plaque at the Sidegate recalls the great heights of floods from the River Tyne. Beyond is the medieval Nungate footbridge, with the Church of St. Mary a little way upstream.

GETTING HERE AND AROUND

From Edinburgh, simply drive east on the A1. Alternatively, take the bus: East Coast Buses 104 and 107 and Perryman's Buses 253 will get you there.

EXPLORING

Lennoxlove House. Majestic Lennoxlove House has been the grand ancestral home of the very grand dukes of Hamilton since 1947, and the Baird family before them. This turreted country house, with parts dating from the 15th century, is a cheerful mix of family life and Scottish history. The beautifully decorated rooms house portraits, furniture, porcelain, and items associated with Mary, Queen of Scots, including her supposed death mask. Sporting activities from falconry to fishing take place on the stunning grounds. ⊠ *E. Port Ave.* ☎ *01620/823720* 🖅 *£8* ☉ *Closed Nov.–mid-Apr. and Fri., Sat., Mon., and Tues.*

GLASGOW

Updated
by Mike
Gonzalez

Trendy stores, a booming cultural life, fascinating architecture, and stylish restaurants reinforce Glasgow's claim to being Scotland's most exciting city. After decades of decline, it has experienced an urban renaissance uniquely its own. The city's grand architecture reflects a prosperous past built on trade and shipbuilding. Today buildings by Charles Rennie Mackintosh hold pride of place along with the Zaha Hadid–designed Riverside Museum.

Glasgow (the "dear green place," as it was known) was founded some 1,500 years ago. Legend has it that the king of Strathclyde, irate about his wife's infidelity, threw a ring he had given her into the River Clyde. (Apparently she had passed it on to an admirer.) When the king demanded to know where the ring had gone, the distraught queen asked the advice of her confessor, St. Mungo. He suggested fishing for it—and the first salmon to emerge had the ring in its mouth. The moment is commemorated on the city's coat of arms.

The vast profits from American cotton and tobacco built the grand mansions of the Merchant City in the 18th century. Tobacco lords financed the building of wooden ships, and by the 19th century the River Clyde had become the center of a vibrant shipbuilding industry, fed by the city's iron and steel works. The city grew again, but its internal divisions grew at the same time. The West End harbored the elegant homes of the newly rich shipyard owners. Down by the river, areas like the infamous Gorbals, with its crowded slums, or Govan, sheltered the laborers who built the ships. They came from the Highlands, expelled to make way for sheep, or from Ireland, where the potato famines drove thousands from their homes.

During the 19th century the city's population grew from 80,000 to more than a million. The new prosperity gave Glasgow its grand neoclassical buildings, such as those built by Alexander "Greek" Thomson, as well as the adventurous visionary buildings designed by Charles Rennie Mackintosh and others who produced Glasgow's Arts and Crafts movement.

The decline of shipbuilding and the closure of the factories in the later 20th century led to much speculation as to what direction the city would take now. The curious thing is that, at least in part, the past gave the city its new lease on life. It was as if people looked at their city and saw Glasgow's beauty for the first time: its extraordinarily rich architectural heritage, its leafy parks, its artistic heritage, and its complex social history. Today Glasgow is a dynamic cultural center and a commercial hub, as well as a launching pad from which to explore the rest of Scotland, which, as it turns out, is not so far away. In fact, it takes only 40 minutes to reach Loch Lomond, where the other Scotland begins.

TOP REASONS TO GO

Design and architecture: The Victorians left a legacy of striking architecture, and Glasgow's buildings manifest the city's love of grand artistic statements—just remember to look up. The Arts and Crafts buildings by Charles Rennie Mackintosh are reason alone to visit.

Art museums: Some of Britain's best art galleries are in Glasgow. The Hunterian Art Gallery, the Kelvingrove Art Gallery and Museum, and the Gallery of Modern Art are worth a visit, even on a sunny day.

Gorgeous parks and gardens: From Kelvingrove Park to the Glasgow Botanic Gardens, the city has more parks per square mile than any other in Europe. Stop by the botanic garden for outdoor theatrical productions in summer, or Bellahouston Park for the annual piping festival.

Pints and great grub: Whether you fancy a Guinness in a traditional old-man's pub like the Scotia or a Pinot Noir in a fashionable wine bar, there's a place to quench all thirsts. Locals love their cafés and tearooms; stop by the Willow Tearooms or Where the Monkey Sleeps for cake and a rest from sightseeing.

Retail therapy: The city has become known for cutting-edge design. Look for everything from Scottish specialties to stylish fashions on the City Centre's hottest shopping streets, Ingram or Buchanan, or at the elegant Princes Square.

ORIENTATION AND PLANNING

GETTING ORIENTED

Glasgow's layout is hard to read at a single glance. The River Clyde, around which Glasgow grew up as a trading city, runs through the center of the city—literally cutting it in two. To the north, the oldest part of Glasgow, the Merchant City, stretches from High Street (the heart of the medieval city) as far as Queen Street, bounded by George Square and Argyle Street to the north and south. The Victorian city, which grew with the shipbuilding boom, stretches from there as far as what is now the M8 motorway and the River Clyde to the south. Beyond the M8 is the West End, originally the wealthy area around Glasgow University. Its main street is Byres Road. Past that are the new bars and restaurants of Finnieston, which has expanded and changed as shipbuilding has given way to riverside concerts and exhibition venues. The opposite bank of the river was the city's poorer quarter, where the workers lived, though beyond it are the park and museum around Pollok Park.

City Centre. If you're interested in how the city blossomed in the 19th century, this is where to start. From Buchanan Street west to Hope Street and beyond, look up to see wonderful Victorian buildings expressing the confidence of an industrial capital. George Square's City Chambers are worth a visit before you trawl the shops, duck into one of the trendy eateries, or explore the bars and music venues.

Merchant City. In the Middle Ages, the city grew up around Glasgow Cathedral. As the city expanded along with the growing transatlantic trade, wealthy tobacco and cotton traders built palatial houses here. They were laid to rest in the glorious tombs of the Necropolis, which overlooks the city. Today the area is busy with high-end restaurants, clubs, and shops, many of them occupying converted mansions.

West End. In the quieter, slightly hillier western part of the city is Glasgow University and the more bohemian side of Glasgow. The West End's treasures include the Glasgow Botanic Gardens, Kelvingrove Park, and the Kelvingrove Art Gallery and Museum. Its social life focuses around the university, where there are well-priced restaurants and lively bars. Byres Road is at its heart, especially when it fills with weekend revelers.

Finnieston. Once lined with shipyards, the River Clyde has been reborn as a relaxing destination that entrances visitors and locals. The Glasgow Science Centre and the Museum of Transport face each other across the water, while the Scottish Exhibition Centre and the new SSE Hydro are major event venues. Argyle Street, once a slightly faded area near Kelvingrove Park, has been transformed into a fashionable strip of restaurants and bars now almost as crowded as the West End.

East End. What was once a neglected corner of Glasgow is being treated to a major face-lift. Glasgow Green's wonderful People's Palace draws visitors throughout the year, and on weekends the nearby Barras market is a reminder of the area's past.

South Side. Often overlooked, this less-visited side of the city includes beautiful Pollok Park as well as Pollok House, with its art collection and its elegant gardens. A couple of architectural gems are here, too.

PLANNING

WHEN TO GO
The best times to visit Glasgow are spring and summer and into early fall. Although you may encounter crowds, the weather is more likely to be warm and dry. In summer the days can be long and pleasant—if the rain holds off—and festivals and outdoor events are abundant. Fall can be nice, although cold weather begins to set in after mid-September and the days grow shorter. From November to February it is cold, wet, and dark. Although thousands of people flock to Glasgow for New Year's celebrations, the winter months are relatively quiet in terms of crowds.

PLANNING YOUR TIME
You could quite easily spend five comfortable days here, although in a pinch, two would do and three would be pleasant. The best strategy for seeing the city is to start at High Street on the east side of Merchant City and work your way west. On the first day explore the city's medieval heritage, taking in Glasgow Cathedral, the Museum of Religious Life, and Provand's Lordship, as well as the Necropolis with its fascinating crumbling monuments. The gentle walk west from here to the Merchant City is also a walk through time, to 17th- and 18th-century Glasgow, and George Square, around which spread the active and crowded shopping areas. For those interested in architect Charles Rennie Mackintosh,

the Mackintosh Trail connects the many buildings designed by this outstanding Glasgow designer and architect. Full information on all his buildings can be found online at ⊕ *www.crmsociety.com*, where you can also purchase tickets, or at the individual sites. Another day could be well spent between the Kelvingrove Art Gallery (you can lunch here and listen to the daily concert on its organ) and the nearby Hunterian Museum and Gallery in the university. From here it's only minutes to lively Byres Road and its shops, pubs, and cafés. The redevelopment of the riverside offers another route—to the Transport Museum and the Science Centre.

If you have a few extra days, head out to Robert Burns country and the extraordinary Burns Birthplace Museum in Ayrshire. It's a scenic 45-minute drive from Glasgow. Most destinations on the Clyde Coast are easily accessible from Glasgow. Direct trains from Central station take you to Paisley, Irvine, and Lanark in less than an hour. These small towns need no more than a day to explore. To get a flavor of island life, take the hour-long train ride to Wemyss Bay and then the ferry to the Isle of Bute.

FESTIVALS

Aye Write. This highly successful literary festival brings together writers from Scotland and the world to discuss their work and exchange ideas. It is held in the Mitchell Library and other venues over one week in spring. ⊠ *Mitchell Library, North St., West End* ☎ *0141/287–2999* ⊕ *www.ayewrite.com* Ⓜ *St. George's Cross.*

Fodor's Choice **Celtic Connections.** Continually expanding, this music festival is held
★ throughout the second half of January in venues across the city. Musicians from Scotland, Ireland, and other countries celebrate Celtic music, both traditional and contemporary. There are a series of hands-on workshops and a popular late-night club at the Royal Concert Hall. ⊠ *Glasgow* ☎ *0141/353–8000* ⊕ *www.celticconnections.com.*

Glasgow Jazz Festival. For five days in late June or early July, Glasgow hosts jazz musicians from around the world in venues throughout the city, though mainly in the City Centre. ⊠ *City Centre* ☎ *0141/552–3552* ⊕ *www.jazzfest.co.uk* ☞ *Tickets from Scottish Music Centre* Ⓜ *Buchanan St.*

GETTING HERE AND AROUND
AIR TRAVEL
Airlines flying from Glasgow Airport to the rest of the United Kingdom and to Europe include Aer Lingus, Air Canada, BMI Regional, British Airways, easyJet, Flybe, Icelandair, Jet 2, and KLM. Several carriers fly from North America, including Air Canada, American Airlines, United, Westjet, and Icelandair (service via Reykjavík).

Ryanair and Vueling offer budget airfares between Prestwick and London and European destinations. Budget-minded easyJet has similar services from Glasgow Airport. Loganair flies to the islands.

AIRPORTS Glasgow Airport (GLA) is about 7 miles west of the City Centre on the M8 to Greenock. The airport serves international and domestic flights, and most major European carriers have frequent and convenient connections to many cities on the continent; it closes overnight.

There's a frequent shuttle service from London, as well as regular flights from Birmingham, Bristol, East Midlands, Leeds/Bradford, Manchester, Southampton, Isle of Man, and Jersey. There are also flights from Wales (Cardiff) and Ireland (Belfast, Dublin, and Londonderry). Local Scottish connections can be made to Aberdeen, Barra, Benbecula, Campbeltown, Inverness, Islay, Kirkwall, Shetland (Sumburgh), Stornoway, and Tiree.

Prestwick Airport (PIK), on the Ayrshire coast about 30 miles southwest of Glasgow, is known mainly as an airport for budget airlines like Ryanair and Vueling.

Airport Contacts Glasgow Airport. ✉ *Caledonia Way, Paisley* ☎ *0844/481–5555* ⊕ *www.glasgowairport.com.* **Prestwick Airport.** ✉ *A79, Prestwick* ☎ *0871/223–0700* ⊕ *www.glasgowprestwick.com.*

TRANSFERS   Although there's a railway station about 2 miles from Glasgow Airport (Paisley Gilmour Street), it is not very accessible. Transport to the City Centre is by bus or taxi and takes about 20 minutes. Metered taxis cost around £22. Express buses depart every 15 minutes from Glasgow Airport to Central and Queen Street stations and to the Buchanan Street bus station. The fare is £7.50 one way, £10 open round-trip per person.

The drive from Glasgow Airport into the City Centre via the M8 motorway (Junction 29) is normally quite easy. Most companies that provide chauffeur-driven cars and tours will also do limousine airport transfers. TBR Global Chauffeuring is a worldwide organization offering chauffeur-driven transport in Glasgow and across the United Kingdom.

There's a rapid half-hourly train service (hourly on Sunday) direct from Prestwick Airport's terminal to Glasgow Central. Strathclyde Passenger Transport and ScotRail offer a discount ticket that allows you to travel for half the standard fare; just show a valid airline ticket for a flight to or from Prestwick Airport. An hourly coach service makes the same trip but takes much longer than the train. Travelers arriving after 11 pm can take a late bus (X99); book this online with Dodds of Troon.

By car, the City Centre is reached from Prestwick via the fast M77 in about 40 minutes. Metered taxis are available at the airport. The fare to Glasgow is about £40.

Airport Transfer Contacts Dodds of Troon. ☎ *01292/288100* ⊕ *www. doddsoftroon.com.* **Little's Chauffeur Drive.** ☎ *0141/883–2111* ⊕ *www. littles.co.uk.* **Strathclyde Passenger Transport Travel Centre.** ✉ *Buchanan Street Bus Station, Killermont St., City Centre* ☎ *0141/332–6811* ⊕ *www.spt. co.uk* Ⓜ *Buchanan St.* **TBR Global Chauffeuring.** ☎ *0141/280–4800* ⊕ *www. tbrglobal.com.*

BIKE TRAVEL

Increasingly cycle-friendly, Glasgow has networks of off-road cycle paths. The city has a public bike-rental scheme run by nextbike; ranks of blue cycles at over 30 stations around the city are available for rent. You provide a credit card number and a £10 deposit on the smartphone app, over the phone, or on the on-bike computer, and give the cycle number. You'll be given the number for the combination lock and off you go. It's a great way to see the city, and you can return the bike at any station. Bikes cost £1 per 30 minutes up to 5 hours or £10 for 5–24 hours. The Glasgow

Cycle Map available at information centers provides comprehensive route information, or see ⊕ *www.glasgow.gov.uk/cycling.*

Bike Contacts nextbike. ☎ *0208/166–9851* ⊕ *www.nextbike.co.uk.*

BUS TRAVEL

The main intercity operators are National Express, Scottish Citylink, and Megabus, which serve numerous towns and cities in Scotland, Wales, and England, including London and Edinburgh. Glasgow's bus station is on Buchanan Street, not far from Queen Street station.

When traveling from the City Centre to either the West End or the South Side, it's easy to use the city's integrated network of buses, subways, and trains. Service is reliable and connections are convenient from buses to trains and the subway. Many buses require exact fare, which is usually around £1.75.

Traveline Scotland provides information on schedules, fares, and route planning, as does the Strathclyde Passenger Transport Travel Centre, which has an information center.

Bus Contacts Buchanan Street Bus Station. ⊠ *Killermont St., City Centre* ☎ *0141/333–3708* ⊕ *www.spt.co.uk* Ⓜ *Buchanan St.* **Megabus.** ☎ *0141/352–4444* ⊕ *uk.megabus.com.* **National Express.** ☎ *0871/781–8181* ⊕ *www. nationalexpress.com.* **Scottish Citylink.** ☎ *0871/266–3333* ⊕ *www.citylink.co.uk.* **Traveline Scotland.** ☎ *0871/200–2233* ⊕ *www.travelinescotland.com.*

CAR TRAVEL

If you're driving to Glasgow from England and the south of Scotland, you'll approach the city via the M6, M74, and A74. From Edinburgh, the M8 leads to the City Centre. From the north, the A82 from Fort William and the A82/M80 from Stirling join the M8 in the City Centre.

You don't need a car in Glasgow, and you're probably better off without one. In the City Centre meters are expensive, running about £2.40 per hour during the day. In the West End they cost 80 pence per hour. Don't park illegally, as fines are upward of £30. Multistory garages are open 24 hours a day at Anderston Centre, George Street, Waterloo Place, Mitchell Street, Cambridge Street, and Concert Square. Rates run between £1 and £2 per hour. More convenient are the park-and-ride operations at some subway stations (Kelvinbridge, Bridge Street, and Shields Road).

SUBWAY TRAVEL

Glasgow's small subway system—it has 15 stations—is useful for reaching all the City Centre and West End attractions. Stations are signposted by a prominent letter "S." You can choose between a flat fare (£1.40) and a one-day pass (£4) that can be used after 9 am on weekdays and all day on weekends. A Smart Card, which you can buy free online or at stations for £3, will give you reduced fares. A Roundabout ticket costs £6.50 a day and covers subway and trains. A Day Tripper ticket is well worth it for families, covering bus, subway, rail, and some ferries. It costs £11.95 for one adult and up to two children or £21 for two adults and up to four kids. The distance between many central stops is no more than a 10-minute walk. More information is available from Strathclyde Passenger Transport Travel Centre or its website, including transportation maps.

TAXI TRAVEL

Taxis are a fast and cost-effective way to get around. You'll find metered taxis (usually black and of the London sedan type) at stands all over the City Centre. Most have radio dispatch. Some have also been adapted to take wheelchairs. You can hail a cab on the street if its "for hire" sign is illuminated. A typical ride from the City Centre to the West End or the South Side costs around £6. Uber is also available in Glasgow.

Taxi Contact Glasgow Taxis. ☎ *0141/429–7070* ⊕ *www.glasgowtaxis.co.uk.*

TRAIN TRAVEL

Glasgow has two main rail stations: Central and Queen Street. Central serves Virgin trains from London's Euston station (five hours). Trains for Ayr and to the south of Glasgow also depart from Central. East Coast trains run from London's Kings Cross (via Edinburgh) to Glasgow's Queen Street station. For details, contact National Rail. All routes heading north from Glasgow depart from Queen Street.

A regular bus service links the Queen Street and Central stations (although you can easily walk if you aren't too encumbered). Queen Street is near the Buchanan Street subway station, and Central is close to St. Enoch. Taxis are available at both stations.

The Glasgow area has an extensive network of suburban railway services. Locals still call them the Blue Trains, even though most are now painted maroon and cream. For more information and a free map, contact the Strathclyde Passenger Transport Travel Centre or National Rail.

Train Contacts National Rail. ☎ *08457/484950* ⊕ *www.nationalrail.co.uk.*

TOURS

BOAT TOURS

Cruises are available on Loch Lomond and to the islands in the Firth of Clyde; contact the Glasgow Tourist Information Centre for details.

FAMILY
Fodor's Choice
★

***Waverley* Excursions.** The last seagoing paddle steamer, the wonderful *Waverley* has retired several times, but the city refuses to let this Glasgow institution fade away. It sails from Glasgow to the Clyde estuary (Glaswegians call it "doon the watter") and the islands of the west coast. The riotous evening jazz cruises remain very popular. The *Waverley* is permanently based at Lancefield Quay, beside the science museum. ⊠ *36 Lancefield Quay, Clyde* ☎ *0845/130–4647* ⊕ *www. waverleyexcursions.co.uk* 🎫 *From £29* ⊘ *Closed Nov.–Apr.*

BUS TOURS

The Glasgow Tourist Information Centre can give information about city tours and about longer tours northward to the Highlands and Islands.

City Sightseeing. Daily hop-on, hop-off bus tours of Glasgow in opentopped double-decker buses are offered by City Sightseeing. The full tour lasts just under two hours, with an English-speaking guide aboard and a multilingual commentary. Tours begin at George Square. ⊠ *153 Queen St., City Centre* ☎ *0141/204–0444* ⊕ *www.citysightseeing-glasgow.co.uk* 🎫 *From £17.*

Rabbie's Trail Burners. Choose from a range of well-regarded one-, two-, and three-day minibus tours with guides to Loch Lomond, Loch Ness, Stirling, and the Highlands. Glasgow-based tours depart from George Street beside the City Chambers, near George Square. ☎ *0131/226–3133* ⊕ *www.rabbies.com.*

PRIVATE GUIDES

Glasgow Taxis. Few people know the city better than taxi drivers. Glasgow Taxis will organize a guided Mackintosh tour around Glasgow, a Burns tour to Ayrshire, or a trip to Loch Lomond, including pickup and drop-off at your place of choice. These black cabs carry up to five passengers. ✉ *City Centre* ☎ *0141/429–7070* ⊕ *www.glasgowtaxis.co.uk* 💷 *From £40 per taxi.*

Little's Chauffeur Drive. You can arrange personally tailored car-and-driver tours, both locally and throughout Scotland. ☎ *0141/883–2111* ⊕ *www.littles.co.uk.*

Scottish Tourist Guides Association. The association provides qualified and accredited Blue Badge Guides with specific areas of expertise; guides also speak a range of languages. Tours start at half a day, and driver guides are available. Book online in advance. ✉ *Glasgow* ☎ *01786/451953* ⊕ *www.stga.co.uk* 💷 *From £140 for half-day tours.*

WALKING TOURS

The Glasgow Tourist Information Centre can provide information on a whole range of self-guided walks around the city.

Glasgow Historic Walks. These themed walks will introduce you to the history and heritage of the city, from its architecture to local history associated with individuals such as St. Patrick and Mary, Queen of Scots. ☎ *No phone* ⊕ *www.glasgowhistoricwalks.com* 💷 *From £8.*

VISITOR INFORMATION

The Glasgow Tourist Information Centre provides information about different types of tours and has an accommodations-booking service. Books, maps, and souvenirs are also available. There's a branch at Glasgow Airport, too.

Contact Glasgow Tourist Information Centre. ✉ *Gallery of Modern Art, Royal Exchange Sq., City Centre* ☎ *0141/566–4083* ⊕ *www.peoplemakeglasgow.com.*

EXPLORING GLASGOW

As cities go, Glasgow is contained and compact. It's set up on a grid system, so it's easy to navigate and explore, and the best way to tackle it is on foot. In the eastern part of the city, start by exploring Glasgow Cathedral and other highlights of the oldest section of the city, then wander through the rest of the Merchant City. From there you can just continue into the City Centre with its designer shops, art galleries, and eateries. From here you can either walk (it takes a good 45 minutes) or take the subway to the West End. If you walk, head up Sauchie-hall Street. Once in the West End, visit the Glasgow Botanic Gardens, Glasgow University, and the Kelvingrove Art Gallery and Museum. A walk through Kelvingrove Park will being you to the Finnieston area.

You can take a taxi to the South Side to experience Pollok House. For Glasgow's East End, walk down High Street from the cathedral to the Tron Cross; from there you can walk to the Barras market and Glasgow Green.

CITY CENTRE

Some of the city's most important historical buildings are found in the City Centre close to George Square, many of them converted to very different purposes now. Along the streets of this neighborhood are some of the best examples of the architectural confidence and vitality that so characterized the burgeoning Glasgow of the turn of the 20th century. There are also plenty of shops, trendy eateries, and pubs.

GETTING HERE

Every form of public transportation can bring you here, from bus to train to subway. Head to George Square and walk from there.

TOP ATTRACTIONS

Fodor's Choice ★ **City Chambers.** Dominating the east side of George Square, this exuberant expression of Victorian confidence, built by William Young in Italian Renaissance style, was opened by Queen Victoria in 1888. Among the interior's outstanding features are the entrance hall's vaulted ceiling, sustained by granite columns topped with marble, the marble-and-alabaster staircases, and Venetian mosaics. The enormous banqueting hall has murals illustrating Glasgow's history. Free guided tours lasting about an hour depart weekdays at 10:30 and 2:30; tours are very popular so pick up a ticket beforehand from the reception desk. The building is closed to visitors during civic functions. ⊠ *80 George Sq., City Centre* ☎ *0141/287–2000* ⊕ *www.glasgow.gov.uk* ⊠ *Free* ۩ *Closed weekends* Ⓜ *Buchanan St.*

Fodor's Choice ★ **Glasgow School of Art.** A 2014 fire badly damaged this iconic Glasgow building exemplifying the genius of architect Charles Rennie Mackintosh, and it is currently undergoing a massive reconstruction to restore its original form—though minus its famous library. The facade still exists, to give a sense of Mackintosh's achievement, but the building will not reopen until 2020. Fortunately, there are other wonderful Mackintosh buildings in and around the city. Stephen Holl's new **Reid Building**, directly opposite the original, is a spectacular modern homage to it; daily walking tours of Mackintosh's Glasgow continue to be organized from the art school shop there. ⊠ *164 Renfrew St., City Centre* ☎ *0141/353–4526* ⊕ *www.gsa.ac.uk/tours* ⊠ *Tours from £7* Ⓜ *Cowcaddens.*

The Lighthouse. Charles Rennie Mackintosh designed these former offices of the *Glasgow Herald* newspaper, with the emblematic Mackintosh Tower, in 1893. On the third floor, the **Mackintosh Interpretation Centre** is a great place to start exploring this groundbreaking architect's work, which is illustrated in a glass wall with alcoves containing models of his buildings. From here you can climb the more than 130 steps up the tower and, once you have caught your breath, look out over Glasgow. (Alternatively, a viewing platform on the sixth floor can be reached by elevator.) Today the Lighthouse serves as Scotland's **Centre**

for **Architecture, Design and the City,** celebrating all facets of architecture and design. The fifth-floor Doocot Cafe is a great place to take a break from sightseeing. ⊠ *11 Mitchell La., City Centre* ☎ *0141/271–5365* ⊕ *www.thelighthouse.co.uk* ⊠ *Free* Ⓜ *St. Enoch.*

Fodor's Choice

★

Tenement House. This ordinary first-floor apartment is anything but ordinary inside: it was occupied from 1937 to 1982 by Agnes Toward (and before that by her mother), both of whom seem never to have thrown anything away. Agnes was a dressmaker, and her legacy is this fascinating time capsule, painstakingly preserved with her everyday furniture and belongings. A small museum explores the life and times of its careful occupant. The red-sandstone building dates from 1892 and is in the Garnethill area near the Glasgow School of Art. ⊠ *145 Buccleuch St., City Centre* ☎ *0141/333–0183* ⊕ *www.nts.org.uk* ⊠ *£6.50* ⊗ *Closed Nov.–Mar.* Ⓜ *Cowcaddens.*

WORTH NOTING

St. Vincent's Street Church. This 1859 church, the work of Alexander Thomson, stands high above the street. The building exemplifies his Greek Revival style, replete with Ionic columns, sphinxlike heads, and rich interior color. Owned by Glasgow City Council, it is currently used by the Free Church of Scotland. You can see the interior by attending a service Sunday at 11 am or 6 pm or by appointment. ⊠ *265 St. Vincent St., City Centre* ⊕ *www.glasgowcityfreechurch.org* ⊠ *Free* ⊗ *Closed Mon.–Sat. except by appointment* Ⓜ *Buchanan St.*

MERCHANT CITY

Near the remnants of medieval Glasgow is the Merchant City, with some of the city's most important 18th-century buildings. Many of them, like the great mansions along Ingram Street, were built by tobacco merchants with profits from the tobacco trade. Today those palatial homes hold restaurants and designer stores; one especially grand example houses the Gallery of Modern Art. Many of Glasgow's young and upwardly mobile have made their home here, in converted buildings ranging from warehouses to the old Sheriff's Court. Shopping is expensive, but the area is worth visiting if you're seeking the youthful Glasgow style.

GETTING HERE

Buchanan Street is the handiest subway station when you want to explore the Merchant City, as it puts you directly on George Square. You can also easily walk from Central station or the St. Enoch subway station.

Gallery of Modern Art (*GoMA*). One of Glasgow's boldest, most innovative galleries occupies the neoclassical former Royal Exchange building. The modern art, craft, and design collections include works by Scottish conceptual artists such as David Mach, and also paintings and sculptures from around the world, including Papua New Guinea, Ethiopia, and Mexico. Each floor of the gallery reflects one of the elements—air, fire, earth, and water—which creates some unexpected juxtapositions and also allows for various interactive exhibits. In the basement is a café, a tourist information center, and an extensive library. The building, designed by David Hamilton (1768–1843) and finished in 1829,

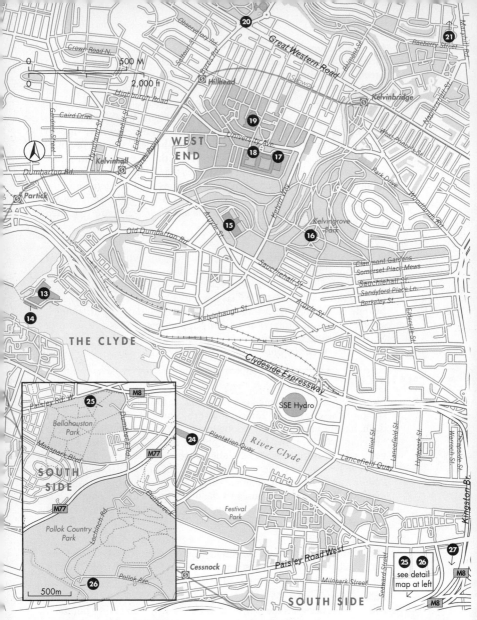

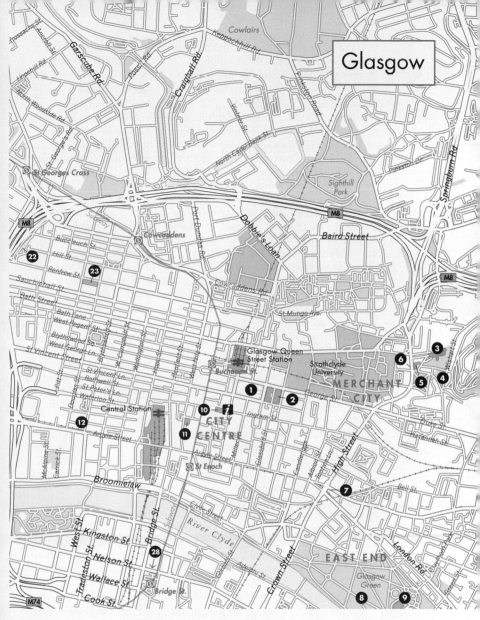

Glasgow

was a meeting place for merchants and traders; later it became Stirling's Library. It incorporates the mansion built in 1780 by William Cunninghame, one of the wealthiest tobacco lords. ⊠ *Queen St., Merchant City* ☎ *0141/287–3050* ⊕ *www.glasgowlife.org.uk* ⊠ *Free* Ⓜ *Buchanan St.*

George Square. The focal point of Glasgow is lined with an impressive collection of statues of worthies: Queen Victoria; Scotland's national poet, Robert Burns (1759–96); the inventor and developer of the steam engine, James Watt (1736–1819); Prime Minister William Gladstone (1809–98); and, towering above them all atop a column, Scotland's great historical novelist, Sir Walter Scott (1771–1832). The column was intended for George III (1738–1820), after whom the square is named, but when he was found to be insane toward the end of his reign, a statue of him was never erected. On the square's east side stands the magnificent Italian Renaissance–style **City Chambers**; the handsome **Merchants' House** fills the corner of West George Street, crowned by a globe and a sailing ship. The fine old Post Office building, now converted into flats, occupies the northern side. There are plenty of benches in the center of the square where you can pause and contemplate. ⊠ *Merchant City* ⊠ *Free* Ⓜ *Buchanan St.*

Fodor's Choice
★ **Glasgow Cathedral.** The most complete of Scotland's cathedrals (it would have been more complete had 19th-century vandals not pulled down its two rugged towers), this is an unusual double church, one above the other, dedicated to Glasgow's patron saint, St. Mungo. Consecrated in 1136 and completed about 300 years later, it was spared the ravages of the Reformation—which destroyed so many of Scotland's medieval churches—mainly because Glasgow's trade guilds defended it. A late-medieval open-timber roof in the nave and lovely 20th-century stained glass are notable features.

In the lower church is the splendid crypt of St. Mungo, who was originally known as St. Kentigern (*kentigern* means "chief word"), but who was nicknamed St. Mungo (meaning "dear one") by his early followers. The site of the tomb has been revered since the 6th century, when St. Mungo founded a church here. Mungo features prominently in local legends; one such legend is about a pet bird that he nursed back to life, and another tells of a bush or tree, the branches of which he used to miraculously relight a fire. The bird, the tree, and the salmon with a ring in its mouth (from another story) are all found on the city's coat of arms, together with a bell that Mungo brought from Rome. ⊠ *Cathedral St., Merchant City* ☎ *0141/552–6891* ⊕ *www.glasgow-cathedral. com* ⊠ *Free* Ⓜ *Buchanan St.*

Fodor's Choice
★ **Necropolis.** A burial ground since the beginning of recorded history, the large Necropolis, modeled on the famous Père-Lachaise Cemetery in Paris, contains some extraordinarily elaborate Victorian tombs. A great place to take it all in is from the monument of John Knox (1514–72), the leader of Scotland's Reformation, which stands at the top of the hill at the heart of the Necropolis. Around it are grand tombs that resemble classical palaces, Egyptian tombs, or even the Chapel of the Templars in Jerusalem. You'll also find a smattering of urns and broken columns, the Roman symbol of a great life cut short. The Necropolis was designed as

a place for meditation, which is why it is much more than just a grave-yard. The main gates are behind the St. Mungo Museum of Religious Life and Art. ■TIP→ **Call ahead for free guided tours.** ✉ *70 Cathedral Sq., Merchant City* ☎ *0141/287–3961* ⊕ *www.glasgownecropolis.org* ✉ *Free* Ⓜ *Buchanan St.*

Provand's Lordship. Glasgow's oldest house, one of only four medieval buildings surviving in the city, was built in 1471 by Bishop Andrew Muirhead. Before it was rescued by the Glasgow City Council, this building had been a pub, a sweetshop, and a soft drinks factory. It is now a museum that shows the house as it might have looked when it was occupied by officers of the church. The furniture is 17th century, and the top floor is a gallery with prints and paintings depicting the characters who might have lived in the surrounding streets. Behind the house is a medicinal herb garden, and the cloisters house rather disturbing carved stone heads. ✉ *3 Castle St., Merchant City* ☎ *0141/276–1625* ⊕ *www.glasgowlife.org.uk* ✉ *Free* ☉ *Closed Mon.* Ⓜ *Buchanan St.*

St. Mungo Museum of Religious Life and Art. An outstanding collection of artifacts, including Celtic crosses and statuettes of Hindu gods, reflects the many religious groups that have settled throughout the centuries in Glasgow and the west of Scotland. A Zen garden creates a peaceful setting for rest and contemplation, and elsewhere stained-glass windows include a depiction of St. Mungo himself. Pause to look at the beautiful Chilkat Blanketwofven, made from cedar bark and wool by the Tlingit people of North America. ✉ *2 Castle St., Merchant City* ☎ *0141/276–1625* ⊕ *www.glasgowlife.org.uk* ✉ *Free* ☉ *Closed Mon.* Ⓜ *Buchanan St.*

WEST END

Glasgow University dominates the West End, creating a vibrant neighborhood. Founded in 1451, the university is the third oldest in Scotland, after St. Andrews and Aberdeen. The industrialists and merchants who built their grand homes on Great Western Road and adjacent streets endowed museums and art galleries and commissioned artists to decorate and design their homes, as a stroll will quickly reveal. In summer the Glasgow Botanic Gardens, with the iconic glasshouse that is the Kibble Palace, becomes a stage for new and unusual versions of Shakespeare's plays. A fun way to save money is to picnic in the park; you can buy sandwiches, salads, and other portable items at shops on Byres Road. Alternatively, stroll past the university and down Gibson Street and Woodlands Road with their cafés and pubs.

GETTING HERE

The best way to get to the West End from the City Centre is by subway; get off at the Hillhead station. A taxi is another option.

TOP ATTRACTIONS

FAMILY **Botanic Gardens.** It is a minor Glasgow miracle how as soon as the
Fodor's Choice sun appears, the Botanics (as they're known to locals) fill with people.
★ Beautiful flower displays and extensive lawns create the feeling that this is a large back garden for the inhabitants of the West End's mainly

apartment homes. At the heart of the gardens is the spectacular circular greenhouse, the **Kibble Palace**, a favorite haunt of Glaswegian families. Originally built in 1873, it was the conservatory of a Victorian eccentric. Kibble Palace and the other greenhouses contain tree ferns, palm trees, and the Tropicarium, where you can experience the lushness of a rain forest or see its world-famous collection of orchids. There is a tearoom, and in June and July the gardens host presentations of Shakespeare's plays (⊕ *www.bardinthebotanics.co.uk*). ⊠ *730 Great Western Rd., West End* 📞 *0141/276–1614* ⊕ *www.glasgowbotanicgardens.com* 🎫 *Free* ۞ *Closed dusk–7 am* Ⓜ *Hillhead.*

Glasgow University. Gorgeous grounds and great views of the city are among the many reasons to visit this university. The Gilbert Scott Building, the university's main edifice, is a lovely example of the Gothic Revival style. **Glasgow University Visitor Centre,** near the main gate on University Avenue, has exhibits on the university and a small coffee bar; one-hour guided walking tours of the campus (Thursday–Sunday at 2) start here. A self-guided tour starts at the visitor center and takes in the east and west quadrangles, the cloisters, Professor's Square, Pearce Lodge, and the not-to-be-missed University Chapel. The university's Hunterian Museum is also well worth a visit. ⊠ *University Ave., West End* 📞 *0141/330–2000* ⊕ *www.glasgow.ac.uk* 🎫 *Free* Ⓜ *Hillhead.*

Hunterian Art Gallery. Opposite Glasgow University's main gate, this gallery houses William Hunter's (1718–83) collection of paintings. You'll also find prints, drawings, and sculptures by Tintoretto, Rembrandt, and Auguste Rodin, as well as a major collection of paintings by James McNeill Whistler, who had a great affection for the city that bought one of his earliest paintings. Also in the gallery is a replica of **Charles Rennie Mackintosh's town house,** which once stood nearby and where Mackintosh and his artist wife, Margaret, lived between 1906 and 1914. These stunning rooms, faithfully rebuilt here, contain Mackintosh's distinctive art nouveau chairs, tables, beds, and cupboards, and the walls are decorated in the equally distinctive style devised by him and his wife. Free guided tours are available. ⊠ *Hillhead St., West End* 📞 *0141/330–5431* ⊕ *www.gla.ac.uk/hunterian* 🎫 *Free; Mackintosh House £5* ۞ *Closed Mon.* Ⓜ *Hillhead.*

Hunterian Museum. Set within Glasgow University, this museum dating from 1807 showcases part of the collections of William Hunter, an 18th-century Glasgow doctor who assembled a staggering quantity of valuable material. Check out Hunter's hoards of coins, manuscripts, scientific instruments, and archaeological artifacts in this striking Gothic building. A permanent exhibit chronicles the building of the Antonine Wall, the Romans' northernmost defense. ⊠ *University Ave., West End* 📞 *0141/330–4221* ⊕ *www.gla.ac.uk/hunterian* 🎫 *Free* ۞ *Closed Mon.* Ⓜ *Hillhead.*

FAMILY
Fodor's Choice
★

Kelvingrove Art Gallery and Museum. Worthy of its world-class reputation, the Kelvingrove Art Gallery and Museum attracts local families as well as international visitors. This combination of cathedral and castle was designed in the Renaissance style and built between 1891 and 1901. The stunning red-sandstone edifice is an appropriate home for works

CLOSE UP

Charles Rennie Mackintosh

Not so long ago, the furniture of innovative Glasgow-born architect Charles Rennie Mackintosh (1868–1928) was broken up for firewood. Today art books are devoted to his distinctive, astonishingly elegant Arts and Crafts—and art nouveau—influenced interiors, and artisans around the world look to his theory that "decoration should not be constructed, rather construction should be decorated" as holy law. Mackintosh's stripped-down designs ushered in the modern age.

AN ARCHITECT'S CAREER

Mackintosh trained in architecture at the Glasgow School of Art and was apprenticed to the Glasgow firm of John Hutchison at the age of 16.

Early influences on his work included the Pre-Raphaelites, James McNeill Whistler (1834–1903), Aubrey Beardsley (1872–98), and Japanese art. But by the 1890s a distinct Glasgow style developed.

The building for the *Glasgow Herald* newspaper, which he designed in 1893, is now the Lighthouse Centre for Architecture, Design and the City. It was soon followed by other major Glasgow buildings: Queen Margaret's Medical College; the Martyrs Public School; the Hill House, in Helensburgh, now owned by the National Trust for Scotland; and Queen's Cross Church, completed in 1899 and now the headquarters of the Charles Rennie Mackintosh Society (🌐 *www.crmsociety.com*). In 1897 Mackintosh began work on a new home for the Glasgow School of Art, recognized as one of his major achievements.

Mackintosh married Margaret Macdonald in 1900, and in later years her decorative work enhanced the buildings' interiors. It was she who inspired the Glasgow Girls group of women artists. In 1904 Mackintosh became a partner in Honeyman and Keppie, and in the same year he designed what is now the Scotland Street School Museum. Until 1913, when he left Honeyman and Keppie and moved to England, Mackintosh's projects included buildings over much of Scotland. He preferred to include interiors as part of his overall design.

Commissions in England after 1913 included design challenges not confined to buildings, such as fabrics, furniture, and even bookbindings. However, after 1904 architectural taste turned against Mackintosh's style; his work was seen as strange. Mackintosh could not conform to the times; he lost commissions, drank heavily, and ended up poor and sick. He died in London in 1928. Mackintosh's reputation revived only in the 1950s and has continued to grow over time; 2018 is the 150th anniversary of his birth.

HOW TO SEE HIS WORK

Glasgow is the best place to admire Mackintosh's work. In addition to the buildings mentioned above, most of which can be visited, the Hunterian Art Gallery contains magnificent reconstructions of the principal rooms at 78 Southpark Avenue, Mackintosh's Glasgow home, and original drawings, documents, and records, plus the re-creation of a room at 78 Derngate, Northampton. The Kelvingrove Art Gallery and Museum also has displays of his creations in several galleries. His iconic Glasgow School of Art building, being reconstructed after a fire, will reopen to visitors in 2020.

3

by Botticelli, Rembrandt, Monet, and others, not to mention the collection of arms and armor. The Glasgow Room houses extraordinary works by local artists. Whether the subject is Scottish culture, design, or storytelling, every room begs you to look deeper; labels are thought-provoking and sometimes witty. You could spend a weekend here, but in a pinch three hours would do one level justice—there are three. Leave time to visit the gift shop and the attractive basement restaurant. Daily free recitals on the massive organ (usually at 1) are well worth the trip. ⊠ *Argyle St., West End* ☎ *0141/276–9599* ⊕ *www.glasgowlife.org.uk* ⊠ *Free (some special exhibitions require admission)* Ⓜ *Kelvinhall.*

FAMILY   **Kelvingrove Park.** Both a peaceful retreat and a well-used playground, the park was purchased by the city in 1852. The River Kelvin flows through its green spaces. The park's numerous statues of prominent Glaswegians include one of Lord Kelvin (1824–1907), the Scottish mathematician and physicist remembered for his pioneering work in electricity. The shady park has a massive fountain commemorating a lord provost of Glasgow from the 1870s, a duck pond, two children's playgrounds, and a skateboard park. The An Clachan café beside the children's play area is an excellent daytime eatery and a boon to parents looking for a refuge. Public bowling greens are free, as are the tennis courts. The Bandstand, a 2,300-seat open-air theater, hosts major concerts in summer. ⊠ *Bounded by Sauchiehall St., Woodlands Rd., and Kelvin Way, West End* ⊕ *www.glasgowlife.org.uk* ⊠ *Free* Ⓜ *Kelvinhall.*

WORTH NOTING

OFF THE BEATEN PATH

Queen's Cross Church. The only church Mackintosh designed houses the Charles Rennie Mackintosh (CRM) Society Headquarters and is the ideal place to learn more about the famous Glasgow-born architect and designer. Although one of the leading lights in the art nouveau movement, Mackintosh died in relative obscurity in 1928. The church has beautiful stained-glass windows and a light-enhancing, carved-wood interior. The center's library and shop provide further insight into Glasgow's other Mackintosh-designed buildings, which include Scotland Street School, the Martyrs Public School, and the Glasgow School of Art. The church sits near the junction of Garscube Road and Maryhill Road. A taxi is probably the best way to get here, but you can also take a bus toward Queen's Cross from stops along Hope Street or walk up Maryhill Road from the St. George's Cross subway station. ⊠ *870 Garscube Rd., West End* ☎ *0141/946–6600* ⊕ *www.crmsociety.com* ⊠ *£4; free Wed. after 1 pm* ☉ *Closed weekends Apr.–Oct and Tues., Thurs., and weekends Nov.–Mar.* Ⓜ *St. George's Cross.*

FINNIESTON

The River Clyde has long been the city's main artery, bearing Clyde-built ships, from warships to ocean liners, to the sea. Few of the yards remain open, and the Finnieston Crane, which once moved locomotives on to ships, is no longer active. But the area around it, bounded by the river on one side and Sauchiehall Street on the other, has undergone a great transformation since the 1990s. The riverside has been reborn, with Zaha Hadid's Transport Museum and the Tall Ship, as well as the Scottish Event Campus (SEC) occupying pride of place on the Finnieston bank and the Science Museum on the opposite side. The SSE Hydro, an ultramodern concert arena, has generated a new fashionable strip of bars and restaurants along Argyle Street.

GETTING HERE

From the Partick subway station it's a 10-minute walk to the Riverside Museum. From that museum it's a short stroll along the river (and across a bridge) to the Glasgow Science Centre. Argyle Street is a short walk from Kelvin Hall subway station or across Kelvingrove Park from Glasgow University.

FAMILY **Glasgow Science Centre.** Fun and engaging, this museum for children has three floors packed with games, experiments, and hands-on machines from pendulums to small-scale whirlpools, soundscapes to optical illusions. Its space-age home on the south side of the Clyde has a whole wall of glass looking out on to the river. The *BodyWorks* exhibition explores every aspect of our physical selves—try and reconstruct a brain. There are daily events and science shows, a lovely play area for under-sevens, a planetarium, an IMAX theater, and the spectacular Glasgow Tower, 400 feet high, from which to survey the whole city from the river to the surrounding hills. Always inquire whether the tower is open—even moderate winds will close it down. ■**TIP→ Admission is expensive, but the tower and planetarium cost less if you buy all the tickets at the same time.** ⊠ *50 Pacific Quay, Finnieston* ✛ *Across the footbridge by the SEC Centre* ☎ *0141/420–5000* ⊕ *www.glasgowsciencecentre.org* ☞ *£10.50, planetarium extra £2.50, tower extra £3.50; tower only £6.50* ⊗ *Closed Mon., Tues., and Thurs. Nov.–Mar.* Ⓜ *Cessnock.*

FAMILY **Riverside Museum: Scotland's Museum of Transport and Travel.** Designed by
Fodor's Choice Zaha Hadid to celebrate the area's industrial heritage, this huge metal
★ structure with curving walls echoes the covered yards where ships were built on the Clyde. Glasgow's shipbuilding history is remembered with a world-famous collection of ship models. Locomotives built at the nearby St. Rollox yards are also on display, as are cars from every age and many countries. You can wander down Main Street, circa 1930, without leaving the building: the pawnbroker, funeral parlor, and Italian restaurant are all frozen in time. Relax with a coffee in the café, wander out onto the expansive riverside walk, or board the Tall Ship that is moored permanently behind the museum. Take Bus 100 from the City Centre, or walk from Partick subway station. ⊠ *100 Poundhouse Pl., Finnieston* ☎ *0141/287–2720* ⊕ *www.glasgowlife.org.uk* ☞ *Free* Ⓜ *Partick.*

FAMILY **Tall Ship at Riverside.** Built in 1896, this fine tall sailing ship now sits on the River Clyde immediately behind the Riverside Museum. The *Glenlee* once belonged to the Spanish Navy (under a different name), but carried cargo all over the world in her day. She returned to Glasgow and the River Clyde in 1993, and now forms part of the museum. You can wander throughout this surprisingly large cargo ship with or without an audio guide, peer into cabins and holds, and stand on the forecastle as you gaze down the river. Bus 100 from George Square brings you here, or you can walk from the Partick subway station in 10 minutes. ⊠ *150 Pointhouse Pl., Finnieston* ☎ *0141/357–3699* ⊕ *www.thetallship.com* ☞ *Free* Ⓜ *Partick.*

EAST END

Glasgow Green has always been the heart of Glasgow's East End, a formerly down-at-heel neighborhood that has seen many changes over time. One of the top attractions is the People's Palace, which tells the story of daily life in the city. On Sunday head to the nearby Barras market to hunt for bargains.

GETTING HERE
To get to the East End, take the subway to the St. Enoch station and walk along Argyle Street to the Tron Cross. From there, London Road takes you to Glasgow Green.

Glasgow Cross. This crossroads was the center of the medieval city. The Mercat Cross (*mercat* means "market"), topped by a unicorn, marks the spot where merchants met, where the market was held, and where criminals were executed. Here, too, was the *tron*, or weigh beam, installed in 1491 and used by merchants to check weights. The Tolbooth Steeple dates from 1626 and served as the civic center and the place where travelers paid tolls. ⊠ *Intersection of Saltmarket, Trongate, Gallowgate, and London Rds., East End* Ⓜ *St. Enoch.*

FAMILY **Glasgow Green.** Glasgow's oldest park has a long history as a favorite spot for public recreation and political demonstrations. Note the Nelson Column, erected long before London's; the McLennan Arch, originally part of the facade of the old Assembly Halls in Ingram Street; and the Templeton Business Centre, a former carpet factory built in the late 19th century in the style of the Doge's Palace in Venice. There is an adventure playground for kids and a small cycle track beside it, with children's bikes for rent. Don't miss the **People's Palace** and the Doulton Fountain that faces it. ⊠ *East End* ✛ *North side of River Clyde between Green St. and Saltmarket St.*

FAMILY **Hampden Park.** A mecca for soccer enthusiasts, who come from far and near to tread the famous turf, the home field for the country's national team was the largest stadium in the world when it was built in 1903. There are stadium tours on nonmatch days at 11, 12:30, 2, and 3. You can then visit the Scottish Football Museum, which traces the history of the game; the museum may close on game days. ⊠ *Letherby Dr., East End* ✛ *Nearest rail stations are Mount Florida and Kings Park. Buses from City Centre* ☎ *0141/616–6139* ⊕ *www.hampdenpark.co.uk* ▣ *Stadium tour £8, museum entrance £8, combined ticket £13.*

FAMILY **People's Palace and Winter Gardens.** The excited conversations among local visitors are a sign that this museum tells the story of everyday lives in Glasgow. There is always something that sparks a memory: a photo, an object, a sound. On display, for example, are the writing desk of John McLean (1879–1923), the famous "Red Clydeside" political activist, and the banana boots worn on stage by Glasgow-born comedian Billy Connolly. On the top floor a sequence of fine murals by Glasgow artist Ken Currie tells the story of the city's working-class citizens. In contrast, the Doulton Fountain opposite the entrance celebrates the British empire. The museum is housed in a Victorian red-sandstone building at the heart of Glasgow Green, and behind it are the restored Winter Gardens (a Victorian conservatory) and a popular café. To get here from the St. Enoch subway station, walk along Argyle Street past Glasgow

Cross. ⊠ *Glasgow Green, Monteith Row, East End* ☎ *0141/276–0788* ⊕ *www.glasgowlife.org.uk* ✉ *Free* ⊘ *Closed Mon.* Ⓜ *St. Enoch.*

SOUTH SIDE

Just southwest of the City Centre in the South Side are two of Glasgow's dear green spaces—Bellahouston Park and Pollok Country Park—which have important art collections: Charles Rennie Mackintosh's House for an Art Lover in Bellahouston, and Pollok House in Pollok Country Park. A respite from the buzz of the city can also be found in the parks, where you can have a picnic or ramble through greenery and gardens. The famous Burrell Collection is also in the area, but the museum will be closed until 2019 for a substantial renovation.

GETTING HERE

Both parks are off Pollokshaws Road, about 3 miles southwest of City Centre. You can take a taxi or car, city bus, or a train from Glasgow Central station to Pollokshaws West station or Dumbreck.

House for an Art Lover. Within Bellahouston Park is a "new" Mackintosh house, based on a competition entry Charles Rennie Mackintosh submitted to a German magazine in 1901. The house was never built in his lifetime, but took shape between 1989 and 1996. It is home to Glasgow School of Art's postgraduate study center, and displays show designs for the various rooms and decorative pieces by Mackintosh and his wife, Margaret. The main lounge is spectacular. There's also a café and shop filled with art. Buses 9, 53, and 54 from Union Street will get you here. Call ahead, as opening times can vary. ⊠ *Bellahouston Park, 10 Dumbreck Rd., South Side* ☎ *0141/353–4770* ⊕ *www.houseforanartlover.co.uk* ✉ *£5.50* ⊘ *Closed weekdays Oct.–Mar.* Ⓜ *Ibrox.*

Pollok House. This classic Georgian house, dating from the mid-1700s, sits amid landscaped gardens and avenues of trees that are now part of Pollok Country Park. It still has the tranquil air of a wealthy but unpretentious country house. The Stirling Maxwell Collection includes paintings by Blake and a strong grouping of Spanish works by El Greco, Murillo, and Goya. Lovely examples of 18th- and early-19th-century furniture, silver, glass, and porcelain are also on display. The house has beautiful gardens that overlook the White Cart River. The downstairs servants' quarters include the kitchen, which is now a café-restaurant. The closest train station is Pollokshaws West, from Central station; or you can take Buses 45, 47, or 57 to the gate of Pollok Country Park. ⊠ *Pollok County Park, 2060 Pollokshaws Rd., South Side* ☎ *0141/616–6410* ⊕ *www.nts.org.uk* ✉ *£6.50.*

OFF THE BEATEN PATH

Scotland Street School Museum. A former school designed by Charles Rennie Mackintosh, this building houses a fascinating museum of education. Classrooms re-create school life in Scotland during Victorian times and World War II, and a cookery room recounts a time when education for Scottish girls consisted of little more than learning how to become a housewife. There's also an exhibition space and a café. The building sits opposite Shields Road underground station. ⊠ *225 Scotland St., South Side* ☎ *0141/287–0513* ⊕ *www.glasgowlife.org.uk* ✉ *Free* ⊘ *Closed Mon.* Ⓜ *Shields Rd.*

WHERE TO EAT

Glasgow's vibrant restaurant culture is constantly renewing itself. Some of Britain's best-known chefs have opened kitchens here, including Jamie Oliver and Yotam Ottolenghi. More recently, the city has responded enthusiastically to the small-plate and sharing-platter trends, but there are still plenty of fine-dining options on the one hand, and steak houses and burger places on the other. The city continues to present the best that Scotland has to offer: grass-fed beef, free-range chicken, wild seafood, venison, duck, and goose, not to mention superb fruits and vegetables. The growing emphasis on organic food is reflected on menus that increasingly provide detailed information about the source of their ingredients. Around the city, an explosion of coffee shops offer artisanal macchiatos and mochas.

You can eat your way around the world in Glasgow. A new generation of Italian restaurants serves updated versions of classic Italian dishes. Chinese, Indian, and Pakistani foods, longtime favorites, are now more varied and sophisticated, and Thai and Japanese restaurants have become popular. Spanish-style tapas are now quite common, and the small-plate trend has extended to every kind of restaurant. Seafood restaurants have moved well beyond the fish-and-chips wrapped in newspaper that were always a Glasgow staple, as langoustines, scallops, and monkfish appear on menus with ever more unusual accompaniments. And Glasgow has an especially good reputation for its vegan and vegetarian restaurants.

Smoking isn't allowed in any enclosed space in Scotland, but more restaurants have placed tables outside under awnings during the warmer summer months, some of which permit smoking. *Use the coordinate (⊕ B2) at the end of each listing to locate a site on the corresponding map.*

PRICES
Eating in Glasgow can be casual or lavish. For inexpensive dining, consider the benefit of lunch or pretheater set menus. Beer and spirits cost much the same as they would in a bar, but wine is relatively expensive in restaurants. Increasing numbers of pubs offer food, but their kitchens usually close early. ■TIP➜ **Some restaurants allow you to bring your own bottle of wine, charging just a small corkage fee. It's worth the effort.**

WHAT IT COSTS IN POUNDS			
$	$$	$$$	$$$$
Restaurants	under £15	£15–£19	£20–£25	over £25

Restaurant prices are the average cost of a main course at dinner or, if dinner is not served, at lunch. Hotel prices are the lowest cost of a standard double room in high season, including 20% V.A.T.

CITY CENTRE

The City Centre has restaurants catering to the 9-to-5 crowd, meaning there are a lot of fine-dining establishments as well as good restaurants catching people as they leave work, drawing them in with pretheater menus. The choice of eateries is extensive.

$$$ STEAKHOUSE 🍴 **Anchor Line.** Occupying the former headquarters of the Anchor Line, whose ships sailed from Scotland to America, this bar and restaurant near St. George Square has been impressively refurbished to create the sense of fine dining aboard a luxury ocean liner. The menu reflects the voyage, too, including Scottish seafood and lamb, and a full range of steaks and their sauces to represent America. **Known for:** high-end cocktails; luxurious fine dining; steak of all kinds. [$] *Average main: £20* ✉ *12 St. Vincent Pl., City Centre* ☎ *0141/248–1434* 🌐 *www.theanchorline.co.uk* [M] *Buchanan St.* ✥ G5.

$ MODERN EUROPEAN 🍴 **Café Rogano.** Filled with photos of Hollywood greats, the brasserie at Glasgow institution Rogano's is more intimate, more relaxed, and a little more crowded than the famous restaurant upstairs. The mellow atmosphere also reflects the slightly more adventurous and less expensive menu, which often includes Moroccan-style lamb tagine and roast belly of pork. **Known for:** fish soup; chilled seafood platter; portraits of film stars on the wall. [$] *Average main: £14* ✉ *11 Exchange Pl.* ☎ *0141/248–4055* 🌐 *www.roganoglasgow.com* [M] *Buchanan St* ✥ F5.

$ THAI Fodor'sChoice ★ 🍴 **Chaophraya.** You can experience dining at its most sumptuous and elegant for a good price in the grand surroundings of what was the Glasgow Conservatoire, where golden Buddhas sit comfortably beside busts of great composers. The delicate flavors of Thai cooking are at their finest here in the chef's wonderful signature Massaman lamb (and beef) curry, flavorsome Fisherman's Soup, and fusion dishes like scallops with black pudding. **Known for:** Massaman lamb curry; luxurious surroundings; extensive menu. [$] *Average main: £12* ✉ *The Town House, Nelson Mandela Pl., City Centre* ☎ *0141/332–0041* 🌐 *www.chaophraya.co.uk* [M] *Buchanan St.* ✥ F4.

$ GREEK 🍴 **Halloumi.** Greek cuisine was one of the few not well represented in Glasgow until Halloumi arrived to fill the gap. Its large windows onto the street invite you in to a simply decorated interior with white walls and wooden tables, where you will find a reassuringly familiar menu of small plates, or meze. **Known for:** meze; moussaka; good lunch deal. [$] *Average main: £11* ✉ *161 Hope St., City Centre* ✥ *Near Central station* ☎ *0141/204–1616* 🌐 *www.halloumiglasgow.co.uk* [M] *Buchanan St.* ✥ F4.

$$ SPANISH 🍴 **Ibérica.** The Spanish small-plates revolution has arrived in Glasgow in this grand former bank, going a step beyond tapas with portions that are larger and encourage sharing and combining flavors at the table. The qualities of each dish are patiently explained: the different kinds of Serrano ham, the flavors of cheese, how aioli (homemade garlic mayonnaise) is made. **Known for:** black-rice dishes; Galician-style octopus; range of Serrano ham. [$] *Average main: £18* ✉ *140 St. Vincent St., City Centre* ☎ *0141/530 7985* 🌐 *www.ibericarestaurants.com* [M] *Buchanan St.* ✥ F4.

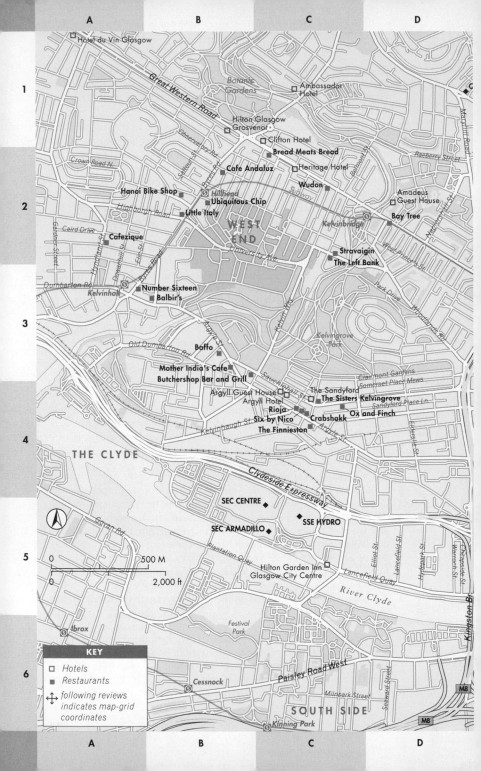

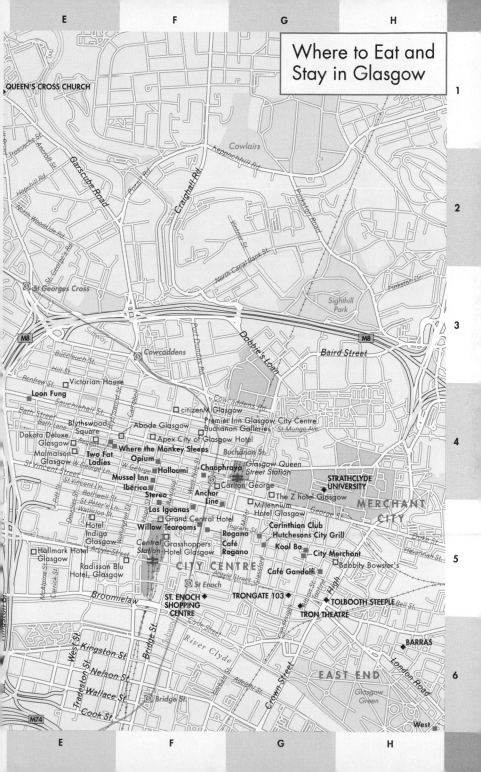

Where to Eat and Stay in Glasgow

$
SOUTH
AMERICAN
✗ **Las Iguanas.** The bright interior of this restaurant, part of a popular chain, echoes the Latin American–themed menu in its vibrant colors and decoration. The extensive menu has the familiar Spanish and Mexican classics like tapas and burritos, but less familiar Brazilian dishes, too—and the cocktail list covers everything from tequila to a pisco sour. **Known for:** Xinxim, a Brazilian stew of chicken and crayfish; colorful cocktails; equally colorful decor. $ *Average main: £14* ✉ *15–20 W. Nile St., City Centre* ☎ *0141/248–5705* ⊕ *www.iguanas.co.uk* Ⓜ *Buchanan St.* ✛ *F5.*

$$
CANTONESE
FAMILY
✗ **Loon Fung.** The pleasant, enthusiastic staff at this huge, popular Cantonese eatery guides you to all the best dishes, including barbecued duck, deep-fried wontons with prawns, and more challenging dishes like pork with jellyfish or king prawn with salted egg, all specialties that have been served here since 1971. On most days you will see local Chinese families seated at the huge round tables enjoying the dim sum for which the restaurant is rightly famous. **Known for:** dim sum; authentic Cantonese cuisine; family atmosphere. $ *Average main: £18* ✉ *417–419 Sauchiehall St., City Centre* ☎ *0141/332–1240* ⊕ *www. loonfungglasgow.com/* Ⓜ *Cowcaddens* ✛ *E4.*

$$
SEAFOOD
Fodor'sChoice
★
✗ **Mussel Inn.** West-coast shellfish farmers own this sleek restaurant and feed their customers incredibly succulent oysters, scallops, and mussels. The pots of mussels, steamed to order and served with any of a number of sauces, are revelatory, and scallops, prawns, and oysters come together in a wonderful seafood pasta. **Known for:** seafood pasta; Queenie oysters; mussels Moroccan style. $ *Average main: £18* ✉ *157 Hope St., City Centre* ☎ *0141/572–1405* ⊕ *www.mussel-inn.com* Ⓜ *Buchanan St.* ✛ *F4.*

$$
ASIAN
✗ **Opium.** This eatery has completely rethought Asian cuisine, taking Chinese, Malaysian, and Thai cooking in new directions and using sauces that are fragrant and spicy but never overpowering. Subdued lighting, neutral tones, and dark wood create a calm setting for specialties including superb dim sum and crisp wontons filled with delicious combinations of crab, shrimp, and chicken. **Known for:** Asian-fusion food; great cocktails; dim sum. $ *Average main: £17* ✉ *191 Hope St., City Centre* ☎ *0141/332–6668* ⊕ *www.opiumrestaurant.co.uk* Ⓜ *Buchanan St.* ✛ *F4.*

$$$
MODERN BRITISH
Fodor'sChoice
★
✗ **Rogano.** It is the surroundings that strike you first in Rogano's beautiful art deco bar, which has all the ambience of a 1930s Clyde-built luxury ocean liner. The restaurant is known for its seafood and has held its own despite the serious competition among fish restaurants that is emerging in the city. **Known for:** art deco bar; Glasgow institution; exquisite cocktails. $ *Average main: £23* ✉ *11 Exchange Pl., City Centre* ☎ *0141/248–4055* ⊕ *www.roganoglasgow.com* Ⓜ *Buchanan St.* ✛ *F5.*

$
VEGETARIAN
✗ **Stereo.** Down a quiet lane near Central station, this ultracool eatery dishes up a fantastic range of vegan food, from paella to gnocchi to a colorful platter with hummus, red-pepper pâté, and home-baked flatbread; roasted sweet-potato chips are the perfect side dish. The decor is homey and relaxed, and there always seems to be someone nearby reading or writing. **Known for:** imaginative vegan food; hipster comes

to Glasgow; good music. $ *Average main: £10* ✉ *20–28 Renfield La., City Centre* ☎ *0141/222-2254* ⊕ *www.stereocafebar.com* Ⓜ *Buchanan St.* ✛ *F5.*

$$$ ✕ **Two Fat Ladies.** From its start in 1989 in a tiny West End space, Two
SEAFOOD Fat Ladies raised the standards of seafood cuisine in the city, and superb fish still dominates the menu. The restaurant is named after two famous TV cooks (or alternatively after the bingo call for number 88, the street number of the original location); the Blythswood Square branch is somewhat larger and airier, but still intimate. **Known for:** seafood; traditional high tea; intimate milieu. $ *Average main: £20* ✉ *118A Blythswood St., City Centre* ✛ *Just off Blythswood Sq.* ☎ *0141/847-0088* ⊕ *www.twofatladiesrestaurant.com* Ⓜ *Cowcaddens* ✛ *E4.*

$ ✕ **Where the Monkey Sleeps.** This quirky basement café, in a series of small
CAFÉ rooms with brightly colored sofas, serves huge sandwiches with amusing names—the "Wytchfinder" has chorizo sausage and cheese, while the "Serious Operation" contains practically everything on the menu. Enjoy your choice with one of the wonderful smoothies. **Known for:** brilliant sandwiches; secret corners; cheerful service. $ *Average main: £6* ✉ *182 W. Regent St., City Centre* ☎ *0141/226-3406* ⊕ *www.monkeysleeps. com* ☾ *Closed weekends. No dinner* Ⓜ *Cowcaddens* ✛ *E4.*

$ ✕ **Willow Tearooms.** Very Scottish breakfasts, lunches, and an array of
BRITISH cakes and scones baked in-house are served in a tearoom that was once part of a department store designed by Charles Rennie Mackintosh. It retains copies of the designer's trademark furnishings, including high-backed chairs with elegant lines and subtle curves. **Known for:** high tea; Mackintosh furniture; St. Andrew's seafood platter. $ *Average main: £10* ✉ *97 Buchanan St., City Centre* ☎ *0141/332-0521* ⊕ *www.willowtearooms.co.uk* ☾ *No dinner* Ⓜ *Buchanan St.* ✛ *F5.*

MERCHANT CITY

Despite covering a relatively small area, the Merchant City has a wide variety of restaurants. The selection of cafés and restaurants includes many budget-friendly options that cater to the working population.

$$ ✕ **Café Gandolfi.** Occupying what was once the tea market, this trendy
MODERN BRITISH café known for its breakfasts draws the style-conscious crowd and can justly claim to have launched the dining renaissance of the Merchant City. Wooden tables and chairs crafted by Scottish artist Tim Stead are so fluidly shaped it's hard to believe they're inanimate. **Known for:** Stornaway black pudding with mushrooms; great breakfasts; unique furniture. $ *Average main: £15* ✉ *64 Albion St., Merchant City* ☎ *0141/552-6813* ⊕ *www.cafegandolfi.com* Ⓜ *Buchanan St.* ✛ *G5.*

$$ ✕ **City Merchant.** If you have a penchant for fresh cuisine and a taste for
MODERN BRITISH intense and flavorful sauces, head to this welcoming spot with simple but traditional furnishings, including white tablecloths, dark wood, soft lighting, and tartan carpets. The secret is the kitchen's use of only local ingredients and its emphasis on Scottish cuisine. **Known for:** intense sauces; traditional Scottish cuisine; Cullen skink soup. $ *Average main: £19* ✉ *97–99 Candleriggs St., Merchant City* ☎ *0141/553-1577* ⊕ *www.citymerchant.co.uk* ☾ *Closed Sun.* Ⓜ *Buchanan St.* ✛ *G5.*

$$$
MODERN BRITISH

✕**Corinthian Club.** Inside what was once the mansion of tobacco merchant George Buchanan, the Corinthian Club includes a restaurant, two bars, a nightclub, and a casino in its maze of rooms. Its main restaurant, the steak-and-seafood-focused Brasserie, makes a dramatic first impression with its glass dome and statues. **Known for:** its extravagant central restaurant; range of menus and spaces; spectacular columns under the roof. Ⓢ *Average main: £20* ✉ *191 Ingram St., Merchant City* ☎ *0141/552–1101* ⊕ *www.thecorinthianclub.co.uk* Ⓜ *Buchanan St.* ✛ *G5.*

$$$
BRITISH

✕**Hutchesons City Grill.** One of the most iconic buildings in the Merchant City, the 17th-century Hutchesons Hospital, has become an elegant, seafood-focused restaurant and bar. Downstairs is divided between the bar area and the café section, its dark-wood decor recalling earlier times; upstairs the dining room has tall windows and beautifully decorated ceilings. **Known for:** Sunday roast with Champagne; weekend and lunch deals; subdued elegance in iconic building. Ⓢ *Average main: £20* ✉ *158 Ingram St., Merchant City* ☎ *0141/552–4050* ⊕ *www. hutchesonsglasgow.com* Ⓜ *Buchanan St.* ✛ *G5.*

$$
ASIAN FUSION

✕**Kool Ba.** Thick wooden tables, tapestries, and soft candlelight make you feel at home in the comfortable dining room of this atmospheric haven serving an intriguing mix of Indian and Persian fare. It's all about healthy, flavorful cooking: chicken tikka masala in a yogurt sauce or lamb korma with coconut cream and fruit or the Persian shashlik are good picks, and the menu describes each dish. **Known for:** Indian-Persian fusion; wide-ranging menu; attentive service. Ⓢ *Average main: £16* ✉ *109–113 Candleriggs, Merchant City* ☎ *0141/552–2777* ⊕ *www. koolba.com* ☉ *Closed Mon.* Ⓜ *Buchanan St.* ✛ *G5.*

TEA TIME

In the Victorian tradition, men went to pubs, and Glasgow women's social interaction took place in the city's many tearooms and cafés. Today *everyone* goes to the café. Glaswegians have succumbed to the worldwide love for espresso-based coffees, but they'll never give up the comfort of a nice cup of tea, so you'll find both at most tearooms, along with scones, Scottish pancakes, and other pastries. The Glasgow tradition of high tea with fish-and-chips, cakes, and tea has been supplanted by afternoon tea, a more genteel affair with sandwiches and cakes on a traditional cake stand.

WEST END

Because of Glasgow University, the eateries in this area were once just the domain of students and professors. In recent years, this elegant residential area has also attracted fine restaurants that appeal to a wide range of visitors.

$$$
INDIAN

✕**Balbir's.** Don't let the tinted windows discourage you: this place is a temple for pure, healthy Indian food that's impressive in taste and presentation. Twinkling chandeliers, immaculate white tablecloths, and perfectly polished silverware set the stage. **Known for:** fast, attentive service; multiple spice (and heat) combinations; everything on a grand scale. $ $\boxed{S}$ Average main: £22 $\boxtimes$ 7 Church St., West End $\boxtimes$ 0141/339–7711 $\oplus$ www.balbirs.co.uk $\odot$ No lunch $\boxed{M}$ Kelvinhall $\oplus$ B3.

$ $ $\times$ **Bay Tree.** This popular small café in the university area is unpretentious and quite cheap. It serves wonderful Middle Eastern food—mostly vegetarian dishes, but there are a few lamb and chicken creations as well. Known for: good meze; Turkish and Lebanese dishes; standard café fare, too. $\boxed{S}$ Average main: £11 $\boxtimes$ 403 Great Western Rd., West End $\boxtimes$ 0141/334–5898 $\oplus$ www.thebaytreewestend.co.uk $\boxed{M}$ Kelvinbridge $\oplus$ D2.

MIDDLE EASTERN

$ $ $\times$ **Bread Meats Bread.** One of a new breed of burger joints that has emerged in the city, this casual spot with long wooden tables, stools, and benches is also a meeting place for coffee or a drink. The many creatively stuffed burgers and sauces are accompanied by different poutines (the basic version of this Canadian dish is fries topped with cheese curds and gravy) and cheese toasties, a variation on the British classic known as rarebit (for reasons unknown). Known for: burgers; poutines; rarebits. $\boxed{S}$ Average main: £10 $\boxtimes$ 701 Great Western Rd., West End $\boxtimes$ 0141/648 0399 $\oplus$ www.breadmeatsbread.com $\boxed{M}$ Hillhead $\oplus$ C2.

BURGER

$$ $ $\times$ **Cafe Andaluz.** With Iberian flair, this lively basement eatery is beautifully decorated using Spanish decorated tiles throughout. The first tapas place to make an impact in Glasgow, it has been followed by others (and has opened a second location in the City Centre) but remains one of the most successful. Known for: Spanish wine; lively but intimate; good paellas. $\boxed{S}$ Average main: £15 $\boxtimes$ 2 Cresswell La., West End $\boxtimes$ 0141/339–1111 $\oplus$ www.cafeandaluz.com $\boxed{M}$ Hillhead $\oplus$ B2.

TAPAS

$$ $ $\times$ **Cafezique.** Small but inviting, this bistro-style café has a vibrant, bustling atmosphere while remaining unhurried. Its changing breakfast, lunch, and dinner menus of British fare are always fresh and exciting. Known for: wonderful breakfasts; sobreasada (a chorizo spread); nearby bakery. $\boxed{S}$ Average main: £15 $\boxtimes$ 66 Hyndland St., West End $\boxtimes$ 0141/339–7180 $\oplus$ www.delizique.com $\boxed{M}$ Hillhead $\oplus$ A2.

BRITISH

$ $ $\times$ **Hanoi Bike Shop.** Glasgow's first Vietnamese canteen offers a different style of dining, which is apparent from the moment you walk through the door and see the rustic setting, low tables, and stools. This is street food: choices include blood sausage with razor clam salad, hot-and-sour fish soup, and versions of pho, the fragrant Vietnamese soup with noodles and sliced meat. Known for: pho; street food in small plates; organic tofu options. $\boxed{S}$ Average main: £14 $\boxtimes$ 8 Ruthven La., West End $\oplus$ Down the alley opposite Hillhead subway station $\boxtimes$ 0141/334–7165 $\oplus$ hanoibikeshop.co.uk $\boxed{M}$ Hillhead $\oplus$ B2.

VIETNAMESE

$$ $ $\times$ **The Left Bank.** Close to Glasgow University, this popular bar and restaurant attracts a more mature student crowd. It's an airy spot with high ceilings, leather sofas, and wood floors, and the specialty is good, eclectic international food at reasonable prices. Known for: small plates; open early until late; brunch. $\boxed{S}$ Average main: £15 $\boxtimes$ 33–35 Gibson St., West End $\boxtimes$ 0141/339–5969 $\oplus$ www.theleftbank.co.uk $\boxed{M}$ Kelvinbridge $\oplus$ C2.

ECLECTIC

$ $ $\times$ **Little Italy.** This busy, noisy, and extremely friendly Italian café sits in the heart of the West End. Its pizzas, made on the premises while you wait with a coffee or a glass of Italian wine, are probably the best

ITALIAN
FAMILY

around, and its house-made pastas are consistently good. **Known for:** pizza; Italian wines; house-made pasta. $ *Average main: £14* ✉ *205 Byres Rd., West End* ☎ *0141/339–6287* ⊕ *littleitalyglasgow.com* Ⓜ *Hillhead* ✛ B2.

$$
BRITISH
✕ **Number Sixteen.** This tiny, intimate restaurant serves only the freshest ingredients, superbly prepared, on a constantly changing menu. Halibut is served with choucroute and a passion-fruit dressing—a typically unpredictable meeting of flavors. **Known for:** excellent set menu; surprising flavor combinations; cozy interior. $ *Average main: £17* ✉ *16 Byres Rd., West End* ☎ *0141/339–2544* ⊕ *www.number16. co.uk* Ⓜ *Kelvin Hall* ✛ A3.

$$
ECLECTIC
Fodor's Choice
★
✕ **Stravaigin.** For many years Stravaigin has maintained the highest quality of cooking, creating adventurous dishes that often combine Asian and local flavors and unusual marriages of ingredients. You can try the *piri piri* quail (the seasoning is used in Africa) or the restaurant's famous haggis and neeps (turnips), symbolizing its commitment to local produce. **Known for:** buzzy bar, quieter restaurant downstairs; haggis and neeps; daily-changing curry. $ *Average main: £18* ✉ *28 Gibson St., West End* ☎ *0141/334–2665* ⊕ *www.stravaigin.co.uk* Ⓜ *Kelvinbridge* ✛ C2.

$$$
MODERN BRITISH
✕ **Ubiquitous Chip.** Occupying a converted stable behind the Hillhead subway station on busy Ashton Lane, this restaurant is a Glasgow institution, with an untarnished reputation for creative Scottish cooking. Its street-level restaurant is a beautiful courtyard protected by a glass roof, and the more informal brasserie upstairs also serves less expensive dishes like haggis with neeps and tatties or a plate of mussels. **Known for:** venison haggis; imaginative fish cookery; lovely courtyard. $ *Average main: £24* ✉ *12 Ashton La., West End* ☎ *0141/334–5007* ⊕ *www. ubiquitouschip.co.uk* Ⓜ *Hillhead* ✛ B2.

$
JAPANESE
✕ **Wudon.** Pleasant and relaxed, this Japanese restaurant with white walls, simple furniture, subdued lighting, and a large window onto the street offers beautifully prepared food presented with great charm by the staff. Whether your taste is for hearty broths, just-made sushi, or savory rice and noodle dishes, the chef will combine the elements to your taste. **Known for:** broth bowls with noodles; huge sushi menu; reasonable prices. $ *Average main: £11* ✉ *535 Great Western Rd., West End* ☎ *0141/357–3033* ⊕ *www.wudon-noodlebar.co.uk* Ⓜ *Kelvinbridge* ✛ C2.

FINNIESTON

A small strip of Argyle has been transformed into an exciting new restaurant area, dominated by fish restaurants (Crabshakk and The Finnieston, for example), newly opened steak houses and old pubs transformed into trendy cocktail bars, and the newest small-plate innovators like Ox and Finch and Six by Nico. It caters to the visitors brought in by the music arena and the riverside development.

$$
ITALIAN
✕ **Baffo.** There has been something of an explosion of new pizzerias in Glasgow, many of them newer chains, but Baffo has made its mark and won approval from a demanding audience. The decor of this busy spot is casual but smart, with exposed brick, white tiles and tables,

black chairs, and wood floors. **Known for:** the half-meter pizza; busy in a friendly way; good pasta at good prices. [$] *Average main: £15* ✉ *1377 Argyle St., Finnieston* ⊕ *Opposite the Kelvingrove Museum* ☎ *0141/583–0000* 🌐 *www.baffo.co.uk* [M] *Kelvin Hall* ⊕ B3.

$$ STEAKHOUSE 🍴 **Butchershop Bar and Grill.** An early arrival in the redeveloping Finnieston area, Butchershop occupies what was once a pub and overlooks the bowling greens in Kelvingrove Park. Modern, open, and airy, it preserves the sociable atmosphere of its predecessor, though it is now a quality steak house offering a range of cuts from rump to T-bone. **Known for:** steaks of every variety; good offers and fixed-price menus; publike atmosphere. [$] *Average main: £19* ✉ *1055 Sauchiehall St., Finnieston* ⊕ *Opposite Kelvingrove Park* ☎ *0141/339–2999* 🌐 *www.butchershopglasgow.com* [M] *Kelvin Hall* ⊕ B3.

$$$ SEAFOOD Fodor's Choice ★ 🍴 **Crabshakk.** Anything but a shack, this intimate dining room has heavy wooden tables and chairs, an elegantly ornate ceiling, and a bar so shiny and inviting that it seems to almost insist you have a drink. The food comes from the sea—oysters, lobster, and squid—and you can have your choice served iced, grilled, roasted, or battered. **Known for:** great seafood cooking; art deco feel; very intimate. [$] *Average main: £20* ✉ *1114 Argyle St., Finnieston* ☎ *0141/334–6127* 🌐 *www.crabshakk.com* ⏲ *Closed Mon.* [M] *Kelvin Hall* ⊕ C4.

$$ SEAFOOD Fodor's Choice ★ 🍴 **The Finnieston.** A 19th-century inn turned into an elegant restaurant, the Finnieston retains the dark wood and narrow cubicles of earlier times, but today it is one of the new high-quality fish restaurants that have transformed the faded Finnieston area into a fashionable district. The menu allows you to choose the fish and how it is prepared, the sauce, and salad or vegetable sides. **Known for:** seafood and fish cuisine; stunning array of cocktails; comfy wooden booths. [$] *Average main: £16* ✉ *1125 Argyle St., Finnieston* ☎ *0141/222–2884* 🌐 *www.thefinniestonbar.com* [M] *Kelvin Hall* ⊕ C4.

$$ INDIAN 🍴 **Mother India's Cafe.** At this progeny of the older Mother India restaurant nearby and early small-plates convert, the style is casual, with an extensive list of very fresh dishes and a no-reservations policy that makes for a (fast-moving) line. What makes this place across from Kelvingrove Art Gallery so popular is the combination of high-quality cooking and an extensive range of tastes that runs from creamy classics, through the vegetarian dal served cold, to spicy ginger chicken. **Known for:** small-plates Indian cuisine; quick service; bring your own wine. [$] *Average main: £15* ✉ *1355 Argyle St., Clyde* ☎ *0141/339–9145* 🌐 *www.motherindiaglasgow.co.uk* [M] *Kelvin Hall* ⊕ B3.

$$$ ECLECTIC Fodor's Choice ★ 🍴 **Ox and Finch.** This immensely popular restaurant shines at every level—service, presentation, and taste. The stripped-back, rustic decor encourages chatter and the sharing of the eclectic small plates that are its specialty. **Known for:** small-plates dining; open kitchen; the buzz of conversation. [$] *Average main: £20* ✉ *920 Sauchiehall St., Finnieston* ☎ *0141/339–8627* 🌐 *www.oxandfinch.com* [M] *Kelvin Hall* ⊕ C4.

$$ SPANISH 🍴 **Rioja.** Rioja belongs to the second generation of tapas restaurants, combining the classics with new and innovative interpretations. At this dark, rustic spot with exposed brick, wood floors and sturdy tables, and dark walls, *patatas riojanas* go a stage beyond *patatas bravas,*

adding pork and chorizo, while the spring lamb with almond crust adds new flavors to the tapas range. **Known for:** contemporary take on tapas; good Spanish wines; late-night dining. $ *Average main: £15* ✉ *1116 Argyle St., Clyde* ☎ *0141/334–0761* ⊕ *www.riojafinnieston. co.uk* Ⓜ *Kelvin Hall* ⊕ C4.

$$$ ✕ **The Sisters Kelvingrove.** Walk up the smooth sandstone steps to this
BRITISH restaurant, which aims to inspire both your palate and your heart with a menu that is locally sourced and always changing: a typical dish is Carluke ham with buttered savoy cabbage and colcannon mash. Douglas Gray tartan pads the pristine room, and polished floorboards reflect the natural light shining in from the long windows around the unusual oval-shape room. **Known for:** fine Scottish cooking carefully sourced; gooseberry fool dessert; being ahead of its time. $ *Average main: £20* ✉ *36 Kelvingrove St., Finnieston* ☎ *0141/564–1157* ⊕ *www.thesisters. co.uk* Ⓜ *Kelvin Hall* ⊕ C4.

$$$ ✕ **Six by Nico.** In a street of adventurous eateries, Six by Nico adds a
BRITISH new dimension of fun and wit. The concept at this intimate, modern restaurant with black tile, wood floors and tables, and black chairs is a six-course tasting menu linked to a theme that changes every six weeks, whether it's fish-and-chips or Route 66, with dishes that deconstruct and reconstruct the familiar. **Known for:** highly original approach to tasting menu; imaginative dishes; adventurous dining out. $ *Average main: £25* ✉ *1132 Argyle St., Finnieston* ☎ *0141/334 5661* ⊕ *www. sixbynico.co.uk* ⊘ *Closed Mon.* Ⓜ *Kelvin Hall* ⊕ C4.

EAST END

The East End is not well furnished with notable places to eat. An exception is West, housed in the Templeton's Carpet Factory opposite the People's Palace.

$ ✕ **West.** This microbrewery serves beer brewed "according to German
GERMAN purity laws of 1516"—in other words, no additives to muddy the flavor. The German theme is continued with the slightly cavernous dining space dotted with large wooden tables, and the food, which includes wursts, Wiener schnitzel, and goulash. **Known for:** wurst and potato salad; variety of its own beers; goulash soup. $ *Average main: £13* ✉ *Templeton Bldg., Templeton St., East End* ☎ *0141/550–0135* ⊕ *www.westbeer. com* Ⓜ *St. Enoch* ⊕ H6.

WHERE TO STAY

Since new or revamped grand hotels such as the Blythswood Square (2009) and Grand Central (2010) opened, a fresh generation of hotels has appeared around the city, from basic budget options to stylish boutique properties. Glasgow's City Centre never sleeps, so downtown hotels may be noisier than those in the leafy and genteel West End or in fashionable Finnieston. Downtown hotels are within walking distance of all the main sights, while West End lodgings are more convenient for museums and art galleries.

Although big hotels are spread out all around the city, B&Bs are definitely a more popular, personal, and cheaper option. For country-house luxury you should look beyond the city—try Mar Hall, near Paisley. Regardless of the neighborhood, hotels are about the same in price. Some B&Bs as well as the smaller properties may also offer discounts for longer stays. Make your reservations in advance, especially when there's a big concert, sporting event, or holiday (New Year's Eve is popular). Glasgow is busiest in summer, but it can fill up when something special is going on. If you arrive in town without a place to stay, contact the Glasgow Tourist Information Centre.

3

PRICES

It is always worthwhile to inquire about special deals or rates, especially if you book online and in advance. Another money-saving option is to rent an apartment. B&Bs are the best-priced short-term lodging option, and you're sure to get breakfast.

Most smaller hotels and all guesthouses include breakfast in the room rate. Larger hotels usually charge extra for breakfast. Also note that the most expensive hotels often exclude V.A.T. (Value-Added Tax, the sales tax) in the initial price quote but budget places include it. *Hotel reviews have been shortened. For full information, visit Fodors.com. Use the coordinate (⊕ B2) at the end of each listing to locate a site on the corresponding map.*

WHAT IT COSTS IN POUNDS

	$	$$	$$$	$$$$
Hotels	under £100	£100–£160	£161–£220	over £220

Restaurant prices are the average cost of a main course at dinner or, if dinner is not served, at lunch. Hotel prices are the lowest cost of a standard double room in high season, including 20% V.A.T.

CITY CENTRE

Here you'll be close to everything—the main sights, shops, theaters, restaurants, and bars—the pulse of the city. You don't have to worry about transportation in the center of town, but it can get noisy on weekend nights.

$ HOTEL 🏨 **Abode Glasgow.** Stylish and modern, this boutique hotel in an Edwardian building was once the home of a prime minister, and it retains architectural features like the wrought-iron elevator and walls lined with 2,000 gold-leaf lions. **Pros:** stylish rooms; great location. **Cons:** limited public areas; some front rooms noisy; pricey parking. [$] *Rooms from: £90* ✉ *129 Bath St., City Centre* ☎ *0141/221–6789,* 🌐 *www.abodeglasgow.co.uk* 🛏 *60 rooms* 🍴 *Breakfast* [M] *Buchanan St.* ⊕ F4.

$$ HOTEL 🏨 **Apex City of Glasgow Hotel.** Its extraordinary projecting floor-to-ceiling windows set this modern chain hotel apart, providing a panoramic view over Glasgow and beyond from the upper floors (sixth and seventh). **Pros:** bright rooms; central location; city views from higher floors. **Cons:** lower-floor rooms overlook other buildings; no parking facility

and nearby lot closes at night. $ Rooms from: £160 ⊠ 110 Bath St., City Centre 🕾 0141/375 3333 ⊕ www.apexhotels.co.uk ⇨ 106 rooms ❋❄ Breakfast Ⓜ Buchanan St. ✦ F4.

$$$ ❈ **Blythswood Square.** History and luxury come together at this smart
HOTEL conversion of the former headquarters of the Royal Automobile Club
Fodor's Choice of Scotland, which occupies a classical building on peaceful Blythswood
★ Square. **Pros:** airy and luxurious; glorious bathrooms; lovely common
areas with the original gold-topped columns. **Cons:** room lighting may
be too dim for some; some street noise. $ Rooms from: £166 ⊠ 11
Blythswood Sq., City Centre 🕾 0141/248–8888 ⊕ www.blythswood-
square.com ⇨ 117 rooms ❋❄ Breakfast Ⓜ Cowcaddens ✦ E4.

$$ ❈ **Carlton George.** A narrow revolving doorway, a step back from busy
HOTEL West George Street, creates the illusion of a secret passageway leading
into this lavish boutique hotel. **Pros:** near City Centre attractions; discounted parking nearby. **Cons:** entrance very small and often crowded;
area sometimes noisy at night. $ Rooms from: £131 ⊠ 44 W. George
St., City Centre 🕾 0141/353–6373 ⊕ www.carlton.nl/george ⇨ 64
rooms ❋❄ Breakfast Ⓜ Buchanan St. ✦ F4.

$$ ❈ **citizenM Glasgow.** There's no lobby at the futuristic citizenM—no
HOTEL reception area at all, because you can only book online—but there
Fodor's Choice are chic "living rooms" with ultramodern furnishings where guests
★ congregate. **Pros:** wonderful design; all the creature comforts; central
location. **Cons:** not for the claustrophobic; breakfast costs more if you
don't book it ahead. $ Rooms from: £119 ⊠ 60 Renfrew St., corner of
Hope St., City Centre 🕾 01782/488–3490 ⊕ www.citizenm.com ⇨ 198
rooms ❋❄ No meals Ⓜ Buchanan St. ✦ F4.

$$ ❈ **Dakota Deluxe Glasgow.** At this extremely stylish addition to Glasgow's
HOTEL hotel scene, the textured, neutral decor creates a restful, subdued
Fodor's Choice atmosphere. **Pros:** beautiful modern design and details; spacious, well-
★ appointed rooms; lovely bathrooms. **Cons:** unexciting views from hotel;
toward edge of City Centre, though near Blythswood Square. $ Rooms
from: £145 ⊠ 179 W. Regent St., City Centre 🕾 0141/404 3680
⊕ glasgow.dakotahotels.co.uk ⇨ 83 rooms ❋❄ Breakfast Ⓜ Cowcaddens ✦ E4.

$$ ❈ **Grand Central Hotel.** This late-19th-century hotel next to Central sta-
HOTEL tion certainly deserves its name, as everything about it, from the mag-
Fodor's Choice nificent marble-floor Champagne bar to the ballroom fully restored
★ to its original glory, is grand. **Pros:** a real air of luxury; generally
spacious rooms; great Champagne bar for lingering. **Cons:** some noise
from street; parking a couple of blocks away; some small rooms.
$ Rooms from: £145 ⊠ 99 Gordon St., City Centre 🕾 0141/240–
3700 ⊕ www.grandcentralhotel.com ⇨ 233 rooms ❋❄ Breakfast
Ⓜ Buchanan St. ✦ F5.

$$ ❈ **Grasshoppers Hotel Glasgow.** Not visible from the street, this hotel
HOTEL occupies a sixth floor above Central station; guest rooms are on the
small side but have expansive windows overlooking the glass roof of
the station on one side and across the rooftops of Glasgow on the
other. **Pros:** bright and clean; quiet atmosphere; central location. **Cons:**
no lobby; rooms are quite small; no parking at hotel site. $ Rooms
from: £128 ⊠ 87 Union St., City Centre ✦ Door marked "Caledonian

Chambers" leads to elevator ☎ *0141/222–2666* ⊕ *www.grasshoppers-glasgow.com* ⤳ *30 rooms* ⊖| *Breakfast* Ⓜ *St. Enoch* ✢ F5.

$ ⛫ **Hallmark Hotel Glasgow.** Behind a rather austere exterior built on to
HOTEL   what was once a mill, the Hallmark clearly sees itself as a family-ori-
FAMILY   ented hotel, with the facilities of a large chain but decor and ambience
that are unpretentious and comfortable. **Pros:** pleasant atmosphere;
good spa and leisure center available to guests; close to City Centre.
Cons: no views; some noise from nearby elevated motorway; hotel
vehicle entrance not easy to find. Ⓢ *Rooms from: £90* ⊠ *27 Washington
St., City Centre* ☎ *0141/222–2929* ⊕ *www.hallmarkhotels.co.uk* ⤳ *129
rooms* ⊖| *Breakfast* Ⓜ *St. Enoch* ✢ E5.

$$ ⛫ **Hotel Indigo Glasgow.** In the center of the city, the fashionable Indigo
HOTEL   is awash with bold colors and modern designs that emphasize comfort
and calm. **Pros:** well-designed rooms; vivid colors, patterns, and light-
ing; no conference rooms. **Cons:** narrow corridors; only showers in
the bathrooms. Ⓢ *Rooms from: £118* ⊠ *75 Waterloo St., City Centre*
☎ *0141/226–7700* ⊕ *www.hinglasgow.co.uk* ⤳ *94 rooms* ⊖| *No meals*
Ⓜ *St. Enoch* ✢ E5.

$$ ⛫ **Malmaison Glasgow.** Housed in a converted church, this modern bou-
HOTEL   tique hotel prides itself on personal service and outstanding amenities
like plasma televisions and high-end stereo systems. **Pros:** stunning
lobby; attention to detail; five-minute walk to Sauchiehall Street. **Cons:**
bland views; dark hallways; no on-site parking. Ⓢ *Rooms from: £135*
⊠ *278 W. George St., City Centre* ☎ *0141/572–1000* ⊕ *www.malmai-
son.com* ⤳ *72 rooms* ⊖| *Breakfast* Ⓜ *Cowcaddens* ✢ E4.

$ ⛫ **Premier Inn Glasgow City Centre Buchanan Galleries.** It would be easy
HOTEL   to miss the big City Centre branch of this popular budget hotel chain,
since its entrance on Renfield Street is quite small, but it's worth seeking
out for its winning location just around the corner from the pedestrian
precinct in Sauchiehall Street. **Pros:** great location; bargain rates; modern rooms. **Cons:** some front rooms a bit noisy; entrance easily missed
at street level; no parking facilities. Ⓢ *Rooms from: £70* ⊠ *Buchanan
Galleries, 141 W. Nile St., City Centre* ☎ *0871/527–9360* ⊕ *www.pre-
mierinn.com* ⤳ *220 rooms* ⊖| *No meals* Ⓜ *Buchanan St.* ✢ F4.

$$ ⛫ **Radisson Blu Hotel, Glasgow.** You can't miss this eye-catching edifice
HOTEL   behind Central station: its glass facade makes the interior, particularly
the lounge, seem as though it were part of the street. **Pros:** kilted door-
man; impeccable service; free Wi-Fi and other amenities. **Cons:** neigh-
borhood can get noisy; most rooms have poor views; no on-site parking.
Ⓢ *Rooms from: £106* ⊠ *301 Argyle St., City Centre* ☎ *0141/204–3333*
⊕ *www.radissonblu.com* ⤳ *250 rooms* ⊖| *Breakfast* Ⓜ *St. Enoch* ✢ F5.

$ ⛫ **Victorian House.** Compared with the bright-yellow entrance hall,
B&B/INN   the rooms in this hotel are rather plain, but its location—on a quiet
residential street only a block from the Charles Rennie Mackintosh–
designed Glasgow School of Art—is prime, and the rates are reasonable.
Pros: appealing and central location; basement rooms very spacious.
Cons: a little expensive for what it offers; no elevator; on-street park-
ing sometimes difficult to find. Ⓢ *Rooms from: £90* ⊠ *212 Renfrew St.,
City Centre* ☎ *0141/332–0129* ⊕ *www.thevictorian.co.uk* ⤳ *60 rooms*
⊖| *Breakfast* Ⓜ *Cowcaddens* ✢ E3.

3

MERCHANT CITY

The hotels in the Merchant City are best for those who plan to spend most of their time out and about. In general, this busy area is not the place to come if you want peace and quiet.

$
B&B/INN
Babbity Bowster's. This warm and welcoming old merchant's house in the heart of the Merchant City is essentially a pub with rooms—simple, no-frills accommodation on its second floor. **Pros:** couldn't be more central; good food; great atmosphere; parking for guests. **Cons:** a bit noisy; no elevator. $ Rooms from: £70 ⊠ 16–18 Blackfriars St., Merchant City ☎ 0141/552–5055 ⊕ www.babbitybowster.com ⋧ 6 rooms ⊠ Breakfast Ⓜ Buchanan St. ✛ G5.

$$
HOTEL
Millennium Hotel Glasgow. This huge hotel in an older building, which occupies almost a whole side of George Square and stretches above the rail station next door, has restrained and comfortable rooms with ample bathrooms. **Pros:** couldn't be more central; ample comfortable public areas. **Cons:** very long corridors; views of the square only from some (more expensive) rooms; can feel very anonymous; some areas are looking a bit tired. $ Rooms from: £135 ⊠ 40 George Sq., City Centre ☎ 0141/332–6711 ⊕ www.millenniumhotels.co.uk ⋧ 116 rooms ⊠ Breakfast Ⓜ Buchanan St. ✛ G5.

$
HOTEL
The Z Hotel Glasgow. Just a few yards from George Square, this good-value modern hotel is one of the newer additions to Merchant City's accommodation options. **Pros:** central location; compact rooms but good beds and bedding; close to Queen Street station. **Cons:** internal rooms have small (or no) windows; no restaurant; no parking facilities. $ Rooms from: £80 ⊠ 36 N. Frederick St., Merchant City ☎ 0141/212 4550 ⊕ www.thezhotels.com ⋧ 104 rooms ⊠ No meals ✛ G4.

WEST END

Many lodgings are on quieter Great Western Road, set apart from busy Byres Road.

$
B&B/INN
Amadeus Guest House. This attractive Victorian town house has comfortably furnished rooms that are flooded with plenty of natural light. **Pros:** near West End attractions; two-minute walk from subway; kids under six free. **Cons:** some rooms small; finding parking sometimes difficult. $ Rooms from: £90 ⊠ 411 N. Woodside Rd., West End ☎ 0141/339–8257 ⊕ www.amadeusguesthouse.co.uk ⋧ 9 rooms ⊠ Breakfast Ⓜ Kelvinbridge ✛ D2.

$
HOTEL
FAMILY
Ambassador Hotel. Opposite the West End's peaceful Glasgow Botanic Gardens and within minutes of busy Byres Road, the Ambassador is part of a terrace of elegant town houses on the banks of the River Kelvin. **Pros:** views of Botanic Gardens; great for families with kids; five-minute walk to public transportation and West End amenities. **Cons:** no elevator; on-street parking difficult after 6 pm. $ Rooms from: £72 ⊠ 7 Kelvin Dr., West End ☎ 0141/946–1018 ⊕ www.ambassador-hotel. net ⋧ 26 rooms ⊠ Breakfast Ⓜ Hillhead ✛ C1.

$
HOTEL
Clifton Hotel. Occupying two of the grand houses along a terrace above Great Western Road, this popular hotel offers wallet-friendly rates and simply furnished rooms done up in cheerful shades. **Pros:** conveniently

located; attentive staff; good budget option. **Cons:** some rooms overlook the parking lot; no elevator. $ *Rooms from: £52* ✉ *26–27 Buckingham Terr., West End* ☎ *0141/334–8080* ⊕ *www.cliftonhotelglasgow.co.uk* ⟿ *26 rooms* ⦿| *Breakfast* Ⓜ *Hillhead* ✛ C1.

$ ⛫ **Heritage Hotel.** This small, unpretentious, but well-established hotel
HOTEL in a very central West End location has cozy, simply decorated rooms at very reasonable rates. **Pros:** very good location; friendly and agreeable staff; very reasonable rates. **Cons:** rooms quite small. $ *Rooms from: £60* ✉ *4/5 Albert Terr., West End* ✛ *Entrance by Hillhead St.* ☎ *0141/339–6955* ⊕ *www.theheritagehotel.net* ⟿ *27 rooms* ⦿| *Breakfast* Ⓜ *Hillhead* ✛ C2.

$$ ⛫ **Hilton Glasgow Grosvenor.** Behind a row of grand terrace houses, this
HOTEL modern hotel overlooks the Glasgow Botanic Gardens. **Pros:** close to Byres Road; some rooms have good views; tasty eatery. **Cons:** rooms at the back overlook a parking lot; a rather institutional feel; parking is extremely limited in the area. $ *Rooms from: £109* ✉ *1–9 Grosvenor Terr., West End* ☎ *0141/339–8811* ⊕ *www3.hilton.com* ⟿ *96 rooms* ⦿| *Breakfast* Ⓜ *Hillhead* ✛ B1.

$$ ⛫ **Hotel du Vin Glasgow.** Once the legendary One Devonshire Gardens
HOTEL hotel, frequented by such celebrities as Luciano Pavarotti and Elizabeth
Fodor's Choice Taylor, the Hotel du Vin Glasgow is still a destination for those in
★ search of luxury. **Pros:** stunning Scottish-style rooms; doting service; complimentary whisky on arrival. **Cons:** no elevator; on-street parking can be difficult after 6 pm. $ *Rooms from: £140* ✉ *1 Devonshire Gardens, West End* ☎ *0330/016–0390* ⊕ *www.hotelduvin.com* ⟿ *49 rooms* ⦿| *Breakfast* Ⓜ *Hillhead* ✛ A1.

FINNIESTON

Besides a handful of interesting museums and a popular cluster of busy bars and restaurants, this up-and-coming area near the river also has a few lodgings, mostly on Sauchiehall Street.

$ ⛫ **Argyll Guest House.** In this budget-minded annex to the Argyll Hotel,
B&B/INN across the road on Sauchiehall Street, the rooms are plainly furnished but scrupulously clean. **Pros:** close to Kelvingrove Park; near public transportation; bargain prices. **Cons:** front rooms noisy on weekends; no elevator; parking on street is metered. $ *Rooms from: £80* ✉ *966–970 Sauchiehall St., Finnieston* ☎ *0141/357–5155* ⊕ *www.argyllhotelglasgow.co.uk* ⟿ *20 rooms* ⦿| *Breakfast* Ⓜ *Kelvin Hall* ✛ C4.

$$ ⛫ **Argyll Hotel.** The tartan in the reception area reflects the clan theme
HOTEL throughout the hotel; each room is named after a clan, but each is also very different from the next. **Pros:** centrally located; comfortable rooms; reasonable prices. **Cons:** street a little noisy; metered parking on the street; downstairs breakfast area and bar need refurbishing. $ *Rooms from: £100* ✉ *973 Sauchiehall St., Finnieston* ☎ *0141/337–3313* ⊕ *www.argyllhotelglasgow.co.uk* ⟿ *38 rooms* ⦿| *Breakfast* Ⓜ *Kelvin Hall* ✛ C4.

$ ⛫ **Hilton Garden Inn Glasgow City Centre.** Overlooking the Clyde, this
HOTEL hotel is within sight of the SSE Hydro entertainment arena and a short walk along the water from the Riverside Museum, and a slightly

longer walk from Argyle Street in Finnieston. **Pros:** beside the Hydro; lovely terrace; some great views. **Cons:** isolated from the rest of the city; no nearby metro. $ *Rooms from:* £89 ✉ *Finnieston Quay, Finnieston* ☎ *0141/240–1002* ⊕ *www3.hilton.com* ⤴ *164 rooms* ⏍*Breakfast* ✛ C5.

$ 🏨 **The Sandyford.** The Victorian exterior of this hotel anticipates the
HOTEL   colorful decor you'll find inside, where the large windows in the reception area let in lots of light. **Pros:** extremely well located; minutes from several good eateries; very competitive prices. **Cons:** front rooms can get late-night noise; no elevator. $ *Rooms from:* £65 ✉ *904 Sauchiehall St., Finnieston* ☎ *0141/334–0000* ⊕ *www.sandyfordhotelglasgow.com* ⤴ *55 rooms* ⏍*Breakfast* Ⓜ *Kelvin Hall* ✛ C4.

NIGHTLIFE AND PERFORMING ARTS

Glasgow's music scene is vibrant and creative, and many successful pop artists began their careers in its pubs and clubs. When it comes to nightlife, the City Centre and the West End are alive with pubs and clubs offering an eclectic mix of everything from bagpipes to salsa to punk. The biweekly magazine *List,* available at newsstands and many cafés and arts centers, is an indispensable guide to Glasgow's bars and clubs.

NIGHTLIFE

Glasgow's busy nightlife scene is impressive and varied. Bars and pubs often close at midnight on weekends, but nightclubs often stay open until 3 or 4 am. Traditional *ceilidh* (a mix of country dancing, music, and song; pronounced *kay*-lee) is not as popular with locals as it used to be (except at weddings), but you can still find it at many more tourist-oriented establishments.

Glasgow's pubs were once hangouts for serious drinkers who demanded few comforts. Today many of these gritty establishments have been transformed into trendy cocktail bars or cavernous spaces with video monitors, though a few traditional bars survive. Bars and pubs vary according to location; many in the City Centre cater to business types, while those in the West End and Finnieston draw in the younger crowd.

As elsewhere in Britain, electronic music—from house to techno to drum and bass—is par for the course in Glasgow's dance clubs. Much of the scene revolves around the City Centre, as a late-night walk down Sauchiehall Street on Friday or Saturday will reveal.

CITY CENTRE
BARS AND PUBS
Baby Grand. One of Glasgow's best-kept secrets, this intimate piano bar is hidden behind the King's Theatre. It serves good food all day (excellent breakfasts), and it manages to be crowded but never overcrowded, even at the busiest times. The pretheater menu is a good value, and tapas are available on weekends. ✉ *3 Elmbank Gardens, City Centre* ☎ *0141/248–4942* ⊕ *www.babygrandglasgow.com* Ⓜ *Cowcaddens.*

Bloc+. Step behind a curious version of the Iron Curtain where burgers and Tex-Mex diner food mix with an eclectic musical mash of DJs and live rock and folk bands. ⊠ *117 Bath St., City Centre* ☎ *0141/574–6066* ⊕ *bloc.ru* Ⓜ *Cowcaddens.*

King Tut's Wah Wah Hut. An intimate venue showcasing up-and-coming independent bands since 1990, King Tut's Wah Wah Hut claims to have been the venue that discovered the U.K. pop band Oasis. Indeed, the list of those who have played here reads like a catalog of indie music history. It's a favorite with students and hosts live music most nights, but the cozy and traditional pub setting draws people of all ages, and the refurbished bar is a pleasant and comfortable place for a drink or a meal. ⊠ *227A St. Vincent St., City Centre* ☎ *0141/221–5279* ⊕ *www. kingtuts.co.uk* Ⓜ *Cowcaddens.*

La Cheetah. A tiny club in the basement of Max's Bar, La Cheetah is popular precisely because it's small and intimate. It plays a variety of dance and electronic music, with some surprising well-known guests who just like the atmosphere. ⊠ *73 Queen St., City Centre* ☎ *0141/221–1379* ⊕ *www.maxsbar.co.uk* Ⓜ *Buchanan St.*

Moskito. For a splash of Mediterranean style, head to Moskito. Amid the cool, aquatic hues you can drink, eat, and watch people dancing to laid-back tunes Thursday to Sunday nights. ⊠ *200 Bath St., City Centre* ☎ *0141/331–1777* ⊕ *www.moskitoglasgow.com* Ⓜ *Buchanan St.*

Fodor'sChoice **Sloans.** One of Glasgow's oldest and most beautiful pubs, the wood-
★ paneled Sloans is always lively and welcoming; it serves traditional pub food like fish-and-chips throughout the day. The upstairs ballroom is a magnificent mirrored affair, and on the floor above there's a dance floor with a ceilidh—traditional music and dancing—every Friday night (booking essential). The pub has a good selection of beers and spirits, and the outdoor area is always lively when the weather cooperates. ⊠ *108 Argyle St., City Centre* ⚓ *Entrance is in an alley off Argyle St.* ☎ *0141/221–8886* ⊕ *www.sloansglasgow.com* Ⓜ *St. Enoch.*

CLUBS

Stereo. The small downstairs music venue gets crowded quickly when bands play Sunday to Thursday night, but that only adds to the electric atmosphere at Stereo. There's also a hopping nightclub where DJs spin on Friday and Saturday nights until the wee hours of the morning. Upstairs, a café-bar serves tasty vegan food and organic drinks. ⊠ *20–28 Renfield La., City Centre* ☎ *0141/222–2254* ⊕ *www.stereocafebar. com* Ⓜ *Buchanan St.*

Sub Club. This atmospheric underground venue has staged cutting-edge music events since its jazz club days in the '50s. Legendary favorites like Saturday's SubCulture (House) and Sunday's Optimo (a truly eclectic mix for musical hedonists) pack in friendly and sweaty crowds. ⊠ *22 Jamaica St., City Centre* ☎ *0141/248–4600* ⊕ *www. subclub.co.uk* Ⓜ *St. Enoch.*

MERCHANT CITY
BARS AND PUBS

Arta. Built on the site of Glasgow's traditional cheese market, Arta has transformed the place into what feels and looks like a Spanish hacienda. It is a labyrinth of different spaces and unexpected rooms on the ground and basement levels, where a live DJ, a salsa night, or a live band might be in action. You can also stay with the cocktails and tapas on the ground floor. ⊠ *62 Albion St., Merchant City* ☎ *0845/166–6018* ⊕ *www.arta.co.uk* Ⓜ *Buchanan St.*

Babbity Bowster's. A busy, friendly spot, Babbity Bowster's serves real ales and excellent, mainly Scottish food, prepared by a French chef who adds his own special touch. The atmosphere is lively and very friendly; there is an outdoor terrace in summer and a fireplace in winter. If you like traditional music, make a point of coming on Saturday and Wednesday afternoon. ⊠ *16–18 Blackfriars St., Merchant City* ☎ *0141/552–5055* ⊕ *www.babbitybowster.com* Ⓜ *Buchanan St.*

Boteco do Brasil. Glasgow's only Brazilian bar-restaurant-club has salsa nights Wednesdays and Latin music to dance to on weekends until 3 am. ⊠ *62 Trongate, Merchant City* ☎ *0141/548–1330* ⊕ *www.botecodobrasil.com* Ⓜ *St. Enoch.*

Fodor's Choice ★ **Scotia Bar.** This longtime bar serves up a taste of an authentic Glasgow pub, with traditional folk music regularly thrown in. Dark wood, a wood-beamed ceiling, and a classic L-shaped bar set the mood. ⊠ *112 Stockwell St., Merchant City* ☎ *0141/552–8681* ⊕ *www.scotiabar-glasgow.co.uk* Ⓜ *St. Enoch.*

CLUBS

Polo Lounge. Oozing with Edwardian style, the Polo Lounge is Glasgow's largest gay club. Upstairs is a bar that resembles an old-fashioned gentlemen's club. On the two dance floors downstairs, the DJs spin something for everyone. ⊠ *84 Wilson St., Merchant City* ☎ *0141/553–1221* ⊕ *www.pologlasgow.co.uk* Ⓜ *Buchanan St.*

Swing. Hidden behind a narrow doorway on Hope Street, Swing comes as a surprise. It is an art deco bar that has survived the city's changes, and jazz bands play here three times a week. Blues and soul are heard other nights. Cocktails enhance the atmosphere, so go ahead and ask for a Manhattan. ⊠ *183A Hope St., City Centre* ☎ *0141/332–2147* ⊕ *www.swingltd.co.uk* Ⓜ *Buchanan St.*

WEST END
BARS AND PUBS

Dram! With mismatched furnishings and the odd stag's head on the wall, the four large rooms here are decorated in a style that can only be described as "ultra eclectic." It's no place for a quiet, intimate evening, but Dram feels like a traditional bar while being brashly youthful and up-to-the-minute. There's a wide range of beers, and the place takes special pride in the 75 whiskies. On Thursday and Sunday, musicians gather in an informal jam session. Food is served every night until 9. ⊠ *232–246 Woodlands Rd., West End* ☎ *0141/332–1622* ⊕ *www.dramglasgow.co.uk* Ⓜ *Kelvinbridge.*

Òran Mór. At the top of Byres Road, Òran Mór is in a massive church that still has its beautiful stained-glass windows as well as an upper hall, once the nave of the church, gloriously decorated by Glasgow artist Alasdair Gray. The bar fills with different crowds at different times of day, but its late license means that it tends to be very full on Friday and Saturday nights. In the basement, the hugely successful lunchtime theater series A Play, a Pie, and a Pint plays to capacity crowds. It also houses a busy bistro, a brasserie, and an evening music venue, as well as a late-night club. The small beer garden fills up quickly in good weather. ✉ *731 Great Western Rd., West End* ☎ *0141/357–6200* ⊕ *www.oranmor.co.uk* Ⓜ *Hillhead.*

Tennents. A spacious corner bar, Tennents prides itself on its comprehensive selection of beers. You can expect lively conversation, as there's a refreshing lack of loud music. ✉ *191 Byres Rd., West End* ☎ *0141/341–1021* ⊕ *www.thetennentsbarglasgow.co.uk* Ⓜ *Hillhead.*

COMEDY CLUBS

Stand Comedy Club. In the basement of a former school, the Stand Comedy Club has live shows every night of the week and is most popular on Thursday and Friday. Prices vary according to who is appearing, and the doors open at 7:30. ✉ *333 Woodlands Rd., at Park Rd., West End* ☎ *0141/212–3389* ⊕ *www.thestand.co.uk* Ⓜ *Kelvingrove.*

FINNIESTON

BARS AND PUBS

Ben Nevis. A traditional pub still holding its own on the trendy Finnieston strip, this eccentric spot is full of Highland artifacts. There are more than 180 whiskies from which to choose and traditional live music on Wednesday, Thursday, and Sunday. ✉ *1147 Argyle St., Finnieston* ☎ *0141/576–5204* ⊕ *www.thebennevis.co.uk* Ⓜ *Kelvinhall.*

78. Enjoy cozy sofas, a real coal fire, and tasty vegan food throughout the day. There's live music every night, with jazz on Sunday. ✉ *10–14 Kelvinhaugh St., Finnieston* ☎ *0141/576–5018* ⊕ *www.the78cafebar.com* Ⓜ *Kelvinhall.*

PERFORMING ARTS

Because the Royal Scottish Conservatoire is in Glasgow, there is always a pool of impressive young talent that's pressing the city's artistic boundaries in theater, music, and film. The city has a well-deserved reputation for its theater, with everything from cutting-edge plays to over-the-top pantomimes. The Citizens Theatre is one of Europe's leading companies, and the Kings and the Theatre Royal play host to touring productions.

TICKETS

Scottish Music Centre. As well as a library, the Scottish Music Centre serves as the main ticket office for all music events at venues like the Royal Concert Hall and for annual events like the Glasgow Jazz Festival. ✉ *Candleriggs, City Centre* ☎ *0141/353–8000* ⊕ *www.scottishmusiccentre.com* Ⓜ *Buchanan St.*

Ticketmaster. Tickets for theatrical performances can be purchased at theater box offices or online through Ticketmaster. ⊕ *www.ticketmaster. co.uk.*

ARTS CENTERS

FAMILY **Tramway.** South of the City Centre, this innovative arts center is well worth seeking out. It hosts regular exhibitions in its two galleries, and plays—often of a very experimental nature—in its flexible theater space. It has a café and a more formal restaurant on the first floor. Don't miss the Hidden Garden, which has transformed an empty lot behind the building into a sculpture park. This is a great place to go with kids. Take the train from Central station to Pollokshields East (one stop). ✉ *25 Albert Dr., South Side* ☎ *0845/330–3501* ⊕ *www.tramway.org.*

Trongate 103. This vibrant contemporary arts center, housed in a converted Edwardian warehouse, is home base for diverse groups producing film, photography, paintings, and prints. It contains the Russian Cultural Centre and the Sharmanka Kinetic Theatre, as well as the Glasgow Print Studio, a well-established outlet for Glasgow artists; Street Level Photoworks, which aims at making photography more accessible; and the Transmission Gallery, a key exhibition space supporting nonconceptual art in the city. ✉ *103 Trongate, Merchant City* ☎ *0141/276–8380* Ⓜ *St. Enoch.*

CONCERTS

City Halls. One of the top music venues in the Merchant City, the stone-fronted City Halls hosts orchestral, jazz, and folk concerts. ✉ *Candleriggs, Merchant City* ☎ *0141/353–8000* ⊕ *www.glasgowconcerthalls.com* Ⓜ *Buchanan St.*

Glasgow Royal Concert Hall. The 2,500-seat Glasgow Royal Concert Hall is the venue for a wide range of concerts, from classical to pop. It also hosts the very popular late-night club during the annual Celtic Connections music festival. ✉ *2 Sauchiehall St., City Centre* ☎ *0141/353–8000* ⊕ *www.glasgowconcerthalls.com* Ⓜ *Buchanan St.*

Old Fruitmarket. A wonderful venue for almost every type of music, this was once the city's fruit and vegetable market. The first-floor balcony, with its intricate iron railings, still carries some of the original merchants' names. It's adjacent to City Halls in the heart of the Merchant City. ✉ *Candleriggs, Merchant City* ☎ *0141/353–8000* ⊕ *www. glasgowconcerthalls.com* Ⓜ *Buchanan St.*

O2 ABC. One of the city's major music venues, O2 ABC is housed inside what was once a cinema. It's the city's main showcase for well-known pop and rock bands. ✉ *300 Sauchiehall St., City Centre* ☎ *0141/332–2232* ⊕ *www.o2abcglasgow.co.uk* Ⓜ *Bridge St.*

Royal Scottish Conservatoire. An important venue for music and drama, the Royal Scottish Conservatoire hosts regular concerts by well-known performers, as well as by its own students. The lunchtime concert series is popular. ✉ *100 Renfrew St., City Centre* ☎ *0141/332–4101* ⊕ *www. rcs.ac.uk* Ⓜ *Cowcaddens.*

SEC Armadillo. The 3,000-seat riverside SEC is known as the Armadillo for its distinctive, curved design by Norman Foster. It hosts large-scale pop concerts and other events. ⊠ *Exhibition Way, Finnieston* ⊹ *Train to Exhibition Centre station from Glasgow Central Low Level station* ☎ *0141/248–3000* ⊕ *www.sec.co.uk.*

SSE Hydro. This dramatic addition to the banks of the Clyde is a 12,000-seat arena under a silver dome. Built for the 2014 Commonwealth Games, it has proved enormously popular as a music and event venue. ⊠ *SEC Exhibition Way, Finnieston* ⊹ *Train to Exhibition Centre from Central station; then walk over the bridge* ☎ *0844/395–4000* ⊕ *www. thessehydro.com.*

St. Andrew's in the Square. A beautifully restored 18th-century church close to Glasgow Cross, the glorious St. Andrew's in the Square is a popular arts venue. Drop by to see fiddle players on Monday evening or take traditional Scottish dance classes on Wednesday night. Concerts are held here from time to time. The downstairs Cafe Source serves a good range of Scottish food for lunch or dinner. ⊠ *1 St. Andrew's in the Square, East End* ☎ *0141/559–5902* ⊕ *www.standrewsinthesquare. com* Ⓜ *St. Enoch.*

DANCE AND OPERA

Theatre Royal. Glasgow is home to the Scottish Opera and Scottish Ballet, both of which perform at the Theatre Royal. Visiting dance and theater companies from many countries appear here as well. ⊠ *282 Hope St., City Centre* ☎ *0141/332–9000* Ⓜ *Cowcaddens.*

FILM

Centre for Contemporary Arts. The center screens classic, independent, and children's films and mounts major art exhibitions and other arts events including talks. It also has a restaurant, the Saramago, which serves vegan dishes; an upstairs bar; and a very good small independent bookshop. ⊠ *350 Sauchiehall St., City Centre* ☎ *0141/352–4900* ⊕ *www.cca-glasgow.com* Ⓜ *Cowcaddens.*

Cineworld Glasgow. An 18-screen facility, this is Glasgow's busiest movie complex. A glass-walled elevator whisks you to the top of the 170-foot-tall building, which is also the world's tallest cinema. ■**TIP**➔ **Book your tickets online and collect them from machines at the venue to avoid the often very long queues.** ⊠ *7 Renfrew St., City Centre* ☎ *0871/200–2000* ⊕ *www.cineworld.co.uk* Ⓜ *Cowcaddens.*

Fodor's Choice ★ **Glasgow Film Theatre.** An independent operation, the three-screen Glasgow Film Theatre hosts the best new releases, documentaries, and classic films. It has several programs for young people and hosts the annual Glasgow Film Festival. ⊠ *12 Rose St., City Centre* ☎ *0141/332–6535* ⊕ *www.glasgowfilm.org* Ⓜ *Cowcaddens.*

Grosvenor. This popular, compact cinema has two screens and extremely comfortable leather seats (some of them big enough for two). It's part of a small complex, immediately behind the subway station, that includes two street-level bars and a spacious upstairs café and bar. ⊠ *Ashton La., West End* ☎ *0845/339–8444* ⊕ *www.grosvenorcafe.co.uk* Ⓜ *Hillhead.*

THEATER

Fodor'sChoice **Citizens' Theatre.** Some of the most exciting theatrical performances take
★ place at the internationally renowned Citizens' Theatre, where productions are often of hair-raising originality. The more experimental work is presented in the smaller studio theater. The theater has always had a strong commitment to working with the community, and tickets for most performances are £15. Behind the theater's striking contemporary glass facade is a glorious red-and-gold Victorian-era auditorium. ⊠ *119 Gorbals St., East End* ☎ *0141/429–0022* ⊕ *www.citz.co.uk* Ⓜ *West St.*

Cottier's Arts Theatre. Contemporary works are staged at this theater, housed in a converted church that also has a bar and restaurant. ⊠ *93 Hyndland St., West End* ☎ *0141/357–5825* ⊕ *www.cottiers.com* Ⓜ *Hillhead.*

King's Theatre. Dramas, variety shows, and musicals are staged at the King's Theatre, open since 1904. Check ticket websites to see what's on. ⊠ *297 Bath St., City Centre* ☎ *0141/240–1111* Ⓜ *Cowcaddens.*

FAMILY **Pavilion Theatre.** This traditional variety theater hosts family-friendly entertainment, some plays, the occasional hypnotist, and concerts, most with a very strong Glasgow flavor. ⊠ *121 Renfield St., City Centre* ☎ *0141/332–1846* ⊕ *www.paviliontheatre.co.uk* Ⓜ *Cowcaddens.*

Fodor'sChoice **A Play, a Pie, and a Pint.** In a former church, Glasgow's hugely success-
★ ful lunchtime theater series called "A Play, a Pie, and a Pint" (and you do get all three) showcases new writing from Scotland and elsewhere. ■ TIP➜ **Performances sell out quickly, particularly late in the week, so book well in advance on the website.** Doors open at 12:15 and shows begin at 1 Monday through Saturday. ⊠ *Òran Mór, 731 Great Western Rd., Byres Rd. and Great Western Rd., West End* ☎ *0141/357–6200* ⊕ *www.playpiepint.com* Ⓜ *Hillhead.*

FAMILY **Sharmanka Kinetic Theatre.** A unique spectacle, Sharmanka Kinetic The-
Fodor'sChoice atre is the brainchild of Eduard Bersudsky, who came to Glasgow from
★ Russia in 1989 to continue making the mechanical sculptures that are his stock in trade. They are witty and sometimes disturbing, perhaps because they are constructed from scrap materials. They move in a kind of ballet to haunting, specially composed music punctuated by a light show. The shows are 45 or 70 minutes. ⊠ *103 Trongate, Merchant City* ☎ *0141/552–7080* ⊕ *www.sharmanka.com* Ⓜ *St. Enoch.*

Tron Theatre. Come here for contemporary theater from Scotland and around the world; there are three performance spaces. ⊠ *63 Trongate, Merchant City* ☎ *0141/552–4267* ⊕ *www.tron.co.uk* Ⓜ *St. Enoch.*

SHOPPING

You'll find the mark of the fashion industry on Glasgow's hottest shopping streets. In the Merchant City, Ingram Street is lined on either side by high-fashion and designer outlets like Cruise. Buchanan Street, in the City Centre, is home to many chains geared toward younger people, including Diesel, Monsoon, and USC, and malls like the elegant Princes Square and Buchanan Galleries. The adjacent Argyle Street Arcade is filled with jewelry stores. Antiques tend be found on and around West

Regent Street in the City Centre. The West End has a number of small shops selling crafts, vintage clothing, and trendier fashions—punctuated by innumerable cafés and restaurants. The university dominates the area around West End, and many shops cater to students.

CITY CENTRE

ANTIQUES AND FINE ART
Compass Gallery. The gallery is something of an institution, having opened in 1969 to provide space for young and unknown artists—a role it continues. It shares space with Cyril Gerber Fine Arts, which specializes in British paintings from 1880 to the present. ⊠ *178 W. Regent St., City Centre* ☎ *0141/221–3095* ⊕ *www.compassgallery. co.uk* Ⓜ *Cowcaddens.*

ARCADES AND SHOPPING CENTERS
Argyll Arcade. An interesting diversion off Argyle Street is the covered Argyll Arcade, the region's largest collection of jewelers under one roof. The L-shape edifice, built in 1827, houses several locally based jewelers and a few shops specializing in antique jewelry. ⊠ *Buchanan St., City Centre* ⊕ *www.argyll-arcade.com* Ⓜ *St. Enoch.*

Buchanan Galleries. Next to the Glasgow Royal Concert Hall, Buchanan Galleries is packed with more than 80 high-quality shops. Its top attraction is the John Lewis department store. ⊠ *220 Buchanan St., City Centre* ☎ *0141/333–9898* ⊕ *www.buchanangalleries.co.uk* Ⓜ *Buchanan St.*

Fodor's Choice ★ Princes Square. The city's best shopping center is the art nouveau Princes Square, a lovely space filled with high-quality shops and pleasant cafés and restaurants. A stunning glass dome was fitted over the original building, which dates back to 1841. ⊠ *48 Buchanan St., City Centre* ☎ *0141/221–0324* ⊕ *www.princessquare.co.uk* Ⓜ *St. Enoch.*

St. Enoch's Shopping Centre. Eye-catching if not especially pleasing, this modern glass building resembles an overgrown greenhouse. It has dozens of stores, including the huge Hamley's toy store. ⊠ *55 St. Enoch Sq., City Centre* ☎ *0141/204–3900* ⊕ *www.st-enoch.com* Ⓜ *St. Enoch.*

BOOKS, PAPER, AND MUSIC
Cass Art Store. One of the country's largest suppliers of art and craft materials operates this store near the Glasgow Gallery of Modern Art. There's plenty to inspire your creativity, and good choices for kids as well. ⊠ *63–67 Queen St., City Centre* ☎ *0141/248–5899* ⊕ *www.cassart.co.uk* Ⓜ *Buchanan St.*

Monorail Music. For the latest on the city's ever-thriving music scene try Monorail Music, inside a café-bar called Mono. The shop specializes in indie music and has a large collection of vinyl with everything from rock to jazz. ⊠ *12 Kings Ct., City Centre* ✛ *Close to the Tron Theatre* ☎ *0141/552–9458* ⊕ *www.monorailmusic.com* Ⓜ *St. Enoch.*

Paperchase. For everything that stationery has to offer—cards, notebooks, books—Paperchase is the place. And there's a café where you can ponder which notebook you want to buy. ⊠ *185–221 Buchanan St., City Centre* ☎ *0141/353–3491* ⊕ *www.paperchase.co.uk* Ⓜ *Buchanan St.*

Waterstones. In an age of online sales, bookstores seem to be becoming scarcer. Waterstones remains as the city's main bookshop, and it has an excellent selection on its four floors. There's also a good basement café. ⊠ *153–57 Sauchiehall St., City Centre* ☎ *0141/248–4814* ⊕ *www. waterstones.com* Ⓜ *Buchanan St.*

CLOTHING

Mr. Ben. A large, funky selection of vintage clothing for men and women is what you'll find at Mr. Ben. ⊠ *6 King's Ct., City Centre* ☎ *0141/553– 1936* ⊕ *mrbenretroclothing.com* Ⓜ *St. Enoch.*

Primark. Invariably crowded, Primark is a huge store where clothing is sold at marked-down prices. It caters to every generation. ⊠ *56 Argyle St., City Centre* ☎ *0141/229–1343* ⊕ *www.primark.co.uk* Ⓜ *St. Enoch.*

Zara. This hugely successful Spanish-owned chain offers high contemporary fashion for men, women, and children at affordable prices. ⊠ *10–16 Buchanan St., City Centre* ☎ *0141/227–4770* ⊕ *www.zara. com* Ⓜ *St. Enoch.*

DEPARTMENT STORES

Debenham's. One of Glasgow's principal department stores, Debenham's has fine china and crystal as well as women's and men's clothing. ⊠ *97 Argyle St., City Centre* ☎ *0844/561–6161* ⊕ *www.debenhams.com* Ⓜ *St. Enoch.*

Fodor'sChoice **House of Fraser.** A Glasgow institution, the House of Fraser stocks wares
★ that reflect the city's material aspirations, including European designer clothing. There are also more locally produced articles, such as tweeds, tartans, glass, and ceramics. The magnificent interior, set off by the grand staircase rising to various floors and balconies, is itself worth a visit. ⊠ *21–45 Buchanan St., City Centre* ☎ *0141/221–3880* ⊕ *www. houseoffraser.co.uk* Ⓜ *St. Enoch.*

John Lewis. This store is a favorite for its stylish mix of clothing, household items, electronics, and practically everything else. John Lewis claims to have "never been knowingly undersold" and prides itself on its customer service. It has a very elegant second-floor balcony café. ⊠ *Buchanan Galleries, 220 Buchanan St., City Centre* ☎ *0141/353–6677* ⊕ *www.johnlewis.com/glasgow* Ⓜ *Buchanan St.*

Marks & Spencer. Selling sturdy, practical clothing and accessories at moderate prices, Marks & Spencer also offers gourmet foods and household goods. There's a second location at 172 Sauchiehall Street. ⊠ *2–12 Argyle St., City Centre* ☎ *0141/552–4546* ⊕ *www.marksand-spencer.com* Ⓜ *St. Enoch.*

HOME FURNISHINGS AND TEXTILES

Linens Fine. Wonderful embroidered and embellished bed linens and other textiles are the specialty of this shop in the Princes Square shopping center. ⊠ *Princes Square, 48 Buchanan St., Unit 6, City Centre* ☎ *0141/248–7082* Ⓜ *St. Enoch.*

SCOTTISH SPECIALTIES

Hector Russell Kiltmakers. Primarily for men, this shop specializes in Highland outfits, wool, and cashmere clothing. ⊠ *110 Buchanan St., City Centre* ☎ *0141/221–0217* ⊕ *www.hector-russell.com* Ⓜ *Buchanan St.*

MacDonald MacKay Ltd. The well-regarded MacDonald MacKay Ltd. makes, sells, and exports Highland dress and accessories for men. ⊠ *161 Hope St., City Centre* ☎ *0141/204–3930* Ⓜ *Buchanan St.*

SHOPPING DISTRICTS

Argyle Street. On the often-crowded pedestrian area of Argyle Street you'll find chain stores like Debenham's and some of the more popular and less expensive chains like Gap, Next, and Schuh as well as Primark and H&M. ⊠ *City Centre* Ⓜ *St. Enoch.*

Buchanan Street. This pedestrian-only street has become increasingly upmarket, with Monsoon, Topshop, Burberry, Jaeger, Pretty Green, and All Saints as well as House of Fraser and other chain stores along its length. Always crowded with shoppers, it has also become a mecca for the growing community of buskers in Glasgow's streets, playing every kind of music. ⊠ *City Centre* Ⓜ *Buchanan St.*

SPORTS GEAR

Tiso Glasgow Outdoor Experience. You'll find good-quality gear and outerwear at Tiso Glasgow Outdoor Experience, handy if you're planning some Highland walks or just need protection from the weather. ⊠ *129 Buchanan St., City Centre* ☎ *0141/248–4877* ⊕ *www.tiso.com* Ⓜ *Buchanan St.*

MERCHANT CITY

Many of Glasgow's young and upwardly mobile types make their home in Merchant City. Shopping here is expensive, but the area is worth visiting if you're seeking the youthful Glasgow style.

ANTIQUES AND FINE ART

Fodor'sChoice **Glasgow Print Studio.** Essentially an artists' cooperative, the Glasgow
★ Print Studio's facilities launched a generation of outstanding painters, printers, and designers. The work of members past and present can be seen (and bought) at the Print Studio Gallery on King Street. ⊠ *103 Trongate, Merchant City* ☎ *0141/552–0704* ⊕ *www.gpsart.co.uk* Ⓜ *St. Enoch.*

CLOTHING

Cruise. As one of the first haute couture stores in central Glasgow, Cruise can claim to have launched a new commercial era in the city. It now has two stores in the Merchant City, where its high-fashion clothes and accessories for men and women are beautifully and characteristically displayed to those who can stretch their budgets to its levels. ⊠ *180 Ingram St., Merchant City* ☎ *0141/332–5797* ⊕ *www.cruisefashion. com* Ⓜ *Buchanan St.*

Jigsaw. You'll find a wide and ever-changing range of fashion items for women and men at Jigsaw, well tailored and glamorous but at accessible prices. A U.K.-based chain, its Glasgow store is especially dramatic, occupying one of the tobacco lords' mansions on Ingram Street. ⊠ *177 Ingram St., Merchant City* ☎ *0141/552–7639* ⊕ *www.jigsaw-uk.co.uk* Ⓜ *Buchanan St.*

JEWELRY

Orro. The beautiful and contemporary jewelry here uses modern designs and new materials in unexpected ways. The shop has a gallery feel, and you can browse uninterrupted. ⊠ *12 Wilson St., Merchant City* ☎ *0141/552–7888* ⊕ *www.orro.co.uk* Ⓜ *Buchanan St.*

WEST END

BOOKS, PAPER, AND MUSIC

Caledonia Books. This well-organized and well-stocked secondhand bookstore fills the gap left by the departure of other bookstores. The owners are knowledgeable and willing to search for even the most obscure volumes. ⊠ *483 Great Western Rd., West End* ☎ *0141/334–9663* ⊕ *www.caledoniabooks.co.uk* Ⓜ *Kelvinbridge.*

Fopp. This funky shop is an extravaganza of music, books, and DVDs. It's a small space, but the selection is huge. The prices are a lot more reasonable than those at most other chain stores. ⊠ *358 Byres Rd., West End* ☎ *0141/222–2128* ⊕ *www.fopp.com* Ⓜ *Hillhead.*

Papyrus. Here you'll find designer cards as well as a selection of books and a trendy kitchen shop in the basement. There's a second location in the City Centre on Sauchiehall Street. ⊠ *374 Byres Rd., West End* ☎ *0141/334–6514* ⊕ *www.papyrusgifts.co.uk* Ⓜ *Hillhead.*

CLOTHING

Charles Clinkard. This traditional shoe store—a rare thing these days—has an impressive range of choices, often unusual lines, principally for women but for men, too. There are also regular bargains here, and the staff knows their shoes. ⊠ *149 Byres Rd., West End* ☎ *0345/241–7742* ⊕ *www.charlesclinkard.co.uk* Ⓜ *Hillhead.*

Glasgow Vintage Co. You can find plenty of genuine bargains here for upmarket vintage clothes at down-market prices. There are choices for men, women, and children from the 1950s to the 1980s. ⊠ *453 Great Western Rd., West End* ☎ *0141/338–6633* ⊕ *www.glasgowvintage.co.uk.*

Strawberry Fields. Designer clothing for children is the specialty of Strawberry Fields. ⊠ *517 Great Western Rd., West End* ☎ *0141/339–1121* Ⓜ *Kelvinbridge.*

FOOD

Demijohn. Specializing in infused wines, spirits, oils, and vinegars, Demijohn calls itself a "liquid deli." ⊠ *382 Byres Rd., West End* ☎ *0141/337–3600* ⊕ *www.demijohn.co.uk* Ⓜ *Hillhead.*

Iain Mellis Cheesemonger. This shop has a superb, seemingly endless selection of fine Scottish cheeses, in addition to others from England and across Europe, as well as bread and olives. ⊠ *492 Great Western Rd., West End* ☎ *0141/339–8998* ⊕ *www.mellischeese.net* Ⓜ *Kelvinbridge.*

HOME FURNISHINGS AND TEXTILES

Nancy Smillie. Local to the floorboards, Nancy Smillie is a one-of-a-kind boutique that sells unique glassware, jewelry, and furnishings. It also runs a jewelry boutique at 425 Great Western Road. ⊠ *53 Cresswell St., West End* ☎ *0141/334–0055* ⊕ *www.nancysmillieshop.com* Ⓜ *Hillhead.*

Time and Tide. Loosely described as a household goods store, Time and Tide sells an eclectic mix of lamps and candleholders and cushions and things you never realized you needed until you see them. ⊠ *398 Byres Rd., West End* ☎ *0141/357–4548* ⊕ *www.timeandtidestores. co.uk* Ⓜ *Hillhead.*

EAST END

Fodor'sChoice ★ **Barras.** Scotland's largest indoor market—named for the barrows, or pushcarts, formerly used by the stallholders—prides itself on selling everything "from a needle to an anchor" and is a must-see for anyone addicted to searching through piles of junk for bargains. The century-old institution, open weekends, consists of nine markets. The atmosphere is always good-humored, and you can find just about anything here, in any condition, from dusty model railroads to antique jewelry. Haggling is compulsory. You can reach the Barras by walking along Argyle Street from the St. Enoch subway station. The Barrowland ballroom, which forms part of the market, was once where Glaswegians went to dance; today it is a venue for concerts of every kind. ■TIP➔ **Across the road is one of Glasgow's oldest pubs, the Saracen's Head; enter with caution—ghosts are said to abound.** ⊠ *Gallowgate, East End* ⊕ *www. theglasgowbarras.com.*

SPORTS AND THE OUTDOORS

You can't go far these days in Glasgow without seeing a runner or cyclist; numerous parks provide plenty of opportunities, and the next-bike (⊕ *www.nextbike.co.uk*) public bike-rental program has been a boon to cyclists. It rains a lot in Glasgow, but don't let the weather stop you. It doesn't deter the locals who play soccer, tennis, hike, bike, run, swim, and walk in the rain.

FOOTBALL

The city has been sports mad, especially for football (soccer), for more than 100 years. The historic rivalry between its two main football clubs, Rangers and Celtic, is legendary. Partick Thistle is a less contentious alternative for football fans. Matches are held usually on Saturday or Sunday in winter. Admission prices start at about £20, and don't go looking for a family-day-out atmosphere. Football remains a fiercely contested game attended mainly by males, though the stadiums at Ibrox and Celtic Park are fast becoming family-friendly.

Celtic. This famous football club wears white-and-green stripes and plays in the east at Celtic Park, or Perkhead as it is know locally. Daily stadium tours must be booked ahead, and the Celtic Museum is also in the stadium. To get here, take a taxi from central Glasgow or a train from Central station to Dalmarnock (10-minute walk from station). ⊠ *Celtic Park, 18 Kerrydale St., East End* ☏ *0871/226–1888* ⊕ *www. celticfc.net* ▭ *Stadium tours £12.50.*

Partick Thistle. Soccer in Glasgow isn't just blue or green, nor is it dominated by international players and big money. Partick Thistle Football Club, known as the Jags, wears red and yellow, and its home field is Firhill Park. ⊠ *80 Firhill Rd., West End* ☏ *0141/579–1971* ⊕ *www.ptfc. co.uk* Ⓜ *St. George's Cross.*

Rangers. The Rangers wear blue and play at Ibrox, on the south side of the Clyde. Stadium tours are on Friday, Saturday, and Sunday; booking ahead is essential. ⊠ *150 Edmiston Dr., South Side* ☏ *0871/702–1972* ⊕ *www.rangers.co.uk* ▭ *Stadium tours £8* Ⓜ *Ibrox.*

GOLF

Several municipal courses are operated within Glasgow proper by the local authorities. Bookings are relatively inexpensive and should be made directly to the course 24 hours in advance to ensure prime tee times (courses open at 7 am). A comprehensive list of contacts, facilities, and green fees of the 30 or so other courses near the city is available from the tourist board.

Douglas Park Golf Club. A charming parkland course at Milngavie, on the western outskirts of Glasgow, this attractive and varied course is set among lush rhododendron bushes and birch and pine trees. Each hole is highly individual, and though shorter than many courses it tests the careful accurate golfer rather than the big swing. The Campsie Fells form a pleasant backdrop. ⊠ *Milngavie Rd., Hillfoot, Bearsden* ☏ *0141/942–0985* ⊕ *www.douglasparkgolfclub.co.uk* ▭ *Apr.–Oct., £33 weekdays, £44 weekends; Nov.–Mar., £15 weekdays, £20 weekends* ⚑ *18 holes, 5981 yards, par 69.*

Lethamhill. The fairways of this city-owned course overlook Hogganfield Loch, in the northeast of Glasgow. It is a parkland course, with trees in some awkward places (around holes for example) and some steep tees, which means it isn't always wise to look for maximum length or to underestimate this public course. To get here, take the M8 north to Junction 12, and drive up the A80 about a quarter mile. ⊠ *1240 Cumbernauld Rd., North City* ☏ *0141/276–0810* ⊕ *www.glasgowlife. org.uk* ▭ *£10.30* ⚑ *18 holes, 5836 yards, par 70.*

Littlehill. One of Scotland's public municipal courses, Littlehill is well used by Glaswegians, especially those learning to play. A fairly flat course with level fairways—many of them tree lined—and well-kept greens, it has the added advantage of being cheap to play. Some of Scotland's finest players began here. It's about 4 miles north of the City Centre. ⊠ *Auchinairn Rd., North City* ☏ *0141/276–0704* ⊕ *www. glasgowlife.org.uk* ▭ *£10 weekdays, £11.50 weekends* ⚑ *18 holes, 6240 yards, par 70.*

SPORTS ARENA

Emirates Arena. Built to host a number of events during the Commonwealth Games of 2014, the arena continues to present sporting events but also contains a gym and spa that are open to the public. It also includes the Sir Chris Hoy Velodrome. The stadium has transformed an East End area that was neglected and abandoned. Trains from Central station go to Dalmarnock, a 10-minute walk from the stadium. ✉ *1000 London Rd., East End* ☎ *0141/287–7000* ⊕ *www.emiratesarena.co.uk.*

3

SIDE TRIPS: AYRSHIRE, CLYDE COAST, AND ROBERT BURNS COUNTRY

The jigsaw puzzle of firths and straits and interlocking islands that you see as you fly into Glasgow Airport harbors numerous tempting one-day excursion destinations. You can travel south to visit the fertile farmlands of Ayrshire or west to the Firth of Clyde. Besides the Burns sites, key treasures in this area include the Marquess of Bute's Mount Stuart House on the Isle of Bute, and Culzean Castle, as famous for its Robert Adam (1728–92) design as it is for its spectacular seaside setting and grounds.

For many people a highlight of this region is Robert Burns country, a 40-minute drive from Glasgow. The poet was born in Alloway, beside Ayr, and the towns and villages where he lived and loved make for an interesting day out. English children learn that Burns (1759–96) is a good minor poet. But Scottish children know that he's Shakespeare, Dante, Rabelais, Mozart, and Karl Marx rolled into one. As time goes by, it seems that the Scots have it more nearly right. As poet and humanist, Burns increases in stature. When you plunge into Burns country, don't forget that he's held in extreme reverence by Scots of all backgrounds. They may argue about Sir Walter Scott and Bonnie Prince Charlie, but there's no disputing the merits of the author of "Auld Lang Syne" and "A man's a man for a' that."

GETTING HERE AND AROUND

From Glasgow you can take the bus or train (from Glasgow Central station) to Ayr for the Burns Heritage Trail; and Troon, Prestwick, and Ayr to play golf. Bus companies also operate one-day guided excursions; for details, contact the tourist information center in Glasgow or the Strathclyde Passenger Transport Travel Centre. Traveline Scotland has helpful information.

If you're driving from Glasgow, there are two main routes to Ayr. The quickest is to take the M77 to the A77, which takes you to Ayr, where Alloway is well signposted. The alternative and much slower route is the coast road; take the M8 to Greenock and continue down the coast on the A78 until you meet the A77 and continue on into Burns Country.

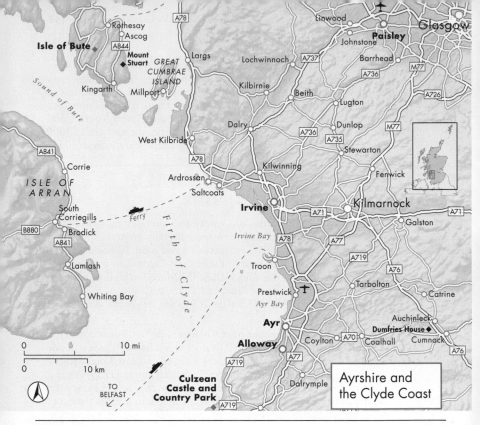

Ayrshire and the Clyde Coast

PAISLEY

7 miles west of Glasgow.

The industrial prosperity of Paisley came from textiles and, in particular, from the woolen paisley shawl. The internationally recognized paisley pattern is based on the shape of a palm shoot, an ancient Babylonian fertility symbol brought from Kashmir. Today you can explore this history at several attractions.

GETTING HERE AND AROUND

Paisley-bound buses depart from the Buchanan Street bus station in Glasgow. Trains to Paisley's Gilour Street depart daily every 5 to 10 minutes from Glasgow Central station. If you're driving, take the M8 westbound and turn off at Junction 27, which is clearly signposted to Paisley.

ESSENTIALS

Visitor Information Paisley Visitor Information Centre. ✉ *9A Gilmore St.* ☎ *0141/889–0711* ⊕ *www.visitscotland.com.*

EXPLORING

Paisley Abbey. Paisley's 12th-century abbey dominates the town center. Founded as a Cluniac monastery and almost completely destroyed by the English in 1307, the abbey was not totally restored until the early

20th century. It's associated with Walter Fitzallan, the high steward of Scotland, who gave his name to the Stewart monarchs of Scotland (Stewart is a corruption of "steward"). Outstanding features include the vaulted stone roof and stained glass of the choir. ✉ *13 High St.* ☎ *0141/889–7654* 🌐 *www.paisleyabbey.org.uk* 🎟 *Free.*

Paisley Museum. The full story of the pattern and of the innovative weaving techniques introduced in Paisley is told in the museum, which has a world-famous shawl collection. ✉ *High St.* ☎ *0141/889–3151* 🌐 *www.renfrewshireleisure.com/paisleymuseum* 🎟 *Free* 🕒 *Closed Mon.*

Sma' Shot Cottages. To get an idea of the life led by textile industry workers, visit the Sma' Shot Cottages. These re-creations of mill workers' houses contain displays of linen, lace, and paisley shawls. Two typical cottages, built 150 years apart, are open to visitors. ✉ *11–17 George Pl.* ☎ *0141/889–1708* 🌐 *www.smashotcottages.co.uk* 🎟 *Free* 🕒 *Closed Oct.–Mar.*

WHERE TO STAY

$$ HOTEL 🏨 **Glynhill Hotel.** This mansion combines old-fashioned living with modern convenience; stylish and bright contemporary furnishings make the bedrooms cheerful and comfortable. **Pros:** elegant rooms; nice pool and sauna; close to transportation. **Cons:** airport noise; lacks atmosphere. [$] *Rooms from: £130* ✉ *169 Paisley Rd., Renfrew* ☎ *0141/886–5555* 🌐 *www.glynhill.com* 🛏 *145 rooms* 🍴 *Breakfast.*

$$$ HOTEL 🏨 **Mar Hall.** This imposing baronial house, now a luxurious golf and spa resort, sits amid formal gardens and overlooks the River Clyde and verdant woodlands. **Pros:** spacious rooms; fantastic pool; wonderful country setting but also near airport. **Cons:** quite remote; an expensive treat. [$] *Rooms from: £165* ✉ *Earl of Mar Estate, Mar Hall Dr., Bishopton* ☎ *0141/812–9999* 🌐 *www.marhall.com* 🛏 *53 rooms* 🍴 *Breakfast.*

ISLE OF BUTE

42 miles west of Glasgow.

The Isle of Bute, a Victorian holiday favorite convenient for Glaswegians, affords a host of relaxing walks and scenic vistas. Mount Stuart, a stately home, is a popular attraction. Rothesay is the main town, and some of its ornate Victorian architecture is striking. In the old Victorian village of Wemyss Bay there's a ferry service to the island. The many handsome buildings, especially the station, are a reminder of the grandeur and style of the era.

GETTING HERE AND AROUND

Take the train from Glasgow Central station to Wemyss Bay, where you can hop aboard the ferry to Rothesay. If you're driving, take the A8/A78 coast road and park at the ferry terminal.

ESSENTIALS

Visitor Information Isle of Bute Discovery Centre. ✉ *The Winter Garden, Victoria St., Rothesay* ☎ *01700/507043* 🌐 *www.visitscotland.com.*

3

EXPLORING

Mount Stuart. Bute's biggest draw is spectacular Mount Stuart, ancestral home of the marquesses of Bute. The massive Victorian Gothic palace, built in red sandstone, has ornate interiors, including the eccentric Horoscope Room and the Marble Hall, with stained glass, arcaded galleries, and magnificent tapestries woven in Edinburgh in the early 20th century. The paintings and furniture throughout the house are equally interesting. You can also appreciate the lovely gardens and grounds. ✉ *Off A844, Rothesay* ✥ *5 miles south of Rothesay; take local bus 490 or 493 from Rothesay* ☎ *01700/503877* 🌐 *www.mountstuart.com* 🎫 *Gardens £6.50; house and gardens £11.50* 🕒 *Closed Nov.–Mar.*

WHERE TO STAY

$ B&B/INN 🏨 **Munro's Bed and Breakfast.** Surrounded by colorful gardens, this small B&B in a peaceful residential area has a home-away-from-home feel. **Pros:** beautiful location; nicely remodeled; environmentally aware. **Cons:** hilltop location is a steep climb; no restaurant; sea-view rooms cost extra. [$] *Rooms from: £95* ✉ *Ardmory Rd., Rothesay* ✥ *North of Rothesay* ☎ *01700/502346* 🌐 *www.visitmunros.co.uk* 🛏 *6 rooms* 🍴 *Breakfast.*

IRVINE

24 miles south of Glasgow.

Beyond Irvine's cobbled streets and grand Victorian buildings, look for a peaceful crescent-shape harbor and fishermen's cottages huddled in solidarity against the Atlantic winds. The Scottish Maritime Museum pays homage to the town's seafaring past. Scotland's national poet, Robert Burns, lived here in 1781. Western Gailes and nearby Royal Troon make the area popular with golfers.

GETTING HERE AND AROUND

By car, take the M8 from Glasgow, then the A726 and the A736 to Irvine. By rail, it's a 40-minute journey from Glasgow Central station.

ESSENTIALS

Visitor Information Irvine Tourist Information Centre. ✉ *New St.* ☎ *01294/313886* 🌐 *www.visitscotland.com.*

EXPLORING

FAMILY Fodor's Choice ★ **Scottish Maritime Museum.** On the waterfront in the coastal town of Irvine, this museum brings together ships and boats—both models and the real thing—to tell the tale of Scotland's maritime history, as well as chronicle the lives of its boatbuilders, fishermen, and sailors. The atmospheric Linthouse Engine Building, part of a former shipyard, hosts most of the displays. The museum also includes a shipyard worker's tenement home that you can explore. In Dumbarton, 35 miles to the north, you can visit the Denny Tank (part of the museum), where ship designs were tested. ■ **TIP→ Children are admitted free.** ✉ *6 Gottries Rd.* ☎ *01294/278283* 🌐 *www.scottishmaritimemuseum.org* 🎫 *£7.50.*

Vennel Art Gallery. The gallery occupies the 18th-century cottage where poet Robert Burns lived and the shed where he learned to heckle—or dress—flax (the raw material for linen). Both buildings have on display paintings, photographs, and sculpture by mainly Scottish artists. ✉ *10 Glasgow Vennel* ☎ *01294/275059* 🎟 *Free* ⏲ *Closed Sun.–Wed.*

WHERE TO STAY

$$ HOTEL 🏨 **Piersland House Hotel.** A late-Victorian mansion on the southern edge of town, formerly the home of a whisky magnate, is now a country-house hotel. **Pros:** gorgeous gardens and grounds; close to golf courses; near Prestwick Airport. **Cons:** helps to have a car to get around; can get crowded with private functions. [$] *Rooms from: £120* ✉ *15 Craigend Rd., Troon* ✣ *7 miles south of Irvine via the A78* ☎ *01292/314747* 🌐 *www.piersland.co.uk* 🛏 *37 rooms* 🍴 *Breakfast.*

GOLF

Fodor's Choice ★ **Royal Troon Golf Clubce.** Of the two courses at Royal Troon, it's the Old or Championship Course—a traditional links course with superb sea views frequently used for the British Open—that is renowned among golfers. The second, Portland, shares the challenges of strong sea breezes and the gorse beside the fairways. Advance payment and a deposit are required, as is a handicap certificate. It is a good idea to check the tournament calendar before you go. ✉ *Craigend Rd., Troon* ✣ *9 miles south of Irvine via the A78* ☎ *01292/311555* 🌐 *www.royaltroon.com* 🎟 *Old Course, £230 mid-Apr.–early Sept, £195 mid-Sept.–mid-Oct.; Portland Course, mid-Apr.–Aug. £85, Sept. and Oct. £70* ⛳ *Old Course: 18 holes, 7208 yards, par 71; Portland Course: 18 holes, 6349 yards, par 72* ☞ *Closed for visitors Nov.–mid-Apr.*

Fodor's Choice ★ **Western Gailes Golf Club.** Known as the finest natural links course in Scotland, Western Gailes is entirely nature-made, and the greens are kept in truly magnificent condition. This is the final qualifying course when the British Open is held at Royal Troon or Trump Turnberry. Tom Watson lists the par-5 6th hole as one of his favorites. Visitors can play Monday, Wednesday, Friday, and weekend afternoons. ✉ *Gailes Rd.* ☎ *01294/311649* 🌐 *www.westerngailes.com* 🎟 *£165 May–Sept., £110 Mar. and Oct., £65 Nov.–Feb.* ⛳ *18 holes, 6640 yards, par 71.*

AYR AND ALLOWAY

10 miles south of Irvine, 34 miles south of Glasgow.

The commercial port of Ayr is Ayrshire's chief town, a peaceful and elegant place with an air of prosperity. Poet Robert Burns was baptized in the Auld Kirk (Old Church) here and wrote a humorous poem about the Twa Brigs (Two Bridges) that cross the river nearby. Burns described Ayr as a town unsurpassed "for honest men and bonny lasses."

If you're on the Robert Burns trail, head for Alloway, on B7024 in Ayr's southern suburbs. A number of sights here are part of the **Burns National Heritage Park**, including the magnificent Robert Burns Birthplace Museum.

GETTING HERE AND AROUND

From Glasgow you can take the bus or train to Ayr; travel time is about an hour (a bit less by train). Drivers can use the A78 and A77 near the coast; a car would provide more flexibility to see the Burns sites around Alloway.

ESSENTIALS

Visitor Information Ayr Visitor Information Centre. ⊠ *22 Sandgate, Ayr* ☎ *01292/288688* ⊕ *www.visitscotland.com.*

EXPLORING

TOP ATTRACTIONS

Burns Cottage. In the delightful Burns Heritage Park, this thatched cottage is where Scotland's national poet lived for his first seven years. It has a living room, a kitchen, and a stable, one behind the other. The life and times of Burns, born in 1759, are beautifully and creatively illustrated in the fly-on-the-wall videos of daily life in the 18th century. The garden is lush with the types of vegetables the poet's father might have grown. Take the Poet's Path through the village to the Robert Burns Birthplace Museum, the spooky churchyard where Tam o'Shanter faced fearsome ghosts, and the Brig o' Doon. ⊠ *Greenfield Ave., Alloway* ☎ *0844/493–2601* ⊕ *www.burnsmuseum.org.uk* ✑ *£9, includes Burns Monument and Robert Burns Birthplace Museum.*

Fodor's Choice ★ **Robert Burns Birthplace Museum.** Besides being a poet of delicacy and depth, Robert Burns was also a rebel, a thinker, a lover, a good companion, and a man of the countryside. This wonderful museum explains why the Scots so admire this complex "man o' pairts." The imaginative displays present each of his poems in context, with commentaries sensitively written in a modern version of the Scots language in which he spoke and wrote. Headsets let you hear the poems sung or spoken. The exhibits are vibrant and interactive, with touch screens that allow you to debate his views on politics, love, taxation, revolution, and Scottishness. An elegant café offers a place to pause, while the kids can play in the adjoining garden. Included in the ticket are the Burns Cottage, a few minutes' walk down a Burns-themed walkway, and the Burns Monument. ⊠ *Murdoch's Lone, Alloway* ☎ *01292/443700* ⊕ *www.burnsmuseum.org.uk* ✑ *£9, includes Burns Cottage and Burns Monument.*

WORTH NOTING

Auld Kirk Alloway. Auld Kirk Alloway is where Tam o' Shanter, in Robert Burns's great epic poem, unluckily passed a witches' revel—with Old Nick himself playing the bagpipes—on his way home from a night of drinking. Tam, in flight from the witches, managed to cross the medieval **Brig o' Doon** (*brig* is Scots for *bridge*; you can still see the bridge) just in time. His gray mare, Meg, lost her tail to the closest witch. (Any resident of Ayr will tell you that witches cannot cross running water.) The church is in ruins, but the graveyard includes the tomb of Burns's father, William. ⊠ *Murdoch's Lone, Alloway* ✑ *Free.*

Bachelors' Club. About 8 miles northeast of Ayr is the Bachelors' Club, the 17th-century house—now fully restored—where Robert Burns learned to dance, founded a debating and literary society, and became a Freemason. ⊠ *Sandgate St., Tarbolton* ☎ *0844/493–2146* ⊕ *www.nts. org.uk* ✑ *Free* ☉ *Closed Oct.–Mar.*

Burns Monument. This neoclassical structure, built in 1823, overlooks the Brig o' Doon. You can climb to the top (with some care!). Entrance is included in the Burns Museum ticket. ⊠ *Murdoch's Lone, Alloway*

🌐 *www.burnsmuseum.org.uk* 🎫 *Free; also included in £9 ticket to Burns Cottage and Robert Burns Birthplace Museum.*

OFF THE BEATEN PATH

Dumfries House. Built in the 1750s by the Adam brothers, Dumfries House has preserved the living conditions of the landed aristocracy of the time. The restored house contains a large collection of furniture by Chippendale that is original to the property, as well as pieces by other great designers of the period. Run by a charity headed by Prince Charles, the surrounding 2,000-acre estate is projected as a site for a new eco-village and centers practicing historic crafts. Entry is by guided tour only; booking is essential. There are 22 guest rooms and some cottages on the property as well. ✉ *Cumnock* ✣ *From Ayr, take the A70 to Cumnock; it's about 10 miles* ☎ *01290/421742* 🌐 *www.dumfries-house.org.uk* 🎫 *Guided tour (required) £9, £13 for extended tour; grounds free* 🕒 *Closed weekdays Nov.–Mar.*

REMEMBERING MR. BURNS

Born in Ayrshire, Robert Burns (1759–96) is one of Scotland's treasures. The poet and balladeer had a style that was his and his alone. His most famous song, "Auld Lang Syne," is heard everywhere on New Year's Day. Burns's talent, charisma, and good looks made him an icon to both the upper and lower classes (and made him quite popular with the ladies). Today his birthday (January 25) is considered a national holiday; on "Burns Night" young and old alike get together for Burns Suppers and recite his work over neeps, tatties, and drams of the country's finest whisky.

WHERE TO EAT AND STAY

$$ BRITISH 🍴 **Brig o' Doon House.** Originally built in 1827, this attractive hotel restaurant often has a piper by the door to greet hungry travelers ready for a Scottish setting and some Scottish fare. Tartan carpets, dark wood paneling, and buck heads mounted on the walls set the mood, and the bar is a shrine to Robert Burns. **Known for:** riverside location; venison casserole; Scottish food and decor. [$] *Average main: £18* ✉ *High Maybole Rd., Alloway* ☎ *01292/442466* 🌐 *www.brigodoonhouse.com.*

$ ITALIAN 🍴 **Cafe Le Monde.** This Italian-style café with alfresco seating for good weather serves lunch and smaller bites to a mainly day-visitor crowd. The ciabattas and soups are well made and substantial, if not enormously adventurous, and the staff is attentive. **Known for:** soup and toasted cheese; good coffee; attentive service. [$] *Average main: £12* ✉ *36 Newmarket St., Ayr* ☎ *01292/611219* 🕒 *No dinner.*

$$$$ HOTEL FAMILY 🏨 **Trump Turnberry.** Turnberry has been synonymous with golf for a century and a half—its three great courses are among the highest rated in the world—and indeed golf is what brings most visitors to this luxury resort, which also caters to the partners and children of golfers with stunning facilities and cuisine. **Pros:** golfer's paradise; high level of luxury in food and accommodation; spa. **Cons:** only for the deepest wallets; advance golf reservations required. [$] *Rooms from: £446* ✉ *Maidens Rd., Turnberry* ✣ *Off A719, 16 miles south of Ayr* ☎ *01655/331000* 🌐 *www.turnberryresort.co.uk* 🛏 *132 rooms* 🍽 *No meals.*

SPORTS AND THE OUTDOORS
GOLF

Girvan. Opened in 1902, scenic Girvan plays along a narrow coastal strip and a lush inland section next to the Water of Girvan—a challenging hazard at the 15th hole unless you're a big hitter. Unlike its illustrious neighbor Turnberry, Girvan is not a championship course, but it is a pleasant combination of links and parkland. And it does share with neighbors fine views of Ailsa Craig and the Clyde Estuary. ✉ *40 Golf Course Rd., Girvan ✛ 20 miles south of Ayr via the A77* ☎ *01465/714346* ⊕ *www.golfsouthayrshire.com* ⌨ *£18 weekdays, £25 weekends* ⚐ *18 holes, 5064 yards, par 64.*

Prestwick Golf Club. Tom Morris helped design this challenging Ayrshire coastal links course, which saw the birth of the British Open Championship in 1860. The first hole is reputed to be among the most challenging in Scotland, since the railway line runs along the length of the hole. But it doesn't get any easier after that. Some of its bunkers are especially threatening, and the bumps at the 5th are high enough to be called the Himalayas. Prestwick has excellent, fast rail links with Glasgow. There are a limited number of tee times on Saturday afternoon. ✉ *2 Links Rd., Prestwick ✛ 4 miles south of Ayr via the A79* ☎ *01292/477404* ⊕ *www.prestwickgc.co.uk* ⌨ *Apr.–Oct., £170 weekdays, £195 weekends; Nov.–Mar., £95* ⚐ *18 holes, 6544 yards, par 71.*

Trump Turnberry. One of the most famous links courses in Scotland, Turnberry now bears the name of its owner, Donald Trump. The main course, the iconic Ailsa Course, is open to the waterside elements, and the 9th hole requires you to hit the ball over the open sea. The British Open was famously hosted here in 1977, and again in 1986, 1994, and 2009. A second course, the King Robert the Bruce, has an 11th hole that overlooks a lighthouse and Ailsa Crag. Opened in 2017, this course redesigned the old Kintyre and Arran courses. ✉ *Trump Turnberry Resort, Maidens Rd., Turnberry ✛ Off A719, 15 miles south of Ayr* ☎ *01655/331000* ⊕ *www.turnberryresort.co.uk* ⌨ *Nonresidents: Ailsa, May–Oct. £325 weekdays, £350 weekends; Nov. and Dec. £200; Robert the Bruce, May–Oct. £120; Nov. and Dec. £70* ⚐ *Ailsa: 18 holes, 7448 yards, par 71; King Robert the Bruce: 18 holes, 7203 yards, par 71.*

CULZEAN CASTLE AND COUNTRY PARK

12 miles south of Ayr, 50 miles south of Glasgow.

There's plenty to do at this popular spot between visiting the Adam-designed house and touring the extensive grounds.

GETTING HERE AND AROUND

Stagecoach buses run from Ayr to the park entrance; the nearest train station from Glasgow is at Maybole, 4 miles to the east, but there is Stagecoach bus service to the park entrance. Note that the park entrance is a mile walk from the castle visitor center.

EXPLORING

FAMILY
Fodor's Choice ★
Culzean Castle and Country Park. The dramatic clifftop castle of Culzean (pronounced ku-*lain*) is the National Trust for Scotland's most popular property. Robert Adam designed the neoclassical mansion, complete with a walled garden, in 1777. The grounds are enormous and beautifully kept, combining parkland, forests, and a beach looking out over the Atlantic Ocean; the surprisingly lush shrubberies reflect the warm currents that explain the mild climate. There are caves in the cliffs; tours are occasionally available. In the castle itself you can visit the armory, luxuriously appointed salons and bedchambers, and a nursery with its lovely cradle in a boat. Adam's grand double spiral staircase is the high point of its design. There's a free audio tour, and guided tours are available daily at 11 and 2:30. A short walk through the woods brings you to the visitor center with shops and a restaurant. ✉ *Culzean Castle, A719, Maybole* ☎ *01655/884455* 🌐 *www.nts.org.uk* 🎫 *Park and castle £15.50, park £10.50* 🕒 *Castle closed Nov.–Mar.*

WHERE TO STAY

$$$$
HOTEL
🏨 **Eisenhower Hotel.** It would be hard to imagine a more spectacular location for an overnight stay than the upper floors of Culzean Castle, which looks out toward Arran and the Atlantic Ocean. **Pros:** beautiful setting; luxurious lodging; a strong sense of history. **Cons:** a little remote; rather formal; not for minimalists. [$] *Rooms from: £250* ✉ *Culzean Castle, A719, Maybole* ☎ *0844/493–2149* 🌐 *www.culzean-eisenhower.com* 🛏 *6 rooms* 🍴 *Breakfast.*

SIDE TRIPS: THE CLYDE VALLEY

The River Clyde is (or certainly was) famous for its shipbuilding, yet its upper reaches flow through some of Scotland's most fertile farmlands, rich with crops of tomatoes and fruit. It's an interesting area with some museums, most notably at New Lanark, that tell the story of the growth of manufacturing.

GETTING HERE AND AROUND

If you're driving from Glasgow, head south on the M74 and turn on to the A72. This is the main road through the Clyde Valley, ending at Lanark. Train service runs from Glasgow Central station to Lanark; for details check National Rail.

NATIONAL MUSEUM OF RURAL LIFE

9 miles south of Glasgow.

The effect of farming on the land and on people's lives is the focus of this museum near Glasgow.

GETTING HERE AND AROUND

From Glasgow, take the M77 and then the A726 at Junction 4 to East Kilbride, or the A725 from Blantyre to East Kilbride; it's a 20-minute drive. You can take the train from Central station to East Kilbride, then taxi or bus. By bus, take First Bus 31 from St. Enoch Centre in Glasgow.

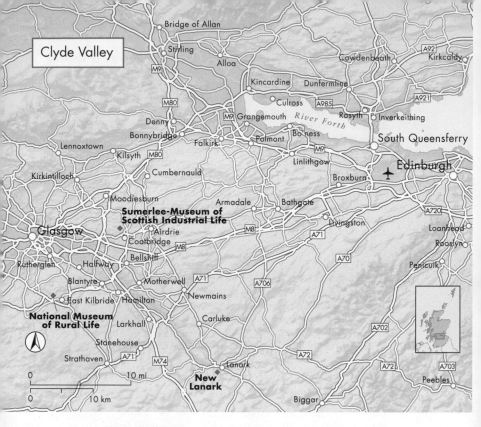

EXPLORING

FAMILY
Fodor's Choice
★

National Museum of Rural Life. Set in a rural area, this lovely museum exploring every aspect of the country's agricultural heritage is slightly off the beaten track but well worth the trip. It is a whole day out. In a modern building resembling a huge barn you learn about how farming transformed the land, experience the life and hardships of those who worked it, and see displays of tools and machines from across the ages. Take a tractor ride to a fully functioning 1950s farmhouse. There are also some great exhibits geared toward children and a range of summer events. ⊠ *Wester Kittochside, Philipshill Rd., East Kilbride* ☎ *0300/123–6789* ⊕ *www.nms.ac.uk/rural* 🖾 *£7.*

SUMMERLEE–MUSEUM OF SCOTTISH INDUSTRIAL LIFE

10 miles east of Glasgow.

A former ironworks is now a museum with a re-created mine and exhibits on both industry and the lives of workers.

GETTING HERE AND AROUND

The museum is a 15-minute drive from Glasgow. Take the M8 Glasgow toward Edinburgh, exiting at Junction 8, and the A89 toward Coatbridge; turn left at the roundabout in the town center.

EXPLORING

FAMILY **Summerlee–Museum of Scottish Industrial Life.** On the site of the old Summerlee Ironworks, this vast and exciting museum re-creates a mine and the miners' rows (the cottages where miners and their families lived); it's a great day out. An electric tram transports you there from the huge hall where industrial machines vie with exhibits about ordinary life. You can take a short trip into a mine (helmets and lamps are provided), and later you can stroll along the canal and take the kids to a fine playground. ✉ *Heritage Way, Coatbridge* ☎ *01236/638460* ⊕ *www.visitlanarkshire. com/summerlee* 🎫 *Free.*

NEW LANARK

25 miles southeast east of Glasgow.

Set in pleasing, rolling countryside, New Lanark was a model workers' community that is now a museum and World Heritage Site. It's about a mile to the south of the old Scottish town of Lanark.

GETTING HERE AND AROUND

If you're driving, take the M74 to the A72. The train from Glasgow Central station to Lanark takes 50 minutes or so; then take a taxi or bus. New Lanark is signposted from Lanark; you drive to the parking lot and walk down into New Lanark.

EXPLORING

FAMILY
Fodor's Choice
★

New Lanark. Now a UNESCO World Heritage Site, New Lanark was home to a social experiment at the beginning of the Industrial Revolution. Robert Owen (1771–1858), together with his father-in-law David Dale (1739–1806), set out to create a model industrial community with well-designed worker homes, a school, and public buildings. Owen went on to establish other communities on similar principles, both in Britain and in the United States. Robert Owen's son, Robert Dale Owen (1801–77), helped found the Smithsonian Institution.

After many changes of fortune, the mills eventually closed. One of the buildings has been converted into a visitor center that tells the story of this brave social experiment. You can also explore Robert Owen's house, the school, and a mill worker's house, and enjoy the Annie McLeod Experience, a fairground ride that takes you through the story of one mill worker's life. Other restored structures hold various shops and eateries; one has a rooftop garden with impressive views of the entire site. Another now houses the New Lanark Mill Hotel. ■TIP→ **It's a good idea to book your ticket ahead in summer to avoid lines.**

The River Clyde powers its way through a beautiful wooded gorge here, and its waters were once harnessed to drive textile-mill machinery. Upstream it flows through some of the finest river scenery anywhere in Lowland Scotland, with woods and waterfalls. ✉ *New Lanark Rd., New Lanark* ☎ *01555/661345* ⊕ *www.newlanark.org* 🎫 *£12.50.*

WHERE TO STAY

$$
HOTEL
New Lanark Mill Hotel. Housed in a converted cotton mill by the river in the 18th-century village of New Lanark, this hotel is decorated in a spare, understated style that allows the impressive architecture of barrel-vaulted ceilings and elegant Georgian windows to speak for itself. **Pros:** beautiful river views; large rooms; impressive spa. **Cons:** bland bar; some rooms can get cold; restaurant is the only one in the vicinity. *Rooms from: £125* ✉ *New Lanark Rd., New Lanark* ☎ *01555/667200* ⊕ *www.newlanarkmillhotel.co.uk* ⇒ *46 rooms* ♒ *Breakfast.*

THE BORDERS AND THE SOUTHWEST

Updated
by Mike
Gonzalez

In the Borders region, south of Edinburgh, are more stately homes, fortified castles, and medieval abbeys than in any other part of Scotland. This is also Sir Walter Scott territory, including his pseudo-baronial home at Abbotsford. The area embraces the whole 90-mile course of one of Scotland's great rivers, the Tweed. Passing woodlands luxuriant with game birds, the river flows in rushing torrents through this fertile land. To the west of the Borders is Dumfries and Galloway, an area of gentle coasts, forests, and lush hills, ideal country for walkers and cyclists.

For centuries the Borders was a battlefield, where English and Scottish troops remained locked in a struggle for its possession. At different times, parts of the region have been in English hands, just as slices of northern England (Berwick-upon-Tweed, for example) have been under Scottish control. The castles and fortified houses as well as the abbeys across the Borders are the surviving witnesses to those times. After the Union of 1707, fortified houses gradually gave way to the luxurious country mansions that pepper the area. And by the 19th century they had become grand country houses built by fashionable architects.

All the main routes between London and Edinburgh traverse the Borders, whose hinterland of undulating pastures, woods, and valleys is enclosed within three lonely groups of hills: the Cheviots, the Moorfoots, and the Lammermuirs. Hamlets and prosperous country towns dot the land, giving valley slopes a lived-in look, yet the total population is still sparse. The sheep that are the basis of the region's prosperous textile industry outnumber human beings by 14 to 1.

To the west is the region of Dumfries and Galloway, on the shores of the Solway Firth. It might appear to be an extension of the Borders, but the southwest has a history all its own. From its ports ships sailed to the Americas, carrying country dwellers driven from their land to make room for sheep. Inland, the earth rises toward high hills, forest, and bleak but captivating moorland, whereas nearer the coast you can find pretty farmlands, small villages, and unassuming towns. The shoreline is washed by the North Atlantic Drift (Scotland's answer to the Gulf Stream), and first-time visitors are always surprised to see palm trees and exotic plants thriving in gardens and parks along the coast.

At the heart of the region is Dumfries, the "Queen o' the South." Once a major port and commercial center, its glamour is now slightly faded. But the memory of poet Robert Burns, who spent several years living and working here and who is buried in the town, remains very much alive.

TOP REASONS TO GO

Ancient abbeys: The great abbeys of the Border regions, and the Whithorn Priory and the wonderful Sweetheart Abbey in the Southwest, are mainly in ruins, but they retain an air of their former grandeur.

Outdoor activities: You can walk, bicycle, or even ride horses across Galloway or through the Borders. Abandoned railway tracks make good paths, and there are forests and moorlands if you prefer wilder country. World-class mountain bike trails cover the region.

Stately homes and castles: The landed aristocracy still lives in these grand mansions, and most of the homes are open to visitors. Try Floors Castle or the wonderful Traquair House in the east. Threave, Drumlanrig, and the magical Caerlaverock Castle near Dumfries evoke grander times.

Literary Scotland: The Borders region has enough monuments dedicated to Sir Walter Scott to make him the focus of a visit. Abbotsford House, which he built for himself, is unmissable. The poet Robert Burns spent much of his working life in Dumfries.

Shopping: The sheep you see everywhere explain why so many locals became involved in textile production. Mill shops are abundant, and are well worth a visit for their wonderful woolens. Craft shops testify to the rebirth of ancient crafts like woodworking and pottery.

4

ORIENTATION AND PLANNING

GETTING ORIENTED

Once a battleground region separating Scotland and England, today the Borders area is a bridge between the two countries. This is a place of upland moors and hills, farmland, and forested river valleys. Yet it also embraces the rugged coastline between Edinburgh and Berwick. It's rustic and peaceful, with textile mills, abbeys, castles, and gardens. The area is a big draw for hikers and walking enthusiasts, too. The Borders region is steeped in history, with Mary, Queen of Scots, a powerful presence despite the relatively short time she spent here.

The Borders. Borders towns cluster around and between two rivers—the Tweed and its tributary, the Teviot. These are mostly textile towns with plenty of personality, where residents take pride in their local municipalities. The cut-down version of rugby (the Sevens), where teams consist of 7 rather than 15 players, brings the Borders towns into fierce (but friendly) rivalry. The Common Ridings, too, are unique, as local people ride through the towns to commemorate a history of defending their local boundaries. The area's top attractions include Jedburgh Abbey, Floors Castle in Kelso, and Abbotsford House just outside Melrose.

Dumfries and Galloway. Easygoing and peaceful, towns in this southwestern region are usually very attractive, with wide streets and colorful buildings. The Solway Firth is a vast nature preserve, and the climate of the west sustains the surprising tropical plants at the Logan Botanic Gardens and the gardens at Threave Castle.

PLANNING

WHEN TO GO

Because many lodgings and some sights are privately owned and shut down from early autumn until early April, the area is less suited to off-season touring than some other parts of Scotland. The best time to visit is between Easter and late September. The region does look magnificent in autumn, especially along the wooded river valleys of the Borders. Late spring is the time to see the rhododendrons in the gardens of Dumfries and Galloway.

PLANNING YOUR TIME

The rail line that began operating in 2015 from Edinburgh's Waverley station to Tweedbank, in the heart of the Borders, is helping to open up a fascinating region. Its 30-mile journey passes through Galashiels (for connections to Traquair House) and ends at Tweedbank, which is near Melrose and Walter Scott's home at Abbotsford. Beyond the Borders Railway, it is still more convenient to explore by car. If you're driving north along the A1 toward Edinburgh, it's easy to take a tour around the prosperous Borders towns. Turn onto the A698 at Berwick-upon-Tweed, which will take you along the Scottish–English border toward Kelso, Jedburgh, Dryburgh, and Melrose. It's 36 miles from Jedburgh to Peebles, a good place to stay overnight. Another day might begin with a visit to Walter Scott's lovely Abbotsford House, and then some shopping in any of these prosperous towns.

To the west, Dumfries and Galloway beckon. If you're traveling north toward Glasgow on the M6/A74, take the A70 west toward Dumfries. From the A1, on the east coast, travel west on the A708 to Moffat and pick up the A70 there. From Glasgow take the A74 south to Beattock and pick up the A701 there. Two days would give you time to explore Burns sites and more in Dumfries. From Dumfries you can visit Sweetheart Abbey (8 miles away), Caerlaverock Castle (9 miles away), and Threave Gardens (20 miles away). Castle Douglas is a good place to stop for lunch. The A710 and A711 take you along the dramatic coastline of the Solway Firth. Farther west along the A75 are the towns of Newton Stewart and Portpatrick, and on the A714, Glen Trool. The region does not have good rail links but there is good bus service, and by car it is a charming and compact region.

FESTIVALS

Common Ridings. More than 10 Borders communities have reestablished their identities through the annual summer gatherings known as the Common Ridings. In medieval times it was essential that each town be able to defend its area by "riding the marches," or patrolling the boundaries. The Common Ridings that celebrate this history are more authentic than the Highland Games concocted by the Victorians. Although this is above all a celebration for native Borderers, you will be welcome to share the excitement of clattering hooves and banners proudly displayed. ⊕ *www.returntotheridings.co.uk* ⊕ *www.visitscotland.com.*

Dumfries & Galloway Arts Festival. Celebrated every year since 1979, this festival with music, theater, dance, and other events is usually held at the

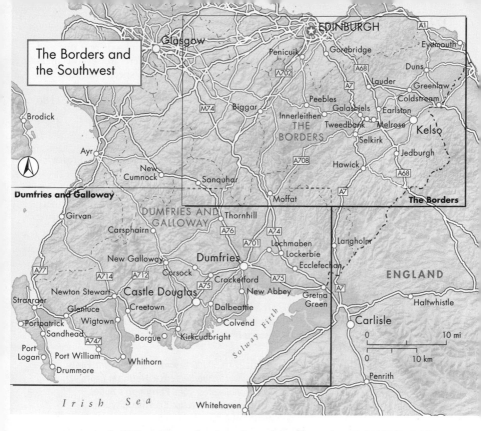

end of May at several venues throughout the region. ☎ *01387/260447* ⊕ *www.dgartsfestival.org.uk.*

SPORTS AND THE OUTDOORS

Dumfries and Galloway Gateway to Golf Pass. There are 25 courses in Dumfries and Galloway. The Gateway to Golf Pass starts at £70 for three rounds on three consecutive days on courses throughout Dumfries and Galloway. The five-round pass over five consecutive days costs £99. Buy it from Dumfries and Galloway Tourist Board or at tourist information centers. ⊠ *Dumries and Galloway Tourist Board, 64 Whitesands, Dumfries* ☎ *01387/253862* ⊕ *www.visitscotland.com.*

Rugby Sevens. The Borders invented the fast and furious, cut-down version of rugby in 1883, though it has now spread worldwide. Teams are made up of 7 players rather than 15, and the matches are shorter. Although the population of the Borders is about 100,000, the region boasts a total of 17 clubs and some of Scotland's best players. Each spring, 10 teams compete for the Kings of the Sevens title. ⊕ *www.kingsofthesevens.net.*

7stanes Mountain Biking. The Dumfries and Galloway region is something of a mecca for mountain bikers, offering trails and routes of every level of difficulty in beautiful and varying landscapes. This outfitter offers full equipment rental, skills training, advice, and local route maps organized by degree of difficulty. You can bring your own bike or rent one and ride gentle forest routes or tough hill climbs. There are seven centers across Dumfries and Galloway and the Borders; specific information on each is available on the comprehensive website. ✉ *Campbell House, Crichton Business Park, Bankend Rd., Dumfries* ☎ *01721/721180* ⊕ *www.7stanesmountainbiking.com.*

GETTING HERE AND AROUND

AIR TRAVEL

The nearest Scottish airports are at Edinburgh, Glasgow, and Prestwick (outside Glasgow).

BOAT AND FERRY TRAVEL

P&O European Ferries and Stena Line operate from Larne, in Northern Ireland, to Cairnryan, near Stranraer, several times daily. The crossing takes one hour on the Superstar Express, two hours on other ferries.

Boat and Ferry Contacts P&O European Ferries. ☎ *0800/130–0030* ⊕ *www. poferries.com.* **Stena Line.** ☎ *08447/707070* ⊕ *www.stenaline.co.uk.*

BUS TRAVEL

If you're approaching from the south, check with Scottish Citylink, National Express, or First about buses from Edinburgh and Glasgow. In the Borders, Firstborders and Perryman's Buses offer service within the region. Stagecoach Western is the main bus company serving Dumfries and Galloway.

Bus Contacts First Bus. ☎ *01224/650000* ⊕ *www.firstgroup.com.* **First-borders.** ☎ *01896/754350* ⊕ *www.firstborders.co.uk.* **National Express.** ☎ *0871/781–8181* ⊕ *www.nationalexpress.com.* **Perryman's Buses.** ☎ *01289/308719* ⊕ *www.perrymansbuses.co.uk.* **Scottish Citylink.** ☎ *0871/266–3333* ⊕ *www.citylink.co.uk.* **Stagecoach Western.** ☎ *0141/552–4961 in Glasgow, 01387/253496 in Dumfries* ⊕ *www.stagecoachbus.com.*

CAR TRAVEL

Traveling by car is the best and easiest way to explore the area, especially if you get off the main, and often crowded, arterial roads and use the little back roads. The main route into both the Borders and Galloway from the south is the M6, which becomes the M74 at the border. You can then take the scenic and leisurely A7 northwestward through Hawick toward Edinburgh, or the A75 and other parallel routes westward into Dumfries, Galloway, and the former ferry ports of Stranraer (nearby Cairnryan is an active ferry port) and Portpatrick.

There are several other possible routes: starting from the east, the A1 brings you from the English city of Newcastle to the border in about an hour. Moving west, the A697, which leaves the A1 north of Morpeth (in England) and crosses the border at Coldstream, is a leisurely back-road option. The A68 is probably the most scenic route to Scotland: after climbing to Carter Bar, it reveals a view of the Borders hills and windy skies before dropping into the ancient town of Jedburgh.

TRAIN TRAVEL

Apart from the main London–Edinburgh line, the Borders had no train service until 2015, when the rail link from Edinburgh to Tweedbank began service. The Borders Railway website has information about using it to explore the area. In the southwest, trains headed from London's Euston to Glasgow stop at Carlisle, just south of the border, and some also stop at Lockerbie. Trains between Glasgow and Carlisle stop at Gretna Green, Annan, and Dumfries. From Glasgow there is service on the coastal route to Stranraer.

First Bus provides connections between Hawick, Selkirk, and Galashiels and train service at Carlisle, Edinburgh, and Berwick.

Train Contacts Borders Railway. ☎ *0344/811–0141* ⊕ *bordersrailway. co.uk.* **National Rail.** ☎ *03457/484950* ⊕ *www.nationalrail.co.uk.* **ScotRail.** ☎ *0344/811–0141* ⊕ *www.scotrail.co.uk.* **Trainline.** ☎ *0871/244–1545* ⊕ *www. thetrainline.com.*

RESTAURANTS

Most good restaurants in the region used to be located in hotels, but today things are changing. Good independent eateries are popping up in small (and sometimes unlikely) towns and villages, and many new establishments specialize in fresh local ingredients. Seasonal menus are now popular. It is important to remember that restaurants here usually serve dinner until 8:30 only.

HOTELS

From top-quality, full-service hotels to quaint 18th-century drovers' inns to cozy bed-and-breakfasts, the Borders has all manner of lodging options. Choices in Dumfries and Galloway may be a little less expensive than in the Borders (with the same full range of services). These days many establishments are willing to lower their rates depending on availability. *Hotel reviews have been shortened. For full reviews, see Fodors.com.*

WHAT IT COSTS IN POUNDS			
$	**$$**	**$$$**	**$$$$**
Restaurants	under £15	£15–£19	£20–£25	over £25
Hotels	under £100	£100–£160	£161–£220	over £220

Restaurant prices are the average cost of a main course at dinner or, if dinner is not served, at lunch. Hotel prices are the lowest cost of a standard double room in high season, including 20% V.A.T.

VISITOR INFORMATION

Visit Scottish Borders has offices in Jedburgh, Hawick, and Peebles. The Dumfries & Galloway Tourist Board can be found in Dumfries and Stranraer. Seasonal information centers are at Castle Douglas, Eyemouth, Galashiels, Gretna Green, Kelso, Kirkcudbright, Langholm, Moffat, Sanquhar, and Selkirk. Liveborders provides online information on cultural and sporting activities in the Borders.

Contacts Dumfries & Galloway Tourist Board. ✉ *64 Whitesands, Dumfries* ☎ *01387/253862* ⊕ *www.visitscotland.com.* **Liveborders.** ✉ *Melrose Rd., Galashiels* ☎ *01896/661166* ⊕ *www.liveborders.org.uk.* **Visit Scottish Borders.** ✉ *Murray's Green, Jedburgh* ☎ *01835/863170* ⊕ *www.visitscotland.com.*

THE BORDERS

Although the Borders has many attractions, it's most famous for being the home base for Sir Walter Scott (1771–1832), the early-19th-century poet, novelist, and creator of *Ivanhoe*. Scott single-handedly transformed Scotland's image from that of a land of brutal savages to one of romantic and stirring deeds and magnificent landscapes. The novels of Scott are not read much nowadays—frankly, some of them are difficult to wade through—but the mystique that he created, the aura of historical romance, has outlasted his books. The ruined abbeys, historical houses, and grand vistas of the Borders provide a perfect backdrop.

A visit to at least one of the region's four great ruined abbeys makes the quintessential Borders experience. The monks in these powerful, long-abandoned religious communities were the first to work the fleeces of their sheep flocks, thus laying the groundwork for what is still the area's main manufacturing industry.

Borders folk take great pride in the region's fame as Scotland's main woolen-goods manufacturing area. Its main towns—Jedburgh, Hawick, Selkirk, Peebles, Kelso, and Melrose—retain an air of prosperity and confidence with their solid stone houses and elegant town squares. Although many mills have closed since the 1980s, the pride in local identity is still evident in the fiercely contested Melrose Sevens rugby competition in April and the annual Common Ridings—local events commemorating the time when towns needed to patrol their borders—throughout June and July.

JEDBURGH

50 miles south of Edinburgh, 95 miles southeast of Glasgow, 14 miles northeast of Hawick.

The town of Jedburgh (*burgh* is always pronounced *burra* in Scots) was for centuries the first major Scottish target of invading English armies. In more peaceful times it developed textile mills, most of which have since languished. The large landscaped area around the town's tourist information center was once a mill but now provides an encampment for the armies of modern tourists. The past still clings to this little town, however. The ruined abbey dominates the skyline, a reminder of the formerly strong governing role of the Borders abbeys.

GETTING HERE AND AROUND

By car from Edinburgh, you can take the A68 (about 45 minutes) or the A7 (about an hour). From Glasgow take the M8, then the A68 direct to Jedburgh (about two hours).

There are fairly good bus connections from all major Scottish cities to Jedburgh. From Edinburgh, direct routes to Melrose take about two hours. From Glasgow it takes 3½ hours to reach Melrose. From Melrose it's just 20 minutes to Jedburgh.

The Borders Railway runs between Edinburgh and Tweedbank, about 15 miles northwest of Jedburgh.

ESSENTIALS

Visitor Information Jedburgh Visitor Centre. ⊠ *Abbey Pl.* ☎ *01835/863170* ⊕ *www.visitscotland.com.*

EXPLORING

TOP ATTRACTIONS

FAMILY **Harestanes Countryside Visitor Centre.** Housed in a former farmhouse 4 miles north of Jedburgh, this visitor center portrays life in the Scottish Borders through art exhibitions and natural history displays. Crafts such as woodworking and tile making are taught here, and finished projects are often on display. Outside are meandering paths, quiet roads for bike rides, and the biggest children's play area in the Borders. There's plenty for children, including a fascinating puzzle gallery full of sturdy wooden games. It is also on one of the best-known walking routes in the Borders, the St. Cuthbert's Path. ⊠ *Junction of A68 and B6400, 4 miles north of Jedburgh* ☎ *01835/830306* ⊕ *www.liveborders.org.uk* ⊠ *Free* ☉ *Closed Nov.–Mar.*

OFF THE BEATEN PATH

Hermitage Castle. To appreciate the famous 20-mile ride of Mary, Queen of Scots, in 1566—she rushed to the side of her wounded lover, the Earl of Bothwell—travel southwest from Jedburgh to this, the most complete remaining example of the bare and grim medieval border castles. Restored in the early 19th century, it was built in the 13th century to guard what was at the time one of the important routes from England into Scotland. Local folklore maintains that the 14th-century Lord Soulis, a descendant of the original owner and notorious for diabolical excess, was captured by the local populace, who wrapped him in lead and boiled him in a cauldron—a much better story than the reality, which is that he died in Dumbarton Jail. ⊠ *2 miles west of B6399, about 21 miles south of Jedburgh, Hawick* ☎ *01387/376222* ⊕ *www. historicenvironment.scot* ⊠ *£5* ☉ *Closed Oct.–Mar.*

Fodor's Choice ★

Jedburgh Abbey. The most impressive of the Borders abbeys towers above Jedburgh. Built by David I, king of Scots in the 12th century, the abbey was nearly destroyed by the English Earl of Hertford's forces in 1544–45, during the destructive time known as the Rough Wooing. This was English king Henry VIII's (1491–1547) armed attempt to persuade the Scots that it was a good idea to unite the kingdoms by the marriage of his young son to the infant Mary, Queen of Scots (1542–87); the Scots disagreed and sent Mary to France instead. The story is explained in vivid detail at the visitor center, which also has information about the ruins and an audio tour. The arched abbey walls, the nave, and the cloisters still give a sense of the power these buildings represented. ⊠ *High St.* ☎ *01835/863925* ⊕ *www.historicenvironment.scot* ⊠ *£6.*

Mary, Queen of Scots Visitor Centre. This *bastel* (from the French *bastille*) was the fortified town house in which, as the story goes, Mary stayed before embarking on her famous 20-mile ride to Hermitage Castle to visit her wounded lover, the Earl of Bothwell (circa 1535–78) in 1566. Displays relate the tale and other episodes in her life, including her doubtful choices of lovers and husbands and her own reflections on her life. Still, Mary's death mask suggests that she was serene at the end. There are tapestries and furniture of the period, and the house's ornamental garden

4

has pear trees leading down to the river. ✉ *Queen St.* ☎ *01835/863331* 🌐 *www.scotborders.gov.uk* 🎫 *Free* 🕑 *Closed Dec.–Feb.*

WORTH NOTING

FAMILY **Jedburgh Castle Jail and Museum.** The site of the Howard Reform Prison was named after 18th-century prison reformer John Howard, who campaigned for improved conditions. Established in 1820, the prison sits where the front of the castle originally stood. Today you can inspect prison cells, rooms with period furnishings, and costumed figures. The audio guide, which recounts the history of the jail and of Jedburgh, is useful. ✉ *Castlegate* ☎ *01835/864750* 🌐 *www.scotborders.gov.uk/museums* 🎫 *Free* 🕑 *Closed Nov.–Mar.*

WHERE TO EAT AND STAY

$$ BRITISH 🍴 **Ancrum Cross Keys.** The quintessential village inn, this storybook traditional pub on the village green has a river running beyond the beer garden at the back. It serves good, hearty pub food that refreshes classics such as game pies and fish-and-chips. **Known for:** craft beer; traditional bar; village setting. [$] *Average main: £15* ✉ *The Green, Ancrum* ☎ *01835/830242* 🌐 *www.ancrumcrosskeys.com* 🕑 *Closed Mon. and Tues. No lunch weekdays.*

$$ BRITISH 🍴 **The Capon Tree Town House.** The interiors of this traditional red sandstone house in central Jedburgh are quite conservative, but the fine-dining menu is adventurous. Food presentation is artistic, and the taste of what is always local produce confirms the artistry. **Known for:** venison three ways; artistic presentation; cheese board. [$] *Average main: £19* ✉ *61 High St.* ☎ *01835/869596* 🌐 *www.thecapontree.com.*

$ B&B/INN FAMILY 🏨 **Hundalee House.** The richly decorated Victorian-style rooms of this 18th-century stone manor house have nice touches such as four-poster beds and cozy fireplaces; 15 acres of gardens and woods surround the B&B. **Pros:** fantastic views of apple orchards; hearty breakfasts; good children's facilities. **Cons:** farm aromas; far from shops and restaurants; small rooms. [$] *Rooms from: £70* ✉ *Off A68* ✣ *1 mile south of Jedburgh* ☎ *01835/863011* 🌐 *www.accommodation-scotland.org* 🕑 *Closed Jan.–Mar.* 🛏 *5 rooms* 🍽 *Breakfast.*

$ B&B/INN 🏨 **Meadhon House.** On a row of medieval buildings in the heart of town, Meadhon House is a charming 17th-century house with a history to match; rooms are bright and clean, with views onto the street or over the large and fragrant garden behind the house. **Pros:** central; pleasant rooms; welcoming atmosphere. **Cons:** rooms on the small side. [$] *Rooms from: £75* ✉ *48 Castlegate* ☎ *01835/862504* 🌐 *www.meadhon.co.uk* 💳 *No credit cards* 🛏 *5 rooms* 🍽 *Breakfast* ☞ *No credit cards.*

SHOPPING

Edinburgh Woollen Mill. The shelves at this shop burst with sweaters, kilts, tartan knitwear, and scarves. It's a good place to stock up on gifts. ✉ *Bankend North, Edinburgh Rd.* ☎ *01835/863773* 🌐 *www.ewm.co.uk.*

SPORTS AND OUTDOORS

Christopher Rainbow Tandem & Bike Hire. You can rent tandem bikes, mountain bikes, and touring bikes at this shop. The location, between Jedburgh and Ancrum, makes it ideal for exploring the area's abbeys, as well as the Tweed Cycleway and Borderloop Cycleway. The company

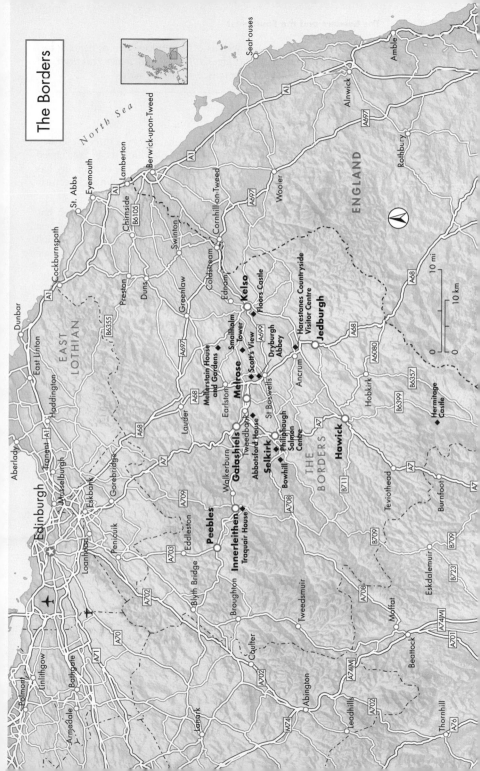

The Borders

North Sea

ENGLAND

EAST LOTHIAN

THE BORDERS

Edinburgh

Berwick-upon-Tweed

Amble

Alnwick

Rothbury

Wooler

Kelso

Floors Castle

Jedburgh

Harestanes Countryside Visitor Centre

Hermitage Castle

Hawick

Melrose

Smailholm Tower

Scott's View

Dryburgh Abbey

Ancrum

Mellerstain House and Gardens

Earlston

St Boswells

Galashiels

Tweedbank

Abbotsford House

Selkirk

Bowhill

Philiphaugh Salmon Centre

Peebles

Innerleithen

Traquair House

Walkerburn

Lauder

Eddleston

Blyh Bridge

Broughton

Tweedsmuir

Moffat

Teviothead

Burnfoot

Eskdalemuir

Beattock

Leadhills

Abington

Thornhill

Coulter

Lanark

Penicuik

Loanhead

Eskbank

Gorebridge

Dalkeith

Musselburgh

Tranent

Haddington

Aberlady

East Linton

Dunbar

Cockburnspath

St. Abbs

Eyemouth

Lamberton

Chirnside

Swinton

Greenlaw

Duns

Preston

Coldstream

Edrom

Cornhill-on-Tweed

Linlithgow

Bathgate

Armadale

Polmont

10 mi

10 km

provides tour itineraries, as well as extra services such as luggage for-warding. ✉ *8 Timpendean Cottages, off A698* ✛ *Between Jedburgh and Ancrum* ☎ *01835/830326* ⊕ *www.chrisrainbow.net.*

KELSO

12 miles northeast of Jedburgh.

One of the most charming Borders burghs, Kelso is often described as having a Continental flavor—some people think its broad, paved square makes it resemble a Belgian market town. The community has some fine examples of Georgian and Victorian Scots town architecture.

GETTING HERE AND AROUND

There are direct bus routes from Jedburgh to Kelso. Edinburgh has direct buses to Jedburgh; buses from Glasgow aren't direct. Your best option is to travel by car. From Jedburgh to Kelso take the A698, which is 12 miles, or about 20 minutes. Alternatively, the A699 is a scenic half-hour drive.

ESSENTIALS

Visitor Information Kelso Tourist Information Centre. ✉ *Town House, The Square* ☎ *01573/221119* ⊕ *www.kelso.bordernet.co.uk.*

EXPLORING

Fodor'sChoice
★

Floors Castle. The palatial Floors Castle, the largest inhabited castle in Scotland, is an architectural extravagance bristling with pepper-mill turrets. Not so much a castle as the ancestral seat of a wealthy and powerful landowning family, the Roxburghes, it stands on the "floors," or flat terrain, on the banks of the River Tweed. The enormous home was built in 1721 by William Adam (1689–1748) and modified by William Playfair (1789–1857), who added the turrets and towers in the 1840s. Rooms are crowded with valuable furniture, paintings, porcelain, and an eerie circular room full of stuffed birds; each has a knowledgeable guide at the ready. The surrounding 56,000-acre estate is home to more than 40 farms. ✉ *A6089* ☎ *01573/223333* ⊕ *www.floorscastle.com* ▣ *Castle and grounds £11.50* ⊘ *Closed Nov.–Mar. and weekdays in Oct.*

Kelso Abbey. The least intact ruin of the four great abbeys, Kelso Abbey is just a bleak fragment of what was once the largest of the group. It was here in 1460 that the nine-year-old James III was crowned king of Scotland. On a main invasion route, the abbey was burned three times in the 1540s alone, on the last occasion by the English Earl of Hertford's forces in 1545, when the 100 men and 12 monks of the garrison were butchered and the structure all but destroyed. ✉ *Bridge St.* ☎ *0131/668–8600* ⊕ *www.historicenvironment.scot* ▣ *Free* ⊘ *Closed Thurs. and Fri. Oct.–Mar.*

Mellerstain House and Gardens. One fine example of the Borders area's ornate country homes is Mellerstain House, begun in the 1720s and finished in the 1770s by Robert Adam (1728–92); it is considered one of his finest creations. Sumptuous plasterwork covers almost all interior surfaces, and there are outstanding examples of 18th-century furnishings, porcelain and china, and paintings and embroidery. The beautiful terraced gardens (open an hour before the house itself) are as renowned as the house. ✉ *Off A6089, 7 miles northwest of Kelso, Gordon* ☎ *01573/410636* 🌐 *www.mellerstain.com* 🎫 *Gardens £5, house and gardens £8.50* 🕓 *Closed Oct.–Apr.*

Fodor's Choice ★ **Smailholm Tower.** Standing uncompromisingly on top of a barren, rocky ridge in the hills south of Mellerstain, this 16th-century peel tower, characteristic of the Borders, was built solely for defense, and its unadorned stones contrast with the luxury of Mellerstain House. If you let your imagination wander at this windy spot, you can almost see the rising dust of an advancing raiding party. Sir Walter Scott found this spot inspiring, and he visited the tower often during his childhood. Anne Carrick's tableaux in the tower illustrate some of Scott's Border ballads, and the ticket includes an audio tour of the building. ✉ *Off B6404, 4½ miles south of Mellerstain House* ☎ *01573/460365* 🌐 *www.historicenvironment.scot* 🎫 *£5* 🕓 *Closed Oct.–Mar.*

WHERE TO EAT AND STAY

$$ BRITISH 🍴 **The Cobbles.** Just off the town's cobbled square, this well-established pub and restaurant with wooden tables and a bustling, cheerful atmosphere seems to be permanently busy. The extensive menu combines generously sized burgers, steaks, and meat pies with more unusual pub items such as homemade artichoke-and-truffle ravioli in a seafood sauce. **Known for:** homemade desserts; friendly atmosphere; generous portions. [$] *Average main: £16* ✉ *7 Bowmont St.* ☎ *01573/223548* 🌐 *www.thecobbleskelso.co.uk.*

$$ B&B/INN 🏨 **Edenwater House.** Overlooking Edenwater, a trout stream that runs into the River Tweed, this handsome stone house has three guest rooms that are luxuriously furnished in a traditional style with flower-pattern fabrics; they offer fine views of the river and the Cheviot hills. **Pros:** excellent food; romantic atmosphere; peaceful surroundings. **Cons:** not good for families with small children; far from urban amenities. [$] *Rooms from: £120* ✉ *Off B6461, Ednam* ☎ *01573/224070* 🌐 *www.edenwaterhouse.co.uk* 🛏 *3 rooms* 🍽 *Breakfast.*

$$$ HOTEL Fodor's Choice ★ 🏨 **Ednam House Hotel.** People return again and again to this stately hotel on the banks of the River Tweed, close to Kelso's grand abbey and sprawling market square. **Pros:** great outdoor activities; atmospheric lobby; impressive restaurant. **Cons:** some rooms need a makeover; popular for weddings and other events so can be crowded; rooms with a river view cost more. [$] *Rooms from: £167* ✉ *Bridge St.* ☎ *01573/224168* 🌐 *www.ednamhouse.com* 🕓 *Closed late Dec.–early Jan.* 🛏 *32 rooms* 🍽 *Breakfast.*

MELROSE

15 miles west of Kelso, 4 miles southeast of Galashiels.

Though it's small, there is nevertheless a bustle about Melrose, the perfect example of a prosperous Scottish market town and one of the loveliest in the Borders. It's set around a square lined with 18th- and 19th-century buildings housing myriad small shops and cafés. Despite its proximity to the much larger Galashiels, Melrose has rejected industrialization. You'll likely hear local residents greet each other by first name in the square.

GETTING HERE AND AROUND

Buses do go to Melrose, and the new Borders Railway ends at Tweedbank, just 2 miles to the northwest. Driving remains the easiest way to get here from the south or east. From Galashiels, take the A6091 (10 minutes).

EXPLORING

TOP ATTRACTIONS

Fodor's Choice ★ Abbotsford House. In this great house overlooking the Tweed, Sir Walter Scott lived, worked, and received the great and the good in luxurious salons. In 1811, the writer bought a farm on this site named Cartleyhole, which was a euphemism for the real name, Clartyhole (*clarty* is Scots for "muddy" or "dirty"). The romantic Scott renamed the property after a ford in the nearby Tweed used by the abbot of Melrose. Scott eventually had the house entirely rebuilt in the Scottish baronial style. It was an expensive project, and Scott wrote feverishly to keep his creditors at bay. John Ruskin, the art critic, disapproved, calling it an "incongruous pile," but most contemporary visitors find it fascinating, particularly because of its expansive views and delightful gardens.

A free audio tour guides you around the salon, the circular study, and the library with its 9,000 leather-bound volumes. Perhaps more than anyone else, Scott redefined Scotland as a place of mystery and romance, and awoke the English, who read him avidly, to its natural beauty and its past—or at least a heavily dramatized version of it. The visitor center houses displays about Scott's life, a gift shop, and a restaurant serving lunch. To get here, take the A6091 from Melrose and follow the signs for Abbotsford. ■ **TIP→ You can also stay on the estate, in the Hope Scott Wing (£120).** ⊠ *B6360* ✚ *Between Melrose and Tweedbank* ☎ *01896/752043* ⊕ *www.scottsabbotsford.co.uk* ✉ *House and gardens £9.60; gardens only £5. Last admission 1 hr before closing* ⊙ *House closed Dec.–Feb.*

Fodor's Choice ★ Melrose Abbey. Just off Melrose's town square sit the ruins of Melrose Abbey, one of the four Borders abbeys: "If thou would'st view fair Melrose aright, go visit it in the pale moonlight," wrote Scott in *The Lay of the Last Minstrel*. So many of his fans took the advice literally that a custodian begged him to rewrite the lines. Today the abbey is still impressive: a red-sandstone shell with slender windows, delicate tracery, and carved capitals, all carefully maintained. Among the carvings high on the roof is one of a bagpipe-playing pig. An audio tour is included in the admission price. The heart of 14th-century national hero Robert the Bruce is rumored to be buried here. ⊠ *Abbey St.* ☎ *01896/822562* ⊕ *www.historicenvironment.scot* ✉ *£6.*

WORTH NOTING

Dryburgh Abbey. The final resting place of Sir Walter Scott and his wife, and the most peaceful and secluded of the Borders abbeys, the "gentle ruins" of Dryburgh Abbey sit on parkland in a loop of the Tweed. The abbey, founded in 1150, suffered from English raids until, like Melrose, it was abandoned in 1544. The style is transitional, a mingling of rounded Romanesque and pointed early English. The north transept, where the Haig and Scott families lie buried, is lofty and pillared,

The World of Sir Walter Scott

Sir Walter Scott (1771–1832) was probably Scottish tourism's best propagandist. Thanks to his fervid Romantic imagination, his long narrative poems—such as "The Lady of the Lake"—and a series of historical novels, including *Ivanhoe* and *Rob Roy*, the world fell in love with the image of heroic Scotland. Scott wrote of Scotland as a place of Highland wilderness and clan romance, shaping outsiders' perceptions of Scotland in a way that to an extent survives even today.

Scott was born in College Wynd, Edinburgh. A lawyer by training, he was an assiduous collector of traditional ballads and tales. "The Lay of the Last Minstrel," a romantic poem published in 1805, brought him fame. In 1811 Scott bought the house that was to become Abbotsford, his Borders mansion near Melrose.

Scott started on his series of Waverley novels in 1814, at first anonymously, and by 1820 had produced *Waverley*, *Guy Mannering*, *The Antiquary*, *Tales of My Landlord*, and *Rob Roy*. Between 1820 and 1825 there followed an additional 11 titles, including *Ivanhoe* and *The Pirate*. Many of his verse narratives and novels had real-life settings, in particular the Trossachs, northwest of Stirling, an area that rapidly became, and still remains, popular with visitors.

Apart from his writing, Scott is also remembered for rediscovering the Honours of Scotland—the crown, scepter, and sword of state of the Scottish monarchs—in 1819. These symbols had languished at the bottom of a chest in Edinburgh Castle since 1707, when Scotland lost its independence. Today they're on display in the castle.

SCOTT SIGHTS

Abbotsford, Scott's home near Melrose in the Borders, is well worth a visit. Other houses associated with Scott can be seen in Edinburgh: 25 George Square, which was his father's house, and 39 Castle Street, where he lived from 1801 to 1826. The site of his birthplace, in College Wynd, is marked with a plaque. The most obvious structure associated with Scott in Edinburgh is the Scott Monument on Princes Street, which looks like a Gothic rocket ship with a statue of Scott and his pet dog as passengers.

4

---

and once formed part of the abbey church. ⊠ *St. Boswell's, B6404* ☎ *01835/822381* ⊕ *www.historicenvironment.scot* 🎫 *£6.*

Priorwood Garden and Harmony Garden. The National Trust for Scotland's Priorwood Garden, next to Melrose Abbey, specializes in flowers for drying, and dried flowers are on sale in the shop. Next to the gardens is an orchard with some old apple varieties. The walled Harmony Garden, belonging to the lovely Georgian house at its heart, sits nearby opposite the abbey. ⊠ *Abbey St.* ☎ *01896/822493* ⊕ *www.nts.org.uk* 🎫 *Free* ☉ *Closed Nov.–Mar.*

Scott's View. This is possibly the most photographed rural view in the south of Scotland. (It's almost as iconic as Eilean Donan Castle, far to the north.) The sinuous curve of the River Tweed and the gentle landscape unfolding to the triple peaks of the Eildons and then rolling out into the shadows beyond are certainly worth seeking out. ⊠ *B6356, 3 miles east of Melrose, Dryburgh.*

Trimontium Museum and Three Hills Roman Heritage Centre. Run by extremely knowledgeable enthusiasts, this museum has such artifacts as tools, weapons, and armor retrieved from the largest Roman settlement in Scotland, which was at nearby Newstead. A blacksmith's shop, several examples of pottery, and scale models of the fort are also on display. A guided four-hour walk along the 5-mile trail to the Newstead site departs at 1:30 on Thursday (also on Tuesday in July and August). ⊠ *The Ormiston, Market Sq.* ☎ *01896/822651* ⊕ *www.trimontium. org.uk* 🗐 *£4* ☉ *Closed Nov.–Mar.*

WHERE TO EAT AND STAY

$$
ECLECTIC

✗ **Hergés on the Loch.** At this light and airy place, a wall of windows allows you to contemplate swans and ducks as they float serenely across Gunknowe Loch, and, if the weather allows, you can dine on the terrace. The elegant but understated food, well presented and served in generous portions, includes familiar dishes like steak-and-ale pie and oat-and-mustard-crusted loin of venison cooked pink and melt-in-your-mouth tender. **Known for:** restful setting with loch view; reasonable prices; familiar food well cooked. Ⓢ *Average main: £15* ⊠ *Tweedbank Dr., Tweedbank* ☎ *01896/759909* ⊕ *www.hergesontheloch.com.*

$$$
BRITISH

✗ **Seasons.** A family-run restaurant in an appealing village setting, Seasons has a reputation for using local produce consistently well in imaginative ways. White walls and wooden tables create an uncluttered setting for a menu that includes steaks, burgers, and fish pie, as well as a couple of set menus (at lunch and dinner) with one dish per course. **Known for:** fresh local produce; attentive service; delicious bread. Ⓢ *Average main: £20* ⊠ *Main St., Gattonside* ☎ *01896/823217* ⊕ *www.seasonsborders.co.uk* ☉ *Closed Mon. and Tues.*

$$
HOTEL

🛏 **Burts Hotel.** Dating from the 18th century, this charming whitewashed building in the center of Melrose has individually decorated and different rooms filled with floral pastels. **Pros:** walking distance to restaurants and pubs; good menu in restaurant. **Cons:** some tiny rooms; slightly overpriced for some rooms. Ⓢ *Rooms from: £145* ⊠ *Market Sq.* ☎ *01896/822285* ⊕ *www.burtshotel.co.uk* ↝ *20 rooms* ⦿| *Breakfast.*

$$
HOTEL

🛏 **Dryburgh Abbey Hotel.** Mature woodlands and verdant lawns surround this imposing, 19th-century mansion-turned-hotel, which is adjacent to the ruins of Dryburgh Abbey on a sweeping bend of the River Tweed. **Pros:** beautiful grounds; romantic setting. **Cons:** some rooms need to be freshened up; service can be on the slow side. Ⓢ *Rooms from: £135* ⊠ *Off B6404, St. Boswells* ☎ *01835/822261* ⊕ *www.dryburgh. co.uk* ↝ *38 rooms* ⦿| *Breakfast.*

SHOPPING

Abbey Mill. Take a break from sightseeing at Abbey Mill, where you'll find handwoven knitwear as well as homemade jams and fudge. The wee tearoom is also popular. ⊠ *Annay Rd.* ☎ *01896/822138.*

SELKIRK

6 miles south of Galashiels, 11 miles north of Hawick.

Selkirk is a hilly outpost with a smattering of antiques shops and an assortment of bakers selling Selkirk bannock (fruited sweet bread) and other cakes. It is the site of one of Scotland's iconic battles, Flodden Field, commemorated here with a statue in the town. Sir Walter Scott was sheriff (judge) of Selkirkshire from 1800 until his death in 1832, and his statue stands in Market Place. Selkirk is also near Bowhill, a stately home.

The town claims its Common Riding (⊕ *returntotheridings.co.uk*) is the largest mounted gathering anywhere in Europe. More than 400 riders take part in the event in June. It's also the oldest Borders festival, with roots back to the Battle of Flodden in 1513.

GETTING HERE AND AROUND
If you're driving, take the A7 south to Galashiels. The scenic journey is less than 7 miles and takes around 10 minutes. First Edinburgh Bus offers a regular service between Galashiels and Selkirk.

ESSENTIALS
Visitor Information Selkirk Visitor Information Centre. ⊠ *Halliwell's House, Market Pl.* ☎ *01750/20054* ⊕ *www.visitscotland.com.*

EXPLORING
TOP ATTRACTIONS
Bowhill. Home of the Duke of Buccleuch, Bowhill dates from the 19th century and houses an outstanding collection of works by Gainsborough, Van Dyck, Canaletto, Reynolds, and Raeburn, as well as porcelain and period furniture. Access is by guided tour on specific days in summer. There is an excellent adventure playground for the kids and a 57-mile country ride for those who prefer horseback riding. A local stable hires out horses. ⊠ *Off A708, 3 miles west of Selkirk* ☎ *01750/22204* ⊕ *www.bowhillhouse.co.uk* ☞ *Grounds £4.50, house and grounds £10* ⊘ *Closed Oct.–Mar. and selected days rest of the year; check website.*

Lochcarron Visitor Centre. You can take an informative guided tour of this world-renowned mill and also purchase some of the best woolen goods on offer, from knitwear to tartans and tweeds. The shop also sells Scottish jewelry. ⊠ *Dinsdale Rd.* ☎ *01750/726100* ⊕ *www.lochcarron. com* ☞ *£9.50 for tour* ⊘ *Closed Sun.*

Sir Walter Scott's Courtroom. The historic courtroom where Sir Walter Scott presided as sheriff from 1804 to 1832 contains a display examining his life, writings, and time on the bench. It uses models to re-create the atmosphere of a 19th-century Scottish court and includes an audiovisual presentation. A statue of the famous writer overlooks the comings and goings outside the court. ⊠ *Market Sq.* ☎ *01750/720761* ⊕ *www. scotborders.gov.uk* ☞ *Free* ⊘ *Closed Nov.–Feb.*

WORTH NOTING

Halliwell's House Museum. Tucked off the main square, Halliwell's House Museum was once an ironmonger's shop, which is now re-created downstairs. Upstairs, an exhibit tells the town's story, illustrates the working lives of its inhabitants, and provides useful background information on the Common Ridings. ✉ *Halliwell's Close, Market Pl.* ☎ *01750/20096* 🌐 *www.scotborders.gov.uk* 🎟 *Free* 🕒 *Closed Nov.–Mar.*

Philiphaugh Salmon Viewing Centre. On the site of a famous battle in 1645 in which the Scottish Covenanters drove off the pro-English armies under the Earl of Montrose, the Philiphaugh Salmon Viewing Centre is devoted to more peaceful pursuits: watching salmon. Its viewing platforms and underwater cameras allow you to follow the life cycle of the salmon. There are also country walks and cycling routes to follow, and a tearoom. The website has a self-guided audio tour of the battlefield. ✉ *A708* ✥ *1 mile outside Selkirk* ☎ *01750/21766* 🌐 *www.salmonviewingcentre.com* 🎟 *Free.*

WHERE TO EAT AND STAY

$ ITALIAN 🍴 **Buon Gusto Ristorante.** A small, busy, and very popular restaurant in central Selkirk, Buon Gusto claims to be genuinely Italian, and its well-made pastas and pizzas attest to this. The predominantly pasta menu includes imaginative variations on the usual fare: pasta with scallops, for example. **Known for:** all-you-can-eat option; superior pizzas; good dessert menu. [$] *Average main: £10* ✉ *73 High St.* ☎ *01750/778174* 🌐 *www.buongustoristorante.co.uk* 🕒 *Closed Mon. and Tues. No lunch.*

$$ HOTEL 🏨 **Best Western Philipburn House Hotel.** West of Selkirk, this alpine-style hotel enjoys a lovely setting among the woods and hills. **Pros:** pleasant rural setting; bright rooms; on-site parking. **Cons:** no elevator; restaurant closes rather early; breakfast is extra. [$] *Rooms from: £140* ✉ *Linglie Rd.* ✥ *Opposite Salmon Viewing Centre* ☎ *01750/720747* 🌐 *www.bw-philipburnhousehotel.co.uk* 🛏 *24 rooms* 🍽 *No meals.*

HAWICK

10 miles south of Selkirk, 14 miles southwest of Jedburgh.

Hawick (pronounced *hoyk*) is a busy town at the center of the region's textile industry, commemorated in the interesting Borders Textile Towerhouse. The Victorian buildings along its High Street recall the town's heyday. The largest community in the Borders, it's a good place to buy the delicate cashmere and wool goods that made the region famous. Hawick's Common Riding festival, held each June, draws onlookers from all over Scotland.

GETTING HERE AND AROUND

Driving here from Selkirk or Jedburgh is no trouble—it's a straight shot on major roads. There is also bus service from many of the other Borders towns.

ESSENTIALS

Visitor Information Hawick Visitor Centre. ✉ *Towermill, Kirkstile* ☎ *01450/373993* 🌐 *www.visitscotland.com.*

EXPLORING

FAMILY **Borders Textile Towerhouse.** In the former Drumlanrig Tower, this museum includes a good exhibition about the textile industry, once the lifeblood of the Borders. Plenty of interactive elements make it interesting for children as well. One room commemorates the demonstrations by textile workers who were demanding the right to vote in the 1880s. On the upper floor are up-to-the-minute fabrics that define the 21st century. Check out the shop, too. ⊠ *1 Tower Knowe* ☎ *01450/377615* ⊠ *Free* ⊗ *Closed Tues. and Sun. Nov.–Mar.*

WHERE TO EAT

$ ✕ **Damascus Drum.** Decorated in muted colors, this lovely little café and

CAFÉ bookshop named for a traditional folktale (you can find it on the tables)

Fodor's Choice provides a tranquil refuge in the town center. It's a perfect spot for a light

★ lunch; choose from a limited menu that includes soup, delicious meze, and burgers with or without meat. **Known for:** meze; vegetarian burgers; quiet atmosphere. ⓢ *Average main: £10* ⊠ *2 Silver St.* ☎ *07707/856123* ⊕ *www.damascusdrum.co.uk* ⊗ *Closed Sun. No dinner.*

SHOPPING

Hawick Factory Visitor Centre. This is a good place to see knitwear in the making—literally. In the shop you can buy knitwear and cashmere goods for discounted prices. ⊠ *Trinity Mills, Duke St.* ☎ *01450/371221* ⊕ *www.hawico.com.*

White of Hawick. There's a room here exclusively dedicated to cashmere, and it's a good place to stock up on warm outerwear. White of Hawick also sells an extensive range of lambswool and knitted garments. ⊠ *Victoria Rd.* ☎ *01450/373206* ⊕ *www.peterscott.co.uk.*

INNERLEITHEN

17 miles northwest of Hawick.

Innerleithen is one of the larger Borders towns; you'll feel that you've entered a hub of activity when you arrive. It's also dramatically beautiful. Surrounded by hills and glens, the town is where the Tweed and Leithen rivers join, then separate. Historically, Innerleithen dates back to pre-Roman times, and there are artifacts all around for you to see. Once a booming industrial town of wool mills, today it's a great destination for outdoor activities including hiking, biking, and fly-fishing.

GETTING HERE AND AROUND

To drive to Innerleithen, take the A7 north from Hawick and then the A707 northwest from Selkirk. There are no trains between the two towns.

EXPLORING

FAMILY **Robert Smail's Printing Works.** Try your hand at printing the way it used to be done: painstakingly setting each letter by hand. Robert Smail's print shop, founded in 1866 to produce materials for nearby factories, boat tickets, theater posters, and the local newspaper, is still a working print shop as well as a museum. Two great waterwheels once powered the presses, and they are still running. The guided tour, which includes making your own bookmark, takes 90 minutes. ⊠ *7–9 High*

St. ☎ *01896/830206* 🌐 *www.nts.org.uk* 🎟 *£6.50* ⏲ *Closed Jan.–Mar.; Apr.–Oct., Tues.–Thurs.; Nov. and Dec., Tues., Wed., and Sun.*

Fodor's Choice ★ **Traquair House.** Said to be the oldest continually occupied home in Scotland (since 1107), Traquair House has secret stairways and passages, a library with more than 3,000 books, and a bed said to be used by Mary, Queen of Scots, in 1566. You can walk freely through the rooms, and there is an explanatory leaflet in each as well as helpful guides. The top floor of the house is an interesting small museum. Outside is a reasonably scary maze, an adventure playground, and some lovely woodland walks as well as pigs, goats, and chickens. The 18th-century brew house still makes highly recommended ale, and there's a café on the grounds near the beautiful walled garden. The Traquair Fair in August is the nearest you are likely to get to a medieval fair, and well worth the visit. You may even spend the night, if you wish. ✉ *B709* ✥ *From the A70 some 6 miles south of Peebles, take the B709 for 7 miles; the car entrance into the house is in the village* ☎ *01896/830323* 🌐 *www.traquair.co.uk* 🎟 *Grounds £4.50, house and grounds £8.80* ⏲ *Closed Dec.–Mar. and weekdays in Nov.*

WHERE TO STAY

$$$ B&B/INN 🏨 **Traquair House.** Staying in one of the guest rooms in the 12th-century wing of Traquair House is to experience a slice of Scottish history. **Pros:** stunning grounds; spacious rooms; great breakfast. **Cons:** nearly 2 miles to restaurants and shops; rooms fill up quickly in summer. [$] *Rooms from: £190* ✉ *B709* ☎ *01896/830323* 🌐 *www.traquair.co.uk* 🛏 *3 rooms* 🍴 *Breakfast.*

$$$ HOTEL 🏨 **Windlestraw Lodge.** This elegant bed-and-breakfast occupies a grand country home surrounded by extensive gardens. **Pros:** beautifully designed rooms; excellent restaurant. **Cons:** a bit expensive for what you get; not all rooms have Tweed views. [$] *Rooms from: £175* ✉ *9 Galashiels Rd., Walkerburn* ✥ *On the A72 between Galashiels and Innerleithen* ☎ *01896/870636* 🌐 *www.windlestraw.co.uk* 🛏 *6 rooms* 🍴 *Breakfast.*

PEEBLES

6 miles west of Innerleithen.

Thanks to its excellent though pricey shopping, Peebles gives the impression of catering primarily to leisured country gentlefolk. Architecturally, the town is nothing out of the ordinary, just a very pleasant burgh. Don't miss the splendid dolphins ornamenting the bridge crossing the River Tweed.

GETTING HERE AND AROUND

Because of its size and location, direct buses run from both Edinburgh and Glasgow to Peebles. There are also buses here from Innerleithen, though driving from here is more direct. (Take the A72; it's about a 10-minute drive.)

ESSENTIALS

Visitor Information Peebles Visitor Information Centre. ✉ *23 High St.* ☎ *01721/728095* 🌐 *www.visitscotland.com.*

EXPLORING

Peebles War Memorial. The exotic, almost Moorish mosaics of the Peebles War Memorial are unique in Scotland, although most towns have a memorial to honor those killed in service. It's a remarkable tribute to the 225 Peebleans killed in World War II. ✉ *Chambers Quadrangle, High St.* ⌨ *Free.*

WHERE TO EAT

$$
BRITISH
FAMILY
Fodor'sChoice
★

✕ Adam Room. With a minstrels' gallery, crystal chandeliers, and tall windows with views over the Tweed, the dining room at the Tontine Hotel has a grand feel. It's a bit surprising, therefore, that it also serves good home cooking for the family at reasonable prices. **Known for:** traditional home cooking; luxurious dining room; wine list. $ *Average main: £18* ✉ *Tontine Hotel, High St.* ☎ *01721/720892* ⊕ *www.tontinehotel.com.*

$$$
DELI

✕ Coltman's Delicatessen and Kitchen. The pleasant white-walled, modern dining room of this bright, airy eatery sits behind the tempting deli counter, and its windows overlook the Tweed. All-day options include salads, platters, and some luxurious sandwiches, while the compact but finely balanced dinner menu (set price of £23.95 or £28.95 for two or three courses) offers choices such as cod with a mussel and saffron broth and a hanger steak with braised shallots. **Known for:** deli lunches; tempting desserts; well-balanced dinner menu. $ *Average main: £24* ✉ *71–73 High St.* ☎ *01721/720405* ⊕ *www.coltmans.co.uk* ✆ *No dinner Sun.–Wed.*

$$$$
BRITISH

✕ Horseshoe Inn. The opulent dining room at the Horseshoe has large gold-framed mirrors and heavy drapes to emphasize its grand style. The prix-fixe menu (at £40 or £50 for two or three courses) is equally grand; you might combine a poached trout starter with a main dish of hake with celeriac or duck breast with carrot and hash brown potatoes. **Known for:** fine dining; Sunday roast menu; luxurious surroundings. $ *Average main: £40* ✉ *Horsehoe Inn, Eddleston* ☎ *01721/730225* ⊕ *www.horseshoeinn.co.uk* ✆ *Closed Mon. and Tues.*

WHERE TO STAY

$$
HOTEL

🏰 Cringletie House. With medieval-style turrets and crow-step gables, this small-scale, peaceful retreat manages to be fancy *and* homey, Victorian (it was built in the 1860s) and modern (flat-screen TVs). **Pros:** elegant bedrooms; cozy fireplaces; decadent dining. **Cons:** some bedrooms have low ceilings; atmosphere can be almost too quiet. $ *Rooms from: £160* ✉ *Edinburgh Rd.* ✚ *Off the A703 north of Peebles* ☎ *01721/725750* ⊕ *www.cringletie.com* ✆ *Closed Nov.–Feb.* ⟳ *13 rooms* �“❑ *Breakfast.*

$$
HOTEL
FAMILY

🏰 Peebles Hydro. One of the great "hydro hotels" built in the 19th century for those anxious to "take the waters," the family-friendly Peebles Hydro has comfortable if rather old-fashioned rooms. **Pros:** plenty of activities; good children's programs; delicious breakfast. **Cons:** can feel impersonal; some rooms have bland decor; air of faded glory but in process of refurbishment. $ *Rooms from: £125* ✉ *Innerleithen Rd.* ☎ *01721/720602* ⊕ *www.peebleshydro.co.uk* ⟳ *132 rooms* �“❑ *Breakfast.*

$$
HOTEL

🏰 Tontine Hotel. A small and charming facade hides a spacious, lovingly refurbished (an ongoing process) hotel that stretches back from Peebles High Street and has lovely views of the Tweed River. **Pros:** centrally

4

located; pleasant rooms; welcoming staff; fine dining. **Cons:** some small rear rooms; old-fashioned decor in some areas. $ *Rooms from: £110* ✉ *High St.* ☎ *01721/729732* 🌐 *www.tontinehotel.com* 🛏 *36 rooms* 🍴 *Breakfast.*

PERFORMING ARTS

Eastgate Theatre. A year-round program of films, concerts, and theater as well as community activities for adults and children are on offer here. The theater also has a very pleasant café. ✉ *1 School Brae* ☎ *01721/725777* 🌐 *www.eastgatearts.com.*

SHOPPING

Be prepared for temptations at every turn as you browse the shops on High Street and in the courts and side streets leading off it.

Brevity. Although it's tiny, this fashion boutique seems to cram an enormous amount of imaginative clothing into a small space. Younger designers, especially Italian ones, have their work on sale here at very reasonable prices; everything is presented with enormous enthusiasm by the owner. ✉ *50 High St.* ☎ *01721/724323.*

Caledonia. For anything and everything Scottish, from kilts to dirks and jams to tablecloths, look no further than Caledonia. You can also rent kilts here. ✉ *57 High St.* ☎ *01721/722343* 🌐 *caledonialifestyle.com.*

Head to Toe. The shop stocks natural beauty products, handmade pine furniture, and handsome linens—from patchwork quilts to silk flowers. ✉ *43 High St.* ☎ *01721/722752* 🌐 *www.headtotoepeebles.co.uk.*

Keith Walter. Among the many jewelers on High Street, Keith Walter is a master of gold and silver who makes his creations on the premises. He also stocks jewelry made by other local designers. ✉ *28 High St.* ☎ *01721/720650* 🌐 *www.keithwalterjeweller.co.uk.*

DUMFRIES AND GALLOWAY

Galloway covers the southwestern portion of Scotland, west of the main town of Dumfries; it's a quiet and less-visited region of Scotland, in general. Here a gentle coastline gives way to farmland and then breezy uplands that gradually merge with coniferous forests. The region now claims two extraordinary public art projects—Charles Jencks's *Crawick Multiverse* and Andy Goldsworthy's *Striding Arches*.

GRETNA GREEN

10 miles north of Carlisle, England, 87 miles south of Glasgow, 92 miles southwest of Edinburgh.

The first town across the English–Scottish border, Gretna Green (not to be confused with nearby Gretna) was historically where runaway couples went to be married by the local blacksmith under Scotland's more lenient laws. No one could accuse the town of failing to exploit its reputation as the place to tie the knot. Although it is highly commercialized, it is still a favorite venue for weddings, even though the original reasons for going have long since changed.

GETTING HERE AND AROUND

From Glasgow you can reach Gretna Green via the M74 and A74; it's an hour-and-a-half drive. From Edinburgh, take the A74 (about two hours). Buses and trains travel daily to Gretna Green from Glasgow and Edinburgh.

ESSENTIALS

Visitor Information Gretna Green Tourist Information Centre. ⊠ *Gretna Gateway Outlet Village, Glasgow Rd., Gretna* ☎ *01461/337834* ⊕ *www. gretnagreen.com.*

EXPLORING

Blacksmith's Shop. Today the 18th-century house of the village blacksmith, known as the "anvil priest," contains a collection of blacksmithing tools, as well as the anvil over which many weddings may have been conducted to symbolize the forging of the link between two people. The village was on the new coaching road from London to Edinburgh when the marriage laws in England became more restrictive than Scotland's, where, for a time at least, boys and girls in their early teens could marry without parental permission. Gretna Green was the first place in Scotland runaway couples reached after crossing the border, hence its fame and the fact that over 1,000 couples a year still go there to marry. Today it also contains a shop and restaurant, as well as the Courtship Maze (£2), two rings that couples enter separately in the hope of finding each other. ⊠ *Headless Cross* ☎ *01461/338441* ⊕ *www.gretnagreen. com* ☑ *Museum £3.75.*

SPORTS AND THE OUTDOORS

Powfoot Golf Club. A pleasant mix of links and parkland holes, this course looks out across the Solway Firth. Its roughs and the tough thorny whins (local bushes with yellow flowers) make the course quite challenging, especially when the wind blows off the firth in summer, but it is the views from here that make it memorable and a pleasure to play. Powfoot is included in the Gateway to Golf Pass. The club is 14 miles west of Gretna Green via the A75. ⊠ *Off B724, Cummertrees, Annan* ☎ *01461/204100* ⊕ *www.powfootgolfclub.com* ☑ *Mid-Mar.– Sept., £40 weekdays, £46 weekends; Oct.–early Mar., £23* ⚑ *18 holes, 6250 yards, par 71.*

DUMFRIES

24 miles west of Gretna Green, 76 miles south of Glasgow, 81 miles southwest of Edinburgh.

The River Nith meanders through Dumfries, and the pedestrian-only center of this town of 31,000 makes wandering and shopping a pleasure. Author J. M. Barrie (1860–1937) spent his childhood in Dumfries, and the garden of Moat Brae House is said to have inspired his boyish dreams in *Peter Pan.* But the town also has a justified claim to Robert Burns, who lived and worked here for several years. His house and his favorite *howff* (pub), The Globe Inn, are here, too, as is his final resting place in St. Michael's Churchyard.

The Borders and the Southwest

The Dumfries & Galloway Tourist Board has a lodging service, and also sells golf passes for the region at £70 for three rounds.

GETTING HERE AND AROUND

Public transportation is a good option for reaching Dumfries—there's a good train station here, and most major Scottish cities have regular daily bus routes to the town. If you're driving from Gretna Green, take the A75; it's a 35-minute drive. From Glasgow, take the M74 to the A701. From Edinburgh, take the A701.

ESSENTIALS

Visitor Information Dumfries & Galloway Tourist Board. ⊠ *64 Whitesands* ☎ *01387/253862* ⊕ *www.visitscotland.com.*

EXPLORING
ROBERT BURNS SIGHTS

Globe Inn. Poet Robert Burns spent quite a lot of time at the Globe Inn, where he frequently fell asleep in the tack room beside the stables; today it's still an active pub where you can eat and drink. Burns later graduated to the upstairs bedroom where he slept with his wife, Jean Armour, and scratched some lines of poetry on the window. The room is preserved (or at least partly re-created), and the bar staff will happily show you around if you ask. ⊠ *56 High St.* ☎ *01387/252335* ⊕ *www. globeinndumfries.co.uk* ☜ *Free.*

Robert Burns Centre. Not surprisingly, Dumfries has its own Robert Burns Centre, housed in a sturdy 18th-century former mill overlooking the River Nith. The center has an audiovisual program and an extensive exhibit about the life of the poet. There's a restaurant upstairs. ⊠ *Mill Rd.* ☎ *01387/264808* ⊕ *www.dumgal.gov.uk/artsandmuseums* ☜ *Free.*

Robert Burns House. Poet Robert Burns (1759–96) lived here, on what was then called Mill Street, for the last three years of his life, when his salary from the customs service allowed him to improve his living standards. Many distinguished writers of the day visited him here, including William Wordsworth. The house contains some of his writings and letters, a few pieces of furniture, and some family memorabilia. ⊠ *Burns St.* ☎ *01387/255297* ⊕ *www.dumgal.gov.uk/artsandmuseums* ☜ *Free.*

St. Michael's Churchyard. When he died in 1796, poet Robert Burns was buried in a modest grave in St. Michael's Churchyard. English poet William Wordsworth, visiting a few years later, was horrified by the small gravestone and raised money to build this much grander monument. ⊠ *39 Cardiness St.* ☎ *01387/253849* ⊕ *www.dumgal.gov.uk/artsandmuseums* ☜ *Free.*

OTHER ATTRACTIONS

Dumfries Museum and Camera Obscura. A camera obscura is essentially a huge reflecting mirror that projects an extraordinarily clear panoramic view of the surrounding countryside onto an internal wall. The one at the Dumfries Museum is housed in the old Windmill Tower, built in 1836. The museum itself covers the culture and daily life of the people living in the Dumfries and Galloway region from the earliest times. ⊠ *Rotchell Rd.* ☎ *01387/253374* ⊕ *www.dumgal.gov.uk/artsandmuseums* ☜ *Museum free; Camera Obscura £2.30* ☉ *Closed Nov.–Mar.*

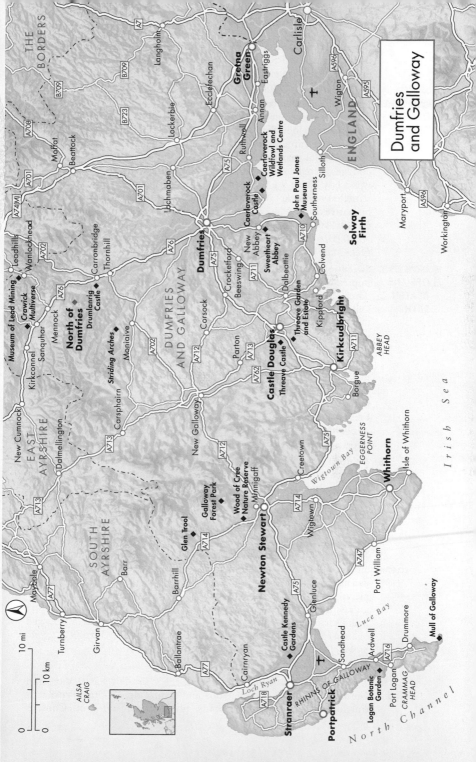

Dumfries and Galloway

Gracefield Arts Centre. With galleries hosting changing exhibits of Scottish art mostly from the 1840s to today, Gracefield Arts Centre also has a well-stocked crafts shop. A café serves lunch and snacks. ✉ *28 Edinburgh Rd.* ☎ *01387/262084* ⊕ *www.exploreart.co.uk* ☞ *Free.*

OFF THE BEATEN PATH

John Paul Jones Museum. The little community of Kirkbean is the backdrop for the bright-green landscape of the Arbigland Estate; in a cottage here, now the John Paul Jones Museum, John Paul (1747–92), the son of an estate gardener, was born. He eventually left Scotland, added "Jones" to his name, and became the founder of the U.S. Navy. The cottage where he was born is furnished as it would have been when he was a boy. There is an informative video, which you watch in a reconstruction of his captain's cabin. Jones returned to raid the coastline of his native country in 1778, an exploit recounted in an adjoining visitor center. ✉ *Off A710, Kirkbean* ✛ *12 miles south of Dumfries on the A710* ☎ *01387/880613* ⊕ *www.jpj.demon.co.uk* ☞ *£4.50* ⊙ *Closed Oct.–Mar.*

OFF THE BEATEN PATH

Sweetheart Abbey. At the center of the village of New Abbey are the impressive red-tinted, roofless remains of Sweetheart Abbey. The odd name is a translation of the abbey's previous name, St. Mary of the Dulce Cor. The abbey was founded in 1273 by the Lady of Galloway, Devorgilla (1210–90), who, it is said, had her late husband's heart placed in a tiny casket that she carried everywhere. After she died, she was laid to rest in Sweetheart Abbey with the casket resting on her breast. The couple's son John Balliol (1249–1315) was the puppet king installed in Scotland by Edward of England when the latter claimed sovereignty over Scotland. After John's appointment the Scots gave him a scathing nickname that would stay with him for the rest of his life: Toom Tabard (Empty Shirt). ✉ *A710, New Abbey* ✛ *7 miles south of Dumfries* ☎ *01387/253849* ⊕ *www.historic-scotland.gov.uk* ☞ *£5.*

WHERE TO EAT

$ ✕ **Cavens Arms.** This lively, welcoming traditional pub in the center of
BRITISH   town has a separate bar and dining area, comfortable seating, and a large selection of beers. It's a magnet for locals at dinnertime and always seems to be busy, a testimony to the quality of its food as well as the large portions. **Known for:** local beers; good food in generous pub portions; vibrant atmosphere. Ⓢ *Average main: £13* ✉ *20 Buccleuch St.* ☎ *01387/252896.*

$$ ✕ **Hullabaloo.** Occupying the top floor of the Robert Burns Centre, itself
ECLECTIC   an old mill, this restaurant serves a substantial, varied lunch and dinner menu. The melts are the highlight of the imaginative, tasty lunch menu, and the dinner menu is equally ambitious, ranging from roe deer loin with tomato pesto to king prawns flambéed in vodka. **Known for:** melts for lunch; creative vegan menu; prawns in vodka. Ⓢ *Average main: £16* ✉ *Robert Burns Centre, Mill Rd.* ☎ *01387/259679* ⊕ *www. hullabaloorestaurant.co.uk* ⊙ *Closed Sun. No dinner Mon.*

WHERE TO STAY

$$ ▦ **Cairndale Hotel.** Centrally located, the Cairndale has a Victorian
HOTEL   Gothic appearance and spacious and comfortable rooms. **Pros:** central location; comfortable rooms; pool, sauna, and gym. **Cons:** a

generally old-fashioned feel. [$] *Rooms from: £143* ✉ *132–6 English St.* ☎ *01387/354111* 🌐 *www.cairndalehotel.co.uk* 🛏 *91 rooms* 🍴 *Breakfast.*

$ HOTEL 🏨 **Holiday Inn.** With the secluded feel of a country hotel, this modern Holiday Inn less than 2 miles from the center of Dumfries is set in the Crichton Estate (owned by the University of the West of Scotland), with its lush plantings, rock gardens, and elegant Victorian buildings. **Pros:** beautiful setting; easy access to Dumfries; rooms for people with disabilities. **Cons:** slightly institutional feel. [$] *Rooms from: £85* ✉ *Bankend Rd., Crichton* ☎ *01387/272410* 🌐 *www.hidumfries.co.uk* 🛏 *71 rooms* 🍴 *Breakfast.*

SHOPPING

Dumfries is the main shopping center for the region, with all the big-name chain stores as well as specialty shops.

Fodor's Choice ★ **Loch Arthur Creamery and Farm Shop.** Known for its high-quality dairy products, this lively and active farm run by the Camphill community in the charmingly named village of Beeswing has an expansive café and retail store selling a range of organic products. Much of what you eat or buy is produced on the farm, where they make their own bread, butcher their meat, and cook the delicious food served here. The building itself has large windows opening directly on to the fields beyond. ✉ *A711, 6 miles south of Dumfries on the A711, Beeswing* ☎ *01387/259669* 🌐 *www.locharthur.org.uk.*

SPORTS AND THE OUTDOORS

G&G Cycle Centre. You can rent bicycles here, and the staff gives good advice on route options. ✉ *10–12 Academy St.* ☎ *01387/259483* 🌐 *www.cycle-centre.co.uk.*

NORTH OF DUMFRIES

18 miles northwest of Dumfries.

Travel north along the A70 from Dumfries for a short trip through time at some very different attractions. Drumlanrig Castle is one of Scotland's grandest houses, set amid hills, moorland, and forest. In contrast, the world of lead miners, explored at the Museum of Lead Mining, was a great deal harsher. A spectacular modern addition to the area, the land artwork *Crawick Multiverse,* transforms the landscape into a mirror of the heavens. Sculptor Andy Goldsworthy's *Striding Arches* frame a natural space and invite the walker to explore them.

GETTING HERE AND AROUND

Trains run from Dumfries to Sanquhar, near *Crawick Multiverse.* You can get a bus from Dumfries to Drumlanrig and Sanquhar along the A701. For Ledhills and the mining museum, it's best to drive. The same is true for *Striding Arches*: Take the A76 from Dumfried to Thornhill, and then the A702 toward Monaive.

EXPLORING

Fodor's Choice ★ ***Crawick Multiverse.*** The extraordinary 2015 land artwork by Charles Jencks, 45 minutes north of Dumfries near the village of Sanquhar, must surely become a focus for visitors to the region for years to come. Jencks has transformed a 55-acre site, once an open-pit mine, into a beautiful and inspiring created landscape, at the heart of which are two grass spiral mounds that represent the Milky Way and the Andromeda Constellation. But they are simply the heart of a site where woodland, moor, mountain, and desert meet. Local rocks have been lifted to form avenues and labyrinths across the site. As you look across from its highest point, it is as if you were looking in a mirror in which the skies were reflected on the earth. Set aside two or three hours at least for the experience. ⊠ *Crawick, off B740, by Sanquhar* ✛ *Take the A75 toward Kirkconnel from Sanquhar, then turn on to the B740 (signposted Crawfordjohn)* ☎ *01659/50242* ⊕ *www.crawickmultiverse.co.uk* ⊠ *£5* ☞ *Nov.–Feb., pedestrian access only; road to site and parking lot are closed.*

FAMILY
Fodor's Choice
★**Drumlanrig Castle.** A spectacular estate, Drumlanrig Castle is as close as Scotland gets to the treasure houses of England—which is not surprising, since it's owned by the dukes of Buccleuch, one of the wealthiest British peerages. Resplendent with romantic turrets, this pink-sandstone palace was constructed between 1679 and 1691 by the first Duke of Queensbury, who, after nearly bankrupting himself building the place, stayed one night and never returned. The Buccleuchs inherited the palace and filled the richly decorated rooms with paintings by Holbein, Rembrandt, and Murillo, among others. Because of the theft of a Leonardo da Vinci painting in 2003, all visits are conducted by guided tour. There's also a playground, a gift shop, and a tearoom. The grounds are varied and good for mountain biking; bikes can be rented at the castle. ⊠ *Off A76, Thornhill* ✛ *18 miles northwest of Dumfries* ☎ *01848/600283* ⊕ *www.drumlanrig.com* ⊠ *Park £6, castle and park £10* ☉ *Castle closed Sept.–mid-Apr. Grounds closed Oct.–Mar.*

Museum of Lead Mining. The Lochnell Mine was abandoned in 1861, after 150 years of operation, and the mine and miners' homes now form part of this museum re-creating their lives. The isolated village of Warnlockhead, where the mine was located, has not changed a great deal since then—there was little alternative employment for the miners and their families. The visitor center, housed in the old smithy, exhibits some of the minerals the mine yielded. The nearby Leadhills and Warnlockhead Narrow Gauge Railway runs on weekends throughout the summer and costs £4, with a 10% reduction for a joint ticket with the museum. ⊠ *Off B797, Wanlockhead* ✛ *32 miles north of Dumfries* ☎ *01659/74387* ⊕ *www.leadminingmuseum.co.uk* ⊠ *£9.50* ☉ *Closed Oct.–Mar.*

Striding Arches. British sculptor Andy Goldsworthy's extraordinary piece of public landscape art enriches the great natural amphitheater at Cairnhead in the southern uplands of Dumfries and Galloway. His three red-sandstone arches stand 13 feet high and mark out the area, "striding" across the landscape. ⊠ *Cairnhead Forest, near Moniaive* ✛ *Take the A702 (off the A76 at Thornhill) to Moniaive, then the road to Benbuie until you reach The Byre. From there it is a walk to the viewpoint* ☎ *07801/232229* ⊕ *www.stridingarches.com* ⊠ *Free.*

SOLWAY FIRTH

10 miles south of Dumfries.

Mostly undiscovered by travelers, the Solway Firth is a must for walkers, cyclists, and bird-watchers. This lovely and protected inlet, guarded by beautiful Caerlaverock Castle, is a haven for a great variety of seabirds. You can see them at the nature reserve behind the castle. Cycling or on foot, you can stroll gentle coastal paths beside the firth that link the villages of Sandyhills, Rockcliffe, and Kippford.

GETTING HERE AND AROUND

There is a bus from Dumfries to Kippford (one hour), but a car is best for visiting this area. Take the A710 from Dumfries and then the A711.

EXPLORING

Fodor's Choice ★ **Caerlaverock Castle.** The stunningly beautiful moated Caerlaverock Castle stands in splendid isolation amid the surrounding wetlands that form the Caerlaverock Nature Reserve. Built in a unique triangular design, this 13th-century fortress has solid-sandstone masonry and an imposing double-tower gatehouse. King Edward I of England (1239–1307) besieged the castle in 1300, when his forces occupied much of Scotland at the start of the Wars of Independence. A splendid residence was built inside in the 1600s. Now largely in ruins, the interior is still atmospheric, and the siege engines on the grounds give some sense of what medieval warfare was like. The castle has a pleasant café for coffee, cakes, or lunch. ✉ *Off B725, Ruthwell* ✣ *10 miles south of Dumfries* ☎ *01387/770244* 🌐 *www.historicenvironment.scot* 🎟 *£6.*

Caerlaverock Wildfowl and Wetlands Centre. You can observe wintering wildfowl, including species of geese, ducks, swans, and raptors, on the wetlands surrounding Caerlaverock Castle. In summer, ospreys patrol the waters of this wild and beautiful place, the northernmost outpost of the Wildfowl and Wetlands Trust. The triops, the tadpole shrimp that is one of the oldest known species, lives in the aquarium here. There are bats and badgers, sparrows, and natterjack toads as well. Free guided walks are available in the afternoons throughout the year. ✉ *Eastpark Farm, Off B725, Dumfries* ✣ *9 miles southeast of Dumfries off the A75* ☎ *01387/770200* 🌐 *www.wwt.org.uk* 🎟 *£7.68.*

WHERE TO STAY

$ B&B/INN 🏨 **Anchor Hotel.** In the picturesque village of Kippford, this small, friendly hotel has wonderful views across the Solway Firth, and while the rooms are small and plainly furnished, all of them gaze out over the water. **Pros:** lovely location; friendly atmosphere; good pub food. **Cons:** small rooms; bar can be noisy at times. [$] *Rooms from: £80* ✉ *Main St., Kippford* ✣ *Take the A710 south from Dalbeattie and turn into Kippford (3 miles)* ☎ *01556/620205* 🌐 *www.anchorhotelkippford.co.uk* 🛏 *6 rooms* 🍴 *Breakfast.*

CASTLE DOUGLAS

18 miles southwest of Dumfries, 25 miles west of Caerlaverock Castle, 84 miles south of Glasgow, 90 miles southwest of Edinburgh.

A quaint town that sits beside Carlingwark Loch, Castle Douglas is a popular base for exploring the surrounding countryside. The loch sets off the town perfectly, reflecting its dramatic architecture of sharp spires and soft sandstone arches. Its main thoroughfare, King Street, has unique shops and eateries.

GETTING HERE AND AROUND

There's no train station in Castle Douglas, and buses from Dumfries make several stops along the way. The best way to get here is by car. From Dalbeattie, take the A711/A745 (10 minutes). From Glasgow, take the A713 (just under two hours). From Edinburgh, take the A70 (a little over 2 hours).

BICYCLING TOURS

Galloway Cycling Holidays. For a slower-paced look at the sights in the region, take a bike tour that begins in Castle Douglas. The small outfit is run by a local resident and former police officer, Robin Hogg, and options range from two- to three-day self-guided tours (with luggage transfer and lodging included) to seven-day guided tours. ⊠ *Castle Douglas* ☎ *1556/502979* ⊕ *gallowaycycling.co.uk* 🖃 *From £135.*

ESSENTIALS

Visitor Information Castle Douglas. ⊠ *Market Hill* ☎ *01556/502611* ⊕ *www.visitscotland.com.*

EXPLORING

Fodor's Choice **Threave Castle.** At this early home of the Black Douglases, who were the earls of Nithsdale and lords of Galloway, the imposing towers reflect well the Lord of Galloway who built it, Archibald the Grim, in the 14th century. Not to be confused with the mansion in Threave Gardens, the castle was dismantled in the religious wars of the mid-17th century, though enough of it remained to have housed prisoners from the Napoleonic Wars two centuries later. It's a few minutes from Castle Douglas by car and is signposted from the main road. To get here, leave your car in a farmyard and make your way down to the edge of the river. Ring the bell (loudly) and, rather romantically, a boatman will come to ferry you across to the great stone tower looming from a marshy island in the river. ⊠ *A75, 3 miles west of Castle Douglas* ☎ *07711/223101* ⊕ *www. historicenvironment.scot* 🖃 *£5 including ferry; buy tickets online or from the NTS Osprey Centre on the site* ۞ *Closed Nov.–Mar.*

Threave Garden and Estate. The National Trust for Scotland cares for the gently sloping parkland and gardens around an 1867 mansion built by William Gordon, a Liverpool businessman. The house, fully restored in the 1930s, gives a glimpse into the daily life of a prosperous 19th-century family. The grounds demand an army of gardeners, and today many of them are students at the National Trust's School of Heritage Gardening, which has developed the variety of gardens here. Bats, ospreys, and other birds and animals share the space. Entry to the house is by timed guided tour, and it's wise to book ahead. There's an on-site restaurant. ✉ *South of A75* ✥ *1 mile west of Castle Douglas* ☎ *01556/502575* 🌐 *www.nts.org.uk/Visits* 🎫 *Gardens £7.50, house and gardens £12.50* 🕒 *House closed Nov.–Mar.*

WHERE TO EAT

$ CAFÉ 🍴 **The Café at Designs Gallery.** For a good balance of art and food, look no further than this café at a contemporary art and crafts gallery in the town center. You'll find the freshest ingredients here, from soup to salads, sandwiches to quiches; everything is made on-site, including the bread, and it's all organic. **Known for:** good lunch menu; homemade soups; lovely garden. [$] *Average main: £9* ✉ *179 King St.* ☎ *01556/504552* 🌐 *www.designsgallery.co.uk* 🕒 *Closed Sun. No dinner.*

SHOPPING

A.D. Livingston and Sons. Fine-furniture restorers and makers in wood and raffia, the Livingstons have a shop in the main street, and some of their work is displayed two doors down under an arch into a charming lane. ✉ *183 King St.* ☎ *01556/504234* 🌐 *www.livingstons-antiques.co.uk.*

By the Book. This well-stocked and (more importantly) well-organized secondhand bookshop on Castle Douglas's main shopping street has large windows that invite you in to browse, which you can do without interruption—there's bound to be something you want, though it may be in a box or under the table. ✉ *201 King St.* ☎ *01556/503338.*

Galloway Gems and Craft Centre and Outback Yarns. In this glittery shop you can purchase mineral specimens, polished stone slices, and a range of Celtic- and Nordic-inspired jewelry, as well as craft materials of every kind. For fiber artists and sewers, it's a real find. ✉ *130–132 King St.* ☎ *01556/503254* 🌐 *www.outbackyarns.co.uk.*

SPORTS AND THE OUTDOORS

BICYCLING

Castle Douglas Cycle Centre. You can rent bicycles for everyone in the family from Castle Douglas Cycle Centre. It also handles repairs and service. ✉ *Church St.* ☎ *01556/504542* 🌐 *www.cdbikes.co.uk.*

BOATING

Galloway Activity Centre. With dinghies, kayaks, and canoes for rent, the Galloway Activity Centre on the banks of Loch Ken specializes in water sports. "Dry" sports include mountain biking, archery, and rock climbing. ✉ *Shirmers Bridge, Loch Ken* ✥ *10 miles northwest of Castle Douglas off A713* ☎ *01556/502011* 🌐 *www.lochken.co.uk.*

GOLF

Southerness Golf Club. Mackenzie Ross designed this course, the first built in Scotland after World War II. Southerness is a long course, played over extensive links with fine views southward over the Solway Firth. The greens are hard and fast, and the frequent winds make for some testing golf. Thursday is reserved for women. The regional Gateway to Golf Pass can be used here. ✉ *Southerness St., Southerness* ✥ *19 miles west of Castle Couglas via the A745 and B793* ☎ *01387/880677* 🌐 *www.southernessgolfclub.com* 🎫 *Summer £55 weekdays, £65 weekends; winter £33 weekdays, £38 weekends* 🏌 *18 holes, 6110 yards, par 69* ✍ *Reservations essential.*

4

KIRKCUDBRIGHT

9 miles southwest of Castle Douglas, 89 miles south of Glasgow, 99 miles southwest of Edinburgh.

Kirkcudbright (pronounced kir-*coo*-bray) is an 18th-century town of Georgian and Victorian houses, some of them washed in pastel shades and roofed with the blue slate of the district. It sits on an inlet from the Solway Firth. In the early 20th century the town became a haven for artists, and its L-shape main street is full of crafts and antiques shops.

GETTING HERE AND AROUND

Driving is your best and only real option. From Castle Douglas, take the A711 (15 minutes). From Glasgow, take the A713 (about two hours). From Edinburgh, take the A701 (about 2½ hours).

ESSENTIALS

Visitor Information Kirkcudbright Tourist Information Centre. ⊠ *Harbour Sq.* ☎ *01557/330494* ⊕ *www.visitscotland.com.*

EXPLORING

Fodor's Choice
★

Broughton House. The 18th-century Broughton House was the home of the artist E. A. Hornel from 1901 until his death in 1933 and remains largely as it was in his time. Hornel was a member of the late-19th-century school of painters called the "Glasgow Boys," who were influenced by the Vienna Secession and art nouveau. You can see many of his paintings in the gallery Hornel built onto the house to impress the guests and buyers who came to see his work. His use and love of color is obvious in the beautiful garden, which combines lawns, ponds, and formal and wildflower beds. The knowledgeable guides will gladly provide information about the life and work of the painter. ⊠ *12 High St.* ☎ *01557/330437* ⊕ *www.nts.org.uk* ⊠ *£6.50* ⊗ *House closed Nov.–Mar. Garden closed Nov.–Jan.*

MacLellan's Castle. Conspicuous in the center of town are the stone walls of MacLellan's Castle, a once-elaborate castellated mansion dating from the 16th century. You can walk around the interior, still atmospheric even though the rooms are bare. The "Lairds Lug," behind the fireplace, allowed the *laird* (lord) to listen in to what his guests were saying about him. You can also get a glimpse of life below stairs in the kitchen vaults beneath the main staircase. The mansion has lovely views over the town. ⊠ *Off High St.* ☎ *01557/331856* ⊕ *www.historicenvironment. scot* ⊠ *£4* ⊗ *Closed Oct. Mar.*

Stewartry Museum. Stuffed with all manner of local paraphernalia, the delightfully old-fashioned Stewartry Museum allows you to putter and absorb as much or as little as takes your interest in the display cases. Stewartry is the former name of Kirkcudbright. ⊠ *St. Mary St.* ☎ *01557/331643* ⊕ *www.dumgal.gov.uk* ⊠ *Free.*

Tolbooth Arts Centre. In the 17th-century tolbooth (a combination town hall–courthouse–prison), the Tolbooth Arts Centre describes how the town attracted famous artists, among them E. A. Hornel, Jessie King, and Charles Oppenheimer. Some of their paintings are on display, as are works by contemporary artists. ⊠ *High St.* ☎ *01557/331556* ⊕ *www. dumgal.gov.uk* ⊠ *Free* ⊗ *Closed Sun. Oct.–May.*

WHERE TO EAT AND STAY

$$ | MODERN BRITISH | ✕ **Artistas at the Selkirk Arms.** Paintings of Scotland, starched white table-cloths, and giant windows overlooking the well-kept garden beckon you into this highly praised eatery. Locals love that the food on the bar and regular menus is locally sourced and full of imagination. **Known for:** local produce; both familiar and more exotic dishes; charming location in town. $ *Average main: £16* ✉ *Selkirk Arms, High St.* ☎ *01557/330402* ⊕ *www.selkirkarmshotel.co.uk.*

$$ | HOTEL | ⊡ **Selkirk Arms.** Bursting with charm, this elegant 18th-century hotel has a lot going for it, including spacious guest rooms that are individually decorated with cozy beds, contemporary wood furniture, and soft lighting. **Pros:** attentive service; massive breakfast; lively traditional pub. **Cons:** rooms closest to restaurant can be noisy; bar gets crowded during sporting events. $ *Rooms from: £112* ✉ *High St.* ☎ *01557/330402* ⊕ *www.selkirkarmshotel.co.uk* ⤳ *16 rooms* ⏐◎⏐ *Breakfast.*

NEWTON STEWART

18 miles northwest of Kirkcudbright, 77 miles southwest of Glasgow, 105 miles southwest of Edinburgh.

The bustling town of Newton Stewart is the place to stop when touring the western region of Galloway. It is the gateway to the Galloway Forest and Glen Trool.

GETTING HERE AND AROUND

Newton Stewart does not have a train station, but the town is served by regular buses from Glasgow and Edinburgh as well as local buses from neighboring towns. By car from Glasgow, take the A77 (about two hours). From Edinburgh, take the A702 (about 2¾ hours).

ESSENTIALS

Visitor Information Newton Stewart Visitor Information. ⊕ *www.newton-stewart.org.*

EXPLORING

Fodor'sChoice ★ **Galloway Forest Park.** You can walk or bicycle along the paths at the Galloway Forest Park through moorland and forests, by lochs and over hills—all contained within the 300 square miles of the forest. The Forestry Commission, which manages the forest, has three visitor centers at Glen Trool, Kirroughtree, and Clatteringshaws, where there are exhibits about the region's wildlife and a reconstruction of an Iron Age dwelling. The forest is designated as a Dark Sky Park; the low light pollution here ensures exceptional stargazing. ✉ *A712, 7 miles northeast of Newton Stewart* ☎ *01671/402420* ⊕ *www.gallowayforestpark.com* ▦ *Free.*

Glen Trool. With high purple-and-green hilltops shorn rock-bare by glaciers, and with a dark, winding loch and thickets of birch trees sounding with birdcalls, Glen Trool's setting almost looks more highland than the real Highlands. Note **Bruce's Stone,** just above the parking lot, marking the site where in 1307 Scotland's champion Robert the Bruce (King Robert I, 1274–1329) won his first victory in the Scottish Wars of Independence. A little road off A714 leads through increasingly wild woodland scenery to a parking lot. The visitor center is open daily.

Only after you have climbed for a few minutes onto a heathery knoll does the full, rugged panorama become apparent. Driving is really the only way to get to Glen Trool, which is part of Galloway Forest Park. From Glasgow, take the A77 (about 2¼ hours). From Edinburgh, take the A702 (about three hours). ✉ *Off A714, Bargrennan ✛ A714 north from Newton Stewart for about 15 mins; turn right at the signpost for Glen Trool* ☎ *01671/840302* ⊕ *www.forestry.gov.uk* ✉ *Free.*

Wood of Cree Nature Reserve. Birders love the Wood of Cree Nature Reserve, managed by the Royal Society for the Protection of Birds. In the reserve you can see such species as the redstart, pied flycatcher, and wood warbler. To get there, take the minor road that travels north from Newton Stewart alongside the River Cree east of the A714. The entrance is next to a small parking area at the side of the road. ✉ *Off A714 ✛ 4 miles north of Newton Stewart* ☎ *01988/402130* ⊕ *www. rspb.org.uk* ✉ *Donations accepted.*

WHERE TO STAY

$$
HOTEL
⬚ **Creebridge House Hotel.** Close to the River Cree and set among gardens and woodland, the Creebridge places the emphasis on comfort and quiet rural surroundings. **Pros:** practical center for exploring the area; comfort in a rural setting; within easy reach of Newton Stewart. **Cons:** slightly conservative feel. Ⓢ *Rooms from: £150* ✉ *Minigaff ✛ Off B7079* ☎ *01671/402121* ⊕ *www.creebridge.co.uk* ➬ *18 rooms* ⦿ *Breakfast.*

WHITHORN

17 miles south of Newton Stewart, 94 miles southwest of Glasgow, 121 miles southwest of Edinburgh.

Known for its early-Christian settlement, Whithorn is full of history. The main street is notably wide, with pretty pastel buildings nestled up against each other, their low doorways and small windows creating images of years long past. It's still mainly a farming community, but is fast becoming a popular tourist destination. Several scenes from the original *Wicker Man* (1973) were shot in and around the area. During the summer months, it's a popular place for festivals. The Isle of Whithorn, just beyond the town, is not an island at all but a fishing village of great charm.

GETTING HERE AND AROUND

There's no train station in Whithorn, and most of the buses are local (getting to main Scottish cities from Whithorn takes careful planning and several transfers). To drive from Newton Stewart, take the A714 and then A746. From Glasgow, take the A77 (about 2½ hours). From Edinburgh, take the A702 (about three hours).

EXPLORING

St. Ninian's Chapel. The Isle of Whithorn (a fishing village on the mainland) holds the ruins of the 14th-century St. Ninian's Chapel, where pilgrims who came by sea prayed before traveling inland to Whithorn Priory. Some people claim that this, and not Whithorn Priory, is the site of the Candida Casa, a 4th-century church. The structure seems to have been constructed on top of a much older chapel built around

1100. It's 4 miles south of Whithorn. ✉ *Isle of Whithorn* ✣ *Take A746 and B7004 from Whithorn* 🌐 *www.historic-scotland.gov.uk* 🎫 *Free.*

Whithorn Priory and Museum. The road that is now the A746 was a pilgrims' path that led to the royal burgh of Whithorn, where sat Whithorn Priory, one of Scotland's great medieval cathedrals, now an empty shell. It was built in the 12th century and is said to occupy the site of a former stone church, the Candida Casa, built by St. Ninian in the 4th century. As the story goes, the church housed a shrine to Ninian, the earliest of Scotland's saints, and kings and barons tried to visit the shrine at least once in their lives. As you approach the priory, observe the royal arms of pre-1707 Scotland—that is, Scotland before the Union with England—carved and painted above the *pend* (covered walkway). The museum houses restored stonework from the period, including crosses. ✉ *Off A746* 🌐 *www.historicenvironment.scot* 🎫 *£5 (includes the Whithorn Story and Visitor Centre)* 🕒 *Closed Nov.–Mar.*

WHERE TO EAT

$ BRITISH 🍴 **Steam Packet Inn.** Lovely and old-fashioned, this inn is always full, mainly because of its good beer and hearty, well-cooked food including fish-and-chips and lamb shanks. Located directly on the harbor, it has few local rivals, but customers come from far and wide to eat here and walk the headland behind the pub to the rocky shore of the Solway Firth. **Known for:** superior pub food; outstanding desserts; fast and friendly service. [$] *Average main: £14* ✉ *Harbour Row, Isle of Whithorn* ☎ *01988/500334* 🌐 *www.thesteampacketinn.biz.*

STRANRAER

31 miles northwest of Whithorn, 86 miles southwest of Glasgow via A77, 131 miles southwest of Edinburgh.

Stranraer was for more than a century the main ferry port between Scotland and Northern Ireland. Its closure, and the transfer of ferry traffic to nearby Cairnryan, is changing the town now and in the future. The city center has had a major face-lift, and there are plans to redevelop the harbor as a leisure centre and transportation hub. Stranraer has a lovely garden.

GETTING HERE AND AROUND

Stranraer's train station is directly accessible from Glasgow; bus services are also good (with many connections to smaller towns). If you're driving, take the A747 from Whithorn (about 45 minutes). From Glasgow, take the M77/A77 (two hours), and from Edinburgh, take the A77 (three hours).

ESSENTIALS

Visitor Information Stranraer Visitor Information Centre. ✉ *28 Harbour St.* ☎ *01776/702595* 🌐 *www.visitscotland.com.*

EXPLORING

Fodor's Choice ★ **Castle Kennedy Gardens.** The lovely Castle Kennedy Gardens surround the shell of the original Castle Kennedy, which burned down in 1716. Parks scattered around the property were built by the second Earl of Stair in 1733. The earl was a field marshal and used his soldiers to help with the heavy work of constructing banks, ponds, and other major landscape features. When the rhododendrons are in bloom (April through July, depending on the variety), the effect is kaleidoscopic. There's also a pleasant tearoom. ✉ *Castle Kennedy* ✥ *3 miles east of Stranraer on the A875* ☎ *01776/702024* 🌐 *www.castlekennedygardens.co.uk* 🎫 *£5.50* 🕒 *Closed Nov.–Jan. and weekdays in Feb. and Mar.*

PORTPATRICK

8 miles southwest of Stranraer, 94 miles southwest of Glasgow, 139 miles southwest of Edinburgh.

The holiday town of Portpatrick lies across the Rhinns of Galloway from Stranraer. Once an Irish ferry port, Portpatrick's harbor eventually proved too small for larger vessels.

GETTING HERE AND AROUND

Direct buses travel between Portpatrick to Stranraer and some of the neighboring towns, but travel to and from the larger Scottish cities can prove more difficult. There is no train station in Portpatrick (though there is one in nearby Stranraer). Driving is probably your best bet. From Stranraer, take the A77; it's about a 15-minute journey. Take the M77/A77 from Glasgow (just over two hours) and the M8/A77 from Edinburgh (about three hours).

EXPLORING

Logan Botanic Garden. One of the four major sites belonging to the Edinburgh-based National Botanic Gardens of Scotland, the spectacular Logan Botanic Garden is a must-see for garden lovers. Displayed here are plants that enjoy the prevailing mild climate, especially tree ferns, cabbage palms, and other Southern Hemisphere exotica. There are free guided walks every second Tuesday of the month at 10:30 am; at other times there is a free audio guide. ✉ *Port Logan* ✥ *On B7065 16 miles south of Portpatrick* ☎ *01776/860231* 🌐 *www.rbge.org.uk* 🎫 *£6.50* 🕒 *Closed Nov.–mid-Mar.*

Mull of Galloway. If you wish to visit the southern tip of the Rhinns of Galloway, called the Mull of Galloway, follow the B7065/B7041 until you run out of land. The cliffs and seascapes here are rugged, and there's a lighthouse and the Mull of Galloway bird reserve. 🌐 *www.rspb.org.uk* 🕒 *Reserve closed Nov.–mid-Mar.*

Southern Upland Way. The village of Portpatrick is the starting point for Scotland's longest official long-distance footpath, the Southern Upland Way, which runs a switchback course for 212 miles to Cockburnspath, on the east side of the Borders. The path begins on the cliffs just north of the town and follows the coastline for 1½ miles before turning inland. 🌐 *www.southernuplandway.gov.uk* 🎫 *Free.*

WHERE TO STAY

$$ HOTEL 🏨 **Crown Portpatrick.** From the terrace of this simple small hotel in a working fishing village, you can look out across the sea to Ireland while eating some delicious seafood. **Pros:** beautiful location; very good restaurant. **Cons:** fairly remote town; extra cost for sea-view rooms. [$] *Rooms from: £120* ✉ *9 N. Crescent* ☎ *01776/810261* 🌐 *www.crown-portpatrick.com* 🛏 *12 rooms* 🍴 *Breakfast.*

5

FIFE AND ANGUS

Updated by
Nick Bruno

Breezy cliff-top walkways, fishing villages, and open beaches characterize Fife and Angus. They sandwich Scotland's fourth-largest city, the rejuvenated city of Dundee. Scotland's east coast has only light rainfall throughout the year; northeastern Fife, in particular, may claim the record for the most sunshine and the least rainfall in Scotland, which all adds to the enjoyment when you're touring the coast or the famous golf center of St. Andrews.

Fife proudly styles itself as a "kingdom," and its long history—which really began when the Romans went home in the 4th century and the Picts moved in—lends some substance to the boast. From medieval times its earls were first among Scotland's nobility and crowned her kings. For many, however, the most historic event in the region was the birth of golf, in the 15th century, which, legend has it, occurred in St. Andrews, an ancient university town with stone houses and seaside ruins. The Royal & Ancient Golf Club, the ruling body of the game worldwide, still has its headquarters here.

Not surprisingly, fishing and seafaring have also played a role in the history of the East Neuk coastal region. From the 16th through the 19th century a large population lived and worked in the small ports and harbors that form a chain around Fife's coast, which James V once called "a beggar's mantle fringed with gold." When the sun shines, this golden fringe—particularly at Tentsmuir, St. Andrews, and Elie—gleams like the beaches of Normandy. Indeed, the houses of the East Neuk villages have a similar character, with color-washed fronts, fishy weather vanes, outdoor stone stairways to upper floors, and crude carvings of anchors and lobsters on their lintels. All the houses are crowded on steep *wynds* (narrow streets), hugging pint-size harbors that in the golden era supported village fleets of 100 ships apiece.

North, across the Firth of Tay, lies the region of Angus, whose charm is its variety: in addition to its seacoast and pleasant Lowland market centers, there's also a hinterland of lonely rounded hills with long glens running into the typical Grampian Highland scenery beyond. One of Angus's interesting features, which it shares with the eastern Lowland edge of Perthshire, is its fruit-growing industry, which includes raspberries.

Known as the "City of Discovery" (after the RRS *Discovery*, a polar exploration vessel that set sail from this port in 1901), and as the United Kingdom's UNESCO City of Design, Dundee has a sophisticated arts and cultural scene and some beguiling sights. The ongoing regeneration of the city's waterfront has created a buzz, with the new cliff-shaped V&A Museum of Design making a bold statement beside the Tay. Today's Dundee makes a superb base for a cultural stay and from which to launch a number of day trips.

TOP REASONS TO GO

St. Andrews: With its medieval streets, ruined cathedral and castle, and peculiarly posh atmosphere, St. Andrews is one of the most incongruous yet beguiling places in Scotland—even without its famous golf course.

Great golf: If you can't get on the Old Course in St. Andrews by ballot or by any other means, Fife and Angus have fabulous fairways aplenty, including the famous links course at Carnoustie.

East Neuk: As you take in crowstep-gabled fishermen's cottages, winding cobbled lanes, seaside harbor scenes, and lovely beaches, you can almost imagine the harsh lives of the hardworking Fifers who lived in tiny hamlets such as Crail, Anstruther, Pittenweem, and Elie. Today artists and visitors make it all pleasantly picturesque.

Dundee: This formerly industrial city is becoming better known for its vibrant arts, music, theater, restaurant, and nightlife scenes. It's in a spectacular natural setting by Britain's most powerful river, the Tay.

The glens: The long Angus glens (such as Glen Clova) that run into the wild Grampian Mountains are magical places beloved by outdoors enthusiasts and those just wanting to rediscover nature.

ORIENTATION AND PLANNING

GETTING ORIENTED

Fife lies north of the Lothians, across the iconic bridges of the Firth of Forth. A headland, Fife's northeastern coast (or East Neuk) is fringed with golden sands, rocky shores, fishermen's cottages, and, of course, the splendor of St. Andrews, home of golf. Northwest of Fife and across the glorious Firth of Tay, the city of Dundee is undergoing a postindustrial reinvention. Its rural hinterland, Angus, hugs the city, which, stretching north toward the foothills of the Grampian Mountains, houses agricultural and fishing communities, and Glamis, one of Scotland's best-loved castles.

St. Andrews and East Neuk. St. Andrews isn't just a playground for golfers. This religious and academic center is steeped in history and prestige, with grand buildings, a palpable air of prosperity, and the cachet of being the place where a riveting 21st-century royal romance began. Beyond St. Andrews the colorful fishing villages of the East Neuk are a day-tripper's (and fish eater's) delight.

Dundee and Angus. Dundee has a knockout setting beside Britain's mightiest river, historical sights—including Captain Scott's ship, RRS *Discovery*—and a vibrant social life. The tree-lined country roads of the Angus heartlands roll through strawberry and raspberry fields to busy market towns, wee villages, and Glamis Castle.

PLANNING

WHEN TO GO

Spring in the Angus glens can be quite captivating, with the hills along Angus's northernmost boundary still covered in snow. Similarly, the moorland colors of autumn are appealing. However, Fife and Angus are really summer destinations, when most of the sights are open to visitors. St. Andrews hosts a number of international golf tournaments that effectively take over the town. Nongolfers may become incredibly frustrated when searching for accommodations or places to eat during these times, so check ahead.

PLANNING YOUR TIME

St. Andrews, 52 miles from Edinburgh, is not to be missed, for its history and atmosphere as much as for the golf; allot an overnight stop and at least a whole day if you can. The nearby East Neuk of Fife has some of Scotland's finest coastline, now becoming gentrified by the Edinburgh second-home set but still evoking Fife's past. A day's drive along A917 (allow for exploring and stops for ice cream and fish) will take you through the fishing villages of Elie, Pittenweem, Anstruther, and Crail. Dundee, with a rich maritime history and a grand museum, is an ideal base for a drive round the Angus towns of Arbroath, Kirriemuir, and Alyth; if you make a three-hour stop at Glamis Castle, this trip will take about a day.

RESTAURANTS

With an affluent population, St. Andrews supports several stylish hotel restaurants. Because it's a university town and popular tourist destination, there are also many good cafés and bistro-style restaurants. Bar lunches are the rule in large and small hotels throughout the region, and in seaside places the carry-*oot* (to-go) meal of fish-and-chips is an enduring tradition.

HOTELS

If you're staying in Fife, the obvious choice for a base is St. Andrews, with ample accommodations of all kinds. Another good option is the Howe of Fife, between Strathmiglo and Cupar, where there are some excellent country-house hotels, many with their own restaurants. Dundee and its hinterlands have a number of diverse accommodations, all of which offer good value. *Hotel reviews have been shortened. For full information, visit Fodors.com.*

WHAT IT COSTS IN POUNDS			
$	$$	$$$	$$$$
Restaurants	under £15	£15–£19	£20–£25	over £25
Hotels	under £100	£100–£160	£161–£220	over £220

Restaurant prices are the average cost of a main course at dinner or, if dinner is not served, at lunch. Hotel prices are the lowest cost of a standard double room in high season, including 20% V.A.T.

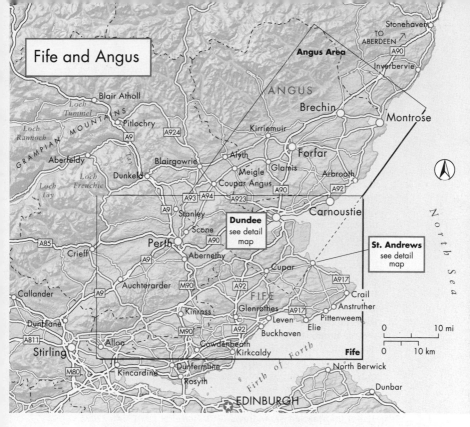

Fife and Angus

VISITOR INFORMATION

The Dundee and St. Andrews tourist offices are open year-round. Smaller tourist information centers operate seasonally in Arbroath, Brechin, Crail, Forfar, Kirriemuir, and Montrose.

ST. ANDREWS AND EAST NEUK

In its western parts Fife still bears the scars of heavy industry, especially coal mining, but these signs are less evident as you move east. Northeastern Fife, around the town of St. Andrews, seems to have played no part in the Industrial Revolution; instead, its residents earned a living from the grain fields or from the sea. Fishing has been a major industry, and in the past a string of Fife ports traded across the North Sea. Today the legacy of Dutch-influenced architecture, such as crowstep gables (the stepped effect on the ends of the roofs)—gives these East Neuk villages a distinctive character.

St. Andrews is unlike any other Scottish town. Once Scotland's most powerful ecclesiastical center as well as the seat of the country's oldest university and then, much later, the very symbol and spiritual home of golf, the town has a comfortable, well-groomed air, sitting almost smugly apart from the rest of Scotland. Its latest boast, being the town where Prince William first kissed Kate Middleton, has boosted university applications from around the world.

ST. ANDREWS

52 miles northeast of Edinburgh, 83 miles northeast of Glasgow.

Fodor's Choice It may have a ruined cathedral and a grand university—the oldest in
★ Scotland—but the modern claim to fame for St. Andrews is mainly its
status as the home of golf. Forget that Scottish kings were crowned here,
or that John Knox preached here and that Reformation reformers were
burned at the stake here. Thousands flock to St. Andrews to play at the
Old Course, home of the Royal & Ancient Club, and to follow in the
footsteps of Hagen, Sarazen, Jones, and Hogan.

The layout is pure Middle Ages: its three main streets—North, Market, and South—converge on the city's earliest religious site, near the
cathedral. Like most of the ancient monuments, the cathedral ruins are
impressive in their desolation—but this town is no dusty museum. The
streets are busy, the shops are stylish, the gray houses sparkle in the
sun, and the scene is particularly brightened during the academic year
by bicycling students in scarlet gowns.

GETTING HERE AND AROUND

If you arrive by car, be prepared for an endless drive round the town
as you look for a parking space. The parking lots around Rose Park
(behind the bus station and a short walk from the town center) are
your best bet. If you arrive by local or national bus, the bus station is a
five-minute walk from town. The nearest train station, Leuchars, is 10
minutes away by taxi (£15) or bus (£3), both of which can be found
outside the station. St. Andrews can be fully enjoyed on foot without
too much exertion.

ESSENTIALS

Visitor Information St. Andrews. ✉ *70 Market St.* ☎ *01334/472021*
⊕ *www.visitstandrews.com.*

EXPLORING

TOP ATTRACTIONS

Fodor's Choice **Bell Pettigrew Museum of Natural History.** Founded by Elsie Bell Pettigrew
★ in memory of her husband James, a former professor of medicine, this
fascinating collection of zoological specimens takes you from sea to
jungle, mountain to sky. The antiquated manner of their presentation
reminds you of their significance in an age when most of these creatures
were still unknown to most people. In the handsome 16th-century St.
Mary's Quadrangle, home to the St. Andrews University's divinity and
psychology departments, it is dominated by a holm oak supposedly
planted by Mary, Queen of Scots. ✉ *Bute Medical Bldg., Queens Gardens, off South St.* ☎ *01334/463608* ⊕ *www.st-andrews.ac.uk/museum/
bellpettigrew* ✆ *Free.*

British Golf Museum. Just opposite the Royal & Ancient Golf Club, this
museum explores the centuries-old relationship between St. Andrews
and golf and displays golf memorabilia from the 18th century to the
21st century. ✉ *Bruce Embankment* ☎ *01334/460046* ⊕ *www.british-
golfmuseum.co.uk* ✆ *£8.*

St. Andrews Castle. On the shore north of the cathedral stands ruined
St. Andrews Castle, begun at the end of the 13th century. The remains

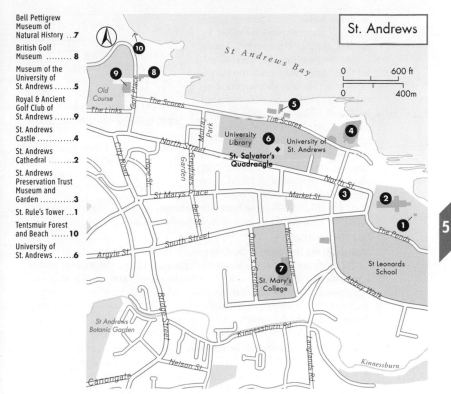

include a rare example of a cold and gruesome bottle-shape dungeon, in which many prisoners spent their last hours. Even more atmospheric is the castle's mine and countermine. The former was a tunnel dug by besieging forces in the 16th century; the latter, a tunnel dug by castle defenders in order to meet and wage battle belowground. You can stoop and crawl into this narrow passageway—an eerie experience, despite the addition of electric light. The visitor center has a good audiovisual presentation on the castle's history. In the summer, the beach below is popular with sunbathers and tide-pool investigators, weather permitting. ⊠ *N. Castle St.* ☎ *01334/477196* ⊕ *www.historicenvironment.scot* 🎫 *£6, £9 with St. Andrews Cathedral and St. Rule's Tower.*

St. Andrews Cathedral. These are the poignant remains of what was once the largest and most magnificent church in Scotland. Work on it began in 1160, and after several delays it was finally consecrated in 1318. The church was subsequently damaged by fire and repaired, but fell into decay during the Reformation. Only ruined gables, parts of the nave's south wall, and other fragments survive. The on-site museum helps you interpret the remains and gives a sense of what the cathedral must once have been like. ⊠ *Off Pends Rd.* ☎ *01334/472563* ⊕ *www. historicenvironment.scot* 🎫 *£5, includes St. Rule's Tower; £9 includes St. Andrews Castle.*

St. Rule's Tower. Local legend has it that St. Andrews was founded by St. Regulus, or Rule, who, acting under divine guidance, carried relics of St. Andrew by sea from Patras in Greece. He was shipwrecked on this Fife headland and founded a church. The holy man's name survives in the cylindrical tower, consecrated in 1126 and the oldest surviving building in St. Andrews. Enjoy dizzying views of town from the top of the tower, reached via a steep staircase. ⊠ *Off Pends Rd.* ☎ *01334/472563* ⊕ *www.historicenvironment.scot* 🖾 *£5, includes St. Andrews Cathedral; £9 includes St. Andrews Castle.*

> **ICE-CREAM TREATS**
>
> In summer the streets of St. Andrews are full of people walking around with a cone or slider (a wafer ice-cream sandwich). Luvians (84 Market Street) is like an old-fashioned sweet shop, while Jannetta's (31 South Street) has a more modern vibe. Which is best? Locals can't decide, so you'll have to try both.

WORTH NOTING

Museum of the University of St. Andrews. With four galleries, the Museum of the University of St. Andrews exhibits more than a few austere paintings from the 1600s all the way up to the present day. You'll also find ecumenical regalia, decorative arts, and early scientific instruments including Humphrey Cole's astrolabe of 1575. It also has sweeping views over St. Andrews Bay. ⊠ *7A the Scores* ☎ *01334/461660* ⊕ *www. st-andrews.ac.uk/musa* 🖾 *Free* ☉ *Closed Mon.–Wed. Nov.–Mar.*

Royal & Ancient Golf Club of St. Andrews. The ruling house of golf worldwide is the spiritual home of all who play or follow the game. Founded in 1754, its clubhouse on the dunes—open to members only, including women from September 2014—is a mix of classical, Victorian, and neoclassical styles; it's adjacent to the famous Old Course. ⊠ *The Scores* ⊕ *www.randa.org.*

St. Andrews Preservation Trust Museum and Garden. Housed in a stone 17th-century house and former fisherfolk dwelling, this charming museum run by friendly volunteers contains furniture, shop fittings, curious objects, and displays relating to St. Andrews's history. The real draw though—especially in bonnie weather—is the flower-filled garden and curious outbuildings including a laundry and twin-bowled privy. ⊠ *12 North St.* ☎ *01334/477629* ⊕ *www.standrewspreservationtrust.co.uk* 🖾 *Free (donations welcome).*

FAMILY
Fodor's Choice
★
Tentsmuir Forest and Beach. Ten miles north of St. Andrews, this wonderful 50-square-mile nature reserve contains a Scots and Corsican pine forest and the birdlife-rich Morton Lochs, fringing dynamic sand dunes and the long, sandy Kinshaldy Beach. Popular with families, beachcombers, and naturalists, the beach is 5 miles long and has enough space for everyone. ⊠ *B945, Leuchars* ⊕ *www.tentsmuir.org* 🖾 *Parking £2.*

University of St. Andrews. Scotland's oldest university is the alma mater of John Knox (Protestant reformer), King James II of Scotland, the Duke and Duchess of Cambridge (William and Kate), and Chris Hoy, Scotland's Olympic cyclist. Founded in 1411, the university's buildings pepper the town. For the quintessential University of St. Andrews experience, **St. Salvator's Quadrangle** reveals the magnificence of this historic institution. Looking out onto this impressive college green is the striking St. Salvator's Chapel, founded in 1450. It bears the marks of a turbulent past: the initials PH, carved into the paving stones under the bell tower, are those of Patrick Hamilton, who was burned alive outside the chapel for his Protestant beliefs. ✉ *St. Mary's Pl.*

WHERE TO EAT

$$$$ CONTEMPORARY Fodor's Choice ★ 🍴 **The Grange Inn.** Fife foodies flock to this beautifully converted 17th-century farmhouse surrounded by verdant fields just 10 minutes outside town. The atmospheric, dark-beamed, stone-walled interior has the warmth of an open fire and stunning views over the green landscape and St. Andrews. **Known for:** stunning location; great lunch deals; quality Scots produce. [$] *Average main: £30* ✉ *Grange Rd.* ☎ *01334/472670* 🌐 *www.thegrangeinn.com* 🕒 *Closed Mon. No dinner Sun.*

$$ CONTEMPORARY FAMILY 🍴 **Playfair's Restaurant and Steakhouse.** If all that sea air has made you ravenous, this restaurant under the Ardgowan Hotel offers quality sustenance elegantly presented at decent prices. Alongside hearty Scots staples like beef stovies (beef boiled with potatoes then mashed) served with oatcakes and haggis and neeps (turnips), there's the local butcher's steak cuts as well as seafood such as Hebredean salmon and Shetland scallops. **Known for:** quality steaks and seafood; thoughtfully presented dishes; relaxed gastropub atmosphere. [$] *Average main: £17* ✉ *2 Playfair Terr., North St.* ✣ *Underneath the Ardgowan Hotel* ☎ *01334/472970* 🌐 *playfairsrestaurant.co.uk.*

$ SEAFOOD 🍴 **Tailend Restaurant.** The line of customers outside might be a bit off-putting, but just focus on the sweet smell of fish-and-chips from St. Andrews's best "chipper." There's a light-filled dining room and modish seating area, or you can carry out and eat on the university grounds (though be wary of the dive-bombing gulls). The menu offers langoustine tails, seared scallops, and a fish of the day, but you can't go wrong with the haddock supper with chips. For a seafood splurge consider the five-course seasonal menu with matching wine flight. **Known for:** the best fish-and-chips in St. Andrews; Arbroath smokies. [$] *Average main: £13* ✉ *130 Market St.* ☎ *01334/474070* 🌐 *www.thetailend.co.uk.*

$ MODERN BRITISH FAMILY 🍴 **West Port Bar & Kitchen.** It's easy to forget that St. Andrews is a university town when the students are on summer break, but this modern bar and eatery remains vibrant and youthful year-round. The reasonably priced menu offers decent modern pub grub—everything from gourmet burgers to smoked haddock fishcakes to pork T-bone—making this a satisfying stop for lunch or dinner. **Known for:** lively beer garden; decent pub grub. [$] *Average main: £14* ✉ *170 South St.* ☎ *01334/473186* 🌐 *www.thewestport.co.uk.*

WHERE TO STAY

$$$$ HOTEL 🏨 **Fairmont St Andrews.** Two miles from St. Andrews, this modern hotel has spectacular views of the bay and two superb golf courses. **Pros:** spacious feel; excellent spa; golf at your doorstep. **Cons:** the huge atrium feels like a shopping center; paintings made to match the decor. [$] *Rooms from: £288* ✉ *A917* ☎ *01334/837000* 🌐 *www.fairmont.com/standrews* 🛏 *209 rooms* 🍽 *Breakfast.*

The Evolution of Golf

The matter of who invented golf has been long debated, but there's no doubt that its development into one of the most popular games in the world stems from Scotland. The first written reference to golf, variously spelled as "gowf" or "goff," was in 1457, when James II (1430–60) of Scotland declared that both golf and football (soccer) should be "*utterly cryit doune and nocht usit*" (publicly criticized and prohibited) because they distracted his subjects from archery practice. Mary, Queen of Scots (1542–87) was fond of golf. When in Edinburgh in 1567, she played on Leith Links and on Bruntsfield Links. When in Fife, she played at Falkland and at St. Andrews itself.

GOLF EXPANDS

Golf clubs (i.e., organizations) arose in the middle of the 18th century. The Honourable Company of Edinburgh Golfers, now residing at Muirfield, was founded in 1744. From then on, clubs sprang up all over Scotland: Royal Aberdeen (1780), Crail Golfing Society (1786), Dunbar (1794), and the Royal Perth Golfing Society (1824).

As for the town of St. Andrews, which now prospers on golf, golf schools, and golf equipment (the manufacture of golf balls is a local industry), locals say that the game was first played here with a piece of driftwood, a shore pebble, and a rabbit hole on the sandy, coastal turf. Residents were playing golf on the town links as far back as the 15th century. Rich golfers eventually formed exclusive clubs. The Royal & Ancient Golf Club of St. Andrews was founded in 1754.

By the early 19th century, clubs had been set up in England, and the game was being carried all over the world by enthusiastic Scots. These golf missionaries spread their knowledge not only of the sport, but also of the courses. Large parts of the Scottish coast are natural golf courses; indeed, the origins of bunkers and the word *links* (courses) are found in the sand dunes of Scotland's shores. Willie Park of Musselburgh, James Braid, and C. K. Hutchison are some of the best known of Scotland's golf-course architects.

CHANGES IN THE GAME

The original balls, called *featheries*, were leather bags stuffed with boiled feathers and often lasted only one round. In 1848, the gutta-percha ball, called a *guttie*, was introduced. It was in general use until the invention of the rubber-core ball in 1901. Clubs were made of wood with shafts of ash (later hickory), and heads of thorn, apple, or pear. Heads were spliced, then bound to the shaft with twine. Later in the 19th century, manufacturers began to experiment with metal in clubfaces and shafts. The technology of golf continues to change, but its addictive qualities are timeless.

$$
HOTEL
 ⚁ **Macdonald Rusacks.** The grand Victorian hotel building with grandstand views of the Old Course's 18th hole and West Sands offers affordable luxury and an unstuffy atmosphere. **Pros:** fabulous views; affordable food options; golf enthusiasts' heaven. **Cons:** service can fall short; bathrooms and bedroom decor lacks the wow factor. ⑨ *Rooms from: £150* ✉ *Pilmour, The Links* ☎ *0344/879–9136* ⊕ *www.macdonaldhotels.co.uk* ⇝ *70 rooms* ⦿ *Breakfast.*

$$$$ HOTEL Fodor's Choice ★ **Old Course Hotel.** Regularly hosting international golf stars and jet-setters, the Old Course Hotel has undergone a renaissance in the last five years—the guest rooms and public spaces have been reinvigorated, and the service has warmed up. **Pros:** fabulous location and lovely views; unpretentious service; golfer's heaven. **Cons:** all the golf talk might bore nongolfers; spa is on the small side; expensive. [$] *Rooms from: £399* ✉ *Old Station Rd.* ☎ *01334/474371* 🌐 *www.oldcoursehotel.co.uk* 🛏 *179 rooms* 🍴 *Breakfast.*

$$$$ HOTEL **Rufflets Country House Hotel.** Ten acres of formal and informal gardens surround this vine-covered country house just outside St. Andrews. **Pros:** attractive gardens; cozy drawing room; popular restaurant. **Cons:** too far to walk to St. Andrews; it's a venue for those celebrating. [$] *Rooms from: £230* ✉ *Strathkinness Low Rd.* ☎ *01334/472594* 🌐 *www.rufflets.co.uk* 🛏 *23 rooms* 🍴 *Breakfast.*

NIGHTLIFE AND PERFORMING ARTS

PUBS

Central Bar. There are still some old-fashioned pubs to be found among the cocktail bars of St. Andrews, and this wood-and-leather-furnished haunt is a good bet for a friendly mingle with a pint in hand. You'll find a good range of beers (bottled and on tap) and decent pub food. ✉ *77 Market St.* ☎ *01334/478296.*

FILM

New Picture House Cinema. A lovely old cinema shows a well-chosen mix of Hollywood and independent films. ✉ *117 North St.* ☎ *01334/474902* 🌐 *nph.nphcinema.co.uk.*

THEATER

Byre Theatre. Experimental plays, small-scale operatic performances, contemporary dance, musical performances, and film screenings are on the bill at the Byre. Its handsome café-bar and bistro serves excellent food. Look out for Byre in the Botanics performance listings in the summer months. ✉ *Abbey St.* ☎ *01334/475000* 🌐 *byretheatre.com.*

SHOPPING

Artery. This well-curated shop sells work by local, Scottish, and British artists, including jewelry, ceramics, paintings, and intriguing handmade clocks. ✉ *183 South St.* ☎ *01334/473153* 🌐 *arterygifts.com.*

Balgove Larder. Here you'll discover a huge selection of Scottish items, from spurtles (for stirring your porridge) to tablet (sugary toffee) to big, thick sausages made in its butchery. Foodies should check out the monthly Night Market, while carnivores can follow their noses to the Steak Barn, where platters piled with huge hunks of beef and sausages are combined with twice-fried chips and onion rings. ✉ *A91* ☎ *01334/898145* 🌐 *www.balgove.com.*

Mellis. This place is truly a cheese-lover's mecca. Look for a soft, crumbly local cheese called Anster. ✉ *149 South St.* ☎ *01334/471410* 🌐 *www.mellischeese.net.*

5

Topping and Company Booksellers. This is a bibliophile's dream haunt, with high ceilings and alcoves lined with over 45,000 titles, knowledgeable staff, and frequent readings and literary events. ⊠ *7 Greyfriars Garden* ☎ *01334/585 111* ⊕ *www.toppingbooks.co.uk.*

GOLF

What serious golfer doesn't dream of playing at world-famous St. Andrews? Seven St. Andrews courses, all part of the St. Andrews Trust, are open to visitors, and more than 40 other courses in the region offer golf by the round or by the day.

Balgove Course. At the beginner-friendly Balgove Course you can turn up and tee off without prior reservation. ⊠ *West Sands Rd., A91* ⊕ *www. standrews.com* ⊠ *£8–£15* ⚑ *9 holes, 1520 yards, par 30.*

Castle Course. Designed by David McLay Kidd in 2008, the Castle Course hugs the rugged coastline and has jaw-dropping views. It's 2 miles from the town center. ⊠ *A917* ⊕ *www.standrews.com* ⊠ *£60–£120* ⚑ *18 holes, 6759 yards, par 71.*

Eden Course. The aptly named Eden Course, designed in 1914 by Harry S. Colt, winds through inland fields bordered with lovely foliage. It's a bit more forgiving compared to other St. Andrews courses. ⊠ *West Sands Rd.* ⊕ *www.standrews.com* ⊠ *£22–£45* ⚑ *18 holes, 6250 yards, par 70.*

Jubilee Course. This windswept course offers quite a challenge even for experienced golfers. When it opened in 1897 it was intended for beginners, but the popularity of its seaside location encouraged the powers that be to convert it into a championship course. Many golfers say the 15th hole is one of the best in the sport. ⊠ *West Sands Rd.* ⊕ *www. standrews.com* ⊠ *£37–£75* ⚑ *18 holes, 6742 yards, par 72.*

New Course. Not exactly new—it opened in 1895—the New Course is rather overshadowed by the Old Course, but it has a firm following of golfers who appreciate the loop design. ⊠ *West Sands Rd.* ⊕ *www. standrews.com* ⊠ *£37–£75* ⚑ *18 holes, 6625 yards, par 71.*

Fodor'sChoice ★ **Old Course.** Believed to be the oldest golf course in the world, the Old Course was first played in the 15th century. Each year, more than 44,000 rounds are teed off, and no doubt most get stuck in one of its 112 bunkers. A handicap certificate and some very early morning waits for a possible tee off are required. ⊠ *West Sands Rd.* ⊕ *www.standrews. com* ⊠ *£88–£175* ⚑ *18 holes, 6721 yards, par 72.*

Strathtyrum Course. Those with a high handicap will enjoy this course, opened in 1993, without the worry or embarrassment of holding up more experienced golfers. ⊠ *West Sands Rd., A91* ⊕ *www.standrews. com* ⊠ *£15–£30* ⚑ *18 holes, 5620 yards, par 69.*

CRAIL

10 miles south of St. Andrews.

Fodor'sChoice ★ The oldest and most aristocratic of East Neuk burghs, pretty Crail is where many fish merchants retired and built cottages. The town landmark is a picturesque Dutch-influenced town house, or *tolbooth,* which contains the oldest bell in Fife, cast in Holland in 1520. Crail may now

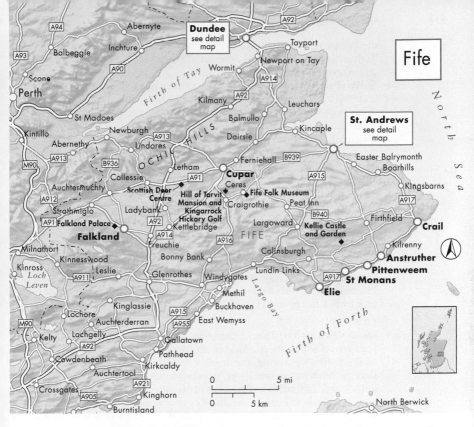

be full of artists, but it remains a working harbor; take time to walk the streets and beaches and to sample fish by the harbor. ■ TIP→ **As you head into East Neuk from this tiny port, look about for market crosses, merchant houses, and little doocots (dovecotes, where pigeons were kept)—typical picturesque touches of this region.**

GETTING HERE AND AROUND

Stagecoach bus No. 95 operates between Crail and St. Andrews. This service also takes you on to Anstruther, Pittenweem St. Monans, and Lower Largo. Crail is about 15 minutes from St. Andrews by car via A917.

EXPLORING

Crail Museum and Heritage Centre. The story of this trading and fishing town can be found in the delightfully crammed Crail Museum and Heritage Centre, entirely run by local volunteers. There is a small tourist information desk within the center. ✉ *62–64 Marketgate* ☎ *01333/450869* ⊕ *www.crailmuseum.org.uk* ✈ *Free* ♡ *Closed Oct.–Mar. Limited hrs Apr. and May.*

WHERE TO EAT AND STAY

$$
SEAFOOD
✕ **Lobster Hut.** This hut on the pier, a hidden gem, sells beautifully cooked lobsters for £12–£20 each (depending on size) and other items at times, including lobster rolls and dressed crab. They'll crack the lobster for you to allow for easy eating on a nearby bench; there is no seating, but

the lobster is wonderful. **Known for:** freshest seafood; alfresco eating. $ *Average main: £15* ✉ *34 Shoregate* ☎ *01333/450476* ⊘ *No dinner* ▭ *No credit cards.*

$
B&B/INN
🛏 **Hazelton.** Beautifully polished wood, exquisitely restored period features, and gentle hues put the Hazelton head and shoulders above the typical seaside B&B. **Pros:** handsome building; excellent location. **Cons:** a couple of rooms on the small side; unreliable communication via email. $ *Rooms from: £85* ✉ *29 Marketgate N* ☎ *01333/450250* ⊕ *www.thehazelton.co.uk* ⊘ *Closed Jan.* ⤳ *5 rooms* ⊙ *Breakfast.*

ANSTRUTHER

4 miles southwest of Crail.

Anstruther, locally called Ainster, has a lovely waterfront with a few shops brightly festooned with children's pails and shovels, a gesture to summer vacationers.

GETTING HERE AND AROUND
Stagecoach bus No. 95 operates between St. Andrews, Crail, Anstruther, Pittenweem, St. Monans, and Lower Largo. Anstruther is 5 to 10 minutes from Crail by car via A917.

EXPLORING

FAMILY
Isle of May Boat Trip. Take to the waves on the compact *May Princess* for a round-trip to the Isle of May, a rocky bird reserve near the mouth of the Forth. Measuring just under a mile long and a third of a mile wide, it harbors 14 species of breeding birds including arctic terns, guillemots, and puffins. The round-trip takes five hours, with three hours on shore to explore the island's history, monastery remains, and the breathtaking sights, sounds, and smells of the avian multitudes. ✉ *Middle Pier, Anstruther Harbour* ☎ *07957/585200* ⊕ *www.isleofmayferry.com* 🎫 *£26.*

FAMILY
Fodor's Choice
★
Scottish Fisheries Museum. Facing Anstruther Harbor, the Scottish Fisheries Museum is inside a colorful cluster of buildings, the earliest of which dates from the 16th century. A charming trail around the various buildings and odd spaces illustrates the life of Scottish fisherfolk: you can spend a couple of hours examining the many documents, artifacts, model ships, paintings, and displays (complete with the reek of tarred rope and net). There are floating exhibits at the quayside and a window onto a working boatyard. ✉ *Harbourhead* ☎ *01333/310628* ⊕ *www.scotfishmuseum.org* 🎫 *£9.*

WHERE TO EAT

$
SEAFOOD
Fodor's Choice
★
✕ **Anstruther Fish Bar and Restaurant.** Next door to the Scottish Fisheries Museum, this popular fish-and-chips shop has a functional space to eat, but most people order takeout. Try local specialties including Pittenweem prawns in batter or the catch of the day, which could be mackerel (line caught by the owners), hake, or local crab. **Known for:** best fish-and-chips in the East Neuk; friendly fryers. $ *Average main: £10* ✉ *42–44 Shore St.* ☎ *01333/310518* ⊕ *www.anstrutherfishbar.co.uk.*

$$$$
EUROPEAN
✕ **The Cellar.** Entered through a cobbled courtyard, this unpretentious, atmospheric restaurant has been run since 2014 by talented head

chef Billy Boyter and family. The three-course prix-fixe meals feature locally sourced seafood and meat such as crab, hake, mussels, beef, lamb, and quail. **Known for:** elegant yet informal dining; exquisite produce; friendly service. Ⓢ *Average main: £60* ✉ *24 E. Green* ☎ *01333/310378* ⏺ *www.thecellaranstruther.co.uk* ⏱ *Closed Mon. and Tues. No lunch Wed.*

NIGHTLIFE AND PERFORMING ARTS

Dreel Tavern. A 16th-century coaching inn, the Dreel Tavern was resurrected and refurbished in 2017 by two sisters who have built on the characterful stone building and added some tasteful improvements. Alongside decent draft beers, there's now an excellent modern menu showcasing local produce such as lobster and smoked fish. The low-ceilinged wood-beamed bar makes for a lively atmosphere, especially during the low-key musical gigs that happen here. It's a fab beer garden for sunshine supping. ✉ *16 High St.* ☎ *01333/279238* ⏺ *www. dreeltavern.co.uk.*

SPORTS AND THE OUTDOORS

East Neuk Outdoors. The back roads of Fife make pleasant places for biking. You can rent bicycles from East Neuk Outdoors, which also has equipment for archery, climbing, kayaking, and canoeing. ✉ *Cellardyke Park* ☎ *01333/310370* ⏺ *www.eastneukoutdoors.co.uk.*

> FIFE COASTAL PATH

Fife's green and undulating landscape includes the Lomond Hills, to the west, which are easy to climb and offer fabulous views of both the Tay and Forth estuaries. The Fife Coastal Path (⏺ www.fifecoastalpath.co.uk) can be bracing or an amble. The 7-mile stretch between East Wemyss and Lower Largo (four to six hours) is the easiest going, with some of it along the beaches of Elie. The 8-mile route between Pittenweem and Fifeness (four to six hours) can be rougher in patches, but takes you through Anstruther and Crail. Be sure to wear the right footwear and take a waterproof jacket.

PITTENWEEM AND ST. MONANS

1½ and 3 miles southwest of Anstruther.

These neighboring harbors are places to wander among lobster creels, fishing nets, and rocks, discovering quirky local artworks and architectural features. Many examples of East Neuk architecture serve as the backdrop for the working harbor at Pittenweem. Look for the crowstep gables, white *harling* (the rough mortar finish on walls), and red *pantiles* (roof tiles with an S-shape profile). The *weem* part of the town's name comes from the Gaelic *uaime*, meaning cave. Nearby St. Monans has an attractive working fishing harbor, small pebbly beach, and a trio of free sights: pop in first to the wonderful, voulnteer-run heritage center by the harbor and curious Wellington boot garden; nearby to the west is the parish church dating from 1265; nearly a mile east along the coastal path is St. Monans Windmill (collect keys from the post office), where Fife salt production is explained.

GETTING HERE AND AROUND

Stagecoach bus No. 95 operates between St. Andrews, Crail, Anstruther, Pittenweem, St. Monans, and Lower Largo. Pittenweem is about five minutes from Anstruther by car via A917.

EXPLORING

Kellie Castle and Garden. Dating from the 16th to 17th century and restored in Victorian times, Kellie Castle stands among the grain fields and woodlands of northeastern Fife. Four acres of pretty gardens surround the castle, which is in the care of the National Trust for Scotland. In summer you can buy berries grown in the walled garden, and baked goods are sold in the tearoom. The garden and estate are open year-round, even when the castle itself is closed. ✉ *B9171* ✥ *3 miles northwest of Pittenweem* ☎ *01337/720271* 🌐 *www.nts.org.uk* 🎫 *£10.50* 🕒 *Castle closed Nov.–Mar. and Fri. Apr.–Oct.*

Pittenweem Arts Festival. There is nothing quite like August's Pittenweem Arts Festival. Exhibitions, which involve hundreds of local and international artists, take place in the town's public buildings and in private homes and gardens. It's a week of events, workshops, and live music. ☎ *01333/313109* 🌐 *www.pittenweemartsfestival.co.uk.*

St. Fillan's Cave. This town's cavern, St. Fillan's Cave, contains the shrine of St. Fillan, a 6th-century hermit who lived here. It's up a *pend* (alleyway) behind the waterfront. If the cave isn't open, ask at the Cocoa Tree on the High Street. Those who can are asked to make a donation of £1 to cover the upkeep of the spooky, spiritual site. ✉ *Cove Wynd* 🎫 *Free* 🕒 *Closed Sun.*

WHERE TO EAT

$$$$ SEAFOOD

🍴 **Craig Millar @ 16 West End.** This eatery overlooking the harbor run by Dundonian chef Craig Millar put St. Monans on Scotland's culinary map. The fixed-price menu has vegetarian and meat options, but with salty fruits of the North Sea on the Fife quayside—such as crab, cod, hake, and mackerel—it's all about Craig's expertise with seafood. **Known for:** elegant seafood dining; gorgeous terrace with sea views;. [$] *Average main: £45* ✉ *16 West End, St. Monans* ✥ *2 miles west of Pittenweem* ☎ *01333/730327* 🕒 *Closed Mon. and Tues. No dinner Sun.*

$ SEAFOOD

🍴 **East Pier Smokehouse.** Painted powder blue, this long harborside building turned eatery and foodie shop is the place to pick up freshly netted and smoked local seafood. After ordering at the shop counter, head up the stairs round the back to feast on lobster, langoustine, and crab accompanied by salads and chips. **Known for:** fresh seafood; imaginative salads; great views. [$] *Average main: £13* ✉ *East Shore, St. Monans* ☎ *01333/405030* 🌐 *www.eastpier.co.uk* 🕒 *Closed Nov.–Mar., weekdays in Apr. and Oct., and Mon. and Tues. in May–Sept. No dinner.*

SHOPPING

Fodor's Choice ★

Pitenweem Chocolate Company. Open daily, this place stocks the most imaginative and comprehensive range of fine chocolates you'll find in this part of the world. Its lovely Cocoa Tree Café serves cakes, drinks, light meals, and, of course, handmade chocolates from the Pittenweem Chocolate Company. ✉ *9 High St.* ☎ *01333/311495* 🌐 *www.pittenweemchocolate.co.uk.*

ELIE

5 miles south of Pittenweem.

To give it its full name, the Royal Burgh of Elie and Earlsferry is an old trading port with a handsome harbor that loops around one of the most glorious stretches of sand in the British Isles. Since Victorian times, when a railway (sadly defunct since the 1960s) linked it with the capital, Elie has been a weekend and summer retreat for the great and the good of Edinburgh. The beach to the south of the harbor is a mile long and has clean sands, clear waters, and tide pools to interest young and old.

WHERE TO EAT

$ BRITISH FAMILY Fodor's Choice ★ 🍴 **Ship Inn.** Overlooking Elie's sandy beach, the Ship Inn combines a new (2016 refurb) wood-filled pub-restaurant with pristine, tastefully revamped rooms. Sports lovers visit Elie on summer Sundays to watch cricket matches played on the beach outside the Ship Inn, and it's a magic spot to dine at any time. **Known for:** beach cricket; sea views; friendly, youthful staff. [$] *Average main: £13* ✉ *The Toft* ☎ *01333/330246* 🌐 *www.shipinn.scot.*

GOLF

Leven Links. A fine Fife course that has been used as a British Open qualifier, Leven Links has a whiff of the more famous St. Andrews, with a hummocky terrain and a tang of salt in the air. The 1st and 18th holes share the same fairway, and the 18th green has a creek running beside it. Saturday play must be booked at least a week in advance. ✉ *The Promenade, Leven* ☎ *01333/428859* 🌐 *www.leven-links.com* 🎟 *£55 weekdays, £60 weekends* ⛳ *18 holes, 6506 yards, par 71* ✍ *Reservations essential.*

Lundin Golf Club. One of a string of fantastic links courses, Lundin Golf Club is a worthy addition to any Scottish golfing itinerary. Designed by the great James Braid, the course is always in prime condition and the greens are a joy. The pick of the holes is the par-3 14th, played from an elevated tee back toward the sea. ✉ *Golf Rd., Lundin Links* ☎ *01333/320202* 🌐 *www.lundingolfclub.co.uk* 🎟 *£65 weekdays, £75 weekends* ⛳ *18 holes, 6371 yards, par 71.*

FALKLAND

24 miles northwest of Pittenweem, 15 miles northwest of Elie.

Fodor's Choice ★ One of the loveliest communities in Scotland, Falkland is a royal burgh of twisting streets and crooked stone houses.

GETTING HERE AND AROUND

Stagecoach bus No. 64 is the only direct service connecting Falkland to St. Andrews as well as Cupar and Ladybank (both of which are train stations on the Edinburgh to Dundee line). Falkland is about 15 minutes from Cupar and a half hour from St. Andrews by car via A91 and A912, or A91 to A914 to A912.

EXPLORING

Falkland Palace. A former hunting lodge of the Stuart monarchs, Falkland Palace dominates the town. The castle is one of the country's earliest examples of the French Renaissance style. Overlooking the main street is the palace's most impressive feature, the walls and chambers on its south side, all rich with buttresses and stone medallions, built by French masons in the 1530s for King James V (1512–42). He died here, and the palace was a favorite resort of his daughter, Mary, Queen of Scots (1542–87). The beautiful gardens behind Falkland Palace contain a rare survivor: a royal tennis court, built in 1539. In the gardens, overlooked by the palace turret windows, you may easily imagine yourself back at the solemn hour when James on his deathbed pronounced the doom of the house of Stuart: "It cam' wi' a lass and it'll gang wi a lass." ✉ *Main St.* ☎ *01337/857397* 🌐 *www.nts.org.uk* 🎟 *£12.50* 🕒 *Closed Nov.–Feb.*

WHERE TO EAT

$ VEGETARIAN FAMILY Fodor's Choice ★ 🍴 **Pillars of Hercules.** Head down a country lane to this organic farm and café-bistro for a tasty vegetarian meal made of produce grown in the wonderful gardens. On a sunny day take your crepe or heaped salad to a bench outside by the nursery, or grab some take-away deli foods from the shop. **Known for:** organic food; inventive dishes; beautiful grounds. [$] *Average main: £7* ✉ *A912* ✣ *1 mile northwest of Falkland* ☎ *01337/857749* 🌐 *www.pillars.co.uk* 🕒 *No dinner.*

CUPAR

21 miles northwest of Loch Leven, 10 miles west of St. Andrews.

Cupar is a busy market town with several interesting sites, including a museum about Fife.

GETTING HERE AND AROUND

Cupar has a train station on the Edinburgh–Aberdeen line (which passes through Dundee), and there are trains almost every hour. Stagecoach buses serve the town as well. By car, you can reach Cupar from Loch Leven via M90 and A91; take A91 if you're traveling from St. Andrews.

EXPLORING

Fife Folk Museum. To learn more about the history and culture of rural Fife, visit the Fife Folk Museum. The life of local rural communities is reflected in artifacts and documents housed in a former weigh house and adjoining weavers' cottages. Refreshments and food are served in the Weigh House Tearoom with views of Ceres Burn. The museum is 3 miles southeast of Cupar via A916 and B939. ✉ *High St., Ceres* ☎ *01334/828180* 🌐 *www.fifefolkmuseum.org* 🎟 *Free (donations welcome)* 🕒 *Closed Mon., Tues., and Nov.–Mar.*

Hill of Tarvit Mansion and Kingarrock Hickory Golf. On rising ground near Cupar stands the National Trust for Scotland's Hill of Tarvit House, a 17th-century mansion that was altered in the high-Edwardian style in the late 1890s and early 1900s by the Scottish architect Sir Robert Lorimer (1864–1929). The extensive wood and parklands offer an enjoyable place for a picnic or stroll, and the house itself is well worth a visit. Golfers will also want to play a round on the old Lorimer family course, the Hickory, which was brought back to life in 2008 after being ploughed up for agricultural use during World War II. ✉ *Off A916 ⊕ 2 miles south of Cupar ☎ 01334/653127 ⊕ www.nts.org.uk ✉ £10.50; golf £45–£75 ⊙ Closed Nov.–Mar.*

FAMILY **Scottish Deer Centre.** At the Scottish Deer Centre, many types of deer can be seen at close quarters or on ranger-guided tours. There are falconry displays every two hours, woodland walks, and a café. The zoolike center, west of Cupar, is one of the few places you can spot the red squirrel, as well as wolves, lynx, wildcat, and European brown bear. ✉ *A91 ☎ 01337/810391 ⊕ www.tsdc.co.uk ✉ £8.50.*

WHERE TO EAT AND STAY

$$$ ✕ **Ostlers Close Restaurant.** Tucked away in an alley off the main street,
BRITISH this cottage-style restaurant has earned a well-deserved reputation for top-quality cuisine that is imaginative without trying to be showy. Elegantly presented in the warm-hued, smart dining room, dishes show off the locally sourced meat and fish, as well as homegrown and foraged produce to best advantage. **Known for:** fine produce; friendly service; handwritten daily menus, which include vegetarian options. Ⓢ *Average main: £24* ✉ *25 Bonnygate* ☎ *01334/655574* ⊕ *www.ostlersclose.co.uk* ⊙ *Closed Sun. and Mon. No lunch.*

$$$$ ⊞ **The Peat Inn.** With eight bright and contemporary two-room suites,
B&B/INN this popular "restaurant with rooms" is perhaps best known for its
Fodor's Choice outstanding, modern, Scottish-style restaurant. **Pros:** exceptional res-
★ taurant; efficient but easygoing staff. **Cons:** booking ahead is essential; you need a car to get here. Ⓢ *Rooms from: £225* ✉ *B941, at intersection of B940* ☎ *01334/840206* ⊕ *www.thepeatinn.co.uk* ⊙ *Closed Sun. and Mon.* ⊅ *8 suites* ⦿ *Breakfast.*

GOLF

Ladybank Golf Club. Fife is known for its coastal courses, but this one provides an interesting inland layout. Although Ladybank, designed by Tom Morris in 1876, is on fairly level ground, the fir and birch trees and heathery rough give it a Highland flavor among the gentle Lowland fields. Qualifying rounds of the British Open are played here when the main championship is played at St. Andrews. ✉ *A92, Annsmuir, Lady-bank* ☎ *01337/830814* ⊕ *www.ladybankgolf.co.uk* ✉ *£25–£65* ⅄ *18 holes, 6580 yards, par 71* ⚑ *Reservations essential.*

DUNDEE AND ANGUS

The small, friendly city of Dundee sits near the mouth of the River Tay surrounded by the farms and glens of rural Angus and the coastal grassy banks and golf courses of northeastern Fife. A vibrant, industrious, and cultural city, it's undergoing a postindustrial renaissance of sorts, with the V&A Museum as the centerpiece of the emerging waterfront regeneration. The first outpost of London's world-famous Victoria and Albert Museum, a repository of the decorative arts and design, is housed in a sculptural building jutting into Britain's most powerful river. Dundee is the United Kingdom's sole UNESCO City of Design, with a large student population, a lively arts and nightlife scene, and several historical and nautical sights.

Angus combines coastal agriculture on rich, red soils with dramatic inland glens that pierce their way into the foothills of the Grampian mountain range to the northwest. ■TIP→ **The main road from Dundee to Aberdeen—the A90—requires special care with its mix of fast cars and unexpectedly slow farm traffic.**

DUNDEE

14 miles northwest of St. Andrews, 58 miles north of Edinburgh, 79 miles northeast of Glasgow.

Dundee makes an excellent base for a cultural stay and Fife and Angus exploration at any time of year. The Dundee Contemporary Arts center gave the city a much-needed boost in 1999; today artsy and foodie hangouts and a vibrant mix of student and creative life make it a beguiling stop. As you explore the streets and new waterfront, including the green expanse of Slessor Gardens, you may glimpse contrasting bold lines of the 2018 V&A Museum of Design, 1966 Tay Road Bridge, and 1888 Tay Rail Bridge. Those ever-changing views of the Tay led actor and wordsmith Stephen Fry to describe Dundee's setting as "ludicrously ideal." Heading southwest down cobbled Roseangle you reach Magdalen Green, where landscape artist James McIntosh Patrick (1907–98) found inspiration from the river and skyscapes. Dundonians' deadpan humor was distilled in the popular comic strips *The Beano* and *The Dandy,* first published here in the 1930s; statues by Scottish sculptors Tony and Susie Morrow depicting characters Desperate Dan, Dawg, and a catapult-wielding Minnie the Minx are in City Square.

GETTING HERE AND AROUND

The East Coast train line runs through the city, linking it to Edinburgh (and beyond, to London), Glasgow (and the West Coast of England), and Aberdeen, with trains to all every hour or half hour at peak times. Cheaper bus service is available to all these locations, as well as St. Andrews and several other towns in Fife and Angus.

If you're traveling by car, the A92 will take you north from Fife to Abroath and the Angus coast towns. The A90, from Perth, heads north to Aberdeen.

Most of the sights in Dundee are clustered together, so you can easily walk around the city. If the weather is bad or your legs are heavy, hail one of the many cabs on the easy-to-find taxi ranks for little more than a few pounds.

ESSENTIALS

Visitor Information Angus and Dundee Tourist Board. ⊠ *16 City Sq.* ☎ *01382/527527* ∰ *www.dundee.com, www.visitangus.com, www.visitscotland.com.*

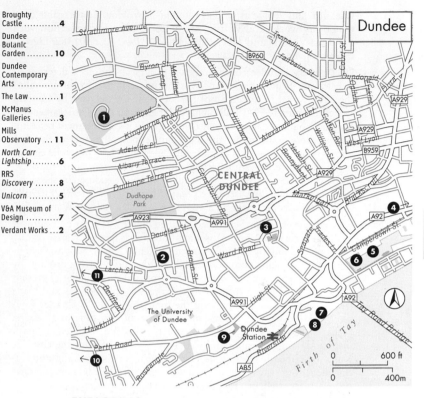

EXPLORING
TOP ATTRACTIONS

FAMILY **Dundee Botanic Garden.** This renowned botanical garden contains an extensive collection of native and exotic plants outdoors and in tropical and temperate greenhouses. There are some beautiful areas for picnicking, as well as a visitor center, an art gallery, and a coffee shop. ✉ *Riverside Dr.* ☎ *01382/381190* ⊕ *www.dundee.ac.uk/botanic* ✆ *£3.90.*

FAMILY **Dundee Contemporary Arts.** Between a 17th-century mansion and a
Fodor's Choice cathedral, this strikingly modern building houses one of Britain's most
★ exciting artistic venues. The two galleries house five shows a year by internationally acclaimed contemporary artists. There are children's and adult's workshops, special events, and meet-the-artist events throughout the year. Two movie theaters screen mainly independent, revival, and children's films. There's also a craft shop and a buzzing café-bar that's open until midnight. ✉ *152 Nethergate* ☎ *01382/909900* ⊕ *www.dca. org.uk* ✆ *Free.*

Fodor's Choice **McManus Galleries.** Dundee's principal museum and art gallery, housed in
★ a striking Gothic Revival–style building, has an engaging collection of artifacts that document the city's history and the working, social, and cultural lives of Dundonians throughout the Victorian period and the 20th century. Its varied fine art collection includes paintings by Rossetti,

Raeburn, and Peploe as well as thought-provoking yet accessible contemporary works and visiting exhibitions, often in connection with London's Victoria and Albert Museum. ⊠ *Albert Sq.* ☎ *01382/432350* ⊕ *www.mcmanus.co.uk* ⊠ *Free.*

FAMILY

Fodor's Choice

★

RRS Discovery. Dundee's urban-renewal program—the city is determined to celebrate its industrial past—was motivated in part by the arrival of the RRS (Royal Research Ship) *Discovery*, the vessel used by Captain Robert F. Scott (1868–1912) on his polar explorations. The steamer was originally built and launched in Dundee; now it's a permanent resident. At Discovery Point, under the handsome cupola, the story of the ship and its famous expedition unfold; you can even feel the Antarctic chill as if you were there. The ship, berthed outside, is the star: wander the deck, then explore the quarters to see the daily existence endured by the ship's crew and captain. ⊠ *Discovery Quay, Riverside Dr.* ☎ *01382/309060* ⊕ *www.rrsdiscovery.com* ⊠ *£9.25, £16 includes Verdant Works.*

Fodor's Choice

★

V&A Museum of Design. Scheduled to open in late 2018, the first outpost of the Victoria and Albert Museum of London is housed in an arresting riverside building by Japanese architect Kengo Kuma. Scotland's first-ever design museum contains seminal works and inspiring displays by Scots and international designers. The Scottish Design Galleries present the past, present, and future through the V&A collections and loans from around the world. Among the many highlights is Charles Rennie Mackintosh's Oak Room, unveiled for the first time in 50 years. Stellar shows, exclusively created for the new V&A galleries, spark inspiration among young and old. This "living room for the city," as Kuma described his design, is worth a visit for the building and setting alone: the vistas in and around its sea-cliff-like edges and perches provide places to linger, mingle, and reflect. ⊠ *Discovery Quay* ⊕ *www. vandadundee.org* ⊠ *Free.*

FAMILY

Verdant Works. In a former jute mill, Verdant Works houses a multifaceted exhibit on the story of jute and the town's involvement in the jute trade. Restored machinery, audiovisual displays, and tableaux all bring to life the hard, noisy life of the jute worker. A light and airy café serves lovely little cakes. ⊠ *W. Hendersons Wynd* ☎ *01382/309060* ⊕ *www. verdantworks.com* ⊠ *£9.25, £16 includes RRS Discovery* ⊘ *Closed Mon. and Tues. Nov.–Mar.*

WORTH NOTING

OFF THE
BEATEN
PATH

Broughty Castle. Originally built to guard the Tay Estuary, Broughty Castle is now a museum focusing on fishing, ferries, and the history of the area's whaling industry. The canons and ramparts make for fine photo opportunities, and inside (up a very narrow stairway) are four floors of displays, including some of the lovely art collection of the Victorian inventor and engineer Sir James Orchar. To the north of the castle lies beautiful Broughty Ferry Beach, which, even in midwinter, is enjoyed by the locals; there is regular bus service from Dundee's city center. ⊠ *Castle Approach, Broughty Ferry* ✛ *4 miles east of city center* ☎ *01382/436916* ⊕ *www.leisureandculturedundee.com/broughty-castle* ⊠ *Free* ⊘ *Closed Mon. Oct.–Mar.*

The Law. For sweeping views of the city, the Angus Glens to the north, and Fife's coastline to the south, head here. This hill (*law* means hill in Scottish) is actually an extinct volcano whose summit reaches 1,640 feet above sea level. A World War II memorial, parking lot, and seating area are at the top. ✉ *Law Rd.*

Mills Observatory. At the top of a thickly forested hill, Mills Observatory is the only full-time public observatory in Britain. There are displays on astronomy, space exploration, scientific instruments, and a 12-inch refracting telescope for night viewing of the stars and planets. **■ TIP→ Dundonians flock here when there's a solar or lunar event. If one happens during your visit, don't miss this universally happy experience.** ✉ *Balgay Hill* ✥ *2 miles west of city center* ☎ *01382/435967* 🌐 *www.leisureandculturedundee.com/mills* 🎟 *Free* 🕒 *Closed Sun.–Tues., Thurs., and Fri. in Apr.–Aug.*

5

North Carr Lightship. Moored next to the *Unicorn*, you'll see a strange red ship, the *North Carr Lightship*. After playing a significant role in World War II, Scotland's only remaining lightship was wrecked on the Fife shore during a storm in 1959; seven crew members were lost. **■ TIP→ The ship is currently closed for refurbishment, but is worth a look from the dock.** ✉ *Broughty Ferry Harbour, Beach Crescent* ☎ *01382/562497.*

FAMILY **Tay River Trips.** Taymara, the nonprofit group that looks after the *North Carr Lightship*, runs exhilarating dolphin-watching trips on its other vessels, the *Badger* and the *Marigot*. Hour-long excursions leave from Broughty Ferry Harbour and tour around the mouth of the delta, where dolphins jump and play. Prior booking is essential. ✉ *Broughty Ferry Harbour, Beach Crescent* ☎ *01382/542516* 🌐 *www.taymara.org* 🎟 *£12.50.*

FAMILY ***Unicorn.*** It's easy to spot this 46-gun wood warship, as it's fronted by a figurehead of a white unicorn. This frigate has the distinction of being the oldest British-built warship afloat, having been launched in 1824 at Chatham, England. You can clamber right down into the hold, or see the models and displays about the Royal Navy's history. In the summer there are often jazz nights on board. The ship's hours vary in winter, so call ahead. ✉ *Victoria Dock, east of Tay Rd. bridge* 🌐 *www.frigateunicorn.org* 🎟 *£5* 🕒 *Closed Mon.–Wed. Nov.–Mar.*

WHERE TO EAT

$$ FRENCH 🍴 **Cafe Montmartre.** A friendly and experienced culinary couple serve delicious French and Mediterranean dishes at this relaxed yet sophisticated eatery, bringing Parisian ganache and panache to the Perth Road. A refined but hearty menu has prix-fixe and à la carte options; baked and grilled fish and meat creations dominate, with classics like duck confit, escargot, and *moules marinière* mainstay favorites. **Known for:** relaxed yet professional service; reliable quality and value; need to book in advance. [$] *Average main: £15* ✉ *91 Perth Rd.* ☎ *01382/204417* 🌐 *www.cafemontmartre.co.uk* 🕒 *Closed Sun. and Mon.*

$$ BRITISH Fodor's Choice ★ 🍴 **Jute.** Downstairs at Dundee Contemporary Arts, this lively eatery serves breakfast at the bar, cocktails and snacks on the terrace in fine weather, or dinner in the open-plan dining area with huge windows that offer views of artists at work in the printmakers studio. There are plenty

of handsomely presented dishes, featuring quality Scots meat, fish, and vegetables. **Known for:** open-plan dining in artsy atmosphere; great set-menu deals; busy bar on weekends. [$] *Average main: £15* ✉ *152 Nethergate* ☎ *01382/909246* 🌐 *www.jutecafebar.co.uk*.

$ CHINESE 🍴 **Manchurian Chinese Restaurant.** This family-run restaurant above a Chinese supermarket will not win any style awards (it feels a little like a hotel conference suite) but thanks to its food it has won a loyal following. Dishes are fresh and light, from plump and fragrant dim sum to more unusual offerings such as bitter melon pork noodles and showstoppers like Taiwanese-style wine chicken pot. **Known for:** authentic Chinese with modern twist; Chinese supermarket downstairs. [$] *Average main: £14* ✉ *15a Gellatly St.* ☎ *01382/228822* 🌐 *www.manchuriandundee.com* 🕑 *Closed Wed.*

$$ ITALIAN 🍴 **Piccolo.** This small basement eatery on the Perth Road, with wooden tables and chairs and a quirky staff, attracts a diverse clientele. It serves surprisingly good pizzas and crepes, and the well-crafted pasta dishes and mains showcase fresh Scots ingredients. **Known for:** candlelit intimacy; immaculate table setting. [$] *Average main: £18* ✉ *21 Perth Rd.* ☎ *01382/201419* 🌐 *www.piccolodundee.co.uk* 🕑 *Closed Sun. and Mon.*

$$$ TAPAS Fodor's Choice ★ 🍴 **Sol y Sombra Tapas Bar.** It looks like an old Scottish pub, and it is, but the tapas and sangria are so authentic they'll make you feel as if you're in España. There's no menu (you are asked if there is anything you don't like) and for £10 lunch or £23 dinner per head you'll be served a steady stream of cracking little dishes. **Known for:** boisterous atmosphere; revelatory tapas. [$] *Average main: £23* ✉ *27 Gray St., Broughty Ferry* ☎ *01382/776941* 🌐 *solysombra.co.*

WHERE TO STAY

$$ HOTEL 🏨 **Apex City Quay.** Scandinavian-style rooms with easy chairs, plump bedding, and flat-screen TVs with DVD players help you unwind at this contemporary quayside hotel. **Pros:** stylish rooms; lively, especially on weekends. **Cons:** outside is popular with seagulls, too; the bar is often mobbed. [$] *Rooms from: £125* ✉ *1 W. Victoria Dock Rd.* ☎ *01382/202404* 🌐 *www.apexhotels.com* 🛏 *151 rooms* 🍽 *Breakfast.*

$$ B&B/INN 🏨 **Duntrune House.** Set among acres of tidy lawns and rustling trees, this mansion is a genteel contrast to the city. **Pros:** owners are keen genealogists and can offer advice to ancestor-seekers; the house and gardens are full of interest; tasty meals. **Cons:** might be too cluttered for some tastes; minimum two-night stay. [$] *Rooms from: £110* ✉ *Off A90, Duntrune* ✥ *5 miles northeast of Dundee* ☎ *01382/350239* 🌐 *www.duntrunehouse.co.uk* 🕑 *Closed Nov.–Feb.* 🛏 *3 rooms* 🍽 *Breakfast.*

$$ HOTEL 🏨 **Malmaison.** British brand Malmaison has brought life to a dilapidated but much-loved Dundee landmark, and done so with style. **Pros:** beautifully restored old building; stylish rooms. **Cons:** pricey restaurant. [$] *Rooms from: £110* ✉ *44 Whitehall Crescent* ☎ *0330/0160380* 🌐 *www.malmaison.com/locations/dundee/* 🛏 *91 rooms* 🍽 *Breakfast.*

$ HOTEL Fodor's Choice ★ 🏨 **Shaftesbury Lodge.** Just off the Perth Road, this Victorian-era villa set among well-tended shrubs is a find for those who like smaller, more intimate hotels. **Pros:** first-rate service; fresh, well-maintained rooms; close, but not too close, to the city. **Cons:** some bathrooms are small.

[$] *Rooms from: £90* ✉ *1 Hyndford St.* ☎ *01382/669216* 🌐 *www.shaftesburylodge.co.uk* 🛏 *12 rooms* 🍴 *Breakfast.*

NIGHTLIFE AND PERFORMING ARTS

BARS AND PUBS

Dundee's pub scene, centered in the West End–Perth Road area, is one of the liveliest in Scotland.

Draffens. Secreted down a wynd (alley), this small speakeasy has stylish, exposed-brick interiors, with decorative nods to the defunct Draffens department store and muckle (a lot in Scots) cocktail shaking going on. ✉ *Couttie's Wynd, Nethergate.*

Fisherman's Tavern. If you find yourself in Broughty Ferry, you can't leave without a tipple in the Fisherman's Tavern, which is also a great place to catch some folk music. ✉ *10–16 Fort St., Broughty Ferry* ☎ *01382/775941* 🌐 *www.fishermanstavern-broughtyferry.co.uk.*

5

Jute Cafe Bar. Better known as the bar at Dundee Contemporary Arts, this places attracts film fans (the art-house cinema's entrance is next door), students, and the well-heeled for European beers, wine, cocktails, or coffee. It serves tasty bar snacks every night until 9:30. ✉ *152 Nethergate* ☎ *01382/909246* 🌐 *www.jutecafebar.co.uk.*

Ship Inn. Right on Broughty Ferry's promenade, this bright and breezy pub has a friendly atmosphere and great bar food. ✉ *121 Fisher St., Broughty Ferry* ☎ *01382/779176* 🌐 *www.theshipinn-broughtyferry.co.uk.*

Fodor's Choice ★ **Speedwell Bar.** Called Mennie's by locals, the Speedwell Bar is in a mahogany-paneled building brimming with Dundonian characters and architectural features. It's renowned for its superb cask beers, choice of malts, and Edwardian interior. ✉ *165–168 Perth Rd.* ☎ *01382/667783* 🌐 *www.speedwell-bar.co.uk.*

MUSIC

Caird Hall. One of Scotland's finest concert halls, Caird Hall stages a wide range of music and events. ✉ *City Sq.* ☎ *01382/434940* 🌐 *www.leisureandculturedundee.com/culture/caird-hall.*

Fodor's Choice ★ **Clarks on Lindsay Street.** This busy bar hosts live music until the early hours. Get in early to avoid the lines. ✉ *80 N. Lindsay St.* ☎ *01382/224925* 🌐 *www.clarksonlindsaystreet.com.*

THEATER

Fodor's Choice ★ **Dundee Repertory Theatre.** This is home to the award-winning Dundee Rep Ensemble and to Scotland's preeminent contemporary-dance group, Scottish Dance Theatre. Popular with locals, the restaurant and bar welcome late-night comedy shows and jazz bands. ✉ *Tay Sq.* ☎ *01382/223530* 🌐 *www.dundeerep.co.uk.*

SHOPPING

COFFEE AND TEA

J. Allan Braithwaite. Established in 1868 and in its current home since 1932, this enticingly aromatic emporium has large old vats of many freshly roasted coffee blends and tea that you can pop into one of the quaint teapots you'll find here. ✉ *6 Castle St.* ☎ *01382/322693.*

JEWELRY

DCA. Just as you enter Dundee Contemporary Arts, the shop on the left sells artist-made jewelry, home ware, books, prints, and gifts. ⊠ *DCA, 152 Nethergate* ☎ *01382/909240* ⊕ *dca.org.uk.*

Gallery Q. A compelling selection of jewelry, ceramics, and paintings by Scottish artists awaits at Gallery Q. ⊠ *160 Nethergate* ☎ *01382/220600* ⊕ *www.galleryq.co.uk.*

MUSIC

Fodor'sChoice   **Groucho's Record Store.** Music lovers, film buffs, and the curious drop by
★   for some crate digging in this store founded by music and jukebox collector Alistair "Breeks" Brodie in 1976. The Victorian interior spins you right around with a dizzying display of rare vinyl, CDs, DVDs, books, T-shirts, and vintage audio supplies. It's also a great place to pick up info, flyers, and tickets for gigs and to chat about the local scene. ⊠ *132 Nethergate* ☎ *01382/228496* ⊕ *www.grouchos.co.uk.*

GOLF

East of Perthshire, near the city of Dundee, lies a string of demanding courses along the shores of the North Sea and inland into the foothills of the Grampian Mountains. Golfers who excel in windy conditions particularly enjoy the breezes blowing westward from the sea.

Camperdown Golf Course. For an alternative to the wild and windy east-coast links, try this magnificent municipal parkland course on the outskirts of Dundee. You can enjoy a game amid tree-lined fairways near the imposing Camperdown House. ■**TIP→ On a fine night in June or July, try the Twilight Session.** ⊠ *Camperdown Park, Coupar Angus Rd.* ☎ *01382/431820* ⊕ *www.golfdundee.com/camperdown-golf-course* ⛳*£19–£27* ⛳ *18 holes, 6548 yards, par 71.*

Fodor'sChoice   **Carnoustie Golf Links.** The venue for the British Open in 1999, 2007,
★   and 2018, the coastal links around Carnoustie have challenged golfers since at least 1527. Winners here have included many of the sport's biggest names: Armour, Hogan, Cotton, Player, and Watson. There are three courses, the most famous of which is the breathtaking Championship Course, ranked among the very best in the world. The choice Burnside course is full of historical interest and local color, as well as being tough and interesting. The Buddon course, designed by Peter Allis and Dave Thomas, is recommended for links novices. ⊠ *20 Links Parade, Carnoustie* ☎ *01241/802270* ⊕ *www.carnoustiegolflinks.co.uk* ⛳*Championship, £175; Buddon, £46; Burnside, £46* ⛳ *Championship Course: 18 holes, 6948 yards, par 72; Buddon Course: 18 holes, 5921 yards, par 68; Burnside Course: 18 holes, 6028 yards, par 68* ⛳ *Reservations essential.*

Panmure Golf Club. Down the road from the famous Carnoustie Golf Links, this traditional course offers an excellent challenge with its seaside setting, undulating greens, and sometimes excruciating—but always entertaining—burrows. The signature 6th is named after British Open Championship winner Ben Hogan, who practiced here prior to his triumphant tournament at Carnoustie in 1953. ⊠ *Burnside Rd., off Station Rd., Carnoustie* ☎ *01241/855120* ⊕ *www.panmuregolfclub.co.uk* ⛳*£30–£95* ⛳ *18 holes, 6551 yards, par 70* ⛳ *Reservations essential.*

ARBROATH

15 miles north of Dundee.

You can find traditional boatbuilding in the fishing town of Arbroath. It has several small curers and processors as well, and shops sell the town's most famous delicacy, Arbroath smokies—whole haddock gutted and lightly smoked. The town is also known for its association with the Declaration of Arbroath, a key document in Scotland's history. A few miles north along the coast is the old fishing village of Auchmithie, with a beautiful little beach that you can walk to via a short path. The jagged, reddish cliffs and caves are home to a flourishing seabird population.

GETTING HERE AND AROUND

The East Coast train line stops at Arbroath. The Abbey and Signal Tower are all within walking distance, but you'll need a car to get to Auchmithie. If you're driving from Dundee, take A92.

ESSENTIALS

Visitor Information Arbroath Tourist Information. ⊠ *Fish Market Quay, A92* ☎ *01241/872609* ⊕ *www.visitscotland.com, www.visitangus.com.*

EXPLORING

Arbroath Abbey. Founded in 1178 and linked to the famous Declaration of Arbroath, Arbroath Abbey is an unmistakable presence in the town center; it seems to straddle whole streets, as if the town were simply ignoring the red-stone ruin in its midst. Surviving today are remains of the church, as well as one of the most complete examples in existence of an abbot's residence. From here in 1320 a passionate plea was sent by King Robert the Bruce (1274–1329) and the Scottish Church to Pope John XXII (circa 1249–1334) in far-off Rome. The pope had until then sided with the English kings, who adamantly refused to acknowledge Scottish independence. The Declaration of Arbroath stated firmly, "It is in truth not for glory, nor riches, nor honours that we are fighting, but for freedom—for that alone, which no honest man gives up but with life itself." Some historians describe this plea, originally drafted in Latin, as the single most important document in Scottish history. The pope advised English king Edward II (1284–1327) to make peace, but warfare was to break out along the border from time to time for the next 200 years. The excellent visitor center recounts this history in well-planned displays. ⊠ *Abbey St.* ☎ *01241/878756* ⊕ *www.historic-environment.scot* ⊠ *£6.*

Signal Tower Museum. In the early 19th century, Arbroath was the base for the construction of the Bell Rock lighthouse on a treacherous, barely exposed rock in the Forth of Tay. A signal tower was built to facilitate communication with the builders working far from shore. That structure now houses the Signal Tower Museum, which tells the story of the lighthouse, built by Robert Stevenson (1772–1850) in 1811. The museum also houses a collection of items related to the history of the town, its customs, and the local fishing industry: look out for the 1813 Book of Signals and the witch's eye, a blue glass buoy hung from the window to ward off evil spirits. ⊠ *Ladyloan* ✢ *West of harbor* ☎ *01241/435329* ⊠ *Free* ☉ *Closed Sun. and Mon.*

5

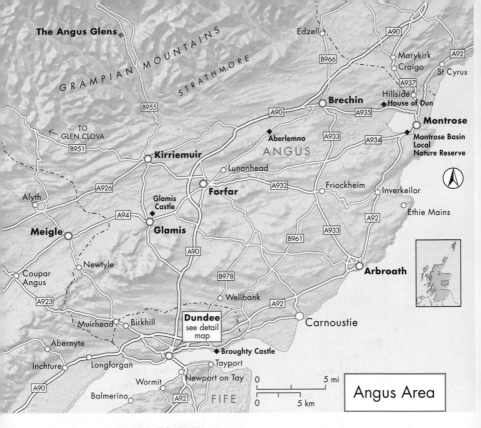

The Angus Glens

GRAMPIAN MOUNTAINS

STRATHMORE

Edzell

A90

B966

Marykirk
Craigo
St Cyrus

A92

A937

Hillside
House of Dun

Brechin

A935

Montrose

Montrose Basin
Local
Nature Reserve

B955

TO
GLEN CLOVA

B951

Kirriemuir

A926

Alyth

Lunanhead

ANGUS

Aberlemno

A90

A933

A934

Forfar

A932

Friockheim

Inverkeilor

Ethie Mains

Glamis
Castle

A94

Glamis

A933

A92

Meigle

B961

A90

Newtyle

B978

Coupar
Angus

A923

Wellbank

Arbroath

Muirhead

Birkhill

A92

Carnoustie

Abernyte

Dundee
see detail
map

Inchture

Longforgan

Broughty Castle

Tayport

Wormit

Newport on Tay

0   5 mi

Balmerino

A92

FIFE

0   5 km

Angus Area

WHERE TO EAT

$ FAST FOOD

✕ **Bellrock.** You can't go to Arbroath and not sample some fish-and-chips. Just across the road from the Signal Museum and painted in nautical white and blue, this local favorite has outside benches for warmer days. You'll find all the classics—breaded or battered—but if you are in the mood for something a little different, the spicy fish (in a spiced batter) has certainly won over discerning locals. **Known for:** great fish suppers; weekday buffet. $ *Average main: £10* ✉ *33 Ladyloan* ☎ *01241/873656* ⊕ *www.thebellrock.com.*

$ BRITISH Fodor'sChoice ★

✕ **But 'n' Ben.** This homey restaurant serves lunches and dinners that offer a taste of quality Scottish home cooking, including Arbroath smokie pancakes, mince and tatties, venison with rowan jelly, and rich moist gingerbread, all at reasonable prices. It's next to Auchmithie's lovely shingle beach; a stroll here is the perfect way to work up an appetite or work off overindulgence. **Known for:** low-ceilinged croft-house surroundings; traditional Scots fare; Sunday high tea. $ *Average main: £13* ✉ *Ethie St., Auchmithie* ✛ *3 miles off A92* ☎ *01241/877223* ⊕ *www.thebutnben.com* ⊙ *Closed Tues. No dinner Sun.*

WHERE TO STAY

$$ **The Brucefield.** This old manor
B&B/INN   house, set among well-tended
grounds, offers luxurious rooms
for very reasonable rates. **Pros:** all
the touches you'd expect in a five-
star hotel; quality bedding; friendly
owners. **Cons:** two-night minimum
in high season; a 20-minute walk to
the city center. $ Rooms from: £120
✉ Cliffburn Rd. ☎ 01241/875393
⊕ www.brucefieldbandb.com ➱ 4
rooms ⦿ Breakfast.

$ **Harbour Nights.** An excellent and somewhat plush budget option, this
B&B/INN   B&B is right on the harbor, affording you the most authentic Arbroath
stay possible. **Pros:** splendid seafront location; delicious breakfasts.
Cons: only one room with a private bathroom; you must book far
in advance. $ Rooms from: £90 ✉ 4 Shore ☎ 01421/434343 ⊕ www.
harbournights.co.uk ➱ 4 rooms ⦿ Breakfast.

> **LIGHTHOUSE BUILDERS**
>
> The name Stevenson is strongly
> associated with the building of
> lighthouses throughout Scotland.
> However, the family's most famous
> son was Robert Louis Stevenson
> (1850–94), who gravely disap-
> pointed his parents by choosing to
> be a writer instead of an engineer.

MONTROSE

14 miles north of Arbroath via A92.

An unpretentious and attractive town with some charming museums
and a selection of shops, Montrose sits beside a wide estuary known
as the Montrose Basin.

GETTING HERE AND AROUND

On the main East Coast train line and local bus route (the Stagecoach
Strathtay 39 and 73 from Dundee and Arbroath), the town is easily
accessed by public transportation. However, you'll need a car to get to
attractions outside town.

ESSENTIALS

Visitor Information **Montrose Tourist Information Point.** ✉ *Montrose
Museum, Panmure Pl.* ☎ *01674/673232* ⊕ *www.visitangus.com, www.visitscot-
land.com.*

EXPLORING

Fodor'sChoice   **House of Dun.** The National Trust for Scotland's leading attraction in
★   this area is the stunning House of Dun, which overlooks the Montrose
Basin. The mansion was built in the 1730s for lawyer David Erskine,
otherwise known as Lord Dun (1670–1755). Designed by architect
William Adam (1689–1748), the house is particularly noted for its mag-
nificently ornate plasterwork and curious Masonic masonry. Showing
everything from Lady Dun's collection of embroidery to the working
kitchens, this house tells the story of the Seat of Dun and the eminent
family's history. The sprawling grounds have a restored hand-loom
weaving workshop, plus an enchanting walled Victorian garden and
wooded den. ✉ *A935* ⊕ *4 miles west of Montrose* ☎ *01674/810264*
⊕ *www.nts.org.uk* ⦿ *£10.50* ⊘ *Closed Dec.–Mar., Thurs. and Fri. in
Apr.–Sept., and weekdays in Oct. and Nov.*

5

BEAUTIFUL BEACHES

Scotland's east coast enjoys many hours of sunshine, compared with its west coast, and is blessed with lots of sandy beaches under the ever-changing backdrop of the sky. Take time to explore the beaches and walk along the coast for a change of pace whatever the time of year.

In Fife, Tentsmuir's Beach near St. Andrews is popular with kite flyers and horseback riders, and the famous and lovely West Sands in St. Andrews is where the running sequences in the movie *Chariots of Fire* were filmed. The small cove beach at Elie, south of Crail, hosts cricket matches in summer.

In Angus the beach at Broughty Ferry, near the city of Dundee, fills with families and children on weekends and during school holidays—even on the most blustery of days.

North of Arbroath lies Auchmithie Beach, more shingly (pebbly) than the others and offering a bracing breath of North Sea air. And finally, near the Montrose Basin you can discover the enchanting crescent of Lunan Bay, home to many species of seabirds.

Montrose Basin Local Nature Reserve. Run by the Scottish Wildlife Trust, the Montrose Basin Local Nature Reserve hosts migrating geese, ducks, and swans. Several nature trails can take you up close to the reserve's residents if you're quiet. In October, at least 20,000 pink-footed geese arrive: come in the morning and the evening to see them fill the sky. ⊠ *Rossie Braes* ☎ *01674/676336* ⊕ *www.montrosebasin.org.uk* ⊠ *£4* ☉ *Closed Tues.–Thurs. Nov.–mid-Feb.*

Montrose Museum. The town's museum—housed in a neoclassical building that also contains the tourist information center—exhibits some fascinating bequests by the local gentry, including an early-19th-century ship carved from bone by French prisoners in the Napoleonic war. ⊠ *Panmure Pl.* ☎ *01674/673232* ⊕ *archive.angus.gov.uk* ⊠ *Free* ☉ *Closed Sun. and Mon.*

Fodor's Choice **William Lamb Studio.** A visit to the studio of renowned Montrosian art-
★ ist and sculptor William Lamb (1893–1951) provides a glimpse into his intriguing life, travels, and obsessions. In the intimate studio you can walk among the heads of 20th-century royalty, society figures, and everyday Montrose folk. The museum is open only in July and August and by appointment; ask the lovely staff at the Montrose Museum. ⊠ *24 Market St.* ☎ *01674/662660* ⊠ *Free* ☉ *Closed Sept.–June.*

WHERE TO EAT

$ ✕ **The Pavilion Cafe.** Bringing new purpose to an old bowling pavilion,
CAFÉ this café's owner freshly painted its clapboard, spruced up the delightful
Fodor's Choice color-glazed fanlights, and gently restored many of the unusual features
★ of this late-Victorian beauty. Expect light meals, breakfasts, salads, buttermilk pancakes, and superfresh home bakes: the seasonal fruit-festooned cream sponges are a treat. **Known for:** bowling-green-scene jollity; scrumptious cakes. $ *Average main: £8* ⊠ *Melville Gardens* ☎ *01674/958188* ☉ *Closed Sun. and Mon.*

BRECHIN

10 miles northwest of Montrose.

The small market town of Brechin has a cathedral that was founded around 1200 and contains an interesting selection of antiquities, including the Mary Stone, a Pictish relic.

GETTING HERE AND AROUND

Brechin is not on the East Coast train line but can be reached by bus from Montrose or Arbroath (Stagecoach StrathtayNo. 30). It's on the A935, just off the main A90 road between Dundee and Aberdeen.

EXPLORING

Brechin Cathedral and Round Tower. The town's 13th-century Brechin Cathedral and Round Tower is on the site of a former Celtic monastery (priory of the Culdee monks) and has some unusual examples of medieval sculpture. The tower is one of only two on mainland Scotland. This type of structure is more frequently found in Ireland. ✉ *6 Church St.* ☎ *01356/629360* 🌐 *brechincathedral.org.uk* 🎟 *Free.*

Brechin Town House Museum. Located in the old courtroom which had cells in its cellars, the Brechin Town House Museum houses a small but interesting collection of objects from inhabitants of the area: from Bronze Age jewelry to a Jacobite sporran to a letter from a World War I soldier. There is a small tourist information desk within the museum. ✉ *28 High St.* ☎ *01356/627458* 🌐 *www.brechintownhouse.org.uk* 🎟 *Free* 🕒 *Closed Sun. and Mon.*

WHERE TO EAT

$ CAFÉ FAMILY 🍴 **Brechin Castle Garden Centre.** Just off the A90, this small country park has a play area for children and an excellent café, serving door-stop-size sandwiches, full breakfasts, tasty soups, and warm scones. **Known for:** hearty food; family-friendly dining. [$] *Average main: £8* ✉ *Haughmuir* ☎ *01356/626813* 🌐 *www.brechincastlecentre.co.uk* 🕒 *No dinner.*

THE ANGUS GLENS

25 miles northwest of Brechin.

You can rejoin the hurly-burly of the A90 for the return journey south from Montrose or Brechin; the more pleasant route, however, leads southwesterly on minor roads (there are several options) that travel along the face of the Grampians, following the fault line that separates Highland and Lowland. The **Angus Glens** extend north from points on A90. Known individually as the glens of Isla, Prosen, Clova, and Esk, these long valleys run into the high hills of the Grampians and some clearly marked walking routes. Those in Glen Clova are especially appealing.

Be aware that Thursday is a half day in Angus; many shops and attractions close at lunch.

GETTING HERE AND AROUND

You really need a car to reach the Angus Glens and enjoy the gentle (and not so gentle) inclines here. Glamis and Kirriemuir are both on the A928 (just off the A90), and the B955—which loops round at Glen

Clova—is one of the loveliest Scottish roads to drive along, especially when the heather is blooming in late summer.

WHERE TO STAY

$$ HOTEL 🏨 **Glen Clova Hotel.** Since the 1850s, the hospitality of this hotel has lifted the spirits of many a bone-tired hill walker, and refurbishment and extension in 2016 have enhanced the comfort. **Pros:** stunning location; great base for outdoor pursuits; spacious accommodations. **Cons:** lack of decent public transportation; bar and live-music nights may be noisy. [$] *Rooms from: £110* ✉ *B955, Glen Clova* ☎ *01575/550350* 🌐 *www.clova.com* 🛏 *10 rooms* 🍴 *Breakfast.*

KIRRIEMUIR

15 miles southwest of Brechin.

Kirriemuir stands at the heart of Angus's red-sandstone countryside and was the birthplace of the writer J.M. Barrie (1860–1937), best known abroad as the author of *Peter Pan* (a statue of whom you can see in the town's square). *Kirrie,* as it's known here, salutes favorite son Bon Scott (1946–80)—the rasping AC/DC vocalist—in a bronze-and-Caithness-rock memorial statue at Bellies Brae. Metal pilgrims gather each springtime for Bonfest.

GETTING HERE AND AROUND

A number of roads lead to Kirriemuir, but A928 (off A90), which also passes Glamis Castle, is one of the loveliest. Stagecoach Strathtay runs buses to this area; Nos. 20 and 22 from Dundee are the most regular.

EXPLORING

FAMILY **Camera Obscura.** J. M. Barrie donated the Camera Obscura to the town. The device—a dark room with a small hole in one wall that projects an image of the outside world onto the opposite wall—is one of only four in the country. In a cricket pavilion, it affords magnificent views of the surrounding area on bright days. ✉ *Kirrie Hill* ☎ *01575/575885* 🌐 *www.kirriemuircameraobscura.com* 🎟 *Free (donations welcome)* 🕒 *Closed Nov.–Mar., and weekdays in Apr.–June, Sept., and Oct.*

J.M. Barrie's Birthplace. At J. M. Barrie's Birthplace, the National Trust pays tribute to the man who sought to preserve the magic of childhood more than any other writer of his age. The house's upper floors are furnished as they might have been in Barrie's time, complete with domestic necessities, while downstairs is his study, replete with manuscripts and personal mementos. The outside washhouse is said to have served as Barrie's first theater. ✉ *9 Brechin Rd.* ☎ *01575/572646* 🌐 *www.nts.org.uk/Property/J-M-Barries-Birthplace/* 🎟 *£6.50* 🕒 *Closed Oct.–Mar., Tues.–Fri. in Apr.–June and Sept., and Tues. and Wed. in July and Aug.*

Kirriemuir Gateway to the Glens Museum. As is the style in Angus, the local museum doubles as the visitor center, meaning you can get all the information you need and admire a few stuffed birds and artifacts at the same time. Rock fans will appreciate the exhibit celebrating local lad made good (or rather bad), the late Bon Scott, original lead singer of the rock band AC/DC. ✉ *32 High St.* ☎ *01575/575479* 🌐 *archive.angus.gov.uk* 🎟 *Free* 🕒 *Closed Sun. and Mon.*

WHERE TO EAT

$ ✕ **88 Espresso.** If you're not in a rush (service can be slow), take time to
CAFÉ   savor excellent coffee, inventive sandwiches, pizzettes, cakes, and hand-
FAMILY   made chocolates at this appealing café and shop selling quality fare. Can't
stop? **Known for:** home baking including sourdough; handmade choco-
lates and truffles. $ *Average main: £7* ✉ *17 High St.* ☎ *07449/345089*
☉ *Closed Mon. and Tues. No dinner* ⊟ *No credit cards.*

FORFAR

7 miles east of Kirriemuir.

Forfar goes about its business of being the center of a farming hinterland
without being preoccupied with (or even that interested in) tourism.

GETTING HERE AND AROUND

Buses are slow here. The quickest route is by car: take the A90 north,
then the A926 turnoff. Alternatively, the A932/A933 route from
Arbroath takes you through farmland and Angus villages.

EXPLORING

OFF THE BEATEN PATH

Aberlemno. You can see excellent examples of Pictish stone carvings
about 5 miles northeast of Forfar alongside the B9134. Carvings of
crosses, angels, serpents, and other animals adorn the stones, which
date from the 7th to the early 9th century. Note the stone in the nearby
churchyard—one side is carved with a cross and the other side depicts
the only known battle scene in Pictish art, complete with horsemen and
foot soldiers. ✉ *Forfar.*

Meffan Museum and Art Gallery. The high point of a visit to Forfar is the
Meffan Museum and Art Gallery, which displays an interesting collection of Pictish carved stones and artifacts from the dark days of burning
witches. Two galleries host frequently changing exhibitions by leading
local and Scottish artists. The museum also houses a tourist information desk. ✉ *20 W. High St.* ☎ *01307/476482* ⊕ *archive.angus.gov.uk/
historyaa/museums/* ☒ *Free* ☉ *Closed Sun. and Mon.*

GLAMIS

5 miles southwest of Forfar, 6 miles south of Kirriemuir.

Set in rolling countryside is the little village of Glamis (pronounced
glahms), the highlight of which is nearby famous Glamis Castle.

GETTING HERE AND AROUND

The drive to Glamis Castle, along beech- and yew-lined roads, is as
majestic as the castle itself. Take the A90 north from Dundee, then off
onto the A928. The village of Glamis can be reached by the Stagecoach
Strathtay No. 22, but service is rather infrequent.

EXPLORING

Fodor's Choice ★   **Glamis Castle.** One of Scotland's best known and most beautiful castles,
Glamis Castle connects Britain's royalty through 10 centuries, from
Macbeth (Thane of Glamis) to the late Queen Mother and her daughter,
the late Princess Margaret, born here in 1930 (the first royal princess
born in Scotland in 300 years). The property of the earls of Strathmore

5

and Kinghorne since 1372, the castle was largely reconstructed in the late 17th century; the original keep, which is much older, is still intact. One of the most famous rooms in the castle is Duncan's Hall, the legendary setting for Shakespeare's *Macbeth*. Guided tours allow you to see fine collections of china, tapestries, and furniture. Within the castle is the delightful Castle Kitchen restaurant; the grounds contain a huge gift shop, a shop selling local produce, and a pleasant picnic area. ■ TIP→ **If you are looking to hear the pipes and see some Highland dancing and games of strength, the Strathmore Highland Games are held here around the second weekend of June. See www.strathmore-highlandgames.co.uk for more information.** ⊠ *A94* ⊹ *1 mile north of Glamis* ☎ *01307/840393* ⊕ *www.glamis-castle.co.uk* ⊠ *£12.50* ⊙ *Closed Nov.–Mar.*

MEIGLE

7 miles southwest of Glamis, 11 miles northwest of Dundee.

The historic village of Meigle, nestled in the rich agricultural land of the Strathmore Valley, is well known to those with an interest in Pictish stones. Said to be built on an 11th-century Pictish monastery, the village has a number of elaborate Victorian buildings.

GETTING HERE AND AROUND

Meigle is an easy and pleasant drive from Glamis on the A94 (or from Dundee on the B954). The hourly Stagecoach Strathtay from Dundee (No. 57) stops here.

EXPLORING

Meigle Sculptured Stone Museum. The town of Meigle, in the wide swathe of Strathmore, has one of the most notable collections of sculpted stones in western Europe, housed at the Meigle Sculptured Stone Museum. It consists of some 25 monuments from the Celtic Christian period (8th to 11th century), nearly all of which were found in or around the local churchyard. The large cross slab known as Meigle 2 shows Daniel in the lions' den. Local legend holds the slab marked the grave of Guinevere, wife of King Arthur; in the story, Arthur sentences her to death by being torn apart by wild animals. ⊠ *A94* ☎ *01828/640612* ⊕ *www.historicenvironment.scot* ⊠ *£5* ⊙ *Closed Oct.–Mar.*

THE CENTRAL
HIGHLANDS

Updated
by Mike
Gonzalez

The Central Highlands are home to superb castles, moody mountains, and gorgeous glens that are best explored at a leisurely pace. The waters of Loch Lomond reflect the crags and dark woods that surround it, and attract those in search of a more romantic and nostalgic Scotland enshrined in the verses of the famous song that bears its name. When you finish a day of exploring, celebrate with a glass of one of the region's top-notch whiskies.

The Carse of Stirling, the wide plain guarded by Stirling Castle, was the scene of many important moments in Scotland's history—from the Roman invasion commemorated by the Antonine Wall, to the castles that mark the site of medieval kingdoms and the battles to preserve them. Look up at Stirling Castle from the valley and you can see why so many battles were fought over its possession.

North from Stirling, past Dunblane, are the birch-, oak-, and pine-covered Highland hills and valleys of the Trossachs, whose high peaks attract walkers and a tougher breed of cyclist. From Callander, a neat tourist town, the hills stretch westward to the "bonnie bonnie banks" of Loch Lomond. The Victorians were drawn here by the lyrical descriptions of the area by Romantic poets like Sir Walter Scott (1771–1832), who set his dramatic verse narrative of 1810, "The Lady of the Lake," in the landscape of the Trossachs. From the peaks of the Trossachs, on a good day, you can see Edinburgh Castle to the east and the tower blocks of Glasgow's housing projects to the west.

Farther north is Perth, once Scotland's capital; its wealthy mansions reflect the prosperous agricultural land that surrounds the city, and it is still an important market town today. Overlooking the River Tay, the city can reasonably claim to be the gateway to the Highlands, sitting as it does on the Highland Fault that divides Lowlands from Highlands. From Perth the landscape begins to change on the road to Pitlochry and the high, rough country of Rannoch Moor.

The region is full of reminders of heroic struggles, particularly against the English, from the monument to William Wallace to the field at Bannockburn (near Stirling), where Robert the Bruce took on the invader. In nearby Callander, Rob Roy MacGregor, the Scottish Robin Hood, lived (and looted and terrorized) his way into the storybooks.

TOP REASONS TO GO

Loch Lomond: You can see the sparkling waters of Scotland's largest loch by car, by boat, or on foot. A popular option is the network of bicycle tracks that creep around Loch Lomond and the Trossachs National Park, offering every conceivable terrain.

Castles: Choosing among Scotland's most splendid fortresses and mansions is a challenge. Among the highlights are Stirling Castle, with its palace built by James V, and Scone Palace, near Perth, with its grand aristocratic acquisitions. By contrast, Doune Castle is an atmospheric reminder of life in a fortification.

Great hikes: The way to experience the Central Highlands is to head out on foot. The fit and well equipped can "bag a Munro" (climb hills over 3,000 feet, named after the mountaineer who listed them). The less demanding woodland paths and gentle rambles of the Trossachs will stir even the least adventurous rambler.

Whisky tours and tastes: The Scots love their whisky, and what better way to participate in Scottish life and culture than to learn about the land's finest? There are some exceptional distilleries in this region, from the Edradour Distillery to Glenturret, home of the Famous Grouse.

Bike trails: This region claims excellent biking trails, ranging from a gentle pedal through Stirling to a wind-in-your-face journey on the Lowland/Highland Trail. Whatever your preference, biking is a beautiful way to tour the countryside.

6

ORIENTATION AND PLANNING

GETTING ORIENTED

The twin reference points for your trip are Stirling, an ancient historic town from whose castle you can see central Scotland laid out before you, and Perth, 36 miles away, the gateway to the Highlands. North from Stirling, you cross the fertile open plain (the Carse of Stirling) dotted with historic cathedral towns like Dunblane and fortified castles like Doune. The Trossachs are the Scotland of the Romantic imagination, lochs and woodland glens, drovers' inns and grand country houses. The small towns of the region, like Callander, Aberfoyle, and Pitlochry, are bases from which to explore this varied countryside. To the west lies Loch Lomond, along whose banks the road leads from industrial Glasgow to the hills and glens of the Highlands.

Stirling. Famous for its castle and vibrant with history, Stirling has a small Old Town on the hill that is worth covering on foot. Look down from the Stirling Castle crag that dominates the plains below and you can see the stages of the city's growth descending from the hill. The town is a good center from which to explore the changing landscape of central Scotland.

The Trossachs and Loch Lomond. This area is small but incredibly varied— from dramatic mountain peaks that attract walkers and climbers, to the gentler slopes and forests that stretch from Perth westward to Aberfoyle

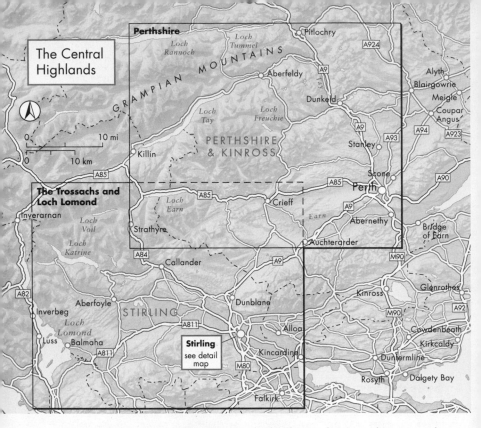

and the shores of Loch Lomond. The glens and streams that pepper the region create a romantic landscape that is a perfect habitat for the figure of Rob Roy McGregor—Robin Hood or bandit according to taste, but undeniably Scottish. Loch Lomond's western side is more accessible, if busier, than the east, but the views across the loch are spectacular.

Perthshire. The prosperous air of Perth, once the capital of Scotland, testifies to its importance as a port exporting wool, salmon, and whisky to the world. Scone Palace serves as a monument to that era. The route northward leads across the Highland Boundary and into the changing landscapes beyond Pitlochry to Rannoch Moor, where the wind sweeps across the hardy heather.

PLANNING

WHEN TO GO

The Trossachs and Loch Lomond are in some ways a miniature Scotland, from the tranquil east shore of Loch Lomond to the hills and glens of the Trossachs and the mountains to the west—and all within a few hours' drive. In spring and summer, despite the erratic weather, the area is always crowded; this is a good time to go. However, the landscape is notably dramatic when the trees are turning red and brown in autumn, and evening skies are spectacular. Scotland in winter has a different kind of beauty, especially for skiers and climbers. ■TIP→ **Carry clothes for wet and dry weather, as the weather can change quickly. Summer evenings attract midges; take some repellent.**

PLANNING YOUR TIME

Scotland's beautiful interior is excellent touring country, though the cities of Stirling and Perth are worth your time, too; Stirling is a good starting point, and exploring its castle can take a half day. Two (slightly rushed) days would be enough to explore the Trossachs loop, to gaze into the waters of Loch Venachar and Loch Achray. The glens, in some places, run parallel to the lochs, including those along Lochs Earn, Tay, and Rannoch, making for satisfying loops and round-trips. Loch Lomond is easily accessible from either Glasgow or Stirling, and is well worth exploring. Don't miss the opportunity to take a boat trip on a loch, especially on Loch Lomond or on Loch Katrine.

SPORTS AND THE OUTDOORS

Lowland/Highland Trail. The region's big attraction for cyclists is the Lowland/Highland Trail, which stretches more than 60 miles and passes through Drymen, Aberfoyle, the Trossachs, Callander, Lochearnhead, and Killin. This route runs along former railroad-track beds, as well as private and minor roads, to reach well into the Central Highlands. Another almost completely traffic-free option is the roadway around Loch Katrine. Almost every town along the route has cycle-hire shops.

Fodor'sChoice
★

West Highland Way. The long-distance walkers' route, the West Highland Way, begins in Glasgow, running 96 miles from the Lowlands of central Scotland to the Highlands at Fort William. Nearly 50,000 people discover the glens each year, climbing the hills and listening to birds singing in the tree canopy. This is not a difficult walk, but keep Scotland's ever-changing weather in mind and go properly prepared. From Milngavie, in Glasgow, the route passes along the banks of Loch Lomond before snaking northward into the more demanding hills beyond, crossing Rannoch Moor, and finishing at Fort William. ⊕ *www.west-highland-way.co.uk.*

GETTING HERE AND AROUND

AIR TRAVEL

Perth and Stirling can be reached easily from the Edinburgh, Dundee, and Glasgow airports by train, car, or bus.

BUS TRAVEL

A good network of buses connects with this area via Edinburgh and Glasgow. For more information, contact Scottish Citylink or National Express. The Perth and Kinross Council supplies a map (available in tourist information centers) showing all public transport routes in Perthshire, marked with nearby attractions.

First, Scottish Citylink, and Stagecoach organize reliable local service on routes throughout the Central Highlands.

Bus Contacts First. ☎ *01224/650100* ⊕ *www.firstgroup.com.* **National Express.** ☎ *08717/818181* ⊕ *www.nationalexpressgroup.com.* **Scottish Citylink.** ☎ *0871/266–3333* ⊕ *www.citylink.co.uk.* **Stagecoach.** ☎ *01292/613502* ⊕ *www.stagecoachbus.com.*

6

CAR TRAVEL

It's easy to access the area from the central belt of Scotland via the motorway network. The M80 connects Glasgow to Stirling, and then briefly joins the M9 from Edinburgh, which runs within sight of the walls of Stirling Castle. From there the A9 runs from Stirling to Perth, and onward to Pitlochry; it is a good road but a little too fast (so take care). Perth can also be reached via the M90 over the Forth Bridge from Edinburgh.

Three signed touring routes are useful: the Perthshire Tourist Route, the Deeside Tourist Route, and the Pitlochry Tourist Route, a beautiful and unexpected trip via Crieff and Loch Tay. Local tourist information centers can supply maps of these routes, or you can check online (⊕ *www. visitscotland.com*). Once you leave the major motorways, roads become narrower and slower, with many following the contours of the lochs. Be prepared for your journey to take longer than distances might suggest.

TRAIN TRAVEL

The Central Highlands are linked to Edinburgh and Glasgow by rail, with through routes to England (some direct-service routes from London take less than five hours). Several discount ticket options are available, although in some cases on the ScotRail system a discount card must be purchased before your arrival in the United Kingdom. Note that families with children and travelers under 26 or over 60 are eligible for significant discounts. Contact Trainline, Traveline Scotland, National Rail, or ScotRail for details.

The West Highland Line runs through the western portion of the area. Services also run to Stirling, Dunblane, Perth, and Gleneagles; stops on the Inverness–Perth line include Dunkeld, Pitlochry, and Blair Atholl.

Train Contacts National Rail Enquiries. ☎ *03457/484950* ⊕ *www. nationalrail.co.uk.* **ScotRail.** ☎ *0344/811–0141* ⊕ *www.scotrail.co.uk.* **Trainline.** ☎ *0871/244–1545* ⊕ *www.thetrainline.com.* **Traveline Scotland.** ☎ *0871/2002233* ⊕ *www.travelinescotland.com.*

RESTAURANTS

Regional country delicacies—loch trout, river salmon, lamb, and venison—appear regularly on even modest menus in Central Highlands restaurants. In all the towns and villages in the area, you will find simple pubs, often crowded and noisy, many of them serving substantial food at lunchtime and in the evening until about 9 (eaten balanced on your knee, perhaps, or at a shared table). The more luxurious restaurants tend to be in upscale hotels, with prices to match. It can be difficult to find a place to eat later in the evening, so plan ahead.

HOTELS

A wide selection of accommodations is available throughout the region, especially in Stirling, Bridge of Allan, Callander, and Pitlochry. They range from bed-and-breakfasts to private houses with a small number of rooms to rural accommodation (often on farms). The grand houses of the past—family homes to the landed aristocracy—have for the most part become country-house hotels. Their settings, often on ample grounds, offer an experience of grand living—but the area also has modern hotels, for those who prefer 21st-century amenities. *Hotel reviews have been shortened. For full information, visit Fodors.com.*

WHAT IT COSTS IN POUNDS				
	$	$$	$$$	$$$$
Restaurants	under £15	£15–£19	£20–£25	over £25
Hotels	under £100	£100–£160	£161–£220	over £220

Restaurant prices are the average cost of a main course at dinner or, if dinner is not served, at lunch, excluding tax. Hotel prices are the lowest cost of a standard double room in high season, including 20% V.A.T.

VISITOR INFORMATION

The tourist offices in Stirling and Perth are open year-round, as are offices in larger towns; others are seasonal (generally from April to October).

STIRLING

26 miles northeast of Glasgow, 36 miles northwest of Edinburgh.

Stirling is one of Britain's great historic towns. An impressive proportion of the Old Town walls can be seen from Dumbarton Road, a cobbled street leading to Stirling Castle, built on a steep-sided plug of rock. From its esplanade there is a commanding view of the surrounding Carse of Stirling. The guns on the castle battlements are a reminder of the military advantage to be gained from its position.

GETTING HERE AND AROUND

Stirling's central position in the area makes it ideal for travel to and from Glasgow and Edinburgh (or north to Perth and the Highlands) by rail or bus. The town itself is compact and easily walkable, though a shuttle bus travels to and from the town center up the steep road to Stirling Castle every 20 minutes. You can stroll the Back Walk on a circuit around the base of the castle walls—set aside at least 30 minutes for a leisurely walk. The National Wallace Monument (2 miles away) is on the outskirts of the town and can be reached by taxi or on foot.

ESSENTIALS

Visitor Information Stirling Visitor Information Centre. ⊠ *Old Town Jail, St. John St.* ☎ *01786/465019* ⊕ *www.visitscotland.com/stirling.*

EXPLORING

TOP ATTRACTIONS

FAMILY

Fodor'sChoice
★

Battle of Bannockburn Visitor Centre. You can almost hear horses' hooves and the zip of arrows in this 21st-century re-creation of the battle that changed the course of Scotland's history in 1314. Robert the Bruce's defeat of the armies of the English king, despite a 2-to1-disadvantage, is the stuff of legend. Using 3-D technology, the battle rages across screens that ring the central hall. Participants on both sides speak directly to you, courtesy of holograms. Later you can play a role in a Bannockburn battle game (reservations essential; age seven and over only). Bruce pursued the Scottish crown, ruthlessly sweeping aside enemies; but his victory here was masterful, as he drew the English horses into marshy

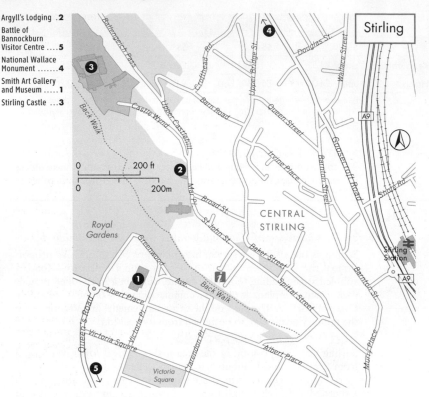

land (now the area around the new center) where they sank in the mud. A circular monument commemorates the battlefield. ■**TIP→ Book ahead; tickets are for timed entry.** ⊠ *Glasgow Rd., Bannockburn* ☎ *01786/812664* ⊕ *www.battleofbannockburn.com* ⊠ *£11.50.*

National Wallace Monument. This Victorian-era shrine to William Wallace (circa 1270–1305), the Scottish freedom fighter reborn as "Braveheart" in Mel Gibson's 1995 film of the same name, was built between 1856 and 1869. It sits on Abbey Craig, from which Wallace watched the English armies struggle across the old Stirling Bridge before attacking them and winning a major victory in 1297. A steep stone spiral staircase leads to the roof gallery, with views of the bridge and the whole Carse of Stirling. A less flamboyant version of Wallace's life is told in an exhibition and audiovisual presentation on the second floor. To reach the monument, follow the Bridge of Allan signs (A9) northward, crossing the River Forth by the New Bridge of 1832, next to the old one. The monument is signposted at the next traffic circle. From the car park a free shuttle will take you to the monument or you can walk (15 minutes). ⊠ *Abbey Craig, Hillfoot Rd.* ☎ *01786/472140* ⊕ *www.nationalwallacemonument.com* ⊠ *£9.99.*

FAMILY
Fodor'sChoice
★

Stirling Castle. Its magnificent strategic position on a steep-sided crag made Stirling Castle the grandest prize in the Scots Wars of Independence in the late 13th and early 14th centuries. Robert the Bruce's victory at Bannockburn won both the castle and freedom from English subjugation for almost four centuries. Take time to visit the **Castle Exhibition** beyond the lower gate to get an overview of its evolution as a stronghold and palace. ■ TIP→ **It's a good idea to book tickets online before your visit.**

The daughter of King Robert I (Robert the Bruce), Marjory, married Walter Fitzallan, the high steward of Scotland. Their descendants included the Stewart dynasty of Scottish monarchs (Mary, Queen of Scots, was a Stewart, though she preferred the French spelling, *Stuart*). The Stewarts were responsible for many of the works that survive within the castle walls. They made Stirling Castle their court and power base, creating fine Renaissance-style buildings that were never completely obliterated, despite reconstruction for military purposes.

Enter the castle through its outer defenses, which consist of a great curtained wall and batteries from 1708. From this lower square the most conspicuous feature is the **Palace,** built by King James V (1512–42) between 1538 and 1542. The decorative figures festooning the ornate outer walls show the influence of French masons. An orientation center in the basement, designed especially for children, lets you try out the clothes and musical instruments of the time. Across a terrace are the **Royal Apartments,** which re-create the furnishings and tapestries found here during the reign of James V and his French queen, Mary of Guise. The queen's bedchamber contains copies of the beautiful tapestries in which the hunt for the white unicorn is clearly an allegory for the persecution of Christ. Overlooking the upper courtyard is the **Great Hall,** built by King James IV (1473–1513) in 1503. Before the Union of Parliaments in 1707, when the Scottish aristocracy sold out to England, this building had been used as one of the seats of the Scottish Parliament.

Among the later works built for regiments stationed here, the **Regimental Museum** stands out; it's a 19th-century baronial revival on the site of an earlier building. Nearby, the **Chapel Royal** is unfurnished. The oldest building on the site is the **Mint,** or **Coonzie Hoose,** perhaps dating as far back as the 14th century. Below it is an arched passageway leading to the westernmost ramparts, the **Nether Bailey,** with a view of the *carselands* (valley plain) of the Forth Valley.

To the castle's south lies the hump of the Touch and the Gargunnock Hills, which diverted potential direct routes from Glasgow and the south. For centuries all roads into the Highlands across the narrow waist of Scotland led through Stirling. If you look carefully northward, you can still see the Old Stirling Bridge, the site of William Wallace's most famous victory. ⊠ *Castlehill* ☎ *01786/450000* ⊕ *www.stirling-castle.gov.uk* ⊠ *£15, includes Argyll's Lodging.*

WORTH NOTING

Argyll's Lodging. A nobleman's town house built in three phases from the 16th century onward, this building is actually older than the name it bears—that of Archibald, the ninth Earl of Argyll (1629–85), who bought it in 1666. It served for many years as a military hospital but has been refurbished to show how the nobility lived in 17th-century Stirling. Specially commissioned reproduction furniture and fittings are based on the original inventory of the house's contents at that time. ✉ *Castle Wynd* ☎ *01786/450000* 🌐 *www.stirlingcastle.gov.uk/discover* 🎟 *£15, includes Stirling Castle.*

FAMILY **Smith Art Gallery and Museum.** This small but intriguing museum in a neoclassical building, founded in 1874, houses "The Stirling Story," a comprehensive social history of the town. It holds the oldest football in the world, as well as the charming 16th-century portraits of the Five Stirling Sybils. Closer to the present are banners and memorabilia from the great miners' strike of 1984–85. The chiming clocks remind us, on the hour, of the present. The museum also holds regular temporary art and historical exhibitions and has a small tearoom. ✉ *Dumbarton Rd.* ✥ *A few mins' walk along Albert Pl. from the town center* ☎ *01786/471917* 🌐 *www.smithartgalleryandmuseum.co.uk* 🎟 *Free* 🕒 *Closed Mon.*

WHERE TO EAT

$ BRITISH FAMILY 🍴 **Allanwater Cafe.** Run by the Bechelli family for four generations, this casual, light, and airy café in Bridge of Allan, just a couple of miles from Stirling, is a popular spot with locals. Try the traditional "fish tea"—here confusingly called "catch of the day"—which consists of fish-and-chips served with tea or coffee and bread and butter. **Known for:** "fish tea"; ice cream; quick service. [$] *Average main: £12* ✉ *15 Henderson St., Bridge of Allan* ☎ *01786/833060* 🌐 *www.allanwatercafe.co.uk.*

$$ BRITISH 🍴 **Brea.** A fresh, welcome addition to Stirling's restaurant scene, this unpretentious place with wooden tables and chairs has a menu that celebrates Scottish food, though well-made burgers and steaks are also permanent features. The food offers some new takes on traditional favorites such as the rolled haddock with salmon, the Cullen skink soup, and haggis in various guises. **Known for:** burgers; good seafood; house-made desserts. [$] *Average main: £18* ✉ *5 Baker St.* ✥ *Down the hill from Stirling Castle* ☎ *01786/446277* 🌐 *www.brea-stirling.co.uk.*

$$ ECLECTIC FAMILY 🍴 **River House.** Behind Stirling Castle, this friendly, light-filled restaurant built in the style of a Scottish *crannog* (ancient loch dwelling) sits by its own tranquil little loch, with tables on a deck overlooking the water. Local produce dominates a menu that includes seafood pie with Arbroath smokies, rump of lamb, and, naturally, haggis and neeps. **Known for:** burgers and steaks; afternoon tea; lochside dining. [$] *Average main: £16* ✉ *Castle Business Park, B8051* ☎ *01786/465577* 🌐 *www.riverhouse-restaurant.co.uk.*

$ CAFÉ 🍴 **Sable and Flea.** Vintage items, housewares, and coffee and homemade cakes are an unusual combination, but a welcome one if it's soup and a sandwich or quiche that you want for lunch. At this charming café, you go through the tempting shop and there's a hidden courtyard, perfect for a break and a piece of cake or a meditative coffee. **Known for:** homemade cakes; light lunches; hidden courtyard. [$] *Average main: £8* ✉ *12 Friars St.* ☎ *07913/340592* 🕒 *Closed Mon. No dinner.*

WHERE TO STAY

$ ⛨ **Castlecroft.** Tucked beneath Stirling Castle, this comfortable modern

B&B/INN house with traditionally furnished guest rooms welcomes you with freshly cut flowers and homemade breakfasts. **Pros:** great location; lovely views; hearty breakfasts. **Cons:** a little hard to find if you are not arriving directly from the motorway. $ *Rooms from: £85* ✉ *Ballengeich Rd.* ☎ *01786/474933* ⊕ *castlecroft-uk.co.uk/* ⇝ *5 rooms* ⓧ *Breakfast.*

$$ ⛨ **Colessio Hotel.** Occupying a large stone, landmark neoclassical build-

HOTEL ing in the center of town and near the castle, this is a modern hotel in the grand style, with 21st-century amenities. **Pros:** great central location; good modern facilities; ample, comfortable bedrooms. **Cons:** difficult parking, though there is a parking lot behind the hotel; black-and-white decor may overpower; limited views in some rooms. $ *Rooms from:* £119 ✉ *33 Spittal St.* ☎ *01786/448880* ⊕ *www.hotelcolessio.com* ⇝ *40 rooms* ⓧ *Breakfast.*

$$ ⛨ **Friars Wynd.** At this small boutique hotel in a restored town house

HOTEL in the heart of Stirling, the rooms have been tastefully modernized and feature some exposed brick and a range of interesting paintings. **Pros:** pleasant and relaxing atmosphere; tasteful decor; reasonably priced. **Cons:** Wi-Fi in public areas only; no parking. $ *Rooms from: £119* ✉ *17 Friars St.* ☎ *01786/447501* ⊕ *www.friarswynd.co.uk* ⇝ *8 rooms* ⓧ *Breakfast.*

$$ ⛨ **Portcullis Hotel.** This small hotel with a lively traditional pub scores

B&B/INN above all on location: it is just outside the walls of Stirling Castle, and the views are spectacular, especially from the upper floors where the guest rooms are located. **Pros:** excellent location close to the castle; fine views. **Cons:** can get noisy; snug rooms; not cheap in high season. $ *Rooms from: £125* ✉ *Castle Wynd* ☎ *01786/472290* ⊕ *www.theportcullishotel.com* ⇝ *4 rooms* ⓧ *Breakfast.*

$$ ⛨ **Victoria Square Guest House.** Looking out over a pleasant grassy

B&B/INN square, this rather grand Victorian house has been completely modernized in tasteful restrained colors; decorative notes such as William Morris wallpaper and brass chandeliers recall the house's origins. **Pros:** spacious, bright rooms; luxurious details; central and quiet location. **Cons:** no children under 12. $ *Rooms from: £122* ✉ *12 Victoria Sq.* ☎ *01786/473920* ⊕ *www.victoriasquareguesthouse.com* ⇝ *7 rooms* ⓧ *Breakfast.*

NIGHTLIFE AND PERFORMING ARTS

Macrobert Arts Centre. On the campus of the University of Stirling, this arts center has a theater, gallery, and cinema with programs that range from films to pantomime. It's off the A9 as you're heading toward Bridge of Allan. ✉ *University of Stirling, W. Link Rd.* ☎ *01786/466666* ⊕ *www.macrobert.org.*

SHOPPING

CLOTHING

House of Henderson. A Highland outfitter, House of Henderson sells tartans, woolens, and accessories, and offers a made-to-measure kilt service. ⊠ *6–8 Friars St.* ☎ *01786/473681* ⊕ *www.houseofhenderson.co.uk.*

Mill Trail. East of Stirling is Mill Trail country, along the foot of the Ochil Hills. A leaflet from any local tourist information center will lead you to the delights of a real textile mill shop and low mill prices—even on cashmere—at Tillicoultry, Alva, and Alloa.

GIFTS

Fotheringham Gallery. The upscale Fotheringham Gallery stocks contemporary Scottish paintings by various artists, as well as striking modern jewelry by Leigh Fortheringham. ⊠ *78 Henderson St., Bridge of Allan* ☎ *01786/832861* ⊕ *www.fotheringhamgallery.co.uk.*

Stirling Bagpipes. This small shop sells bagpipes of every type and at every price, including antiques by legendary craftspeople that are displayed in glass cases. In the room behind the shop, the owner lovingly turns the chanters and drones, but he will happily take time to talk you through the history of these instruments. ⊠ *8 Broad St.* ☎ *01786/448886* ⊕ *www.stirlingbagpipes.com.*

SIDE TRIP: FALKIRK

14 miles southeast of Stirling, along the M9 motorway.

Falkirk has a fascinating history and some striking attractions. It was here, at the impressive Antonine Wall, that the Roman occupiers drove back the warlike Picts. You can visit parts of the wall and imagine the fierce battles over this strategic location.

In the late 18th century Falkirk was an important industrial town because of its network of canals linking Glasgow and Edinburgh, but with the arrival of the railways, the town's fortunes flagged. The canals have been brought back to life with the Millennium Link Project, which added cycling and walking routes, the new Kelpies nature park, and the spectacular Falkirk Wheel, a boat lift that has become a major visitor draw.

GETTING HERE AND AROUND

The M9 from Stirling to Falkirk follows the widening estuary of the River Forth, the view dominated by the huge Grangemouth oil refinery in the distance.

EXPLORING

Antonine Wall. West of Falkirk, Bonnybridge is home to the most extensive remains of the Antonine Wall, a 37-mile-long Roman earthwork fortification that marked the northernmost limit of the Roman Empire. Built around AD 140 as a defense against the warlike Picts of the north, it was abandoned some 20 years later. A UNESCO World Heritage Site, the wall was site of a famous battle in 1298, when William Wallace was defeated by the English. To get here from Falkirk, take the A803 west. ■ **TIP→** You can download a walking map of the wall from ⊕ **visitfalkirk. com.** ⊠ *Off A803, Bonnybridge* ✥ *2 miles west of Falkirk off the A803* ⊕ *www.historicenvironment.scot* 🎫 *Free.*

FAMILY **Falkirk Wheel.** The only rotating boat lift in the world, the Falkirk Wheel
Fodor'sChoice links two major waterways, the Forth and Clyde Canal and the Union
★ Canal, between Edinburgh and Glasgow. Opened in 2001, this extraordinary engineering achievement lifts and lowers boats using four giant
wheels shaped like Celtic axes; it can transport eight or more boats at
a time from one canal to the other in about 45 minutes. The Falkirk
Wheel replaced 11 locks. You can take a 50-minute trip as the wheel
turns, and you're transported up or down to the other canal. The site
offers children's play areas, as well as children's canoes and bicycle
rentals. An on-site office has information on canal boat cruises. There
are also several canal path walkways and cycleways. The excellent Heritage Centre provides plenty of information and has a good café and
gift shop. ■ TIP→ **Booking your trip ahead is recommended in summer.**
⊠ *Lime Rd., Tamfourhill* ✢ *Signposted off the A803* ☎ *08700/500208*
⊕ *www.thefalkirkwheel.co.uk* ☑ *£12.95.*

FAMILY **The Kelpies.** The Helix, a country park on the edges of Falkirk with cycle
Fodor'sChoice and walking paths, play areas, and a wetland, is home to sculptor Andy
★ Scott's extraordinary *The Kelpies*, horse heads forged in steel, 85 and
98 feet high respectively. The largest works of art in Scotland, they sit
at the center of the park, their beautiful heads framed against the Ochil
Hills behind, paying homage to Falkirk's industrial past. The heads are
modeled on Clydesdales, the huge draft horses that hauled barges along
the canals before the advent of the railways. A special guided tour (book
online for convenience) gives you an insight into the area's past and
takes you inside the sculptures, and there is a visitor center with a café
and gift shop. ⊠ *The Helix, A9 and Falkirk Rd.* ✢ *From the A9, the M9,
or through Falkirk, where the route is well signposted* ☎ *01324/506850*
⊕ *www.thehelix.co.uk* ☑ *Park free; £7.50 tour.*

6

THE TROSSACHS AND LOCH LOMOND

Immortalized by Wordsworth and Sir Walter Scott, the Trossachs (the
name means "bristly country") contains some of Scotland's loveliest
forest, hills, and glens, well justifying the area's designation as a national
park. The area has a special charm, combining the wildness of the Highlands with the prolific vegetation of an old Lowland forest. Its open
ground is a dense mat of bracken and heather, and its woodland is of
silver birch, dwarf oak, and hazel—trees that fasten their roots into the
crevices of rocks and stop short on the very brink of lochs. There are
also many small towns to visit along the way, some with their roots in
a medieval world; others sprang up and expanded in the wake of the
first tourists who came to Scotland in the late 19th century in search of
wild country or healing waters. Dunblane has a magnificent cathedral;
Doune's castle will make you stare in awe.

The most colorful season is fall, particularly October, a lovely time
when most visitors have departed, and the hares, deer, and game birds
have taken over. Even in rainy weather the Trossachs of "darksome
glens and gleaming lochs" are memorable: the water filtering through
the rocks by Loch Lomond comes out so pure and clear that the loch
is like a sheet of glass.

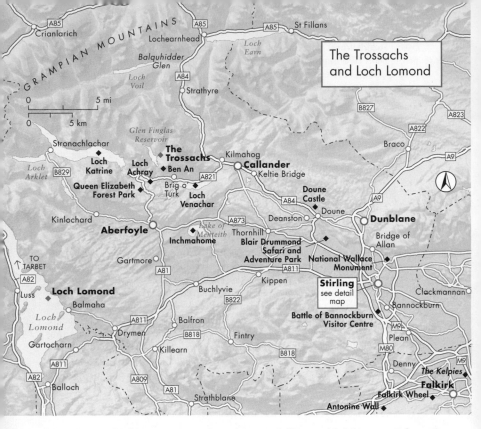

The best way to explore this area is by car, by bike, or on foot; the latter two depend, of course, on the weather. Keep in mind that roads in this region of the country are narrow and winding, which can make for dangerous conditions in all types of weather.

DUNBLANE

6 miles north of Stirling.

The small, quiet town of Dunblane has long been an important religious center; it is dominated by its cathedral, which dates mainly from the 13th century. The town also boasts one of Scotland's most impressive libraries, the Leighton Library.

GETTING HERE AND AROUND

Dunblane station is on the main line to Perth and Inverness, and regular bus service links the town to Stirling. For drivers it is easily reached along the main A9 artery.

EXPLORING

FAMILY **Blair Drummond Safari and Adventure Park.** As unlikely as it might seem in this gentle valley, the Blair Drummond Safari and Adventure Park is the place to see sea lions bobbing their heads above the water or monkeys swinging from the branches. Take a footbridge to Lemur Land or watch hawks and falcons in the "Birds of Prey" exhibit. Beware the llamas, who are more bad-tempered than they may appear. The enclosures are spacious, so the place doesn't feel like a zoo. There are rides, slides, and an adventure playground for the kids. ✉ *Blair Drummond, Doune* ✛ *Off the A84* ☎ *01786/841456* ⊕ *www.blairdrummond.com* ☐ *£16.50* ⊘ *Closed Nov.–Feb.*

Doune Castle. The castle may seem eerily familiar because it is a favorite with filmmakers: *Monty Python and the Holy Grail* was filmed here, and more recently it was used in the *Game of Thrones* and *Outlander* series. In 1361 it became the seat of Robert Stewart, the Duke of Albany and Governor of Scotland, who embarked on various building projects. The semi-ruined Doune is grim and high-walled, with a daunting central keep and echoing, drafty stairways up to the curtain-wall walk. Climb the wall; the views over the countryside will make it worthwhile. There is a good audio guide narrated by Monty Python's Terry Jones. ■ **TIP→ The best place to photograph this squat, walled fort is from the bridge, a little way upstream.** In the past, Doune was known for its gunsmiths, and no self-respecting Highland chief's attire was complete without an ornate pair of pistols made here. ✉ *Castle Rd., Doune* ✛ *5 miles west of Dunblane* ☎ *01786/841742* ⊕ *www.historicenvironment.scot* ☐ *£6.*

Dunblane Cathedral. The oldest part of Dunblane—with its narrow winding streets—huddles around this church's square. Bishop Clement built the cathedral in the early 13th century on the site of St. Blane's tiny 8th-century cell; with the Reformation of the 16th century, it ceased to be a cathedral. In 1996 it was the scene of a moving memorial service for the 15 children and one teacher killed in the local school by Thomas Hamilton. ✉ *The Cross* ☎ *01667/460232* ⊕ *www.dunblanecathedral.org.uk* ☐ *Free.*

WHERE TO EAT AND STAY

$$
BRITISH
✕ **Juniper Restaurant.** Housed in a row of 18th-century cottages directly overlooking the cathedral, this pleasant and atmospheric restaurant with a wood-beamed ceiling serves traditional Scottish dishes side by side with creative modern cooking such as venison bourguignon. There's also an extensive and excellent vegetarian menu. **Known for:** homemade steak pie; vegetarian menu; "Flavors of Scotland" starter. Ⓢ *Average main: £16* ✉ *1 Kirk St.* ☎ *01786/823663* ⊕ *www.oldchurcshouse.com.*

$$$$
HOTEL
Fodor's Choice
★
☷ **Cromlix House.** A grand Victorian country house set amid beautiful grounds, Cromlix House has been tastefully refurbished by its owner, Scottish tennis champion Andy Murray, to maintain its atmosphere and create a sense of restrained luxury. **Pros:** luxurious facilities; lovely grounds for walking; comfortable beds. **Cons:** not much for children; a little hard to find. Ⓢ *Rooms from: £295* ✉ *Kinbuck* ✛ *Off B8033, beyond the village of Kinbuck; keep looking for the entrance; 4½ miles north of Dunblane* ☎ *01786/822125* ⊕ *www.cromlix.com* ⇗ *16 rooms* ⦿ *Breakfast.*

$$
HOTEL
☷ **DoubleTree by Hilton Dunblane Hydro.** One of the grandes dames where Victorians would come to "take the waters," this hotel on sprawling grounds has retained its original building and the high style of its interior. **Pros:** fine views; lovely grounds; leisure center included in the rates. **Cons:** slightly old-fashioned feel; some rooms are small; charge for Wi-Fi. Ⓢ *Rooms from: £129* ✉ *Perth Rd.* ☎ *01786/822551* ⊕ *www. doubletreedunblane.com* ⇗ *200 rooms* ⦿ *No meals.*

6

CALLANDER

8 miles northwest of Doune.

A traditional Highland-edge resort, the little town of Callander bustles throughout the year, even during off-peak times, simply because it's a gateway to Highland scenery and Loch Lomond and the Trossachs National Park. As a result, there's plenty of window-shopping here, plus nightlife in pubs and a selection of mainly bed-and-breakfast accommodations.

GETTING HERE AND AROUND

You can access Callander by bus from Stirling, Glasgow, or Edinburgh. If you're traveling by car from Stirling, take the M8 to Dunblane, then the A820 (which becomes the A84) to Callander. If you are coming from Glasgow, take the A81 through Aberfoyle to Callander; an alternative route (longer but more picturesque) is to take the A821 around Loch Venachar, then the A84 east to Callander.

ESSENTIALS

Visitor Information Callander Visitor Information Centre. ✉ *52–54 Main St.* ☎ *01877/330342* ⊕ *www.visitscotland.com.*

EXPLORING

FAMILY **Hamilton Toy Collection.** One of those eccentric museums born of one person's (or one family's) passionate obsession, this small, crowded house and shop on Callander's main street contains one of the most extensive toy collections in Britain. The rooms throughout the house are filled with everything from Corgi cars and an enormous number of toy soldiers, carefully organized by regiment, to Amanda Jane dolls and Beatles memorabilia. The collection of model railways has extended into tracks in the back garden. The museum is jammed and quirky, but full of reminders of everyone's childhood. ✉ *111 Main St.* ☎ *01877/330004* ⊕ *www.thehamiltontoycollection.co.uk* 🎟 *£3* ⊘ *Closed Nov.–Mar.*

WHERE TO EAT

$ **✕ Deli Ecosse.** Don't miss it: in one corner of the square, a narrow door

CAFÉ opens into a high-ceilinged old church hall crowded with good things to eat there or take away. You can order tasty soups, homemade cakes, and plump sandwiches from the counter, or try the excellent coffee or a glass of wine. **Known for:** homemade cakes; excellent breakfast; inexpensive lunch. $ *Average main: £10* ✉ *10 Ancaster Sq.* ☎ *01877/331220* ⊘ *No dinner.*

$ **✕ MHOR Fish.** Simple white walls and black-and-white floors provide the

SEAFOOD backdrop for great fish at this very superior "chippy" (fish-and-chips shop) owned by the people who run the Monachyle MHOR hotel; there's also a takeaway next door. It's somehow reassuring that the restaurant doubles as a fishmonger; you know the fish is fresh and sustainable, so it might be pollock or coley rather than cod or haddock. **Known for:** sustainable fish; great chips (fried in beef fat); homemade bread. $ *Average main: £12* ✉ *75 77 Main St.* ☎ *01877/330213* ⊕ *www.mhor.net.*

$$ **✕ Venachar Lochside.** There is a special pleasure in dining overlooking a

MODERN BRITISH loch, and this restaurant's glass wall affords a lovely panorama of the

Fodor's Choice water and surrounding hills—a pleasant surprise given that all you see

★ from the road is what seems to be a large shed. The menu lives up to its

ROB ROY MACGREGOR

Scotland produces legends, and that of Rob Roy MacGregor (1671–1734) is one of the most enduring. He joined the Jacobite rebellion in 1689, but the MacGregors were excluded from the amnesty of 1717. Two years later he was wounded in the battle of Glen Shiel. In later life MacGregor became a cattleman who was cheated of his herd and his money and evicted from his home. He became an outlaw and a Jacobite hero whose final home was Balquhidder, near Callander. Rob Roy MacGregor was rescued from obscurity by Sir Walter Scott's 1817 novel, *Rob Roy*; the 1995 film starred Liam Neeson. In 2002 the Rob Roy Way (🌐 *www.robroyway.com*), a multiday walk from Drymen to Pitlochry, was inaugurated.

surroundings, with an emphasis on fish—mussels, scallops, the excellent smoked-fish selection to start, and the trout with roast chorizo. **Known for:** smoked-fish platter; fine seafood; lochside dining. [$] *Average main: £15* ✉ *Loch Venachar* ✥ *On the A821 about 6 miles from Callander, at Brig o' Turk* ☎ *01877/330011* 🌐 *www.venachar-lochside.co.uk.*

WHERE TO STAY

$ B&B/INN FAMILY 🏨 **Auchenlaich Farmhouse.** This unpretentious house on a working farm sits just outside Callander, with bright, comfortable rooms and lovely views. **Pros:** fine views; especially good for cyclists and walkers; economical. **Cons:** not all rooms are en suite; basic, practical accommodation; cash only. [$] *Rooms from: £80* ✉ *Keltie Bridge* ✥ *Just past Keltie Bridge at the end of a short farm road* ☎ *01877/331683* 🌐 *www.auchenlaich-farmhouse.co.uk* 🛏 *5 rooms* 🍴 *Breakfast* 💳 *No credit cards.*

$ B&B/INN FAMILY 🏨 **MHOR 84.** For walkers and cyclists Balquhidder Glen is the perfect place, and this modest but casually chic hotel has been designed with them in mind. **Pros:** beautiful setting; great quality for the price; game room for kids. **Cons:** a rather isolated spot. [$] *Rooms from: £80* ✉ *Balquhidder* ✥ *Off the A84 from Callander to Crianlarich, turn at Kingshouse; 11 miles north of Callender* ☎ *01877/384646* 🌐 *www.mhor84.net* 🛏 *7 rooms* 🍴 *No meals.*

$$$ HOTEL Fodor's Choice ★ 🏨 **Monachyle MHOR.** Splendidly isolated, this beautiful converted farmhouse with contemporary interiors is set amid forests and moorland, looking out on to Lochs Voil and Doine. **Pros:** stunning scenery; delicious food; complimentary salmon and trout fishing. **Cons:** remote location; rooms are on the small side. [$] *Rooms from: £190* ✉ *Off A84, Balquhidder* ✥ *17 miles (a 40-min drive) northwest of Callander* ☎ *01877/384622* 🌐 *www.mhor.net* 🛏 *14 rooms* 🍴 *Breakfast.*

$$ B&B/INN Fodor's Choice ★ 🏨 **Roman Camp.** Within a hundred yards of Callander's main street, pass through an unpretentious arch and you'll find this 17th-century hunting lodge surrounded by ornate gardens. **Pros:** beautiful grounds; luxurious rooms; close to everything in town. **Cons:** restaurant is expensive; no Internet in rooms. [$] *Rooms from: £160* ✉ *Off Main St.* ☎ *01877/330003* 🌐 *www.romancamphotel.co.uk* 🛏 *15 rooms* 🍴 *Breakfast.*

SHOPPING

Trossachs Woollen Mill. The Edinburgh Woollen Mill Group owns this mill shop in Kilmahog, a mile west of Callander. It has a vast selection of woolens on display, including luxurious cashmere and striking tartan throws, and will provide overseas mailing and tax-free shopping. ⊠ *Main St., Kilmahog* ☎ *01877/330178* ⊕ *www.ewm.co.uk.*

SPORTS AND THE OUTDOORS

BICYCLING

Wheels. You can rent bikes of every sort by the hour, the half day, or the day from this friendly firm. Most popular are the mountain bikes, which go for £20 per day. The staff can also help you find the best mountain-bike routes around the Trossachs. ⊠ *Invertrossachs Rd.* ☎ *01877/331100* ⊕ *www.wheelscyclingcentre.com.*

GOLF

Callander Golf Club. Designed by Tom Morris in 1890 and extended to 18 holes in 1913 by Willie Fernie, Callander has a scenic upland feel in a town well prepared for visitors. Pine and birch woods and hilly fairways afford fine views, especially toward Ben Ledi, and the tricky moorland layout demands accurate hitting off the tee. The challenging 15th is one of Scotland's most famous holes. ⊠ *Aveland Rd.* ☎ *01877/330090* ⊕ *www.callandergolfclub.co.uk* ⊠ *£30 weekdays, £40 weekends* ⅃ *18 holes, 5208 yards, par 66.*

HIKING

Bracklinn Falls. A walk is signposted from the east end of Callander's main street to the Bracklinn Falls, over whose lip Sir Walter Scott once rode a pony to win a bet.

Callander Crags. It's a 1½-mile walk through the woods up to the Callander Crags, with views of the Lowlands as far as the Pentland Hills behind Edinburgh. The walk begins at the west end of Callander's main street.

Pass of Leny. Just north of Callander, the mountains squeeze both the road and rocky river into the narrow Pass of Leny. An abandoned railway—now a pleasant walking or biking path—also goes through the pass, past Ben Ledi and Loch Lubnaig.

THE TROSSACHS

10 miles west of Callander.

The Trossachs has been a popular touring region since the late 18th century, at the dawn of the age of the Romantic poets. Influenced by the writings of Sir Walter Scott, early visitors who strayed into the Highlands from the central belt of Scotland admired this as the first "wild" part of Scotland they encountered. Perhaps because the Trossachs represent the very essence of what the Highlands are supposed to be, the whole of this area, including Loch Lomond, is now protected as a national park. Here you can find birch and pine forests, vistas down lochs where the woods creep right to the water's edge, and, in the background, peaks that rise high enough to be called mountains, though they're not as high as those to the north and west.

GETTING HERE AND AROUND

To reach the Trossachs, take the A84 from Callander through the Pass of Leny, then on to Crianlarich on the A85; from here you can continue down the western shore of Loch Lomond or carry on toward Fort William. Alternately, turn onto the A821 outside Callander and travel past Loch Katrine through the Duke's Pass to Aberfoyle.

EXPLORING

TOP ATTRACTIONS

Fodor'sChoice
★

Ben An. The parking lot by Loch Achray is near the beginning of the path that ascends steep, heathery Ben An, which affords some of the best Trossachs views. The climb requires a couple of hours and good lungs. ⊠ *A821, Aberfoyle.*

FAMILY
Fodor'sChoice
★

Loch Katrine. This loch was a favorite among Victorian visitors—mysterious and wide and, at times, quite wild. Today it's the source of Glasgow's freshwater. Take a cruise around the loch if time permits, as the shores remain undeveloped and scenic. The steamship *Sir Walter Scott* and the motor launch *Lady of the Lake* sail from the lake's eastern end several times a day in season. You can make the round-trip journey around the loch, or head directly across to Stronachlachar and return by bicycle on the lochside road. There are café facilities and cycle-hire shops at the head of the loch; reservations are required if you're taking a bike on the boat. ⊠ *Trossachs Pier, Aberfoyle* ⊹ *Off A821* ☎ *01877/376316* ⊕ *www.lochkatrine.com* ☒ *Sir Walter Scott £16.50 round-trip, £13.50 one way; Lady of the Lake £14.50 round-trip, £11.50 one way* ☉ *Closed Oct.–May.*

WORTH NOTING

Loch Achray. Stretching west of the small community of Brig o' Turk, Loch Achray dutifully fulfills expectations of what a verdant Trossachs loch should be: small, green, reedy meadows backed by dark plantations, rhododendron thickets, and lumpy hills, thickly covered with heather. ⊠ *A821, Brig o'Turk.*

Loch Venachar. The A821 runs west together with the first and gentlest of the Trossachs lochs, Loch Venachar. A sturdy gray-stone building, with a small dam at the Callander end, controls the water that feeds into the River Teith (and, hence, into the Forth). ⊠ *A821, Brig o'Turk.*

ABERFOYLE

11 miles south of Loch Katrine, in the Trossachs.

This small tourist-oriented town has a somewhat faded air, but the surrounding hills (some snowcapped) and the green slopes visible from the town are the reason so many people pause here before continuing up to Duke's Pass or on to Inversnaid on Loch Lomond. Access to nearby Queen Elizabeth Forest Park is another reason to visit.

GETTING HERE AND AROUND

The main route out of Glasgow, the A81, takes you through Aberfoyle and on to Callander and Stirling. There are regular buses from Stirling and Glasgow to Aberfoyle.

ESSENTIALS

Visitor Information Trossachs Discovery Centre. ✉ *Main St.* ☎ *01877/382352* 🌐 *www.visitscotland.com.*

EXPLORING

FAMILY **Go Ape High Wire Forest Adventure.** Near the David Marshall Lodge, this is an exhilarating experience for thrill seekers age 10 and over. After a short orientation course, you can travel 40 feet above the forest via ziplines and rope ladders on a sort of midair assault course. ✉ *Queen Elizabeth Forest Park, A821, 1 mile north of Aberfoyle* ☎ *0845/643–9215* 🌐 *www.goape.com* 🎫 *£31 (3 hrs), £25 (2 hrs)* 🕒 *Closed weekdays in Nov., Feb., and Mar.*

Fodor's Choice ★ **Inchmahome.** The 13th-century ruined priory on the tiny island of Inchmahome, on the Lake of Menteith, is a lovely place for a picnic after you explore the building's chapter house and other remains. It was a place of refuge in 1547 for the young Mary, Queen of Scots. In season, a seven-minute ferry takes passengers to the island, now owned by the National Trust for Scotland. The ferry jetty is just past the Port of Menteith (a village). ✉ *Off A81* ✥ *Take the A81 to the B8034; it's 4 miles east of Aberfoyle* ☎ *01786/385294* 🌐 *www.historicenvironment.scot* 🎫 *Ferry £7.50* 🕒 *Closed. Nov.–Mar.*

Fodor's Choice ★ **Queen Elizabeth Forest Park.** For exquisite nature, drive north from Aberfoyle on the A821 and turn right at signposts to Queen Elizabeth Forest Park. Along the way you'll be heading toward higher moorland blanketed with conifers. The conifers hem in the views of Ben Ledi and Ben Venue, which can be seen over the spiky green waves of trees as the road snakes around heathery knolls and hummocks. There's another viewing area, and a small parking lot, at the highest point of the road. Soon the road swoops off the Highland edge and leads downhill.

At the heart of the Queen Elizabeth Forest Park, the **Lodge Forest Visitor Centre** leads to four forest walks, a family-friendly bicycle route, and the 7-mile 3 Lochs Forest Drive, open April to October. Or you can sit on the terrace of the Bluebell Cafe and scan the forests and hills of the Trossachs. The visitor center has a wildlife-watch room where you can follow the activities of everything from ospreys to water voles. ✉ *Off A821, 1 mile north of Aberfoyle* ☎ *01877/382383* 🌐 *www.forestry.gov.uk/qefp* 🎫 *Free, parking £3.*

FAMILY **Scottish Wool Centre.** Besides selling a vast range of woolen garments and knitwear, the Scottish Wool Centre has a small café and some activities. Three times a day from April to September it presents an interactive "gathering" during which dogs herd sheep and ducks in the large amphitheater, with a little help from the public. ✉ *Off Main St.* ☎ *01877/382850* 🌐 *www.ewm.co.uk* 🎫 *Free.*

WHERE TO EAT AND STAY

$ BRITISH 🍴 **Pier Café.** At the historic Stronachlachar Pier, this light-filled coffee shop has a satisfying lunch menu (burgers and sandwiches) and a deck with expansive views over Loch Katrine. Cakes, scones, and soups are made on the premises. **Known for:** home baking; good coffee; loch views. [$] *Average main: £10* ✉ *B829, Stronachlachar* ☎ *01877/386374* 🌐 *www.thepiercafe.com* 🕒 *No dinner Mon.–Wed.*

$$
HOTEL
Fodor'sChoice
★
⊞ Lake of Menteith Hotel. At this beautifully located hotel overlooking the Lake of Menteith, muted colors and simple but elegant rooms create a restful air, enhanced, perhaps, by the silent hills that ring the hotel and the tranquil lake. **Pros:** elegant, unpretentious bedrooms; beautiful setting. **Cons:** not well signposted; not all rooms have lake views and those that do are more expensive. $ *Rooms from: £145* ⊠ *Off A81* ☎ *01877/385258* ⊕ *www.lake-hotel.com* ➟ *17 rooms* ⦿ *Breakfast.*

$$$
HOTEL
⊞ Macdonald Forest Hills Hotel. This is a traditional Scottish country hotel for families and those who simply want to take it easy, though it also offers numerous sporting activities. **Pros:** stunning views; 20-plus acres of grounds to explore; good children's programs. **Cons:** restaurant is pricey; some of the building looks run-down; feels slightly anonymous. $ *Rooms from: £179* ⊠ *B829, Kinlochard* ✛ *4 miles west of Aberfoyle* ☎ *08448/799057* ⊕ *www.macdonaldhotels.co.uk/foresthills* ➟ *56 rooms* ⦿ *No meals.*

GOLF

Aberfoyle Golf Club. Queen Elizabeth Forest Park provides the backdrop for this hilly course. One of the area's many James Braid–designed parkland courses, it dates back to 1890. There are views of Ben Lomond and Stirling Castle from different points on the course, which is relatively short but varied and challenging even for quite experienced players, with several uphill shots and undulating ground. ⊠ *Braeval* ✛ *Off A821* ☎ *01877/382493* ⊕ *www.aberfoylegolf.co.uk* ⊠ *£20 weekdays, £25 weekends* 🏌 *18 holes, 5158 yards, par 66.*

LOCH LOMOND

14 miles west of Aberfoyle.

The waters of Scotland's largest loch, which also happens to be one of its most beautiful, create a perfect reflection of the surrounding hills. You can cruise among its small islands or follow the low road that carries you from Glasgow to the beginning of the Highlands.

GETTING HERE AND AROUND

To reach Loch Lomond from Aberfoyle, take the A81 toward Glasgow, then the A811 to Drymen and then the B837 as far as it will take you. From Glasgow, take the A82 to the Balloch roundabout and either go right through Balloch for Drymen and the eastern shore, or continue along the A82 as it hugs the west bank all the way to Crianlarich.

You can drive, cycle, or walk along the 32 miles of Loch Lomond along its western shores, and watch the changing face of the loch as you go, or look up toward the shifting slopes of Ben Lomond.

ESSENTIALS

Visitor Information Loch Lomond and the Trossachs National Park Headquarters. ⊠ *Carrochan Rd., Balloch* ☎ *01389/722600* ⊕ *www.lochlomond-trossachs.org.*

EXPLORING

Fodor's Choice ★ **Loch Lomond.** Known for its "bonnie, bonnie banks," Loch Lomond is Scotland's largest loch in terms of surface area, and its waters reflect the crags that surround it. The song "The Banks of Loch Lomond" is said to have been written by a Jacobite prisoner incarcerated in Carlisle, England.

On the western side of the loch, the A82 follows the shore for 24 miles, continuing a farther 7 miles to Crianlarich, passing picturesque Luss, which has a pier where you can hop aboard boats cruising along the loch, and Tarbert, the starting point for the *Maid of the Loch*. On the eastern side of the loch, take the A81 to Drymen, and from there the B837 signposted toward Balmaha, where you can hire a boat or take the ferry to the island of Inchcailloch. Once you're there, a short walk takes you to the top of the hill and a spectacular view of the loch. Equally spectacular, but not as wet, is the view from Conic Hill behind Balmaha. If you continue along the B837 beyond Rowardennan to where it ends at a car park, you can join the walkers at the beginning of the path up Ben Lomond. Don't underestimate this innocent-looking hill; go equipped for sudden changes in the weather. Hikers can also try part of the 96-mile West Highland Way (⊕ *www.west-highland-way.co.uk*) that runs along the shore of Loch Lomond on its way north.

WHERE TO EAT

$ BRITISH Fodor's Choice ★ **✕ Coach House Coffee Shop.** This lively restaurant and café serving Scottish classics fits perfectly into its surroundings with its cheerful, over-the-top Scottishness. Long wooden tables, a large chimney with an open fire in the winter months, and a cabinet full of mouthwatering cakes baked by the owner create the atmosphere. **Known for:** teapots; stovies; Scottish style. $ *Average main: £11 ⊠ Church Rd., Luss ✛ Off A82 ☎ 01436/860341 ⊗ No dinner.*

$ BRITISH **✕ Drovers Inn.** Knowing its clientele, this quirky, noisy, friendly inn serves huge, hearty portions that are what you need after a day's walking on the nearby West Highland Way. Scottish staples like sausage and mash, minced beef, and haggis jostle for a place beside occasionally more adventurous dishes. **Known for:** big portions; old stuffed animals; good bar. $ *Average main: £12 ⊠ A82, Balloch ✛ On the A82 toward Crianlarich, north of Ardlui, just north of Loch Lomond ☎ 01301/704234 ⊕ www.thedroversinn.co.uk.*

WHERE TO STAY

$ HOTEL **Balloch House.** Cute, cozy, and very Scottish, this small hotel offers tasty breakfasts and good, hearty pub meals like fish-and-chips and local smoked salmon for reasonable prices. **Pros:** beautiful building; peat fires; near shopping. **Cons:** noisy pinball machine next to bar; not all rooms have views. $ *Rooms from: £98 ⊠ Balloch Rd., Balloch ☎ 01389/752579 ⊕ www.innkeeperslodge.com/loch-lomond ⊐ 12 rooms ⊘ Breakfast.*

$$$$ HOTEL **Cameron House.** There is little that you cannot do at this luxury resort hotel beside Loch Lomond, including taking to the water in a motorboat or riding a seaplane above the trees. **Pros:** beautiful grounds; away-from-it-all feel; good dining. **Cons:** prices are high; slightly difficult

access from A82. [$] *Rooms from: £310* ✉ *Loch Lomond, off A82, Alexandria* ☎ *01389/755565* 🌐 *www.cameronhouse.co.uk* 🛏 *103 rooms* 🍴 *Breakfast.*

SHOPPING

Loch Lomond Shores. This lakeside shopping complex contains restaurants, pubs, and a visitor center. ✉ *Ben Lomond Way, Balloch* ☎ *01389/751031* 🌐 *www.lochlomondshores.com.*

SPORTS AND THE OUTDOORS

BOATING

FAMILY **Cruise Loch Lomond.** You can take tours year-round with this company. From April to October boats depart from various ports around the loch, including Tarbet, Luss, Balmaha, and Inversnaid. There is also a Two-Loch Tour taking in Loch Lomond and Loch Katrine. From November to March the boats operate on demand. ✉ *A82, Tarbet* ☎ *01301/702356* 🌐 *www.cruiselochlomond.co.uk* 🎫 *From £10.*

Macfarlane and Son. At this longtime favorite, boats with outboard motors rent for £60 per day. Rowboats rent for £10 per hour or £40 per day. From Balmaha, it is a short trip to the lovely island of Incailloch. Macfarlane's also runs a ferry to the island for £5 per person. ✉ *Balmaha Boatyard, B837, Balmaha* ☎ *01360/870214* 🌐 *www.balmahaboatyard.co.uk* 🎫 *From £40 per day.*

Sweeney's Cruises. This operator runs trips and tours on Loch Lomond from Balloch, Luss, and Tarbert. ✉ *Riverside, Balloch Rd., Balloch* ☎ *01389/752376* 🌐 *www.sweeneyscruises.com* 🎫 *From £10.50.*

PERTHSHIRE

If Perthshire's castles invoke memories of past conflicts, the grand houses and spa towns here are testimony to the continued presence of a wealthy landed gentry. This is also a place for walking, cycling, and water sports. In some ways Perthshire is a crossing point where Lowlands and Highlands, two Scottish landscapes and two histories, meet. Perthshire itself is rural, agricultural Scotland, fertile and prosperous. Its woodlands, rivers, and glens (and agreeable climate and strategic position) drew the Romans and later the Celtic missionaries. In fact, the motto of the capital city, Perth, is "the perfect center."

PERTH

36 miles northeast of Stirling, 43 miles north of Edinburgh, 61 miles northeast of Glasgow.

For many years Perth was Scotland's capital, and central to its history. One king (James I) was killed here, and the Protestant reformer John Knox preached in St. John's Kirk, where his rhetoric moved crowds to burn down several local monasteries. Perth's local whisky trade and the productive agriculture that surrounds the town have sustained it through the centuries. Its grand buildings, especially on the banks of the River Tay, testify to its continued wealth. The open parkland within the city (the Inches) gives the place a restful air, and shops range from

6

small crafts boutiques to department stores. Impressive Scone Palace is nearby.

GETTING HERE AND AROUND

Perth is served by the main railway line to Inverness, and regular and frequent buses run here from Glasgow, Edinburgh, and Stirling. The central artery, the A9, passes through the city en route to Pitlochry and Inverness, while a network of roads opens the way to the glens and hills around Glen Lyon, or the road to Loch Lomond (the A85) via Crianlarich.

ESSENTIALS

Visitor Information Perth Visitor Centre. ⊠ *45 High St.* 🕾 *01738/450600* ⊕ *www.visitscotland.com.*

EXPLORING PERTH
TOP ATTRACTIONS

Elcho Castle. Built around 1560 by the River Tay, the castle marks a transition period when these structures began to be built as grand houses rather than fortresses, and it's easy to see that Elcho was built for both comfort and defense. The well-preserved but uncluttered rooms let you imagine how life might have been here in the 17th century. The staircases still give access to all floors, and a flashlight is provided for the darker corners. From the battlements of the castle you can see the river stretching east and west. ⊠ *Off A912* ✛ *Close to Rhynd* 🕾*01738/639998* ⊕ *www.historicenvironment.scot* ⊠ *£5* ⊘ *Closed Oct.–Mar.*

FAMILY
Fodor's Choice
★

Scone Palace. The current residence of the Earl of Mansfield, Scone Palace (pronounced *skoon*) is much more cheerful than the city's other castles. Although it incorporates various earlier works, the palace today has mainly a 19th-century theme, with mock castellations that were fashionable at the time. There's plenty to see if you're interested in the acquisitions of an aristocratic Scottish family: magnificent porcelain, some sumptuous furniture, a fine collection of ivory, clocks, and 16th-century needlework. Each room has a guide who will happily talk you through its contents and their associations. In one bedroom hangs a portrait of Dido Elizabeth Belle, a young black slave adopted by the family, who became a well-known society beauty in the 1760s. A coffee shop, restaurant, gift shop, and play area are on-site. The palace has its own mausoleum nearby, on the site of a long-gone abbey on **Moot Hill,** the ancient coronation place of the Scottish kings. To be crowned, they sat on the Stone of Scone, which was seized in 1296 by Edward I of England, Scotland's greatest enemy, and placed in the coronation chair at Westminster Abbey, in London. The stone was returned to Scotland in November 1996 and is now on view in Edinburgh Castle. ⊠ *Braemar Rd.* ✛ *2 miles north of Perth* 🕾 *01738/552300* ⊕ *www.scone-palace.co.uk* ⊠*£11.50* ⊘ *House closed Nov.–Mar. Grounds closed Mon.–Thurs. Nov.–Mar.*

WORTH NOTING

Fergusson Gallery. Originally a waterworks, this gallery with a magnificent dome and rotunda shelters a collection of 6,000 works—paintings, drawings, and prints—by the Scottish artist J. D. Fergusson (1874–1961) and his wife, Margaret Morris, an artist in her own right and a pioneer of modern dance. Fergusson was the longest-lived member

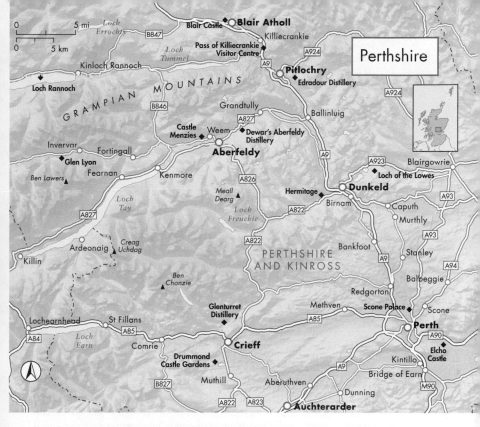

of the group called the Scottish Colourists, who took their inspiration from the French impressionist painters in their use of color and light. ⊠ *Marshall Pl.* ☎ *01738/783425* ⊕ *www.culturepk.org.uk* ⊠ *Free* ☯ *Closed Mon.*

Perth Art Gallery and Museum. This museum has a wide-ranging collection including exhibits on natural history, local history, archaeology, and art, as well as an important glass collection. It also includes work by the great painter of animals Sir Edwin Landseer and some botanical studies of fungi by Beatrix Potter, and presents temporary exhibitions from its own collection and elsewhere. ⊠ *78 George St.* ☎ *01738/632488* ⊕ *www.culturepk.org.uk* ⊠ *Free* ☯ *Closed Mon.*

Regimental Museum of the Black Watch. Some will tell you the Black Watch was a Scottish regiment whose name is a reference to the color of its tartan. An equally plausible explanation, however, is that the regiment was established to keep an undercover watch on rebellious Jacobites. The Gaelic word for black is *dubh,* meaning, in this case, "hidden" or "covert." A wide range of uniforms, weaponry, and marching banners are displayed in this museum in Balhousie Castle, and there's a very good café and shop. ⊠ *Balhousie Castle, Hay St.* ☎ *01738/638152* ⊕ *www. theblackwatch.co.uk* ⊠ *£7.50, guided tour (book ahead) £12.50.*

St. John's Kirk. In this impressive cruciform-plan church dating from the 12th century, religious reformer John Knox preached a fiery sermon in May 1559 against idolatry. An enraged crowd stripped the church and poured into the street to attack the wealthy religious institutions; this helped start the Reformation in Scotland. The interior was divided into three parts at the Reformation, but was restored to something closer to its medieval state by Sir Robert Lorimer in the 1920s. ✉ *St. John St.* ☎ *01738/633192* 🌐 *www.st-johns-kirk.co.uk* 🎫 *Free* 🕒 *Closed Oct.–Mar. except for services.*

WHERE TO EAT AND STAY

$$ BRITISH 🍴 **Deans Restaurant.** The varied clientele reflects the broad appeal of noted chef Willie Deans's imaginative and satisfying cuisine, including a dinner menu with starters such as ceviche of sea bream, passion fruit, and lime, and Shetland fish curry and delicious Orkney steak for main courses. Deans is airy and pleasant, merging warm colors and light woods with comfortable sofas perfect for a predinner drink. **Known for:** pretheater menu; good lunch menu; Shetland fish curry. [$] *Average main: £19* ✉ *77–79 Kinnoull St.* ☎ *01738/643377* 🌐 *www.letseatperth.co.uk.*

$$ BRITISH Fodor's Choice ★ 🍴 **63 Tay Street.** Dine looking out on to the River Tay in this elegant but relaxed restaurant with tall windows, gray-and-white walls, and wooden tables. Known for imaginative fare with an emphasis on seasonal and local produce, chef Graeme Pallister produces combinations that are adventurous, such as the "witch sole" with curry and sprouting broccoli or red deer with pear, parsnips, and licorice. **Known for:** imaginative use of seasonal ingredients; excellent tasting menu; wine list. [$] *Average main: £19* ✉ *63 Tay St.* ☎ *01738/441451* 🌐 *www.63taystreet.com.*

$$ HOTEL 🏨 **Huntingtower Hotel.** Less than 5 miles from Perth, this tranquil, traditional country hotel with an air of understated elegance has a spacious garden and trees that make it feel more rural than it really is. **Pros:** restful setting; amply sized rooms. **Cons:** no elevator; perhaps a slight excess of tartan. [$] *Rooms from: £110* ✉ *Crieff Rd.* ☎ *01738/583771* 🌐 *www.huntingtowerhotel.co.uk* 🛏 *34 rooms* 🍽 *Breakfast.*

$ B&B/INN 🏨 **Sunbank House Hotel.** This handsome early Victorian gray-stone mansion near Perth's Branklyn Gardens overlooks the River Tay and the city of Perth. **Pros:** reasonably priced; friendly staff; delicious local cuisine. **Cons:** some rooms are very small; some traffic noise from the main road. [$] *Rooms from: £90* ✉ *50 Dundee Rd.* ☎ *01738/624882* 🌐 *www.sunbankhouse.com* 🛏 *9 rooms* 🍽 *Breakfast.*

NIGHTLIFE AND PERFORMING ARTS

Perth Concert Hall. The city's main concert venue hosts musical performances of all types. ✉ *Mill St.* ☎ *017384/621031* 🌐 *www.horsecross.co.uk.*

Perth Theatre. After a major face-lift of its Edwardian building in 2017, this respected repertory theater continues to present a varied program. It also offers musical events. ✉ *185 High St.* ☎ *017384/621031* 🌐 *www.horsecross.co.uk.*

SHOPPING

JEWELRY AND ANTIQUES

Cairncross of Perth. The Romans coveted freshwater pearls from the River Tay. If you do, too, then head to Cairncross of Perth, where you can admire a display of some of the more unusual shapes and colors. Some of the delicate settings take their theme from Scottish flowers. ⊠ *18 St. John's St.* ☎ *01738/624367* ⊕ *www.cairncrossofperth.co.uk.*

Timothy Hardie. Stunning antique jewelry and silver, including a few Scottish items, can be found here, as well as modern pieces. ⊠ *25 St. John's St.* ☎ *01738/633127* ⊕ *www.timothyhardie.co.uk.*

Whispers of the Past. This lovely shop has a collection of jewelry, china, and other gift items, some vintage and some new. ⊠ *15 George St.* ☎ *01738/635472* ⊕ *whispers-of-the-past.weebly.com.*

DUNKELD

14 miles north of Perth.

The historic town of Dunkeld remains intact and beautifully preserved with its rows of white houses around the town square. The original village was destroyed in 1689 in a ferocious battle during the Jacobite rebellion and was rebuilt after its defeat by the Atholl family. Today it survives as part of the National Trust for Scotland's Little Houses Project, which helps maintain the houses. The town is overlooked by the grand but semiruined 12th-century cathedral (still used for services). Atholl Street, leading down to the River Tay, has several crafts shops and a hotel.

The bridge across the River Tay takes you to Birnam Wood, where Shakespeare's Macbeth met the three witches who issued the prophecy about his death. Witty wooden notices lead you to the right tree, a gnarled hollow oak.

GETTING HERE AND AROUND

Dunkeld is on the A9 between Perth and Pitlochry. The town is also on the main train line to Inverness.

ESSENTIALS

Visitor Information Dunkeld and Birnam Tourist Information Centre. ⊠ *The Cross* ☎ *01350/727688* ⊕ *www.visitscotland.com.*

EXPLORING

FAMILY **Beatrix Potter Exhibition and Garden.** The garden and exhibition celebrates the life and work of this much-beloved children's writer who, for many years, spent her family holidays in the area. You're free to walk around the enchanting garden where you can peep into the homes of Peter Rabbit and Mrs. Tiggy-Winkle, her best-known characters. The visitors center has a well-stocked shop, a small café, and an imaginative small exhibition on the writer's life and work. The garden is a mile south of Dunkeld, in Birnam. ⊠ *Birnam Arts Centre, Station Rd., Birnam* ☎ *01350/727674* ⊕ *www.birnamarts.com* ⊠ *£3 exhibition, garden free.*

Hermitage. On the outskirts of Dunkeld, the Hermitage is a 1½-mile woodland walk that follows the River Braan. In the 18th century, the dukes of Atholl constructed two follies (fantasy buildings) here, **Ossian's Cave** and the awesomely decorated **Ossian's Hall,** above a spectacular—and noisy—waterfall. (Ossian was a fictional Celtic poet invented by James MacPherson in the 18th century for an era fascinated by the "primitive" past.) You'll also be in the presence of Britain's tallest tree, a Douglas fir measuring 214 feet. ✉ *Hermitage Car Park, off A9, 2 miles west of Dunkeld* 🌐 *www.nts.org.uk* 🎟 *Free, parking lot £2.*

FAMILY **Loch of the Lowes.** From the lochside hides at this Scottish Wildlife Trust reserve near Dunkeld, you can observe the area's rich birdlife through a powerful telescope. The main attractions are always the ospreys, one of Scotland's conservation success stories, which can be observed between March and August. But there is much to see throughout the year, like the great crested grebe at feeding stations. The enthusiastic staff will willingly describe what is happening around the center. ✉ *Off A923* ✣ *About 2 miles northeast of Dunkeld off the A9* ☎ *01350/727337* 🌐 *scottishwildlifetrust.org.uk* 🎟 *£4* 🕒 *Closed Mon.–Thurs. Nov.–Feb.*

WHERE TO EAT

$ BRITISH ✕ **The Taybank.** This lovely spot overlooking the River Tay is a musical meeting place owned by Scottish singer Dougie MacLean. It serves unpretentious but plentiful traditional pub food, like haggis, Cullen skink (fish soup), and stovies (a beef-and-potato dish) in the friendly, rough-and-ready bar; the more elegant dinner menu uses local produce and changes daily. **Known for:** traditional Scottish fare; excellent music; beer garden. [$] *Average main: £13* ✉ *Tay Terr.* ☎ *01350/727340* 🌐 *www.thetaybankdunkeld.com.*

SHOPPING

Jeremy Law of Scotland. Here you can purchase deerskin shoes and moccasins, as well as leather items including jackets, gloves, shoes, and wallets. ✉ *City Hall, Atholl St.* ☎ *0800/146780* 🌐 *www.moccasin.co.uk.*

PITLOCHRY

15 miles north of Dunkeld.

In the late 19th century Pitlochry was an elegant Victorian spa town, famous for its mild microclimate and beautiful setting. Today it is a busy tourist town, with wall-to-wall gift shops, cafés and B&Bs, large hotels, and a huge golf course. The town itself is oddly nondescript, but it's a convenient base from which to explore the surrounding hills and valleys.

GETTING HERE AND AROUND

The main route through central Scotland, the A9, passes through Pitlochry, as does the main railway line from Glasgow/Edinburgh to Inverness. From here the B8019 connects to the B846 west to Rannoch Moor or south to Aberfeldy.

ESSENTIALS

Visitor Information Pitlochry Visitor Information Centre. ✉ *22 Atholl Rd.* ☎ *01796/472215* 🌐 *www.visitscotland.com.*

EXPLORING

TOP ATTRACTIONS

Edradour Distillery. If you have a whisky-tasting bent, visit Edradour Distillery, which claims to be the smallest single-malt distillery in Scotland (but then, so do others). There's a fun, informative tour of the distillery where you get to see how the whisky is made; you also get to savor a free dram at the end of the tour. ⊠ *Pitlochry* ✢ *Off A924, 2½ miles east of Pitlochry* ☎ *01796/472095* ⊕ *www.edradour.com* ☎ *Tours £7.50* ⊙ *Closed Sun. and Nov.–Mar.*

Fodor's Choice
★
Loch Rannoch. With its shoreline of birch trees framed by dark pines, Loch Rannoch is the quintessential Highland loch, stretching more than 9 miles from west to east. Fans of Robert Louis Stevenson (1850–94), especially of *Kidnapped* (1886), will not want to miss the last, lonely section of road. Stevenson describes the setting: "The mist rose and died away, and showed us that country lying as waste as the sea, only the moorfowl and the peewees crying upon it, and far over to the east a herd of deer, moving like dots." ⊠ *Pitlochry* ✢ *B846, 20 miles west of Pitlochry.*

WORTH NOTING

Pass of Killiecrankie Visitor Centre. Set among the oak woods and rocky river just north of Pitlochry, the Pass of Killiecrankie was the site of a famous battle won by the Jacobites in 1689. The battle was noted for the death of the central Jacobite leader, John Graham of Claverhouse (1649–89), also known as Bonnie Dundee, who was hit by a stray bullet. After his death the rebellion petered out. The National Trust for Scotland's visitor center at Killiecrankie explains the significance of this battle, which was the first attempt to restore the Stewart monarchy. ⊠ *B8079* ✢ *3 miles north of Pitlochry* ☎ *01796/473233* ⊕ *www.nts. org.uk* ☎ *Free* ⊙ *Closed Nov.–Mar.*

WHERE TO EAT

$$
BRITISH
✕ **Moulin Hotel and Brewery.** At this traditional pub, you can eat in the airy, pleasant dining room or at the lively bar, with its dark, wooden interiors and some stuffed animals on the walls. Expect standard Scottish fare in generous quantities, including venison, scallops, and mussels; local produce is favored. **Known for:** Scottish cuisine; ales made on-site; choice of lively or quiet dining. $ *Average main: £15* ⊠ *11–30 Kirkmichael Rd.* ✢ *Between Pitlochry and Edradour* ☎ *01796/472196* ⊕ *www.moulinhotel.co.uk.*

$$
BRITISH
FAMILY
✕ **Two Sisters Restaurant.** This well-regarded and bright, airy restaurant is within East Haugh House, a country hotel in a turreted 17th-century stone house set in gardens just outside Pitlochry. Two Sisters serves mainly local produce in these charming surroundings, with a well-balanced menu that includes a good range of fish dishes, such as hake with black olive mash, game (in season), and local lamb, as well as some curry dishes. **Known for:** seafood and game; country-house setting; Sunday roast. $ *Average main: £18* ⊠ *East Haugh House* ✢ *Off A924, 1 mile south of Pitlochry* ☎ *01796/473121* ⊕ *www.easthaugh.co.uk.*

6

WHERE TO STAY

$ B&B/INN **Claymore Guest House.** One of the large Victorian houses set back from the main road, this B&B is a quiet refuge with spacious, updated rooms with large windows. **Pros:** large, well-lit rooms with comfortable seating areas; dog-friendly. **Cons:** no children; slightly old-fashioned feel. *$ Rooms from: £95 ✉ 162 Atholl Rd. ☎ 01796/472888 🌐 www.claymorehotel.com 🛏 10 rooms 🍴 Breakfast.*

$$$$ HOTEL Fodor's Choice ★ **Green Park Hotel.** Set among woods and on the shores of Loch Faskally, Green Park is a genuinely luxurious country house hotel; most guest rooms have views over the loch or the gardens, and the most sought-after are those with a balcony on the second floor. **Pros:** great location; very attentive staff; country house comfort. **Cons:** a slightly conservative feel; very popular so books up early. *$ Rooms from: £236 ✉ Clunie Bridge Rd. ✣ 5 mins north of Pitlochry center on A924 ☎ 01796/473248 🌐 www.thegreenpark.co.uk 🛏 51 rooms 🍴 Breakfast.*

$$$$ HOTEL **Killiecrankie Hotel.** A neat oasis, this hotel is set amid the wooded hills and streams of the Pass of Killiecrankie. **Pros:** lovely location; pleasant rooms. **Cons:** books up fast; rate generally includes dinner (though it's good). *$ Rooms from: £280 ✉ B8079, Killiecrankie ✣ 3 miles north of Pitlochry ☎ 01796/473220 🌐 www.killiecrankiehotel.co.uk 🛏 10 rooms 🍴 Breakfast.*

$$ HOTEL FAMILY **Pitlochry Hydro Hotel.** A grand hotel in the best Victorian style, the Pitlochry Hydro is a 19th-century vision of a medieval castle on 50 acres with views of hills and valleys. **Pros:** lovely grounds; lots for kids to do; high comfort. **Cons:** old-fashioned feel; long, anonymous corridors. *$ Rooms from: £125 ✉ A924 ☎ 01796/472400 🌐 www.coastandcountryhotels.com 🛏 73 rooms 🍴 Breakfast.*

NIGHTLIFE AND PERFORMING ARTS

Pitlochry Festival Theatre. The theater presents six plays each season, hosts Sunday concerts, and holds art exhibitions. It also has a café and restaurant overlooking the River Tummel. *✉ Port Na Craig ☎ 01796/484626 🌐 pitlochryfestivaltheatre.com.*

SPORTS AND THE OUTDORS

GOLF

Blairgowrie Golf Club. Well known to area golfers looking for a challenge, the Blairgowrie Golf Club's Rosemount Course is laid out on rolling land in the pine, birch, and fir woods, which bring a wild air to the scene. There are, however, wide fairways and at least some large greens. If Rosemount is hosting a tournament, you can play on Lansdowne, another 18-hole course, or Wee, a 9-hole course. *✉ Golf Course Rd., Blairgowrie ☎ 01250/872622 🌐 www.theblairgowriegolfclub.co.uk 🎫 Rosemount, £59.50; Lansdowne, £59.50; Wee, £17.50 🏌 Rosemount: 18 holes, 6630 yards, par 72; Lansdowne: 18 holes, 6886 yards, par 72; Wee: 9 holes, 2327 yards, par 32.*

Pitlochry Golf Course. A decent degree of stamina is needed for the first three holes at Pitlochry, where steep climbs are involved. The reward is magnificent Highland scenery. Despite its relatively short length, this beautiful course has more than its fair share of surprises. The course offers golf with food packages. *✉ Golf Course Rd. ☎ 01796/472792*

⊕ *www.pitlochrygolf.co.uk* ✉ *Mar., Apr., Oct., and Nov.: £32 week-days, £40 weekends; May–Sept.: £40 weekdays, £50 weekends* ⚐ *18 holes, 5681 yards, par 69.*

BLAIR ATHOLL

10 miles north of Pitlochry.

Located where the Tilt and Garry rivers flow together, this small town sits in the middle of the Grampian Mountains. Here you'll find Blair Castle, one of Scotland's grandest grand houses.

GETTING HERE AND AROUND

Popular Blair Castle is just off the A9 Pitlochry-to-Inverness road, beyond the village of Blair Atholl. The village has a railway station that is on the main Inverness line.

EXPLORING

Fodor'sChoice
★

Blair Castle. Its setting among woodlands and gardens, together with its war-torn past, make Blair Castle one of Scotland's most highly rated sights. The turreted white castle was home to successive dukes of Atholl and their families, the Murrays, one of the most powerful in the land. During the Jacobite rebellion of 1745 the loyalties of the Atholls were divided—a preserved piece of floor shows the marks of red-hot shot fired when the castle was under siege. In the end the supporters of the English king held off the rebels and were well rewarded for it. The dukes were allowed to retain a private army, the Atholl Highlanders. The castle entrance hall presents some of the dukes' collections of weapons, while a rich collection of furniture, china, and paintings occupies the family rooms. The grounds contain a 9-acre walled garden, an 18th-century folly, and a play area for children. ✉ *Off B8079* ☎ *01796/481207* ⊕ *www.blair-castle.co.uk* ✉ *Castle and gardens £11, grounds only £6* ⊙ *Closed Nov.–Mar.*

SHOPPING

House of Bruar. An upscale shopping complex, the House of Bruar has a heavy emphasis on traditional tweeds and cashmeres. A large supermarket sells local produce and food, and a restaurant serves breakfast and lunch. When you're done shopping, take a walk up the path that crosses Bruar Falls, behind the complex. ✉ *Off A9* ✛ *3 miles west of Blair Castle* ☎ *01796/483236* ⊕ *www.houseofbruar.com.*

ABERFELDY

15 miles southwest of Pitlochry, 25 miles southwest of Blair Castle.

The most dramatic thing about Aberfeldy is the high humpbacked bridge into the town, built by William Adam in 1733 and commissioned by General Wade, who marched through Scotland suppressing local resistance after the Jacobite rebellion. The town itself is rather sleepy, but this is a popular base for exploring the region. There's also a whisky distillery and plenty of local golf courses.

6

GETTING HERE AND AROUND

To get here from Pitlochry, take the A9 and then the A827. You can also reach Aberfeldy from Dunkeld via the A9 and the A827. A longer but very pretty route is the A85 from Crieff, then through Killin on the A827. Aberfeldy is served by regular buses from Perth and Pitlochry.

ESSENTIALS

Visitor Information Aberfeldy Tourist Information Centre. ✉ *The Square* ☎ *01887/820276* 🌐 *www.visitscotland.com.*

EXPLORING

Castle Menzies. A 16th-century fortified tower house, Castle Menzies contains the **Clan Menzies Museum,** which displays many relics of the clan's history. The rooms have been carefully restored, including the bedroom where Bonnie Prince Charlie once took refuge. The castle stands west of Aberfeldy, on the opposite bank of the River Tay. ✉ *Aberfeldy Rd., Weem* ✣ *Off the B846* ☎ *01887/820982* 🌐 *www.castlemenzies.org* 🎫 *£6.50* 🕓 *Closed Nov.–Mar.*

Dewar's Aberfeldy Distillery. This established distillery offers tours that demonstrate how Aberfeldy single-malt whisky is made (with a tasting at the end, of course); audio guides and interactive screens add to the appeal. There's also a worthwhile Heritage Center and a pleasant restaurant. The basic tours are £9.50, but there are more expensive tours for whisky experts, including cask tastings. Dewar's also makes blended whiskies. ✉ *A827* ☎ *01887/822010* 🌐 *www.dewars.com* 🎫 *Basic tour £9.50; cask tasting tour £17* 🕓 *Closed Sun. Nov.–Mar.*

Glen Lyon. One of central Scotland's most attractive glens, 34-mile-long Glen Lyon is also one of its longest. It has a rushing river, thick forests, and the typical big house hidden on private grounds. There's a dam at the head of the loch, a reminder that little of Scotland's scenic beauty is unadulterated. The winding road lends itself to an unrushed, leisurely drive, past the visitor center (🌐 *www.nts.org.uk* www.nts.org.uk) at the access to Ben Lawers, a popular climb. ✉ *A827, 15 miles west of Aberfeldy* 🎫 *Free.*

WHERE TO EAT

$ CAFÉ 🍴 **Habitat Cafe.** This café with handmade wooden tables and windows overlooking the main town square offers excellent coffee and tea, sandwiches and burgers, platters, and soup in the central square of Aberfeldy. Habitat takes great pride in its coffee making and has awards to prove it; it works closely with sustainable farmers. **Known for:** double burgers; excellent coffee; lunch platters. [$] *Average main: £10* ✉ *The Square* ☎ *01877/822944* 🌐 *www.habitatcafe.co.uk* 🕓 *No dinner.*

SHOPPING

John A Lacey. Watch for this house on the road between Killin and Aberfeldy: its front room is a treasure trove of horn carving, from a full-masted galleon to knives in their sheaths. There are also deerskins for sale. Carver John Lacey has worked here since 1984; he says the egg spoons are still the most popular items. ✉ *A827* ✣ *15 miles west of Aberfeldy on north side of Loch Tay* ☎ *01567/820561* 🌐 *www.horncarver.co.uk.*

The Watermill. At this converted mill you can visit an excellent independent bookshop with a large children's section, a gallery with frequently changing exhibitions, a home-goods store (called Homer), and a café. ⊠ *Mill St.* ☎ *01887/822896* ⊕ *www.aberfeldywatermill.com.*

SPORTS AND THE OUTDOORS

FAMILY **Highland Safaris.** This center just outside Aberfeldy offers a full range of outdoor activities, from encounters with the red deer in the neighboring field to off-road driving, fishing, bike rental, and "safaris" into the nearby hills in Land Rovers or on foot. Activities come in a range of prices and lengths, or you can create your own experience. There is a shop and café on the site. ⊠ *Aberfeldy* ✛ *2½ miles west of Aberfeldy on B846* ☎ *01887/820071* ⊕ *www.highlandsafaris.net* ⊠ *Activities from £8.*

CRIEFF

24 miles south of Aberfeldy

Crieff retains the prosperous air of its Victorian heyday as a place to take the waters. Its central square, where local farmers may once have gathered to trade, is still a lively focus. For a different view of the town, you could climb Knock Hill, which is signposted from the town center.

GETTING HERE AND AROUND

Crieff once prospered because of the arrival of the railway. There is no station here today, but there are regular buses from Stirling and Glasgow. By car, take the A85 from Perth, or the A9 from Stirling, turning onto the A822 after Dunblane. From Aberfeldy, take the A826 and A822 for a direct route, or explore the longer, scenic A827/A85 route.

ESSENTIALS

Visitor Information Crieff Visitor Information Centre. ⊠ *Muthill Rd.* ☎ *01764/654065* ⊕ *www.visitscotland.com.*

EXPLORING

Fodor'sChoice **Drummond Castle Gardens.** These formal Victorian gardens, regarded as
★ some of the finest of their kind in Europe, celebrate family and Scottish heraldry. Combining the formal French and more relaxed Italian styles, the flower beds are planted and trimmed in the shapes of various heraldic symbols, such as a lion rampant and a checkerboard, associated with the coat of arms of the family that owns the castle. The gardens even made an appearance in the film *Rob Roy.* ⊠ *Off A822, 6 miles southwest of Crieff* ☎ *01764/681433* ⊕ *www.drummondcastlegardens. co.uk* ⊠ *£5* ☉ *Closed Nov.–Apr.*

Glenturret Distillery. To discover the delights of whisky distilling, sign up for the "Famous Grouse Experience" at the Glenturret Distillery, which claims to be Scotland's oldest. Here you learn how whisky is made and why time, water, soil, and air are so important to the taste. A guide takes you through the distillery and to the bar where you can have a glass of Famous Grouse Finest (a blended whisky) and try your skill at "nosing." You might cap your tour with lunch in the Wild Thyme café and restaurant. Signs lead to the distillery on the west side of the town. ⊠ *The Hosh, Comrie Rd.* ☎ *01764/656565* ⊕ *www.thefamousgrouse-experience.com* ⊠ *£10.*

WHERE TO STAY

$$ HOTEL FAMILY **Crieff Hydro.** One of Scotland's great Victorian hydropathy centers (treating illnesses using water), this grand hotel on 900 acres has been owned by the same family for more than 100 years; today it focuses on outdoor activities, though it has a pampering spa. **Pros:** extensive grounds; variety of activities; spa. **Cons:** some rooms are rather dull; some activities are quite expensive. [$] *Rooms from: £148* ✉ *Off A85* ☎ *01764/655555* 🌐 *www.crieffhydro.com* 🛏 *220 rooms* 🍴 *Breakfast.*

SHOPPING

Caithness Glass at Crieff Visitor Centre. You can watch the glassblowing process (weekdays only) and then browse the sales gallery here for paperweights and other gift items. There's also a garden center and a restaurant. ✉ *Muthill Rd.* ☎ *01764/654014* 🌐 *www.crieff.co.uk.*

AUCHTERARDER

11 miles southeast of Crieff.

Famous for the Gleneagles Hotel (including its restaurant by Andrew Fairlie) and nearby golf courses, Auchterarder also has a flock of tiny antiques shops to amuse Gleneagles's golf widows and widowers.

GETTING HERE AND AROUND

Gleneagles station is on the main Inverness line, while the A9 gives direct access to Gleneagles and Auchterarder via the A823.

ESSENTIALS

Visitor Information Auchterarder Visitor Information Centre. ✉ *90 High St.* ☎ *01764/663450* 🌐 *www.visitscotland.com.*

WHERE TO STAY

$$$$ HOTEL Fodor's Choice ★ **Gleneagles Hotel.** One of Britain's most famous hotels, Gleneagles is the very essence of modern grandeur, a vast palace that stands hidden in breathtaking countryside amid its world-famous golf courses. **Pros:** luxurious rooms; famous Andrew Fairlie restaurant; the three courses are a golfer's paradise. **Cons:** steep price. [$] *Rooms from: £495* ✉ *Off A823* ☎ *01764/662231* 🌐 *www.gleneagles.com* 🛏 *258 rooms* 🍴 *Breakfast.*

SPORTS AND THE OUTDOORS

GOLF

Fodor's Choice ★ **Gleneagles.** Its superb courses have made Gleneagles a part of golfing history. The 18 holes of the King's Course, designed by James Braid in 1919, have quirky names—many golfers have grappled with the tough 17th hole, known as the Warslin' Lea (Wrestling Ground). The Queen's Course mixes varied terrain, including woods and moors. Jack Nicklaus designed the PGA Centenary Course (host of the 2014 Ryder Cup), which sweeps into the Ochil Hills and has views of the Grampians. The 9-hole Wee Course provides challenges for beginners and pros. Gleneagles is also home to the PGA National Academy, a good place to improve your skills. ✉ *A823* ☎ *01764/662231* 🌐 *www.gleneagles.com* 🎫 *King's, Queen's, and PGA Centenary courses, £195; Wee Course, £35* ⛳ *King's: 18 holes, 6790 yards, par 71; Queen's: 18 holes, 6790 yards, par 68; PGA Centenary: 18 holes, 6815 yards, par 72; Wee Course: 9 holes, 1418 yards, par 27.*

ABERDEEN AND THE NORTHEAST

Updated by
Robin Gauldie

Here, in this granite shoulder of Grampian, are some of Scotland's most enduring travel icons: Royal Deeside, the countryside that Queen Victoria made her own; the Castle Country route, where fortresses stand hard against the hills; and the Malt Whisky Trail, where peaty streams embrace the country's greatest concentration of distilleries. The region's gateway is the city of Aberdeen. Once a prosperous merchant port, it became a boomtown in the 1970s with the discovery of oil beneath the North Sea, but as oil and gas reserves dwindle the city is looking in new directions for its wealth.

More than 125 miles north of the central belt of Glasgow and Edinburgh, Aberdeen has historically been a fairly autonomous place. Even now it's perceived by many U.K. inhabitants as lying almost out of reach in the northeast. In reality, it's a 90-minute flight from London or a little more than two hours by car from Edinburgh. Its 18th- and early-19th-century city center amply rewards exploration. Yet even if this popular base for travelers vanished from the map, an extensive portion of the northeast would still remain at the top of many travelers' wish lists.

Balmoral, the Scottish baronial–style house built for Queen Victoria as a retreat, is merely the most famous castle in the area, and certainly not the oldest. There are so many others that in one part of the region a Castle Trail has been established. In later structures, such as Castle Fraser, you can trace the changing styles and tastes of each of their owners over the centuries. Grand mansions such as 18th-century Haddo House, with its symmetrical facade and elegant interior, surrender any defensive role entirely.

A trail leading to a more ephemeral kind of pleasure can be found south of Elgin and Banff, where the glens embrace Scotland's greatest concentration of malt-whisky distilleries. With so many in Morayshire, where the distilling is centered on the valley of the River Spey and its tributaries, there's now a Malt Whisky Trail. Follow it, and visit other distilleries as well, to experience a surprising wealth of flavors.

The northeast's chief topographical attraction lies in the gradual transition from high mountain plateau—by a series of gentle steps through hill, forest, and farmland—to the Moray Firth and North Sea coast, where the word "unadulterated" is redefined. Here you'll find some of the United Kingdom's most perfect wild shorelines, both sandy and sheer cliff, and breezy fishing villages like Cullen on the Banffshire coast and Stonehaven, south of Aberdeen. The Grampian Mountains, to the west, contain some of the highest ground in the nation, in the area of the Cairngorms. In recognition of this area's special nature, Cairngorms National Park was created in 2003.

TOP REASONS TO GO

Glorious castles: With more than 75 castles, some Victorian and others dating back to the 13th century, this area has everything from ravaged ruins like Dunnottar to opulent Fyvie Castle. They still evoke the power, grandeur, and sometimes the cruelty of Scotland's past.

Fine distilleries: The valley of the River Spey is famous for its single-malt distilleries, including those connected by the signposted Malt Whisky Trail. You can choose from bigger operations such as Glenfiddich to the iconic Strathisla, where Chivas Regal is blended.

Seaside cities and towns: The fishing industry may be in decline, but the big-city port of Aberdeen and the colorful smaller fishing towns of Stonehaven and Cullen in the northeast are great (and very different) places to soak up the seagoing atmosphere—and some seafood.

Great walking: There are all types of walking for all kinds of walkers, from the bracing but spectacular inclines of the Grampian Hills to the wooded gardens and grounds of Balmoral and Haddo House, to breath-stealing golden sands near towns such as Cullen.

Superb golf: The northeast has more than 50 golf clubs, some of which have championship courses. Less famous clubs, both inland and by the sea, have some amazing courses as well.

ORIENTATION AND PLANNING

GETTING ORIENTED

Aberdeen, on the North Sea in the eastern part of the region, is Scotland's third-largest city; many people start a trip here. Once you have spent time in the city, you may be inclined to venture west into rural Deeside, with its royal connections and looming mountain backdrop. To the north of Deeside is Castle Country, with many ancient fortresses. Speyside and the Whisky Trail lie at the western edge of the region and are equally accessible from Inverness. From Speyside you might travel back east along the pristine coastline at Scotland's northeastern tip.

Aberdeen. Family connections or Royal Deeside often take travelers to this part of Scotland, but many are surprised by how grand and rich in history Aberdeen is. The august granite-turreted buildings and rose-lined roads make this a surprisingly pleasant city to explore; don't miss Old Aberdeen in particular.

Royal Deeside and Castle Country. Prince Albert designed Balmoral Castle for Queen Victoria, and so began the royal family's love affair with Deeside—and Deeside's love affair with it. However, this area has long been the retreat or the fortress of distinguished families, as the clutter of castles throughout the region shows. The majesty of the countryside also guarantees a superlative stop for everyone interested in history and romance.

The Northeast and the Malt Whisky Trail. For lovers of whisky, this is a favored part of Scotland to visit. Unique in their architecture, their ingredients, and the end product, the distilleries of Speyside are keen to share with you their passion for "the water of life." This region also has rolling hills and, to the north, the beautiful, wild coastline of the North Sea.

PLANNING

WHEN TO GO

May and June are probably the loveliest times to visit, but many travelers arrive from late spring to early fall. The National Trust for Scotland tends to close its properties in winter, so many of the northeast's castles are not open for off-season travel, though you can always see them from the outside. The distilleries are open much of the year, but some close during winter months, so check before visiting.

PLANNING YOUR TIME

How you allocate your time may depend on your special interests—castles or whisky, for example. But even if you can manage only a morning or an afternoon, do not miss a walk around the granite streets of Old Aberdeen, and take in St. Nicholas Kirk and a pint in the Prince of Wales pub. A trip southward to the fishing town of Stonehaven and the breathtaking cliff-top fortress of Dunnottar makes a rewarding afternoon. Royal Deeside, with a good sprinkling of castles and grandeur, needs a good two days; even this might be tight for those who want to lap up every moment of majesty at Balmoral, Crathes, Fraser, and Fyvie, the best of the bunch. A visit to malt-whisky country should include tours of Glenfiddich, Glenfarclas, Glenlivet, and Glen Grant distilleries, and although it's not technically a maker of malt whisky, Strathisla. Real enthusiasts should allot two days for the distilleries, and they shouldn't pass up a visit to Speyside Cooperage, one of the few remaining cooperages in Scotland. Cullen and Duff House gallery in Banff, on the coast, can be done in a day before returning to Aberdeen.

GETTING HERE AND AROUND

AIR TRAVEL

The city is easy to reach from other parts of the United Kingdom as well as Europe. British Airways, bmi, Eastern Airways, EasyJet, Flybe, Loganair, and Ryanair are some of the airlines with service to other parts of Britain. Aberdeen Airport—serving both international and domestic flights—is in Dyce, 7 miles west of the city center on the A96 (Inverness). The drive to the center of Aberdeen is easy via the A96 (which can be busy during rush hour).

Airport Contact Aberdeen Airport. ⊠ *Dyce Dr., Dyce* ☎ *0844/481–6666* ⊕ *www.aberdeenairport.com.*

BOAT AND FERRY TRAVEL

Northlink Ferries has service between Aberdeen, Lerwick (Shetland), and Kirkwall (Orkney).

Boat and Ferry Contact Northlink Ferries. ⊠ *Jamieson's Quay, Aberdeen* ☎ *0845/600–0449* ⊕ *www.northlinkferries.co.uk.*

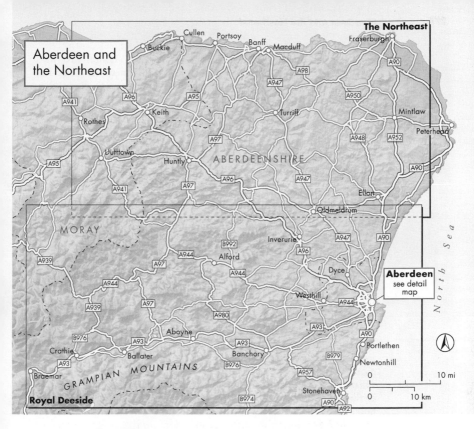

BUS TRAVEL

Long-distance buses run to Aberdeen from most parts of Scotland, England, and Wales. Contact Megabus, National Express, and Scottish Citylink for bus connections with English and Scottish towns. There's a network of local buses throughout the northeast run by Stagecoach, but they can take a long time and connections are not always well timed.

Bus Contacts Megabus. ☎ 0900/160–0900 ⊕ uk.megabus.com. **National Express.** ☎ 08717/818178 ⊕ www.nationalexpress.com. **Scottish Citylink.** ☎ 0871/266–3333 ⊕ www.citylink.co.uk. **Traveline.** ☎ 0871/200–2233 ⊕ www.travelinescotland.com.

CAR TRAVEL

A car is the best way to see the northeast. If you are coming from the south, take the A90, continuing on from the M90 (from Edinburgh) or the M9/A9 (from Glasgow), which both stop at Perth. The coastal route, the A92, is a more leisurely alternative, with its interesting resorts and fishing villages. The most scenic route, however, is the A93 from Perth, north to Blairgowrie and into Glen Shee. The A93 then goes over the Cairnwell Pass, the highest main road in the United Kingdom. This route isn't recommended in winter, when snow can make driving difficult.

Around the northeast roads can be busy, with speeding and erratic driving a problem on the main A roads.

TRAIN TRAVEL

You can reach Aberdeen directly from Edinburgh (2½ hours), Inverness (2½ hours), and Glasgow (3 hours). ScotRail timetables have full details. There are also London–Aberdeen routes that go through Edinburgh and the east-coast main line connecting Aberdeen to all corners of the United Kingdom. The Caledonian Sleeper, a luxury overnight train, runs nightly between London and Aberdeen, taking just over 10 hours.

Train Contact Caledonian Sleeper. ✉ *Aberdeen railway station, Guild St., Aberdeen* ☎ *0330/060–0500* ⊕ *www.sleeper.scot.* **ScotRail.** ✉ *Aberdeen railway station, Guild St., Aberdeen* ☎ *0344/811–0141* ⊕ *www.scotrail.co.uk.*

RESTAURANTS

As in much of the rest of Scotland, Aberdeen and the northeast have rediscovered the quality and versatility of the local produce. Juicy Aberdeen Angus steaks, lean lamb, and humanely reared pork appear on local menus, and there's a great choice of locally sourced seafood, from old-school fish-and-chips to dishes that fuse Mediterranean, Asian, and Latin influence. Traditional favorites like *Cullen skink* (a creamy smoked-fish soup) are on many menus.

HOTELS

The northeast has some splendid country hotels with log fires and old Victorian furnishings, where you can also be sure of eating well. Many hotels in Aberdeen are in older buildings that have a baronial feel. The trend for serviced apartments has caught on here, with some extremely modish and good-value options for those who want a bit more privacy. This trend is now extending into Deeside, where it's been notoriously difficult to find good accommodations beyond some country-house hotels, even though it's a popular tourist spot. *Hotel reviews have been shortened. For full information, visit Fodors.com.*

WHAT IT COSTS IN POUNDS			
$	**$$**	**$$$**	**$$$$**
RESTAURANTS under £15	£15–£19	£20–£25	over £25
HOTELS under £100	£100–£160	£161–£220	over £220

Restaurant prices are the average cost of a main course at dinner or, if dinner is not served, at lunch. Hotel prices are the lowest cost of a standard double room in high season, including 20% V.A.T.

VISITOR INFORMATION

The tourist information center in Aberdeen supplies information on all of Scotland's northeast. There are also year-round tourist information offices in Braemar and Elgin. In summer, also look for tourist information centers in Alford, Ballater, Banchory, Braemar, Elgin, and Stonehaven.

Contact Aberdeen Visitor Information Centre. ✉ *23 Union St., Aberdeen* ☎ *01224/269180* ⊕ *www.visitscotland.com, www.visitabdn.com.*

ABERDEEN

As a gateway to Royal Deeside and the Malt Whisky Trail, Aberdeen attracts visitors, though many are eager to get out into the countryside. Today, though, the city's unique history is finally being recognized as more impressive than many Scots had previously realized, and Aberdeen is being rediscovered. Distinctive architecture, some fine museums, universities, and good restaurants, nightlife, and shopping add to the appeal of Scotland's third-largest city (population 217,000). Union Street is the heart of the city, but take time to explore the university and the pretty streets of Old Aberdeen.

In the 18th century local granite quarrying produced a durable silver stone that would be used boldly in the glittering blocks, spires, columns, and parapets of Victorian-era Aberdonian structures. The city remains one of the United Kingdom's most distinctive, although some would say it depends on the weather and the brightness of the day. The mica chips embedded in the rock look like a million mirrors in the sunshine. In rain (and there is a fair amount of driving rain from the North Sea) and heavy clouds, however, their sparkle is snuffed out.

The city lies between the Dee and Don rivers, with a working harbor that has access to the sea; it has been a major fishing port and is the main commercial port in northern Scotland. The North Sea has always been important to Aberdeen. In the 1850s the city was famed for its sleek, fast clippers that sailed to India for cargoes of tea. In the 1970s, exploitation of newly discovered offshore oil and gas turned Aberdeen into a world energy capital. As reserves dwindle and the oil industry winds down, the city is seeking new ways to diversify its economy.

GETTING HERE AND AROUND
AIR TRAVEL
Stagecoach Bluebird Jet Service 727 and First Aberdeen Bus 16 operate between the airport terminal and Union Square in the center of Aberdeen. Buses (£3.20 and £2.50 respectively) run frequently at peak times, less often at midday and in the evening; the journey time is approximately 40 minutes.

Dyce is on ScotRail's Inverness–Aberdeen route. The rail station is a short taxi ride from the terminal building (£10). Alternatively, the Jet Connect Service 80 operates between 6:06 am and 6:27 pm (£1.75). The ride takes 12 minutes, and trains run approximately every two hours.

BUS TRAVEL
First Aberdeen has easy and reliable service within the city of Aberdeen. Timetables are available from the tourist information center in Union Street.

Contact First Aberdeen. ☎ *01224/650000* ⊕ *www.firstgroup.com.*

CAR TRAVEL

Aberdeen is a compact city with good signage. Its center is Union Street, the main east–west thoroughfare, which tends to get crowded with traffic. Anderson Drive is an efficient ring road on the city's west side; be extra careful on its many traffic circles. It's best to leave your car in one of the parking garages (arrive early to get a space) and walk around, or use the convenient park-and-ride stop at the Bridge of Don, north of the city. Street maps are available from the tourist information center, newsstands, and booksellers.

TAXI TRAVEL

You can find taxi stands throughout the center of Aberdeen: at the railway station and at Back Wynd, Chapel Street, Dee Street, and Hadden Street. The taxis have yellow plates, meters, and might be saloon cars (sedans) or black cabs. They are great ways to travel between neighborhoods.

TRAIN TRAVEL

Aberdeen has good ScotRail service.

AROUND UNION STREET

Aberdeen centers on Union Street, with its many fine survivors of the Victorian and Edwardian streetscape. Marischal College, dating from the late 16th century, is a city-center landmark, and has many grand buildings that are worth exploring.

EXPLORING
TOP ATTRACTIONS

Aberdeen Art Gallery. Scheduled to reopen late in 2017 after a major restoration, the museum contains excellent paintings, prints, drawings, sculpture, porcelain, costumes, and much else—from 18th-century art to major contemporary British works by Lucien Freud and Henry Moore. Scottish artists are well represented in the permanent collection and special exhibits. Local stone has been used in interior walls, pillars, and the central fountain, designed by the acclaimed British sculptor Barbara Hepworth. Look for the unique collection of Aberdeen silver on the ground floor. The museum also has a cake-filled café and well-stocked gift shop. ■TIP→ **Until the museum's reopening, some of the most important works in its collection can be seen at Drum Castle and in the Aberdeen Maritime Museum.** ⊠ *School-hill* ☎ *01224/523700* ⊕ *www.aagm.co.uk* ⧆ *Free.*

FAMILY **Aberdeen Maritime Museum.** This excellent museum, which incorporates Fodor's Choice the 1593 Provost Ross's House, tells the story of the city's relation-★ ship with the sea, from early inshore fisheries to tea clippers and the North Sea oil boom. The information-rich exhibits include the bridge of a fishing boat and the cabins of a clipper, in addition to models, paintings, and equipment associated with the fishing, shipbuilding, and oil and gas industries. The Gateway to the North gallery on the top floor, installed in 2016, is a lively introduction to the archaeology of the region, with exhibits spanning the years 1136–1660. ⊠ *Ship Row* ☎ *01224/337700* ⊕ *www.aagm.co.uk* ⧆ *Free* ⊙ *Closed Mon.*

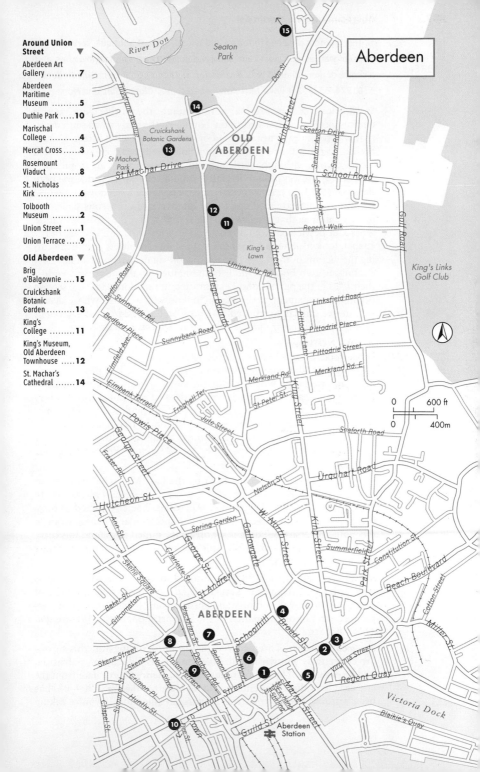

Ti. This tearoom attached to Teasel and Tweed, a smart boutique, serves a menu of waffles with sweet and savory toppings, snacks and sandwiches, and a choice of more than 40 teas. Known for: waffles. ✉ *85 Rosemount Viaduct* ☎ *01224/652352* ⊕ *www.teaselandtweed.com* ⊗ *Closed Sun. and Mon.*

St. Nicholas Kirk. The original burgh church, the Mither Kirk, as this edifice is known, is not within the bounds of the early town settlement; that was to the east, near the end of present-day Union Street. During the 12th century the port of Aberdeen flourished, and there wasn't room for the church within the settlement. Its earliest features are its pillars—supporting a tower built much later—and its clerestory windows: both date from the 12th century. The East Kirk is closed for renovation work, which has been extended due to the discovery of numerous skeletons, mainly children, that date back to the 12th century; the post-excavation work can be viewed from a large window in the Drum's Aisle. In the chapel, look for Shona McInnes's stained-glass window commemorating the victims of the 1989 Piper Alpha oil-rig disaster and a glass case containing two books. One lists the names of all those who've lost their lives in the pursuit of oil exploration in the North Sea; the second is empty, a testament to the many "unknown" workers whose deaths were never officially recorded. ✉ *Union St.* ☎ *01224/643494* ⊕ *www. kirk-of-st-nicholas.org.uk* ✍ *Free, but donations welcome.*

WORTH NOTING

Duthie Park. These 44 acres were donated to the people of Aberdeen by a Miss Elizabeth Crombie Duthie in 1880. An excellent place to while away an afternoon, whether it be the sunniest or foulest day, it has a boating pond, a bandstand, playgrounds, and a popular conservatory café selling creamy ice cream. In the beautifully tended Winter Gardens (tropical and arid conservatories) are fishponds, free-flying birds, and turtles and terrapins among the luxuriant foliage and flowers. The park borders Aberdeen's other river, the Dee. ✉ *Polmuir Rd., about 1 mile south of city center* ✍ *Free.*

Marischal College. Founded in 1593 by the Earl Marischal (the keeper of the king's mares), Marischal College was a Protestant alternative to the Catholic King's College in Old Aberdeen. The two joined to form the University of Aberdeen in 1860. The spectacularly ornate work of the main university building is set off by the gilded flags, and this turn-of-the-20th-century creation is still one of the world's largest granite buildings. ✉ *Broad St.*

Mercat Cross. Built in 1686 and restored in 1820, the Mercat Cross (the term stems from "marketplace"), always the symbolic center of a Scottish medieval burgh, stands just beyond King Street. Along its parapet are 12 portrait panels of the Stewart monarchs. ✉ *Justice and Marischal Sts.*

Rosemount Viaduct. Three silvery, handsome buildings on this bridge are collectively known by all Aberdonians as Education, Salvation, and Damnation. The **Central Library** and **St. Mark's Church** date from the last decade of the 19th century, and **His Majesty's Theatre** (1904–08) has been restored inside to its full Edwardian splendor. If you're taking photographs, you can choose an angle that includes the statue of Scotland's first freedom fighter, Sir William Wallace (1270–1305), in the foreground pointing majestically to Damnation. ⊠ *Aberdeen.*

FAMILY **Tolbooth Museum.** The city was governed from this 17th-century building, which was also the burgh court and jail, for 200 years. Now a museum of crime and punishment, highly entertaining tour guides take you around its cells and dungeons and bring life and death to the various instruments of torture—including the "Maiden," a decapitating machine—making it a must-see for older kids. ⊠ *Castle St.* ☎ *01224/621167* ⊕ *www.aagm.co.uk* ⌧ *Free.*

Union Street. This great thoroughfare is to Aberdeen what Princes Street is to Edinburgh: the central pivot of the city plan and the product of a wave of enthusiasm to rebuild the city in a contemporary style in the early 19th century. ⊠ *Aberdeen.*

Union Terrace. In the 19th-century development of Union Terrace stands a statue of Robert Burns (1759–96) addressing a daisy. Behind Burns are the **Union Terrace Gardens.** Proposals for a £140 million "transformation" of this much-loved public green space were dropped after a public outcry in 2013, but in 2017 the city council approved a scaled-down development, a move that will either be to Aberdeen's aesthetic benefit or its disgrace, depending on your viewpoint. ⊠ *Aberdeen.*

OLD ABERDEEN

Very much a separate area of the city, Old Aberdeen is north of the modern center, clustered around St. Machar's Cathedral and the many fine buildings of the University of Aberdeen. Take a stroll on College Bounds; handsome 18th- and 19th-century houses line this cobbled street in the oldest part of the city.

EXPLORING
TOP ATTRACTIONS
Cruickshank Botanic Garden. Built on land bequeathed by Miss Anne Cruickshank in memory of her beloved brother Alexander, the 11-acre Cruickshank Botanic Garden at the heart of Old Aberdeen has a peaceful water garden and lush greens ideal for lounging—when the weather allows—and beautifully tended subtropical and alpine collections. Botanical tours are available. ⊠ *St. Machar Dr., at the Chanonry* ☎ *01224/272704* ⊕ *www.abdn.ac.uk/botanic-garden* ⌧ *Free.*

King's College. Founded in 1494, King's College is now part of the University of Aberdeen. Its **chapel,** built around 1500, has an unmistakable flying (or crown) spire. That it has survived at all was because of the zeal of the principal, who defended his church against the destructive fanaticism that swept through Scotland during the Reformation, when the building was less than a century old. Today the renovated chapel plays an important role in university life. Don't miss the tall oak screen that separates the nave from the choir, the ribbed wooden ceiling, and the stalls, as these constitute the finest medieval wood carvings found anywhere in Scotland. ⊠ *25 High St.* ☎ *01224/272137* ⊕ *www.abdn. ac.uk* ⊗ *Closed weekends.*

King's Museum, Old Aberdeen Townhouse. Across from the archway leading to King's College Chapel, this plain but handsome Georgian building was the center of all trading activity in the city before it became a grammar school, a Masonic lodge, and then a library. Now housing the university's museum, it hosts constantly changing exhibitions. It presents some impressive and often strange curiosities from the university's collection, from prehistoric flints to a tiger's penis. ⊠ *17 High St.* ☎ *01224/274300* ⊕ *www.abdn.ac.uk/kingsmuseum* ⊠ *Free* ☉ *Closed Sun. and Mon.*

NEED A BREAK

✕ **St. Machar Bar.** St. Machar Bar, aka The Machar, is a small, vibrant pub in the middle of the university campus, selling not just pints but also real *stovies* (a potato-based beef stew) or haggis bon bons (deep-fried panko-encrusted haggis balls). **Known for:** stovies; choice of ales. ⊠ *97 High St.* ☎ *01224/483079* ⊕ *www.adamsfamilypubs.com.*

Fodor's Choice
★

St. Machar's Cathedral. It's said that St. Machar was sent by St. Columba to build a church on a grassy platform near the sea, where a river flowed in the shape of a shepherd's crook. This beautiful spot, now the still-beating heart of Old Aberdeen, fits the bill. Although the cathedral was founded in AD 580, most of the existing building dates from the 15th and 16th centuries. Built as a fortified kirk, its twin towers and thick walls give it a sturdy standing. The former can be seen up close by climbing the spiral staircases to the upper floors, which also affords an admirable view of the "body of the kirk" inside and graveyard outside. It lost its status as a cathedral during the Reformation and has since been part of the Church of Scotland. The stained-glass windows depicting the martyrdom of the saints and handsome heraldic ceiling are worth noting. ⊠ *Chanonry* ☎ *01224/485988* ⊕ *www.stmachar.com.*

NEED A BREAK

✕ **Kilau Coffee.** Popular with students and academics alike, this cheerful café across from the cathedral offers loungy seating downstairs and table and chairs upstairs. Expertly made coffee is on offer, as well as cakes and snacks. **Known for:** fresh-brewed coffee; toothsome cakes and snacks. ⊠ *55–57 High St.* ☎ *01224/485510* ⊕ *www.kilaucoffee.wordpress.com* ☉ *Closed Sun. No dinner.*

WORTH NOTING
Brig o'Balgownie. Until 1827, the only northern route out of Aberdeen was over the River Don on this single-arch bridge. It dates from 1314 and is thought to have been built by Richard Cementarius, Aberdeen's first provost. ⊠ *Seaton Park.*

WHERE TO EAT

$
BRITISH
FAMILY

✕ **Ashvale.** Ask anyone about this long-established place and the response will probably be overwhelmingly positive. Fish-and-chips is the specialty, and the secret-recipe batter is now the stuff of legend. **Known for:** perfectly crunchy battered cod; gluten-free options. $ *Average main: £12* ⊠ *42–48 Great Western Rd.* ☎ *01224/575842* ⊕ *theashvale.co.uk.*

$ | **✕ Café 52.** This artsy café-restaurant has an innovative menu, an atmo-
MODERN BRITISH | spheric dining room with open kitchen, and covered outdoor seating. Mackerel and watermelon salad, Persian marinated chicken, and bramble panna cotta are just a few of the options. **Known for:** Middle Eastern–Mediterranean-fusion menu; old-school Scottish desserts with a twist. Ⓢ*Average main: £13* ⊠ *52 The Green* ☎ *01224/590094* ⊕ *www.cafe52.co.uk* ☾ *No dinner Sun.*

$ | **✕ Foodstory.** A friendly, homespun café-eatery, Foodstory pulls in a loyal
BRITISH | crowd to graze on its healthy, freshly made breakfasts, lunches, and
FAMILY | wonderful cakes. Expect organic breakfast and brunch choices such as superfood porridge, scones, Aberdeenshire bacon rolls, and Ellon pork sausage. **Known for:** oatmeal enriched with nuts, fruit, and berries; sinfully delicous bacon and sausage rolls. Ⓢ*Average main: £7* ⊠ *13–15 Thistle St.* ☎ *01224/611717* ⊕ *www.foodstorycafe.co.uk.*

$$ | **✕ Moonfish.** This elegant yet relaxed seafood restaurant can be found along
BRITISH | a medieval lane next to St. Nicholas Kirk. Mains may include freshly caught sea trout, halibut, or hake served with imaginative accompaniments such as celeriac with seaweed. **Known for:** perfectly presented seafood; artisanal gin-based cocktails. Ⓢ*Average main: £16* ⊠ *9 Correction Wynd* ☎ *01224/644166* ⊕ *www.moonfishcafe.co.uk* ☾ *Closed Sun. and Mon.*

$$$ | **✕ Silver Darling.** Huge windows overlook the harbor and beach at this
SEAFOOD | quayside favorite in a former customshouse, long one of Aberdeen's
Fodor'sChoice | most acclaimed restaurants. The French-inspired menu focuses on
★ | fish: try the crab bisque with samphire to start, then move on to a lavish seafood platter of scallops, mussels, langoustes, prawns, and cockles. **Known for:** classic seafood, sensitively prepared; French-inspired entrées. Ⓢ*Average main: £25* ⊠ *North Pier, Pocra Quay* ☎ *01224/576229* ⊕ *thesilverdarling.co.uk* ☾ *Closed Sun. No lunch Sat.*

$$ | **✕ Yatai Izakaya.** The slick facade and glowing red interior might be
JAPANESE | a little intimidating at first, but the smiling staff are approachable and happy to help you choose the right blend of flavors and textures from a menu that includes dishes like *kushiyaki*-style skewers of aged sirloin steak, sushi, miso soup, and salad. **Known for:** aged steak; sushi platters. Ⓢ*Average main: £15* ⊠ *53 Langstane Pl.* ☎ *01224/592355* ⊕ *www.yatai.co.uk* ⊟ *No credit cards* ☾ *Closed Sun. and Mon.*

WHERE TO STAY

$$ | **▦ Atholl Hotel.** With its many turrets and gables, this granite hotel
HOTEL | recalls a bygone era but has modern amenities. **Pros:** family-run establishment; tasty restaurant; very pleasant staff. **Cons:** some rooms are a little generic; some bathrooms need updating. Ⓢ*Rooms from: £145* ⊠ *54 Kings Gate* ☎ *01224/323505* ⊕ *www.atholl-aberdeen.com* ⬐ *34 rooms* ⏻❘ *Breakfast.*

$$ | **▦ Bauhaus Hotel.** This 1960s-era office-turned-hotel's clean, modern
HOTEL | lines pay homage to the Bauhaus architectural movement, but there's nothing sterile about this smart property, where comfort has not been sacrificed to style. **Pros:** great design; comfortable rooms; tasty eatery. **Cons:** beware the furniture's sharp corners; fake art on the walls—in a city with a great art school; nightlife noise on weekends. Ⓢ*Rooms from:*

7

£140 ✉ *52–60 Langstane Pl.* ☎ *01224/212122* 🌐 *www.thebauhaus.co.uk* 🛏 *39 rooms* 🍴 *Breakfast.*

$ HOTEL FAMILY 🏨 **Craibstone Suites.** On one of Aberdeen's most attractive squares, these 18 modern and comfortable suites come with fully equipped kitchens. **Pros:** great central location; feels more like an apartment than a hotel room. **Cons:** executive suites are small—go for the grand or superior suites if you need elbow room; breakfast is pretty basic. [$] *Rooms from: £68* ✉ *15 Bon Accord Sq.* ☎ *01224/857950* 🌐 *www.craibstone-suites.co.uk* 🛏 *18 suites* 🍴 *Breakfast.*

$ B&B/INN 🏨 **The Jays Guest House.** Alice Jennings or her husband, George, will greet you at the front door of this granite house, a homey bed-and-breakfast they've run for more than 30 years. **Pros:** immaculate rooms; expert advice on city's sites; near Old Aberdeen and the university. **Cons:** no public areas; popular so book ahead. [$] *Rooms from: £52* ✉ *422 King St.* ☎ *01224/612771* 🌐 *www.jaysguesthouse.co.uk* 🛏 *10 rooms* 🍴 *Breakfast.*

$ HOTEL Fodor's Choice ★ 🏨 **Malmaison.** Part of a British minichain, this boutique hotel with fabulously comfy rooms and suites—some with terraces from which you can watch the sunset—sets the standard by which all rivals in Aberdeen are judged. **Pros:** stylish rooms; excellent restaurant; delightful staff; spa and minigym. **Cons:** not very central. [$] *Rooms from: £89* ✉ *45–93 Queen's Rd.* ☎ *01224/507097* 🌐 *www.malmaison.com/locations/aberdeen* 🛏 *77 rooms* 🍴 *All meals.*

$$$ HOTEL 🏨 **Marcliffe Hotel and Spa.** Offering a perfect combination of town and country outside the city center, this elegant hotel stands on 11 acres of wooded grounds and combines old and new to impressive effect. **Pros:** the wooded environs means a stunning dawn chorus; well-trained and friendly staff. **Cons:** if you struggle to sleep, the dawn chorus; a little out of town. [$] *Rooms from: £170* ✉ *N. Deeside Rd.* ☎ *01224/861000* 🌐 *www.marcliffe.com* 🛏 *42 rooms* 🍴 *Breakfast.*

NIGHTLIFE AND PERFORMING ARTS

Aberdeen has a fairly lively nightlife scene revolving around pubs and clubs. Theaters, concert halls, arts centers, and cinemas are also well represented. The principal newspapers—the *Press and Journal* and the *Evening Express*—and *Aberdeen Leopard* magazine can fill you in on what's going on anywhere in the northeast. Aberdeen's tourist information center has a monthly publication with an events calendar.

NIGHTLIFE

With a greater club-to-clubber ratio than either Edinburgh or Glasgow, Aberdeen offers plenty of loud music and dancing for a night out. There are also pubs and pool halls for those with two left feet. Pubs close at midnight on weekdays and 1 am on weekends; clubs go until 2 or 3 am.

BARS AND PUBS

Bottle Cap Brewery. Craft brews and feisty in-house ales are served alongside good pub grub. The handsome old stone warehouse stages frequent live music gigs. ✉ *10 Littlejohn St.* ☎ *01224/478080.*

BrewDog. Aberdeen's pioneering craft brewery turned global brand runs its flagship bar with suitable gusto and no lack of style. A bare-brick warehouse interior with lots of steel means there's lots of noise and chatter flying around the cavernous space, oiled by a choice of over 100 craft beers. ✉ *17 Gallowgate* ☎ *01224/631223* ⊕ *www.brewdog.com.*

CASC Bar. A fine selection of malt whiskies and Cuban cigars (which can be smoked in the outside seating area) makes this one of Aberdeen's more sophisticated watering holes. CASC, which stands for cigars, ale, Scotch, and coffee, is popular for its craft beers (more than 150 of them) and cool industrial interior. It can seem a bit crowded and noisy on weekends. ✉ *7 Stirling St.* ☎ *01224/212373* ⊕ *www.cascbar.co.uk.*

Cellar 35. This intimate bar and club space (capacity 80) is known for its almost nightly live music, DJ sets, and comedy. ✉ *35 Rosemount Viaduct* ☎ *01224/640483* ⊕ *www.thenooseandmonkey.com.*

Fittie Bar. Some pubs spend a fortune trying to re-create the warm atmosphere that the Fittie Bar comes by naturally. Located where the harbor stops and the old fishing village of Footdee (Fittie) begins, the pub tells the story of Aberdeen's fishing past, as will any of the salty dogs who drink there. ✉ *18 Wellington St.* ☎ *01224/582911.*

Musa. Combining postindustrial chic with a hint of heresy—it's housed in adjoining buildings that were once, respectively, a warehouse and a church—Musa offers live music, cutting-edge art exhibitions, and quirky dining options in atmospheric surroundings. ✉ *33 Exchange St.* ☎ *01224/571771* ⊕ *www.musaaberdeen.com.*

Old Blackfriars. With a nice location near the end of Union Street, Old Blackfriars has dim lighting and a big fireplace to warm things up on a chilly evening, although it can get crowded as the night goes on. This cask-ale pub has a great selection—Belhaven St. Andrews Ale and Caledonian 80 top the list. ✉ *52 Castle St.* ☎ *01224/581922* ⊕ *www. oldblackfriars-aberdeen.co.uk.*

The Prince of Wales. Dating from 1850, the Prince of Wales has retained its paneled walls and wooden tables. Still regarded as Aberdeen's most traditional pub, it's hardly regal, but good-quality food and reasonable prices draw the regulars back. ✉ *7 St. Nicholas La.* ☎ *01224/640597* ⊕ *www.princeofwales-aberdeen.co.uk.*

The Tippling House. Aberdonian *bon viveurs* have taken this subterranean and sophisticated late-night drinking den to their hearts and stomachs. It's a great place to escape and mingle and offers casual dining, innovative cocktails, craft beers, and spirits. ✉ *4 Belmont St.* ⊕ *www. thetipplinghouse.com.*

PERFORMING ARTS

Aberdeen is a rich city, both financially and culturally.

FAMILY **Aberdeen International Youth Festival.** In August the world-renowned Aberdeen International Youth Festival attracts 80 international acts—orchestras, choirs, dance troupes, and theater companies—who over nine days perform in 50 venues across the city and the region. ☎ *01224/213800* ⊕ *www.aiyf.org.*

ARTS CENTERS

FAMILY   **ACT Aberdeen (Arts Centre and Theatre Aberdeen).** This midscale venue hosts plays, musicals, poetry readings, and exhibitions by professional, amateur, and youth companies. ⊠ *33 King St.* ☎ *01224/635208* ⊕ *www. act-aberdeen.org.uk.*

Lemon Tree. This intimate theater has an innovative and international program of dance, stand-up comedy, and puppet theater, as well as folk, jazz, and rock music. ⊠ *5 W. North St.* ☎ *01224/641122* ⊕ *www. aberdeenperformingarts.com.*

Peacock Visual Arts. This gallery displays photographic, video, and slide exhibits of contemporary art and architecture. ⊠ *21 Castle St.* ☎ *01224/639539* ⊕ *www.peacockvisualarts.com.*

CONCERT HALLS

His Majesty's Theatre. The Edwardian His Majesty's Theatre hosts performances on par with those in some of the world's biggest cities. It's a regular venue for musicals and operas, as well as classical and modern dance. The restaurant, called 1906, is popular with audiences and cast members alike. ⊠ *Rosemount Viaduct* ☎ *01224/641122* ⊕ *www.aberdeenperformingarts.com.*

FILM

The Belmont. Independent, foreign language, and classic films are screened at the Belmont. The basement café bar is a stylish place to hang out. ⊠ *49 Belmont St.* ☎ *01224/343500* ⊕ *www.belmontfilmhouse.com.*

SHOPPING

You can find most of the large national department stores in Union Square. The Bon Accord & St. Nicholas Mall and Trinity Shopping Centre host chain stores, but Aberdeen has a few good specialty shops as well: Rosemount Viaduct and Belmont Street are worth a meander.

Aberdeen Art Gallery Shop. Scheduled to reopen in 2017 when the museum's reconstruction is complete, the Aberdeen Art Gallery Shop always has something of interest, and there are pretty postcards of the city from times gone by. ⊠ *Schoolhill* ☎ *01224/523695.*

Fodor'sChoice   **Aitkens.** You can't leave Aberdeen without trying one of its famous
★   *rowies* (or *butteries*), the fortifying morning roll. Aitkens Bakery is considered the finest purveyor of this local speciality. ⊠ *14–16 Menzies Rd.* ☎ *01224/899124* ⊕ *www.aitkens-bakery.co.uk/the-bakery.*

Alex Scott & Co. For Scottish kilts, tartans, crests, and other traditionally Scottish clothes (including a stunning "Scotland" hoodie), a good place to start is Alex Scott & Co. ⊠ *43 Schoolhill* ☎ *01224/674874* ⊕ *www. kiltmakers.co.uk.*

Books and Beans. This independent bookshop has its own Internet café (one of the few surviving such places in the city center) and sells a good range of flavored coffees. You're welcome to browse, sip, and surf the Web at the same time. ⊠ *22 Belmont St.* ☎ *01224/646438* ⊕ *www. booksandbeans.co.uk.*

Candle Close Gallery. This shop has some strange and wonderful mirrors, clocks, ceramics, and jewelry that you're unlikely to see elsewhere. ⊠ *123 Gallowgate* ☎ *01224/624940* ⊕ *www.candleclosegallery.co.uk.*

Cocoa Ooze. Enjoy a cup of tea and a chocolate fondue before tasting and buying handmade chocolate gifts, such as chocolate-drenched cinder toffee and hand-rolled truffles. ⊠ *24/28 Belmont St.* ☎ *01224/467212* ⊕ *www.cocoa-ooze.co.uk.*

Colin Wood Antiques. This shop is the place to go for small antiques, interesting prints, and regional maps. ⊠ *25 Rose St.* ☎ *01224/643019* ⊕ *www.colinwood-antiques.com.*

Juniper. Here you'll find gifts, housewares, and souvenirs, perfect for friends and family back home. ⊠ *35 Belmont St.* ☎ *01224/640480* ⊕ *www.juniperaberdeen.co.uk.*

Peapod. Check out vintage and retro clothing and housewares: think Bakelite, chichi cups and saucers, and 1920s cocktail dresses. ⊠ *144 Rosemount Pl.* ☎ *01224/874087.*

Fodor's Choice ★ **Teasel & Tweed.** If you are in need of a Harris tweed iPod cover, this is your place. All manner of housewares and accessories made by Scottish designers and craftspeople are on offer. Downstairs Ti (formerly Yvi's House of Tea) serves delicious waffles and connoisseur teas. ⊠ *85 Rosemount Viaduct* ☎ *01224/652352.*

SPORTS AND THE OUTDOORS

GOLF

With challenging dunes links swept by North Sea breezes, northeast Scotland is known for good golf.

You can expect to pay more than £100 for a round of world-class golf at courses in and around Aberdeen.

Murcar Links Golf Club. Sea views and a variety of rugged terrain—from sand dunes to tinkling burns—are the highlights of this course, founded in 1909. It's most famous for breathtaking vistas at the 7th hole, appropriately called the Serpentine. Designer Archibald Simpson considered this course to be one of his finest. ⊠ *Bridge of Don* ☎ *01224/704354* ⊕ *www.murcarlinks.com* ⊠ *£105 weekdays, £130 weekends* ⚑ *18 holes, 6314 yards, par 73.*

Fodor's Choice ★ **Royal Aberdeen Golf Club.** This venerable club, founded in 1780, is the archetypal Scottish links course: tumbling over uneven ground, with the frequently added hazard of sea breezes. Prickly gorse is inclined to close in and form an additional hurdle. The two courses are tucked behind the rough, grassy sand dunes, and there are surprisingly few views of the sea. One historical note: in 1783 this club originated the five-minute-search rule for a lost ball. A handicap certificate and letter of introduction are required. Visitors are only allowed on weekdays. ⊠ *Links Rd., Bridge of Don* ☎ *01224/702571* ⊕ *www.royalaberdeen-golf.com* ⊠ *Balgownie, £172; Silverburn, £70* ⚑ *Balgownie: 18 holes, 6900 yards, par 71; Silverburn: 18 holes, 4021 yards, par 64* ⚑ *Reservations essential.*

7

ROYAL DEESIDE AND CASTLE COUNTRY

Deeside, the valley running west from Aberdeen down which the River Dee flows, earned its "royal" appellation when discovered by Queen Victoria. To this day, where royalty goes, lesser aristocracy and freshly minted millionaires follow. Many still aspire to own a grand shooting estate in Deeside, and you may appreciate this yearning when you see the piney hills, purple moors, and blue river intermingling. As you travel deeper into the Grampian Mountains, Royal Deeside's gradual scenic change adds a growing sense of excitement.

There are castles along the Dee as well as to the north in Castle Country, another region that illustrates the gradual geological change in the northeast: uplands lapped by a tide of farms. All the Donside and Deeside castles are picturesquely sited, with most fitted out with tall, slender turrets, winding stairs, and crooked chambers that epitomize Scottish baronial style. All have tales of ghosts and bloodshed, siege and torture. Many were tidied up and "domesticated" during the 19th century. Although best toured by car, much of this area is accessible either by public transportation or on tours from Aberdeen.

STONEHAVEN

15 miles south of Aberdeen.

Stonehaven's golden sands made this historic town near spectacular Dunnottar Castle a popular holiday destination, until Scots began vacationing in sunnier climates. The surrounding red-clay fields were made famous by Lewis Grassic Gibbon (real name James Leslie Mitchell), who attended school in the town and wrote the seminal Scottish trilogy *A Scots Quair,* about the people, the land, and the impact of World War I. Stonehaven is now famous for its Hogmanay (New Year's Eve) celebrations, where local men swing huge balls of fire on chains before tossing them into the harbor, and as the birthplace of a quirky Scots delicacy, the deep-fried Mars bar.

GETTING HERE AND AROUND

Most trains heading south from Aberdeen stop at Stonehaven; there's at least one per hour making the 15-minute trip. Stagecoach Bluebird runs bus services between Stonehaven and Aberdeen; the fastest, the X70, takes around 40 minutes. Drivers should take A90 south and turn off at A957.

ESSENTIALS

Visitor Information Stonehaven Visitor Information Centre. ⊠ *66 Allardyce St.* ☎ *01569/762806* ⊕ *www.visitscotland.com.*

EXPLORING

Fodor's Choice **Dunnottar Castle.** It's hard to beat the cinematic majesty of the magnifi-
★   cent cliff-top ruins of Dunnottar Castle, with its panoramic views of the North Sea. Building began in the 14th century, when Sir William Keith, Marischal of Scotland, decided to build a tower house to demonstrate his power. Subsequent generations added to the structure, and important visitors included Mary, Queen of Scots. The castle is most famous

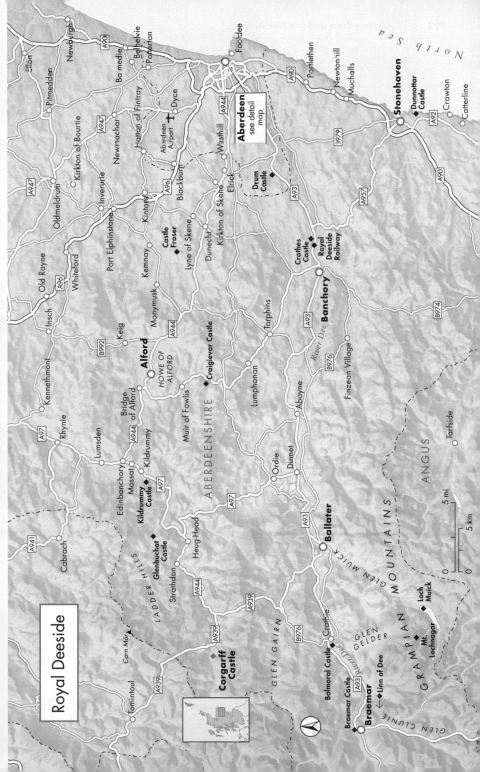

for holding out for eight months against Oliver Cromwell's army in 1651 and 1652, thereby saving the Scottish crown jewels, which had been stored here for safekeeping. Reach the castle via the A90; take the Stonehaven turnoff and follow the signs. Wear sensible shoes, and allow about two hours. ✉ *Off A92* ☎ *01569/762173* 🌐 *www.dunnottarcastle.co.uk* 🎟 *£7.*

FAMILY **Stonehaven Open-Air Swimming Pool.** A vintage art deco gem, Stonehaven Open-Air Swimming Pool is the only remaining outdoor heated pool in Scotland. Seawater is pumped in and warmed up to a balmy 29°C (82°F). Run by a local trust, this place is perfect for families. Wednesday's midnight swims (£7.10) let you float under the stars. ✉ *Queen Elizabeth Park, off A90* ☎ *01569/762134* 🌐 *www.stonehavenopenairpool.co.uk* 🎟 *£5.40* 🕒 *Closed Oct.–May.*

WHERE TO EAT AND STAY

$$ SEAFOOD 🍴 **The Ship Inn.** This former coaching inn is exactly where you want to take nourishment after a bracing walk from Dunnottar Castle. Refurbishment has taken away much of the history, but wood paneling and rattan chairs make it comfortable, and huge new windows provide views of the harbor. **Known for:** knowledgeably prepared harbor-fresh seafood; tempting Scottish desserts. [$] *Average main: £16* ✉ *5 Shore Head* ☎ *01569/762617* 🌐 *www.shipinnstonehaven.com.*

$$ B&B/INN 🏨 **Bayview B&B.** This contemporary bed-and-breakfast couldn't be in a more convenient location or have better views. **Pros:** spic-and-span rooms; right on the beach; fresh, modern design. **Cons:** standard rooms are smallish. [$] *Rooms from: £125* ✉ *Beachgate La.* ✣ *On the beach, down the lane from the town square* ☎ *07791/224227* 🌐 *www.bayviewbandb.co.uk* 🛏 *4 rooms* 🍽 *Breakfast.*

SHOPPING

FAMILY **Aunty Betty's.** Even if the weather is lousy, this coffee, sweets, and ice-cream shop confirms you are on your summer holidays. Grown-ups will love the gin-and-tonic or Champagne sorbets, kids the complimentary sprinkles. ✉ *The Promenade* ☎ *01569/763656.*

BANCHORY

15 miles west of Stonehaven, 19 miles west of Aberdeen.

Banchory is an immaculate town filled with pinkish granite buildings. It's usually bustling with ice-cream-eating strollers, out on a day trip from Aberdeen. Nearby are Crathes and Drum castles.

GETTING HERE AND AROUND

A car is by far the best way to get around the area; A93 is one of the main roads connecting the towns.

For those reliant on public transport, Stagecoach buses operate a number of services for towns along or just off A93 (Drum Castle, Banchory, Kincardine, Aboyne, Ballater, Balmoral, and Braemar).

ESSENTIALS

Visitor Information Banchory Visitor Information Centre. ✉ *Bridge St.* ☎ *01330/822000* 🌐 *www.visitbanchory.com.*

Which Castle Is Right for You?

We admit it there are almost too many castles in this part of Scotland. Because it's nearly impossible to see all of them, we've noted the prime characteristics of each to help you decide which you'd most like to visit.

■ **Balmoral:** The queen's home, this is where Queen Victoria and the royal family fell in love with Scotland and all things Scottish. Expect baronial largesse and groomed grounds, though you don't see much inside.

■ **Balvenie:** This ruined castle is known for its indomitable bearing and verdant surroundings, right in the midst of the Malt Whisky Trail.

■ **Braemar:** Offering memorable insight into the lives of the Scottish landed gentry, this castle heaves with memorabilia and mementos of the fascinating Farquharsons, who still hold their clan gathering here.

■ **Corgarff:** You'll find a sober solitude out on the moorland, as well as 18th-century graffiti and the reconstructed barracks used by Jacobite troops in 1746 as they retreated north.

■ **Craigievar:** Highlights of this 17th-century castle are a magical forest, fairy-tale turrets, and the furnishings and possessions of the Forbes family that fill the house.

■ **Crathes:** Expect tight quarters, notable family portraits, and a network of walled gardens at this well-preserved seat of the Burnett family. Its adventure park keeps the kids occupied.

■ **Drum:** A fusion of architectural styles and some historic roses are notable at this castle, but it's the medieval chapel that stirs the senses.

■ **Dunnottar:** The dramatic, scene-stealing, cliff-top location of Mel Gibson's *Hamlet* (1991), the ruins of this 14th-century tower house by the sea are unbeatable.

■ **Fraser:** Considered the grandest castle in Aberdeenshire, Castle Fraser has opulent period furnishings and woodland walks that make for a rewarding day.

■ **Fyvie:** This 14th-century castle underwent a luxurious Edwardian makeover. Come here for an awesome art collection, rich interiors, and haunting history.

■ **Kildrummy:** This is the place for evocative ruins, some from the 13th century, and tales of a treacherous past. Its austere but poignant chapel is a must-see.

EXPLORING

Crathes Castle. About 16 miles west of Aberdeen, Crathes Castle was once the home of the Burnett family and is one of the best-preserved castles in Britain. Keepers of the Forest of Drum for generations, the family acquired lands here by marriage and later built a castle, completed in 1596. The National Trust for Scotland cares for the castle, which is furnished with many original pieces and family portraits. Outside are grand yet lovingly tended gardens with calculated symmetry and flower-rich beds. Make sure you browse the Horsemill bookshop and sample the tasty baked goods in the tearoom. There's an adventure park for kids, and the staff organizes activities that are fun and educational. ✉ *Off A93* ☎ *01330/844525* 🌐 *www.nts.org.uk* 🎟 *£12.50* 🕒 *Closed weekdays Nov.–Mar.*

Fodor's Choice ★ **Drum Castle.** This foursquare tower has an evocative medieval chapel that dates from the 13th century; like many other castles, it also has later additions up to Victorian times. Note the tower's rounded corners, said to make battering-ram attacks more difficult. Nearby, fragments of the ancient Forest of Drum still stand, dating from the days when Scotland was covered by great stands of oak and pine. The Garden of Historic Roses, open from April to October, lays claim to some old-fashioned roses not commonly seen today. ✉ *Drumoak, by Banchory* ✣ *Off the A93, 8 miles east of Banchory and 11 miles west of Aberdeen* ☎ *01330/700334* 🌐 *www.nts.org.uk* 🎟 *£12.50* 🕒 *Closed weekdays Oct.–Mar.; closed Tues. and Wed. in Apr.–June and Sept.*

FAMILY **Royal Deeside Railway.** Built for Queen Victoria, this historic station and its railway line now serve passengers using veteran steam and diesel locomotives to haul vintage carriages along a short scenic route; the journey takes only 15–20 minutes. ✉ *Milton of Crathes* ☎ *01330/844416* 🌐 *www.deeside-railway.co.uk* 🎟 *Round-trip £4 for diesel, £6 for steam* 🕒 *Closed mid-Oct.–Nov. Closed weekdays Dec.–mid-Oct.*

WHERE TO STAY

$ HOTEL Fodor's Choice ★ 🏨 **Banchory Lodge.** Right on the River Dee, this Georgian lodge offers the lovely touches you expect at a luxury hotel, but at a moderate cost. **Pros:** a warm welcome; great bar; excellent food and afternoon teas. **Cons:** popular for weddings. [$] *Rooms from: £69* ✉ *Dee St.* ☎ *01330/822625* 🌐 *www.banchorylodge.com* 🛏 *28 rooms* 🍴 *Breakfast.*

$$ HOTEL Fodor's Choice ★ 🏨 **Raemoir House Hotel.** Dating from the 16th to 19th century, this baronial home 2 miles north of Banchory makes you feel as if you're on the set of a period drama. **Pros:** charming old building with extensive grounds; popular restaurant; staff is informal and efficient. **Cons:** inconvenient location for those without a car. [$] *Rooms from: £150* ✉ *Off A980, Raemoir* ☎ *01330/824884* 🌐 *www.raemoir.com* 🛏 *18 rooms* 🍴 *Breakfast.*

NIGHTLIFE AND PERFORMING ARTS

Fodor's Choice ★ **Woodend Barn.** Holding art exhibitions, film nights, and live performances, this arts venue packs a mean cultural punch for a renovated barn. Its excellent café-bar serves simple modern dishes. ✉ *Burn O'Bennie* ☎ *1330/825431 box office, 1330/826520* 🌐 *www.thebarn-arts.co.uk.*

BALLATER

25 miles west of Banchory, 43 miles west of Aberdeen.

The handsome holiday resort of Ballater, once noted for the curative properties of its waters, has profited from the proximity of the royals, nearby at Balmoral Castle. You might be amused by the array of "by royal appointment" signs proudly hanging from many of its various shops (even monarchs need bakers and butchers).

The locals have long taken the town's royal connection in stride. To this day, the hundreds who line the road when the Queen and her family arrive for services at the family's parish church at Crathie are invariably visitors to Deeside—one of Balmoral's attractions for the monarch has always been the villagers' respect for royal privacy.

GETTING HERE AND AROUND

There's good train service to Aberdeen, but you'll need to catch a bus to get to this and other towns near A93. Stagecoach Bluebird Buses 201 and 202 operate hourly to all the main towns, including Ballater. Otherwise, it's an easy car trip.

ESSENTIALS

Visitor Information Ballater Visitor Information Centre. ⊠ *Albert Memorial Hall, Station Sq.* ☎ *01339/755306* ⊕ *www.visitscotland.com.*

EXPLORING

Fodor'sChoice

★

Balmoral Castle. The British royal family's favorite vacation spot is a fabulous fake-baronial pile, with emphasis on the "fake." Compared with Scotland's most authentic castles, Balmoral is a right royal upstart, designed in the 19th century by Queen Victoria's German-born consort, Prince Albert. That doesn't stop it being one of Scotland's most visited castles, though only the formal gardens, the ballroom, and the carriage hall, with their exhibitions of royal artifacts, commemorative china, and stuffed native wildlife, are on view.

When members of the royal family are in residence, usually from mid-August to the end of September, Balmoral is closed to visitors, including the grounds. You can take a guided tour in November and December; if the weather is crisp and bright, the estate is at its most dramatic and romantic. You're only allowed a peek inside, but the Royal Cottage is where Queen Victoria spent much of her time. You can see the table where she took breakfast and wrote her correspondence.

Around and about Balmoral are some notable spots—Cairn O'Mount, Cambus O'May, and the Cairngorms from the Linn of Dee—that are home to golden eagles, red squirrels, red deer, black and red grouse, snow bunting, and the United Kingdom's only free-roaming reindeer, some of which may be seen on the quintessentially queenlike Land Rover Safari Tour. Tempted by the setting? Balmoral Castle has a number of cottages (some very large) for rent by the week at certain times. These are atmospheric but can be basic (which, believe it or not, is how the royal family likes its holidays to be—though the late Diana, Princess of Wales, who vacationed here before the breakup of her marriage to Prince Charles, hated Balmoral's lack of luxury). ⊠ *A93* ✛ *7 miles west of Ballater* ☎ *01339/742534* ⊕ *www.balmoralcastle.com* ⌨ *£11.50* ⊙ *Closed when royals are in residence, normally July and Aug.*

Loch Muick. A three- or four-hour walk takes you around glorious Loch Muick (Gaelic for "pig") and past Glas-alt Shiel, a favorite retreat of Queen Victoria's that you might recognize from the film *Mrs. Brown.* From Ballater, take the B976 over the River Dee before turning off at the sign for Glen Muick. Park at the Spittal of Loch Muick car park. The path around the loch is well signposted, although good boots are necessary for the stony beach at the far side of the loch. ■**TIP→ The native red deer are quite common throughout the Scottish Highlands, but here is one of the best places to see them.** ⊠ *Ballater.*

CLOSE UP

Balmoral, Queen Victoria's Retreat

Some credit Sir Walter Scott with having opened up Scotland for tourism through his poems and novels. But it was probably Queen Victoria (1819–1901) who gave Scottish tourism its real momentum when, in 1842, she first came to Scotland and when, in 1847—on orders of a doctor, who thought the relatively dry climate of upper Deeside would suit her—she bought Balmoral. The pretty little castle was knocked down to make room for a much grander house designed by her husband, Prince Albert (1819–61), in 1855. In full-blown Scottish baronial style, the new structure had a veritable rash of tartanitis. Before long the entire Deeside and the region north were dotted with country houses and mock-baronial châteaux.

"It seems like a dream to be here in our dear Highland Home again," Queen Victoria wrote. "Every year my heart becomes more fixed in this dear Paradise." Victoria loved Balmoral more for its setting than its house, so be sure to take in its pleasant gardens. Year by year Victoria and Albert added to the estate, taking over neighboring houses, securing the forest and moorland around it, and developing deer stalking and grouse shooting here.

In consequence, Balmoral is now a large property, with grounds that run 12 miles along the Deeside road. Its privacy is protected by belts of pinewood, and the only view of the castle from the A93 is a partial one, from a point near Inver, 2 miles west of the gates.

There's an excellent bird's-eye view of Balmoral from an old military road, now the A939, which climbs out of Crathie, northbound for Cockbridge and the Don Valley. This view embraces the summit of Lochnagar, in whose *corries* (hollows) the snow lies year-round and whose boulder fields the current Prince of Wales, Charles Windsor, so fondly and frequently treads.

EN ROUTE

As you continue west into Highland scenery past Balmoral Castle, further pine-framed glimpses appear of the "steep frowning glories of dark Lochnagar," as it was described by the poet Lord Byron (1788–1824). The mountain (3,786 feet) was made known to an audience wider than hill walkers by the current Prince of Wales, who published a children's story, *The Old Man of Lochnagar.*

WHERE TO EAT

$ ECLECTIC

🍴 **Rocksalt & Snails.** This cheeky little contemporary café-bar, with its fancy metalwork interiors and solid wooden tables, has an interesting take on local produce, serving Heidi (goat meat) and Deerstalker (venison) pies and the abundant Rocksalt & Snails platter (with all kinds of salmon and trout). For sweetness try huge scones or cakes with very good coffee or loose-leaf tea. **Known for:** game pies; trout and salmon; cakes and pastries. [$] *Average main: £10* ✉ *2 Bridge St.* ☎ *07834/452583.*

WHERE TO STAY

$$ B&B/INN

🏨 **Auld Kirk.** This strikingly renovated old church makes for an interesting stay, with guest rooms that are simply furnished, but are functional and have large shower rooms. **Pros:** helpful team looks after you;

pin-tidy bedrooms and public rooms. **Cons:** bar is popular with locals, so can get noisy; restaurant has reduced hours in winter. $ *Rooms from: £115* ✉ *Braemar Rd.* ☎ *01339/755762* ⊕ *www.theauldkirk.com* ⇆ *7 rooms* ⦾ *Breakfast.*

\$\$
HOTEL
FAMILY
Fodor's Choice
★

⊡ **Hilton Grand Vacations at Craigendarroch Suites.** This grand mansion has been turned into a resort with a luxury spa and country club, combining Victorian style with modern comforts. **Pros:** a great pool and decent gym facilities; good amenities for kids; rooms and suites have kitchenettes. **Cons:** if there's a conference, nonattending guests can feel lost among the crowds. $ *Rooms from: £136* ✉ *Braemar Rd.* ☎ *01339/755558* ⊕ *www.hiltongrandvacations.com/scotland/hgvc-craigendarroch-suites/* ⇆ *51 rooms* ⦾ *Breakfast.*

\$
B&B/INN

⊡ **No 45.** With plenty of period charm, this Victorian-era house offers old-fashioned hospitality and simple, understated comfort. **Pros:** unpretentious feel; good price; relaxing lounge. **Cons:** a few bedrooms on the small side. $ *Rooms from: £90* ✉ *45 Braemar Rd.* ☎ *01339/755420* ⊕ *www.no45.co.uk* ⇆ *8 rooms* ⦾ *Breakfast.*

SHOPPING

Atholl Countrywear. At either location of Countrywear, men (and women) can find everything that's necessary for Highland country living, including fishing tackle, natty tweeds, and that flexible garment popular in Scotland between seasons: the body warmer. ✉ *13 Bridge St.* ☎ *01339/755453* ⊕ *www.athollcountrywear.com* ⊙ *Closed Sun.–Tues.*

Deeside Books. Beyond the gifts section, veer to the right and you will find an interesting collection of old, out-of-print, and hard-to-find books about Scotland, which make splendid gifts for lovers of all things Scots. ✉ *18–20 Bridge St.* ☎ *01339/754080* ⊕ *www.deesidebooks.com.*

McEwan Gallery. A mile west of Ballater, the McEwan Gallery displays fine paintings, watercolors, prints, and books (many with a Scottish or golf theme) in an unusual house built by the Swiss artist Rudolphe Christen in 1902. ✉ *A939* ☎ *01339/755429* ⊕ *www.mcewangallery.com* ⊙ *Closed Mon.*

7

BRAEMAR

17 miles west of Ballater, 60 miles west of Aberdeen, 51 miles north of Perth via A93.

Synonymous with the British monarchy, due to its closeness to Balmoral, and with the famous Highland Games, this village is popular year-round as a base for walkers and climbers enjoying the Grampian Mountains.

GETTING HERE AND AROUND

The town is on A93; there's bus service here, as to other towns on the road.

ESSENTIALS

Visitor Information Braemar Visitor Information Centre. ✉ *The Mews, Mar Rd.* ☎ *01339/741600* ⊕ *braemarscotland.co.uk, www.visitscotland.com.*

THE HIGHLAND GAMES

They might not all be as royally attended as the Braemar Highland Gathering, but from spring to late summer across a wide swath of northern Scotland competitors gather to toss, pull, fling, and sing at various Highland events. No two games are the same, but many incorporate agricultural shows, sporting competitions, clan gatherings, or just beer in the sun. VisitScotland (⊕ *www.visitscotland.com*) has a list of them.

Which one to attend? Braemar stands tall on ceremony and tradition, and the chance of seeing royalty up close means it attracts visitors from far and wide. Dufftown Games (⊕ *www. dufftownhighlandgames.org*) is the most competitive, with its race up the nearby Ben Rinnes, while the most picturesque is the Lochcarron Games (⊕ *www.lochcarrongames.org. uk*), which are played and danced out under the massif of the Torridon hills.

EXPLORING

Braemar Castle. On the northern outskirts of town, Braemar Castle dates from the 17th century, although its defensive walls, in the shape of a pointed star, came later. At Braemar (the *braes*, or slopes, of the district of Mar), the standard, or rebel flag, was first raised at the start of the unsuccessful Jacobite rebellion of 1715. About 30 years later, during the last Jacobite rebellion, Braemar Castle was strengthened and garrisoned by government troops. From the early 1800s the castle was the clan seat of the Farquharsons, who hold their clan reunion here every summer.

Thanks to the commitment of local volunteers, a remarkable 2008 renovation restored Braemar to the home it would have been in the early 20th century, complete with all the necessary comforts and family memorabilia. A dozen rooms are on view, including the laird's day room with a plush daybed and the kitchen. ⊠ *Off A93* ☎ *01339/741219* ⊕ *www.braemarcastle.co.uk* ⊡ *£8* ⊙ *Closed Nov.–Easter. Closed Mon. and Tues. in Apr.–June, Sept., and Oct.*

FAMILY **Braemar Highland Gathering.** The village of Braemar is associated with the Braemar Highland Gathering, held the first Saturday in September. Although there are many such gatherings celebrated throughout Scotland, this one is distinguished by the presence of the royal family. Competitions and events include hammer throwing, caber tossing, and bagpipe playing. If you plan to attend, book your accommodations months in advance and be sure to buy tickets and, if necessary, your car parking ticket about six months in advance, as they do sell out. ⊠ *Princess Royal and Duke of Fife Memorial Park, Broombank Terr.* ⊕ *www.braemargathering.org.*

OFF THE BEATEN PATH

Linn of Dee. Although the main A93 slinks off to the south from Braemar, a little unmarked road will take you farther west into the hilly heartland. The road offers views over the winding River Dee and the blue hills before passing through the tiny hamlet of Inverey and crossing a bridge at the Linn of Dee. *Linn* is a Scots word meaning "rocky narrows," and the river's gash here is deep and roaring. Park beyond the bridge and walk back to admire the sylvan setting.

WHERE TO EAT AND STAY

$
CAFÉ
✕ **Taste.** Tasty and fresh soups and sandwiches made with local ingredients like venison pâté and Cambus O' May artisanal cheeses adorn the menu at this chalet-style café. You can order moist cakes and tasty lattes here, too. **Known for:** homemade soups; fresh-baked bread. $ *Average main: £6* ✉ *Auchendryne Sq.* ☎ *01339/741425* ⊕ *www.taste-braemar. co.uk* ⊘ *Closed Sun.*

$
B&B/INN
☷ **Ivy Cottage.** Everything at this 19th-century inn, from the silky bedding to the bright bathroom fittings, is of the highest standard and done with good taste. **Pros:** relaxing rooms; owners who go out of their way to make you feel at home; facilities for walkers and cyclists. **Cons:** next to the church, so expect bells on Sunday morning. $ *Rooms from: £75* ✉ *Cluniebank Rd.* ☎ *01339/741642* ⊕ *www.ivycottagebraemar.co.uk* ⇆ *5 rooms* ❍ *Breakfast.*

GOLF

Braemar Golf Course. It's worth playing the tricky 18-hole Braemar Golf Course if only to say you've played the highest 18-hole course in Scotland. Founded in 1902, it is laden with foaming water hazards. ✉ *Cluny Bank Rd.* ☎ *01339/741618* ⊕ *www.braemargolfclub.co.uk* ▦ *£25 weekdays, £30 weekends* ⚑ *18 holes, 4935 yards, par 65.*

CORGARFF CASTLE

23 miles northeast of Braemar, 14 miles northwest of Ballater.

This castle has a striking setting on the moors and some rebuilt military features that recall its strategic importance.

GETTING HERE AND AROUND

By car, take A939 and then follow signs.

EXPLORING

Corgarff Castle. Eighteenth-century soldiers paved a military highway north from Ballater to Corgarff Castle, an isolated tower house on the moorland with a star-shape defensive wall that's a curious replica of Braemar Castle. Corgarff was built as a hunting lodge for the earls of Mar in the 16th century. After an eventful history that included the wife of a later laird being burned alive in a family dispute, the castle ended its career as a garrison for Hanoverian troops. The troops were responsible for preventing illegal whisky distilling. Reconstructed barracks show what the castle must have been like when the Redcoats arrived in 1746. ✉ *Off A939, Corgarff* ☎ *01975/651460* ⊕ *www.historicenvironment. scot* ▦ *£6* ⊘ *Closed Oct.–Mar.*

EN
ROUTE
Castle Trail. If you return east from Corgarff Castle to the A939/A944 junction and make a left onto the A944, the signs indicate that you're on the Castle Trail. The A944 meanders along the River Don to the village of Strathdon, where a great mound by the roadside turns out to be a *motte*, or the base of a wooden castle, built in the late 12th century. Although it takes considerable imagination to become enthusiastic about a grass-covered heap, surviving mottes have contributed greatly

Language and the Scots

Until quite recently, many Scots were made to feel uncomfortable—even within Scotland—about using their native regional dialects. After the Union of England and Scotland in 1707, Scotland's professional middle class, including its politicians, adopted an only mildly accented form of "standard English." Even today, the voices of the Scottish aristocracy— usually educated in elite English schools—are almost indistinguishable from those of their English counterparts. Liz Lochhead, Scotland's Makar (poet laureate) from 2011 to 2016 and a champion of spoken and written Scots, put it like this in her poem *Kidspoem/Bairnsang*: "Oh saying it was one thing / but when it came to writing it / in black and white / the way it had to be said / was as if you were posh, grown-up, male, English and dead." But in recent generations, Scots urban accents and rural dialects have become accepted once again. The creation of the post of Makar (first held by Edwin Morgan from 2004 to 2010 and now by Jackie Kay) signaled that Scots is once again to be taken seriously. Taking up the mantle of Robert Burns, whose poems drew on the *Lallans* (Lowlands) of his native southwest, contemporary authors such as Irvine Welsh and William McIlvanney and others write in the voices of working-class Scots city dwellers.

LOWLAND SCOTS

The Scots language (that is, Lowland Scots, not Gaelic), a northern form of Middle English influenced by Norse, Gaelic, French, and Dutch, was used in the court and in literature until the late 16th century. After the Scottish court moved to London in 1603 it declined as a literary or official language. But Scots survives in various forms, some of which—like the broadest urban accents of Dundee and Glasgow—are almost impenetrable to an ear used to "standard" English.

Some Scottish words are used and understood across the entire country (and world), such as *wee* (small), *aye* (yes), *lassie* (girl), and *bonny* (pretty). You may even find yourself exporting a few useful words, such as *dreich* (gloomy), *glaikit* (acting and looking foolish), or *dinna fash* (don't worry), all of which are much more expressive than their English equivalents. Doric, the regional dialect of Aberdeenshire, is the purest direct descendant of the old Scots tongue. It's loaded with borrowings from Norse, such as *quine* (a young woman) and *loon* (a young man), while "what" becomes "fit," "who" becomes "faa," and "which" becomes "fitna." The local version of "How do you do?" is "Fit like?" A country dweller might refer to an urban Aberdonian as a *toonser*; his city cousin might call him a *teuchter*. Neither term is entirely complimentary.

GAELIC

Scottish Gaelic—an entirely different language—is not, despite what many still think, Scotland's national tongue. This Celtic language is incomprehensible to 99% of Scots and spoken by fewer than 60,000 people. Most live in the Western Isles (*Eilean Siar* in Gaelic), with a handful in the Highlands and Argyll. All speak English as well as their mother tongue. Gaelic was frowned upon after the failure of the 1745 Jacobite rebellions, and numbers of Gaelic speakers have declined ever since, though the decline has slowed in recent years.

to the understanding of the history of Scottish castles. The A944 then joins the A97, and a few minutes later a sign points to **Glenbuchat Castle,** a plain Z-plan tower house. ⊕ *www.visitscotland.com/see-do/ itineraries/castles/scotlands-castle-trail.*

ALFORD

28 miles west of Aberdeen, 41 miles northeast of Braemar.

A plain and sturdy settlement in the Howe (Hollow) of Alford, this town gives those who have grown somewhat weary of castle-hopping a break: it has a museum instead. Craigievar Castle and Castle Fraser are nearby, though.

GETTING HERE AND AROUND

The town is on A944.

EXPLORING

Fodor'sChoice **Castle Fraser.** The massive Castle Fraser is the ancestral home of the
★ Frasers and one of the largest of the castles of Mar; it's certainly a contender as one of the grandest castles in the northeast. Although the well-furnished building shows a variety of styles reflecting the taste of its owners from the 15th through the 19th century, its design is typical of the cavalcade of castles in the region, and for good reason. This—along with many others, including Midmar, Craigievar, Crathes, and Glenbuchat—was designed by a family of master masons called Bell. There are plenty of family items, but don't miss the two Turret Rooms—one of which is the trophy room—and Major Smiley's Room. He married into the family but is famous for having been one of the escapees from Colditz (a high-security prisoner-of-war camp) during World War II. The walled garden includes a 19th-century knot garden, with colorful flower beds, box hedging, gravel paths, and splendid herbaceous borders. Have lunch in the tearoom or the picnic area. ⊠ *Off A944 ✛ 8 miles southeast of Alford* ☎ *01330/833463* ⊕ *www.nts.org. uk* ✍ *£10.50* ⊗ *Closed Nov.–Mar.*

Craigievar Castle. Pepper-pot turrets make Craigievar Castle an outstanding example of a tower house. Striking and well preserved, it has many family furnishings, and the lovely grounds are worth exploring, too. Craigievar was built in relatively peaceful times by William Forbes, a successful merchant in trade with the Baltic Sea ports (he was also known as Danzig Willie). ⊠ *A980 ✛ 5 miles south of Alford* ☎ *01339/883635* ⊕ *www.nts.org.uk* ✍ *£12.50* ⊗ *Closed Oct.–Mar.*

FAMILY **Grampian Transport Museum.** The entertaining and enthusiastically run Grampian Transport Museum specializes in road-based means of locomotion, backed up by archives and a library. Its collection of buses and trams is second to none, but the Craigievar Express, a steam-driven creation invented by the local postman to deliver mail more efficiently, is the most unusual. Look out for the Hillman Imp: if Scotland has a national car, this is it. There's a small café that offers tea, baked goods, and ice cream. ⊠ *Montgarrie Rd.* ☎ *01975/562292* ⊕ *www.gtm.org. uk* ✍ *£10 (includes 2 children)* ⊗ *Closed Oct.–Mar.*

7

THE NORTHEAST AND THE MALT WHISKY TRAIL

North of Deeside another popular area of this region lies inland, toward Speyside—the valley, or strath, of the River Spey—famed for its whisky distilleries, some of which it promotes in another signposted trail. Distilling Scotch is not an intrinsically spectacular process. It involves pure water, malted barley, and sometimes peat smoke, then a lot of bubbling and fermentation, all of which cause a number of odd smells. The result is a prestigious product with a fascinating range of flavors that you may either enjoy immensely or not at all.

Instead of closely following the Malt Whisky Trail, dip into it and blend visits to distilleries with some other aspects of the county of Moray, particularly its coastline. Whisky notwithstanding, Moray's scenic qualities, low rainfall, and other reassuring weather statistics are worth remembering. You can also sample the northeastern seaboard, including some of the best but least-known coastal scenery in Scotland.

DUFFTOWN

54 miles west of Aberdeen.

On one of the Spey tributaries, Dufftown was planned in 1817 by the Earl of Fife. Its simple cross layout with a square and a large clock tower (originally from Banff and now the site of the visitor center) is typical of a small Scottish town built in the 19th century. Its simplicity is made all the more stark by the brooding, heather-clad hills that rise around it. Dufftown is convenient to a number of distilleries.

GETTING HERE AND AROUND

To get here from Aberdeen, drive west on A96 and A920; then turn west at Huntly. It's not easy or quick, but you can take the train to Elgin or Keith and then the bus to Dufftown.

EXPLORING

TOP ATTRACTIONS

Balvenie Distillery. As soon as you step into the old manager's office at Balvenie Distillery—now gently restored and fitted with knotted-elm furniture—you realize Balvenie wants to make sure that all visitors get to see, smell, and feel the magic of the making of this malt. Balvenie is unusual because it has its own cooperage with six coopers hard at work turning the barrels. Tours show the mashing, fermentation, and distillation process and end with a tasting. ■TIP➔ **Visitors must be 18 or older.** ⊠ *Balvenie St.* ☎ *01340/822210* ⊕ *www.thebalvenie.com* ☒ *£40* ⊙ *Closed weekends.*

Fodor's Choice ★ **Glenfiddich Distillery.** Many make Glenfiddich Distillery their first stop on the Malt Whisky Trail. The independent company of William Grant and Sons Limited was the first to realize the tourist potential of the distilling process. The company began offering tours around the typical pagoda-roof malting buildings and subsequently built an entertaining visitor center. Besides a free 20-minute tour of the distillery there are various tours for more discerning visitors that include nosing and

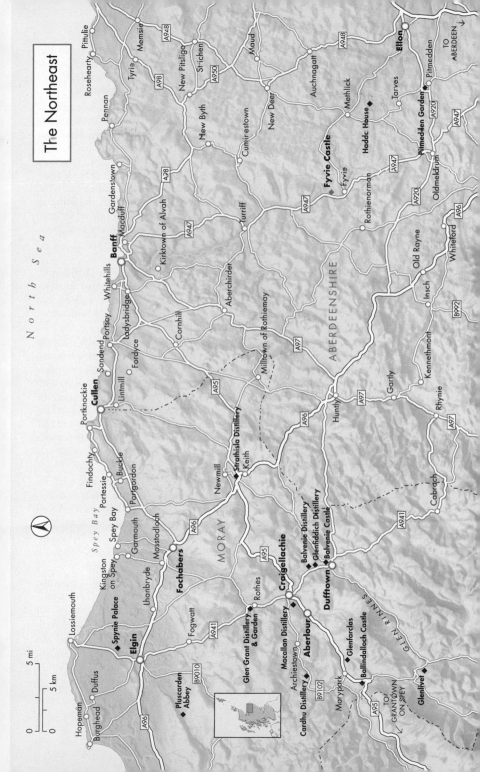

tasting sessions. Check out the Malt Barn Bar, serving a limited but tasty menu, and look out for viewings of the current Glenfiddich Distillery Artists in Residence's work. ✉ *A941* ✣ *½ mile north of Dufftown* ☎ *01340/820373* 🌐 *www.glenfiddich.com* 🎫 *Tours from £10.*

Strathisla Distillery. Whisky lovers should take the B9014 11 miles northeast from Dufftown—or alternatively, ride the Keith Dufftown Railway—to see one of Scotland's most iconic distilleries, the Strathisla Distillery, with its cobblestone courtyard and famous double pagoda roofs. Stretching over the picturesque River Isla, the Strathisla Distillery was built in 1786 and now produces the main component of the Chivas Regal blend. Guided tours, for those 18 and over only, take you to the mash house, tun room, and still house—all pretty much the same as they were when production began. The tour ends with a tasting session. ✉ *Seafield Ave., Keith* ☎ *01542/783044* 🌐 *www.maltwhiskydistilleries.com* 🎫 *£7.50* 🕒 *Closed weekends mid-Nov.–mid.-Mar.*

WORTH NOTING

Balvenie Castle. On a mound just above the Glenfiddich Distillery is this grim, gray, and squat curtain-walled castle. This ruined fortress, which dates from the 13th century, once commanded the glens and passes toward Speyside and Elgin. ✉ *A941* ☎ *01856/761616* 🌐 *www.historicenvironment.scot* 🎫 *£4.50* 🕒 *Closed Oct.–Mar.*

FAMILY **Keith and Dufftown Railway.** Leaving from Dufftown three times a day on weekends then returning from Keith, this restored locomotive lets you return to the age when trains were exciting, chugging 11 miles through forests, fields, and across rivers. It passes Drummuir Castle on its way to Keith, home of the Strathisla Distillery. The Buffer Stop restaurant car at the Dufftown station serves snacks, scones, and tea. Reservations are a good idea. ✉ *Dufftown station, Station Rd.* ☎ *01340/821181* 🌐 *keith-dufftown-railway.co.uk* 🎫 *£7* 🕒 *Closed Oct.–Easter and weekdays Easter–Sept.*

WHERE TO STAY

$ B&B/INN 🏨 **The Fife Arms Hotel.** This 18th-century coaching inn offers a whiff of atmosphere and acceptable accommodations for a one-night stay in motel-style rooms attached to an old-school pub popular with locals. **Pros:** full Scottish breakfast; off-street parking; very central. **Cons:** some noise from adjoining pub. [$] *Rooms from: £70* ✉ *2 The Square* ☎ *01340/820220* 🌐 *www.fifearmsdufftown.co.uk* 🛏 *6 rooms* 🍴 *Breakfast.*

SHOPPING

Collector's Cabin. Two adjoining shops—one with Scottish silver, fossils, and book illustrations, the other with kilts, ceramics, and other curiosities—are filled with conversation starters. This is truly a trove worth delving into. ✉ *22 and 24 Balvenie St.* ☎ *01340/821393* 🕒 *Closed Wed.*

Dufftown Glassworks. This light and airy gallery sells interesting fused and painted glass, as well as prints and crafts by local makers. The adjoining café sells the best coffee in Dufftown, leaf tea, and a good selection of cakes from scones to lemon drizzle to gooey chocolate. ✉ *16 Conval St.* ☎ *01340/821534* 🌐 *dufftownglassworks.com.*

Whisky, the Water of Life

Conjured from an innocuous mix of malted barley, water, and yeast, malt whisky is for many synonymous with Scotland. Lowlanders and Highlanders produced whisky for hundreds of years before it emerged as Scotland's national drink and major export. Today those centuries of expertise result in a sublimely subtle drink with many different layers of flavor. Each distillery produces a malt with—to the expert—instantly identifiable, predominant notes peculiarly its own.

WHISKY TYPES AND STYLES
There are two types of whisky: malt and grain. Malt whisky, generally acknowledged to have a more sophisticated bouquet and flavor, is made with malted barley—barley that is soaked in water until the grains germinate and then is dried to halt the germination, all of which adds extra flavor and a touch of sweetness to the brew. Grain whisky also contains malted barley, but with the addition of unmalted barley and maize.

Blended whiskies, which make up many of the leading brands, usually balance malt- and grain-whisky distillations; deluxe blends contain a higher percentage of malts. Blends that contain several malt whiskies are called "vatted malts." Whisky connoisseurs often prefer to taste the single malts: the unblended whisky from a single distillery.

In simple terms, malt whiskies may be classified into "eastern" and "western" in style, with the whisky made in the east of Scotland, for example in Speyside, being lighter and sweeter than the products of the Western Isles, which often have a taste of peat smoke or even iodine.

The production process is, by comparison, relatively straightforward: just malt your barley, mash it, ferment it, and distill it, then mature to perfection. To find out the details, join a distillery tour, and be rewarded with a dram. Check out ⊕ *www.scotlandwhisky.com* for more information.

TASTING WHISKY
When tasting whisky, follow these simple steps. First, pour a dram. Turn and tilt the glass to coat the sides. Smell the whisky, "nosing" to inhale the heady aromas. If you want, you can add a little water and turn the glass gently to watch it "marry" with the whisky, nosing as you go. Take a wee sip and swirl it over your tongue and sense what connoisseurs call the "mouthfeel." Swallow and admire the finish. Repeat until convinced it's a good malt!

7

CRAIGELLACHIE

4 miles northwest of Dufftown via A941.

Renowned as an angling resort, Craigellachie, like so many settlements on the River Spey, is sometimes enveloped in the malty reek of the local industry. Glen Grant is one of the distilleries nearby. The Spey itself is crossed by a handsome suspension bridge, designed by noted engineer Thomas Telford (1757–1834) in 1814 and now bypassed by the modern road.

GETTING HERE AND AROUND

The town is on A491; it's best to drive here, as public transportation is infrequent and complicated.

EXPLORING

Fodor's Choice ★ **Glen Grant Distillery & Garden.** James Grant founded this distillery in 1840 when he was only 25, and it was the first in the country to be electrically powered. This place will come as a welcome relief to companions of dedicated Malt Whisky Trail followers, because in addition to the distillery there's a large and beautiful garden. It's planted and tended as Grant envisioned, with orchards and woodland walks, log bridges over waterfalls, a magnificent lily pond, and azaleas and rhododendrons in profusion. Using peculiarly tall stills and special purifiers that follow a design introduced over a century ago, Glen Grant produces a distinctive pale-gold whisky with an almost floral or fruity finish. The tour is excellent value, with perhaps the friendliest guides and certainly the most generous tastings. There's a coffee shop, too, selling huge scones. ✉ *A941, Rothes* ✢ *North of town, left at junction of A941 and B9015* ☎ *01340/832118* 🌐 *www.glengrant.com* 🎫 *£5.*

Macallan Distillery. On the sprawling Easter Elchies Estate, Macallan Distillery offers unique whisky matured in sherry casks and, more recently, in oak bourbon casks. The tour lasts an hour and 45 minutes and, aiming to give you a full understanding of the six pillars of whisky making, it takes you from the still house to the warehouse where maturation takes place, finishing off with a nosing and tasting session. Booking is essential. ✉ *Easter Elchies* ✢ *About 1 mile west of Craigellachie, off B9102* ☎ *01304/872280* 🌐 *www.themacallan.com* 🎫 *£15* 🕒 *Closed Sun. Easter–Sept. and weekends Oct.–Easter.*

Speyside Cooperage and Visitor Centre. A major stop on the Malt Whisky Trail, the huge Speyside Cooperage and Visitor Centre is a must for all whisky fans. Retired coopers will talk you through the making of the casks, a surprisingly physical and dramatic process that uses the same tools and skills employed for hundreds of years. Inside you can watch highly skilled craftspeople make and repair oak barrels used in the local whisky industry. The Acorn to Cask exhibit tells all about the ancient craft of coopering. There's a cottage café with huge cakes and sandwiches for those in need of sustenance. ✉ *Dufftown Rd.* ☎ *01340/871108* 🌐 *www.speysidecooperage.co.uk* 🎫 *£3.50* 🕒 *Closed weekends.*

WHERE TO EAT AND STAY

$$ BRITISH 🍴 **Copper Dog.** With its reclaimed woodwork and mismatched wooden chairs, rows of malt whisky bottles, decorative oak barrel-ends, and walls hung with prints, the Craigellachie Hotel's bar-restaurant is an edgy blend of cozy and shabby chic. The menu is equally relaxed, with dishes such as locally produced gourmet sausages, rumbledethumps (a casserole of baked potato, cabbage, and onions), and an outstanding platter of Scottish cheeses with homemade chutney, all of which can be matched with regional craft beers. **Known for:** local produce; malt whiskies; craft beers. [$] *Average main: £15* ✉ *Craigellachie Hotel, Victoria St.* ☎ *01340/881204* 🌐 *www.craigellachiehotel.co.uk.*

$$ HOTEL **Craigellachie Hotel.** Who would expect a rock-chic hideaway in the heart of sleepy Speyside? But that's what this stylish old town house has become. **Pros:** stylish decor down to the details; perfectly pitched service; huge range of malt whiskies. **Cons:** popular for wedding parties. [$] *Rooms from: £150* ✉ *Victoria St.* ☎ *01340/881204* 🌐 *www.craigellachiehotel.co.uk* 🛏 *26 rooms* 🍴 *Some meals.*

$ B&B/INN **Highlander Inn.** Don't be fooled by the rather alpine exterior: this very Scottish hotel prides itself on its whisky bar and its friendly welcome. **Pros:** simple accommodations; warm atmosphere; great bar. **Cons:** dated decor; could be rather too lively for some. [$] *Rooms from: £90* ✉ *Victoria St.* ☎ *01340/881446* 🌐 *www.whiskyinn.com* 🛏 *8 rooms* 🍴 *Breakfast.*

ABERLOUR

2 miles southwest of Craigellachie.

Aberlour, often listed as Charlestown of Aberlour on maps, is a handsome little burgh, essentially Victorian in style, though actually founded in 1812 by the local landowner. The names of the noted local whisky stills are Cragganmore, Aberlour, and Glenfarclas; Glenlivet and Cardhu are also nearby. Also in Aberlour is Walkers, famous for producing shortbread, tins of buttery, crumbly goodness, since 1898.

7

GETTING HERE AND AROUND

Aberlour is on A95; public transportation here is infrequent.

EXPLORING

Ballindalloch Castle. The family home of the Macpherson-Grants since 1546, Ballindalloch Castle is every visitor's idea of what a Scots laird's lair should look like. You can wander around the beautifully kept rooms and meticulously tended gardens at your leisure; you may even bump into the lord and lady of the manor, who live here all year. There's also a splendid tea shop offering large slices of cake. ✉ *Off A95* ✣ *8 miles southwest of Craigellachie* ☎ *01807/500205* 🌐 *www.ballindallochcastle.co.uk* 🎫 *£11.50* 🕒 *Closed Sept.–Easter.*

Cardhu Distillery. The striking outline of Cardhu Distillery, whose main product lies at the heart of Johnnie Walker blends, is set among the heather-clad Mannoch Hills. Established by John and Helen Cumming in 1811, it was officially founded in 1824 after distilling was made legal by the Excise Act of 1823. Guides take you to the mashing, fermenting, and distilling halls, and they explain the malting process, which now takes place on the coast at Burghead. ✉ *B1902, Knockando* ✣ *10 miles north of Glenlivet and 7 miles west of Aberlour* ☎ *01340/875635* 🌐 *www.discovering-distilleries.com/cardhu/find-us/* 🎫 *£5* 🕒 *Closed weekends Oct.–Mar.*

Glenfarclas. Glenfarclas is one of Scotland's few remaining family-owned distilleries, passed down from father to son since 1865. That link to the past is most visible among its low buildings, where the retired still sits outside: if you didn't know what it was, you could mistake it for part of a submarine. The tours end with tastings in the superlative Ship

Room, the intact lounge of an ocean liner called the *Empress of Australia.* ✉ *Off A95, Ballindalloch* ☎ *01807/500345* 🌐 *www.glenfarclas.co.uk* 🎟 *£7.50* 🕒 *Closed weekends Oct.–June and Sun. in July–Sept.* ☞ *In-depth tasting tours from £100.*

Glenlivet. The famous Glenlivet was the first licensed distillery in the Highlands, founded in 1824 by George Smith. Today it produces one of the best-known 12-year-old single malts in the world. The 75-minute Classic Tour offers an introduction to malt whisky making, explains the distillery's history, and includes a free dram; more in-depth tours are available. There's a coffee shop with baked goods and, of course, a whisky shop. Visitors must be 18 or over. ✉ *Off B9008, Ballindalloch* ✣ *10 miles southwest of Aberlour via A95 and B9008.* ☎ *01340/821720* 🌐 *www.glenlivet.com* 🎟 *£10* 🕒 *Closed mid-Nov.–mid-Mar.*

WHERE TO STAY

$$ B&B/INN 🏨 **Cardhu Country House.** This once-abandoned manse (minister's house) looks as if it has always been loved and lived in: huge bedrooms with wooden floors, antique fireplaces, and large beds dressed in Harris tweed throws are married to contemporary bathrooms. **Pros:** period charm and modern comforts; tasty meals. **Cons:** you need a car to get here. [$] *Rooms from: £120* ✉ *Off B9102, Knockando* ☎ *01340/810895* 🌐 *www.cardhucountryhouse.co.uk* 🛏 *6 rooms* 🍴 *Breakfast.*

$$ B&B/INN 🏨 **Mash Tun.** Curvy yet sturdy, this former station hotel, now a smart B&B with a popular restaurant, is the social hub of the village. **Pros:** superb accommodations; tasty meals; great atmosphere in the restaurant and bar. **Cons:** book well ahead in summer. [$] *Rooms from: £115* ✉ *8 Broomfield Sq.* ☎ *01340/881771* 🌐 *www.mashtun-aberlour.com* 🛏 *5 rooms* 🍴 *Breakfast.*

ELGIN

15 miles north of Craigellachie, 69 miles northwest of Aberdeen, 41 miles east of Inverness.

As the center of the fertile Laigh (low-lying lands) of Moray, Elgin has been of local importance for centuries. Sheltered by great hills to the south, the city lies between two major rivers, the Spey and the Findhorn. Beginning in the 13th century, Elgin became an important religious center, a cathedral city with a walled town growing up around the cathedral and adjacent to the original settlement.

Elgin prospered, and by the early 18th century it became a mini-Edinburgh of the north and a place where country gentlemen spent their winters. It even echoed Edinburgh in carrying out wide-scale reconstruction in the 18th century. Many fine neoclassical buildings survive today despite much misguided demolition in the late 20th century for better traffic flow. However, the central main-street plan and some of the older little streets and *wynds* (alleyways) remain.

GETTING HERE AND AROUND

Elgin is on the A96 road from Aberdeen to Inverness. The A941 runs north from the distillery area to the city. There's a train stop here on the line that links Aberdeen and Inverness: Aberdeen is 90 minutes away.

ESSENTIALS

Visitor Information Elgin Visitor Information Point. ✉ *Elgin Library, Cooper Park* ☎ *01343/562608* 🌐 *www.morayspeyside.com/elgin.*

EXPLORING

Elgin Cathedral. Cooper Park contains a magnificent ruin, the Elgin Cathedral, consecrated in 1224. Its eventful story included devastation by fire: a 1390 act of retaliation by warlord Alexander Stewart (circa 1343–1405), the Wolf of Badenoch. The illegitimate son of King David II (1324–71) had sought revenge for his excommunication by the bishop of Moray. The cathedral was rebuilt but finally fell into disuse after the Reformation in 1560. By 1567 the highest authority in the land, the regent earl of Moray, had stripped the lead from the roof to pay for his army. Thus ended the career of the religious seat known as the Lamp of the North. Some traces of the cathedral settlement survive—the gateway Pann's Port and the Bishop's Palace—although they've been drastically altered. ✉ *Cooper Park* ☎ *01343/547171* 🌐 *www.historicenvironment.scot* 🎫 *£7.50; £9 with Spynie Palace* 🕒 *Closed Thurs.–Sun. Oct.–Mar.*

OFF THE BEATEN PATH

Pluscarden Abbey. Given the general destruction caused by the 16th-century upheaval of the Reformation, abbeys in Scotland tend to be ruinous and deserted, but at the 13th-century Pluscarden Abbey the ancient way of life continues. Monks from Prinknash Abbey near Gloucester, England, returned here in 1948, and the abbey is now a Benedictine community. Mass is at 9 (10 on Sunday) and is sung by the monks using Gregorian chant. ✉ *Off B9010* ✣ *6 miles southwest of Elgin* 🌐 *www.pluscardenabbey.org.*

Spynie Palace. Just north of Elgin sits Spynie Palace, the impressive 15th-century former headquarters of the bishops of Moray. It has now fallen into ruin, though the top of the tower has good views over the Laigh of Moray. Find it by turning right off the Elgin–Lossiemouth road. ✉ *Off A941* ☎ *01343/546358* 🌐 *www.historicenvironment.scot* 🎫 *£7.50, £9 with Elgin Cathedral* 🕒 *Closed weekdays Oct.–Mar.*

St. Giles Church. At the center of Elgin, the most conspicuous structure is St. Giles Church, which divides High Street. The grand foursquare building, constructed in 1828, exhibits the Greek Revival style: note the columns, the pilasters, and the top of the spire, surmounted by a representation of the Monument of Lysicrates. ✉ *High St.* 🌐 *www.elginstgileschurch.co.uk.*

WHERE TO STAY

$$ HOTEL

🏨 **Mansfield Hotel.** Four-poster beds add a touch of class to the very comfortable double rooms and suites in this modern hotel in the center of Elgin. **Pros:** comfortable rooms; free off-street parking; good food and beverage options. **Cons:** bland decor; popular wedding and conference venue. [$] *Rooms from: £115* ✉ *2 Mayne St.* ☎ *01343/540883* 🌐 *www.themansefield.com* 🛏 *42 rooms* 🍴 *Breakfast.*

7

SHOPPING

Gordon and MacPhail. An outstanding delicatessen and wine merchant, Gordon and MacPhail also stocks rare malt whiskies. This is a good place to shop for gifts for your foodie friends. ⊠ *58–60 South St.* ☎ *01343/545110* ⊕ *www.gordonandmacphail.com* ☉ *Closed Sun.*

Johnstons of Elgin. This woolen mill has a worldwide reputation for its luxury fabrics, especially cashmere. The large shop stocks not only the firm's own products, but also top-quality Scottish crafts. There's a coffee shop on the premises. ■ TIP→ **Tours of the mill are free and must be booked in advance.** ⊠ *Heritage Centre, Newmill Rd.* ☎ *01343/554099* ⊕ *www.johnstonscashmere.com.*

SPORTS AND THE OUTDOORS
GOLF

Moray Golf Club. Discover the relatively mild microclimate of what vacationing Victorians dubbed the Moray Riviera, as Tom Morris did in 1889 when he was inspired by the lay of the natural links. Henry Cotton's New Course (1979) has tighter fairways and smaller greens. A handicap certificate is required for the Old Course. ⊠ *Stotfield Rd., Lossiemouth* ☎ *01343/812018* ⊕ *www.moraygolf.co.uk* ⌨ *Old Course, £100; New Course, £45* ⚲ *Old Course: 18 holes, 6995 yards, par 71; New Course: 18 holes, 6008 yards, par 69.*

FOCHABERS

9 miles east of Elgin.

With its hanging baskets of fuchsia in summer and its perfectly mowed village square, Fochabers has a cared-for charm that makes you want to stop here, even just to stretch your legs. Lying just to the south of the River Spey, the former market town was founded in 1776 by the Duke of Gordon. The duke moved the village from its original site because it was too close to Gordon Castle. Famous today for being home to the Baxters brand of soups and jams, Fochabers is near some of the best berry fields: come and pick your own in the summer months.

GETTING HERE AND AROUND

Fochabers is not on the Inverness-to-Aberdeen train line, but there is an hourly bus service (Stagecoach Bluebird No. 10) from Fochabers to Elgin. It's near the junction of A98 and A96.

EXPLORING

Baxters Highland Village. Legendary Scottish food brand Baxters of Fochabers makes gourmet products here on the banks of the River Spey for worldwide export. From Tokyo to New York, upmarket stores stock the company's soups, jams, and chutneys. Watch cooking demonstrations, have a look at a re-creation of the Baxters' first grocery shop, or browse around the Best of Scotland, specializing in all kinds of Scottish products. A restaurant serves up an assortment of delectables. ⊠ *A96* ☎ *01343/820666* ⊕ *www.baxters.com.*

FAMILY **Fochabers Folk Museum & Heritage Centre.** Once over the Spey Bridge and past the cricket ground (a very unusual sight in Scotland), you can find the symmetrical, 18th-century Fochabers village square. The old Pringle Church is now the home of the Fochabers Folk Museum, which boasts a fine collection of items relating to past life of all types of residents in the village and surrounding area. Exhibits include carts and carriages, farm implements, domestic labor-saving devices, and an exquisite collection of Victorian toys. ✉ *High St.* ☎ *01343/821204* 🌐 *www.fochabers-heritage.org.uk* 🕒 *Closed Oct.–mid-May.*

Gordon Chapel. One of the village's lesser-known treasures is the Gordon Chapel, which has an exceptional set of stained-glass windows by Pre-Raphaelite artist Sir Edward Burne-Jones. Look out for the Good Shepherd, carrying a newborn lamb around his neck. ✉ *Church of St. Elizabeth, Castle St.*

WHERE TO EAT

$$ BRITISH 🍴 **Gordon Castle Walled Garden Cafe.** With light streaming through the large windows onto the wooden tables and rattan chairs, there is an airiness and freshness to this eatery. Fish landed just a few miles away on the Moray coast is a good bet, as are the long-aged steaks. **Known for:** local steak and seafood; fresh summer fruit desserts. [$] *Average main: £15* ✉ *Fochabers* ✥ *Just off A96, Fochabers Bypass Rd.* ☎ *01343/612317* 🌐 *www.gordoncastlescotland.com.*

$ BRITISH 🍴 **The Quaich.** The friendly Quaich is a local favorite, serving great cakes and other baked goods, outstanding full Scottish breakfasts, warming porridge, and a plethora of snacks and sandwiches. Unusual dishes include a salmon omelet and haggis panini. **Known for:** imaginative omelets; tempting cakes and pastries. [$] *Average main: £6* ✉ *85 High St.* ☎ *01343/820981* 🕒 *Closed Mon.*

SHOPPING

Watt's Antiques. This shop has small collectibles, jewelry, ornaments, and china. ✉ *45 High St.* ☎ *01343/820077* 🌐 *www.wattsantiques.com.*

CULLEN

21 miles east of Elgin, 13 miles east of Fochabers.

Fodor's Choice ★ Look for some wonderfully painted homes at Cullen, in the old fishing town below the railway viaduct. The real attractions of this charming little seaside resort, however, are its white-sand beach (the water is quite cold, though) and the fine view west toward the aptly named Bowfiddle Rock. In summer Cullen bustles with families carrying buckets and spades and eating ice cream and chips.

A stroll past the small but once busy harbor reveals numerous fishers' cottages, huddled together with small yards where they dried their nets. Beyond these, the vast stretch of beach curves gently round the bay. Above are the disused Victorian viaduct—formerly the Peterhead train line—and the 18th-century town.

GETTING HERE AND AROUND

Cullen is on A98, on Cullen Bay.

EXPLORING

Seafield Street. The town has a fine *mercat* (market) cross and one main street—Seafield Street—that splits the town. It holds numerous specialty shops—antiques and gift stores, an ironmonger, a baker, a pharmacy, and a locally famous ice-cream shop among them—as well as several cafés. ✉ *Cullen.*

NEED A BREAK

🍴 Cullen Ice Cream Shop. In summer it can seem as if everyone you see in Cullen is licking a cone from the Ice Cream Shop. There's only a handful of flavors but they are all made on-site. Known for: homemade ice cream; weird vintage candies. ✉ *40 Seafield St.* ☎ *01542/840484.*

WHERE TO EAT AND STAY

$ SEAFOOD FAMILY

🍴 **Linda's Fish & Chips.** This casual place serves the freshest fish, caught in nearby Buckie and cooked to crispy perfection (gluten-free batter is available, too). There's a seating area inside, but it's best for takeout. **Known for:** fish battered to perfection; crispy fries. [$] *Average main: £10* ✉ *54 Seafield St.* ☎ *01542/840202.*

$ SEAFOOD

🍴 **Rockpool.** This modish fish restaurant has remarkably reasonable prices for the quality of the food and size of the servings. Try the rich Cullen skink (a creamy smoked-haddock soup), a pint glass of fat prawns served with mayo and oat bread, or some freshly fried squid with a lime sauce, all beautifully presented on wooden boards. **Known for:** Cullen skink; yummy prawns; zesty shellfish. [$] *Average main: £10* ✉ *10 The Square* ☎ *01542/841397* 🌐 *www.rockpool-cullen.co.uk* 🕒 *Closed Mon. No dinner.*

$ B&B/INN

🏨 **Academy House.** In the picturesque village of Fordyce, this luxurious bed-and-breakfast in a handsomely preserved Victorian house was once the headmaster's house for a famous local secondary school. **Pros:** good home cooking; delightful setting; helpful owners eager to help you find your way around. **Cons:** rooms book up fast. [$] *Rooms from: £90* ✉ *School Rd., Fordyce* ☎ *01261/842743* 🌐 *www.fordyceaccommodation.com* 🛏 *2 rooms* 🍽 *Breakfast* ☞ *Dinner on request.*

SHOPPING

Abra Antiques. With surprisingly pleasing prices, Abra Antiques overflows with all kinds of trinkets, Victoriana, antiquarian books, and Scottish miscellany. ✉ *6 Seafield St.* ☎ *01542/840605* 🕒 *Closed Wed.*

BANFF

36 miles east of Elgin, 47 miles north of Aberdeen.

Midway along the northeast coast, overlooking Moray Firth and the estuary of the River Deveron, Banff is a dour fishing town, huddled around a small harbor, with a bleak but sometimes lovely coastline of crags, cliffs, and sandy coves to either side. Sixteenth-century houses huddle around the harbor, while surprisingly grand Georgian streets are reminders of its glory years as a hub of the fishing industry.

GETTING HERE AND AROUND

Banff is on the A98 coastal road and at the end of the tree-lined A947 to Aberdeen. If you are relying on public transportation, Bus 325 from Aberdeen bus station takes two hours and gets you into Low Street, just five minutes from Duff House.

ESSENTIALS

Visitor Information Banff Visitor Information Centre. ⊠ *Collie Lodge, Low St.* ☎ *01261/812419* ⊕ *www.visitscotland.com.*

EXPLORING

Fodor's Choice
★

Duff House. The jewel in Banff's crown is the grand mansion of Duff House, a splendid William Adam–designed (1689–1748) Georgian mansion. It's now an annex of the National Galleries, housing works by El Greco, Sir Henry Raeburn, and Thomas Gainsborough. A good tearoom and a gift shop are on the ground floor. ⊠ *Off A98* ☎ *01261/818181* ⊕ *www.duffhouse.org.uk* ⊠ *£7.50* ☉ *Closed Nov.–Mar.*

SPORTS AND THE OUTDOORS

GOLF

Duff House Royal Golf Club. Just moments from the sea, this club combines a coastal course with a parkland setting. Close to the center of Banff, it's on the grounds of Duff House, a country-house art gallery in a William Adam–designed mansion. The club has inherited the ancient traditions of seaside play; golf records here go back to the 17th century. ⊠ *The Barnyards, off A98* ☎ *01261/812062* ⊕ *www.duffhouseroyal. com* ⊠ *£45 weekdays, £50 weekends* ⚘ *18 holes, 6031 yards, par 68* ⚘ *Reservations essential* ☞ *Closed Oct.–Mar.*

FYVIE CASTLE

18 miles south of Banff.

This castle mixes ancient construction with Edwardian splendor and includes excellent art. The grounds are also worth exploring.

GETTING HERE AND AROUND

If you're driving from Banff, take the A947 south for 20 minutes or so until you see the turnoff.

EXPLORING

Fodor's Choice
★

Fyvie Castle. In an area rich with castles, Fyvie Castle stands out as the most complex. Five great towers built by five successive powerful families turned a 13th-century foursquare castle into an opulent Edwardian statement of wealth. Some superb paintings are on view, including 12 works by Sir Henry Raeburn. There are myriad sumptuous interiors—the circular stone staircase is considered one of the best examples in the country—and delightfully laid-out gardens. A former lady of the house, Lillia Drummond, was apparently starved to death by her husband, who entombed her body inside the walls of a secret room. In the 1920s, when the bones were disrupted during renovations, a string of such terrible misfortunes followed that they were quickly returned and the room sealed off. Her name is carved into the windowsill of the Drummond Room. ⊠ *Off A947, Turriff* ☎ *01651/819226* ⊕ *www.nts. org.uk* ⊠ *£12.50* ☉ *Closed Oct.–Mar.*

7

ELLON

32 miles southeast of Banff, 14 miles north of Aberdeen.

Formerly a market center on what was then the lowest bridging point of the River Ythan, Ellon, a bedroom suburb of Aberdeen, is a small town at the center of a rural hinterland. It's also well placed for visiting Fyvie Castle and Haddo House.

GETTING HERE AND AROUND

To get to Ellon, take the A947 from Banff or the A90 from Aberdeen; both routes take half an hour.

EXPLORING

Haddo House. Built in 1732, this elegant mansion has a light and graceful Georgian design, with curving wings on either side of a harmonious, symmetrical facade. The interior is late-Victorian ornate, filled with magnificent paintings (including works by Pompeo Batoni and Sir Thomas Lawrence) and plenty of objets d'art. Pre-Raphaelite stained-glass windows by Sir Edward Burne-Jones grace the chapel. Outside is a terrace garden with a fountain, and a few yards farther is Haddo Country Park, which has walking trails leading to memorials about the Gordon family. ■ TIP→ Visits to the house are by prebooked tour only, which are held at 11 and 2. ⊠ *Off B999* ✢ *8 miles northwest of Ellon* ☎ *01651/851440* ⊕ *www.nts.org.uk* ⊠ *£10.50* ☉ *Closed Nov.–Mar.*

Pitmedden Garden. Five miles west of Ellon, at Pitmedden Garden is an exquisite re-creation of a 17th-century garden. It is best visited in summer, from July onward, when annual bedding plants—framed by precision-cut box hedging—form intricate formal patterns. The 100-acre estate also has woodland and farmland walks, as well as the Museum of Farming Life. ⊠ *Off A920, Pitmedden* ☎ *01651/843188* ⊕ *www.nts. org.uk* ⊠ *£6.50* ☉ *Closed Oct.–Apr.*

NIGHTLIFE AND PERFORMING ARTS

Haddo House. Aristocratic Haddo House hosts a range of events in summer, from performances by the Haddo Choral and Operatic Society to opera, recitals, ballet, Shakespearean drama, and puppet shows in the grounds and salons of the mansion. The season runs from spring through fall. ⊠ *Off B999, Tarves* ✢ *8 miles northwest of Ellon* ☎ *01651/851440* ⊕ *www.nts.org.uk.*

SPORTS AND THE OUTDOORS

GOLF

Cruden Bay Golf Club. This historic golf course, sheltered among extensive sand dunes, offers a quintessential Scottish golf experience. Narrow channels and deep valleys on challenging fairways ensure plenty of excitement, making Cruden Bay one of the northeast's most outstanding courses. ⊠ *Aulton Rd., Cruden Bay* ☎ *01779/812285* ⊕ *www.crudenbaygolfclub.co.uk* ⊠ *Championship, £110; St. Olaf, weekdays £25, weekends £35* ✵ *Championship: 18 holes, 6287 yards, par 70; St. Olaf: 9 holes, 2463 yards, par 32* ⌂ *Reservations essential* ☞ *Book months in advance for a round on weekends.*

8

ARGYLL AND
THE ISLES

8

Visit Fodors.com for advice, updates, and bookings

Updated by
Robin Gauldie

Argyll's rocky seaboard looks out onto islands that were once part of a single prehistoric landmass. Its narrow roads slow travel but give time to admire its lochs and woods, and the ruins that recall the region's dramatic past. Here, too, are grand houses like Brodick and Inveraray castles and elegant gardens such as Crarae. This is whisky country, too: the peaty aroma of Islay's malts is unmistakable. Yet all this is within three hours of Glasgow.

Western Scotland has a complicated, splintered coastline where you'll observe the interplay of sea, loch, and rugged green peninsula. The islands are breathtakingly beautiful, though they often catch the extremely wet weather arriving here from the Atlantic. It is common to experience four seasons in a day, as cliffs and woods suddenly and dramatically disappear in sea mists then reappear just as suddenly.

Ancient castles like Dunstaffnage and the ruined towers on the islands of Loch Awe testify to the region's past importance. Prehistoric peoples left their mark here in the stone circles, carved stones, and Bronze and Iron Age burial mounds around Kilmartin and on Islay and Arran. The gardens of Inveraray and Brodick castles, nourished by the temperate west-coast climate, are the pride of Argyll while the paths of Crarae's, south of Inveraray, wind through plantings of magnolias and azaleas.

The working people of Glasgow traditionally spent their family holidays on the Clyde estuary, taking day trips by steamer down the Firth, or making longer journeys to Rothesay on the Isle of Bute or to Arran and the Ayrshire coast. From Ardrossan, farther down the coast, ferries cruise to the prosperous and varied Isle of Arran.

Western Scotland's small islands have jagged cliffs or tongues of rock, long white-sand beaches, fertile pastures where sheep and cattle graze, fortresses, and shared memories of clan wars and mysterious beasts. Their cliff paths and lochside byways are a paradise for walkers and cyclists, and their whisky the ideal reward after a long day outside. While the islands' western coasts are dramatic, their more sheltered eastern seaboards are the location for pretty harbor towns like brightly painted Tobermory on Mull, or Port Ellen on Islay, with its neat rows of low whitewashed houses.

TOP REASONS TO GO

Whisky, whisky, whisky: With 14 distilleries—9 on Islay, 1 each on Jura and Mull, and just 3 on the mainland—the region has been nicknamed Scotland's whisky coast. The unmistakable peaty smell of the whiskies of Islay contrasts with the lighter whiskies of Arran and Oban.

Iona and its abbey: Maybe it's the remoteness that creates the almost mystical sense of history on Iona. From this early center of Scottish Christianity, evangelists traveled throughout Europe from the 6th century onward. It was also the burial place of Scottish kings, including Macbeth.

The great outdoors: Salmon and trout fill the lochs and rivers, while even bigger trophy fish await farther out to sea. Golfers have more than two dozen courses to choose from, and cyclists and walkers will find every kind of terrain at hand.

Cool castles: Often poised on cliffs overlooking the sea, the region's castles tell the story of eight centuries of occupations, sieges, and conflicts between warring clan chiefs and nobles. Vikings, Scots, and the English fought for their possession.

Glorious gardens: Plants flourish in the mild Gulf Stream that brushes against this broken, western coastline. For vivid flowers, trees, birds, and butterflies, visit Crarae Garden, southwest of Inveraray.

ORIENTATION AND PLANNING

GETTING ORIENTED

8

With long sea lochs carved into its hilly, wooded interior, Argyll is a beguiling interweaving of water and land. The Mull of Kintyre, a narrow finger of land, points south towards nearby Ireland, separating the Firth of Clyde and its islands from the Atlantic and the isles of the Inner Hebrides. Arran, largest of the Clyde isles, looms near the mouth of the Clyde, separated from Kintyre by Kilbrannan Sound. Ferry services allow all kinds of interisland tours and can shorten mainland trips as well.

Linking the region with Glasgow, the A82 runs along the west shore of Loch Lomond to connect with the A83. That road follows the north shore of Loch Fyne, a long fjordlike inlet known for some of Scotland's finest seafood, all the way to Campbeltown near the tip of Kintyre. Along the way is Kennacraig, departure point for ferries to Islay and Jura. Coming from the east, the A85 runs through equally spectacular scenery between Perth and Oban, the main port for ferries to Mull and other islands. From Oban, the A828 runs north to Fort William and the Great Glen.

Argyll. The linked peninsulas of Knapdale and Kintyre—separated by the Crinan Canal at Tarbert—are areas of moorland and forest dotted with small lochs. From Inveraray at the head of Loch Fyne, you can take in Auchindrain's re-created fishing village on the way to the Arran ferry. Or turn west toward Crinan and the prehistoric sites around Kilmartin, then travel northward toward Loch Awe and its intriguing island ruins. A short drive away is Oban, an active ferry and fishing port.

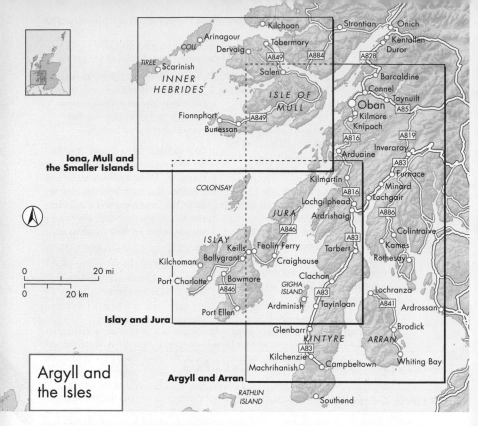

Argyll and
the Isles

Arran. Touring this island will give you a glimpse in a day or two of the whole of Scotland in miniature. In the north, the forbidding Goatfell is a challenge that draws walkers and climbers. The island's wilder west coast attracts bird-watchers and naturalists, while the fertile south of the island contains nine lovely golf courses, leisurely walks, and Brodick Castle.

Islay and Jura. The smell of peat that hangs in the air on Islay is bottled in its famous whiskies. Aside from distilleries, the island's historical sites evoke a past in which these islands were far less remote. The whitewashed cottages along the coast of Islay line clean and beautiful beaches, many of them visited by a variety of wildlife. Jura is wilder and more dramatic, its twin mountains (the Paps) dominating its infertile moorland.

Isle of Mull and Iona. The pretty harbor of Tobermory, with its painted houses, is a relaxing base from which to explore the varied and beautiful island of Mull. Along Mull's west coast, spectacular cliffs and rocky beaches look out on to the Atlantic. From Craignure, the road crosses the sweeping green valleys of the Ross of Mull to Fionnphort and the ferry to the meditative island of Iona.

The Smaller Islands. These islands seem more akin to the remoter Outer Hebrides than to the greener pastures of Mull or Arran. Abandoned by many of their original inhabitants, they are havens for birdlife, particularly Coll's giant dunes or the cliffs of Tiree. Colonsay's Kiloran Bay is open to the Atlantic's breakers, while Tiree's waves draw surfers from around the world.

PLANNING

WHEN TO GO

This part of the mainland is close enough to Glasgow to make it accessible year-round. Oban is just over two hours from the city by car (three hours by bus), but getting to the isles via ferries takes longer, and the crossings are less frequent out of season. You can take advantage of quiet roads and plentiful accommodations in early spring and late autumn. The summer months of July and August can get very busy indeed; book accommodations and restaurants in advance during high season. In winter, short daylight hours and winds can make island stays rather bleak, but add allure to the prospect of sipping malt whisky by a log fire. Birding enthusiasts can observe vast flocks of migrant Arctic wildfowl arriving and leaving Islay in autumn and spring. At any time, come prepared with adequate clothing for fast-changing weather.

PLANNING YOUR TIME

You could easily spend a week exploring the islands alone, so consider spending at least a few nights in this region. Argyll and some island excursions make pleasant and easy side trips from Glasgow and Loch Lomond. Driving anywhere here takes a little longer than you'd think, so allow ample travel time. A leisurely day will take you to Inveraray, its castle, and the surrounding gardens (don't miss the folk museum at Auchindrain) before driving on to Kennacraig to take the ferry for Islay and Jura. Two or three days here will give you a sense of the history and varied landscapes of these stunning islands—and time for a distillery or two. If you have time to visit just one island, sail from Oban to Mull, returning the same day or the next to take in the Scottish Sea Life Sanctuary. If you can, drive around beautiful Loch Awe on your way back to Glasgow. If time is really tight, consider flying from Glasgow to Islay or Tiree.

Plan ahead: car ferries fill up in the summer months (there is usually no problem for foot passengers), and some of the smaller islands are served only once or twice a week. Bear in mind that it is not easy to find places to eat after 9 pm at any time of year—though you can usually find a place that will sell you a whisky until much later.

GETTING HERE AND AROUND

AIR TRAVEL

Flybe operates flights from Glasgow to Campbeltown, Islay, Tiree, and Mull. Hebridean Air Services flies from Oban to Islay, Coll, Colonsay, and Tiree.

Air Travel Contacts Flybe. ☎ *0371/700–2000* ⊕ *www.flybe.com.* **Hebridean Air Services.** ☎ *0845/805–7465* ⊕ *www.hebrideanair.co.uk.*

BOAT AND FERRY TRAVEL

Caledonian MacBrayne (CalMac) operates car-ferry and passenger services to and from the main islands. It is important to plan ahead when traveling to the islands in order to coordinate the connecting ferries; CalMac can advise you on this. Multiple-island tickets are available and can significantly reduce the cost of island-hopping.

CalMac ferries run from Oban to Mull, Lismore, Coll, and Tiree; from Kennacraig to Islay, Jura, and Gigha; from Ardrossan to Arran; and from Port Askaig on Islay to Feolin on Jura; as well as a number of shorter routes. Western Ferries operate between Dunoon, in Argyll, and Gourock, west of Glasgow. The ferry passage between Dunoon and Gourock is one frequented by locals; it saves a lot of time, and you can take your car across as well. Jura Passenger Ferry operates between Tayvallich (on the mainland) and Craighouse on Jura.

Ferry reservations are needed if you have a car; passengers traveling by foot do not need to make reservations.

Boat and Ferry Travel Contacts Caledonian MacBrayne (*CalMac*)
. ☎ *0800/066–5000* ⊕ *www.calmac.co.uk.* **Jura Passenger Ferry.**
☎ *07768/450000* ⊕ *www.jurapassengerferry.com.* **Western Ferries.**
☎ *01369/704452* ⊕ *www.western-ferries.co.uk.*

BUS TRAVEL

You can travel throughout the region by bus, but service here tends to be less frequent than elsewhere in Scotland. Scottish Citylink runs daily service from Glasgow's Buchanan Street station to the mid-Argyll region and Kintyre; the trip to Oban takes about three hours. Several other companies provide local services within the region.

Bus Contacts Garelochhead Coaches. ☎ *01436/810200* ⊕ *www.garelochheadcoaches.co.uk.* **Islay Coaches.** ☎ *01496/840273* ⊕ *www.bmundell.co.uk.* **Scottish Citylink.** ☎ *0871/266–3333* ⊕ *www.citylink.co.uk.* **Stagecoach West Scotland.** ☎ *01770/302000* ⊕ *www.stagecoachbus.com.* **West Coast Motors.** ☎ *01586/552319* ⊕ *www.westcoastmotors.co.uk.*

CAR TRAVEL

Negotiating this area is easy except in July and August, when the roads around Oban may be congested. There are a number of single-lane roads, especially on the east side of the Kintyre Peninsula and on the islands, which require special care. Remember that white triangles indicate places where you can pass. You'll probably have to board a ferry at some point during your trip; nearly all ferries take cars as well as pedestrians.

From Glasgow, take the A82 and the A85 to Oban, the main ferry terminal for Mull and the islands (about 2½ hours by car). From the A82, take the A83 at Arrochar; it rounds Loch Fyne to Inveraray. From there you can take the A819 from Inveraray around Loch Awe and rejoin the Glasgow–Oban road. Alternatively, you can stay on the A83 and head down Kintyre to Kennacraig, the ferry terminal for Islay. Farther down the A83 is Tayinloan, the ferry port for Gigha. You can reach Brodick on Arran by ferry from Ardrossan, on the Clyde coast (M8/A78 from Glasgow); in summer you can travel to Lochranza from Claonaig on the Kintyre Peninsula, but there are very few crossings.

TRAIN TRAVEL

Oban and Ardrossan are the main rail stations; it's a three hour trip from Glasgow to Oban. For information call ScotRail. All trains connect with ferries.

Train Contact ScotRail. ☏ *0344/811–0141* ⊕ *www.scotrail.co.uk.*

RESTAURANTS

Argyll and the Isles have earned a reputation for excellent gastropubs and restaurants (many of which also offer accommodations) that use superb locally sourced produce, including luscious seafood, lamb, wild and farmed venison, and game of many kinds. Most hotels and many guesthouses offer evening meals, and it may often be your best option to look to hotel restaurants, though the quality can vary. Most restaurants and pubs stop serving food by 9 pm; lunch usually ends at 2:30.

HOTELS

Accommodations in Argyll and on the Isles range from country-house hotels to private homes offering a bed and breakfast. Most small, traditional, provincial hotels in coastal resorts have been updated and modernized, while still retaining personalized service. And though hotels often have a restaurant offering evening meals, the norm is to offer breakfast only. *Hotel reviews have been shortened. For full information, visit Fodors.com*

WHAT IT COSTS IN POUNDS				
	$	$$	$$$	$$$$
Restaurants	under £15	£15–£19	£20–£25	over £25
Hotels	under £100	£100–£160	£161–£220	over £220

Restaurant prices are the average cost of a main course at dinner or, if dinner is not served, at lunch. Hotel prices are the lowest cost of a standard double room in high season, including 20% V.A.T.

TOURS

BOAT TOURS

Getting out on the water is a wonderful way to see the landscape of the islands and also sea life.

FAMILY
Fodor's Choice
★

Sea Life Surveys. Dolphins, seals, porpoises, and (if you're fortunate) minke whales and basking sharks are among the stars of the show on a Sea Life Surveys cruise from pretty Tobermory. Seabirds abound too, and you may spot huge white-tailed eagles, once extinct here but reintroduced to this part of Scotland in recent years. Several cruises are offered: if time is short, choose the two-hour Ecocruz. ⊠ *A848, Tobermory* ⊕ *Cruises leave from floating pontoons opposite Mull Aquarium* ☏ *01688/302916* ⊕ *www.sealifesurveys.com* ⊠ *From £25.*

FAMILY
Staffa Tours. This company organizes a number of tours to the smaller islands, with the emphasis on wildlife. Tours run from Mull, Ardnamurchan on the mainland, or from Iona. The three-hour trip to uninhabited Staffa includes Fingal's Cave, commemorated by Mendelssohn in his famous overture. With luck you may encounter dolphins on the way.

Staffa also runs tours to the Treshnish islands, famous for the puffin colonies on Lunga. ⊠ *The Boat Shed, Iona, Iona* ☎ *07732/912370* ⊕ *www.staffatours.com* ✉ *From £30.*

FAMILY **Turus-Mara.** Based on the island of Mull, Turus-Mara runs trips to Staffa, Iona, and the Treshnish islands, with an emphasis on wildlife. There are puffins and guillemots through the summer, seals until late in the year, and sometimes even basking sharks. Tours depart from Ulva Ferry on the west coast of Mull, but there is a courtesy bus from Tobermory. ⊠ *Penmore Mill, Dervaig* ☎ *01688/400242* ⊕ *www.turusmara.com* ✉ *From £32.50.*

BUS TOURS
Many of the bus companies in the area also arrange sightseeing tours, so check with them.

West Coast Tours. A range of bus tours in and around Oban and on Mull are available through West Coast Tours. The company can also arrange combined bus and boat tours. ⊠ *1 Queenspark Pl., Oban* ☎ *01631/566809* ⊕ *www.westcoasttours.co.uk* ✉ *From £7.*

VISITOR INFORMATION
The tourist offices in Tarbert and Tobermory (Mull) are open April through October only; other offices are open year-round.

ARGYLL

Topographical grandeur and rocky shores are what make Argyll special. Try to take to the water at least once, even if your time is limited. The sea and the sea lochs have played a vital role in the history of western Scotland since the time of the war galleys of the clans. Oban is the major ferry gateway and transport hub, with a main road leading south into the Kintyre Peninsula.

OBAN

96 miles northwest of Glasgow, 125 miles northwest of Edinburgh, 50 miles south of Fort William, 118 miles southwest of Inverness.

It's almost impossible to avoid Oban when touring the west. Its waterfront has some character, but the town's main role is as a launch point for excursions into Argyll and for ferries to the islands. A traditional Scottish resort town, Oban has many music festivals, *ceilidhs* with Highland dancing, as well as all the usual tartan kitsch and late-night revelry in pubs and hotel bars. The Oban Distillery offers tours and a shop. Still, there are more exciting destinations just over the horizon, on the islands and down into Kintyre.

GETTING HERE AND AROUND
From Glasgow, the A82 along Loch Lomond meets the A85 at Crianlarich. Turn left and continue to Oban. In summer the center of Oban can become gridlocked with ferry traffic, so leave yourself time for the wait. Alternatively, the A816 from Lochgilphead enters Oban from the less crowded south. Train services run from Glasgow to Oban (ScotRail); Scottish Citylink runs buses from Glasgow to Oban several times a day.

ESSENTIALS

Visitor Information **Oban Tourist Information Centre.** ✉ *3 North Pier* ☎ *01631/563122* 🌐 *www.oban.org.uk.*

EXPLORING

Dunstaffnage Castle. Standing high atop volcanic rock, Dunstaffnage commands the hills and lochs that surround it. That is why this 13th-century castle was so strategic and contested by those battling for control of Argyll and the Isles. From the walk along the walls you have outstanding views across the **Sound of Mull** and the **Firth of Lorne.** A small well-illustrated guidebook (£2.50) lets you take your own guided tour, but there are storyboards throughout the building that give you a sense of how it was used across the ages. In the woods is the ruined chapel of St. Cuthbert, built by the Macdougall clan at the same time as the castle. ✉ *Off A85* ☎ *01631/562465* 🌐 *www.historicenvironment.scot* 🎟 *£6* 🕒 *Closed Oct.–Apr.*

Oban Distillery. One of Scotland's oldest and smallest distilleries was founded in 1794, several years before the town where it now stands. It produces a well-known 14-year-old malt which, according to those who know, has a taste somewhere between the smoky Islay whiskies and the softer, sweeter Highland varieties—a distinctive West Highland flavor. ✉ *Stafford St.* ✥ *Opposite North Pier* ☎ *01631/572004* 🌐 *www.discovering-distilleries.com/oban* 🎟 *Basic tour £8* 🕒 *Closed weekends in Dec.*

FAMILY **Ocean Explorer Centre.** On the Firth of Lorn, this imaginative venture lets you get a look under the sea. Hands-on exhibits include microscopes where you can observe tiny algae and a live undersea camera where you can see what's happening below the waves. Part of a scientific research center, it's educational, but also accessible and fun. There is a bright little café and a shop with books on marine science and other topics. It's 2 miles from Oban—follow the signs for nearby Dunstaffnage Castle. ✉ *Kirk Rd.* ☎ *01631/559123* 🌐 *www.oceanexplorercentre.org* 🎟 *Free* 🕒 *Closed weekends.*

FAMILY **Scottish Sea Life Sanctuary.** On the shores of Loch Creran, this marine sanctuary is part aquarium, where you can get an up-close look at everything from sharks to stingrays, and part animal-rescue facility. Adorable otters and seals receive rehabilitation here before being released back into the wild. Kids will appreciate the adventure playground. The restaurant serves morning coffee, a full lunch menu, and afternoon tea. To get here, drive 10 miles north from Oban on the A828; West Coast Motors also provides regular bus service. ■ **TIP→ Book online for significantly cheaper tickets.** ✉ *Barcaldine, off A828, Connel* ☎ *01631/720386* 🌐 *www.visitsealife.co.uk/oban* 🎟 *£13.40* 🕒 *Closed Tues.–Thurs. Nov.–Mar.*

WHERE TO EAT

$$$ SEAFOOD Fodor's Choice ★

🍴 **Ee-usk.** This clean-lined restaurant's name means "fish" in Gaelic, and it has earned quite a reputation for serving excellent dishes made with the freshest fish and shellfish delivered directly from Oban's harbor. The signature creations use appealingly simple sauces; try oven-baked wild halibut with creamed leeks or the full-scale seafood platter. **Known for:** lobster and crab; Mull scallops; Loch Linnhe oysters and langoustines. [$] *Average main: £20* ✉ *North Pier* ☎ *01631/565666* 🌐 *www.eeusk.com* 🕒 *Closed Sun.*

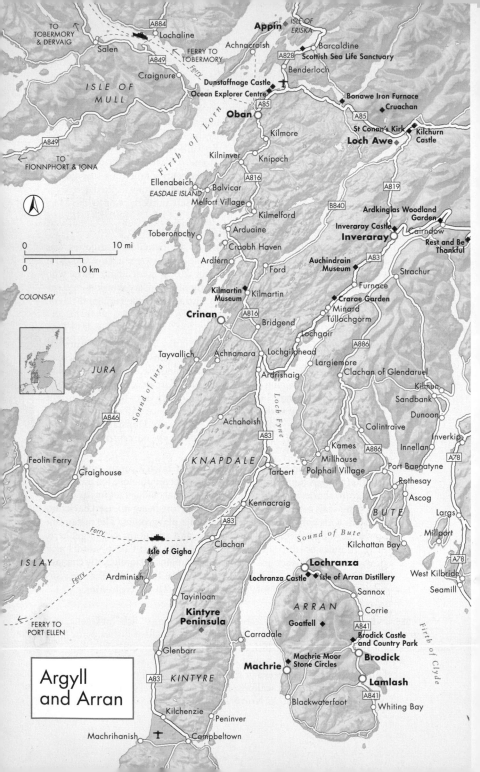

$$ BRITISH 🍴 **Hawthorn Restaurant.** Fish shares the menu here with local lamb, pork, and game. Although it's just a few miles from Oban (whence it sources its seafood), the setting is rural, surrounded by crofts that are still working farms. **Known for:** Oban seafood; Argyll lamb. [$] *Average main: £19* ✉ *Keil Crofts, Benderloch* ✢ *6 miles north of Oban off the main A816, after crossing the Connel Bridge* ☎ *01631/720777* 🌐 *www.hawthorn-restaurant.co.uk* 🕒 *Closed Dec.–Apr. and Mon. in May–Nov.*

$ CAFÉ 🍴 **Kitchen Garden.** This delicatessen serves good homemade soups, paninis, and sandwiches, as well as freshly baked cakes. If you're visiting in summer and pushed for time it's best to book your table in advance or take your order to go. **Known for:** home-baked cakes; tasty panini and sandwiches. [$] *Average main: £10* ✉ *North Pier, 14 George St.* ☎ *01631/566332* 🌐 *www.kitchengardenoban.co.uk* 🕒 *No dinner.*

$ SEAFOOD 🍴 **Oban Seafood Hut.** Serving arguably the best-value seafood in Oban, ex-fisherman John Ogden's quayside fish shack is a local legend. Look for a green-painted shed on the pier, then join the line of cognoscenti waiting for simply sautéed scallops, grilled langoustine and lobster, oysters, and mussels. **Known for:** superbly fresh shellfish, langoustine, crab, and lobster; simple, sublime preparations. [$] *Average main: £8* ✉ *CalMac Pier* ☎ *07881/418565* 🕒 *Closed Nov.–Apr.* 💳 *No credit cards.*

WHERE TO STAY

$$ B&B/INN 🏨 **Glenburnie House.** At this typical seafront guesthouse in a Victorian house with fine views over Oban Bay, most rooms are spacious and comfortable, if slightly overdecorated in traditional style. **Pros:** centrally located; good sea views. **Cons:** too many flowery fabrics for some tastes. [$] *Rooms from: £100* ✉ *Esplanade* ☎ *01631/562089* 🌐 *www.glenburnie.co.uk* 🕒 *Closed Dec.–Feb.* 🛏 *12 rooms* 🍽 *Breakfast.*

$ B&B/INN 🏨 **Kilchrenan House.** Just a few minutes from the town center, this Victorian-era stone house has been transformed into a lovely bed-and-breakfast. **Pros:** great sea views; tasteful attention to detail. **Cons:** some bedrooms may be too colorfully decorated for some tastes; attic rooms have a slanting roof; credit cards not accepted for one-night stays. [$] *Rooms from: £75* ✉ *Corran Esplanade* ☎ *01631/562663* 🌐 *www.kilchrenanhouse.co.uk* 🕒 *Closed Dec. and Jan.* 🛏 *13 rooms* 🍽 *Breakfast.*

$$$ HOTEL Fodor's Choice ★ 🏨 **Manor House Hotel.** On the coast near Oban, this 1780 stone house—once the home of the Duke of Argyll—has sea views and a convenient location. **Pros:** excellent restaurant; near all necessary amenities; nice garden overlooking the bay. **Cons:** smallish bedrooms; no children under 12. [$] *Rooms from: £185* ✉ *Gallanach Rd.* ☎ *01631/562087* 🌐 *www.manorhouseoban.com* 🛏 *11 rooms* 🍽 *Breakfast.*

SPORTS AND THE OUTDOORS

BICYCLING

Oban Cycles. This shop rents bikes of various sorts starting at £15 for a full day. The area round Oban is good cycling country, and the staff is happy to advise you on routes. ✉ *89 George St.* ☎ *01631/566033* 🌐 *www.obancyclescotland.com.*

8

APPIN

17 miles north of Oban.

GETTING HERE AND AROUND

From Oban, follow the A828 around Loch Creran and take the left turn to Port Appin just beyond Tynribbie. Continue for just over 2 miles to the old pier. From the port, the passenger ferry runs to the island of Lismore throughout the year. Steamers once plied the waters of Loch Linnhe, but today the largest boats here are those taking workers to the quarries of Kingairloch.

WHERE TO EAT AND STAY

$$$ SEAFOOD Fodor's Choice ★ 🍴 **Pierhouse Hotel and Restaurant.** The round towers of the old pier mark the entrance to this restaurant, appealingly situated on the water's edge. The restaurant serves the freshest seafood; try its signature platter of lobster, scallops, mussels, and langoustine. **Known for:** ultrafresh lobster; lively atmosphere. [$] *Average main: £25* ✉ *Port Appin* ☎ *01631/730302* 🌐 *www.pierhousehotel.co.uk.*

$$$$ HOTEL 🏨 **Airds Hotel and Restaurant.** This luxurious small hotel (once a travelers' inn) has stylish rooms with superb views. **Pros:** fabulous views from the breakfast room; spare boots for the unprepared; beautiful location. **Cons:** expensive. [$] *Rooms from: £340* ✉ *A828, Port Appin* ☎ *01631/730236* 🌐 *www.airds-hotel.com* 🛏 *12 rooms* 🍽 *Some meals.*

$$$$ HOTEL FAMILY Fodor's Choice ★ 🏨 **Isle of Eriska.** On one of Scotland's few private islands, this sybaritic enclave conceals luxury facilities like a spa, pool, gym, golf course, and a Michelin-starred restaurant behind a severe baronial facade. **Pros:** exceptional food; good service; superb leisure facilities; families actively welcomed. **Cons:** remote; dining out not an easy option. [$] *Rooms from: £340* ✉ *Off A828, Benderloch* ✣ *Island signposted from Benderloch village and connected to mainland by short bridge* ☎ *01631/720371* 🌐 *www.eriska-hotel.co.uk* 🛏 *27 rooms* 🍽 *Breakfast.*

LOCH AWE

18 miles east of Oban.

Measuring more than 25 miles long, Loch Awe is Scotland's longest stretch of freshwater. Its northwest shore is quiet; forest walks crisscross the Inverliever Forest here. At the loch's northern end tiny islands, many with ruins, pepper the water. One, Inishail, is home to a 13th-century chapel.

GETTING HERE AND AROUND

From Oban the A85 will bring you to the head of Loch Awe and the small village of the same name. Turn onto the B845 at Taynuilt to reach the loch's northern shore, or continue through the forbidding Pass of Brander and turn onto the A819 to get to the southern shore. From here you can continue on to Inveraray, or drive along the loch on the B840.

EXPLORING

TOP ATTRACTIONS

FAMILY Fodor's Choice ★ **Bonawe Iron Furnace.** Seemingly out of place in this near-wilderness setting, Bonawe is a fascinating relic from the dawn of Britain's Industrial Revolution. In the mid-18th century, Argyll's virgin forests attracted ironmasters from England, where such valuable fuel sources were harder to find. Business boomed when wars with France boosted demand for pig iron and cannonballs, and in its heyday Bonawe employed up to 600 unskilled local wood gatherers and skilled southern foundrymen. ✉ *Off B845, Bonawe* ☎ *01866/822432* 🌐 *www.historicenvironment.scot* 🎫 *£5* 🕒 *Closed Oct.–Mar.*

FAMILY **Cruachan.** Like the lair of a classic James Bond villain, this triumph of 20th-century British technology lurks deep within a vast man-made cavern. Hidden 3,000 feet beneath the slopes of Ben Cruachan, the colossal water-driven turbines of this subterranean power station, completed in 1965, supply clean energy to much of Scotland. The ½-mile bus ride from the surface to the generating hall is a surreal experience, made all the more so by the subtropical plants that thrive under artificial light in the warm, humid atmosphere. ✉ *A85, Dalmally* ☎ *01866/822618* 🌐 *www.visitcruachan.co.uk* 🎫 *£7* 🕒 *Closed weekends Nov.–Mar.*

Rest and Be Thankful. This viewpoint at the highest point of the route from Loch Lomond to Inveraray is one of the few places where you can pull off the road to enjoy the spectacular panorama. It's an ideal place to take some selfies, and it's easy to imagine how it earned its name in the days when the only travelers on this trail went on foot or on horseback. ✉ *A83* ✥ *10 miles northwest of Tarbert.*

WORTH NOTING

Kilchurn Castle. This is one of Argyll's most evocative ruins, with its crumbling lochside towers and high ramparts. Built by the Campbells in the 15th century, Kilchurn was rebuilt as a government garrison after the troubles of the late 17th century. The castle was abandoned after peace came to the Highlands following the final defeat of the Jacobite cause in 1746. ✉ *Lochawe, Dalmally* ✥ *2½ miles west of Dalmally* 🌐 *www.historic-scotland.gov.uk/places* 🕒 *Closed Oct.–Mar.*

St. Conan's Kirk. St. Conan's may look medieval, but in fact, it's less than 100 years old. Built in 1930 from local boulders, it features modern stained glass and wood and stone carvings, including an effigy of Robert the Bruce. ✉ *A85, Lochawe* ✥ *About 18 miles from Oban* ☎ *01838/200298* 🌐 *www.stconanskirk.org.uk* 🎫 *Free.*

WHERE TO STAY

$ HOTEL Fodor's Choice ★ 🏨 **Taychreggan Hotel.** Peace and quiet are the big selling points of this lovely country-house hotel beside Loch Awe. Once a drovers' inn, the whitewashed building is surrounded by lawns and wooded gardens. **Pros:** lovely setting; activities including fishing and kayaking; wonderful meals. **Cons:** off the beaten track. [$] *Rooms from: £99* ✉ *Off B845, Kilchrenan* ☎ *01866/833211* 🌐 *www.taychregganhotel.co.uk* 🛏 *18 rooms* 🍴 *Breakfast.*

INVERARAY

21 miles south of Loch Awe, 61 miles north of Glasgow, 29 miles west of Loch Lomond.

Fodor's Choice ★ Inveraray's star attraction is the grandiose seat of the Campbell Dukes of Argyll, for centuries the most powerful magnates of the Highlands. It's a trim little township, planned and built in the mid-18th century at the behest of the third duke. There are fine views of Loch Fyne, and there are gardens and museums to see nearby.

GETTING HERE AND AROUND

Driving from Oban, take the A85 and the A819 beyond Loch Awe (the village). From Glasgow, take the A82, turn on to the A83 at Arrochar, and make the long drive around Loch Fyne.

ESSENTIALS

Visitor Information Inveraray Tourist Information Centre. ⊠ *Front St.* ☎ *01499/302063* ⊕ *www.visitscotland.com.*

EXPLORING

TOP ATTRACTIONS

Ardkinglas Woodland Garden. Rambling over 12,000 acres, one of Britain's finest collections of conifers is set off by rhododendron blossoms in early summer. You can find the garden around the head of Loch Fyne, about 10 miles east of Inveraray. There's a wild woodland walk beyond the garden; both are open all year. The house, regarded as architect Sir Robert Lorimer's masterpiece, is only open to visitors on Fridays between April and October. ⊠ *Ardkinglas Estate, Cairndow* ☎ *01499/600261* ⊕ *www.ardkinglas.com* ☜ *£5.*

FAMILY
Fodor'sChoice
★

Auchindrain Museum. Step a few centuries back in time at this open-air museum, a rare surviving example of an 18th-century communal-tenancy farm. About 250 years ago, there were several thousand working communities like Auchindrain. Auchindrain was the last of them, its final tenant leaving in 1963. Today the bracken-thatch and iron-roof buildings, about 20 in all, give you a feel for early farming life in the Highland communities. Several houses are furnished and tell the story of their occupants. A tearoom is open morning to afternoon. ⊠ *Auchindrain* ✣ *Off A83 about 6 miles south of Inveraray* ☎ *01499/500235* ⊕ *auchindrain.org.uk* ☜ *£7.50* ☉ *Closed Nov.–Mar.*

Crarae Garden. Exotic Himalayan plants flourish in the gentle microclimate of this 100-acre garden, where the Crarae Burn, a small stream, cascades through a rocky gorge. Rhododendrons, azaleas, and magnolias lend color, and native flowers and trees attract birds and butterflies. ⊠ *A83* ✣ *10 miles southwest of Inveraray* ☎ *01546/886614* ⊕ *www. nts.org.uk* ☜ *£6.50* ☉ *Closed Nov.–Mar.*

Inveraray Castle. The current seat of the Chief of the Clan Campbell is a smart, grayish-green turreted stone house with a self-satisfied air. Set among well-tended grounds, it contains displays of luxurious furnishings and interesting art, as well as a huge armory. Built between 1743 and 1789, the castle has spires on the four corner turrets that give it a vaguely French look. Tours of the castle follow the history of the powerful Campbell family and how it acquired its considerable wealth. There is a tearoom for snacks and light lunches. You can hike around the extensive estate grounds, but wear sturdy footwear. ⊠ *Off A83* ☎ *01499/302203* ⊕ *www.inveraray-castle.com* ☜ *£11* ☉ *Closed Nov.–Mar.*

WORTH NOTING

FAMILY **Inveraray Jail.** In this old jail, realistic courtroom scenes, carefully re-created cells, and other paraphernalia give you a glimpse of life behind bars in Victorian times—and today. Actors represent some of the jail's most famous occupants. The site includes a Scottish crafts shop. ✉ *Main St.* ☎ *01499/302381* 🌐 *www.inverarayjail.co.uk* 🎟 *£11.50.*

WHERE TO EAT AND STAY

$$ SEAFOOD Fodor's Choice ★ 🍴 **Loch Fyne Oyster Bar and Restaurant.** The legendary flagship of a chain of seafood restaurants that now stretches across the United Kingdom, this restaurant continues to please with its emphasis on ultrafresh, locally sourced seafood, simply prepared. Oysters, are, of course, a keynote, but the menu also features mussels, lobster, prawns, salmon, and much more from the sea, accompanied by perfect crunchy green vegetables such as peas, beans, and asparagus. **Known for:** plump oysters perfectly prepared; meltingly tender smoked salmon. [$] *Average main: £19* ✉ *Clachan Farm, A83, Cairndow* ☎ *01499/600482* 🌐 *www.lochfyne.com.*

$$ SEAFOOD 🍴 **Samphire Seafood Restaurant.** This small, cozy, unpretentious restaurant in the center of Inveraray has earned a reputation for excellently prepared seafood, though it also serves meat and vegetarian dishes. Favorites include the seafood pie, and the Taste of the Loch medley of shellfish and crustaceans is a special treat. **Known for:** lavish seafood platters; hearty seafood pie. [$] *Average main: £18* ✉ *6A Arkland* ☎ *01499/302321* 🌐 *www.samphireseafood.com* 🕒 *Closed Sun. and Mon.*

$ HOTEL Fodor's Choice ★ 🏨 **The George Hotel.** The George has been Inveraray's social hub since the 18th century, when it was a coaching inn, and it still reeks of history. **Pros:** excellent restaurant; atmospheric bars. **Cons:** too much tartan for some; unattractive reception area. [$] *Rooms from: £85* ✉ *Main St. E* ☎ *01499/302111* 🌐 *www.thegeorgehotel.co.uk* 🛏 *25 rooms* 🍽 *Breakfast.*

CRINAN

32 miles southwest of Inveraray.

Crinan is synonymous with its canal, the reason for this tiny community's existence and its mainstay. The narrow road beside the Crinan Hotel bustles with yachting types waiting to pass through the locks, bringing a surprisingly cosmopolitan feel to such an out-of-the-way corner of Scotland.

GETTING HERE AND AROUND

To reach Crinan, follow the A83 from Inveraray along the north shore of Loch Fyne through Lochgilphead, take the A816 Oban road north for about a mile, then turn left on to the B841 at Cairnbaan.

EXPLORING

Crinan Canal. This canal opened in 1801 to let fishing vessels reach Hebridean fishing grounds without making the long haul south around the Kintyre Peninsula. At its western end the canal drops to the sea in a series of locks, the last of which is beside the Crinan Hotel. Today it's popular with pleasure boats traveling to the west coast. ✉ *Crinan.*

8

Kilmartin Museum. To see a little of the region's prehistoric past, start at this museum 8 miles north of Crinan and then explore some of the more than 300 ancient remnants within a 6-mile radius. Exhibits provide information about stone circles, burial mounds, and carved stones dating from the Bronze Age and earlier. ✉ *A816, Kilmartin* ☎ *01546/510278* 🌐 *www.kilmartin.org* 🎟 *£6.50* 🕒 *Closed Jan.–Mar.*

WHERE TO STAY

$$ B&B/INN 🏨 **Allt-Na-Craig.** Overlooking Loch Fyne, this stone Victorian house is set in lovely gardens. **Pros:** atmospheric; views. **Cons:** children not accepted; pricey for what it is. [$] *Rooms from: £115* ✉ *Tarbert Rd., Ardrishaig* ✣ *9 miles southeast of Crinan* ☎ *01546/603245* 🌐 *www.allt-na-craig.co.uk* 🛏 *6 rooms* 🍴 *Breakfast.*

$$$$ HOTEL 🏨 **Crinan Hotel.** A dramatic location overlooking the Sound of Jura is this hotel's big selling point, along with bright, maritime-themed public areas and guest rooms. **Pros:** elevator; above-average choice of restaurants; art gallery. **Cons:** Wi-Fi in public areas only. [$] *Rooms from: £230* ✉ *Off B841* ☎ *01546/830261* 🌐 *www.crinanhotel.com* 🛏 *20 rooms* 🍴 *Breakfast.*

KINTYRE PENINSULA

57 miles south of Crinan (to Campbeltown).

Rivers and streams crisscross this long, narrow strip of green pasturelands and hills stretching south from Lochgilphead.

GETTING HERE AND AROUND

Continue south on the A83 (the road to Campbeltown) to Tarbert. Some 4 miles farther along the A83 is Kennacraig, where you catch the ferry to Islay. Beyond that is the pier at Tayinloan; CalMac ferries run from here to the Isle of Gigha.

Flybe operates flights from Glasgow to Campbeltown.

ESSENTIALS

Air Travel Contact Campbeltown Airport. ✉ *Off A83, Campbeltown* ✣ *At Machrihanish, 3 miles west of Campbeltown* ☎ *01586/553797* 🌐 *www.hial.co.uk.*

Visitor Information Campbeltown Information Centre. ✉ *Mackinnon House, The Pier, Campbeltown* ☎ *01586/556162* 🌐 *www.visitscotland.com.* **Tarbert Information Centre.** ✉ *Harbour St.* ☎ *01880/820429* 🌐 *www.tarbertlochfyne.com.*

EXPLORING

Isle of Gigha. Barely 7 miles long, this sheltered island between Kintyre and Islay has sandy beaches and rich wildlife. Ferries make the 20-minute trip from Tayinloan on the mainland. ✉ *Isle of Gigha* ☎ *01583/505390* 🌐 *www.gigha.org.uk.*

GOLF

Machrihanish Golf Club. For many Scots golfers (and they should know) Machrihanish's out-of-the-way location makes it a place of pilgrimage. Laid out in 1876, it's an intimidatingly memorable links course by a sandy bay. There is also a 9-hole course, The Pans. ✉ *Off B843, Machrihanish* ☎ *01586/810213* 🌐 *www.machgolf.com* 🎟 *£65 Apr.–Oct., £30 Nov.–Mar.* 🏌 *Championship Course: 18 holes, 6235 yards, par 70; The Pans: 9 holes (out), 2376 yards, par 34* ✍ *Reservations essential.*

ARRAN

Approaching Arran by sea, you'll first see forbidding Goatfell (2,868 feet) in the north, then the green fields of the south. These varied landscapes earn the island its sobriquet: "Scotland in Miniature." A temperate microclimate attracted ancient settlers whose stone circles still stand on the island. This weather also explains why it has long been a favorite getaway for Glaswegians, who come here to walk, climb Goatfell, or play golf.

GETTING HERE AND AROUND

Caledonian MacBrayne runs regular car and passenger ferries that cross the Firth of Clyde from Ardrossan (near Saltcoats) to Brodick throughout the year; crossing takes just under an hour. There is also a small ferry from Claonaig on the Kintyre Peninsula to Lochranza during the summer months.

Connecting trains run to the ferry at Ardrossan from Glasgow's Queen Street station. Stagecoach runs regular local bus services around the island. Exploring the island by car is easy, as the A841 road circles it.

BRODICK

1 hour by ferry from Ardrossan.

Arran's largest village, Brodick, has a main street that is set back from the promenade and the lovely bay. Beyond that, it is really little more than a gateway to the rest of the island.

GETTING HERE AND AROUND

You can reach Brodick from Ardrossan by ferry. From Brodick the A841 circles the island; head south to reach Lamlash, north to reach Lochranza. The String Road crosses the island between Brodick and Machrie.

ESSENTIALS

The information center, opposite the landing point for the Ardrossan Ferry, has an accommodation desk as well as tourist information.
Brodick Information Centre. ⊠ *The Pier* ☎ *01770/303774* ⊕ *www.visitscotland.com.*

EXPLORING

Brodick Castle and Country Park. On the north side of Brodick Bay, this red sandstone mansion with typical Scottish-baronial features was built in the 16th century and was the seat of the dukes of Hamilton, who added to it extensively during the 19th century. ■ **TIP→ The castle is closed for repairs until 2019, but you can explore the expansive gardens, which are open all year.** In summer they are ablaze with azaleas and rhododendrons.

The country park that surrounds the castle embraces Arran's most striking scenery, rising to the 2,867-foot summit of Goatfell, the island's highest peak. The beautiful upland landscape is more challenging to explore than it seems, so it's important to go prepared with sturdy footwear and waterproof clothing. From the summit there is a stunning panoramic view of the Firth, Kintyre, and the Ayrshire coast, and on a clear day you can just see Ireland. ⊠ *Off A841, 1 mile*

8

north of Brodick Pier ☎ *0844/493–2152* 🌐 *www.nts.org.uk* 🕒 *Castle closed until 2019.*

Isle of Arran Heritage Museum. A typical Arran cottage, a re-created 1940s schoolroom, and farm buildings filled with antiquated implements that were in use within living memory make this lively little museum a must-see for anyone interested in the island's social history. ✉ *Rosaburn, A841* ☎ *01770/302636* 🌐 *www.arranmuseum.co.uk* 🎟 *£4* 🕒 *Closed Nov.–Mar.*

WHERE TO EAT AND STAY

$$ BRITISH

🍴 **Brodick Bar and Brasserie.** This lively bar and restaurant serves fixed-price lunch and dinner menus featuring popular if unadventurous seafood favorites such as monkfish, halibut, and scallops, and adds spice to the mix with an array of Asian-influenced dishes. Like many places in the west of Scotland, hours are restricted so it is well worth booking ahead. **Known for:** perfect grilled scallops; surprising seafood curries. [$] *Average main: £16* ✉ *Alma Rd.* ☎ *01770/302169* 🌐 *www.brodickbar.co.uk.*

$$$$ RESORT FAMILY Fodor's Choice ★

🏨 **Auchrannie Resort.** With outstanding indoor and outdoor leisure facilities (including two pools and a spa), well-designed modern rooms, and three restaurants and bars, Auchrannie is by far the best place to stay on Arran. **Pros:** choice of restaurants; good for families; excellent outdoor activities. **Cons:** could be anywhere. [$] *Rooms from: £269* ✉ *Auchrannie Rd.* ☎ *01770/30234* 🌐 *www.auchrannie.co.uk* 🛏 *115 rooms* 🍽 *Breakfast.*

SHOPPING

Arran's shops are well stocked with locally produced goods. The Home Farm is a popular shopping area with several shops and a small restaurant.

Arran Aromatics. This is one of Scotland's best-known suppliers of scents, soaps, and perfumes of every kind. The shop is filled with pleasant smells, and between May and September a tour of the soap factory is available every Thursday evening. ✉ *Home Farm, A841* ☎ *01770/302595* 🌐 *www.arranaromatics.com.*

Isle of Arran Cheese Company. Arran is famous for its cheeses, especially its cheddar and its Arran blue; stop here to sample and buy handmade Scottish cheeses. ✉ *The Home Farm, A841* ☎ *01770/302788* 🌐 *www.arranscheeseshop.co.uk.*

SPORTS AND THE OUTDOORS

Arran Adventure at Auchrannie Resort. Mountain biking, sea kayaking, hill and gorge walking, and climbing are among the activities offered by Arran Adventure. Gentler guided strolls along the coast and on the slopes of Goatfell are also on offer. ✉ *Shore Rd.* ☎ *01770/302244* 🌐 *auchrannie.co.uk* 🎟 *From £15* 🕒 *Closed Nov.–Mar.*

LAMLASH

4 miles south of Brodick.

With views offshore to Holy Isle, which is now a Buddhist retreat, Lamlash has a breezy seaside-holiday atmosphere. To reach the highest point accessible by car, go through the village and turn right beside the bridge onto Ross Road, which climbs steeply from a thickly planted valley, **Glen Scorrodale,** and yields fine views of Lamlash Bay. From Lamlash you can explore the southern part of Arran: 4 miles to the southwest, **Whiting Bay** has a pleasant well-kept waterfront and a range of hotels and guest-houses. If you travel another 6 miles, you'll reach the little community of **Lagg**, which sits peacefully by the banks of the Kilmory Water.

GETTING HERE AND AROUND

You can reach Lamlash by driving south from Brodick on the A841. The town is also served by Stagecoach buses.

WHERE TO STAY

$

B&B/INN

Lagg Hotel. Arran's oldest inn is an 18th-century lodge with fire-places in the common rooms and 11 acres of gardens and grounds that meander down to the river. **Pros:** beautiful gardens; warming fireplaces; nice local feel. **Cons:** floral designs everywhere; some rooms are small; Wi-Fi in public areas only. $ *Rooms from: £95* ⊠ *A841, Kilmory* ✛ *12 miles south of Lamlash* ☎ *01770/870255* ⊕ *www.lagghotel.com* ↄ *13 rooms* ⧫ *Breakfast.*

MACHRIE

10 miles west of Brodick, 11 miles north of Lagg.

The area surrounding Machrie, home to a popular beach, is littered with prehistoric sites: chambered cairns, hut circles, and standing stones dating from the Bronze Age.

GETTING HERE AND AROUND

The quick route to Machrie is via the String Road (B880) from Brodick; turn off onto the Machrie Road 5 miles outside Brodick. A much longer but stunning journey will take you from Brodick, north to Lochranza, around the island to Machrie, and down the island's dramatic west coast, a distance of some 28 miles.

EXPLORING

Machrie Moor Stone Circles. Six ancient circles of boulders and head-high sandstone pillars are scattered across Machrie Moor. These relics of a prehistoric culture are as old as Egypt's pyramids, if not quite as impres-sive, and the site evokes a dim and distant past. ✛ *1½ miles north of Machrie* ⊕ *www.historicenvironment.scot.*

WHERE TO EAT

$

TURKISH

✕ **Cafe Thyme.** This bright and pleasant restaurant offers a combination of Scottish and Turkish flavors (an expression of the owners' back-grounds) as well as fine views out to sea. Look for meze as well as *pides* (Turkish pizza)—try the haggis-and-cheese or crayfish-and-olive combinations. **Known for:** Turkish-style meze; unusual East-West fusion dishes. $ *Average main: £12* ⊠ *Machrie* ✛ *Next to Old Byre Visitor Centre* ☎ *01770/840608* ⊕ *www.oldbyre.co.uk/cafethyme.irs* ⊗ *No dinner Oct.–Apr. and Sun. in May–Sept.*

SHOPPING

Old Byre Showroom. This shop sells sheepskin goods, hand-knit sweaters, leather goods, and rugs. ⊠ *Auchencar Farm, A841* ✛ *2 miles north of Machrie* ☎ *01770/840227* ⊕ *www.oldbyre.co.uk.*

8

LOCHRANZA

13 miles north of Machrie, 14 miles north of Brodick.

Lochranza shows Arran's wilder northern side, with rocky seashores and sweeping slopes leading to the stark granite peaks of Goatfell and Caisteal Abahail (2,735 feet), which dominate the skyline.

Arran's only distillery, the sparkling Isle of Arran Distillery, nestles in the hills overlooking Lochranza Bay.

GETTING HERE AND AROUND

Lochranza is north of Brodick via the A841.

EXPLORING

Fodor's Choice ★ **Isle of Arran Distillery.** The open aspect and closeness to the sea explains the taste of Arran's well-respected single malt, light and airy and with the scent of sea and fields. The round white building housing the distillery sits comfortably among fields and hills in the northernmost part of the island. The tours take the visitor through the process of creating whisky, with a small or slightly larger tasting depending on the level. The basic tour ends with a dram. The CASKS café-restaurant is a comfortable place for a long lunch. ✉ *Distillery Visitor Centre* ☎ *01770/830264* 🌐 *www.arranwhisky.com* 🎫 *Tours from £8.*

Fodor's Choice ★ **Lochranza Castle.** Perched above the bay, Lochranza is Arran's most picturesque ruin and occupies a special place in Scotland's history. It was here that Robert the Bruce, after years of dithering, returned from exile to commit himself to the war for Scotland's independence. ✉ *Off A841* ☎ *0131/668–8800* 🌐 *www.historicenvironment.scot* 🕒 *Closed Oct.–Mar.*

WHERE TO STAY

$ B&B/INN 🏨 **Butt Lodge.** Set in 2 acres of private woods and gardens overlooking Kilbrannan Sound, this onetime Victorian shooting lodge offers a personalized welcome from owners who really make guests feel at home with hearty (but healthy) Scottish breakfasts and complimentary afternoon tea, served in a cozy lounge. **Pros:** peace and quiet; luxurious rooms and suites; great views. **Cons:** a little hard to find, up a farm track; no bar. [$] *Rooms from: £95* ✉ *off Newton Rd.* ✣ *½ mile east of Lochranza* ☎ *01770/830333* 🌐 *www.buttlodge.co.uk* 🛏 *6 rooms* 🍴 *Breakfast.*

ISLAY AND JURA

Islay is an island of rolling fields and pastures, heather-covered uplands where red deer roam and rutting stags clash antlers in spring, and white-sand beaches that on a summer day can look as enticing as any Caribbean strand. Huge flocks of Arctic wildfowl migrate to Islay in fall, leaving again in spring, when their wings literally darken the sunset sky. This was the long-ago seat of the Macdonald Lords of the Isles, a mongrel Celtic-Norse dynasty that held sway over the southern Hebrides for almost three centuries. Some of their heritage can still be seen. But it's a different inheritance that draws many visitors, namely the smoky, peaty malt whisky produced here by eight world-famous distilleries. Two more independent distilleries are poised to join that list, but are unlikely to start production until 2018, so you won't be able to sample their wares for some years yet. In sharp contrast to Islay's gaggle of villages set among rolling moorland and fertile pastures, thinly populated Jura is ruggedly beautiful, with a hilly landscape dominated by twin summits, the Paps of Jura, so named because of their silhouette, reminiscent of shapely bosoms.

BOWMORE

On Islay: 11 miles north of Port Ellen.

Bowmore, Islay's capital, is a good base for touring because it's central to Islay's main routes. A tidy town, its grid pattern was laid out in 1768 by local landowner Daniel Campbell, of Shawfield. Main Street stretches from the pier head to the commanding parish church, built in 1767 in an unusual circular design—so the devil could not hide in a corner.

GETTING HERE AND AROUND

Flybe flights from Glasgow to Islay Airport take 40 minutes; the airport is 5 miles north of Port Ellen. The trip by CalMac ferry from Kennacraig to Port Ellen takes about 2½ hours; ferries also travel less frequently to Port Askaig. From Port Ellen it is 10 miles on the A846 to reach Bowmore; drivers should use caution during the first mile out of Port Ellen, as the road is filled with sharp turns. The rest of the route is straight but bumpy, because the road is laid across peat bog.

Bus service is available on the island through Islay Coaches; comprehensive timetables are available from the tourist information center.

ESSENTIALS

Air Travel Contact Islay Airport. ⊠ *A846, Glenegedale* ☎ *01496/302022* ⊕ *www.hial.co.uk.*

Visitor Information Bowmore Visitor Information Centre. ⊠ *The Square* ☎ *01496/305165* ⊕ *www.visitscotland.com.*

EXPLORING

Fodor's Choice ★ **Bowmore Distillery.** Bowmore is the grand old lady of Islay's distilleries, and a tour is a must for any visitor. In business since 1779, the distillery, like all Islay whisky makers, stands by the sea. Standard tours include a walk around the malting areas and the stills, and connoisseurs can opt for in-depth tours that include tutored tastings. ⊠ *School St.* ☎ *01496/810441* ⊕ *www.bowmore.com* ⊠ *From £7* ⊙ *Closed Sun. Nov.–Mar.*

Islay Woollen Mill. Gorgeous tweed, plaid, and tartan clothing, wraps, and throws—woven at this historic mill and dyed in subtle, traditional tones—are sold here. ⊠ *A846* ⊕ *4 miles outside Bowmore on the A846* ☎ *01496/810563* ⊕ *www.islaywoollenmill.co.uk* ⊠ *Free* ⊙ *Closed Sun.*

WHERE TO EAT

$$
SEAFOOD
Fodor's Choice ★ ✕ **Harbour Inn.** An adjunct of the Bowmore distillery, the Harbour Inn has a bar frequented by locals and a more upscale restaurant with a menu that emphasizes oysters, langoustines, mussels, and other local seafood. The elegant dining room looks out onto the water. **Known**

8

ISLAY'S WHISKIES

With 3,500 inhabitants and eight working distilleries—with two more due by the 2020s—Islay claims more stills per person than anywhere in the world. Yet, considering the island's size, there's remarkable variety here. Malts from the southeast coast, like Laphroaig, Lagavulin, and Ardbeg, reek of peat and iodine. Peat is still the keynote of malts from the western distilleries, such as Bowmore, Bruichladdich, and Caol Ila, but old-school aging in sherry casks gives these a lighter, more floral nose.

The Islay Festival of Music and Malt 🌐 *www.islayfestival.com*, the last week in May, brings large numbers of whisky lovers to the island.

for: imaginative seafood combinations; North African–influenced vegetarian dishes. [$] *Average main: £18* ✉ *The Square* ☎ *01496/810330* 🌐 *www.bowmore.com/harbour-inn* 🛏 *7 rooms* 🍴 *Breakfast.*

SHOPPING

Islay Whisky Shop. If you don't have time to visit all of Islay's distilleries, let alone those elsewhere, you can do worse than visit this shop with its enormous collection of whiskies. ✉ *Shore St.* ☎ *01496/810684* 🌐 *www.islaywhiskyshop.com.*

PORT CHARLOTTE

On Islay: 11 miles west of Bowmore.

Planned by a benevolent 19th-century laird (and named after his mom), Port Charlotte is an unusually (for Scotland) pretty village, with wild landscapes and sandy beaches nearby. South of the village, the A847 road leads to **Portnahaven** and **Port Wemyss**, where pleasing white cottages stand in a crescent around the headland.

GETTING HERE AND AROUND

To reach Port Charlotte from Bowmore, take the A846 via Bridgend and then the A847, Portnahaven Road. Islay Coaches and Royal Mail buses also travel here from Bowmore.

EXPLORING

Museum of Islay Life. A converted church is home to this local museum, a haphazard collection of local artifacts, photographs, and memorabilia. There is also a local history archive. ✉ *A847* ☎ *01496/850358* 🌐 *www.islaymuseum.org* 🎟 *£3.50* 🕒 *Closed weekends and Nov.–Mar.*

FAMILY **Natural History Centre.** With its exhibits about the island's wildlife, the Natural History Centre has lots of hands-on activities for kids. It's a great stop on rainy days, and tickets are valid for a week. On Monday and Friday there are nature rambles, and family activities are offered throughout July and August. ✉ *Main St.* ☎ *01496/850288* 🌐 *www.islaynaturalhistory.org* 🎟 *£3.50* 🕒 *Closed Oct.–Apr.*

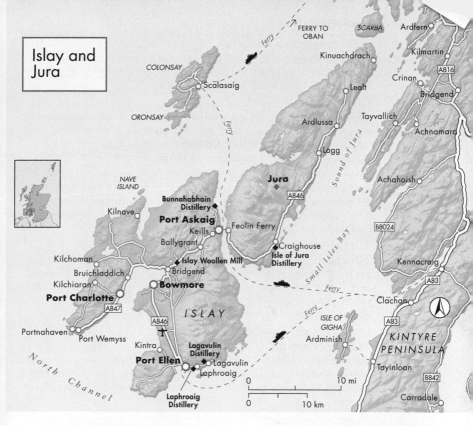

Islay and Jura

WHERE TO STAY

$$$$
HOTEL
Fodor's Choice
★

🏨 Port Charlotte Hotel. Once a row of fishermen's cottages and with views over a sandy beach, this whitewashed Victorian hotel has been lovingly restored. **Pros:** beautiful location; lovely restaurant; views over the water. **Cons:** can be a little noisy from the bar; rooms are quite small. **$** *Rooms from: £230* ⊠ *Main St.* ☎ *01496/850360* ⊕ *www.portcharlottehotel.co.uk* ⇆ *10 rooms* ⏐⊙⏐ *Breakfast.*

PORT ELLEN

On Islay: 11 miles south of Bowmore.

Islay's sturdy community of Port Ellen was founded in the 1820s, and much of its architecture dates from the following decades. It has a harbor (ferries stop here), a few shops, and a handful of inns. The road traveling east from Port Ellen (the A846 to Ardbeg) passes three top distilleries and makes a pleasant afternoon's "whisky walk." All three distilleries offer tours, but you should call ahead for an appointment; there may be no tours on weekends at times. The last week in May, large numbers of whisky lovers descend on the island for the Islay Festival of Music and Malt, the heart of which is Port Ellen.

GETTING HERE AND AROUND

It is likely that Port Ellen will be your port of arrival on Islay. From here you can travel north to Bowmore, along the A846 before turning northwest towards Bridgend and Port Askaig.

EXPLORING

Lagavulin Distillery. Many malt whisky connoisseurs say the Lagavulin is the strongest nosed of all Islay's peaty malt whiskies. You can find out why, and how, with a distillery tour and tasting here. ✉ *A846* ☎ *01496/302400* 🌐 *www.discovering-distilleries.com* 🎫 *From £6.*

Laphroaig Distillery. Laphroiag (say la-*froig*) is Islay's most distinctive malt, redolent of peat, seaweed, and iodine. You can take a tour of the distillery, then settle in for a spell of sipping at the new whisky bar, which opened in 2017. ✉ *A846* ☎ *01496/302418* 🌐 *www.laphroaig.com* 🎫 *From £10* 🕒 *No tours weekends Jan.–Mar.*

WHERE TO STAY

$$$ HOTEL 🏨 **The Islay Hotel.** This charming hotel overlooking Port Ellen's harbor has large, bright rooms decorated in muted contemporary colors. **Pros:** central location; bright, welcoming interior; friendly staff. **Cons:** can get crowded. [$] *Rooms from: £190* ✉ *Charlotte St.* ☎ *01496/300109* 🌐 *www.theislayhotel.com* 🛏 *13 rooms* 🍴 *Breakfast.*

SPORTS AND THE OUTDOORS

HORSEBACK RIDING

Ballivicar Pony Trekking. The company leads horseback-riding trips on nearby beaches and into the surrounding countryside. ✉ *Ballivicar Farm, off A846* ☎ *01496/302251* 🌐 *www.islay-farm-accommodation.co.uk.*

PORT ASKAIG

On Islay: 11 miles northeast of Bowmore.

Serving as the ferry port for Jura and receiving ferries from Kennacraig, Port Askaig is a mere cluster of cottages. Uphill, just outside the village, a side road travels along the coast, giving impressive views of Jura on the way. There are distilleries near here, too; make appointments for tours.

GETTING HERE AND AROUND

Traveling from Bowmore, you can reach Port Askaig (where the road ends) via A846. The village is also served by local buses.

EXPLORING

Fodor's Choice ★ **Bunnahabhain Distillery.** Established in 1881, the Bunnahabhain (pronounced *Boon*-a-*ha*-bin) Distillery sits on the shore, with dramatic views across to the Paps of Jura. This is one of Scotland's most picturesque and evocative malt whisky distilleries, redolent of a preindustrialized era. ✉ *A846* ☎ *01496/840646* 🌐 *www.bunnahabhain.com* 🎫 *From £7* 🕒 *Closed Nov.–Mar. and Sun. in Apr.*

WHERE TO STAY

$$ **Kilmeny Country House.** This luxurious bed-and-breakfast is on
B&B/INN a 300-acre farm, but the rooms are so elegantly furnished that the
place feels more like a hotel. **Pros:** elegant and quiet; great breakfast.
Cons: easy to miss. $ *Rooms from: £140* ✉ *A846, Ballygrant* ✚ *Sign-posted off the A846 to Port Askaig just before the village of Ballygrant* ☎ *01496/840668* ⊕ *www.kilmeny.co.uk* ⤳ *5 rooms* |◎| *Breakfast.*

JURA

5 minutes by ferry from Port Askaig.

The rugged, mountainous landscape of the island of Jura—home to
only about 200 people—looms immediately east of Port Askaig, across
the Sound of Islay: a perfect landscape for walkers. Jura has only
one single-track road (the A846), which begins at Feolin, the ferry
pier. It climbs across moorland, providing scenic views of the island's
most striking feature, the Paps of Jura, three breast-shaped rounded
peaks. The ruined Claig Castle, on an island just offshore, was built
by the Lords of the Isles to control the sound. The island has no cash
machines, so plan ahead.

GETTING HERE AND AROUND

The Port Askaig–Feolin car ferry takes five minutes to cross the Sound
of Islay, and there is a passenger-only ferry during the summer from
Tayvallich on Argyll to Craighouse. Bus service is also available from
Craighouse and Inverlussa.

EXPLORING

Isle of Jura Distillery. The community of Craighouse has the island's only
distillery, producing malt whisky since 1810. Tours must be booked in
advance by phone or online. ✉ *Craighouse* ☎ *01496/820385* ⊕ *www.
jurawhisky.com* ⤳ *Tours from £6* ⊘ *Closed mid-July–mid-Aug., week-ends in Nov.–Mar., and Sun. in Apr.–Oct.*

WHERE TO STAY

$$ **Jura Hotel.** Jura's only hotel, next to the island's renowned distillery,
HOTEL has simple but cozy no-frills rooms, and its pleasant gardens are attrac-
tive on a summer day. **Pros:** convenient location; good, unpretentious
restaurant; lively bar. **Cons:** some shared bathrooms. $ *Rooms from:
£100* ✉ *A846, Craighouse* ☎ *01496/820243* ⊕ *www.jurahotel.co.uk*
⤳ *17 rooms* |◎| *Breakfast.*

ISLE OF MULL AND IONA

Mull is one of the most beguiling of Scotland's isles, and happily it's
also one of the easiest to get to. The island's landscapes range from the
pretty harbor of Tobermory and the gentle slopes around Dervaig to
dramatic Atlantic beaches on the west. In the south, the long road past
the sweeping green slopes of the Ross of Mull leads to Iona, Scotland's
holy island and a year-round attraction.

GETTING HERE AND AROUND

Ferries to Mull are run by the ubiquitous Caledonian MacBrayne. Its most frequent car-ferry route to Mull is from Oban to Craignure (45 minutes). Two shorter routes are from Lochaline on the Morvern Peninsula to Fishnish (15 minutes), or Kilchoan (on the Adrnamurchan Peninsula) to Tobermory (15 minutes). The Kilchoan-Lochaline ferry is not bookable. West Coast Tours serves the east coast, running between Tobermory, Craignure, and Fionnphort (for the ferry to Iona).

CRAIGNURE

On Mull: 40-minute ferry crossing from Oban, 15-minute ferry crossing to Fishnish (5 miles northwest of Craignure) from Lochaline.

Craignure, little more than a pier and some houses, is close to the well-known Duart Castle. Reservations for the year-round ferries that travel from Oban to Craignure are advisable in summer. The ferry from Lochaline to Fishnish, just northwest of Craignure, does not accept reservations and does not run on Sunday.

GETTING HERE AND AROUND

The arrival point for the 40-minute ferry crossing from Oban, Craignure is the starting point for further travel on Mull northwest toward Salen and Tobermory, or toward Fionnphort and the Iona ferry to the southwest.

ESSENTIALS

Visitor Information Craignure Information Centre. ✉ *The Pierhead* ☎ *01680/812377* 🌐 *www.visitscotland.com.*

EXPLORING

Fodor's Choice ★ **Duart Castle.** The 13th-century Duart Castle stands dramatically atop a cliff overlooking the Sound of Mull. The ancient seat of the Macleans, it was ruined by the Campbells, their archenemies, in 1691 but restored by Sir Fitzroy Maclean in 1911. Inside you can visit the dungeons and state rooms, then climb the keep for a view of the waterfront. Nearby stands the **Millennium Wood,** planted in 2000 with indigenous trees. To reach Duart by car, take the A849 and turn left around the shore of Duart Bay. From Craignure's ferry port, there is a direct bus that takes you to the castle in about 10 minutes. ✉ *A849, 3 miles southeast of Craignure* ☎ *01680/812309* 🌐 *www.duartcastle.com* 🎟 *£6.50* 🕒 *Closed Nov.–Mar.*

WHERE TO STAY

$ B&B/INN 🏨 **Craignure Inn.** Snug bedrooms with exposed beams, polished wood furniture, and views of the Sound of Mull make this 18th-century inn very appealing. **Pros:** lively bar scene; hearty local food; expansive views. **Cons:** live music can get loud; bar can get very busy. [$] *Rooms from: £82* ✉ *A849, near the ferry pier* ☎ *01680/812305* 🌐 *www.craignure-inn.co.uk* 🛏 *3 rooms* 🍴 *Breakfast.*

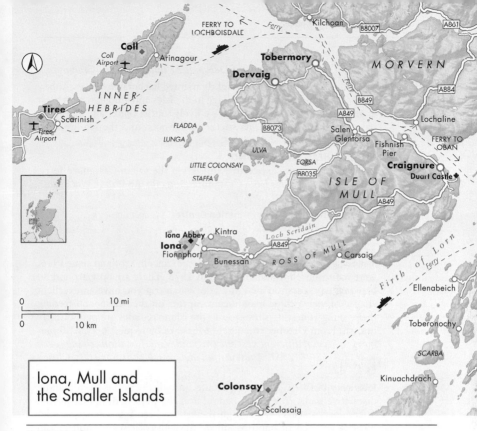

Iona, Mull and
the Smaller Islands

DERVAIG

On Mull: 27 miles northwest of Craignure, 60 miles north of Fionnphort.

A pretty riverside village, Dervaig has a circular, pointed church tower that is reminiscent of the Irish-Celtic style of the 8th and 9th centuries. The Bellart is a good trout- and salmon-fishing river, and Calgary Bay, 5 miles away, has one of the best beaches on Mull.

GETTING HERE AND AROUND

You can reach Dervaig from Craignure via the A849. From Salen, take the B8073, and from Tobermory, take the B8073.

EXPLORING

Old Byre Heritage Centre. At this museum, an audiovisual presentation on the history of the region is one of the highlights. The tearoom's wholesome fare, particularly the homemade soup, is a boon to travelers, as is the craft shop. You'll see signs for the center on the B8073, just before Dervaig. ⊠ *Off B8073* ☎ *01688/400229* ⊕ *www.old-byre.co.uk* 🎫 *£4* ⊙ *Closed Mon., Tues., and Nov.–Easter.*

TOBERMORY

On Mull: 5 miles northeast of Dervaig, 21 miles north of Craignure.

Fodor's Choice ★ With its rainbow crescent of brightly painted harborside houses, Tobermory is the most photogenic village in the Isles and among the prettiest in all Scotland. Unsurprisingly, it's a lively tourist center and a popular base for exploring Mull, its smaller neighbors, and the sea-life-filled surrounding waters.

GETTING HERE AND AROUND

The most frequent service to Mull is via the Oban-Craignure ferry. Tobermory is 21 miles from Craignure along the A849/848 (via Salen).

ESSENTIALS

Visitor Information **Mull Information Centre.** ✉ *Ledaig Car Park* ☎ *01683/302875* 🌐 *www.isle-of-mull.net.*

EXPLORING

Mull Eagle Watch. White-tailed sea eagles, extinct in Scotland since 1916, were reintroduced to the Hebrides in 1975. There are now around 80 breeding pairs, and on a Mull Eagle Watch trip you have an excellent chance of seeing these magnificent raptors on their nests and feeding their young at nesting sites around the island. Guides are paid directly in cash. From October to March, tours are by request only. ✉ *Tobermory* ✣ *Several different nest sites around Mull. Locations change each year* ☎ *01680/812556* 🌐 *www.mulleaglewatch.com* 🎫 *£10* 🕓 *Closed Oct.–Mar.*

Fodor's Choice ★ **Tobermory Distillery.** Tobermory's cute little distillery has been making distinctive malts (the peaty Ledaig and the unpeated, lighter-tasting Tobermory) since 1798, though there have been intervening decades when it was "silent" and produced no whisky. It was relaunched in 1993, and a tour here is a more personal experience than is offered by some bigger, better-known distilleries. ✉ *Bad-Daraich House, Ledaig* ✣ *Off Main St. on south side of harbor* ☎ *01688/302647* 🌐 *www.tobermorydistillery.com* 🎫 *Tours from £8.*

Fodor's Choice ★ **Whale Watch With Us.** High-speed boats carrying 12 passengers leave from Tobermory's harbor on scenic cruises, wildlife sea safaris, and whale-watching trips lasting up to four hours. You'll have a good chance of spotting dolphins, porpoises, and minke whales. If you're lucky, basking sharks and some of the sound's orcas may also put in an appearance. ✉ *Raraig House, Raeric Rd.* ✣ *Ledaig pontoons, opposite car park and Tobermory Harbor Authority on Tobermory waterfront* ☎ *01688/302875* 🌐 *whalewatchwithus.com* 🎫 *From £30.*

WHERE TO EAT AND STAY

$$ SEAFOOD Fodor's Choice ★ 🍴 **Café Fish.** This restaurant's location has certainly contributed to its success—it's perched on the pier at the end of Tobermory. The owners pride themselves on the freshness of their fish; they have their own boat and bring in their own seafood each day. **Known for:** hand-dived scallops; very fresh lobster. [$] *Average main: £18* ✉ *The Pier* ☎ *01688/301253* 🌐 *www.thecafefish.com* 🕓 *Closed Jan.–mid-Mar.*

$$ B&B/INN 🏨 **Highland Cottage.** Set on the hill above the harbor, this family-run hotel prides itself on its elegant rooms and the imaginative dishes in its

dining room. **Pros:** comfortable hotel; attentive owners; high-quality dining. **Cons:** rooms are a bit small; no children under 10. [$] *Rooms from: £155* ✉ *Breadalbane St.* ☎ *01688/302030* 🌐 *www.highlandcottage.co.uk* 🛏 *6 rooms* 🍴 *Breakfast.*

$$ HOTEL FAMILY 🏨 **Tobermory Hotel.** Made up of five former fishermen's cottages, this lodging on Tobermory's waterfront has a warm, intimate feel. **Pros:** adorable cottage setting with fireplace; toys for children. **Cons:** small rooms; small bathrooms. [$] *Rooms from: £146* ✉ *Main St.* ☎ *01688/302091* 🌐 *www.thetobermoryhotel.com* 🕒 *Closed Nov.–Mar.* 🛏 *18 rooms* 🍴 *Breakfast.*

$$ HOTEL 🏨 **Western Isles Hotel.** This grand hotel from the Victorian era looks down on Tobermory from its idyllic location overlooking the Sound of Mull. **Pros:** the view is brilliant; spacious public rooms; great food. **Cons:** some rooms look onto the car park; rooms vary in size. [$] *Rooms from: £130* ✉ *Off B882* ☎ *01688/302012* 🌐 *www.westernisleshotel.co.uk* 🛏 *26 rooms* 🍴 *Breakfast.*

NIGHTLIFE AND PERFORMING ARTS

Mull Theatre. The renowned Mull Theatre, founded in 1966, once prided itself on being the smallest theater in the United Kingdom. Today it has grown in size and in stature, and its productions tour not only the islands, but the whole of Scotland. It's wise to book ahead. ✉ *Druimfin, Salen Rd.* ☎ *01688/302828* 🌐 *www.comar.co.uk/about/mull-theatre.*

IONA

5 minutes by ferry from Fionnphort (Mull), which is 36 miles west of Craignure.

The ruined abbey on Iona gives little hint that this was once one of the most important Christian religious centers in the land. The priceless *Book of Kells* (now in Dublin) was illustrated here, and it was the monks of Iona who spread Christian ideas across Scotland and the north. The abbey was founded in the year 563 by the fiery and argumentative Columba (circa 521–97) after his expulsion from Ireland. Until the 11th century, many of Scotland's kings and rulers were buried here, their tombstones still visible inside the abbey. While few visitors venture beyond the pier and the abbey, there are several tranquil paths around the island.

GETTING HERE AND AROUND

Caledonian MacBrayne's ferry from Fionnphort departs at regular intervals throughout the year (£4.50 round-trip). Timetables are available on the Caledonian MacBrayne website. Note that cars are not permitted; there's a parking lot by the ferry at Fionnphort.

EXPLORING

Fodor's Choice ★ **Iona Abbey.** Overseen by St. Columba, who traveled here from Ireland, Iona was the birthplace of Christianity in Scotland in the 6th century. It survived repeated Norse sackings before falling into disuse around the time of the Reformation. Restoration work began at the beginning of the 20th century. Today the restored buildings serve as a spiritual center under the jurisdiction of the Church of Scotland. Guided tours by the

Iona Community, an ecumenical religious group, begin every half hour in summer and on demand in winter. ✉ *Iona* ☎ *01681/700512* 🌐 *www.iona.org.uk* 🎟 *£7.50.*

WHERE TO STAY

$$ HOTEL 🏨 **St. Columba Hotel.** As befits a religious retreat, rooms in this 1846 minister's home are simple to the point of being spartan, but those in the front make up for it with glorious views across the Sound of Iona to Mull. **Pros:** impressive views; nice log fires; Wi-Fi throughout the hotel. **Cons:** no TVs; basic decor. [$] *Rooms from: £135* ✉ *Next to cathedral* ✣ *About ¼ mile from the ferry pier* ☎ *01681/700304* 🌐 *www.stcolumba-hotel.co.uk* 🕒 *Closed Nov.–Mar.* 🛏 *27 rooms* 🍴 *Breakfast.*

SHOPPING

Iona Community Shop. The shop carries Celtic-inspired gift items, as well as sheet music, songbooks, and CDs. It also sells local crafts and the Wild Goose publications of the Iona Community. ✉ *Across from Iona Abbey* ☎ *01681/700404* 🌐 *www.iona.org.uk.*

Low Door. This shop attached to the St. Columba Hotel sells locally produced jams, chutneys, and other artifacts as well as cookbooks. **■ TIP→ The store is only open April to October.** ✉ *Beside St. Columba Hotel* ☎ *01681/700483* 🌐 *www.stcolumba-hotel.co.uk.*

THE SMALLER ISLANDS

The smaller islands, sometimes known as the Southern Hebrides, may seem quite remote, but were once important centers of power and production. Successively depopulated by force or by emigration to Glasgow's industries or the promise of the Americas, the islands still survive on fishing, cattle and sheep raising, and tourism. Their populations remain small, though, and many residents are "incomers" from the mainland or from England. For the visitor, the experience is one of open, often barely populated landscapes and a slightly brooding sense of history.

TIREE

4-hour sail from Oban, via Coll.

Archaeological sites and good surfing make this windy island popular in summer.

GETTING HERE AND AROUND

Caledonian MacBrayne runs ferries to Tiree via Coll, four times a week (Tuesday, Thursday, Saturday, and Sunday). You can also fly here from Glasgow on Flybe or from Oban on Hebridean Air Services. Tiree has a shared taxi service (☎ *01879/220311*), which you should book ahead of your arrival. An alternative is to rent a bike from **Skerryvore House** (☎ *01879/220268*).

ESSENTIALS

Air Travel Contact Tiree Airport. ✉ *Off B8065* ☎ *01879/220456* 🌐 *www.hial.co.uk.*

EXPLORING

Tiree. A fertile, low-lying island with its own microclimate, Tiree is windswept, but has long hours of sunshine in summer. Long, rolling Atlantic swells make it a favorite with surfers, and in summer, when an influx of wealthy visitors arrives, the posh accents of southern England sometimes drown out native voices. Among Tiree's several archaeological sites are a large boulder near Vaul covered with more than 50 Bronze Age cup marks, and an excavated *broch* (stone tower) at Dun Mor Vaul. Tiree has two hotels and an assortment of self-catering accommodations, including a hostel with shared dorm rooms. The island is served by CalMac ferry from Oban. ⊕ *www.isleoftiree.com.*

COLL

3-hour sail from Oban.

Good birding and a number of ancient sites are among the attractions on Coll.

GETTING HERE AND AROUND

Caledonian MacBrayne runs ferries to Coll on Tuesday, Thursday, Saturday, and Sunday. You can also fly here from Oban on Hebridean Air Services. There is no public transportation on Coll, but you can rent a bike at the post office (☎ *01879/2303395*) or use the island's one taxi (☎ *01879/230402*).

EXPLORING

Coll. Unlike their neighbors in nearby Tiree, Coll's residents were not forced to leave the island in the 19th century. Today half of the island's sparse population lives in its only village, Arinagour. Its coasts offer extraordinarily rich birdlife, particularly along the beautiful sandy beaches of its southwest. Coll is even lower lying than Tiree but also rockier and less fertile. The island is rich in archaeology, with standing stones at Totronald, a cairn at Annagour, and the remains of several Iron Age forts around the island. ⊕ *www.visitcoll.co.uk.*

8

COLONSAY

2½-hour sail from Oban.

Less bleak than Coll and Tiree, Colonsay is one of Scotland's quietest, most unspoiled, and least populated islands. It is partly wooded, with a fine 20-acre rhododendron garden surrounding Colonsay House, private home of Baron Strathcona. The island also boasts a great variety of wildlife on land and in the surrounding waters.

GETTING HERE AND AROUND

CalMac ferries run to Colonsay on Monday, Wednesday, Friday, and Sunday. The island of Oronsay lies half a mile away and can be reached at certain times across a natural causeway. There is no public transport on Colonsay; bikes can be rented from **Archie's Bike Hire** (☎ *01951/200355*).

EXPLORING

Colonsay. The beautiful beach at Kiloran Bay on Colonsay is an utterly peaceful place even at the height of summer. The standing stones at Kilchattan Farm are known as Fingal's Limpet Hammers. Fingal, or Finn, MacCool (Fionn mac Cumhaill) is a warrior of massive size and strength in Celtic mythology. Standing before the stones, you can imagine Fingal wielding them like hammers to cull equally large limpets from Scotland's rocky coast. The island's social life revolves around the bar at the 19th-century Colonsay Hotel, 100 yards from the ferry pier. The adjacent island of Oronsay with its ruined cloister can be reached at low tide via a 1½-mile wade across a sandy sound. ⊕ *www.colonsay.org.uk.*

INVERNESS AND AROUND THE GREAT GLEN

Updated
by Eilidh
McCabe

Defined by its striking topography, the Great Glen brings together mountains and myths, history and wild nature—then lets you wash it all down with a dram of the world's finest whisky. Inverness is the gateway to an area in which the views from almost every twist and bend in the circuitous roads may take your breath away. There's also plenty here for history buffs, including Culloden Moor, where the last battle fought on British soil ended the hopes of the tragically outgunned Jacobite rebels in 1746.

The Great Glen Fault runs diagonally through the Highlands of Scotland and was formed when two tectonic plates collided, shoving masses of the crust southwest toward the Atlantic Ocean. Over time the rift broadened into a glen, and a thin line of lochs now lies along its seam. The most famous of these is deep, murky Loch Ness, home to the elusive Loch Ness monster.

The city of Inverness has a growing reputation for excellent restaurants, and from here nearly everything in the Great Glen is an easy day trip. Just south of the city the 13th-century ruined Urquhart Castle sits on the shores of Loch Ness. In Fort Augustus, the Caledonian Canal joins Inverness to Fort William via a series of 29 locks. At the western end of the canal, Ben Nevis, Britain's highest mountain, rises sharply. The Nevis Range, like Cairngorms National Park to the east, is ideal for walking, climbing, and mountain biking through the hills and glens.

Fort William makes a good base for exploring Glencoe, an awe-inspiring region that was also the scene of another notoriously murky episode in Scottish history: the Glencoe Massacre of 1692. It's an area where history seems to be imprinted on the landscape, and it remains desolate, with some of the steepest, most atmospheric hills in Scotland.

Just north of Fort William the Road to the Isles offers impressive coastal views. The Small Isles of Rum and Eigg create a low rocky skyline across the water. Near the start of this road lies Glenfinnan, where in 1745 Bonnie Prince Charlie rallied his Jacobite troops. The surrounding Morayshire coast is home to a more pastoral landscape, and 14th-century Cawdor Castle and its gardens have an opulent air. Nearby Brodie Castle has an awe-inspiring library and art collection.

Impressive long, sandy beaches stretch out along the coast from the towns of Nairn and Findhorn. Finally, the Malt Whisky Trail begins in Forres and follows the wide, fast River Spey south until it butts against the Cairngorm Mountains and the old Caledonian forests, with their diverse and rare wildlife.

TOP REASONS TO GO

Castles, fortresses, and battle-fields: Hear stories of the Highland people and famous figures like Bonnie Prince Charlie, and absorb the atmosphere of castles and battlefields, at Culloden Moor, Cawdor and Brodie castles, Fort George, and Glencoe.

Hill walking and outdoor activities: The Great Glen is renowned for its hill walking. Some of the best routes are around Glen Nevis, Glencoe, and on Ben Nevis, the highest mountain in Britain. It's not just hiking: Glenmore Lodge in the Cairngorms offers everything from kayaking to mountain biking to ice climbing.

Wild landscapes and rare wildlife: Spot rare plants and beasts including tiny least willow trees and golden eagles in the near-arctic tundra of Cairngorms National Park.

Whisky tours: The two western-most distilleries on the Malt Whisky Trail are in Forres. Benromach is the smallest distillery in Moray and has excellent tours; Dallas Dhu is preserved as a museum. You can strike out from here to nearby distilleries in Speyside (⇨ see Chapter 7).

Boat trips: There are many ferries to the Small Isles (or to Skye) from Arisaig and Mallaig. You can also go Nessie-watching on Loch Ness or hire a small boat and travel the Caledonian Canal.

ORIENTATION AND PLANNING

GETTING ORIENTED

If Inverness is the center point of a compass, the Great Glen spreads out to the east, south, and west. To the east stretches the Morayshire coast, populated with castles, distilleries, and beaches. Head southeast and you hit the Cairngorms National Park and other nature preserves. The A82 heads south from Inverness, hugging the west side of Loch Ness. Nearby are the contemplative ruins at Urquhart Castle and the interesting locks of the Caledonian Canal. Farther southwest, Fort William can be a good base for day trips to the foreboding and steep mountain pass of Glencoe.

Inverness and Nearby. From the small city of Inverness, just about anywhere in the Great Glen is a day trip. Spend your days exploring Culloden Moor, Brodie Castle, or Cawdor Castle. There are long, walkable beaches at Nairn and Findhorn.

Speyside and the Cairngorms. Speyside is best known for its whisky distilleries, and those who enjoy a good dram often follow the Whisky Trail. In and around the Cairngorms there are mountains, lochs, rivers, and dozens of cycling and walking paths that make it tailor-made for outdoors enthusiasts.

Loch Ness, Fort William, and Nearby. Have a go trying to spot Nessie from the banks of Loch Ness. For something wilder, base yourself at Fort William and take in the spectacular scenery of Glencoe and Glen Nevis. If you dare, climb Britain's highest peak, Ben Nevis. The Road

9

to the Isles, known for larger-than-life figures both old (Bonnie Prince Charlie) and new (Harry Potter), has classic views across water to rocky islands perched on blue seas.

PLANNING

WHEN TO GO

Late spring to early autumn is the best time to visit the Great Glen. If you catch good weather in summer, the days can be glorious. Unfortunately summer is also when you will encounter midges (tiny biting insects: keep walking, as they can't move very fast). Winter can bring a damp chill, gusty winds, and snow-blocked roads, although many Scots value the open fires and the warming whisky that make the off-season so appealing.

PLANNING YOUR TIME

The Great Glen is an enormous area that can easily be broken into two separate trips. The first would be based in or near Inverness, allowing an exploration of Speyside, the Cairngorms, Cawdor and Brodie castles, and perhaps a few whisky-distillery tours. The second moves through the cloud-laden Glencoe and down through the moody Rannoch Moor, or toward the Road to the Isles; you could stay near Glencoe or in Fort William. To do the area justice you probably need at least three days.

For those with more time, a trip around the Great Glen could be combined with forays north into the Northern Highlands, east toward Aberdeen and the rest of the Malt Whisky Trail, southeastward to the Central Highlands, or south to Argyll.

GETTING HERE AND AROUND

AIR TRAVEL

Inverness Airport has flights from London, Edinburgh, and Glasgow. Domestic flights covering the Highlands and islands are operated by easyJet and Flybe. Fort William has bus and train connections with Glasgow, so Glasgow Airport can be a good access point.

BUS TRAVEL

A long-distance Scottish Citylink service connects Glasgow and Fort William. Inverness is also well served from the central belt of Scotland. Discount carrier Megabus (book online to avoid phone charges) has service to Inverness from various cities.

Traveling around the Great Glen area without a car is challenging if not impossible, especially in the more rural areas. Stagecoach Highlands serves the Great Glen and around Fort William. A handful of postbus services (run by the postal service) can help get you to a few of the more remote corners of the area, although just a few seats are available on each bus.

Bus Contacts Megabus. ☎ *0900/160–0900* ⊕ *www.megabus.com.* **Royal Mail Post Buses.** ☎ *0345/774–0740* ⊕ *www.royalmail.com.* **Scottish Citylink.** ☎ *0871/266–3333* ⊕ *www.citylink.co.uk.* **Stagecoach Highlands.** ☎ *01463/233371* ⊕ *www.stagecoachbus.com.*

CAR TRAVEL

As in all areas of rural Scotland, a car is a great asset for exploring the Great Glen, especially because the best of the area is away from the main roads. You can use the main A82 from Inverness to Fort William,

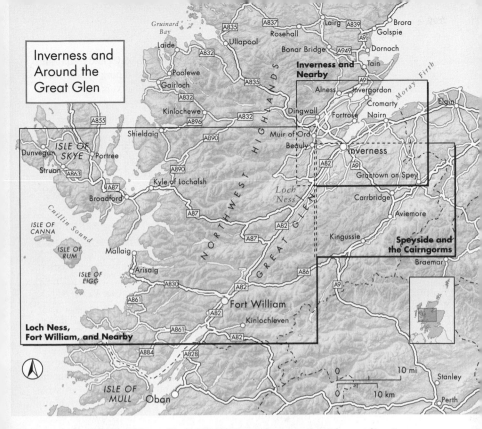

or use the smaller B862/B852 roads to explore the much quieter east side of Loch Ness. Mallaig, west of Fort William, is reached via a new road, but there are still a few narrow and winding single-lane roads, which require slower speeds and concentration.

In the Great Glen the best sights are often hidden from the main road, which is an excellent reason to favor peaceful rural byways and to avoid as much as possible the busy A96 and A9, which carry much of the traffic in the area.

TRAIN TRAVEL

ScotRail has connections from London to Inverness and Fort William (including overnight sleeper service), as well as reliable links from Glasgow and Edinburgh. There's train service between Glasgow (Queen Street) and Inverness, via Aviemore, which gives access to the heart of Speyside.

Although there's no rail connection among towns within the Great Glen, this area has the West Highland Line, which links Fort William to Mallaig. This train, run by ScotRail, remains the most enjoyable way to experience the rugged hills and loch scenery between these two places. The Jacobite Steam Train is an exciting summer (mid-May to mid-October) option on the same route.

Train Contacts Jacobite Steam Train. ☎ 0844/850–4685 ⊕ www.westcoas-trailways.co.uk. **ScotRail.** ☎ 0344/811–0141 ⊕ www.scotrail.co.uk.

RESTAURANTS

Inverness, Aviemore, and Fort William have plenty of cafés and restaurants in all price ranges. Inverness has particularly diverse dining options. Outside the towns there are many country-house hotels serving superb meals.

HOTELS

In the Great Glen, towns have accommodations ranging from cozy inns to expansive hotels; in more remote areas your choice will usually be limited to smaller establishments. Book as far in advance as you can; the area is very busy in the peak season and the best places fill up early. In Inverness, you may find it more appealing to stay outside the city center or in the pretty countryside nearby. *Hotel reviews have been shortened. For full information, visit Fodors.com.*

WHAT IT COSTS IN POUNDS				
	$	$$	$$$	$$$$
Restaurants	under £15	£15–£19	£20–£25	over £25
Hotels	under £100	£100–£160	£161–£220	over £220

Restaurant prices are the average cost of a main course at dinner or, if dinner is not served, at lunch. Hotel prices are the lowest cost of a standard double room in high season, including 20% V.A.T.

TOURS

Inverness Tours. This outfitter runs the occasional boat cruise, but it's mainly known for very good tours around the Highlands in well-equipped vehicles, led by expert guides and heritage enthusiasts. However, the price is per minibus, not per person, so while it's quite a bargain for parties of six or seven, it's less appealing for small groups. It may be possible to get single tickets if another group will sell its unused space. ☎ *01667/455699* ⊕ *www.invernesstours.com* ✉ *From £150.*

J.A. Johnstone. At the more luxurious end of the scale, this company offers chauffeur-driven tours of the Highlands in air-conditioned Mercedes sedans. Tours are completely tailored to what you want to see, and the guides have an encyclopedic knowledge of the region. The company also runs multiday tours of the Scottish regions, and can help book accommodations along the way. ☎ *01463/798372* ⊕ *www.jajcd.com* ✉ *Prices on request.*

INVERNESS AND NEARBY

At the center of this region is Inverness, a small but appealing city that makes a useful gateway to the Great Glen. It has an increasingly strong range of restaurants and accommodations, but its cultural offerings remain more or less limited to what is happening at the Eden Court Theatre and the live music at a few good pubs.

East of Inverness, the infamous Culloden Moor still looks desolate on most days, and you can easily imagine the fierce, brief, and bloody battle that took place here in 1746 that ended in final, catastrophic defeat for the Jacobites and their quest to restore the exiled Stewarts to the British throne. Because Jacobite tales are interwoven with landmarks throughout this entire area, you will get much more out of this storied landscape if you first learn something about this thorny but colorful period of Scottish history. The Morayshire coast boasts many long beaches and some refined castles (Cawdor and Brodie) that are definitely worth a visit. Moving east along the inner Moray Firth, you might be tempted by Benromach distillery in Forres, a taste of what you can find farther south if you follow the Malt Whisky Trail.

INVERNESS

176 miles north of Glasgow, 109 miles northwest of Aberdeen, 161 miles northwest of Edinburgh.

It's not the prettiest or the most charming Scottish city, but with a few attractions and some reliably good hotels and restaurants, Inverness makes a practical base for exploring a region that has a lot to offer. From here you can fan out in almost any direction for interesting day trips: east to Moray and the distilleries near Forres, southeast to the Cairngorms, and south to Loch Ness. Throughout its past the town was burned and ravaged by Highland clans competing for dominance.

GETTING HERE AND AROUND

You can easily fly into Inverness Airport, as there are daily flights from London, Bristol, Birmingham, Manchester, and Belfast. However, there are also easy train and bus connections from Glasgow Airport. Scottish Citylink has service here, and Megabus has long-distance bus service from Edinburgh and Glasgow. ScotRail runs trains here from London, Edinburgh, Glasgow, and other cities.

Once you're here, you can explore much of the city on foot. A rental car makes exploring the surrounding area much easier. But if you don't have a car, there are bus and boat tours from the city center to a number of places in the Great Glen.

An unusual option from Inverness is a day trip to Orkney. John O'Groats Ferries runs day tours from Inverness to Orkney, daily from June through August. They cost £37 round-trip.

ESSENTIALS

Airport Contact Inverness Airport. ⊠ *Dalcross* ☎ *01667/464000* ⊕ *www.invernessairport.co.uk.*

Boat Contact John O'Groats Ferries. ☎ *01955/611353* ⊕ *www.jogferry.co.uk.*

Bus Contact Inverness Bus Station. ⊠ *Margaret St.* ☎ *01463/233371.*

Visitor Information Inverness. ⊠ *Castle Wynd* ☎ *01463/252401* ⊕ *www.inverness-scotland.com.*

EXPLORING

Fort George. After the fateful battle at Culloden, the nervous government in London ordered the construction of a large fort on a promontory reaching into the Moray Firth. Fort George was started in 1748 and completed some 20 years later. It's one of the best-preserved

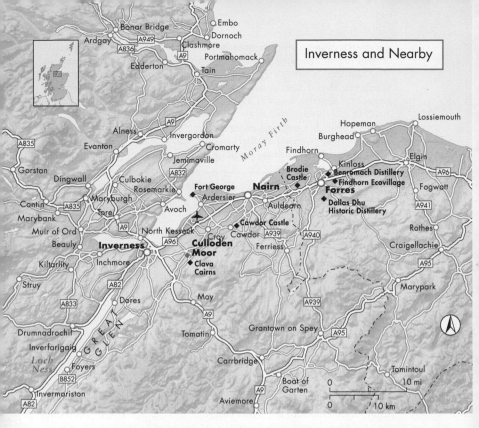

18th-century military fortifications in Europe. At its height it housed 1,600 men and around 30,000 pounds of gunpowder. The on-site Highlanders Museum gives you a glimpse of the fort's history. The fort is 14 miles northeast of Inverness. ✉ *Old Military Rd., Ardersier* ☎ *01667/460232* ⊕ *www.historicenvironment.scot* 💷 *£9.*

Inverness Castle. One of Inverness's few historic landmarks is reddish sandstone Inverness Castle (now the local Sheriff Court), nestled above the river off Castle Road on Castle Hill. The current structure is Victorian, built after a former fort was blown up by the Jacobites in the 1745 campaign. The castle isn't open to the public, but you are free to wander the grounds. ✉ *41 Castle St.*

Inverness Cathedral. This handsome Victorian cathedral, dating from 1869, has two unique claims to fame; in addition to being the northernmost cathedral in the British Isles, it was, more significantly, the first cathedral to be built in Britain after the Reformation. The twin-turreted exterior of the building is made from characteristically reddish local Tarradale stone. Inside it follows a medieval layout, with the addition of an unusual patterned wooden floor. Check out the beautiful white marble font, carved in the shape of a seated angel. ✉ *Ardross St.* ☎ *01463/233535* ⊕ *www.morayepiscopalchurch.scot/inverness-cathedral* 💷 *Free.*

FAMILY   **Inverness Museum and Art Gallery.** The small but excellent Inverness Museum and Art Gallery covers archaeology, art, local history, and the natural environment in its lively displays. The museum is also home to the Highland Photographic Archive. ⊠ *Castle Wynd* ☎ *01463/237114* ⊕ *www.highlifehighland.com/inverness-museum-and-art-gallery* ⊠ *Free* ⊘ *Closed Sun. and Mon.*

WHERE TO EAT

$$ ✕ **Cafe 1.** Consistently recommended by locals as one of the best res-
MODERN BRITISH   taurants in the area, Cafe 1 really practices what it preaches in terms of
Fodor'sChoice   sustainable, local produce. Taking inspiration from such big names as
★   Blue Hill in New York, the restaurant rears its own herds to provide the Hebridean lamb and Highland beef on the menu, maybe served with a simple order of chips (thick-cut fries) and rich garlic butter. **Known for:** castle views; melt-in-your-mouth lamb; ethically sourced ingredients. Ⓢ *Average main: £18* ⊠ *75 Castle St.* ☎ *01463/226200* ⊕ *www.cafe1. net* ⊘ *Closed Sun.*

$$$ ✕ **Chez Roux.** The menu is as sleek as the service at this restaurant in the
MODERN BRITISH   Rocpool Reserve Hotel, with clean modern design throughout (think
Fodor'sChoice   monochrome walls, straight lines, and a whole lot of upholstery in taste-
★   ful accent colors). Expect indulgent yet creative dishes, such as Loch Duart salmon set off with Keta caviar, and a lavish signature soufflé that is far more filling than a lighter-than-air starter ought to be. **Known for:** exceptional service; inventive dishes; beautiful presentation. Ⓢ *Average main: £22* ⊠ *Rocpool Reserve Hotel, Culduthel Rd.* ☎ *01463/240089* ⊕ *www.rocpool.com/dining.*

$$ ✕ **Dores Inn.** Off a pretty country road on the eastern shore of Loch
BRITISH   Ness, this low-slung, white-stone eatery is the perfect place to stop for lunch or dinner. The menu is a combination of well-prepared old favorites—fish-and-chips, perhaps, or neeps and tatties (turnips and potatoes)—together with steaks, lamb, and seafood. **Known for:** well-prepared Scottish classics; excellent range of whiskies; gluten-free options. Ⓢ *Average main: £16* ⊠ *Off B862, Dores* ☎ *01463/751203* ⊕ *www.thedoresinn.co.uk.*

$$ ✕ **Fig and Thistle Bistro.** This intimate little restaurant has been packing
BISTRO   in the crowds nightly since it opened in 2015. Modern bistro fare is
FAMILY   presented stylishly but without fuss—goat cheese and fig tart on a bed of oakleaf lettuce to start, perhaps, followed by seared local salmon infused with Thai flavors, or steak with a decadent red-wine-and-thyme sauce. **Known for:** contemporary classics; tasty homemade desserts. Ⓢ *Average main: £16* ⊠ *4A Stephens Brae* ☎ *01463/712422* ⊘ *Closed Sun. and Mon. No lunch Tues.*

$$$ ✕ **River House.** Head chef and owner Alfie Little draws heavily on local
SEAFOOD   inspiration to shape the menu at this tiny riverside seafood restaurant, which has an interior as stylish as its appealing gray and white exterior. Start with mussels or oysters from the Scottish islands, then take your pick from mains based on native fish such as Shetland halibut and Scrabster hake, and wash it all down with a local beer. **Known for:** intimate atmosphere; fresh, sustainable local seafood. Ⓢ *Average main: £22* ⊠ *1 Greig St.* ☎ *01463/222033* ⊕ *www.riverhouseinverness.co.uk* ⊘ *Closed Sun. and Mon. No lunch.*

9

$$$ BRASSERIE Fodor's Choice ★ 🍴 **Rocpool Restaurant.** Another perennial, the Rocpool has a frequently changing menu of modern bistro classics, with a few international twists. Local seafood is a specialty, and the wine list is excellent. **Known for:** outstanding wine selection; contemporary twists on traditional dishes; quality meat and seafood. [$] *Average main: £20* ✉ *1 Ness Walk* ☎ *01463/717274* 🌐 *www.rocpoolrestaurant.com* 🕒 *Closed Sun.*

> **FISHING**
>
> The Great Glen is laced with rivers and lochs where you can fly-fish for salmon and trout. The fishing seasons are as follows: salmon and sea trout, from early February through September or even into October and November (depending on the area); brown trout, from March 15 to October 6; rainbow trout year-round. Sea angling from shore or boat is also possible. Tourist centers can provide information on locations, permits, and fishing rights.

WHERE TO STAY

There are many places to stay in Inverness, but if your goal is to explore the countryside, a hotel outside the center may be a good choice.

$ B&B/INN 🏨 **Avalon.** A 20-minute walk from the city center, this neat and modern B&B is a rare find. **Pros:** friendly and well run; good-size rooms. **Cons:** slightly far outside the city; minimum stay on some dates; not for families with very young kids (they must be "old enough to sleep in a room of their own"). [$] *Rooms from: £90* ✉ *79 Glenarquhart Rd.* ☎ *01463/239075* 🌐 *www.inverness-loch-ness.co.uk* 🛏 *6 rooms* 🍽 *Breakfast.*

$ B&B/INN 🏨 **Bluebell House.** Each room at Bluebell House has sturdy oak furnishings, including a downstairs bedroom with a full-curtained four-poster bed and a curved chaise lounge. **Pros:** large rooms; decadent furnishing; great hosts. **Cons:** smallish bathrooms; no windows in bathrooms. [$] *Rooms from: £95* ✉ *31 Kenneth St.* ☎ *01463/238201* 🌐 *www.bluebell-house.com* 🛏 *4 rooms* 🍽 *Breakfast.*

$$$$ HOTEL 🏨 **Bunchrew House Hotel.** This 17th-century baronial mansion, its turrets reflected in a glassy lake, looks like something from a Scottish fairy tale. **Pros:** beautiful setting; atmospheric building; good restaurant. **Cons:** some rooms could do with refurbishment; quite expensive. [$] *Rooms from: £345* ✉ *Off A862* ✥ *About 3 miles west of Inverness* ☎ *01463/234917* 🌐 *www.bunchrew-inverness.co.uk* 🛏 *16 rooms* 🍽 *Breakfast.*

$ B&B/INN 🏨 **Moyness House.** On a quiet residential street with well-trimmed hedges a few minutes from downtown Inverness, this lovely Victorian villa was once the home of Scottish author Neil M. Gunn (1891–1973), known for short stories and novels that evoke images of the Highlands, such as *Morning Tide, Highland River,* and *Butcher's Broom*. **Pros:** beautiful building; lovely garden; great location near the river. **Cons:** public rooms a bit fussy for some; books up quickly; harsh cancellation policy. [$] *Rooms from: £92* ✉ *6 Bruce Gardens* ☎ *01463/233836* 🌐 *www.moyness.co.uk* 🛏 *6 rooms* 🍽 *Breakfast.*

$$ B&B/INN 🏨 **Strathness House.** Standing on the banks of the River Ness, this 12-room guesthouse is a quick walk from the well-regarded Eden Court Theatre and the rest of the attractions of the city center. **Pros:** overlooks the river; close to the city center; free Wi-Fi. **Cons:** parking can

be difficult. $ *Rooms from: £107* ⊠ *4 Ardross Terr.* ☏ *01463/232765* ⊕ *www.strathnesshouse.com* ⇨ *12 rooms* ¶◎¶ *Breakfast.*

$$ **⊞ Trafford Bank.** A 15-minute walk from downtown Inverness, this
B&B/INN delightful little B&B makes for a practical but stylish base. Pros: welcoming atmosphere; stylish rooms; relaxing vibe. Cons: rooms on the small side. $ *Rooms from: £130* ⊠ *96 Fairfield Rd.* ☏ *01463/241414* ⊕ *www.traffordbankguesthouse.co.uk* ⇨ *5 rooms* ¶◎¶ *Breakfast.*

NIGHTLIFE AND PERFORMING ARTS
BARS AND LOUNGES
Hootananny. An odd combination of Scottish pub, concert hall, and Thai restaurant, Hootananny is one of the best places in the region to hear live music. The excellent pub has a warm atmosphere and serves food that comes highly recommended by locals. Several bands play each Saturday evening and a few during the week, too—check the website for listings. ⊠ *67 Church St.* ☏ *01463/233651* ⊕ *www.hootananny-inverness.co.uk.*

THEATER
Eden Court Theatre. The varied program at this popular local theater includes films, music, comedy, ballet, and even pantomime. Check out the art gallery and the bright café, and take a walk around the magnificent Bishop's Palace. ⊠ *Bishops Rd.* ☏ *01463/234234* ⊕ *www.eden-court.co.uk.*

SHOPPING
Although Inverness has the usual indoor shopping malls and department stores, the most interesting goods are in the specialty outlets in and around town.

BOOKSTORES
Leakey's Secondhand Bookshop. This shop claims to be the biggest secondhand bookstore in Scotland. When you get tired of leafing through the 100,000 or so titles, climb to the mezzanine café and study the cavernous church interior. Antique prints and maps are housed on the balcony. ⊠ *Greyfriars Hall, Church St.* ☏ *01463/239947.*

CLOTHING
Duncan Chisholm. This shop specializes in Highland dress and tartans. Mail-order and made-to-measure services are available. ⊠ *47–51 Castle St.* ☏ *01463/234599* ⊕ *www.kilts.co.uk.*

GALLERIES
Castle Gallery. The excellent Castle Gallery sells contemporary paintings, sculpture, prints, and crafts. It also hosts frequently changing exhibitions by up-and-coming artists. ⊠ *43 Castle St.* ☏ *01463/729512* ⊕ *www.castlegallery.co.uk.*

LOCAL SPECIALTIES
Inverness Coffee Roasting Co. An ideal place to pick up a gift, this beautifully presented little coffee shop stocks a good selection of locally roasted beans to enjoy on the premises or take away with you. Indulgent handmade treats made in Inverness by luxury chocolatiers The Chocolate Place are also available here. ⊠ *15 Chapel St.* ☏ *01463/242555* ⊕ *www.invernesscoffeeroasting.co.uk.*

9

SHOPPING CENTER

Victorian Market. Don't miss the colorful Victorian Market, built in 1870. The atmospheric indoor space houses more than 40 privately owned specialty shops. ⊠ *Academy St.* ☎ *01463/724273.*

SPORTS AND THE OUTDOORS

GOLF

Fodor's Choice
★ **Castle Stuart Golf Links.** Opened in 2009, this course overlooking the Moray Firth is already considered one of Scotland's finest, hosting the Scottish Open in 2011. Expect undulating fairways and extensive bunkers that test your mettle. The 210-yard 17th hole provides perilous cliff-top play; the wind can defeat the canniest player. The art deco–inspired clubhouse offers stunning views of the water. ⊠ *B9039* ☎ *01463/796111* ⊕ *www.castlestuartgolf.com* ≋ *£195 May–Oct., £140 Apr. and Nov.* ⚑ *18 holes, 6553 yards, par 72* ⟲ *Closed mid-Nov.–Mar.*

Inverness Golf Club. Established in 1883, and partly designed by famous British Open champion and course designer James Braid, Inverness Golf Club welcomes visitors to its parkland course 1 mile from downtown. The tree-lined course overlooking the Beauly Firth presents some unique challenges to keep even experienced golfers on their toes. ⊠ *Culcabock Rd.* ☎ *01463/239882* ⊕ *www.invernessgolfclub.co.uk* ≋ *£38 Apr., £50 May–Sept., £28 Oct., £20 Nov.–Mar.* ⚑ *18 holes, 6102 yards, par 69.*

Torvean Golf Course. This municipal course has one of the longest par-5 holes (565 yards) in the north of Scotland. There are quite a few water hazards, including the Caledonian Canal. One of the most challenging sections is Torvean Hill, a famous local landmark colloquially known as the "Hill of Bean"—partly in reference to its history (the "Bean" is thought to be the 11th-century St. Bean)—but also as a wry nod to what the foolhardy may assume its gradient amounts to. ⊠ *Glenurquhart Rd.* ☎ *01463/225651* ⊕ *www.torveangolfclub.co.uk* ≋ *£35 weekdays, £40 weekends May–Sept., £30 Apr. and Oct., £25 Mar. and Nov., £17 Dec.–Feb.* ⚑ *18 holes, 5784 yards, par 68.*

CULLODEN MOOR

8 miles east of Inverness.

Culloden Moor was the scene of the last battle fought on British soil—and to this day its name is enough to invoke raw and tragic feelings in Scotland. Austere and windswept, it's also a place of outstanding natural beauty.

GETTING HERE AND AROUND

Driving along the B9006 from Inverness is the easiest way to Culloden Moor, and there's a large car park to handle many visitors. Local buses also run from Inverness to the battlefield.

EXPLORING

Clava Cairns. Not far from Culloden, on a narrow road southeast of the battlefield, are the Clava Cairns, dating from the Bronze Age. In a cluster among the trees, these stones and monuments form a large ring with underground passage graves that are reached via a tunnel. Helpful placards put everything into historical context. ⊠ *B851, Culloden* ≋ *Free.*

Fodor's Choice
★
Culloden Moor. Here, on a cold April day in 1746, the hopelessly out-gunned Jacobite forces of Bonnie Prince Charlie were destroyed by King George II's army. The victorious commander, the Duke of Cumberland (George II's son), earned the name of the "Butcher" of Cumberland for the bloody reprisals carried out by his men on Highland families, Jacobite or not, caught in the vicinity. In the battle itself, the duke's army—greatly outnumbering the Jacobites—killed up to 2,000 soldiers. (The victors, by contrast, lost just 50). It was the last battle to be fought on British soil. The National Trust for Scotland has re-created a slightly eerie version of the battlefield as it looked in 1746 that you can explore with a guided audio tour. An innovative visitor center enables you to get closer to the sights and sounds of the battle and to interact with the characters involved. A viewing platform helps (literally) put things into perspective from on high. Academic research and technology have helped re-create the Gaelic dialect, song, and music of the time. There's also a good on-site café. ✉ *B9006, Culloden* ☎ *0844/493–2159* ⊕ *www.nts.org.uk/Culloden* ⊡ *£11* ☉ *Visitor center closed late Dec.–Feb.*

NAIRN

12 miles east of Culloden Moor, 17 miles east of Inverness, 92 miles west of Aberdeen.

This once-prosperous fishing village is now more likely to lure golfers than sailors. Nearby is Cawdor Castle, loaded with history. East of Nairn pier is a long beach, great for a stroll.

GETTING HERE AND AROUND
A car gives you the most flexibility, but Nairn is close to Inverness (via A96), and regular local buses serve the town.

EXPLORING
FAMILY
Fodor's Choice
★
Cawdor Castle. Shakespeare's Macbeth was the Thane of Cawdor (a local officer of the crown), but the sense of history that exists within the turreted walls of Cawdor Castle is certainly more than fictional. Cawdor is a lived-in castle, not an abandoned, decaying structure. The earliest part is the 14th-century central tower; the rooms contain family portraits, tapestries, fine furniture, and paraphernalia reflecting 600 years of history. Outside the walls are sheltered gardens and woodland walks. Children will have a ball exploring the lush and mysterious Big Wood, with its wildflowers and varied wildlife. There are lots of creepy stories and fantastic tales amid the dank dungeons and drawbridges. If the castle sounds appealing, keep in mind that the estate has cottages to rent. ✉ *B9090, Cawdor* ✛ *5 miles southwest of Nairn* ☎ *01667/404401* ⊕ *www.cawdorcastle.com* ⊡ *Castle £11.20; grounds only £6.50* ☉ *Closed mid-Oct.–Apr.*

Nairn Museum. The fishing boats have moved to larger ports, but Nairn's historical flavor has been preserved at the Nairn Museum, in a hand-some Georgian building in the center of town. Exhibits emphasize artifacts, photographs, and model boats relating to the town's fishing past. A genealogy service is also offered. A library in the same building has a strong local-history section. ✉ *Viewfield House, Viewfield Dr.* ☎ *01667/456791* ⊕ *www.nairnmuseum.co.uk* ⊡ *£4* ☉ *Closed Sun. and Nov.–Mar.*

9

CLOSE UP

Bonnie Prince Charlie

His life became the stuff of legend. Charles Edward Louis John Casimir Silvester Maria Stuart—better known as Bonnie Prince Charlie, or the Young Pretender—was born in Rome in 1720. The grandson of ousted King James II of England, Scotland, and Ireland (King James VII of Scotland) and son of James Stuart, the Old Pretender, he was the focus of Jacobite hopes to reclaim the throne of Scotland. Charles was charming and attractive, and he enjoyed more than the occasional drink.

In 1745 Charles led a Scottish uprising to restore his father to the throne. He sailed to the Outer Hebrides with only a few men but with promised support from France. When that support failed to arrive, he sought help from the Jacobite supporters, many from the Highland clans, who were faithful to his family. With 6,000 men behind him, Charles saw victory in Prestonpans and Falkirk, but the tide turned when he lied to his men about additional Jacobite troops waiting south of the border. When these fictitious troops did not materialize, his army retreated to Culloden where, on April 16, 1746, they were massacred.

Charles escaped to the Isle of Benbecula, where he met and is rumored to have fallen in love with Flora MacDonald. After he had hidden there for a week, Flora dressed him as her maid and brought him to sympathizers on the Isle of Skye, who helped him escape to France.

Scotland endured harsh reprisals from the government after the rebellion. As for Charles, he spent the rest of his life in drunken exile, taking the title Count of Albany. In 1772 he married Princess Louise of Stolberg-Gedern, only to separate from her eight years later. He died a broken man in Rome in 1788.

Phoenix Boat Trips. With one-hour and two-hour trips by boat from Nairn harbor into the Moray Firth, Phoenix Boat Trips offers you the chance to see dolphins in their breeding areas. The daily departure times for the modern, ex-naval SWIFT vessels vary depending on the tides and the weather. Evening trips are offered on certain dates in summer. ✉ *Nairn Harbour* ☎ *0770/316–8097* 🌐 *www.dolphin-trips-nairn.co.uk* 🎫 *Tours from £18.*

WHERE TO STAY

$$$$ B&B/INN Fodor's Choice ★ 🏨 **Boath House.** Built in the 1820s, this stunning Regency manor house is surrounded by 20 acres of lovingly nurtured gardens. **Pros:** excellent dining; beautiful 20-acre grounds; relaxed atmosphere. **Cons:** some airplane noise; pricey. [$] *Rooms from: £325* ✉ *Off A96, Auldearn* ☎ *01667/454896* 🌐 *www.boath-house.com* 🛏 *8 rooms* 🍴 *Breakfast.*

SHOPPING

Auldearn Antiques. It's easy to spend an hour wandering around an old church filled with furniture, fireplaces, architectural antiques, and linens. The converted farmsteads have tempting antique (or just old) chinaware and textiles. ✉ *Dalmore Manse, Lethen Rd., Auldearn* ✣ *3 miles east of Nairn* ☎ *01667/453087* 🌐 *www.auldearnantiques.co.uk.*

Brodie Countryfare. Visit Brodie Countryfare only if you're feeling flush: you may covet the unusual knitwear, quality designer clothing and shoes, gifts, and toys, but they are *not* cheap. The excellent restaurant, on the other hand, is quite inexpensive. ⊠ *On A96, Brodie, Forres* ☎ *01309/641555* ⊕ *www.brodiecountryfare.com.*

GOLF

Nairn's courses are highly regarded by golfers and are very popular, so book far in advance.

Nairn Dunbar Golf Club. Founded in 1899, Nairn Dunbar Golf Club is a difficult course with gorse-lined fairways and lovely sea views. ■ TIP→ **Ask about the special-rate Nairn ticket, which allows you to play both this and the similarly named Nairn Golf Club for the bargain rate of £160 from April to October.** The special tickets are valid for four days. ⊠ *Lochloy Rd.* ☎ *01667/452741* ⊕ *www.nairndunbar.com* ⚐ *£40 (£30 after 1 pm) Apr. and Oct., £55 (£45 after 2 pm) May–Sept., £27 Nov.–Mar.* ⚑ *18 holes, 6765 yards, par 72.*

Nairn Golf Club. Well regarded in golfing circles, the Nairn Golf Club dates from 1887 and is the regular home of Scotland's Northern Open. Huge greens, aggressive gorse, a beach hazard for five of the holes, a steady prevailing wind, and distracting views across the Moray Firth make play on the Championship Course unforgettable. The adjoining 9-hole Cameron Course is ideal for a warm-up or a fun round for the family. ⊠ *Seabank Rd.* ☎ *01667/453208* ⊕ *www.nairngolfclub. co.uk* ⚐ *Championship Course, £135 (£85 off-peak) Apr.–Oct., £50 Nov.–Mar.; Cameron Course, £20* ⚑ *Championship Course: 18 holes, 6774 yards, par 72; Cameron Course: 9 holes, 1634 yards, par 29* ⚑ *Reservations essential.*

FORRES

10 miles east of Nairn.

The burgh of Forres is everything a Scottish medieval town should be, with a handsome tolbooth (the former courthouse and prison) and impressive gardens as its centerpiece. It's remarkable how well the old buildings have adapted to their modern retail uses. With two distilleries—one still operating, the other preserved as a museum—Forres is a key point on the Malt Whisky Trail. Brodie Castle is also nearby. Just 6 miles north you'll find Findhorn Ecovillage, and a sandy beach stretches along the edge of the semi-enclosed Findhorn Bay, which is excellent bird-watching territory.

GETTING HERE AND AROUND

Forres is easy to reach by car or bus from Inverness on the A96. Daily ScotRail trains run here from Inverness and Aberdeen.

EXPLORING

TOP ATTRACTIONS

Brodie Castle. This medieval castle was rebuilt and extended in the 17th and 19th centuries. Fine examples of late-17th-century plasterwork are preserved in the Dining Room and Blue Sitting Room; an impressive library and a superb collection of pictures extend into the 20th century.

The castle is about 24 miles east of Inverness, making it a good day trip. ✉ *Off A96, Brodie* ☎ *01309/641371* 🌐 *www.nts.org.uk* 🎟 *Castle £10.50, grounds free* ⏲ *Castle closed mid-Oct.–Mar. Grounds open all year.*

Dallas Dhu Historic Distillery. The final port of call on the Malt Whisky Trail, the Dallas Dhu Historic Distillery was the last distillery built in the 19th century and was still in operation until the 1980s. Today it holds a small museum that tells the story of Scotland's national drink. ✉ *Mannachie Rd.* ☎ *01309/676548* 🌐 *www.historicenvironment.scot* 🎟 *£6* ⏲ *Closed Thurs. and Fri. Oct.–Mar.*

WORTH NOTING

Benromach Distillery. The smallest distillery in Moray, Benromach was founded in 1898. It's now owned by whisky specialist Gordon and MacPhail, and it stocks a vast range of malts. An informative hourly tour ends with a tutored nosing and tasting. ✉ *Invererne Rd.* ☎ *01309/675968* 🌐 *www.benromach.com* 🎟 *£6* ⏲ *Closed late Dec.–early Jan.*

Findhorn Ecovillage. This education center is dedicated to developing "new ways of living infused with spiritual values." Drawing power from wind turbines, locals farm and garden to sustain themselves. A tour affords a thought-provoking glimpse into the lives of the ultra-independent villagers. See homes made out of whisky barrels, and the Universal Hall, filled with beautiful engraved glass. The Phoenix Shop sells organic foods and handmade crafts, and the Blue Angel Café serves organic and vegetarian fare. ✉ *The Park, off B9011, Findhorn* ✣ *6 miles from Forres* ☎ *01309/690311* 🌐 *www.findhorn.org* 🎟 *Free; tours £5* ⏲ *No tours Tues., Thurs., some Sun., and Dec.–mid-Apr.*

Sueno's Stone. At the eastern end of town stands Sueno's Stone, a 22-foot-tall pillar of stone carved with the ranks of soldiers from some long-forgotten battle. Nobody can quite agree on how old it is or what battle it marked, but it is generally believed to have been erected between AD 600 and 1000. ✉ *Findhorn Rd.* 🎟 *Free.*

WHERE TO STAY

$$ HOTEL 🏨 **Cluny Bank Hotel.** Take one look at any of this pretty Victorian hotel's unique bedrooms, filled with personal touches, and you could easily guess that this is a family-run venture. **Pros:** lovely hosts; tranquil residential area. **Cons:** some bathrooms a bit small. [$] *Rooms from: £130* ✉ *69 St Leonard's Rd.* ☎ *01309/674304* 🌐 *www.clunybankhotel.co.uk* 🛏 *7 rooms* 🍴 *Breakfast.*

SPORTS AND THE OUTDOORS

Findhorn Bay Beach. Along the edge of Findhorn Bay you'll find a long stretch of beach, great for an afternoon by the sea. You can reach the beach through the dunes from the northern end of the Findhorn Ecovillage, or park at the edge of the village of Findhorn for a shorter stroll. There are public restrooms, but few other amenities. **Amenities:** toilets. **Best for:** solitude; walking. ✉ *Off B89011, Findhorn.*

SPEYSIDE AND THE CAIRNGORMS

The Spey is a long river, running from Fort Augustus to the Moray Firth, and its fast-moving waters make for excellent fishing at many points along the way. They also give Speyside malt whiskies a softer flavor than those made with peaty island water. The area's native and planted pine forests draw many birds each spring and summer, and people come for miles to see the capercaillies and ospreys.

Defining the eastern edge of the Great Glen, Cairngorms National Park provides sporty types with all the adventure they could ask for, including walking, kayaking, rock climbing, and even skiing, if the winter is cold enough. The park has everything but the sea: craggy mountains, calm lochs, and swift rivers. While the unremarkable town of Aviemore may put off some travelers, the Cairngorms are truly stunning.

BOAT OF GARTEN

6 miles northeast of Aviemore.

In the peaceful village of Boat of Garten, the scent of pine trees mingles with an equally evocative smell—that of steam trains. You can take a nostalgic trip on the Strathspey Steam Railway between Aviemore and Boat of Garten. Close to Cairngorms National Park, Boat of Garten is building a reputation as a great place to stay while exploring the region.

GETTING HERE AND AROUND

This charming town is an easy drive from Inverness or Aviemore via the A9 and the A95. It's also serviced by local buses, and some people travel here on the Strathspey Steam Train.

EXPLORING

FAMILY **Landmark Forest Adventure Park.** About 4 miles northwest of Boat of Garten, the Landmark Forest Adventure Park has nature trails, a fire tower you can climb, and plenty of more adventurous attractions to keep younger ones entertained. Among the amusements are the Wonder Wood, where tricks like forced perspective are used to befuddle your senses; a heart-stopping parachute jump simulator; and raft rides of varying degrees of, well, wetness. You could easily spend half a day here. The park is open year-round, but most attractions close in winter. To get to Carrbridge, take the quiet B9153 rather than the crowded A9. ✉ *B9153, Carrbridge* ☎ *0800/731–3446* ⊕ *www.landmarkpark.co.uk* ✑ *Apr.–Oct., £20; Nov.–Mar., £6.75.*

Loch Garten Nature Reserve. Set in the heart of Abernethy Forest, the Loch Garten Nature Reserve offers a glimpse of the osprey, a large fishing bird that comes here to breed. The reserve, one of the last stands of ancient Scots pines in Scotland, attracts a host of birds, including the bright crossbill and the crested tit. You might also spot the rarely seen red squirrel. The sanctuary is administered by the Royal Society for the Protection of Birds. ✉ *Off B970, 1 mile east of Boat of Garten, Nethy Bridge* ☎ *01479/831476* ⊕ *www.rspb.org.uk* ✑ *Reserve free; Osprey Centre £5* ⊘ *Osprey Centre closed early Sept.–Mar.*

9

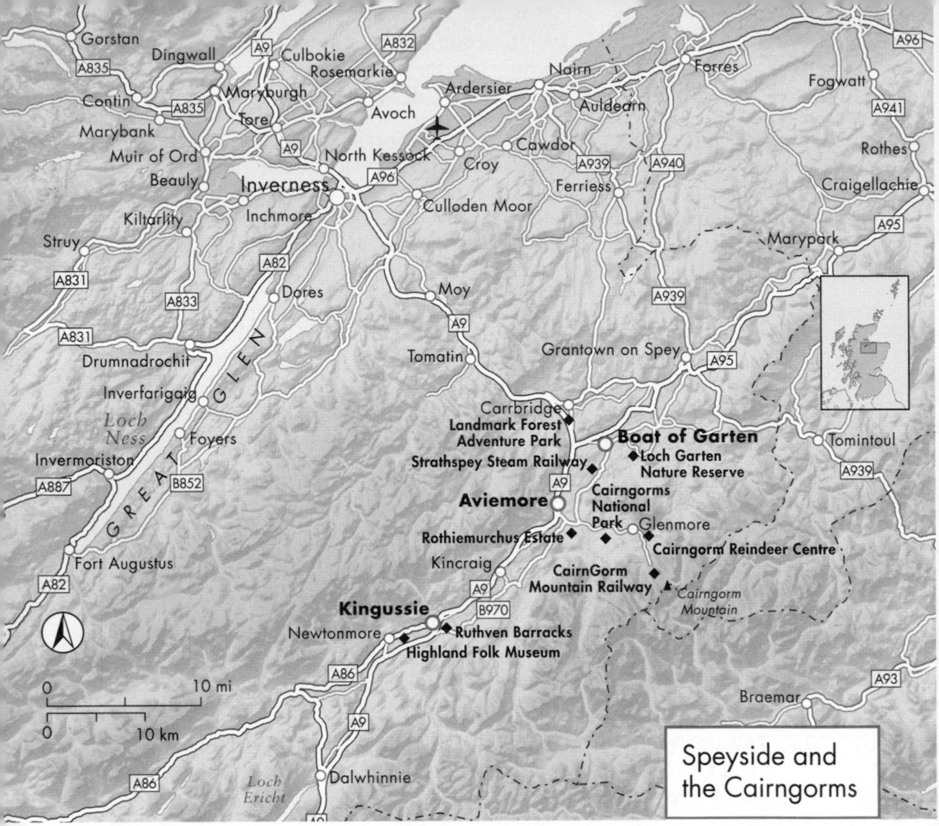

[FAMILY] **Strathspey Steam Railway.** The oily scent of smoke and steam hangs faintly in the air near the authentically preserved train station in Boat of Garten. Travel in old-fashioned style and enjoy superb views of the high and often white domes of the Cairngorm Mountains. Breakfasts, lunches, and special dinners are served on board from March to October and in December. ⚠ **For the full experience, check the details carefully before you book, especially outside of the high season—less romantic diesel engines are used on certain days.** ✉ *Boat of Garten station, Spey Ave.* ☎ *01479/810725* 🌐 *www.strathspeyrailway.co.uk* 🎫 *£14.25 round-trip.*

WHERE TO STAY

$$ HOTEL 🏨 **The Boat Hotel.** Great views of the Strathspey Steam Railway, welcoming traditional decor, and a wide variety of room types make this hotel much more than just a base for exploring the Cairngorms. **Pros:** good views; peaceful location; garden access an option. **Cons:** not all rooms are family-friendly; some shared spaces need a lick of paint. [$] *Rooms from: £120* ✉ *Spey Ave.* ☎ *01479/831258* 🌐 *www.boathotel.co.uk* 🛏 *34 rooms* 🍴 *Breakfast.*

$$ HOTEL 🏨 **Mountview Hotel.** An old hunting lodge perched in the hills of Nethybridge, this hotel boasts great views out over the valley. **Pros:** stunning setting; pretty views; good restaurant. **Cons:** some shared bathrooms.

$ *Rooms from: £140* ✉ *B970, Nethy Bridge* ☎ *01479/821248* ⊕ *www.mountviewhotel.co.uk* ⟿ *12 rooms* ⋈ *Breakfast.*

SPORTS AND THE OUTDOORS

GOLF

Fodor's Choice ★ **Boat of Garten Golf Club.** This is one of Scotland's greatest "undiscovered" courses. The club, which dates to the late 19th century, was redesigned and extended by James Braid in 1932, and each of its 18 holes has a strong Highland feel. Some cut through birch wood and heathery rough, and most have long views to the Cairngorms. An unusual feature is the preserved steam railway that runs alongside part of the course. ✉ *Nethybridge Rd.* ☎ *01479/831282* ⊕ *www.boat-golf.com* 🎫 *£47* ⅄ *18 holes, 5876 yards, par 70* ⟝ *Reservations essential.*

BOAT OF GARTEN'S FERRY

A ferry that once linked both sides of the River Spey gave its name to Boat of Garten. The first official record of the ferry is in 1662, although it had probably been there longer. The village itself did not appear until the coming of the railway, in 1868, when cottages sprang up between the railway line and the ferry crossing. When it was time to pick a name, the ferry seemed like a good symbol for the locale. Not long after that, bridges were built across the River Spey, and demand for the little ferry disappeared. The name, on the other hand, stuck.

AVIEMORE

6 miles southwest of Boat of Garten, 30 miles south of Inverness.

At the foot of the Cairngorms, once-quiet Aviemore now has all the brashness and boxiness of a year-round holiday resort. In the summer months it's filled with walkers, cyclists, and rock climbers, so it's a convenient place for stocking up on supplies. However, many of the smaller villages nearby are quieter places to stay. ■ **TIP→ Be forewarned: this region can get very cold above 3,000 feet, and weather conditions can change rapidly, even in the middle of summer.**

GETTING HERE AND AROUND

The A9, Scotland's major north–south artery, runs past Aviemore. From Boat of Garten, take the A95. The town is serviced by regular trains and buses from Inverness, Edinburgh, and Glasgow.

ESSENTIALS

Visitor Information Aviemore Visitor Information Centre. ✉ *7 Grampian Rd.* ☎ *01479/810930* ⊕ *visitcairngorms.com.*

EXPLORING

Fodor's Choice ★ **CairnGorm Mountain Railway.** A funicular railway to the top of Cairn Gorm (the mountain that gives its name to the region), the CairnGorm Mountain Railway operates daily, year-round, and affords sweeping views across the Cairngorms and the broad valley of the Spey. At the top is a visitor center and restaurant. The round-trip journey takes about half an hour. Reservations are recommended. ✉ *B970* ☎ *01479/861261* ⊕ *www.cairngormmountain.co.uk* 🎫 *£13.50.*

9

FAMILY   **Cairngorm Reindeer Centre.** On the high slopes of the Cairngorms, you may see the reindeer herd that was introduced here in the 1950s. The reindeer are docile creatures that seem to enjoy human company. Ranger-led visits to the herd are offered at least once a day from February to December, weather permitting. From June to August you can also accompany rangers on gentle half-day treks through the mountains. From April through December a small herd of young reindeer are cared for at a paddock near the visitor center; you can visit (and pet them) for a small fee. Bring waterproof gear, as conditions can be wet and muddy. ⊠ *Glenmore Forest Park, B970 ✛ 6 miles east of Aviemore* ☎ *01479/861228* ⊕ *www.cairngormreindeer.co.uk* ⊠ *£14; paddock £3.50* ☺ *Closed Jan.–early Feb.*

Fodor's Choice   **Cairngorms National Park.** A rugged wilderness of mountains, moorlands,
★   glens, and lochs, the sprawling Cairngorms National Park, established in 2003, takes in more than 1,700 square miles. Past Loch Morlich, at the high parking lot on the exposed shoulders of the Cairngorm Mountains, are dozens of trails for hiking and cycling. This is a massive park, encompassing small towns as well as countryside, but a good place to start exploring is the main visitor center in Aviemore. The staff can dispense maps, expert advice on the best trails, and also information on guided walks and other activities. (There are additional Cairngorms visitor centers in Braemar, Glenmore, Ballater, Tomintoul, Newtonmore, and Grantown-on-Spey.) Because much of the best scenery in the park is off-road—including ancient pine forests and open moorland—a particularly good way to cover ground in the park is on a pony trek. The **Rothiemurchus Estate** leads guided hacks for riders of all ability levels. The park is a haven for rare wildlife: a full 25% of Britain's endangered species have habitats in the park. Birding enthusiasts come here to look (and listen) for the Scottish crossbill—the only bird completely unique to Britain. Weather conditions in the park change abruptly, so be sure to bring cold-weather gear, particularly if you plan on hiking long distance. ⊠ *Visitor Information Centre, 7 The Parade, Grampian Rd.* ☎ *01479/810930* ⊕ *cairngorms.co.uk.*

FAMILY   **Rothiemurchus Estate.** This excellent activity center is among the best in
Fodor's Choice   the Cairngorms. It offers a host of organized outdoor diversions, includ-
★   ing guided pony rides, mountain biking, fishing, gorge swimming, and white-water rafting. It also offers ranger-guided safaris to see the park's rare and endangered wildlife, including red squirrels and "hairy heilan coos" (Highland slang for Highland cattle—docile, yaklike creatures). The Rothiemurchus Centre is the best place to get oriented and book activities; it also has a handy restaurant and a well-stocked shop selling plenty of fresh produce from the estate. One of the most beautiful parts of the estate is a nature reserve called **Loch an Eilein.** There are great low-level paths around the tree-rimmed loch—perfect for bikes—or longer trails to Glen Einich. A converted cottage beside Loch an Eilein serves as a visitor center, art gallery, and craft store. ⊠ *Rothiemurchus Centre, on B970, Inverdruie* ☎ *01479/812345* ⊕ *www.rothiemurchus. net* ⊠ *Free* ☺ *Gallery closed Oct.–Easter.*

WHERE TO EAT

$ CAFÉ 🍴 **Mountain Café.** On the main street in Aviemore, the Mountain Café is a useful pit stop for a hearty lunch or afternoon snack. Crowned Best Café in Scotland at the 2017 Scottish Food Awards, this small place has a big reputation that means it's rarely empty. **Known for:** lively atmosphere (be prepared to wait); award-winning baked goods. [$] *Average main: £10* ✉ *111 Grampian Rd.* ☎ *01479/812473* 🌐 *mountaincafe-aviemore.co.uk* 🕒 *No dinner.*

$$ MODERN BRITISH 🍴 **Old Bridge Inn.** Across a pedestrian bridge from Aviemore station, this old-style bar and conservatory restaurant serves what many locals call the best pub food in Aviemore. The menu changes with the seasons, but you can always expect simple dishes built around quality ingredients such as local lamb chops or Angus beef, as well as a variety of fresh fish. **Known for:** classic British fare; spirited live music. [$] *Average main: £17* ✉ *Dalfaber Rd.* ☎ *01479/811137* 🌐 *www.oldbridgeinn.co.uk.*

$ CAFÉ Fodor's Choice ★ 🍴 **The Potting Shed.** Seasonal fruits and smooth cream top many of the delectable desserts at this cake shop in a scenic garden south of Aviemore. Taught by his Norwegian mother, John Borrowman makes light sponges that contain no butter or fat (although you can't say the same thing about the rich cream they're topped with). **Known for:** outrageously tasty cakes; beautiful garden setting. [$] *Average main: £5* ✉ *Inshriach Nursery, B970* ☎ *01540/651287* 🌐 *www.inshriachnursery.co.uk* 🕒 *Closed Mon., Tues., and Nov.–Feb.*

WHERE TO STAY

$$ HOTEL 🏨 **Cairngorm Hotel.** Walk past the suit of armor standing guard at the entrance and you should already have a good idea of what awaits within this grand old house, the first building you'll see on exiting the train station. **Pros:** practical location; simple, traditional rooms; family rooms offered. **Cons:** not scenic; interior needs a refresh. [$] *Rooms from: £104* ✉ *77 Grampian Rd.* ☎ *01479/810233* 🌐 *www.cairngorm.com* 🛏 *31 rooms* 🍽 *Breakfast.*

$$ B&B/INN 🏨 **The Old Ministers Guest House.** Small but perfectly formed, this B&B offers a quality stay with a personal touch. **Pros:** welcoming feel; large rooms. **Cons:** no restaurant; a mile from Aviemore. [$] *Rooms from: £140* ✉ *B970* ☎ *01479/812181* 🌐 *www.theoldministershouse.co.uk* 🛏 *5 rooms* 🍽 *Breakfast.*

SPORTS AND THE OUTDOORS

Glenmore Lodge. In Cairngorms National Park, this is a good center for day and residential courses on rock and ice climbing, hiking, kayaking, ski touring, mountain biking, and more. Some classes are aimed at under-18s. There are superb facilities, such as an indoor climbing wall. ✉ *Signposted on B970, Glenmore* ✣ *About 9 miles east of Aviemore* ☎ *01479/861256* 🌐 *www.glenmorelodge.org.uk.*

G2 Outdoor. The wide range of adventures at G2 Outdoor includes white-water rafting, gorge walking, and rock climbing. The company offers a family float trip on the River Spey in summer, and in winter runs ski courses. ✉ *The Hatchery, Alvie Estate, off A9* ☎ *01540/651784* 🌐 *www.g2outdoor.co.uk.*

Mikes Bikes. This small bike shop stocks all the gear you might need to take advantage of the many paths around Aviemore. It also rents and repairs bikes. Prices start at £17 for four hours. ⊠ *Myrtlefield Shopping Centre, Grampian Rd.* ☎ *01479/810478* ⊕ *www.aviemorebikes.co.uk.*

KINGUSSIE

13 miles southwest of Aviemore.

Set in a wide glen, Kingussie is a pretty town east of the Monadhliath Mountains. With great distant views of the Cairngorms, it's perfect for those who would prefer to avoid the far more hectic town of Aviemore.

GETTING HERE AND AROUND

From Aviemore, Kingussie is easy to reach by car via the A9 and the A86. There are also good bus and train services between the two towns.

EXPLORING

FAMILY

Fodor'sChoice
★

Highland Folk Museum. Explore reconstructed Highland buildings, including a Victorian-era school-house, and watch tailors, clock makers, and joiners demonstrating their trades at this museum. Walking paths (or old-fashioned buses) take you to the 18th-century township that was a setting for the hit TV show *Outlander* and includes a peat house, made of turf, and a weaver's house. Throughout the museum there are hands-on exhibits like a working quern stone for grinding grain. ⊠ *Kingussie Rd., Newtonmore* ☎ *01540/673551* ⊕ *www.highlandfolk.com* ⊠ *Free* ⊗ *Closed Nov.–late Mar.*

> ### BIKING THE GLEN
>
> A dedicated bicycle path, created by Scotland's National Cycle Networks, runs from Glasgow to Inverness, passing through Fort William and Kingussie. Additionally, a good network of back roads snakes around Inverness and toward Nairn. The B862/B852, which runs by the southeast side of Loch Ness, has little traffic and is a good bet for cyclists. Stay off the A9, however, as it's busy with vehicular traffic on both sides of Aviemore. The very busy A82 main road, along the northwest bank of Loch Ness via Drumnadrochit, is for the same reason not recommended for cyclists.

Ruthven Barracks. Looking like a ruined castle on a mound, Ruthven Barracks is redolent with tales of "the '45" (as the last Jacobite rebellion is often called). The defeated Jacobite forces rallied here after the battle at Culloden, but then abandoned and blew up the government outpost they had earlier captured. You'll see its crumbling, yet imposing, stone outline as you approach. ⊠ *B970* ⊹ *½ mile south of Kingussie* ☎ *01667/460232* ⊕ *www.historic-scotland.gov.uk* ⊠ *Free.*

WHERE TO EAT AND STAY

$$$$

BRITISH

Fodor'sChoice
★

✕ **The Cross at Kingussie.** This former tweed mill, with a narrow river running alongside its stone walls, is set in 4 acres of woodlands. With stone walls painted a creamy white, the intimate dining room is warmed by a crackling fireplace. **Known for:** perfectly curated set menus; stunning location; effortlessly beautiful interior. Ⓢ *Average main: £55* ⊠ *Tweed Mill Brae, Ardbroilach Rd.* ☎ *01540/661166* ⊕ *www.thecross.co.uk* ⊗ *Closed Jan. No dinner Sun. and Mon.*

$ B&B/INN 🏨 **Coig Na Shee.** This century-old Highland lodge has a warm and cozy atmosphere, and each of its spacious bedrooms is unique, with well-chosen furnishings and soothing color schemes. **Pros:** quiet location; great walks from house; kids aged 8–16 can share with parents for £20 (including breakfast). **Cons:** tricky to get to without a car; no children under eight. [$] *Rooms from: £75* ✉ *Laggan Rd., Newtonmore* ☎ *01540/670109* 🌐 *www.coignashee.co.uk* 🛏 *5 rooms* 🍴 *Breakfast.*

$$ B&B/INN Fodor'sChoice ★ 🏨 **Sutherlands Guest House.** Finding that sweet spot where contemporary meets cozy is no mean feat, but the husband-and-wife team behind this welcoming guesthouse make it look simple. **Pros:** lovely rooms; great value. **Cons:** hilltop location best accessed by car. [$] *Rooms from: £105* ✉ *Old Distillery Rd.* ☎ *01540/661155* 🌐 *www.sutherlandskingussie.co.uk* 🛏 *5 rooms* 🍴 *Breakfast.*

LOCH NESS, FORT WILLIAM, AND NEARBY

Compared with other lochs, Loch Ness is by no means known for its beauty, but it draws attention for its famous monster. Heading south from Inverness, you can travel along the loch's quiet east side or the more touristy west side. A pleasant morning can be spent at Urquhart Castle, in the tiny town of Drumnadrochit, or a bit farther south in the pretty town of Fort Augustus, where the Caledonian Canal meets Loch Ness. As you travel south and west, the landscape opens up and the Nevis Range comes into view.

From Fort William you can visit the dark, cloud-laden mountains of Glencoe and the desolate stretch of moors and lochans at Rannoch Moor. Travelers drive through this region to experience the landscape, which changes at nearly every turn. It's a brooding, haunting area that's worth a visit in any season.

The Road to the Isles, less romantically known as the A830, leads from Fort William to the coastal towns of Arisaig, Morar, and Mallaig, with access to the Small Isles of Rum, Eigg, Canna, and Muck. From here you can also visit the Isle of Skye (⇨ *see Chapter 10*) via the ferry at Mallaig.

9

DRUMNADROCHIT

14 miles south of Inverness.

A tourist hub at the curve of the road, Drumnadrochit is not known for its style or culture, but it attracts plenty of people interested in searching for mythical monsters. There aren't many good restaurants, but there are some decent-enough hotels.

GETTING HERE AND AROUND

It's easy to get here from Fort Augustus or Inverness via the A82, either by car or by local bus. However, a more leisurely alternative is driving the B862 south from Inverness and along the east bank of Loch Ness. Take the opportunity to view the waterfalls at Foyers and the peaceful, reedy Loch Tarff. Descend through forests and moorland until the road runs around the southern tip of Loch Ness. The half-hidden track beside the road is a remnant of the military road built by General Wade.

EXPLORING

TOP ATTRACTIONS

Loch Ness. From the A82 you get many views of the formidable and famous Loch Ness, which has a greater volume of water than any other Scottish loch, a maximum depth of more than 800 feet, and—perhaps you've already heard?—a monster. Early travelers who passed this way included English lexicographer Dr. Samuel Johnson (1709–84) and his guide and biographer, James Boswell (1740–95), who were on their way to the Hebrides in 1783. They remarked at the time about the poor condition of the population and the squalor of their homes. Another early travel writer and naturalist, Thomas Pennant (1726–98), noted that the loch kept the locality frost-free in winter. Even General Wade—remembered for destroying much of Hadrian's Wall in England—came here, his troops blasting and digging a road up much of the eastern shore. None of these observant early travelers ever made mention of a monster. Clearly, they had not read the local guidebooks. ⊠ *Drumnadrochit.*

FAMILY **Loch Ness Centre & Exhibition.** If you're in search of the infamous monster, the Loch Ness Centre & Exhibition documents the fuzzy photographs, the unexplained sonar readings, and the sincere testimony of eyewitnesses. It's said that the loch's huge volume of water has a warming effect on the local weather, making the loch conducive to mirages in still, warm conditions—but you'll have to make up your own mind. From Easter to October you can also take hourly cruises of the loch (£14). The cruises leave from the little craft store at the Loch Ness Lodge Hotel in Drumnadrochit; no prebooking allowed. ⊠ *On A82* ☎ *01456/450573* ⊕ *www.lochness.com* ⌑ *£7.95.*

Urquhart Castle. About 2 miles southeast of Drumnadrochit, this castle is a favorite Loch Ness monster–watching spot. This romantically broken-down fortress stands on a promontory overlooking the loch, as it has since the Middle Ages. Because of its central and strategic position in the Great Glen line of communication, the castle has a complex history involving military offense and defense, as well as its own destruction and renovation. The castle was begun in the 13th century and was destroyed before the end of the 17th century to prevent its use by the Jacobites. A visitor center gives an idea of what life was like here in medieval times. ⊠ *A82* ☎ *01456/450551* ⊕ *www.historic-scotland.gov. uk/places* ⌑ *£9.*

WORTH NOTING

Fort Augustus. The best place to see the Caledonian Canal's 29 locks in action is at Fort Augustus, at the southern tip of Loch Ness and around a half-hour drive from Drumnadrochit. At the visitor center in this scenic village you can learn all about this historic marvel of engineering, and set off on a picturesque walk that takes in the stunning vistas along the canal: mountains, lochs, and glens, and to the south, the profile of Ben Nevis. Fort Augustus itself was captured by the Jacobite clans during the 1745 rebellion. Later the fort was rebuilt as a Benedictine abbey, but the monks no longer live here. ⊠ *Fort Augustus.*

Jacobite Cruises. The company runs morning and afternoon cruises on Loch Ness to Urquhart Castle and other destinations throughout the

CLOSE UP

"Nessie": The Loch Ness Monster

Tall tales involving some kind of beast inhabiting the dark waters of Loch Ness go all the way back to St. Columba in the 7th century AD—but, for the most part, the legend of "Nessie" is a disappointingly modern one. In 1933, two vacationing Londoners gave an intriguing account to a newspaper, describing a large, unidentifiable creature that slithered in front of their car before plunging into the loch. Later that year, a local man, Hugh Gray, took the first purported photograph of the monster—and Nessie fever was born. The pictures kept coming—none of them *too* clear, of course—and before long the resident monster turned into a boon for the local tourism industry. Fortunately for them, the age of camera phones has not dented Nessie's popularity; you don't have to search far on the Internet to find all sorts of photos of something—*anything*—that must surely be the monster, if you only squint a little. But does anybody seriously believe in it? Well... no. But like all good legends, there is just enough doubt to keep the campfire tales alive. In 2006 declassified documents even revealed that, in the 1980s, Prime Minister Margaret Thatcher considered plans to declare the Loch Ness monster a protected species, as a safeguard against the hordes of bounty hunters she feared would descend should it ever be proven to exist.

region. The harbor is 5 miles northeast of Drumnadrochit via the A82. ✉ *Clansman Harbour, A82* ☎ *01463/233999* 🌐 *www.jacobite.co.uk* 🎟 *Tours from £14.*

WHERE TO STAY

$$ HOTEL Fodor's Choice ★ 🏨 **Glengarry Castle Hotel.** Tucked away in Invergarry, this rambling baronial mansion is just south of Loch Ness and within easy reach of the Great Glen's most popular sights. **Pros:** atmospheric building and gardens; good-value take-out lunches; family rooms available. **Cons:** no elevator. [$] *Rooms from: £145* ✉ *Off A82, Invergarry* ✥ *26 miles south of Drumnadrochit* ☎ *01809/501254* 🌐 *www.glengarry.net* ⏲ *Closed mid-Nov.–mid-Mar.* 🛏 *26 rooms* 🍴 *Breakfast.*

$$$ B&B/INN Fodor's Choice ★ 🏨 **Loch Ness Lodge.** Run by siblings Scott and Iona Sutherland, Loch Ness Lodge is an exquisite place: opulent, classy, and welcoming. **Pros:** excellent staff; superb views; lovely rooms. **Cons:** near a busy road; no restaurant; don't confuse it with a (lesser) hotel of the same name in Drumnadrochit. [$] *Rooms from: £210* ✉ *A82, Brachla* ☎ *01456/459469* 🌐 *www.loch-ness-lodge.com* 🛏 *7 rooms* 🍴 *Breakfast.*

EN ROUTE

A more leisurely alternative to the fast-moving traffic on the busy A82, and one that combines monster-spotting with peaceful road touring, is the **B862** south from Inverness and along the east bank of Loch Ness. Take the opportunity to view the waterfalls at Foyers and the peaceful, reedy Loch Tarff. Descend through forests and moorland until the road runs around the southern tip of Loch Ness. The half-hidden track beside the road is a remnant of the military road built by General Wade.

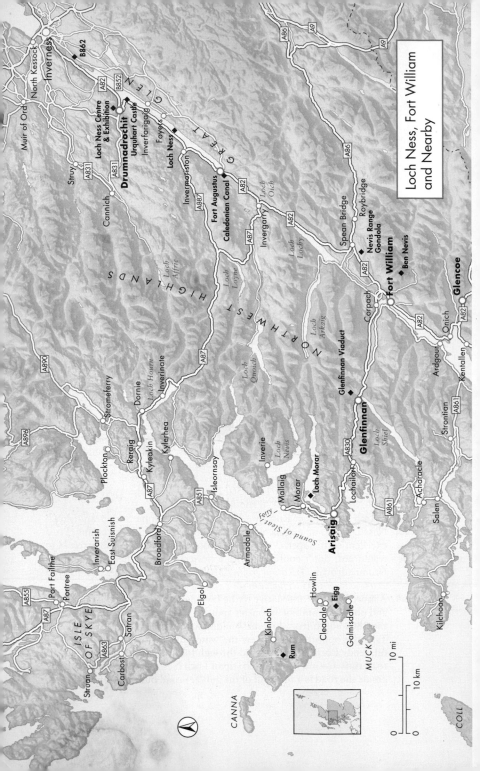

Loch Ness, Fort William and Nearby

FORT WILLIAM

32 miles southwest of Fort Augustus, 69 miles southwest of Inverness, 108 miles northwest of Glasgow, 138 miles northwest of Edinburgh.

As its name suggests, Fort William originated as a military outpost, first established by Oliver Cromwell's General Monk in 1655 and refortified by George I (1660–1727) in 1715 to help combat an uprising by the turbulent Jacobite clans. It remains the southern gateway to the Great Glen and the far west. It's not Scotland's most charming or authentic town, but it's got several good hotels and makes a convenient base for exploring the surrounding countryside.

GETTING HERE AND AROUND

From Glasgow (to the south) and Inverness (to the north), the A82 takes you the entire way. From Edinburgh, take the M9 to the A84. This empties into the A85, which connects to the A82 that takes you to Fort William. Roads around Fort William are well maintained, but mostly one lane in each direction. They can be very busy in summer.

A long-distance Scottish Citylink bus connects Glasgow and Fort William. ScotRail has trains from London, as well as connections from Glasgow and Edinburgh. It also operates a train service three times a day between Fort William and Mallaig.

ESSENTIALS

Visitor Information Fort William Tourist Information Centre. ✉ *15 High St.* ☎ *01397/701801* ⊕ *www.visitfortwilliam.co.uk, www.visitscotland.com.*

EXPLORING

Ben Nevis. The tallest mountain in the British Isles, 4,406-foot Ben Nevis looms over Fort William, less than 4 miles from Loch Linnhe. A trek to its summit is a rewarding experience, but you should be fit and well prepared—food and water, map and compass, first-aid kit, whistle, hat, gloves, and warm clothing (yes, even in summer) for starters—as the unpredictable weather can make it a hazardous hike. Ask for advice at the local tourist office before you begin.

FAMILY
Fodor's Choice
★

Jacobite Steam Train. The most relaxing way to take in the landscape of birch- and bracken-covered wild slopes is by rail. The best ride is on the Jacobite Steam Train, a spectacularly scenic 84-mile round-trip that runs between Fort William and Mallaig. You'll see mountains, lochs, beaches, and islands along the way. There are two trips a day (weekdays only outside high season). ✉ *Station Sq.* ☎ *0844/850–4685* ⊕ *www.westcoastrailways.co.uk* 🎫 *£35* 🕙 *Closed late Dec.–late Apr.*

Nevis Range Gondola. Those who want to climb a mountain, without the need for hiking boots and an iron will, will prefer to make the journey in a gondola. These cable cars rise nearly 2,000 feet to the summit of Aonach Mor, part of the Nevis range. The journey takes about 15 minutes, and needless to say the views of the Great Glen are incredible—but definitely not for those without a head for heights. Call ahead for times, especially in winter—the published opening hours are a little confusing. ✉ *A82* ☎ *01397/705825* ⊕ *www.nevisrange.co.uk* 🎫 *£14* 🕙 *Closed mid-Nov.–mid-Dec.*

9

Fodor'sChoice ★ **West Highland Museum.** In the town center, the small but fascinating West Highland Museum explores the history of Prince Charles Edward Stuart and the 1745 rebellion. Included in the museum's folk exhibits are a costume and tartan display and an excellent collection of Jacobite relics. One of the most intriguing objects here is a tray decorated with a distorted image of Bonnie Prince Charlie that only becomes visible when reflected in a wine glass or goblet. This elaborate ruse enabled clandestine supporters among the nobility to raise a (treasonous) toast without fear of discovery. ✉ *Cameron Sq.* ☎ *01397/702169* 🌐 *www.westhighlandmuseum.org.uk* 🎟 *Free* 🕒 *Closed Sun. in Sept.–June, and Mon.–Sat. in July and Aug.*

WHERE TO EAT

$$ SEAFOOD Fodor'sChoice ★ 🍴 **Crannog Seafood Restaurant.** With a reputation for quality and simplicity, this restaurant on the town pier serves outstanding seafood. Fishing boats draw up on the shores of Loch Linnhe and deliver their catch straight to the kitchen. **Known for:** small but well-curated menu; idyllic lochside location. [$] *Average main: £19* ✉ *The Pier* ☎ *01397/705589* 🌐 *www.crannog.net.*

$$ MODERN BRITISH 🍴 **The Lime Tree.** One of Fort William's most upscale culinary spots, this restaurant is unfussy and modern inside, with low-hanging lamps, rich jewel-toned walls, and solid wood furniture. Expect filling dishes that, while not overly complex, are given an edge with embellishments such as fennel sauerkraut or marrowbone crumble. **Known for:** some of Fort William's most interesting food; inspired desserts. [$] *Average main: £19* ✉ *The Old Manse, Achintore Rd.* ☎ *01397/701806* 🌐 *www.limetreefortwilliam.co.uk* 🕒 *No lunch.*

$ CAFÉ 🍴 **Lochaber Farm Shop Cafe.** The lovely café at this friendly farm-and-crafts store makes for a perfect pit stop if you're visiting Ben Nevis. The shop, which overlooks the mountain, sells produce from Lochaber farm, also put to great use in tasty light lunches—free-range-chicken soup, perhaps, or sandwiches filled with local beef or ham. **Known for:** Ben Nevis views; home-baked treats. [$] *Average main: £7* ✉ *Lochaber Rural Complex, Torlundy* ☎ *01397/708686* 🌐 *www.lochaberfarmshop.com* 🕒 *Closed Mon. and Tues. (Mon. only in summer). No dinner.*

WHERE TO STAY

$$ B&B/INN Fodor'sChoice ★ 🏨 **Crolinnhe.** An elegant Victorian house with colorful gardens, this exceptionally comfortable B&B overlooks Loch Linnhe, yet is only a 10-minute walk from town. **Pros:** stunning loch views; great breakfasts; comfortable rooms. **Cons:** final payment only by cash or check. [$] *Rooms from: £140* ✉ *Grange Rd.* ☎ *01397/702709* 🌐 *www.crolinnhe.co.uk* 💳 *No credit cards* 🕒 *Closed Nov.–Easter* 🛏 *3 rooms* 🍽 *Breakfast.*

$$$ B&B/INN Fodor'sChoice ★ 🏨 **The Grange.** This meticulously renovated Victorian villa stands in pretty gardens a 10-minute walk from downtown. **Pros:** amazing location; great attention to detail; elegant lounge with plenty of books. **Cons:** no restaurant; not suitable for families with younger children. [$] *Rooms from: £180* ✉ *Grange Rd.* ☎ *01397/705516* 🌐 *www.grangefortwilliam.com* 🕒 *Closed Oct.–Mar.* 🛏 *2 rooms* 🍽 *Breakfast.*

$$$$ HOTEL 🏨 **Inverlochy Castle Hotel.** A red-granite Victorian mansion turned luxury boutique hotel, Inverlochy Castle stands on 50 acres of woodlands in the shadow of Ben Nevis, with striking scenery on every side; prices are high, but you could have a meal here to take in the ambience. **Pros:** spectacular setting; sumptuous public areas; top restaurant; children under seven free

(when sharing with parents). **Cons:** very expensive; must dress up for dinner. [$] *Rooms from: £490* ✉ *A82* ☎ *01397/702177* 🌐 *www.inverlochycastlehotel.com* ⏲ *Closed Jan. and Feb.* 🛏 *17 rooms* 🍴 *Breakfast.*

$ B&B/INN **Myrtle Bank Guest House.** This sweet, cheerful guesthouse is in a converted Victorian villa on the banks of Loch Linnhe. **Pros:** great views; friendly owners; convenient location. **Cons:** ground-floor rooms don't have such nice views; breakfast finishes early; some shared bathrooms. [$] *Rooms from: £75* ✉ *Achintore Rd.* ☎ *01397/702034* 🌐 *www.myrtlebankguesthouse.co.uk* 🛏 *25 rooms* 🍴 *Breakfast.*

SPORTS AND THE OUTDOORS

BICYCLING

Nevis Range Mountain Bike Track. For a thrilling ride down Ben Nevis, take the gondola up to the beginning of the Nevis Range Mountain Bike Track and then shoot off on a 2,000-foot descent. The lift costs £14.50. It's open mid-May to mid-September, weather permitting. (Also closed on certain dates for races; call ahead to check). Bike rentals are available near the gondola. ⚠ **Remember, though, that this is seriously mountainous territory and is only recommended for hard-core cyclists.** ✉ *A82* ☎ *01397/705825* 🌐 *bike.nevisrange.co.uk.*

GOLF

Fort William Golf Club. This excellent course has spectacular views of Ben Nevis (indeed, it partly occupies its lower slope). The Highland course appeals to beginners and experts alike, drawn as much for the beautiful setting as the thoroughly reasonable green fees. Watch out for the treacherous 4th hole—it looks simple, but a fierce prevailing wind will test even the most practiced swing. ✉ *Torlundy* ☎ *01397/704464* 🌐 *www.fortwilliamgolf.co.uk* 🎫 *£30, full day £40* ⛳ *18 holes, 6217 yards, par 70.*

HIKING

This area—especially around Glen Nevis, Glencoe, and Ben Nevis—is popular with hikers; however, routes are not well marked, so contact the Fort William tourist information center before you go. The center will provide you with expert advice based on your interests, level of fitness, and hiking experience.

Fodor's Choice ★ **Glen Nevis.** For a walk in Glen Nevis, drive north from Fort William on the A82 toward Fort Augustus. On the outskirts of town, just before the bridge over the River Nevis, turn right up the road signposted Glen Nevis. About 8 miles along this road is a parking lot where a footpath leads to waterfalls and a steel-cable bridge (1 mile), and then to Steall, a ruined croft beside a boulder-strewn stream (a good picnic place). You can continue up the glen for some distance without danger of becoming lost, so long as you stay on the path and keep the river to your right. Watch your step going through the tree-lined gorge. The return route is back the way you came.

GLENCOE

16 miles south of Fort William, 92 miles north of Glasgow, 44 miles northwest of Edinburgh.

Fodor's Choice ★ Glencoe is both a small town and a region of stunning grandeur, with high peaks and secluded glens. Dramatic scenery is the main attraction here;

9

it's as awesomely beautiful for a drive as it is for a hike. The A82—the main route through Glencoe—can get surprisingly crowded in high season, but it's one of the great scenic drives in Scotland. This area, where wild, craggy buttresses loom darkly over the road, has a special place in the folk memory of Scotland: the glen was the site of an infamous massacre in 1692, still remembered in the Highlands for the treachery with which soldiers of the Campbell clan, acting as a government militia, treated their hosts, the MacDonalds. According to Highland code, in his own home a clansman should give shelter even to his sworn enemy. In the face of bitter weather, the Campbells were accepted as guests by the MacDonalds. Apparently acting on orders from the British crown, the Campbells turned on their hosts and murdered them. The Massacre of Glencoe has gained an unlikely resurgence of fame in recent years, since it was revealed to be the historical basis for the so-called "Red Wedding" in George R.R. Martin's popular books (and HBO series) *Game of Thrones*.

GETTING HERE AND AROUND

Glencoe is easily accessed by car via the A82. ScotRail trains and regional buses arrive from most of Scotland's major cities.

EXPLORING

Visitor Center at Glencoe. The National Trust for Scotland's Visitor Center at Glencoe tells the story of the MacDonald massacre and has excellent displays about this area of outstanding natural beauty. You can also get expert advice about hiking trails. ✉ *Off A82* ✥ *1 mile south of Glencoe Village* ☎ *01855/811307* 🌐 *www.glencoe-nts.org.uk* 🎫 *Exhibition £6.50* ⏲ *Closed Mon.–Wed. Nov.–late Mar.*

WHERE TO STAY

$$$$ B&B/INN Fodor's Choice ★ 🏨 **Glencoe House.** Peaceful surroundings, arresting views, and the friendliest of welcomes await you at this former Victorian hunting lodge. **Pros:** beautiful landscape; superb restoration; lovely hosts. **Cons:** expensive; few facilities. [$] *Rooms from: £340* ✉ *Glencoe Lochan* ☎ *01855/811179* 🌐 *www.glencoe-house.com* 🛏 *13 rooms* 🍴 *No meals.*

SPORTS AND THE OUTDOORS

FAMILY **Glencoe Activities.** This popular outdoor center west of Ballachulish offers a long list of high-energy activities, from rock climbing to white-water rafting, and even hair-raising vertical canyon explorations complete with 500-foot descents. However, there's a welcome twist here—it also caters to those with more limited mobility (or less adventurous souls). Guided Segway tours (£35) last 50 minutes and take you through some spectacular scenery, with stunning mountain views and even a trail along a stretch of Loch Leven. ✉ *Dragon's Tooth Golf Course, off A828* ✥ *4 miles west of Glencoe* ☎ *01855/811695* 🌐 *www.glencoeactivities.com.*

GLENFINNAN

10 miles west of Fort William, 33 miles northwest of Glencoe.

Perhaps the most visitor-oriented stop on the route between Fort William and Mallaig, Glenfinnan has much to offer if you're interested in Scottish history. Here the National Trust for Scotland has capitalized on the romance surrounding the story of the Jacobites and their attempts to return a Stewart monarch and the Roman Catholic religion to a country that had become staunchly Protestant. It was at Glenfinnan that the rash adventurer Bonnie Prince Charlie gathered his meager forces for the final Jacobite rebellion of 1745–46.

GETTING HERE AND AROUND

If you're driving from Fort William, travel via the A830. For great views, take a ride on the Jacobite Steam Train, which you can catch in Fort William.

EXPLORING

Glenfinnan Monument. One of the most striking monuments in Britain, the Glenfinnan Monument commemorates the place where Bonnie Prince Charlie raised his standard. The tower, which was built in 1815, overlooks Loch Shiel; note, however, that the figure on the top is a Highlander, not the prince himself. The story of his ill-fated campaign is told in the nearby visitor center. You have to pay a small access fee, which includes a tour, when the center is open, but in truth the monument is just as picturesque when seen from the car park. ■ **TIP→ The view down Loch Shiel from the Glenfinnan Monument is one of the most photographed in Scotland.** ✉ *A830* ☎ *01397/722250* 🌐 *www.nts.org.uk* 🎟 *Exhibition free; guided tour £3.50* 🕒 *Visitor center closed Nov.–Mar.*

Glenfinnan Viaduct. The 1,248-foot-long Glenfinnan Viaduct was a genuine wonder when it was built in 1897, and remains so today. The railway's contractor, Robert MacAlpine (known among locals as "Concrete Bob") pioneered the use of concrete for bridges when his company built the Mallaig extension, which opened in 1901. In more recent times the viaduct became famous for its appearance in the Harry Potter films. The viaduct can be seen on foot; about half a mile west of the railway station in Glenfinnan, on the A380 road, is a small parking lot. Take the footpath from here; you'll reach the viaduct in about ½ mile. ✉ *A380.*

9

WHERE TO STAY

$$ HOTEL

🏨 **Glenfinnan House.** This handsome hotel on the shores of Loch Shiel was built in the 18th century as the home of Alexander MacDonald VII of Glenaladale, who was wounded fighting for Bonnie Prince Charlie; it was transformed into an even grander mansion in the 19th century. **Pros:** fabulous setting; atmospheric dining experience. **Cons:** some shared bathrooms. [$] *Rooms from: £140* ✉ *A830* ☎ *01397/722235* 🌐 *www.glenfinnanhouse.com* 🕒 *Closed mid-Nov.–mid-Mar.* 🛏 *14 rooms* 🍴 *Breakfast.*

EN ROUTE

As you get closer to **Arisaig** along A830, you'll be able to spot Eigg, a low island marked by the dramatic black peak of An Sgurr. Beyond Eigg is the larger Rum, with its range of hills and the Norse-named, cloud-capped Rum Coullin looming over the island. The breathtaking seaward views should continue to distract you from the road beside Loch nan Uamh (from Gaelic, meaning "cave" and pronounced *oo*-am). This loch is associated with Bonnie Prince Charlie's nine-month stay on the mainland, during which he gathered a small army, marched as far south as Derby in England, alarmed the king, retreated to unavoidable defeat at Culloden, and then spent a few months as a fugitive in the Highlands. A cairn by the shore marks the spot where the prince was rescued by a French ship; he never returned to Scotland.

ARISAIG

15 miles west of Glenfinnan.

Considering its small size, Arisaig, gateway to the **Small Isles,** offers a surprising choice of high-quality options for dining and lodging. To the north of Arisaig the road cuts across a headland to reach a stretch of coastline where silver sands glitter with the mica in the local rock; clear water, blue sky, and white sand lend a tropical flavor to the beaches—when the sun is shining.

From Arisaig try to visit a couple of the Small Isles: **Rum, Eigg, Muck,** and **Canna,** each tiny and with few or no inhabitants. Rum serves as a wildlife reserve, while Eigg has the world's first solely wind-, wave-, and solar-powered electricity grid.

GETTING HERE AND AROUND

From Glenfinnan, you reach Arisaig on the A830, the only road leading west. The Fort William–Mallaig train also stops here.

EXPLORING

Arisaig Marine. Along with whale-, seal-, and bird-watching excursions, Arisaig Marine runs a boat service from the harbor at Arisaig to the islands from May to September. There's also a handy gift shop and café. ✉ *Arisaig Harbour* ☎ *01687/450224* 🌐 *www.arisaig.co.uk* 🎟 *Round-trip fares from £18.*

Loch Morar. A small, unnamed side road just south of Mallaig leads east to an even smaller road that will bring you to Loch Morar, the deepest of all the Scottish lochs (more than 1,000 feet). The next deepest point is miles out into the Atlantic, beyond the continental shelf. The loch is said to have a resident monster, Morag, which undoubtedly gets less recognition than its famous cousin Nessie. Whether that means you have more chance of getting her to appear for a photograph, we can't say. ✉ *Loch Morar, Mallaig.*

WHERE TO EAT AND STAY

$$ FRENCH — 🍴 **Old Library.** On the waterfront, this 1722 barn has been converted into a fine, reasonably priced restaurant. Expect fairly simple, but tasty plates of local fish and meats, prepared in a French-bistro style—lamb shank, sirloin, or perhaps a fillet of buttery hake, served with seasonal veggies. **Known for:** hearty meals; ultrafresh produce; local character. [$] *Average main: £17* ✉ *B8008* ☎ *01687/450651* 🌐 *www.oldlibrary.co.uk.*

$$ B&B/INN — 🏨 **Arisaig Hotel.** A coaching inn built in 1720, this hotel is close to the water and has magnificent views of the Small Isles. **Pros:** good-value restaurant; lots of life and music in the bar; amazing views of the bay. **Cons:** the main bar is noisy for some. [$] *Rooms from: £110* ✉ *B8008* ☎ *01687/450210* 🌐 *www.arisaighotel.co.uk* 🛏 *13 rooms* 🍽 *Breakfast.*

$$$ HOTEL — Fodor's Choice ★ — 🏨 **Arisaig House.** An open-arms welcome and stunning views of the Isle of Skye await you at this wonderful mansion. **Pros:** beautiful views; lovely hosts; outstanding food. **Cons:** a bit isolated. [$] *Rooms from: £175* ✉ *Beasdale* ☎ *01687/450730* 🌐 *www.arisaighouse.co.uk* 🛏 *12 rooms* 🍽 *Breakfast.*

THE NORTHERN HIGHLANDS AND THE WESTERN ISLES

Updated by
Joseph Reaney

Wild and remote, the Northern Highlands and the Western Isles of Scotland have a timeless grandeur. Dramatic cliffs, long beaches, and craggy mountains that rise up out of moorland like islands in a sea heighten the romance and mystery. Well-preserved Eilean Donan Castle marks a kind of gateway to the Isle of Skye, famous for the brooding Cuillin Mountains and forever associated with Bonnie Prince Charlie. Jurassic-era sites, prehistoric ruins, crumbling castles, and abandoned crofts (small farms) compress the whole span of history in the islands.

The Northern Highlands is a region where roads hug the coast, dipping down toward beaches and back up for stunning views over the clear ocean, across to the dramatic mountains, or along stunning heather moorland. These twisted, undulating roads—many of them single-track—demand that you shift down a gear, pause to let others pass, and take the time to do less and experience more of the rough-hewn beauty. If you're lucky, you may see a puffin fishing below the cliffs, an eagle swooping for a hare, or perhaps even a pod of dolphins or whales swimming off the coast. Adorable Highland *coos* (cows) are sure to make an appearance, too.

Sutherland was once the southern land belonging to the Vikings, and some names reflect this. Cape Wrath got its name from the Viking word *hvarth,* meaning "turning point," and Suilven translates as "pillar." The Isle of Skye and the Outer Hebrides are referred to as the Western Isles, and remain the stronghold of the Gaelic language. Skye is often called Scotland in miniature because the terrain shifts from lush valleys in the south, to the rugged girdle of the Cuillin Mountains, and then to the steep cliffs that define the northern coast. A short ferry journey away, the moody island of Lewis and Harris lays claim to the brilliant golden sands of Luskentyre and incredible prehistoric sites, from the lunar-aligned Calanais Standing Stones to the Iron Age Doune Broch.

Depending on the weather, a trip to the Northern Highlands and the Western Isles can feel like a tropical getaway or a blustery, rain-drenched holiday. Just remember: "There's no such thing as bad weather, just inappropriate clothing."

TOP REASONS TO GO

Skye: Scotland in miniature, the landscape of Skye ranges from the lush, undulating hills and coastal tracks of Sleat to the deep glens and saw-toothed peaks of the Cuillin Mountains. Farther north are stunning geological features like the Old Man of Storr and Kilt Rock.

Seafood: Sample fresh seafood like Bracadale crab, Dunvegan Bay langoustines, and Sconser king scallops, as well as the local smoked salmon, lobster, and oysters.

Coastal walks: There are no wilder places in Britain to enjoy an invigorating coastal walk than on the islands of the Uists and Lewis and Harris. Expect vast swaths of golden sand set against blue bays, or—when

the weather is rough—giant waves crashing against the rocks.

Wildlife viewing: Seals, deer, otters, dolphins, and an abundance of birdlife can be seen throughout the Northern Highlands and Western Isles. Don't miss a boating foray to the Handa Island bird reserve, off Scourie.

Single-lane roads: In the Northern Highlands, take a drive on one-lane roads such as Destitution Road, north of Gairloch, for some of the most dramatic scenery in Britain. Discover a primeval landscape where strange craggy mountains, with Gaelic and Nordic names like An Teallach, Suilven, and Stac Pollaidh, jut out of vast, desolate moorlands dotted with *lochans* (small lakes).

ORIENTATION AND PLANNING

GETTING ORIENTED

Moving north and west from Inverness toward John O'Groats, this rugged landscape includes the old counties of Ross and Cromarty (sometimes called Easter and Wester Ross), Sutherland, and Caithness; together they constitute the northernmost portion of mainland Scotland. Farther to the west, you can get to Skye by traveling across the bridge from Kyle of Lochalsh, or by taking a short summer ferry ride from Mallaig to Armadale. From Skye you can connect to Lewis and Harris with a ferry from Uig to Tarbert, and from Leverburgh on Lewis and Harris you can catch a ferry south to Lochmaddy on North Uist.

The Northern Landscapes. North of Inverness, northwest Scotland is known for its dramatic coastlines and craggy hills. To explore these landscapes, you should travel by car, and preferably 4x4 (though you can manage without). You'll want to explore Stoer Point Lighthouse, the beaches north of Lochinver, and spectacular islandlike hills such as Suilven. The single-track road from Lairg up to Tongue, near Durness, is particularly scenic.

Torridon. A few hours' drive west of Inverness, Torridon has cool glens, mirrorlike lochs, impressive mountains, and tantalizing glimpses across to the Isle of Skye. Single-track roads lead to Glen Torridon and to lighthouses on sea-lashed headlands.

Isle of Skye. Scotland's most famous island is home to the 11 peaks of the Cuillin Mountains, the quiet gardens of Sleat, and the dramatic

10

peninsulas of Waternish and Trotternish. You can take a day trip to Skye, but it's worth spending a few days exploring its shores if you can. **The Outer Hebrides.** Extending about 130 miles from north to south, this archipelago is reached by ferry from the mainland and from the Isle of Skye. Lewis and Harris has wonderful historic attractions, such as the Calanais Standing Stones, traditional "black houses," and glorious, untouched beaches. The Uists are dotted with old cairns and ruined forts and chapels. Barra is so small you can easily walk from one end to the other.

PLANNING

WHEN TO GO

The Northern Highlands and islands are best seen from May to September. The earlier in the spring or later in the fall you go, the greater the chances of your encountering the elements in their extreme form, and the fewer attractions and accommodations you will find open (even Skye closes down almost completely by the end of October.) Then again, you'll also find fewer tourists. Winter is best avoided altogether, unless taking a ferry in a relentless gale is your idea of fun.

PLANNING YOUR TIME

The rough landscape of the Highlands and islands, as this region is sometimes called, means this isn't a place you can rush through. It could take eight busy days to do a coastal loop and also see some islands. Single-lane roadways, undulating landscapes, and eye-popping views will slow you down. You can base yourself in a town like Ullapool or Portree, or choose a B&B or hotel (of which there are many) tucked into the hills or sitting at the edge of a sea loch. If you have only a couple of days, head directly to the Isle of Skye and the other islands off the coast. They attract hordes of tourists, and for good reason, yet you don't have to walk far to find yourself in wild places, often in solitude. Sunday is a day of minimal activity here; restaurants, bars, and shops are closed, as are many sites.

You could combine a trip to the Northern Highlands with forays into the Great Glen (including Inverness and Loch Ness) or up to Orkney (there are day trips from John O'Groats) and the Shetland Islands.

GETTING HERE AND AROUND
AIR TRAVEL

On a map, this area may seem far from major urban centers, but it's easy to reach. Inverness has an airport with direct links to London, Edinburgh, Glasgow, and Amsterdam.

The main airports for the Northern Highlands are Inverness and Wick (both on the mainland). Loganair and Flybe have direct air service from Edinburgh and Glasgow to Inverness and from Edinburgh to Wick. You can fly from London Gatwick, Luton Airport (near London), or Bristol to Inverness on one of the daily easyJet flights. British Airways also has a service from Gatwick. Loganair operates flights to and among the islands of Barra, Benbecula, and Lewis and Harris in the Outer Hebrides.

Airport Contact Inverness Airport. ☎ *01667/464000* ⊕ *www.invernessairport. co.uk.*

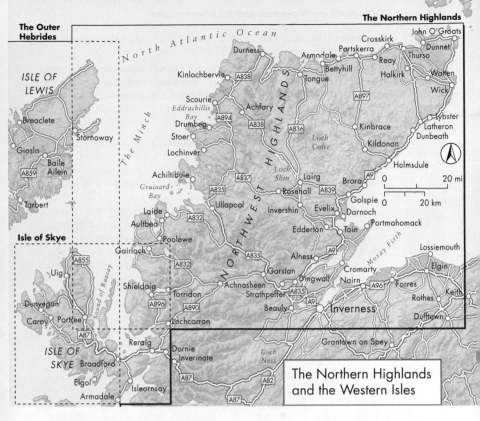

The Northern Highlands
and the Western Isles

BOAT AND FERRY TRAVEL

Ferry services are generally reliable, weather permitting. Car and passenger ferries run from Ullapool to Stornoway (Lewis and Harris), from Oban to Castlebay (Barra), from Mallaig to Lochboisdale (South Uist), and from Uig (Skye) to Tarbert (Lewis and Harris) and Lochmaddy (North Uist). The Hopscotch planned-route ticket by Caledonian MacBrayne (known locally as CalMac) gives considerable reductions on interisland ferry fares; it is worth calling ahead and asking for the best route plan.

Boat and Ferry Contact Caledonian MacBrayne (*CalMac*). ☎ *0800/066–5000* ⊕ *www.calmac.co.uk.*

10

BUS TRAVEL

Scottish Citylink runs two main routes in the Northern Highlands; one heading west to Ullapool and the other up the east coast to Scrabster (via Dornoch, Wick, and Thurso). It also has a route across the Isle of Skye to Uig, as does National Express. These buses can be a good way to see the region, but they don't run frequently.

Once you're in the Northern Highlands, Stagecoach has some routes up the east coast of the mainland to Brora. It also has regular services on Skye. In the Outer Hebrides, several small operators run regular routes to most towns and villages. Traveline Scotland, a handy website, provides timetables and a journey planner to help you navigate around Scotland. There's an app, too.

Bus Contacts National Express. ☎ *0871/781–8181* ⊕ *www.nationalexpress. com.* **Scottish Citylink.** ☎ *0871/266–3333* ⊕ *www.citylink.co.uk.* **Stagecoach.** ☎ *01463/233371* ⊕ *www.stagecoachbus.com.* **Traveline Scotland.** ☎ *0871/200–2233* ⊕ *www.travelinescotland.com.*

CAR TRAVEL

Because of infrequent bus and train services, a car is definitely the best way to explore this region. The winding single-lane roads demand a degree of driving dexterity, however. Local rules of the road require that when two cars meet, whichever driver reaches a passing place first must stop and allow the oncoming car to continue (this may entail a bit of backing up). Drivers always wave, as a courtesy and as a genuine greeting. Cars driving uphill have priority, and small cars tend to yield to large commercial vehicles. Never park in passing places, and remember you can also pull into them to allow traffic behind you to pass. On bad days, you can encounter trucks at the most awkward of spots. On good days, single-track driving can be relaxing, with a lovely pace of stopping, waving, moving on. Note that in this sparsely populated area distances between gas stations can be considerable, so it is wise to fill your tank when you see one. You can reach Inverness (the natural starting point for an exploration of the Northern Highlands) in 3½ hours from Edinburgh or Glasgow; it's around 4½ hours to Skye.

TRAIN TRAVEL

Main railway stations in the area include Oban (for ferries to Barra and the Uists) and Kyle of Lochalsh (for Skye) on the west coast, as well as Inverness (for points north to Thurso and Wick). There's direct service from London to Inverness and connecting service from Edinburgh and Glasgow. For information contact National Rail or ScotRail.

Train Contacts National Rail. ☎ *03457/484950* ⊕ *www.nationalrail.co.uk.* **ScotRail.** ☎ *0344/811–0141* ⊕ *www.scotrail.co.uk.*

TOURS

There are fascinating boat tours from a number of places around the coast, including seal- and bird-watching trips. Inland, tours of castles, distilleries, fishing lochs, and hill-walking routes are available locally.

Rabbie's. This popular tour operator organizes tours throughout the Highlands, starting from Edinburgh, Glasgow, or Inverness. In small, comfortable, 16-seater minibuses, tours range from 1 to 17 days. ☎ *0131/226–3133* ⊕ *www.rabbies.com* ⌑ *From £34.*

Scotland Tours. Choose from a wide range of bus tours for a wide range of budgets, taking anything from one to eight days. The company is Highland-owned, and the guides know their region well. ☎ *0131/226– 1414* ⊕ *www.scotlandtours.com* ⌑ *From £42.*

RESTAURANTS

Northern Scotland has many fine restaurants, where talented chefs use locally grown produce. Most country-house inns and pubs serve reliable, hearty seafood and tasty meat-and-potatoes meals. The Isle of Skye has the most, and the most expensive, restaurants, many of them quite good.

But you can find tasty meals almost everywhere, though in more remote regions you may have to drive some distance to find them. Remember that locals eat early, so most restaurants stop serving dinner at 9.

HOTELS

Charming B&Bs, inexpensive inns, and a few excellent luxury hotels are all here to welcome you after a day touring the Highlands. Much of the available accommodation books up far in advance in high season, when some require a minimum two-day stay.

In the more remote parts of Scotland your best lodging option may be to rent a cottage or house. Besides allowing you to make your own meals and to come and go as you please, it can also be less expensive. VisitScotland (⊕ *www.visitscotland.com*), the official tourism agency, lists many cottages and even rates them with stars, just like hotels. *Hotel reviews have been shortened. For full information, visit Fodors.com.*

WHAT IT COSTS IN POUNDS			
$	**$$**	**$$$**	**$$$$**
Restaurants	under £15	£15–£19	£20–£25	over £25
Hotels	under £100	£100–£160	£161–£220	over £220

Restaurant prices are the average cost of a main course at dinner or, if dinner is not served, at lunch. Hotel prices are the lowest cost of a standard double room in high season, including 20% V.A.T.

VISITOR INFORMATION

There are VisitScotland iCentres open year-round at Durness and Thurso (Northern Highlands), Portree (Skye), and Stornoway (Lewis and Harris)). VisitScotland iCentres are open seasonally (from around Easter to around October) at Lochinver and Ullapool (Northern Highlands), Tarbert (Lewis and Harris)), Castlebay (Barra), and Lochmaddy (North Uist).

Information VisitScotland. ☎ *01463/252401 Inverness center* ⊕ *www. visitscotland.com.*

10

THE NORTHERN LANDSCAPES

The northernmost part of Scotland, from Inverness all the way up to John O'Groats in the east and Cape Wrath in the west, has some of the most distinctive mountain profiles and coastal stretches in all of Scotland. The rim roads around the wilds of Durness overlook rocky shores, and the long beaches are as dramatic as the awe-inspiring and desolate cross-country routes like Destitution Road in Wester Ross. Follow the North Coast 500 loop from Inverness to see the very best of the region. If you head counter-clockwise up the east coast, along the north coast, and down the west coast, the spectacular landscape gets more and more dramatic at every turn. Travel clockwise, and you might find the east coast down from John O'Groats feels a bit anticlimactic.

DINGWALL

10 miles northwest of Inverness, 180 miles north of Glasgow.

This pretty market town and royal burgh (a Scottish town granted a royal charter) makes for a very pleasant stop if you're heading north from Inverness. While it may not have the headline-grabbing attractions of some other Northern Highland towns—notwithstanding its excellent museum—Dingwall's historic center, replete with alluring architecture, charming cafés, and quaint little shops, makes it well worth a stop. What's more, it's a convenient place to stock up on fuel and supplies before venturing farther up the east coast; opportunities become scarcer and scarcer after this point.

GETTING HERE AND AROUND

From Inverness, take the A9 north to Dingwall, turning off onto the A835. From the north, take the A9 south, turning off onto the A862.

EXPLORING

Dingwall Museum. Set inside the old town council building (topped by the pretty Townhouse Tower), this small museum offers real insight into local life throughout the 20th century. Exhibits include re-creations of a 1920s kitchen and a local *smiddy* (blacksmiths), a section on military life in the town, and details of historical crimes and punishments. Upstairs has a re-creation of a town council meeting with information on the walls, though the creepy mannequins around the table may make you wary of turning your back. ✉ *High St., Inverness* ☎ *01349/865366* 🌐 *www.dingwallmuseum.co.uk* 🎟 *Free (donations welcome)* 🕒 *Closed Sun. and Oct.–mid-May.*

WHERE TO STAY

$$$ HOTEL 🏨 **Tulloch Castle Hotel.** For hundreds of years, Tulloch Castle has watched over the town of Dingwall and the Cromarty Firth, first as the home of the Bain family and Clan Davidson, now as a grand, historic hotel. **Pros:** characterful accommodation; comfy beds and armchairs; good breakfasts. **Cons:** a whiff of faded glory. [$] *Rooms from: £205* ✉ *Tulloch Castle Dr., Inverness* ☎ *0843/178–7143* 🌐 *www.bespokehotels.com/tullochcastlehotel* 🛏 *20 rooms* 🍴 *Breakfast.*

DORNOCH

25 miles northwest of Dingwall.

A town of sandstone houses, tiny rose-filled gardens, and a 13th-century cathedral with stunning traditional and modern stained-glass windows, Dornoch is well worth a visit. It's noted for golf (you may hear it referred to as the St. Andrews of the North), but because of the town's location so far north, the golf courses here are delightfully uncrowded. Royal Dornoch is the jewel in its crown, praised by the world's top golfers.

GETTING HERE AND AROUND

From Dingwall or Inverness, take the A9 north to Dornoch. Note that this stretch of the road can get busy with ferry traffic.

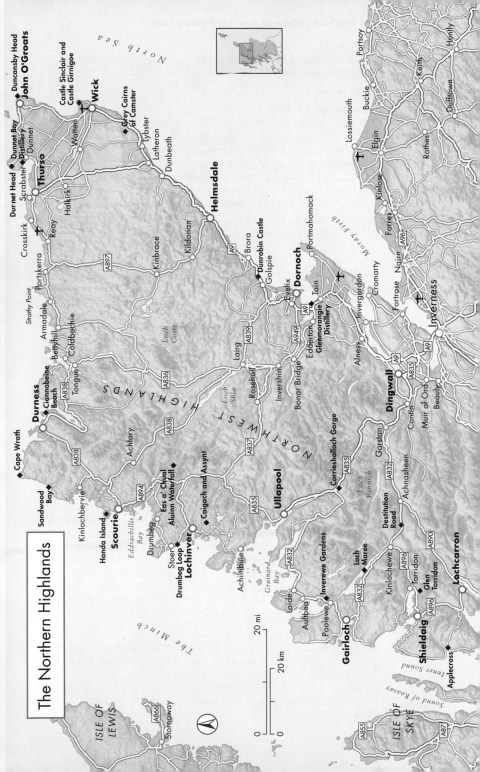

The Northern Highlands

ESSENTIALS

Visitor Information Dornoch Visitors Centre. ✉ *Carnegie Courthouse, Castle St.* ☎ *01349/886606* 🌐 *www.visitdornoch.com.*

EXPLORING

Fodor's Choice ★ **Glenmorangie Distillery.** The light color and delicate floral taste of the Speyside whiskies is exemplified in Glenmorangie, one of the best known of the Highland whiskies. The picturesque distillery in Tain, 8 miles south of Dornoch, offers fascinating tours that reveal how the taste is achieved (the secret's in the exceedingly tall stills). The Original Tour includes a dram, and the Signet Tour (£30) offers a chance to sample the rare, chocolatey Glenmorangie Signet in a unique audio tasting experience. ✉ *Tain* ☎ *01862/892477* 🌐 *www.glenmorangie.com* 🎫 *Tours from £7.*

OFF THE BEATEN PATH

Dunrobin Castle. Situated 12 miles north of Dornoch, flamboyant Dunrobin Castle is an ancient seat that became the home of the dukes of Sutherland, at which point it was transformed into the 19th-century white-turreted behemoth you see today. As well as its grand palatial facade and lavish interiors, the property also has summer falconry demonstrations and Versailles-inspired gardens. The first duke, who was fascinated by trains, built his own railroad in the park and staffed it with his servants. Yet for all this frivolity, the duke has a controversial legacy; he was responsible for the Sutherland Clearances of 1810 to 1820, when people were forcibly removed from their farms to make room for sheep to graze. ✉ *Off A9, Golspie* ☎ *01408/633177* 🌐 *www.dunrobincastle.co.uk* 🎫 *£11* ⏲ *Closed mid-Oct.–Apr.*

WHERE TO EAT AND STAY

$ BRITISH 🍴 **Sutherland House.** Just off the main square, Sutherland House restaurant has a feeling of intimacy in its two separate rooms, reinforced by the enthusiastic reception and delicious food. The menu is imaginative, with some unusual combinations dreamed up by the chef. **Known for:** imaginative seafood; chicken with Glenmorangie whisky sauce. [$] *Average main: £13* ✉ *Argyle St.* ☎ *01862/811023* 🌐 *www.sutherland-house.net.*

$$$$ RESORT Fodor's Choice ★ 🏨 **Glenmorangie House.** Situated 10 miles southeast from the distillery, Glenmorangie House offers luxurious but casual stays in a spectacular 17th-century country home. **Pros:** wonderfully rural location; superb service; extensive whisky collection. **Cons:** puny showers that take a while to heat up. [$] *Rooms from: £390* ✉ *Fearn by Tain, Tain* ☎ *01862/871671* 🌐 *www.theglenmorangiehouse.com* 🛏 *9 rooms* 🍽 *Some meals.*

$ B&B/INN 🏨 **Strathview Lodge.** A few miles north of Dornoch, this B&B sits high above the road with a wonderful view of Loch Fleet. **Pros:** beautiful location; comfortable and warm rooms; attentive owners. **Cons:** a little way out of Dornoch. [$] *Rooms from: £84* ✉ *Cambusavie* ☎ *01408/634286* 🌐 *www.strathview-dornoch.co.uk* 🛏 *3 rooms* 🍽 *Breakfast.*

SHOPPING

Jail Dornoch. It's rare for people to voluntarily walk into jail, but this place is the exception, as an old prison has been converted in a popular fashion store. The onetime cells are now home to a range of elegant clothes and accessories, toiletries, housewares, and interesting gifts. It's so popular that there's now a second outlet at Inverness Airport. ✉ *Castle St.* ☎ *01862/810555* 🌐 *www.jail-dornoch.com.*

SPORTS AND THE OUTDOORS
GOLF

Fodor's Choice ★ **Royal Dornoch Golf Club.** The legendary Championship Course, laid out by Tom Morris in 1886, challenges even the very best golfers with its fast, raised greens. It also inspires them with views of white sandy beaches and tall mountains carpeted in wild yellow gorse each spring. The Struie Course provides even more sea views and demanding golf for players of every level. ⊠ *Golf Rd.* ☎ *01862/810219* ⊕ *www.royal-dornoch.com* ✉ *Championship: £145; Struie: £45* ⚘*. Championship: 18 holes, 6748 yards, par 70; Struie: 18 holes, 6265 yards, par 71* ⚘ *Reservations essential.*

HELMSDALE

28 miles north of Dornoch.

Helmsdale is a fascinating fishing village with a checkered past. It was once a busy Viking settlement, later became the scene of an aristocratic poisoning plot, and then was transformed into a Victorian village, used to house some of the poor souls removed from their land to make way for sheep. These "clearances," perpetrated by the Duke of Sutherland, were among the Highlands' most inhumane.

GETTING HERE AND AROUND

Helmsdale is one of the few towns on this part of the coast that has daily train service from Inverness. However, a car will allow you to see more in the surrounding area. Get here via the coastal A9 in each direction, or the inland A897.

EXPLORING

FAMILY **Timespan.** This thought-provoking mix of displays, artifacts, and audio-visual materials portrays the history of the area, from the Stone Age to the 1869 gold rush in the Strath of Kildonan. There's a geology exhibit in the garden and a tour of the Kildonan gold-rush site. The complex also includes a café and an art gallery that often hosts visiting artists and changing exhibitions. ⊠ *Dunrobin St.* ☎ *01431/821327* ⊕ *www. timespan.org.uk* ✉ *£4.*

10

WICK

35 miles north of Helmsdale.

Wick is a substantial town that was built on its fishing industry. The town itself is not especially noteworthy, but it does have a handful of worthwhile sights.

GETTING HERE AND AROUND

From Helmsdale, follow the A99 north. From Thurso, take the A882 that cuts diagonally southwest.

EXPLORING

Fodor's Choice ★ **Pulteney Distillery.** Unusually for a distillery, Pulteney is situated very close to the town center, and it has been for almost 200 years. The spirit produced here, known as "gold," was once in the shadow of the town's other big "silver" industry—herring fishing. But, despite a hairy period of prohibition, it has easily outlasted its competition. The brooding brick distillery is open for tours and tastings, so join the standard one-hour tour (£8) for a behind-the-scenes look at the facilities and a taste of the award-winning 12-year-old Old Pulteney—famed for its smooth, faintly briny character with lingering butterscotch sweet finish. Or, for £20, experience all this plus additional tastings of the 17- and 21-year-old expressions. ⊠ *Huddart St* ☎ *01955/602371* ⊕ *www.oldpulteney.com* ✉ *Tours from £8* ⊙ *Closed Sun. May–Sept. and weekends Oct.–Apr.*

OFF THE BEATEN PATH

Castle Sinclair and Castle Girnigoe. Dramatically perched on the edge of the cliff, this ruined castle—or rather, castles—is a spectacular sight. Situated 3 miles northwest of Wick, this site comprises the remains of the 15th-century Castle Girnigoe and the 17th-century Castle Sinclair, set among stunning scenery. The precipitous location, with old walls teetering inches from the cliff edge, means it has a limited lifespan, so go take a look while you can. ⊠ *Wick* ⊕ *www.castlesinclairgirnigoe.org* ✉ *Free.*

Wick Heritage Museum. The locals who run this lovely town museum are real enthusiasts, and they will take you through Wick's history from its founding by the Vikings to its heyday in the 1860s as a leading herring port. The collection includes everything from ancient fossils and a 19th-century cooperage to the Johnston Photographic Collection, a set of 40,000 images that show more than a century of life in Wick through one local family's eyes. There's also an art gallery and lovely terraced gardens that overlook the town. ⊠ *18–27 Bank Row* ☎ *01955/605393* ⊕ *www.wickheritage.org* ✉ *£4* ⊙ *Closed Sun. and Nov.–Easter.*

EN ROUTE

Grey Cairns of Camster. The remarkable Grey Cairns of Camster, two Neolithic chambers made of rough stones, were built more than 5,000 years ago and are among the best preserved in Britain. **Camster Round Cairn** is 20 yards in diameter and 13 yards high, while **Camster Long Cairn** stretches an extraordinary 77 yards. Some 19th-century excavations revealed skeletons, pottery, and flint tools in the round cairn's internal chamber. They are in an isolated location, around 8 miles southwest of Wick and without a visitor center in sight, so if you feel adventurous and don't mind dirty knees, you can crawl into the chambers (the metal grills over the entrances mean they appear locked, but they aren't). To get here, you'll need to drive 5 miles along an unnamed road; once you're just north of Lybster on the A99, look out for the brown signposts pointing the way. ⊠ *Off A9* ⊕ *www.historicenvironment.scot* ✉ *Free.*

JOHN O'GROATS

15 miles north of Wick.

The windswept little outpost of John O'Groats is usually taken to be the northernmost point on the Scottish mainland, though that is not strictly true, as a short drive to Dunnet Head will reveal. From the harbor, you can take a boat to see the dolphins and seals that live beneath the coastal cliffs—or head farther afield with a ferry to Orkney. The little town has charms of its own, including a row of colorful wooden houses (part of the Inn at John O' Groats) and a crafts center with high-quality shops selling knitwear, candles, and gifts.

GETTING HERE AND AROUND

Traveling north from Wick, take the A99. From the east, take the coast-hugging A836.

EXPLORING

Duncansby Head. Head to Duncansby Head for spectacular views of cliffs and sea stacks by the lighthouse, as well as seabirds like guillemots and (if you're lucky) puffins. It's on the coastal road east of town. ⊠ *John O'Groats* 🖾 *Free.*

John O'Groats Ferries. Sailing from John O'Groats Harbor, this company offers 90-minute wildlife cruises past spectacular cliff scenery and birdlife into the Pentland Firth, to Duncansby Stacks, and to the island of Stroma. Trips cost £18 and are available daily at 2:30 between mid-June and August. The company also offers a "Maxi Day" tour of Orkney between May and September. It leaves at 8:45 am and costs £56. ⊠ *County Rd., John O'Groats* ☎ *01955/611353* ⊕ *www.jogferry. co.uk* 🖾 *Tours from £18.*

WHERE TO STAY

$$

RENTAL

Fodor's Choice

★

🖼 **Natural Retreats John O'Groats.** A local landmark in their own right, the brightly colored lodges here are the region's best self-catering accommodation—not to mention the most photogenic. **Pros:** very comfy beds; good Wi-Fi (a rarity here); natural light all day long. **Cons:** can feel understaffed. $ *Rooms from: £125* ⊠ *John O'Groats* ✛ *Just west of ferry terminal* ☎ *01625/416430* ⊕ *www.naturalretreats.com* 🛏 *23 rooms* 🍽 *No meals.*

NIGHTLIFE AND PERFORMING ARTS

Lyth Arts Centre. Housed in a Victorian-era school building with a modern interior, the Lyth Arts Centre serves as a cultural hub for the region. From April to November, professional music and theater companies fill the schedule and locals fill the seats. There are also exhibitions of contemporary fine art. Lyth is 11 miles southwest of John O'Groats. ⊠ *Lyth* ☎ *01955/641434* ⊕ *www.lytharts.org.uk* 🖾 *By event.*

THURSO

10

19 miles west of John O'Groats.

The town of Thurso is quite substantial for a community so far north. In town are the Thurso Heritage Museum and Old St. Peter's Kirk, which dates back to the 12th century. There are also fine beaches, particularly at Dunnet Bay, and great seabird watching at Dunnet Head.

GETTING HERE AND AROUND

A car remains the best way to see this region, although local buses run most days. From John O'Groats, simply follow the A836 west.

ESSENTIALS

Visitor Information VisitScotland Thurso iCentre. ⊠ *Caithness Horizons, Old Town Hall, High St.* ☎ *01847/893155* ⊕ *www.visitscotland.com.*

EXPLORING

Caithness Horizons. This rich museum, set within the beautiful Old Town Hall, explores life in the county of Caithness from the dawn of time to the present day; that's everything from Picts and Vikings to the highly controversial Dounreay Nuclear Power Development Establishment. There is also a pleasant café and shop. ✉ *Old Town Hall, High St.* ☎ *01847/896508* 🌐 *www.caithnesshorizonsmuseum.com* 🎫 *£4* ⏲ *Closed Sun. Oct.–Apr.*

Dunnet Bay Distillery. This small north coast distillery proves that Scotland's craft distilling boom has stretched to the very edges of the mainland. It also proves that Scotland has far more to offer than just whisky. Dunnet Bay Distillery has gained plaudits and prizes galore for its Rock Rose gin (notable for its use of sea buckthorn and other coastal botanicals), and it also produces a superb vodka called Holy Grass. You can tour the "wee" distillery every summer; reservations are advised. ✉ *Off A836* ☎ *01847/851287* 🌐 *www.dunnetbaydistillers.co.uk* 🎫 *£6* ⏲ *Closed Tues., Thurs., Sun., and Oct.–Apr.*

Dunnet Head. Most people make the trip to Dunnet Head to stand at the northernmost point of mainland Britain. But it's also worth a visit for the pretty Dunnet Head Lighthouse (built 1831), the dramatic sea cliffs, and the fine views over the water to Orkney. The Royal Society for the Protection of Birds also runs a nature reserve here, due to the number of seabirds nesting in the cliffs. ✉ *Brough* 🌐 *www.dunnethead.co.uk* 🎫 *Free.*

WHERE TO STAY

$$$ B&B/INN Fodor's Choice ★

🏨 **Forss House.** Don't be fooled by the stark exterior, as this house dating from 1810 is a charming place to stay. **Pros:** large guest rooms; lots of outdoor activities; hearty meals. **Cons:** heavy old doors make a racket. [$] *Rooms from: £205* ✉ *Forss* ✣ *4 miles west of Thurso* ☎ *01847/861201* 🌐 *www.forsshousehotel.co.uk* 🛏 *14 rooms* 🍴 *Breakfast.*

BICYCLING

The Bike Shop. This cycle-repair shop has a friendly staff and a handful of hybrid bikes to rent. You can also get advice on the best local routes. ✉ *35 High St.* ☎ *01847/895385.*

DURNESS

70 miles west of Thurso.

The sudden patches of green surrounding the village of Durness, on the north coast, are caused by the richer limestone outcrops among the acid moorlands. The town is the jumping-off point for several natural highlights, from a beautiful sandy beach to the country's highest cliff.

GETTING HERE AND AROUND

From Thurso, simply head west along the A836, which will turn into A838 at Tongue.

ESSENTIALS

Visitor Information VisitScotland Durness iCentre. ✉ *Sango* ☎ *01971/511368* 🌐 *www.visitscotland.com.*

EXPLORING

Cape Wrath. If you've made it this far north, you'll probably want to go all the way to Cape Wrath, a rugged headland at the northwest tip of Scotland. The white-sand beaches, impressive dunes covered in marram grass, and crashing seas of nearby Balnakeil Bay make it an exhilarating place to visit. As this land is owned by the Ministry of Defence (it is listed as an area for air force training), you can't drive your own vehicle. From May through September, a small boat ferries people here from Keoldale, 2 miles outside Durness. En route look out for Clo Mor; at 920 feet, they're the United Kingdom's highest sea cliffs. Once you're across the sea inlet, a minibus will take you to the lighthouse. Call ahead or check departure times on the board at the jetty. ☎ *01971/511284* 🌐 *www.visitcapewrath.com* 🎫 *£12 boat/bus return* 🕒 *No boat Oct.–Apr.*

Fodor's Choice ★ **Smoo Cave.** This atmospheric cavern, hollowed out of the limestone by rushing water, feels like something out of a fantasy novel. The combined sea-and-freshwater cave, complete with gushing waterfall, can be reached via a steep cliff stairway from the Smoo Cave car park. However, don't start your descent before reading the explanatory boards at the top of the stairs, which tell the history of those who lived and used the caves in much earlier times. ✉ *Durness* 🎫 *Free.*

OFF THE BEATEN PATH

Sandwood Bay. The very definition of off the beaten path, Sandwood Bay is one of Scotland's most spectacular—and most isolated—beaches. The only way to reach it is to walk 4 miles each way across sheep fields and sand dunes. It's a lovely, fairly easy walk, which may just end with you having a long, sandy beach, with its dramatic sea stack Am Buachaille, all to yourself. To get here, turn off the A838 onto the B801 at Rhiconich (14 miles southwest of Durness), then turn off at Kinlochbervie to Balchrick. Just before you reach the latter, look for a tiny white sign to "Sandwood," then follow this single-track lane to its end, where you can park and start walking. ✉ *Durness.*

WHERE TO EAT AND STAY

$ CAFÉ **Cocoa Mountain.** A must for those with a sweet tooth, this "chocolate bar" serves up world-class truffles and stunningly rich hot chocolate made in its specialist "chocolate factory," which sources the beans from around the world. There are also sandwiches, cakes, and coffee available, in case the chocolate gets to be too much. **Known for:** sublime chocolate truffles; house-made hot chocolate. [$] *Average main: £9* ✉ *Balnakeil* ☎ *01971/511233* 🌐 *www.cocoamountain.co.uk.*

$$ HOTEL 🏨 **Tongue Hotel.** With open fireplaces, tartan rugs, and floral wallpaper, this traditional Highland hotel is a great base for exploring the northern coast of the Scottish mainland. **Pros:** warm and friendly staff; beautiful location with stunning views; deliciously creamy porridge at breakfast. **Cons:** Wi-Fi only in public areas; TV sets from the '80s. [$] *Rooms from: £105* ✉ *Tongue* ☎ *01847/611206* 🌐 *www.tonguehotel.co.uk* 🛏 *19 rooms* 🍴 *Breakfast.*

10

SHOPPING

Balnakeil Craft Village. Artisans sell pottery, leather, weavings, paintings, and more from their studios at Balnakeil Craft Village. It is a rather odd place, housed as it is on an unnamed road running northwest from Durness in a collection of shabby former military buildings framed by dramatic views of Balnakeil Bay. There are galleries, workshops, and a range of crafts for sale. The village is open during the summer, with most shops open daily from 10 to 5. ⊠ *Balnakeil* ☎ *01971/511777* ⊕ *www.balnakeilcraftvillage.weebly.com.*

Sculpture Croft. This odd garden of delights provokes a double-take from most drivers traveling along the A838, thanks to its incongruous ceramic-topped gates. Park opposite and take a stroll down into Lotte Glob's pottery wonderland, where ceramic and metal sculptures are scattered across the gardens. Several paths lead down to the coast, and there are hundreds of pieces en route, including a library of ceramic books. Her work reflects and adds to the landscape, using natural shapes and forms and building patterns into the rocks themselves. End your visit with a trip to the studio and pottery shop. ⊠ *105 Laid* ☎ *01971/511727* ⊕ *www.lotteglob.co.uk.*

SPORTS AND THE OUTDOORS

Ciannabeine Beach. Situated 10 miles east of Durness, Ciannabeine is one of Scotland's most achingly beautiful beaches, a spectacular sweep of sand caught in the embrace of 10,000-year-old rocks. There is a car park opposite and a path down to the beach itself. You will recognize it by the white house just beyond, once the village school. **Amenities:** parking (no fee). **Best for:** swimming; walking. ⊠ *Lairg.*

SCOURIE

27 miles southwest of Durness.

Scourie is a small coastal settlement catering to visitors—particularly fisherfolk—with a good range of accommodations. The bay-side town makes a good base for a trip to the bird sanctuary on Handa Island.

GETTING HERE AND AROUND

From Durness, head south on the A838, turning onto the A894.

EXPLORING

Fodor's Choice
★ **Handa Island.** Just off the coast of Scourie is Handa Island, a bird sanctuary that shelters huge seabird colonies, especially impressive at nesting time. You can gaze at more than 200,000 birds nesting on dramatic cliffs here, including guillemots, razorbills, great skuas, kittiwakes, and, of course, crowd-pleasingly colorful puffins. This remarkable reserve, administered by the Scottish Wildlife Trust, is open only in spring and summer, and can be reached by a small open boat from Tarbert; contact the tourist information center in Lochinver or Durness for details. ■ TIP→ **Note that ferries don't run on Sunday.** Sturdy boots, a waterproof jacket, and a degree of fitness are needed to walk the path around the island. ⊕ *scottishwildlifetrust.org.uk* ☉ *Closed Oct.–Mar.*

WHERE TO EAT AND STAY

$$ **✕ Shorehouse Restaurant.** If you're feeling peckish after a trip to Handa
SEAFOOD Island, make a stop at this exceptional seafood restaurant overlook-
Fodor'sChoice ing Tarbet Harbor. It serves freshly caught seafood specialties, from
★ hand-dived scallops and hot smoked mackerel to whole lobsters, in a
quaint, maritime-theme setting. **Known for:** spectacular seafood; gor-
geous views; friendly and attentive service. [$] *Average main: £15* ✉ *Tigh
Na Mara, Tarbet* ☎ *01971/502251* ⊘ *Closed Sun. and Oct.–Easter.*

$$ ☷ **Eddrachilles Hotel.** With one of the most spectacular vistas of any
B&B/INN hotel in Scotland—out toward the picturesque islands of Badcall Bay—
Fodor'sChoice Eddrachilles sits on a huge plot of private moorland just south of the
★ Handa Island bird sanctuary. **Pros:** attractive garden; stunning shoreline
nearby; close to bird sanctuary. **Cons:** needs a lick of paint. [$] *Rooms
from: £125* ✉ *Off A894* ☎ *01971/502080* ⊕ *www.eddrachilles.com*
⊘ *Closed Nov.–Mar.* ⟿ *10 rooms* ℺*Breakfast.*

$$ ☷ **Kylesku Hotel.** This charming hotel, looking out over Loch Glendhu
HOTEL and toward Eas Coul Aulin (Scotland's highest waterfall), has great
Fodor'sChoice service, excellent food, and a warm, relaxed atmosphere. **Pros:** stunning
★ views; great staff; delicious food. **Cons:** some old-building quirks; two
tiny (but cheap) attic rooms. [$] *Rooms from: £125* ✉ *Off A894* ✛ *10
miles south of Scourie* ☎ *01971/502231* ⊕ *www.kyleskuhotel.co.uk*
⟿ *11 rooms* ℺*Breakfast.*

LOCHINVER

28 miles south of Scourie.

Lochinver is a very pretty, quiet, shoreside community of whitewashed
cottages, with lovely beaches to the north, a harbor used by the west-
coast fishing fleet, and a couple of good dining and lodging options.
Behind the town the mountain Suilven rises abruptly. Take the cul-de-
sac, **Baddidarroch Road,** for a great photo opportunity. Lochinver is a
perfect base for exploring Sutherland.

GETTING HERE AND AROUND

To get to Lochinver from Scourie, head south, then turn off the A894
to the A837.

ESSENTIALS

Visitor Information VisitScotland Lochinver iCentre. ✉ *The Mission, Culag
Park* ☎ *01571/841073* ⊕ *www.visitscotland.com.*

EXPLORING

Fodor'sChoice **Drumbeg Loop.** Bold souls spending time at Lochinver may enjoy the
★ interesting single-track B869 Drumbeg Loop to the north of Lochin-
ver—it has several challenging hairpin turns along with breathtaking
views. The junction is on the north side of the River Inver bridge on
the outskirts of the village, signposted as "Stoer" and "Clashnessie."
Just beyond the scattered community of Stoer, a road leads west to **Stoer
Point Lighthouse.** If you're an energetic walker, you can hike across the
short turf and heather along the cliff top for fine views west towards the
Isle of Skye. There's also a red-sandstone sea stack: the **Old Man of Stoer**
(not to be confused with the Old Man of Storr on Skye). This makes a
pleasant excursion on a long summer evening.

10

Eas a' Chual Aluinn Waterfall. With a drop of 685 feet, this is the longest waterfall in the United Kingdom. A rugged hike leads to the falls, which are at the head of Loch Glencoul. Start from the car park off A894, approximately 17 miles east and north from Lochinver. In summer, cruises (£25) from Kylesku Old Ferry Pier offer a less taxing alternative. ✉ *A894, 3 miles southeast of Kylesku Bridge.*

WHERE TO EAT AND STAY

$ BRITISH 🍴 **Lochinver Mission Cafe.** An abandoned fishermen's mission (a place where fishermen stayed while in port), situated at the far end of town near the harbor, now houses this pleasant café serving lunch, soup, sandwiches, and home baking. The specials often include fish freshly delivered from the harbor. **Known for:** delicious homemade soup; great fish-and-chips; friendly staff. [$] *Average main: £9* ✉ *Culag Park* ☎ *01571/844324* 🌐 *www.lochinvermission.org.uk* 💳 *No credit cards* 🕒 *Closed Sun.*

$$$$ HOTEL 🏨 **Inver Lodge Hotel.** In a commanding location on a hillside above Lochinver, this modern luxury hotel has stunning views of the coast, as well as smart guest rooms that are decorated in contemporary colors and traditional mahogany furniture. **Pros:** cozy public room with a fireplace; refreshing sauna; great fishing nearby. **Cons:** slightly drab exterior; not good for families with children. [$] *Rooms from: £275* ✉ *Iolaire Rd.* ☎ *01571/844496* 🌐 *www.inverlodge.com* 🛏 *21 rooms* 🍽 *Breakfast.*

$ B&B/INN 🏨 **Tigh Na Sith.** Set just above the bay at Lochinver, this family-run B&B wins rave reviews for its warm welcome. **Pros:** great hosts; fantastic views. **Cons:** room at back doesn't have a view. [$] *Rooms from: £85* ✉ *Off A837* ☎ *01571/844588* 🌐 *www.tighnasith.com* 🛏 *3 rooms* 🍽 *Breakfast.*

SHOPPING

Highland Stoneware. The huge sofa and television composed entirely of broken crockery are a witty introduction to the beautiful ceramic works of art made at Highland Stoneware. The potters and decorators busy themselves in a studio behind the shop, and visitors are encouraged to watch as they create pieces incorporating Highland themes. If you miss this one, there's a second Highland Stoneware store in Ullapool. ✉ *Baddidarroch* ☎ *01571/844376* 🌐 *www.highlandstoneware.com.*

ULLAPOOL

35 miles south of Lochinver, 238 miles north of Glasgow, 57 miles northwest of Inverness.

Ullapool is an ideal base for hiking throughout Sutherland and taking wildlife and nature cruises, especially to the Summer Isles. By the shores of salty Loch Broom, the town was founded in 1788 as a fishing station to exploit the local herring stocks. There's still a smattering of fishing vessels, as well as visiting yachts and foreign ships. When their crews fill the pubs, Ullapool has a surprisingly cosmopolitan feel. The harbor area comes to life when the Lewis and Harris ferry arrives and departs.

GETTING HERE AND AROUND

A desolate but well-maintained stretch of the A835 takes you from Inverness to Ullapool, with a connection to Torridon via the A832.

ESSENTIALS

Visitor Information VisitScotland Ullapool iCentre. ⊠ *Argyle St.*
☎ *01854/612486.*

EXPLORING

The Ceilidh Place. Ullapool's cultural focal point is The Ceilidh Place, an excellent venue for concerts and other events all through the year (*ceilidh* is a Scottish social gathering with traditional music and dance). It started out as a small café, but over the years has added space for local performers, an excellent bookshop specializing in Scottish writing, and a handful of comfortable rooms (as well as a basic bunkhouse) for those who want to spend the night. It's a great place for afternoon coffee or a wee dram in the evening. ⊠ *12–14 W. Argyle St.* ☎ *01854/612103* ⊕ *www.theceilidhplace.com.*

Coigach and Assynt. North of Ullapool lies a different kind of landscape, one of brooding mountains and languid lochs, where peaks punch their way out of heathered terrain and appear to constantly shift positions. Even their names have a more mysterious air than those of the *bens* (mountain peaks or hills) elsewhere: Cul Mor, Cul Beag, Stac Pollaidh, Canisp, Suilven. Some hark back to Norse rather than to Gaelic—a reminder that Vikings used to sail this northern shore. ■**TIP**➔ **This vast empty region, within the North West Highlands Geopark, is spectacular from top to bottom, but the highlight is the eerily pretty Loch Assynt, peppered with tiny wooded isles.** ✛ *15 miles north of Ullapool on the A835.*

Corrieshalloch Gorge. For a thrilling touch of vertigo, don't miss Corrieshalloch Gorge, 12 miles south of Ullapool, just off the A835. Draining the high moors, the Falls of Measach plunge into a 200-foot-deep, thickly wooded gorge. There's a suspension-bridge viewpoint and a heady atmosphere of romantic grandeur, like an old Scottish print come to life. A short walk leads from a parking area to the viewpoint. ⊕ *www. nts.org.uk.*

Ullapool Museum. Films, photographs, and audiovisual displays tell the story of the area from the Ice Age to modern times, including the "klondyking" period between 1970 and 1990 when foreign boats filled the loch to fish the mackerel. There's an ongoing exhibition on weather, climate change, and the environment. The building was designed by Thomas Telford and dates from the early 19th century. ⊠ *7–8 W. Argyle St.* ☎ *01854/612987* ⊕ *www.ullapoolmuseum.co.uk* 🎫 *£4* ⊙ *Closed Sun. and Nov.–Mar.*

SPORTS AND THE OUTDOORS

Stac Pollaidh. For a great afternoon of walking, ascend the dramatic hill of Stac Pollaidh (pronounced "stack polly"), about 14 miles north of Ullapool. The clearly marked path climbs for a bit and then curves around to the right and takes you on a loop with incredible views over Sutherland, north to Suilven, and west to the Summer Isles. About halfway around the hill, a steeper path takes you to the start of the ridge. ⚠ **Only very experienced rock climbers should continue from here, as the route requires rock climbing in very exposed conditions.** But not to worry, because from the west side of the looped path you can see the pinnacled

10

pitch of Stac Pollaidh. To get here, take the A835 to Drumrunie, then a minor road off to the west (there's a sign for "Achiltibuie"). Five miles along the road, there's a car park; start your walk from here. ⊠ *Off A835, Dornie.*

WHERE TO EAT AND STAY

$ ✕ **The Arch Inn.** On the face of it,
BRITISH this popular restaurant isn't doing anything particularly remarkable; its simple pub-style menu of steaks, burgers, and fish-and-chips hardly pushes the envelope. But its use of fresh, local ingredients, its pretty presentation of dishes, and its appealing waterside seating make it a favorite dining spot among locals. **Known for:** fresh and tasty pub grub; waterside seating. $ *Average main: £13* ⊠ *10–11 W. Shore St.* ☎ *01854/612454* ⊕ *www.thearchinn.co.uk.*

$ ✕ **The West Coast Delicatessen.** This charming family-run deli serves
CAFÉ delicious homemade sandwiches, pies, soups, salads, and hummus to
Fodor's Choice a long line of locals and tourists. It also has great cakes and baked
★ goods. **Known for:** great homemade soups; excellent coffee; an array of artisanal products. $ *Average main: £8* ⊠ *Argyle St.* ☎ *01854/613450* ⊕ *www.westcoastdeli.co.uk* ☉ *Closed Sun. No dinner.*

$$ 🏨 **Royal Hotel.** This longtime favorite has a great location and beautiful
HOTEL views over Ullapool Harbor and Loch Broom, so be sure to request a balcony room in advance. **Pros:** a short walk to Ullapool; good breakfasts. **Cons:** sometimes very crowded; rear rooms have no views. $ *Rooms from: £110* ⊠ *Garve Rd.* ☎ *01854/612181* ⊕ *www.royalhotelullapool.co.uk* ⊷ *54 rooms* ⦿*Breakfast.*

$ 🏨 **Tanglewood House.** Sitting on a headland above a rocky beach, with
B&B/INN spectacular views across Loch Broom toward Ullapool, one of Scot-
Fodor's Choice land's most unique and appealing B&Bs feels wonderfully remote while
★ only being a short drive (or even a walk) into town. **Pros:** truly unique property; beautiful setting; fast and reliable Wi-Fi. **Cons:** a steep drive down to the house. $ *Rooms from: £99* ⊠ *Off A835* ☎ *01854/612059* ⊕ *www.tanglewoodhouse.co.uk* ⊷ *3 rooms* ⦿*Breakfast.*

> ## GET HOOKED IN THE HIGHLANDS
>
> The possibilities for fishing are endless in Sutherland, as a glance at the loch-covered map suggests. Brown trout and salmon are abundant. You can fish from the banks of Loch Garve, 35 miles south of Ullapool, or Loch Assynt, 5 miles east of Lochinver, from March to October. Boat fishing is popular on Loch Maree, southeast of Gairloch and north of Poolewe, from May to October. Fishing permits are available at local post offices and shops; some hotels have their own fishing rights but most will arrange fishing permits for you.

TORRIDON

Located far to the west of Scotland, Torridon has a grand, rugged, and wild air that feels especially remote, yet it's just an hour's drive from Inverness before you reach Kinlochewe, near the east end of Glen Torridon. The western side is equally spectacular, with walking trails and mountain panoramas galore. Torridon is a wonderful place to visit if you want to tackle one of the legendary peaks here—Beinn Alligin, Liathach, and Beinn Eighe—or if you enjoy outdoor activities like kayaking, climbing, or mountain biking. The A890, which runs from the A832 into the heart of Torridon, is a single-lane road in some stretches, with plenty of open vistas across the deserted heart of northern Scotland.

GAIRLOCH

55 miles southwest of Ullapool.

Aside from its restaurants and lodgings, peaceful Gairloch has one further advantage: it often escapes the rain clouds that can cling to the high summits. You can enjoy a round of golf here and perhaps stay dry, even when the nearby Torridon Hills are deluged.

GETTING HERE AND AROUND

From Ullapool, this coastal town can be reached via the winding A832.

EXPLORING

Destitution Road. The road south between **Corrieshalloch Gorge** (a very worthwhile stop) and Gairloch passes through wild woodlands around Dundonnell and Loch Broom, then takes in stunning coastal scenery with views of Gruinard Bay and its white beaches. Look out for the toothed ramparts of the mountain **An Teallach** (pronounced tyel-lack), visible on the horizon for miles. The moorland route you travel is known, rather chillingly, as Destitution Road; a holdover from the terrible potato famines of the 1840s.

Fodor's Choice ★ **Inverewe Gardens.** A highlight of the area, Inverewe Gardens has lush plantings tucked away behind a dense barrier of trees and shrubs. This is all thanks to the warm North Atlantic Drift, which takes the edge off winter frosts. Inverewe is sometimes described as subtropical, but this inaccuracy irritates the head gardener; do not expect coconuts and palm trees here. Instead, look for rarities like the blue Himalayan poppy. ✉ *A832, 6 miles northeast of Gairloch, Poolewe* ☎ *01445/781229* 🌐 *www.nts.org.uk/visit/inverewe* 🎟 *£10.50.*

Fodor's Choice ★ **Loch Maree.** Southeast of Gairloch stretches one of Scotland's most scenic lochs, Loch Maree. Its harmonious setting, with tall Scots pines and the mountain Slioch looming as a backdrop, is regularly visited by red deer, as well as the endangered pine marten (a member of the weasel family)—though they're just as likely to be hanging around the trash cans as in the trees. There are few official parking places along the loch, but these are nestled between the trees with limited views, so be prepared to park and climb to a better vantage point. ✉ *Gairloch.*

WHERE TO STAY

$$ HOTEL 🏨 **The Dundonnell.** Thirty miles from Gairloch, this lovely family-run hotel, set on the roadside by Little Loch Broom with the mountains of An Leachall rising up behind, couldn't be more picturesque. **Pros:** fabulous scenery; plenty of outdoor activities; good dining options. **Cons:** bland exterior. [$] *Rooms from: £100* ✉ *A832, 30 miles northeast of Gairloch, Dundonnell* ☎ *01854/633204* 🌐 *www.dundonnellhotel.com* 🛏 *28 rooms* 🍴 *Breakfast.*

10

SPORTS AND THE OUTDOORS

GOLF

Gairloch Golf Club. This lovely 9-hole course is one of the few to be found on this stretch of coast, but it is the coastal location that gives it its charm—as well as its challenges. There has been a golf club here since 1898, and local records show that putters of more than a century ago played on the golden sand dunes, long since been replaced by rolling greens. While you are waiting for your turn at the tee, take a moment to drink in fine views of the Minch and Skye. ✉ *Off A832* ☎ *01445/712407* 🌐 *www.gairlochgolfclub.co.uk* 🎟 *£15 for 9 holes, £25 for 18 holes* ⛳ *9 holes, 2167 yards, par 31.*

SHIELDAIG

37 miles south of Gairloch.

Just west of the southern coast of Upper Loch Torridon is Shieldaig, a village that sits in an attractive crescent overlooking a loch of its own, Loch Shieldaig. For an atmospheric evening foray, walk north toward Loch Torridon, at the northern end of the village by the church. The path—fairly well made, though hiking shoes are recommended—leads to exquisite views and tiny, rocky beaches.

GETTING HERE AND AROUND

From Gairloch head south on the A832 then turn onto the A896 at Kinlochewe; Shieldaig is around halfway to Lochcarron.

EXPLORING

OFF THE BEATEN PATH

Applecross. The tame way to reach this small community facing Skye is by a coastal road from near Shieldaig. The exciting route turns west off the A896 a few miles farther south and then a series of hairpin turns corkscrews up the steep wall at the head of a corrie (a glacier-cut mountain valley), over the **Bealach na Ba** (Pass of the Cattle). There are spectacular views of Skye from the bare plateau on top, and you can brag afterward that you've been on what is probably Scotland's highest drivable road.

Fodor's Choice ★

Glen Torridon. The scenic spectacle of Glen Torridon lies east of Shieldaig as you follow the A896 between Kinlochewe and Shieldaig. Some say that Glen Torridon has the finest mountain scenery in Scotland. It consists mainly of the long, gray, quartzite flanks of **Beinn Eighe** and **Liathach,** with its distinct ridge profile that looks like the keel of an upturned boat.

WHERE TO STAY

$$$$ HOTEL

🏨 **The Torridon.** The Victorian Gothic turrets of this former hunting lodge promise atmosphere and grandeur—and the Torridon doesn't disappoint. **Pros:** wonderful location; center for outdoor activities; more than 300 malts in the bar. **Cons:** quite pricey. [$] *Rooms from: £380* ✉ *A896* ☎ *01445/700300* 🌐 *www.thetorridon.com* 🛏 *18 rooms* 🍴 *Breakfast.*

$$ B&B/INN

🏨 **Torridon Inn.** A more affordable option than the grand Torridon Hotel, this bright and sparkling clean lodging makes a great base for exploring the area. **Pros:** pleasant wood-clad decor; eco-friendly vibe; reasonable rates. **Cons:** service sometimes erratic; can be noisy. [$] *Rooms from: £130* ✉ *A896* ☎ *01445/791242* 🌐 *www.thetorridon.com/inn* 🛏 *12 rooms* 🍴 *Breakfast.*

LOCHCARRON

14 miles southeast of Shieldaig, 23 miles northeast of Skye, 62 miles west of Inverness.

Strung along the shore, the village of Lochcarron has some attractive croft buildings, a couple of churches (one an 18th-century ruin set in a graveyard), a golf club, and some handy shops.

GETTING HERE AND AROUND

To drive here from Shieldaig, take A896 south; the single-lane road skirts both steep mountains and lochs. From Skye, take the A87 and turn northwards onto the A890, then turn east onto the A896.

WHERE TO EAT

$ CAFÉ 🍴 **Bealach Café.** This lovely café offers sandwiches, soups, and fine home baking against a background of mountains and the steepest road ascent in Britain, the Bealach na Ba (from which it gets its name). All this can be viewed through the café's large windows or from the outside deck, if weather allows. **Known for:** lovely home-baked cakes; friendly hosts; views to die for. [$] *Average main: £9* ✉ *A896* ☎ *01520/733436* 🌐 *www.thebealach.co.uk* ⏲ *Closed Mon. No dinner.*

SHOPPING

Lochcarron Weavers. Watch a weaver producing pure-wool tartans that can be bought here or at the company's other outlets in the area. There's also a café. ✉ *Lochcarron* ☎ *01520/722212* 🌐 *www.lochcarron.co.uk.*

ISLE OF SKYE

Fodor's Choice ★ The misty Isle of Skye is awash with romance and myth, lush green gardens, and steep, magnetic mountains. Its extraordinary natural beauty and royal connections see it rank highly on most visitors' must-see lists, while its proximity to the mainland makes it one of Scotland's most easily accessible islands.

Skye has a dramatic, mysterious, and mountainous landscape, where sunsets linger brilliantly until late at night and otherworldly mists roll gently through the valleys. Much photographed are the old crofts, one or two of which are still inhabited today. It also has an impressive range of accommodation, and restaurants that showcase the best of the island's produce and culinary talent.

To reach Skye, cross over the bridge spanning the narrow channel of Kyleakin, between Kyle of Lochalsh and Kyleakin. Or, if you're visiting in the summer, take a romantic boat trip between Mallaig and Armadale or between Glenelg and Kylerhea. You can tour comfortably around the island in two or three days, but a bit longer will allow extra time for hiking or sea kayaking.

Orientation is easy: in the north, follow the roads that loop around the peninsulas of Waternish and Trotternish; in the south, enjoy the road running the length of the Sleat Peninsula. There are some stretches of single-lane road, but for careful drivers these shouldn't pose a problem.

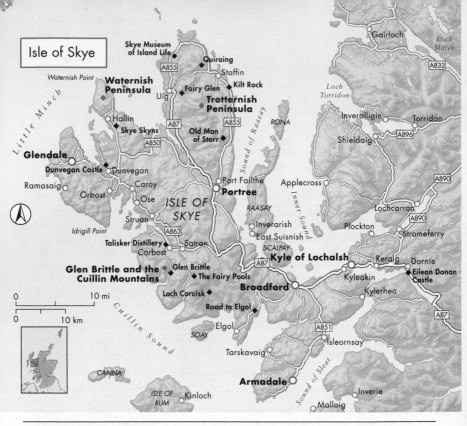

Isle of Skye

KYLE OF LOCHALSH

55 miles west of Inverness, 120 miles northwest of Glasgow.

This little town is the mainland gateway to Skye. Opened in 1995, the bridge transformed not only travel to Skye but the very seascape itself. The most noticeable attraction, though (in fact, almost a cliché), is not in Kyle at all, but 8 miles farther east at Dornie—Eilean Donan Castle.

GETTING HERE AND AROUND

From the north, you reach Kyle of Lochalsh via the A890; from the south, take the A87. There are four direct trains a day from Inverness.

EXPLORING

FAMILY **Bright Water Visitor Centre.** Discover *Ring of Bright Water*, Gavin Maxwell's much-loved account of his work with otters on the island of Eilean Ban. This center, in Kyleakin at the northern tip of Skye, has an exhibit illustrating his work; wildlife tours that promise otters, seals, and birdlife; and a whole host of interactive activities. The center itself is just over the bridge from Kyle of Lochalsh, and includes a 155-year-old lighthouse designed by Robert Louis Stevenson's father. ⊠ *The Pier, Kyleakin* ☎ *01599/530040* ⊕ *www.eileanban.org* ⊠ *Free* ⊗ *Closed Oct.–Easter and weekends.*

Fodor'sChoice ★ **Eilean Donan Castle.** Guarding the confluence of lochs Long, Alsh, and Duich stands the most picturesque of all Scottish castles. Eilean Donan Castle, perched on an islet connected to the mainland by a stone-arched bridge, dates from the 14th century and has all the dramatic stone walls, timber ceilings, and winding stairs you could possibly desire. Empty and neglected for years after being bombarded by frigates of the Royal Navy during an abortive Spanish-Jacobite landing in 1719, this romantic Scottish icon was almost entirely rebuilt from a ruin in the early 20th century. The kitchen re-creates the busy scene before a grand banquet, and the upper floors show how the castle was transformed into a grand house. The picturesque cover of a thousand travel brochures, Eilean Donan has also appeared in a number of Hollywood movies and TV shows, from *The Wicker Man* to *Highlander*. There's a shop and a coffeehouse for the many visitors. ✉ *A87, Dornie* ☎ *01599/555202* 🌐 *www.eileandonancastle.com* 🎫 *£7.50* 🕓 *Closed Jan.*

EN ROUTE **Plockton.** Once a fishing and crofting center, Plockton today attracts visitors for its natural beauty and its warm microclimate, which allows palms to grow all along the main Harbour Street. Situated just 6 miles northeast of Kyle of Lochalsh, its natural bay is an ideal space for the small yachts that make their leisurely way to the coast and beyond, where gray seals can often be seen. Park at the car park at the entrance to the village and stroll along the main street, ideally with an ice cream as your companion. ✉ *Kyle of Lochalsh* ✥ *6 miles northeast of Kyle of Lochalsh.*

WHERE TO STAY

$$ B&B/INN 🏨 **Glenelg Inn.** Looking out over the Sound of Sleat, the Glenelg Inn's pleasant, contemporary rooms are furnished in wood and cane and are bright and clean. **Pros:** lively atmosphere; pretty views; excellent local seafood. **Cons:** no sea views in some rooms; out-of-the-way location. [$] *Rooms from: £110* ✉ *Kirkton* ☎ *01599/522273* 🌐 *www.glenelg-inn.com* 🛏 *7 rooms* 🍴 *Breakfast.*

BROADFORD

8 miles west of Kyle of Lochalsh via Skye Bridge.

One of the larger of Skye's settlements, Broadford lies along the shore of Broadford Bay, which has been known to welcome whales to its sheltered waters.

GETTING HERE AND AROUND

Broadford is on the A87, the main road crossing the Isle of Skye.

ESSENTIALS

Visitor Information Broadford Visitor Information Centre. ✉ *The car park, off A87* ☎ *01471/822361* 🌐 *www.visitscotland.com.*

EXPLORING

FAMILY Fodor'sChoice ★ **Misty Isle Boat Trips.** For fantastic views of the Cuillin Mountains and the Inner Hebrides, book a place on one of the Misty Isle Boat Trips. The expansive scenery around Loch Coruisk is some of the most spectacular in Scotland. Round-trip journeys depart from the town of Elgol, and booking ahead is essential. Prices vary, but a cruise to a seal colony

10

costs £17.50. Private charters are available. ✉ *Elgol jetty, Sealladh na Mara, Elgol* ☎ *01471/866288* 🌐 *www.mistyisleboattrips.co.uk* 🎫 *From £12.50* ⏲ *Closed Nov.–Mar. and Sun.*

OFF THE BEATEN PATH

Road to Elgol. The B8083 leads from Broadford to one of the finest vistas anywhere in Scotland. This road passes by **Strath Suardal** and little **Loch Cill Chriosd** (Kilchrist), and also takes in breathtaking views of the mountain **Bla Bheinn** en route. As the A881 continues to Elgol, see a gathering of traditional crofts that descends to a pier, then admire the heart-stopping profile of the Cuillin peaks from the shore. Seek out the path, around halfway down the hill, that leads across rough grasslands into the mountains. ✉ *Elgol.*

OFF THE BEATEN PATH

Bella Jane. Take a boat trip on the *Bella Jane* to see playful seals frolicking in the water. The three-hour round-trip excursions to Loch Coruisk are generally available April to October, though lucky winter visitors may find boat trips running on sunny days. ✉ *Elgol jetty, Elgol* ☎ *01471/866244* 🌐 *www.bellajane.co.uk* 🎫 *From £26 round-trip* ⏲ *Closed Nov.–Mar.*

WHERE TO EAT AND STAY

$$ SEAFOOD Fodor's Choice ★

🍴 **Creelers of Skye.** Don't be fooled by its humble appearance; Creelers is a celebrated French seafood restaurant. From its pan-roasted sea bass to its seafood gumbo, it is a compulsory stop for all passing gourmands. **Known for:** excellent bouillabaisse; sea views. [$] *Average main: £18* ✉ *Lower Harrapool* ☎ *01471/822281* 🌐 *www.skye-seafood-restaurant.co.uk* ⏲ *Closed Sun.*

$$$ HOTEL

🏨 **Broadford Hotel.** Watch over Broadford Bay in comfort and style with a stay at this well-appointed hotel, which takes pride in being the place where Drambuie was invented. **Pros:** quintessentially Scottish; convenient location; free Wi-Fi. **Cons:** no elevator; poorly lit public areas. [$] *Rooms from: £164* ✉ *Torrin Rd.* ☎ *01471/822204* 🌐 *www.broadfordhotel.co.uk* 🛏 *11 rooms* 🍽 *Breakfast.*

ARMADALE

17 miles south of Broadford, 43 miles south of Portree, 5 miles (ferry crossing) west of Mallaig.

Rolling moorlands, scattered with rivers and lochans, give way to enchanting hidden coves and scattered waterside communities. Welcome to **Sleat,** Skye's southernmost peninsula.

GETTING HERE AND AROUND

The Mallaig-Armadale ferry arrives here. There's a short (and beautiful) road to the southwest, while the main road heads east following the stunning coast.

EXPLORING

Armadale Castle, Gardens & Museum of the Isles. As the name suggests, this attraction has three distinct strings to its bow: a romantic, ruined castle; a lush, flower-filled estate; and a fascinating museum of local history. The castle is a windswept 17th-century mansion house built by the influential Clan Donald, while the extensive gardens cover 40 acres, offering magnificent views across the Sound of Sleat to Knoydart and the

Mallaig Peninsula. The highlight, however, is the fascinating museum, which tells the story of the clan and their proud title, the Lords of the Isles, with the help of an excellent audiovisual presentation. There's a gift shop, restaurant, library, and center for genealogy research. Also on the grounds are high-quality accommodations in the form of seven cottages, complete with kitchen facilities. Access is from Armadale Pier, where signs indicate the different forest walks that are available. ✉ *Off A851* ✣ *½ mile north of Armadale Pier* ☎ *01471/844305* 🌐 *www.clan-donald.com* 🎫 *Gardens free, museum £8.50* 🕐 *Closed Nov.–Mar.*

WHERE TO STAY

$$$$ HOTEL 🏨 **Duisdale House Hotel.** Set in 35 acres of mature woodlands and gardens, this former mansion with a lovely hillside location and ocean views is boutique chic at its very best. **Pros:** finely furnished rooms; expansive views; attentive staff. **Cons:** nautical decor is an acquired taste; expensive. [$] *Rooms from: £280* ✉ *Off A851, Isleornsay* ☎ *01471/833202* 🌐 *www.duisdale.com* 🛏 *18 rooms* 🍴 *Breakfast.*

$$$$ HOTEL Fodor's Choice ★ 🏨 **Hotel Eilean Iarmain.** Built on a small peninsula dotted by a quiet lighthouse, this hotel has an unforgettable location and an enchanting collection of wood paneling, chintz fabrics, and country-style antiques. **Pros:** spectacular waterfront location; plenty of sporting activities; excellent wine list. **Cons:** temperamental Wi-Fi. [$] *Rooms from: £235* ✉ *Off A851, Isleornsay* ☎ *01471/833332* 🌐 *www.eileaniarmain.co.uk* 🛏 *16 rooms* 🍴 *Breakfast.*

$$$$ HOTEL 🏨 **Kinloch Lodge.** An upmarket hotel with an equally upmarket restaurant, Kinloch Lodge peacefully overlooks the tidal Loch na Dal. The historic buildings date from the 17th century, while the newer South House has the best views, built from the ground up with comfort and relaxation in mind. **Pros:** historic property; characterful interior; sublime afternoon tea. **Cons:** expensive rooms and dining. [$] *Rooms from: £380* ✉ *Off A851, Isleornsay* ☎ *01471/833333* 🌐 *www.kinloch-lodge.co.uk* 🛏 *19 rooms* 🍴 *Breakfast.*

SHOPPING

Fodor's Choice ★ **Ragamuffin.** This well-stocked shop specializes in designer knitwear and has some of the nicest staff you could hope to meet. On cold winter days, they might make you coffee while you browse, then mail your purchases back home for you. ✉ *Armadale Pier, off A851* ☎ *01471/844217* 🌐 *www.ragamuffinloves.blogspot.co.uk.*

PORTREE

42 miles northwest of Armadale.

Portree, the population center of the island, is a pleasant place clustered around a small and sheltered bay. Although not overburdened by historical features, it's a fine touring base with a number of good shops and an excellent bakery.

GETTING HERE AND AROUND

The biggest town on Skye, Portree is well served by local buses and by a well-maintained road, the A87.

ESSENTIALS

Visitor Information VisitScotland Portree iCentre. ✉ *Bayfield House, Bayfield Rd.* ☎ *01478/612992* 🌐 *www.visitscotland.com.*

EXPLORING

Aros. On the outskirts of town, Aros is a community center that screens films, exhibits artworks, and hosts live music, dance, and theater productions. It's the cultural hub of the Isle of Skye. ✉ *Viewfield Rd.* ☎ *01478/613649* 🌐 *www.aros.co.uk* 🎟 *Free.*

WHERE TO EAT

$ BRITISH 🍴 **Café Arriba.** Up a steep flight of stairs, the laid-back café has window seats with great views over Portree Harbour. Using only local produce (whatever is "fresh, local, and available"), this is a good option for no-frills eating. **Known for:** delicious homemade cakes; mildly treacherous stairs. [$] *Average main: £8* ✉ *Quay Brae, Quay St.* ☎ *01478/611830* 🌐 *www.cafearriba.co.uk.*

$$$ BRITISH 🍴 **Scorrybreac Restaurant.** It may be tiny, but this 20-seater restaurant has made big waves since opening in 2013. The vibe is relaxed and informal, while the cooking is imaginative and varied, creating unexpected marriages such as coffee-crusted venison or coconut and hake. **Known for:** intimate dining; inventive dishes. [$] *Average main: £20* ✉ *7 Bosville Terr.* ☎ *01478/612069* 🌐 *www.scorrybreac.com* 🕒 *Closed Mon. No lunch.*

WHERE TO STAY

$$$ HOTEL 🏨 **Cuillin Hills Hotel.** This Victorian-era hunting lodge looks down on Portree and the brightly painted houses around the harbor. **Pros:** a short stroll from Portree; good breakfast menu; attentive service. **Cons:** rooms at back overpriced; restaurant can be full; no elevator. [$] *Rooms from: £215* ✉ *Off A855* ☎ *01478/612003* 🌐 *www.cuillinhills-hotel-skye.co.uk* 🛏 *29 rooms* 🍽 *Breakfast.*

$$$ B&B/INN 🏨 **Peinmore House.** A former manse (the minister's residence), Peinmore House has panoramic views to die for: to the north, Portree Bay (on a clear day, all the way to the Old Man of Storr); to the south, the moody Cuillin mountains. **Pros:** tranquil location; great breakfast; impeccable rooms. **Cons:** rather pricey; car required to get here. [$] *Rooms from: £165* ✉ *Off B883, 2 miles south of Portree* ☎ *01478/612574* 🌐 *www.peinmorehouse.co.uk* 🛏 *4 rooms* 🍽 *Breakfast.*

SHOPPING

Isle of Skye Soap Company. This charming little shop handcrafts its own soaps, aromatherapy oils, candles, and other pleasingly fragranced gifts. Founder (and soap-maker in chief) Fiona is an aromatherapist. ✉ *Somerled Sq.* ☎ *01478/611350* 🌐 *www.skye-soap.co.uk.*

TROTTERNISH PENINSULA

16 miles north of Portree.

Travel north from Portree on the A855 and you'll see cliffs rising to the left. These are the closest edge of an ancient lava flow, set back from the road and running the length of the peninsula. Fossilized dinosaur

Clans and Tartans

The Scottish clans have a long and varied history. Some clans claim Norman roots and later married into Celtic society; others were of Norse origin, the product of Viking raids on Scotland; while others still may have been descended from Pictish tribes. Whatever their origins, by the 13th century the clan system was at the heart of Gaelic tribal culture. By the 15th century, clan chiefs of the Scottish Highlands were even a threat to the authority of the Stewart monarchs.

The word *clann* means "family" or "children" in Gaelic, and it was customary for clan chiefs to board out their sons among nearby families, a practice that helped to bond the clan unit and create strong allegiances.

THE CLAN SYSTEM

The clan chiefs' need for strong men-at-arms, fast-running messengers, and bards for entertainment, and the preservation of clan genealogy, was the probable origin of the Highland Games, with their unusual mix of sports, music, and dance. Highland Games are celebrated annually across Highland communities to this day.

Gradually, by the 18th century, increasing knowledge of Lowland agricultural improvements, and better roads into the Highlands that improved communication of ideas and "southern" ways, began to weaken the clan system. The Battle of Culloden marked the death of the clan system, as the victorious English armies banned the kilt and the pipes and claimed the land of the rebellious clan chiefs. And when the new landowners introduced the hardy Cheviot breed of sheep and changed farming activity, the Highlands were transformed forever. Many Highlanders, and especially islanders, began to emigrate in the 1750s, and by the 1820s, landowners were paying people to leave.

TARTAN REVIVAL

Tartan's own origins as a part of the clan system are disputed; the Gaelic word for striped cloth is *breacan*—piebald or spotted—so even the word itself is not Highland. However, when cloth was locally spun, woven, and dyed using plant derivatives, each neighborhood would use different colorings. In this way, combinations of colors and favorite patterns of the local weavers could become associated with an area and therefore its dominant clans. Between 1746 and 1782, the wearing of tartan was generally prohibited, and by the time the ban was lifted, many recipes for dyes and weaving patterns had been forgotten.

It took the influence of Sir Walter Scott, with his romantic (and fashionable) view of Highland history, to create the "modern myth" of clans and tartan. Sir Walter engineered George IV's visit to Scotland in 1822, which turned into a tartan extravaganza. The idea of one tartan or group of tartans "belonging" to one particular clan was created at this time—literally created, with new patterns dreamed up and "assigned" to particular clans. Queen Victoria and Prince Albert reinforced the tartan culture later in the century—and with it, the revival of the Highland Games.

10

bones have been uncovered at the base of these cliffs, while overhead, you might just spot a sea eagle, identifiable by the flash of its white tail.

GETTING HERE AND AROUND
From Portree, take the twisting, undulating A855 as it follows the coast.

EXPLORING
TOP ATTRACTIONS

Fodor'sChoice **Fairy Glen.** Out of the way and little visited, Fairy Glen is a magical
★   place—an enchanting, otherworldly valley of strange green hillocks, eerily still pools, crumbling cottages, and roaming sheep. To get here, take a small road just south of Uig signed "Sheader and Balnaknock" and drive for about a mile. ✢ *11 miles southwest of Staffin* ☒ *Free.*

Old Man of Storr. Along the dramatic road around the Trotternish Peninsula, a gate beside a car park marks the beginning of the climb to the Old Man of Storr, one of Skye's most iconic landmarks. At 2,000 feet, this volcanic pinnacle is the highest point on the peninsula, so give yourself at least three hours to explore and enjoy the spectacular views from the top. ⚠ **The weather here changes very quickly, so be prepared.**

Fodor'sChoice **Quiraing.** A spectacular geological formation of rocky crags and tower-
★   ing stacks, Quiraing dominates the horizon of the Trotternish Peninsula. It is situated about 5 miles beyond Kilt Rock, so for a closer look, make a left onto a small road at Brogaig by Staffin Bay. There's a parking lot near the point where this road breaches the ever-present cliff line. The road is very narrow and rough, so drive cautiously. The rambler's trail is on uneven, stony ground, and it's a steep scramble up to the rock formations. In ages past, stolen cattle were hidden deep within the Quiraing's rocky jaws.

Skye Museum of Island Life. Discover the old crofting ways of the local population at this museum, situated close to the tip of the Trotternish Peninsula. Informative displays and exhibits show life as it was on the island merely a century ago, from reconstructed interiors with traditional tools and implements to historical photographs and documents. ☒ *Off A855, Kilmuir* ☎ *01470/552206* ⊕ *www.skyemuseum.co.uk* ☒ *£2.50* ☾ *Closed Nov.–Easter and Sun.*

WORTH NOTING

Kilt Rock. No drive between Portree and Staffin is complete without a sojourn at Skye's most famous sea cliff. Named for the shape of its sheer rock face, which is ridged like a pleated kilt and swoops out to sea at the "hem," soaring Kilt Rock (and its gushing waterfall) can be seen from a specially built viewing platform. ☒ *Staffin* ✢ *1½ miles south of Staffin.*

FAMILY **Staffin Ecomuseum.** Billed as "a museum without walls," the Staffin Ecomuseum is a collection of 13 open-air geological and social exhibits dotted along the landscape of the peninsula. Follow the map along the coastal route and you will discover dinosaur footprints, a healing well, a deserted village, and more. This is not to be confused with Staffin Museum, Dugald Ross's nearby exhibition. ☒ *Staffin Community Trust, 3 Ellishadder, Staffin* ⊕ *www.skyecomuseum.co.uk.*

WHERE TO EAT AND STAY

$
BRITISH
⤬ **Skye Pie Café at Glenview.** For a gourmet pie made using locally sourced, organic ingredients, look no further than this sweet café. Housed in a renovated, whitewashed croft building, complete with wooden floors and cheerfully painted walls. the café serves every style of pie imaginable, from savory meat or fish to sweet apple or toffee. **Known for:** delicious pies; specialty sausage rolls; comfortable rooms. $ *Average main: £5* ✉ *A855, Culnacnoc, Staffin* ☎ *01470/562248* ⊕ *skyepiecafe. co.uk* ☉ *Closed Nov.–Easter and weekends. No dinner.*

$
B&B/INN
⛺ **Corran House.** Set back off the A87 near Kingsburgh, this cozy B&B is a convenient, good-value stay at the base of the Trotternish Peninsula, 7 miles northwest of Portree. **Pros:** great location between sights; splendid views; good value. **Cons:** not close to any one particular attraction. $ *Rooms from: £80* ✉ *1 Eyre, Portree* ✛ *Set back from the road; look out for the small white sign* ☎ *01470/532699* ⊕ *www.corranhouseskye. co.uk* ⇱ *6 rooms* ⎮⊚⎮ *Breakfast.*

$$$
HOTEL
⛺ **The Flodigarry Hotel.** With spectacular coastal views and antique furnishings throughout, the Flodigarry Hotel retains the feel of a grand country manor. **Pros:** spectacular views; a good base for walking; free Wi-Fi. **Cons:** steep road down; expensive rooms. $ *Rooms from: £210* ✉ *A855, Staffin* ☎ *01470/552203* ⊕ *www.hotelintheskye.co.uk* ⇱ *18 rooms* ⎮⊚⎮ *Breakfast.*

WATERNISH PENINSULA

20 miles northwest of Portree.

The northwest corner of Skye has scattered crofting communities and magnificent coastal views. In the Hallin area, look westward for a sea loch with small cliffs rising from the water like miniature models of full-size islands.

GETTING HERE AND AROUND

From Portree, follow the A87 north then head west on the A850 to the Waternish Peninsula.

EXPLORING

Skye Skyns. A 10-minute tour of this working tannery gives visitors excellent insight into the process of salting, washing, and preparing sheepskins. You'll learn the source of such phrases as "on tenterhooks" and "stretched to the limits," and you can buy sheepskins from the on-site shop. ✉ *17 Lochbay, Waternish* ☎ *01470/592237* ⊕ *www.sky-eskyns.co.uk* 🎟 *Free.*

WHERE TO EAT

$$$$
SEAFOOD
⤬ **Loch Bay Restaurant.** Situated right on the waterfront, this distinctive black-and-white restaurant is a Skye foodie favorite. It's where the island's top chefs unwind on their nights off, so you know it must be good. **Known for:** sublime yet simple seafood; beautiful bay views. $ *Average main: £35* ✉ *1 Macleods Terr., Stein* ☎ *01470/592235* ⊕ *www.lochbay-restaurant.co.uk* ☉ *Closed Jan., Feb., and Mon. and Tues. Easter–Oct. No lunch Sat. and Oct.–Easter. No dinner Sun.*

10

SHOPPING

Edinbane Pottery. This store, which specializes in quirky handmade ceramics and watercolors of local wildlife, is a great place to pick up a distinctive souvenir from your time on Skye. ⊠ *Off A850, Edinbane* ☎ *01470/582234* ⊕ *www.edinbane-pottery.co.uk.*

GLENDALE

14 miles southwest of Waternish.

Glendale is a region rich in flora and fauna: otters, seals, and dolphins can be spotted off its rocky coast, while white-tailed sea eagles soar overhead. Dunvegan Castle is just at the region's eastern edge.

GETTING HERE AND AROUND

Traveling south from Dunvegan, the B884 road twists and curves along the coast. It can feel rather isolated in bad weather or after dark.

EXPLORING

Fodor's Choice ★ **Dunvegan Castle.** In a commanding position looming over a sea loch, Dunvegan Castle has been the seat of the chiefs of Clan MacLeod for more than 700 years. Though the structure has been greatly changed over the centuries, a gloomy ambience prevails, and there's plenty of family history on display; most notable is the Fairy Flag—a silk banner, thought to be originally from Rhodes or Syria, which is credited with protecting the clan from danger. Enthusiastic guides take you through several rooms, and an interesting collection of photos hangs in the lower corridors. Make time to visit the gardens, with their water garden and falls, fern house, walled garden, and various viewing points. There's a café beside the car park. Boat trips from the castle to the nearby seal colony run mid-April through September. ⊠ *Junction of A850 and A863, Dunvegan* ☎ *01470/521206* ⊕ *www.dunvegancastle.com* ⊠ *Castle and gardens £13; gardens only £11; seal trips £7.50.*

WHERE TO EAT AND STAY

$$$$
MODERN BRITISH
Fodor's Choice ★ ✕ **Three Chimneys.** Perhaps the Isle of Skye's biggest culinary draw, this old stone-walled restaurant on the banks of Loch Dunvegan serves consistently daring, well-crafted food. The chef's belief in quality Scottish ingredients is evident in every dish, from the locally sourced game to the sublime Scottish seafood, and when aligned with the simple but chic interior—all crisp white walls and exposed brickwork—it makes for a luxury dining experience you won't soon forget. Too full to move? **Known for:** inventive seafood dishes; faultless service. $ *Average main: £65* ⊠ *Colbost House, B884, Colbost* ☎ *01470/511258* ⊕ *www.three-chimneys.co.uk* ☾ *Closed mid-Dec.–mid-Jan.* ☞ *No children under 8 at dinner.*

$
B&B/INN
☲ **Roskhill House.** A 19th-century croft house that once housed the local post office, this pretty Glendale hotel feels like a home away from home. **Pros:** friendly and helpful hosts; cozy lounge with fireplace; free Wi-Fi. **Cons:** very small place; need to reserve far in advance. $ *Rooms from: £93* ⊠ *A863, Roskhill ✦ 3 miles south of Dunvegan* ☎ *01470/521317* ⊕ *www.roskhillhouse.co.uk* ⇋ *5 rooms* ❑ *Breakfast.*

SHOPPING

Skye Silver. Distinctive gold and silver jewelry with Celtic themes is the bread and butter of Skye Silver. From pendants to rings, bracelets to earrings, you'll find beautiful and unique pieces inspired by the surrounding natural landscapes of sea and countryside, with motifs of island wildlife. ⊠ *The Old School, B884, Colbost* ☏ *01470/511263* ⊕ *www.skyesilver.com.*

GLEN BRITTLE AND THE CUILLIN MOUNTAINS

28 miles southeast of Glendale.

Fodor's Choice The gentle slopes of this valley are a gateway to the dramatic peaks and
★ ridges of the Cuillin Mountains. Glen Brittle's lower slopes are fine for walkers and weekend climbers, but the higher ridges are strictly for serious mountaineers.

GETTING HERE AND AROUND

Glen Brittle extends off the A863/B8009 on the west side of the island.

EXPLORING

Fodor's Choice **Fairy Pools.** One of the most magical sights in Scotland, the Fairy Pools
★ are a spectacularly beautiful collection of waterfalls and plunge pools in the midst of Glen Brittle. The rocky gray landscape contrasts with the vivid blue-green of the pools, the colorful plant life, and visiting wildlife (including, occasionally, red deer) to give the environment a fairy-tale feel. You can walk to the pools from a parking lot 20 minutes away. Come at sunrise or sunset for a truly enchanting swim—just don't expect the water to be warm. ⊠ *Glenbrittle* ☞ *Free.*

Glen Brittle. Enjoy spectacular mountain scenery in Glen Brittle, including some unforgettable views of the Cuillin Mountains (these are not for the casual walker, due to steep and dangerous cliff faces). The drive from Carbost along a single-track road is one of the most dramatic in Scotland and draws outdoorsy types from across the globe. At the southern end of the glen is a murky-color beach, a campground, and gentle foothills that were made for strolling. ⊠ *Off A863 and B8009.*

10

Talisker Distillery. The only distillery on the Isle of Skye is one of the best in Scotland. Talisker produces a sweet, light single malt that has the distinctive peaty aroma of island whiskies, yet with less intensity—making it a great introductory dram for newcomers to Scotch. Robert Louis Stevenson called Talisker "the king of drinks," and the inhabitants of Skye are very proud of it. Classic tours here take about 45 minutes, while tasting tours (available weekdays) take two hours. Book ahead, as tours are very popular. ⊠ *B8009, Carbost* ☏ *01478/614308* ⊕ *www.discovering-distilleries.com/talisker* ☞ *Tours from £10* ⊗ *Closed mid-Feb.–mid-Mar., Sun. in Apr., May, and Oct., and weekends in Nov.–Mar.*

THE OUTER HEBRIDES

The Outer Hebrides—the Western Isles in common parlance—stretch about 130 miles from end to end and lie roughly 50 miles from the Scottish mainland. This splintered archipelago extends from the Butt of Lewis in the north (no giggling) to Barra Head in the south, whose lighthouse has the greatest arc of visibility in the world. In the Hebrides, clouds cling to the hills, and rain comes in squalls. Any trip here requires protection from the weather and a conviction that a great holiday does not require constant sunshine.

It may have two names, but Lewis and Harris is one single island, the third largest in the United Kingdom, in fact, after Great Britain and Ireland. Lewis is the term used to refer to the northern two-thirds of the island, with Harris representing the southern third. The island's only major town, Stornoway, is on a nearly landlocked harbor on the east coast of Lewis; it's the most convenient starting point for a driving tour of the island (assuming you arrive, like most visitors, by ferry from the mainland or by plane). Lewis and Harris has some fine historic attractions, including the Calanais Standing Stones—a truly magical glimpse of an ancient civilization—as well as an abundance of natural beauty.

Just south of the Sound of Harris is the Isle of North Uist, rich in monoliths, chambered cairns, and other reminders of a prehistoric past. Benbecula, sandwiched between North and South Uist, is in fact less bare and neglected-looking than its bigger neighbors to the north. The Isle of South Uist, once a refuge of the old Catholic faith, is dotted with ruined forts and chapels; in summer its wild gardens burst with alpine and rock plants. Eriskay Island and a scattering of islets almost block the 6-mile strait between South Uist and Barra, an island you can walk across in an hour.

Harris tweed is available at many outlets on the islands, including some of the weavers' homes; keep an eye out for signs directing you to weavers' workshops. Sunday on the islands is observed as a day of rest, and nearly all shops and visitor attractions are closed. This includes most restaurants, with the exception of some island hotels, so make dinner plans in advance.

ISLE OF LEWIS

53 miles from Ullapool via ferry.

The history of Lewis stretches back 5,000 years, as archaeological sites scattered across the island attest. Here, the Highland past persists in the Gaelic that is spoken everywhere, and the clan names are still borne by most of its inhabitants. The main town on Lewis is Stornoway.

GETTING HERE AND AROUND

Three main routes radiate from Stornoway to give access to the rest of the island. The A859 leads south all the way to Harris; the A857 leads north to Port of Ness, the island's northernmost point; and the A858 leads west, looping up and round to meet the A857 near Brue.

STORNOWAY

2½-hour ferry trip from Ullapool.

The port capital for the Outer Hebrides is Stornoway, the only major town on Lewis. As the island's cultural center, it has a few interesting attractions and an increasing number of good restaurants. Keep an eye out for seals bobbing about in the harbor.

The ferry docks at Stornoway, and there's an airport within easy reach of the center. It's best to have a car to explore the island, but there are also infrequent local buses to attractions including the Calanais Standing Stones and the Blackhouse at Arnol.

Airport Contact Stornoway Airport. ✉ *A866, Stornoway* ☎ *01851/702256* 🌐 *www.hial.co.uk/stornoway-airport/.*

Visitor Information Stornoway VisitScotland iCentre. ✉ *26 Cromwell St., Stornoway* ☎ *01851/703088* 🌐 *www.visitscotland.com.*

EXPLORING

An Lanntair Arts Centre. This fabulous arts center hosts exhibitions of contemporary and traditional art and frequent traditional musical and theatrical events in the impressive auditorium. There's also a cinema, a gift shop, and a café bar serving coffee and snacks alongside fine international and Scottish fare. ✉ *Kenneth St., Stornoway* ☎ *01851/703307* 🌐 *www.lanntair.com* 🕑 *Closed Sun.*

WHERE TO EAT AND STAY

$$$ MODERN BRITISH Fodor's Choice ★

🍴 **Digby Chick.** Lewis's best seafood restaurant, this informal local favorite is an ideal destination for a rainy evening's meal. The solid wood floors and white tablecloths are guaranteed to brighten your outlook, while the sublime seasonal food will lighten the spirits. **Known for:** inventive seafood dishes; informal atmosphere; having to book by phone. [$] *Average main: £23* ✉ *5 Bank St., Stornoway* ☎ *01851/700026* 🌐 *www.digbychick.co.uk* 🕑 *Closed Sun.*

$$$ B&B/INN

🏨 **Broad Bay House.** It may be a little out of town, but the view alone makes Broad Bay House a worthwhile detour. **Pros:** stunning views; great coastal walks; fine evening meals. **Cons:** no kids under 12; car required; expensive. [$] *Rooms from: £179* ✉ *B895, 7 miles north of Stornoway, Stornoway* ☎ *01851/820990* 🌐 *www.broadbayhouse.co.uk* 🛏 *4 rooms* 🍽 *Breakfast.*

BICYCLING

Alex Dan's Cycle Centre (*AD Cycle Centre*). With a range of bikes to hire, AD Cycle Centre is also a place to pick up valuable advice on where to ride, including a route to Tolsta that takes in five stunning beaches before reaching the edge of moorland. Bike rental is £5 per hour or £20 for 24 hours. ✉ *67 Kenneth St., Stornoway* ☎ *01851/704025* 🌐 *www.ad-cycles.co.uk.*

PORT OF NESS

30 miles north of Stornoway.

The stark, windswept community of Port of Ness cradles a small harbor squeezed in among the rocks.

From Stornoway, drive up the A857 or take Bus W1.

EXPLORING

Butt of Lewis Lighthouse. At the northernmost point of Lewis stands the Butt of Lewis Lighthouse, which was first illuminated in 1862. Designed by David and Thomas Stevenson, it's one of many Scottish lighthouses built by the prominent Stevenson engineering family, whose best-known member was not an engineer at all, but novelist Robert Louis Stevenson. The adjacent cliffs provide a good vantage point for viewing seabirds, whales, and porpoises. ⊠ *B8014, Port of Ness ✛ Northwest of Port of Ness.*

SHOPPING

Borgh Pottery. Pick up a range of attractive hand-thrown studio pottery made on the premises, including lamps, vases, mugs, and dishes. ⊠ *Fivepenny House, A857, Borve* ☎ *01851/850345* ⊕ *www.borghpottery.co.uk.*

CARLOWAY
15 miles northwest of Stornoway.

This old crofting town is surrounded by historic sights that give real insight into island life.

Travel west on the A858, or take the W2 bus from Stornoway.

EXPLORING

Fodor's Choice
★

The Blackhouse. In the small community of Arnol, the Blackhouse is a well-preserved example of an increasingly rare type of traditional Hebridean home. Common throughout the islands as recently as the mid-20th century, these dwellings were built without mortar and thatched on a timber framework without eaves. Other characteristic features include an open central peat hearth and the absence of a chimney (hence "blackhouse," from all the soot). Inside you'll find half the house designated for family life, complete with many original furnishings, and the other half a stable for animals. Opposite is the White House, built later when houses were no longer allowed to accommodate humans and animals together. ⊠ *Off A858, Arnol* ☎ *01851/710395* ⊕ *www. historic-scotland.gov.uk* 🖾 *£4* ⊘ *Closed Sun. Closed Wed. Oct.–Mar.*

Doune Broch (*Dun Carloway Broch*). Discover one of the country's best-preserved Iron Age *brochs* (circular stone towers). These fortified residences are exclusive to Scotland, and Doune Broch dominates the scattered community of Carloway. The mysterious tower was probably built around 2,000 years ago as protection against seaborne raiders; the nearby Doune Broch Centre explains all about the broch, its history, and its setting. ⊠ *Off A857, Carloway* ⊕ *www.visitscotland.com* 🖾 *Free.*

Gearrannan Blackhouse Village (*Garenin*). Situated at the end of a side road north from Carloway, Gearrannan is an old coastal crofting village that has been brought back to life as a living museum with excellent guided tours evoking its past. For a unique self-catering cottage stay, rent one of the restored blackhouses here. There is also a small gift shop and café here. ⊠ *5a Gearrannan, Carloway* ☎ *01851/643416* ⊕ *www. gearrannan.com* 🖾 *Free.*

10

CALANAIS STANDING STONES

15 miles west of Stornoway.

The mysterious arrangement of stones at this ancient site is Lewis's top attraction.

Take the A858 to reach Calanais by car, or pick up the W2 bus from Stornoway.

EXPLORING

Fodor's Choice **Calanais Standing Stones** (*Callanish Stones*). The west coast of Lewis is ★ rich in prehistoric sites, and the most famous of these is the Calanais Standing Stones. Believed to have been positioned in several stages between 3000 BC and 1500 BC, this arrangement consists of an avenue of 19 monoliths extending northward from a circle of 13 stones, with other rows leading south, east, and west. Ruins of a cairn sit within the circle on the east side. Researchers believe they may have been used for astronomical observations, but you're free to cook up your own theories. The visitor center has an interesting exhibit on the stones, a very pleasant tearoom, and a gift shop. ⊠ *Calanais Visitor Centre, Callanish* ☎ *01851/621422* ⊕ *www.callanishvisitorcentre.co.uk* ⊠ *Free; £2.50 for exhibition* ⊙ *Closed Sun. Closed Mon. Nov.–Mar.*

ISLE OF HARRIS

40 miles south of Stornoway.

For most people, Harris is forever linked to tweed. Woven here and on nearby islands, the tweed has colors that echo the tones of the landscape. The dramatic mountains of the northern part of Harris give way in the south to *machairs*, grassy plains typical of this region, and a series of spectacular sandy beaches.

GETTING HERE AND AROUND

The A859 is the main artery through Harris. From Tarbert you can follow the A859 south to Leverburgh (21 miles), where you can catch ferries bound for Newtonferry in North Uist. The single-track road down the east coast is known as the Golden Road.

TARBERT

47 miles south of Calanais.

The main port of Harris, Tarbert has some good shops and a few worthwhile sights. **Traigh Luskentyre,** roughly 5 miles southwest of Tarbert, is a spectacular example of a Harris beach—2 miles of pristine white sand flanked by dunes. Across the bay lies another beautiful beach, **Traigh Seilebost**; both of these would be crowded with holidaymakers if in warmer climes. The narrow Golden Road, which runs along the east coast, offers some glorious views of a rocky, otherworldly landscape.

The ferry from Uig on the Isle of Skye arrives at Tarbert once or twice daily. Having a car makes travel on Harris much easier, but with careful planning, it's possible to see the area with local buses.

Visitor Information Tarbert VisitScotland iCentre. ⊠ *Pier Rd., Tarbert* ☎ *01859/502011* ⊕ *www.visitscotland.com.*

EXPLORING

Fodor's Choice ★ **Isle of Harris Distillery.** Opened in 2015, this island distillery has already gained a reputation for its distinctive gin, infused with coastal botanicals including sugar kelp. Their first malt whisky, called The Hearach (the Gaelic term for an inhabitant of Harris), should be ready in late 2019. The distillery holds guided tours every weekday during the summer months—call to book in advance. ✉ *Tarbert* ☎ *01859/502212* 🌐 *www.harrisdistillery.com* 🎫 *Free* 🕒 *Closed Oct.–mid-May.*

THE BONNIE PRINCE

At the Battle of Culloden, King George II's army outnumbered that of Prince Charles Edward Stuart (aka Bonnie Prince Charlie). After the battle, Charles wandered over the Highlands, escaping to the isles of Harris and South Uist. It's here that he met Flora Macdonald, who took him, disguised as her maid, "over the sea to Skye."

OFF THE BEATEN PATH **Traigh Luskentyre.** One of Scotland's most spectacular beaches, Traigh Luskentyre is flanked by rolling sand dunes on one side and the shimmering sea on the other. Add in the distant peaks, the lush grassland, and the rocky islets and there are few better places on Lewis and Harris for a windswept walk. To reach the beach, drive 8 miles south of Tarbert on the A859, then turn right at the sign to "Losgaintir" (Gaelic for Luskentyre). **Amenities:** parking (no fee); toilets. **Best for:** solitude; sunset; walking. ✉ *Off A859, Tarbert.*

WHERE TO EAT AND STAY

$$$$ BRITISH Fodor's Choice ★ 🍴 **Scarista House.** Enjoy hearty, pleasingly presented fish and game dishes served in an elegant dining room complete with stunning views out to a crescent-shape beach. Scarista House, previously a manse, sits in splendid isolation but is made cozy with heavy curtains, sturdy sofas and chairs, and an open fire. **Known for:** locally sourced ingredients; an extensive wine list; pricey set menus. [$] *Average main: £45* ✉ *A859, Sgarasta Gheag* ✥ *15 miles south of Tarbert* ☎ *01859/550238* 🌐 *www.scaristahouse.com* 🕒 *No lunch.*

$ CAFÉ 🍴 **Skoon Art Café.** This renovated croft house café, which is tucked just off the twisting Golden Road running south from Tarbert to Leverburgh, has a simple, delicious menu that changes daily. You'll find everything from filling homemade soups to sumptuous smoked salmon to mouthwatering cakes. **Known for:** simple but delicious fare; good tea and coffee. [$] *Average main: £8* ✉ *4 Geocrab, Tarbert* ☎ *01859/530268* 🌐 *www.skoon.com* 🕒 *Closed Sun. and Mon. No dinner* 💳 *No credit cards.*

$$ HOTEL 🏨 **Hotel Hebrides.** A small boutique hotel with lovely gardens and views across the loch and harbor, Hotel Hebrides is an oasis of luxury in unassuming Tarbert. **Pros:** wonderful location; comfortable bedrooms. **Cons:** some rooms small; sea views from only some rooms. [$] *Rooms from: £140* ✉ *Pier Rd., Tarbert* ☎ *01859/502364* 🌐 *www.hotel-hebrides.com* 🛏 *21 rooms* 🍽 *Breakfast.*

10

LEVERBURGH

21 miles south of Tarbert.

Named after Lord Leverhulme, who bought Lewis and Harris in 1917 with an eye to developing its local industries, Leverburgh is now the departure and arrival port for North Uist. Nearby Northton and Rodel have several attractions, with St. Clement's Church a particular highlight.

Leverburgh is on the A859 between Tarbert and Rodel.

EXPLORING

Seallam! Visitor Centre and Co Leis Thu? Genealogical Research Centre. Trace your Western Isles ancestry at this informative visitor center. Photographs and interpretive signs reveal the long and turbulent history of Harris and its residents, with the owners organizing guided walks and cultural evenings every week between May and September. ✉ *Off A859, Northton* ☎ *01859/520258* 🌐 *www.hebridespeople.com* 🎫 *£2.50* 🕒 *Closed Sun.*

Fodor's Choice ★ **St. Clement's Church** (*Eaglais Roghadail*). At the southernmost point of Harris, in the village of Rodel, lies St. Clement's Church—the most impressive pre-Reformation House of God in the Outer Hebrides. The large cruciform church, which sits atop a small hillock, was built around 1500. Head inside to see the magnificently sculpted 16th-century wall tomb of the church's builder, clan chief Alasdair Crotach MacLeod of Dunvegan Castle. ✉ *A859, Rodel* 🌐 *www.historic-scotland.gov.uk* 🎫 *Free.*

OFF THE BEATEN PATH

St. Kilda. About 55 miles to the west of Harris lies the abandoned island of St. Kilda. The residents of this island lived in harsh and unforgiving conditions, forced to climb cliffs to hunt fulmar, a cliff-dwelling seabird that was their main source of sustenance. In 1930, the remaining 30 inhabitants left St. Kilda, and it has been deserted ever since. Cruises to this frozen-in-time isle depart from Leverburgh and take three hours; you then have four hours to wander the island. A unique experience with a hefty price tag (between £185 and £210), tours are operated by Kilda Cruises (🌐 *www.kildacruises.co.uk*) and Sea Harris (🌐 *www.seaharris.co.uk*).

WHERE TO EAT AND STAY

$ MODERN BRITISH

🍴 **Anchorage Restaurant.** Situated along the southern coast of Harris, this lively restaurant looks across the Sea of Hebrides toward North Uist. It's a great place to grab a bite before hopping aboard the ferry, which departs from the harbor nearby. **Known for:** cheap and tasty dishes; open until fairly late. [$] *Average main: £13* ✉ *Pier Rd., Leverburgh* ☎ *01859/520225* 🕒 *Closed Nov.–Mar.*

$$ B&B/INN

🏨 **Pairc an t-Srath Guest House.** Set back from the main road and with splendid views of the beach, this rural B&B is comfortable and quirky, with elegant and unpretentious rooms. **Pros:** lovely views of the coast; very good breakfasts. **Cons:** rooms quite small; overkill with the animal statues. [$] *Rooms from: £108* ✉ *Off A859, Borve* ☎ *01859/550386* 🌐 *www.paircant-srath.co.uk* 🛏 *4 rooms* 🍽 *Breakfast.*

NORTH UIST

7 miles southwest of Leverburgh.

Stunning coastal scenery and ancient ruins are the main draws on North Uist. You'll find art everywhere on the island, from the ends of roads and paths to the edge of the coast, only visible from a boat. Be sure to visit the camera obscura (an old-fashioned projector) at the Uist Outdoor Centre just beyond the ferry terminal. Its watery images are evocative and unsettling.

GETTING HERE AND AROUND

You can get to North Uist by ferry from Leverburgh on Harris and from Uig on the Isle of Skye, or you can drive from South Uist and Benbecula on the A865. Public transport is infrequent, so a car (or a bike) is the most reliable way to get around.

EXPLORING

Balranald Nature Reserve. Run by the Royal Society for the Protection of Birds, the Balranald Nature Reserve shelters large numbers of waders and seabirds who inhabit the rock foreshore and marshland. Listen for corncrakes, whose distinctive rasping cry sounds not unlike a plastic drink lid being unscrewed. ⊠ *Hougharry ✛ 3 miles northwest of Bayhead* ☎ *01876/560287* ⊕ *www.rspb.org.uk* ☞ *Free.*

Barpa Langass. Dating back around 5,000 years, Barpa Langass is a chambered cairn (a Neolithic burial monument), the only one in the Western Isles to retain a fully intact inner chamber. You can peek inside, but don't venture too far without a light. You'll find Barpa Langass just off the A867, a third of the way between Clachen and Lochmaddy. ⊠ *Off A687, Lochmaddy.*

Dun an Sticir. Near Port nan Long in the very north of North Uist stands the remains of Dun an Sticir, reputed to be the last inhabited broch on the island. This defensive tower, reached by a causeway over the loch, was built in the Iron Age but abandoned when the Vikings arrived in the 9th century. In 1602, it was reoccupied by Hugh Macdonald, a descendant of Macdonald of Sleat, but since he reached an unpleasant end (starved to death in a castle dungeon on the Isle of Skye), it has been slowly crumbling into the sea. ⊠ *Off B893* ☞ *Free.*

Taigh Chearsabhagh. Set right on the shore, the well-run Taigh Chearsabhagh is an informative museum and arts center, complete with two exhibition spaces, a working printshop, and a permanent exhibition that reveals what life is really like on North Uist. The café serves a selection of cakes and soup, as well as excellent French-press coffee. ⊠ *Lochmaddy* ☎ *01870/603970* ⊕ *www.taigh-chearsabhagh.org* ☞ *£3 museum; galleries free* ☉ *Closed Sun.*

10

SOUTH UIST

12 miles south of Carinish (on North Uist) via Grimsay, Benbecula, and three causeways.

Carpets of wildflowers in spring and early summer, superb deserted beaches, and historical connections to Flora Macdonald and Bonnie Prince Charlie head the list of reasons to visit this island.

GETTING HERE AND AROUND

You can travel the length of South Uist along the A865, making short treks off this main road on your way to Lochboisdale in the southeast. At Lochboisdale you can catch ferries to Barra, the southernmost of the Outer Hebrides' main islands, or to Oban on the mainland.

EXPLORING

Kildonan Museum. This small museum has a number of interesting artifacts on the Uists and their people. The small details, like how locals filled their mattresses or the names for the tools they used in their houses, are what make this place interesting. There is also a craft shop and café renowned for its home-baked cakes. ✉ *A865, Kildonan* ☎ *01878/710343* 🌐 *www.kildonanmuseum.co.uk* 🎟 *£2* 🕓 *Closed Nov.–Mar.*

Our Lady of the Isles. This 30-foot-high granite statue of the Madonna and child is a symbol of island resistance. In the 1950s, the Ministry of Defense proposed building a missile-testing facility on South Uist, but islanders opposed the plans, fearing it would destroy their way of life, culture, and language. So they raised the funds for this ambitious work of art and erected it on land earmarked for development by the MOD. Today, it is a listed monument, making any future building proposals even less likely to succeed. ✉ *Off A865.*

WHERE TO EAT AND STAY

$ BAKERY 🍴 **Lochboisdale Cafe.** A lovely stop for coffee, cake, or a light lunch, this charming pink-roofed café is a favorite with locals and tourists alike. The delicious and filling homemade soups and the wonderful array of colorful cakes are the culinary highlights here. **Known for:** delicious cakes; great coffee (available for takeout). [$] *Average main: £6* ✉ *Kenneth Dr., Lochboisdale* ☎ *01878/700313* 🕓 *No dinner.*

$$ B&B/INN 🏨 **Polochar Inn.** Set within a 300-year-old property, this secluded inn at the southern end of South Uist offers basic but pleasant rooms with a good seafood restaurant and sea views. **Pros:** wild and remote location; reasonable rates; free and reliable Wi-Fi. **Cons:** some small rooms. [$] *Rooms from: £100* ✉ *Bottom of B888, Lochboisdale* ☎ *01878/700215* 🌐 *www.polocharinn.com* 🛏 *11 rooms* 🍽 *Breakfast.*

SHOPPING

Hebridean Jewellery. Handcrafted Celtic-influenced silver and gold earrings, brooches, and pendants are the order of the day at Hebridean Jewellery. Come for a tour of the workshop and stay for an espresso and cake in the on-site café. ✉ *Bualadubh, Iochdar* ☎ *01870/610288* 🌐 *www.hebrideanjewellery.co.uk.*

ORKNEY AND SHETLAND ISLANDS

Updated by
Shona Main
and Nick
Bruno

A Scandinavian heritage gives the 170 islets that make up Orkney and Shetland a history and an ambience different from that of any other region of Scotland. Both Orkney and Shetland are essentially austere and bleak, but they have awe-inspiring seascapes, fascinating seabirds, remarkable ancient ruins, and genuinely warm, friendly people. Although a trip to these remote islands requires time and effort, your reward will be a unique experience.

An Orcadian has been defined as a crofter (farmer) with a boat, whereas a Shetlander has been called a fisherman with a croft. Orkney, the southern archipelago, is greener and is rich with artifacts that testify to the many centuries of continuous settlement here: stone circles, burial chambers, ancient settlements, and fortifications. UNESCO has recognized the key remains as a World Heritage Site called the Heart of Neolithic Orkney.

North of Orkney, Shetland, with its ocean views and sparse landscapes—trees are a rarity because of ever-present wind—seems even more remote. However, don't let Shetland's desolate countryside fool you: it has a wealth of historic interest and is far from being a backwater. Oil money from local mineral resources and its position as a crossroads in the northern seas for centuries have helped make Shetland a busy, thriving community that wants for little.

For mainland Scots, visiting these islands is a little like traveling abroad without having to worry about a different language or currency. Neither has yet been overrun by tourism, but the people of Orkney and Shetland will be delighted that you have come so far to see their islands and learn a little of their extraordinary past.

ORIENTATION AND PLANNING

GETTING ORIENTED

Ten miles from Caithness in Scotland, Orkney is made up of 70 islands, of which 10 are inhabited. A number of ferries travel to ports on the Mainland, the main island of Orkney, including its administrative center, Kirkwall, where an airport serves Scotland's larger cities. The primary road is essentially a loop that passes near the key historic sites. The Mainland is linked to the southern island of South Ronaldsay by way of the Barricades.

About 125 miles north of Orkney lies the spiny outline of Shetland, comprising 100 islands. Sumburgh has the main airport, and 25 miles north is Lerwick, the island's "capital" and a port linking the island to Scotland and Orkney. South Mainland, half an hour from Lerwick,

TOP REASONS TO GO

Standing stones and ancient sites: Among the many Neolithic treasures in Orkney are the Ring of Brodgar, a 3,000-year old circle of standing stones, and Skara Brae, the remarkable remains of a village uncovered on the grounds of delightful Skaill House. In Shetland, Jarlshof has been the home to different societies since the Bronze Age. Don't miss Mousa Broch and Clickimin Broch in Shetland, two Iron Age towers.

Music and arts festivals: The Shetland Folk Festival in late April/ May is a fiddling shindig that attracts musicians and revelers from around the world. Orkney's St. Magnus International Festival is a more highbrow celebration of classical music, poetry, and performance.

Seabirds, seals, and more: These islands have some of the planet's most important colonies of seabirds, with millions clinging to colossal cliffs. You're guaranteed to see seals and may spot dolphins, orcas, or porpoises. In Shetland, Noss, and Eshaness, nature reserves are prime spots, or you can check out the puffins by Sumburgh Head.

Pure relaxation: There's a much more laid-back approach to life on these islands than on the mainland. Shetlanders are particularly renowned for their hospitality and are often happy to share stories and tips that will enrich your adventure.

Outdoor activities by the coast and ocean: The rugged terrain, beautiful beaches, and unspoiled waters make a perfect backdrop for invigorating strolls, sea fishing, diving, or exploring the coastline and sea lochs by boat.

has prehistoric sites. Less than an hour north of Lerwick are dramatic landscapes such as Eshaness. Ferries go beyond the Mainland to Yell and Unst, the latter Britain's most northerly point.

Orkney. The towns of Stomness and Kirkwall have sights and museums testifying to Orkney's rich past, including Kirkwall's Norman St. Magnus Cathedral. For many people, though, they're a prelude to impressive Neolithic sites around the Mainland: Maeshowe, Skara Brae, the Ring of Brodgar, and others. Beyond the Mainland, explore sights such as Scapa Flow on Hoy, which reveals the islands' role in two world wars.

Shetland. A descent at Sumburgh's airport provides stunning views of a shining white lighthouse, bird-crammed cliffs, and golden bays. Lerwick has the excellent Shetland Museum, and nearby on the South Mainland are the prehistoric sites of Jarlshof, Old Scatness, and Mousa Broch. Worth exploring to the north are the lunarlike Ronas Hill and wave-lashed Eshaness. Unst, the island farthest north, is worth the journey for wide-open ocean views and superb bird-watching at Hermaness National Nature Reserve.

PLANNING

WHEN TO GO

Although shivering, wind-flattened visitors braving Orkney and Shetland's winter are not unheard of, the travel season doesn't really start until May, and it runs until September. June is one of the most popular months for both islands. The bird colonies are at their liveliest in early summer, which is also when the long northern daylight hours allow you plenty of sightseeing time. Shetland's northerly position means that it has only four or five hours of darkness around the summer solstice, and on a clear night it doesn't seem to get dark at all. Beware the changeable weather even in summer: it could be 75°F one day and then hail the next. Many sights close in September, and by October wilder gales will be mixed with snow flurries one minute and glorious sunshine the next. If you are determined to brave the elements, take into account that there are only six hours of daylight in winter months. More importantly, there can be thick mist and high winds at Sumburgh and Kirkwall airports even in July, meaning flights cannot take off for days, although they will put you on the Northlink boat if there's space. Bear this in mind when planning flight connections.

Shetland's festival of fire, Up-Helly-Aa, is held the last Tuesday of each January. The spectacle of Lerwick overrun by Vikings, with torches aflame and a huge Viking longship, is wildly popular. Book at least a year in advance if you want to get a bed for the night.

FESTIVALS

In the middle of the long winter, at the end of January, Shetlanders celebrate their Viking culture with the **Up-Helly-Aa Festival**, which—for the men—involves dressing up as Vikings, parading with flaming torches, and then burning a replica of a Viking longship, followed by one or sometimes two nights of carousing. Women play hostess in the halls, feeding and quenching the thirsts of those involved, and dancing with them. The **Shetland Folk Festival**, held in late April/May, and October's **Shetland Accordion and Fiddle Festival** both attract large numbers of visitors. Orkney's **St. Magnus International Festival**, a celebration focusing on classical music, is based in Kirkwall and is usually held the third week in June. Orkney also hosts a jazz festival in April, an annual folk festival at the end of May, the unique **Boys' Ploughing Match** in mid-August, and **The Ba'** (ball; street rugby-football played by the Uppies and Doonies residents of Kirkwall) on Christmas and New Year's Day.

PLANNING YOUR TIME

Orkney and Shetland require at least a couple of days each if you're to do more than just scratch the surface. The isles generate their own laidback approach to life, and once here, you may want to take it slowly.

A good clutch of the key sites of Mainland Orkney can be seen in a day, if you have a car and are disciplined, but to really get the most out of them, take two days. You can do the Kirkwall sights in a morning before heading to the Italian Chapel on South Ronaldsay in the afternoon. This allows a whole day for Stomness, a town caught in the most poignant of time warps, and the archaeological sites of Maeshowe, the Ring of Brodgar, Skara Brae and Skaill House, and Gurness Broch. To include Birsay, plan your day round the tides.

Since getting to Shetland isn't easy, you may want to spend three or four days here. The sites on the South Mainland—Jarlshof, Old Scatness, the Shetland Crofhouse Museum, St. Ninian's Isle, and Mousa Broch—take the best part of a day, although sailing times for Mousa must be factored into your schedule. Lerwick, with its lanes and spectacular museum, is a good day, and can be supplemented with a trip to the Bonhoga Gallery in Weisdale. It's a good idea to take a whole day to explore the north of the islands, including Eshaness and Tangwick Haa, although a car or a guide who drives will be necessary. Ferry times allow for a mad dash round the northern islands of Yell and Unst, but you will see more if you book an overnight stay.

GETTING HERE AND AROUND
AIR TRAVEL
Both Flybe and Loganair, Scotland's national airline, provide regular service to Sumburgh in Shetland and Kirkwall in Orkney from Edinburgh, Glasgow, Aberdeen, and Inverness. Tickets are very expensive, even if booked well in advance, but if you register with both airlines you will get notice of reduced prices. Because of the isolation of Orkney and Shetland, there's also a network of interisland flights, through Airtask in Shetland and Loganair in Orkney. These flights are run by a friendly staff and are as reliable as the weather allows them to be.

Airline Contacts Airtask. ☏ *01595/840246* ⊕ *www.airtask.com.* **Flybe.** ☏ *0371/700–2000, 0207/308–0812 outside U.K.* ⊕ *www.flybe.com.* **Loganair.** ☏ *0344/800–2855* ⊕ *www.loganair.co.uk.*

BOAT AND FERRY TRAVEL
Northlink operates ferries—locally known as "the boat"—from Aberdeen to Kirkwall in Orkney and Lerwick in Shetland. These leave Aberdeen Harbor each evening (or every second night for Kirkwall), arriving at Kirkwall at 11 pm and Lerwick at 7:30 am the next day. These top-notch services with excellent staff have recliner seats for the budget traveler, pods for those wanting more comfort, and clean, compact cabins in single, double, or four-berth combinations. There's a shop, a cinema, two bars, and two restaurants (one self-service and one table service) on each boat.

If you're arriving in Aberdeen on Sunday morning and plan on meeting a train, note that the station does not open until 9 am. Northlink allows you to stay in your cabin or the restaurant until 9:30 am.

An alternate way of reaching Orkney is the Northlink ferry from Scrabster to Stromness. There is also a ferry from John O'Groats to Burwick, operated by John O'Groats Ferries, with up to three daily departures May through September. The fastest and smoothest sail is by catamaran from Gills Bay, Caithness, to St. Margaret's Hope on Orkney. Operated by Pentland Ferries, it has three daily departures.

In both Orkney and Shetland, the local council runs the interisland ferry networks (Orkney Ferries and Shetland Island Ferries) to the outer islands. Northlink Ferries has service between Lerwick on Shetland and Kirkwall on Orkney. ■TIP→ **These are lifeline services, so not just for visitors: always book ferry tickets in advance.**

Ferry Contacts John O'Groats Ferries. ☎ *01955/611353* ⊕ *www.jogferry. co.uk.* **Northlink Ferries.** ☎ *0845/600–0449* ⊕ *www.northlinkferries.co.uk.* **Orkney Ferries.** ☎ *01856/872044* ⊕ *www.orkneyferries.co.uk.* **Pentland Ferries.** ☎ *0800/688–8998* ⊕ *www.pentlandferries.co.uk.* **Shetland Island Ferries.** ☎ *01595/745804 for Unst, Fetlar, Yell, Whalsay, Skerries, and Papa Stour, 01595/760363 for Fair Isle* ⊕ *www.shetland.gov.uk/ferries.*

BUS TRAVEL

National Express, Scottish Citylink, and Stagecoach operate buses to Aberdeen where you can get a plane, ferry, or connecting bus to the ferries at John O'Groats, Gills Bay, or Scrabster. John O'Groats Ferries operates the Orkney Bus, a direct express coach from Inverness to Kirkwall (via ferry) that runs daily from June to early September, making a day tip to Orkney a definite—if hurried—possibility.

The main bus service on Orkney is operated by Stagecoach and on Shetland by ZetTrans (although buses are run by small operators).

Bus Contacts John O'Groats Ferries. ☎ *01955/611353* ⊕ *www.jogferry. co.uk.* **National Express.** ☎ *08717/818178* ⊕ *www.nationalexpress.com.* **Scottish Citylink.** ☎ *0871/266–3333* ⊕ *www.citylink.co.uk.* **Stagecoach.** ☎ *01856/878014* ⊕ *www.stagecoachbus.com.* **ZetTrans.** ☎ *01595/744868* ⊕ *www.zettrans.org.uk.*

CAR TRAVEL

The most convenient way of getting around these islands is by car, especially if your time is limited. Roads are well maintained and traffic is nearly nonexistent, although speeding cars can be a problem. Orkney has causeways—the Barricades—connecting some of the islands, but in some cases these roads take fairly roundabout routes.

You can transport your rental car from Aberdeen, but for fewer than five days it's usually cheaper to rent a car from one of Shetland and Orkney's agencies. Most are based in Lerwick, Shetland, and Kirkwall, Orkney, but airport pickups are easily arranged.

Local Car Rental Contacts Bolts Car and Minibus Hire. ✉ *26 North Rd., Lerwick* ☎ *01595/693636* ⊕ *www.boltscarhire.co.uk.* **Orkney Car Hire.** ✉ *Junction Rd., Kirkwall* ☎ *01856/872866* ⊕ *www.orkneycarhire.co.uk.* **Star Rent-a-Car.** ✉ *22 Commercial Rd., Lerwick* ☎ *01595/692075 Lerwick, 01950/460444 Sumburgh Airport* ⊕ *www.starrentacar.co.uk.* **W. R. Tullock.** ✉ *Castle Garage, Castle St., Kirkwall* ☎ *01856/875500* ⊕ *www.orkneycarrental.co.uk.*

TRAIN TRAVEL

There are no trains on Orkney or Shetland, but you can take the train to Aberdeen or Thurso and then take a ferry to the islands.

Train Contact ScotRail. ☎ *0344/811–0141* ⊕ *www.scotrail.co.uk.*

RESTAURANTS

Kirkwall has an increasing number of good cafés and restaurants, as does Lerwick, but both islands now have memorable spots beyond the main towns, from cafés and fish-and-chips spots to some fancier restaurants. Orkney and Shetland have first-class seafood, and in pastoral Orkney the beef is lauded and in Shetland the heather- or seaweed-fed lamb. Orkney is famous for its cheese and its fudge; a glug of its

Highland Park malt whisky or some Skull Splitter Ale is also worth trying. Shetlanders are also now brewing their own and make much of their natural edible resources of seaweed-fed lamb and mussels, while making ice cream and smoking fish in a variety of ways. Some bakeries create their own version of bannocks—a scone-type baked item you eat with salt beef, mutton, or jam—but Johnson and Wood (otherwise known as the Voe bakery), available in shops across the islands, takes the biscuit.

HOTELS

Accommodations in Orkney and Shetland are on par with mainland Scotland, with a growing range of stylish bed-and-breakfasts that might suit some travelers better than the bigger hotels that rely and therefore focus on business customers, which in Shetland—with the oil and the building of a major gas plant—are many. Although standards are improving, the islands still do not offer luxury accommodations. To experience a simpler stay, check out the unique "camping *böds*" in Shetland—old cottages providing inexpensive, basic lodging (log fires, cold water, and sometimes no electricity). For details, contact the Shetland Tourist Information Centre. *Hotel reviews have been shortened. For full information, visit Fodors.com.*

WHAT IT COSTS IN POUNDS				
	$	$$	$$$	$$$$
Restaurants	under £15	£15–£19	£20–£25	over £25
Hotels	under £100	£100–£160	£161–£220	over £220

Restaurant prices are the average cost of a main course at dinner or, if dinner is not served, at lunch. Hotel prices are the lowest cost of a standard double room in high season, including 20% V.A.T.

TOURS

Cycharters. John Tulloch offers a day trip to Foula, a remote Shetland island, on his boat, the MV *Cyfish*, on Wednesday. ⊠ *Scalloway Harbour, Scalloway* ☎ *01595/810887* ⊕ *www.cycharters.co.uk* 🖾 *From £60.*

Dawn Star Boat Trips. All aboard Laurence Tait's *Dawn Star II* pilot boat for bespoke trips mid-May through July. A three-hour wildlife and history exploration of Scapa Flow is popular. ⊠ *Holm Pier, St. Mary's* ☎ *07759/944015* ⊕ *www.orkneyboattrips.co.uk* 🖾 *From £120.*

Fodor's Choice ★ **Island Trails.** Local tour guide and crofter James Tait offers tours steeped in the social history of Shetland, giving you a lively account, and no doubt many an introduction, to Shetland and its people. Opt for a guided tour around St. Ninian's Isle or a bespoke day's tour of the island. ☎ *01950/950228* ⊕ *www.island-trails.co.uk* 🖾 *From £25.*

Shetland Nature. Here you'll find richly informed tours that cover a lot of ground while quietly tracking Shetland's otters, birds, and the unique wildflowers of the islands. Photographers are specially catered to. ☎ *01957/710000* ⊕ *www.shetlandnature.net* 🖾 *From £60.*

Wildabout Orkney. Well-organized and informative tours, including Treasures of Orkney and Megalithic Masterpieces, run daily April to September. ☎ *01856/877737* ⊕ *www.wildaboutorkney.com* ✉ *From £59.*

VISITOR INFORMATION

The Orkney visitor center in Kirkwall is open all year. The Shetland visitor center, in Lerwick, stays open year-round; there's also a desk for Visit Shetland in the Sumburgh Airport.

Visitor Information Visit Orkney. ✉ *W. Castle St.* ☎ *01856/230300* ⊕ *www. visitorkney.com.* **Visit Shetland.** ☎ *01595/989898* ⊕ *www.shetland.org.*

ORKNEY

If you're touring the north of Scotland, the short boat trip to Orkney offers the chance to step outside the Scottish history you've experienced on the mainland. Prehistoric sites such as the Ring of Brodgar, and the remnants of Orkney's Viking-influenced past, are in dramatic contrast to that of the mainland. The Orkney Islands may have a population of just 20,000, but a visit reveals the islands' cultural richness. In addition, Orkney's continued reliance on farming and fishing reminds you how some things can stay the same despite technological advances. At Maeshowe, for example, it becomes evident that graffiti is not solely an expression of today's youths: the Vikings left their marks here way back in the 12th century. ■TIP➔ **You can purchase the Historic Scotland Orkney Explorer Pass joint-entry ticket (£18) at the first site you visit; the ticket costs less than paying separately for entry into each site.**

STROMNESS AND THE NEOLITHIC SITES

1 ¾ hrs north of Thurso on Scotland's mainland, via ferry from Scrabster.

On the southwest of the Mainland, on the shore of the old Norse anchorage Hamnavoe, is Stromness, a remarkably attractive fishing town seemingly so unsullied by modernity that it evokes an uncomplicated way of life long gone. Walk past the old-fashioned shops and austere cottages that line the main street and you'll understand why local poet and novelist George Mackay Brown (1921–96) was inspired and moved by its sober beauty.

With its ferry connection to Scrabster in Caithness, Stromness makes a good base for visiting the western parts of Orkney, and the town holds several points of interest. It was once a key trading port for the Hudson's Bay Company, and the Stromness Museum displays artifacts from those days. Nearby are three spectacular ancient sites, the Ring of Brodgar, Maeshowe, and Skara Brae at Skaill House.

GETTING HERE AND AROUND

Stromness is at the end of the A965 and can be reached by one of the many buses from Kirkwall.

Stagecoach Buses 7 and 8S link Kirkwall, the Ring of Brodgar, and Skara Brae and Skaill House with Kirkwall. Altogether there are three bus services there and three back per day except Sunday, so plan accordingly.

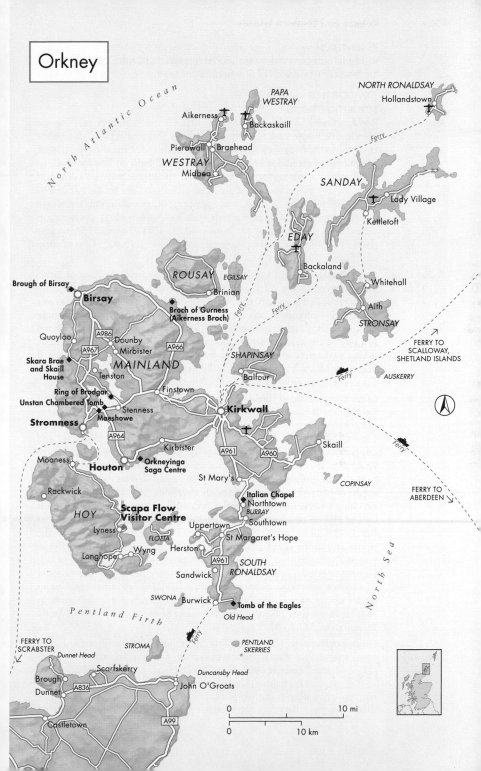

ESSENTIALS

Visitor Information Stromness Tourist Information Centre. ⊠ *Pier Head, Stromness* ☎ *01856/850716* ⊕ *www.visitorkney.com.*

EXPLORING
TOP ATTRACTIONS

Fodor's Choice
★
Pier Arts Centre. At the striking Pier Arts Centre, a gallery in a former merchant's house and adjoining buildings, huge sheets of glass offer tranquil harborside views and combine with space-maximizing design to make the best use of every shard of natural light and inch of wall to display the superb permanent collection. The more than 100 20th- and 21st-century paintings and sculptures include works by Barbara Hepworth and Douglas Gordon, and edgy temporary exhibitions showcase international contemporary artists such as Damien Hirst. A chic shop sells design products and art books. ⊠ *28–30 Victoria St., Stromness* ☎ *01856/850209* ⊕ *www.pierartscentre.com* ⊠ *Free* ⊘ *Closed Sun. and Mon.*

Fodor's Choice
★
Ring of Brodgar. About 5 miles northeast of Stromness, the Ring of Brodgar is a magnificent circle of 36 Neolithic standing stones (originally 60) surrounded by a henge, or deep ditch. When the fog descends over the stones—a frequent occurrence—their looming shapes seem to come alive. The site dates to between 2500 and 2000 BC. Though the original use of the circle is uncertain, it's not hard to imagine strange rituals taking place here in the misty past. The stones stand between Loch of Harray and Loch of Stenness. ⊠ *B9055, Stromness* ☎ *01856/841815* ⊕ *www.historicenvironment.scot* ⊠ *Free.*

Fodor's Choice
★
Skara Brae and Skaill House. After a fierce storm in 1850, the laird of Breckness, William Graham Watt, discovered this cluster of Neolithic houses at the bottom of his garden. The houses, first occupied around 3000 BC and containing stone beds, fireplaces, dressers, and cupboards, are the most extensive of their kind in northern Europe and provide real insight into this ancient civilization. A reconstruction of one house can be seen in the visitor center, which displays artifacts from the site and hosts an excellent café. Skara Brae stands on the grounds of **Skaill House,** a splendid, intriguing mansion built by the Bishop of Orkney in the 1600s. His descendants, the lairds of Breckness, along with the various ladies of the manor, added to the house and to the eclectic furnishings. These sites offer a joint ticket in summer months that's well worth the price: the juxtaposition of different societies thousands of years apart that shared the same corner of Orkney makes a fascinating visit. ⊠ *B9056, Stromness* ✛ *8 miles north of Stromness* ☎ *01856/841815* ⊕ *www.historicenvironment. scot* ⊠ *Skara Brae £6.50, Skara Brae and Skaill House £7.50* ⊘ *Skaill House closed Oct.–Mar.*

FAMILY
Fodor's Choice
★
Stromness Museum. The enchanting Stromness Museum has the feel of some grand Victorian's private collection but has, in fact, been community owned since it opened in 1837. Its crammed but utterly fascinating exhibits on fishing, shipping, and whaling are full of interesting trinkets from all over the world that found their way to this small Orcadian town because of its connections with the Hudson's Bay Shipping

Company. The company recruited workers in Stromness between the late 18th and 19th century as they were considered more sober and therefore more reliable than other Scots. Also here are model ships and displays on the German fleet that was scuttled on Scapa Flow in 1919. Upstairs, don't miss the beguiling, traditionally presented collection of birds and butterflies native to the British Isles. ✉ *52 Alfred St., Stromness* ☎ *01856/850025* 🎟 *£5 (allows as many visits as you like within a week)* ⏲ *Closed Sun. Nov.–Mar.*

QUICK BITE

🍴 **Julia's Café Bistro.** Right on the quayside, this casual spot serves the cakes that make you forget about calories. Expect huge slices of lemon drizzle, coffee layer, raspberry cream, and other cakes, as well as scones and traybakes (cakes baked in pans and cut up). **Known for:** delicious cakes; vibrant decor and sunny harbor views. ✉ *20 Ferry Rd., Stromness* ☎ *01856/850904* 🌐 *www.juliascafe.co.uk* ⏲ *No dinner.*

WORTH NOTING

Maeshowe. The huge burial mound of Maeshowe, circa 2500 BC, measures 115 feet in diameter and contains an enormous burial chamber. It was raided by Vikings in the 12th century, and Norse crusaders found shelter here, leaving a rich collection of runic inscriptions. Outside you see a large, grassy mound; the stunning interior of the chambered tomb has remarkably sophisticated stonework. This site is 6 miles northeast of Stromness and 1 mile from the Ring of Brodgar. **■ TIP→ As space is limited, buy tickets for guided tours online or call to check availability.** Tours start at the new visitor center at Stenness. ✉ *A965, Stromness* ☎ *01856/851266* 🌐 *www.historicenvironment.scot* 🎟 *£6.*

WHERE TO STAY

$$ HOTEL 🏨 **Ferry Inn.** This traditional inn with rooms and restaurant is handy for the ferry and other transport links for Orkney's sights. **Pros:** good restaurant; friendly pub; handy location for ferry. **Cons:** no elevator; can get very busy. [$] *Rooms from: £100* ✉ *10 John St., Stromness* ☎ *01856/850280* 🌐 *www.ferryinn.com* 🛏 *20 rooms* 🍴 *Breakfast.*

$$ HOTEL 🏨 **Merkister Hotel.** Popular with anglers, this family-run hotel overlooks the gentle lap of Loch Harray—its experienced *ghillies* (guides) know the choicest spots and provide instruction for novices. **Pros:** endless coffee in the lounge and library; notable restaurant; fishing experts. **Cons:** some small rooms; very dated decor; some curious house rules. [$] *Rooms from: £158* ✉ *A965, Harray, Birsay* ☎ *01856/771366* 🌐 *www.merkister.com* 🛏 *16 rooms* 🍴 *Breakfast.*

$$ B&B/INN Fodor's Choice ★ 🏨 **Mill of Eyrland.** White-painted stone walls, country antiques, and the rippling sound of a stream running beneath the windows make for an evocative stay at this former mill dating from 1861. **Pros:** the old grinding stones are a stunning focal point in the lounge; beautiful views out to Scapa Flow; notable breakfasts and packed lunches. **Cons:** difficult to find; breakfast is served at one big table, so be prepared to socialize. [$] *Rooms from: £130* ✉ *Off A964, Stenness* ☎ *01856/850136* 🌐 *www.millofeyrland.co.uk* 🛏 *4 rooms* 🍴 *Breakfast.*

SPORTS AND THE OUTDOORS
DIVING

The cool, clear waters of Scapa Flow and eight sunken ships that were part of Germany's fleet during World War I make for an unparalleled diving experience. Several companies organize trips to Scapa Flow—including shore and offshore dives among the Churchill Barriers—and other nearby dive sites.

Scapa Scuba. Dives with Scapa Scuba are from its boat, the MV *Radiant Queen*. Two dives around wrecks near the Churchill Barriers cost £150. ⊠ *Lifeboat House, Dundas St., Stromness* ☎ *01856/851218* ⊕ *www.scapascuba.co.uk.*

BIRSAY

12 miles north of Stromness, 25 miles northwest of Kirkwall.

Birsay itself is a small collection of houses, but some interesting historic and natural sites are nearby.

GETTING HERE AND AROUND
The village is on A966; a car is the easiest way to see the nearby sites.

EXPLORING
Broch of Gurness (Aikerness Broch). An Iron Age tower built between 500 BC and 200 BC, the Broch of Gurness stands more than 10 feet high and is surrounded by stone huts, indicating that this was a village. The tower's foundations and dimensions suggest that it was one of the biggest brochs in Scotland, and the remains of the surrounding houses are well preserved. ⊠ *A966* ✛ *8 miles east of Birsay* ☎ *01856/751414* ⊕ *www.historicenvironment.scot* 🎫 *£6* ⊘ *Closed Nov.–Mar.*

Brough of Birsay. A Romanesque church can be seen at the Brough of Birsay, a tidal island with the remains of an early Pictish and then Norse settlement. (*Brough* is another word for burgh.) The collection of roofless stone structures on the tiny island, close to Birsay, is accessible only at low tide by means of a concrete path that winds across the seaweed-strewn bay. The path is slippery, so boots are essential. To ensure you won't be swept away, check the tides with the tourism office in Kirkwall or Stromness before setting out. ⚠ **The cliffs at the far side of the island are stunning but be very careful as you look for puffins.** ⊠ *A966* ☎ *01856/841815* ⊕ *www.historicenvironment.scot* 🎫 *£5* ⊘ *Closed Oct.–mid-June.*

KIRKWALL

16 miles east of Stromness.

In bustling Kirkwall, the main town on Orkney, there's plenty to see in the narrow, winding streets extending from the harbor. The cathedral and some museums are highlights.

GETTING HERE AND AROUND
Kirkwall is a ferry port and also near Orkney's main airport. Its sights are all near one another, though visitors to the Highland Park Distillery might want to hop on the T11 Kirkwall Circular or get a taxi (about £7).

ESSENTIALS

Fodor'sChoice ★ **St. Magnus International Festival.** The region's cultural highlight is Kirkwall's St. Magnus International Festival, usually held the third week in June. Its impressive program includes distinguished orchestral, operatic, and choral artists. Orkney also hosts an annual folk festival at the end of May. ☎ *01856/871445* ⊕ *www.stmagnusfestival.com.*

Visitor Information Kirkwall Visitor Information Centre. ✉ *Travel Centre, W. Castle St.* ☎ *01856/872856* ⊕ *www.visitorkney.com.*

EXPLORING
TOP ATTRACTIONS

OFF THE BEATEN PATH

Italian Chapel. During World War II, 550 Italian prisoners of war were captured in North Africa and sent to Orkney to assist with the building of the Churchill Barriers, four causeways that blocked entry into Scapa Flow, Orkney's great natural harbor. Using two corrugated-iron Nissan huts, the prisoners, led by Domenico Chiocchetti, a painter-decorator from the Dolomites, constructed this beautiful and inspiring chapel in memory of their homeland. The elaborate interior frescoes were adorned with whatever came to hand, including bits of metal, colorful stones, and leftover paints. ✉ *A961 ✛ 7 miles south of Kirkwall* ⛯ *Free.*

FAMILY **Orkney Museum.** With artifacts from the Picts, the Vikings, and other ancient peoples, this museum in Tankerness House (a former residence) has the entire history of Orkney crammed into a rabbit warren of rooms. It's not easily accessible for those with disabilities, but with the help of staff, can be done. The setup may be old-fashioned, but some artifacts—especially those from everyday Orcadian life in the 19th century—are riveting. Lovely gardens around the back provide a spot to recoup after a history lesson. ✉ *Broad St.* ☎ *01856/873191* ⊕ *www.orkney.gov.uk* ⛯ *Free* ☾ *Closed Sun.*

Orkney Wireless Museum. The lifetime collection of Jim MacDonald, a radio operator during World War II, tells the story of wartime communications at Scapa Flow, where thousands of service members were stationed; they used the equipment displayed to protect the Home Fleet. Run by volunteers, the museum also contains many handsome 1930s wireless radios and examples of the handicrafts produced by Italian prisoners of war. ✉ *Kiln Corner, Junction Rd.* ☎ *01856/871400* ⊕ *www.owm.org.uk* ⛯ *£3* ☾ *Closed Oct.–Mar.*

St. Magnus Cathedral. Founded by the Norse earl Jarl Rognvald in 1137 and named for his uncle, this grand red-and-yellow sandstone cathedral was mostly finished by 1200, although more work was carried out during the following 300 years. The cathedral is still in use and contains some fine examples of Norman architecture, although traces of later styles are found here and there. The ornamentation on some of the tombstones in the church is particularly striking. At the far end to the left is the tomb of the tragically discredited Dr. John Rae, the Victorian-era Orcadian adventurer and unsung hero who discovered the final section of the Northwest Passage in Canada but was decried for his reporting that the British men of the Franklin expedition, overwhelmed by starvation, had resorted to cannibalism: an assertion that has since been proved true. ✉ *Broad St.* ☎ *01856/874894* ⊕ *www.stmagnus.org* ☾ *Closed weekends Oct.–Mar.*

Tomb of the Eagles. In 1958, while looking for stones for diking, local farmer Ronnie Simison found and excavated this chambered cairn, packed with 340 human skulls that were 5,000 years old. The lack of other bones suggests that the skulls were taken after the bones had been picked clean by birds. The tomb, however, gets its name from the 70 talons of sea eagles and their remains found among the skulls. The walk to the tomb is a mile through fields and then along spectacular cliffs. Access to the tomb is by way of a trolley. This can be messy if it's muddy and a no-go for those with mobility problems, but it's not as uncomfortable or claustrophobic as you'd imagine. The visitor center, still run by Ronnie Simison's family, is full of exhibits. ⊠ *Off A961, St. Margaret's Hope* ✛ *22 miles south of Kirkwall* ☎ *01856/831339* ⊕ *www.tomboftheeagles.co.uk* ⊡ *£7.50* ⊗ *Closed Nov.–Feb.*

WORTH NOTING

Bishop's and Earl's Palaces. The Bishop's Palace dates to the 12th century when St. Magnus Cathedral was built. In 1253 this was the site of King Hakon IV of Norway's death, marking the end of Norwegian rule over Sudreyjar (the Southern Hebrides). It was rebuilt in the late 15th century, and a round tower was added in the 16th century. The nearby Earl's Palace was built in 1607 for Earl Patrick Stewart, the much despised Earl of Orkney and Shetland who bound the people of both into terrible, inescapable poverty. While his name is still mud, his Orcadian residence is considered one of the finest examples of Renaissance architecture in Scotland. The great hall with its magnificent fireplace may be a ruin, but it evokes the splendor of its age. ⊠ *Palace Rd.* ☎ *01856/871918* ⊕ *www.historicenvironment.scot* ⊡ *£5* ⊗ *Closed Nov.–Mar.*

Fodor's Choice
★
Highland Park Distillery. Having come this far, you'll have earned a dram of the local single malt at Scotland's northernmost distillery. It was founded around the turn of the 19th century by Magnus Eunson, a church officer who dabbled in illicit stilling. The Viking Soul tour is highly recommended and takes you through the essential aspects of this near-sacred process, from the ingredients to the hand turning of the malt, the peating in the peat kilns, the mashing, and finally the maturation in oak casks. This smoky, peaty malt can be purchased all over Orkney, as well as from the distillery's austere shop. ⊠ *Holm Rd.* ☎ *01856/874619* ⊕ *www.highlandpark.co.uk* ⊡ *Tours from £10* ⊗ *Closed weekends Sept.–Apr.*

▌OFF THE BEATEN PATH
Orkneyinga Saga Centre. A good starting point for an exploration of Orkney's Norse heritage, the center examines the Orkneyinga Saga, an oral history first written down in the 13th century that tells of the Norse conquest of Orkney, with murders and battles galore. Panels discuss the saga and Viking life (with, rather amusingly, Hollywood hunks pasted into the Norse family tree). Exhibits include the remains of the 12th-century Orphir Church, Scotland's only circular medieval church, and the outline of a Viking drinking hall. Check ahead before visiting, as the center may not be open every year. ⊠ *Off A964* ✛ *8 miles southwest of Kirkwall* ☎ *01856/811319* ⊡ *Free* ⊗ *Closed Oct.–Mar.*

Unstan Chambered Tomb. This intriguing burial chamber lies within a 5,000-year-old cairn. Excavations here uncovered a collection of similarly designed pottery bowls, subsequently found in other Orcadian Neolithic tombs. Access to the tomb by trolley can be awkward for those with mobility problems. ✉ *A964* ✣ *7½ miles west of Kirkwall* ☎ *01856/841815* 🌐 *www.historicenvironment.scot* 🎟 *Free.*

WHERE TO EAT

$ MODERN BRITISH 🍴 **Archive Coffee.** Opened in 2017 within the handsome former Carnegie Free Library, the Old Library cultural venue houses this spacious high-ceilinged café. Take a pew in one of the quirky Orkney diner-style booths and ask the friendly staff about the daily specials and upcoming music gigs. **Known for:** wonderful renovation; attached Sound Archive music venue and Grooves record shop; bountiful cakes and packed lunches. [$] *Average main: £8* ✉ *8 Laing St.* ☎ *01856/872239* 🕑 *No dinner.*

$ CAFÉ 🍴 **Cafelolz.** If you've been indulging in too much fish-and-chips, this café with its bountiful and inventive salads will make you feel healthy and nourished yet full. For those seeking something sweet, its award-winning baking—with huge muffins, tall cakes, and crunchy macaroons, much of which is gluten-free—and excellent coffee will liven up even the dankest Orkney afternoon. **Known for:** heaping healthy salads; superlative in-house baking. [$] *Average main: £11* ✉ *21 Albert St.* ☎ *01856/877714* 🕑 *No dinner.*

$ ITALIAN FAMILY Fodor's Choice ★ 🍴 **Lucano.** This modern trattoria-style Italian restaurant has been taken to the heart of Orcadians, and rightly so, as it delivers an abundant menu of good Italian food. Decor is clean and stylish, with a tile floor, wooden tables, red chairs, and chalkboard menus on the wall. **Known for:** café by day; healthy choice of classic Italian dishes; good children's menu. [$] *Average main: £14* ✉ *31–33 Victoria St.* ☎ *01856/875687* 🌐 *www.lucanokirkwall.com.*

$ CAFÉ 🍴 **The Reel.** Orkney's musical tradition is alive and fiddling, but never more so than at this café and restaurant. As you eat, young Orcadians run up the stairs with their violin cases to the music school, where all sorts of sprees and shindigs are held in the performance spaces. **Known for:** Orcadian craft beer; gluten-free choices; music venue, shop, and lessons. [$] *Average main: £7* ✉ *3 Castle St.* ☎ *01856/871000* 🌐 *www.wrigleyandthereel.com.*

WHERE TO STAY

$$ HOTEL 🏨 **Ayre Hotel.** This large, functional hotel by the harbor offers ample accommodation choice—including a wing of nine spacious, self-catering apartments—plus a good bar-restaurant. **Pros:** great for families and groups; elevator; near the harbor. **Cons:** uninspiring parking lot views from some rooms; feels like a chain hotel; used by tour groups. [$] *Rooms from: £130* ✉ *Ayre Rd.* ☎ *01856/873001* 🌐 *www.ayrehotel.co.uk* 🛏 *60 rooms* 🍴 *Breakfast.*

$$ HOTEL 🏨 **Foveran Hotel.** About 34 acres of grounds surround this modern, ranch-style hotel overlooking Scapa Flow, about 3 miles southwest of Kirkwall. **Pros:** expansive grounds; efficient service; food that's cooked to perfection. **Cons:** exterior looks a bit institutional; you must book the popular restaurant ahead. [$] *Rooms from: £120* ✉ *Off A964* ☎ *01856/872389* 🌐 *www.thefoveran.com* 🛏 *8 rooms* 🍴 *Breakfast.*

$$ B&B/INN [icon] **West End Hotel.** Built in 1824 by a retired sea captain, the West End Hotel once served as Kirkwall's first hospital and is now a small, affably run hotel. **Pros:** great location; friendly owners. **Cons:** no tubs, just showers; some rooms are small. [$] *Rooms from: £120* ✉ *Main St.* ☎ *01856/872368* 🌐 *www.westendkirkwall.co.uk* 🛏 *10 rooms* 🍴 *Breakfast.*

SHOPPING

Judith Glue. Not only can you purchase designer knitwear with traditional patterns, as well as handmade crafts and hampers of local produce at Judith Glue: the shop is also home to the Orkney Real Food Cafe. ✉ *25 Broad St.* ☎ *01856/874225* 🌐 *www.judithglue.com.*

The Longship. Don't miss this eclectic shop, open since the 19th century, which sells a huge array of Ola Gorrie's original designs in gold and silver jewelry with Celtic and Norse themes. It also stocks knitwear, under-the-radar designer clothes labels, and quirky housewares. Its wineshop in the courtyard has a large selection, plus locally brewed craft beers and quality deli staples from Italy. ✉ *11 Broad St.* ☎ *01856/888790* 🌐 *www.thelongship.co.uk.*

The Orcadian Bookshop. The publisher of the local newspaper, *The Orcadian,* also manages this store, a good place to find books about the history of Orkney, its wildlife, and folklore. Look out for the occasional book reading and cultural event held here. ✉ *50 Albert St.* ☎ *01856/878888* 🌐 *www.orcadian.co.uk.*

SPORTS AND THE OUTDOORS

BICYCLING

Cycle Orkney. For £15 a day bicycles can be rented from Cycle Orkney, which is open year-round. ✉ *Tankerness La.* ☎ *01856/875777* 🌐 *www.cycleorkney.com.*

FISHING

Merkister Hotel. The Merkister Hotel, on Loch Harray, arranges fishing trips. All your equipment, including boats, is available to rent, and ghillies provide instruction. ✉ *A965, Harray, Birsay* ☎ *01856/771366* 🌐 *www.merkister.com.*

SCAPA FLOW VISITOR CENTRE

On Hoy, 14 miles southwest of Kirkwall, 6 miles south of Stromness.

On the beautiful island of Hoy, Scapa Flow Visitor Centre explores the strategic and dramatic role that this sheltered anchorage played in two world wars.

GETTING HERE AND AROUND

The car ferry from Houton (7 miles east of Stromness) takes 25 minutes to reach Lyness on Hoy and the visitor center. The ferry costs around £28 round-trip for a regular-size car and £8.50 round-trip per passenger.

ESSENTIALS

Ferry Contacts **Orkney Ferries.** ☎ *01856/872044* 🌐 *www.orkneyferries.co.uk.*

11

EXPLORING

Scapa Flow Visitor Centre. Military history buffs will appreciate the Scapa Flow Visitor Centre, which displays military vehicles and guns from both world wars. You'll also find equipment salvaged from the German boats scuttled off the coast. In the plain but poignant graveyard here, British and German personnel both rest in peace. If you want to take your car over to Hoy, book well in advance with Orkney Ferries, as this is a popular route. The visitor center is a short walk from the ferry terminal on the island of Hoy. ✉ *Off B9047, Lyness* ☎ *01856/791300* ⊕ *www.scapaflow.co.uk* 🎫 *Free* ☉ *Closed Nov.–Feb. and weekends in Mar., Apr., and Oct.*

SHETLAND

The Shetland coastline is an incredible 900 miles because of the rugged geology and many inlets; there isn't a point on the islands farther than 3 miles from the sea. Lerwick is the primary town, but the population of 22,000 is scattered across the 15 inhabited islands.

In general, the prehistoric treasures such as Jarlshof and Mousa Broch are in the South Mainland. For the geological marvels of the islands, Ronas Hill and Eshaness, visit the North Mainland. The social history of the islands is told most comprehensively in the Shetland Museum and in the lanes of Lerwick. Wherever your interest, you'll see and hear an island that buzzes with music, life, and history.

LERWICK

14 hrs by ferry from Aberdeen.

Founded by Dutch fishermen in the 17th century, Lerwick today is a busy town and administrative center. Handsome stone buildings—known as lodberries—line the old harbor; they provided loading bays for goods, some of them illegal. The town's twisting flagstone lanes once heaved with activity, and Lerwick is still an active port today. This is also where most visitors to Shetland dock, spilling out of cruise ships to walk around the town.

GETTING HERE AND AROUND

The town center of Lerwick is 1 mile south of Holmsgarth, the terminal for the ferry from Aberdeen. You can take a bus from Holmsgarth to the center or to the bus station for travel to Sumburgh or Scalloway. Car rentals can be arranged to meet you at the ferry terminal. Lerwick is small and compact, and the bus network, overseen by ZetTrans, offers hourly bus service around town.

ESSENTIALS

Transportation Contacts Boddam Cabs. ☎ *01950/460111* ⊕ *www.boddam-cabs.co.uk.*

Visitor Information Lerwick Visitor iCentre. ✉ *Market Cross* ☎ *01595/693434* ⊕ *www.shetland.org.*

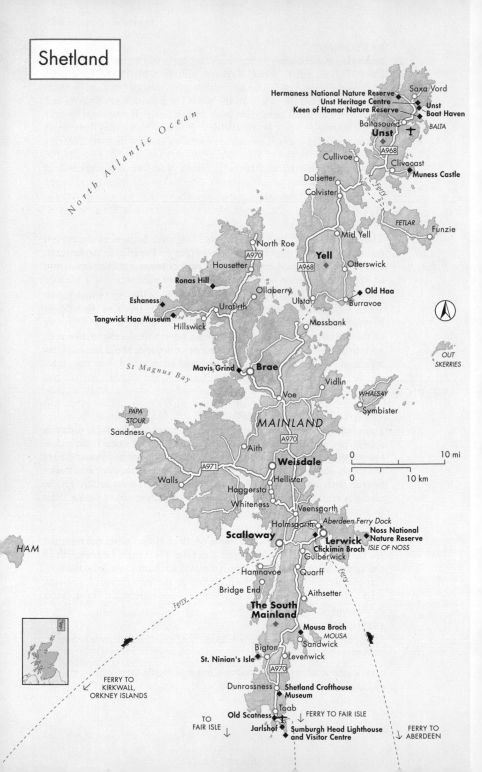

EXPLORING
TOP ATTRACTIONS

Fodor's Choice ★ **Clickimin Broch.** A stone tower on the site of what was originally an Iron Age fortification, Clickimin Broch makes a good introduction to these mysterious buildings. It was possibly intended as a place of retreat and protection in the event of attack. South of the broch are vivid views of the cliffs at the south end of the island of Bressay, which shelters Lerwick Harbor. ⊠ *Off A970 ✛ 1 mile south of Lerwick* ⊕ *www.historicenvironment.scot* ⊑ *Free.*

Fort Charlotte. This artillery fort was built in 1665 to protect the Sound of Bressay from the invading Dutch. They seized it in 1673 and razed the fort to the ground. They were soon chased out of Shetland and the fort was rebuilt in 1781. ⊠ *Market St.* ⊕ *www.historicenvironment.scot* ⊑ *Free.*

Fodor's Choice ★ **Mareel.** Next to the Shetland Museum, the bold and beautiful—although somewhat brutal around the back—Mareel is Shetland's adventurous and ambitious arts center. It has a live performance space attracting national and international musicians, two cinemas showing art-house and mainstream films, and a café and bar area that showcases local crafts, acoustic musicians, and some very drinkable Shetland beers. ⊠ *North Ness* ☎ *01595/745500* ⊕ *www.mareel.org.*

FAMILY
Fodor's Choice ★ **Shetland Museum.** On the last remaining stretch of the old waterfront at the restored Hay's Dock, the striking Shetland Museum, with its sail-like tower, is the area's cultural hub and a stimulating introduction to local history. The two-story space is filled with displays about archaeology, textiles, and contemporary arts. Standout exhibits include depictions of the minutiae of everyday Shetland life across the centuries, the last remaining *sixareen* (a kind of fishing boat), and the collection of lace shawls donated by Shetland families. Its informal spaces make this a wonderful place to hang out; look for vintage vessels moored in the dock and seals that pop up to observe everyone at the glass-fronted café-restaurant terrace. The museum shop is a must-visit, with a beautiful selection of nicely priced postcards and useful things inspired by the museum's collection. ⊠ *Hay's Dock, Commercial Rd.* ☎ *01595/695057* ⊕ *www.shetlandmuseumandarchives.org.uk* ⊑ *Free.*

WORTH NOTING

OFF THE
BEATEN
PATH

Noss National Nature Reserve. The island of Noss (which means "nose" in old Norse) rises to a point called the Noup. The smell and noise of the birds that live on the vertiginous cliffs can assault the senses. Residents nest in orderly fashion: black-and-white guillemots (45,000 pairs) and razorbills at the bottom; gulls, gannets, cormorants, and kittiwake in the middle; fulmars and puffins at the top. If you get too close to their chicks, some will dive-bomb from above. To get here, take a ferry from Lerwick to Bressay, then (weather permitting) an inflatable boat to Noss. It's a four- to five-hour walk around the reserve, so allow plenty of time if the walk is the draw. Mid-May to mid-July is the best time to view breeding birds. No matter when you visit, be sure to wear waterproof clothing and sensible shoes. ⊠ *Noss* ☎ *01595/693345* ⊕ *www.nnr-scotland.org.uk/noss* ⊑ *Free.*

WHERE TO EAT

$$ CAFÉ Fodor's Choice ★ 🍴 **Fjarå.** Sitting on rocks on the ebb (or *fjara* in Faroese) of Brewick Bay, the views from this large wood-and-glass house allow you to look at otters and seals between courses. The menu is very simple: big breakfasts, coffees, and cake—including an array of gluten-free items—soup and huge salads, as well as Shetland mussels or fish-and-chips for lunch. **Known for:** local lamb cooked to pefection; gorgeous views. [$] *Average main: £16* ✉ *Sea Rd.* ☎ *01595/697388.*

$$$ BRITISH Fodor's Choice ★ 🍴 **Hay's Dock.** In the Shetland Museum, chunky wooden tables fitted with glass panels allow you to see the detail of Shetland knitting. Good lunch picks include the celebrated seafood chowder; in the evening, try the Shetland lamb shoulder marinated in spiced yogurt or the North Atlantic wolffish with an herb risotto. **Known for:** fish dishes; popular, so book in advance. [$] *Average main: £20* ✉ *Hay's Dock, off Commerical Rd.* ☎ *01595/741569* 🌐 *www.haysdock.co.uk* 🕒 *No dinner Sun. or Mon.*

$ CAFÉ Fodor's Choice ★ 🍴 **The Peerie Shop Cafe.** Who would believe you could get such good cappuccino at 60 degrees north? In back of the popular Lerwick knitwear shop is a modish, consistently good café that sells filled sponge cakes, lip-smackingly good soups, and, yes, the best coffee on the islands. **Known for:** excellent coffee; nicely priced breakfasts. [$] *Average main: £6* ✉ *Esplanade* ☎ *01595/692817* 🌐 *www.peerieshop.co.uk* 🕒 *Closed Sun. No dinner.*

SHETLAND FIDDLING

Held in high regard both here and afar, Shetland's musicians attract global audiences traveling vast distances for their folk fix. At the Shetland Folk Festival, Fiddle Frenzy, and the Shetland Accordion and Fiddle Festival you can catch big names like Fiddlers' Bid and Hom Bru, and, if you're lucky, the internationally known Shetland fiddler Aly Bain and accordionist Phil Cunningham. For something more informal outside of these festivals, just wander into one of Lerwick's pubs: The Lounge (✉ *4 Mounthooly St.* ☎ *01595/692231*) is legendary.

WHERE TO STAY

$ B&B/INN 🏨 **Alder Lodge Guest House.** Occupying a bank building dating from the 1830s, this consistently good guesthouse sits on a quiet street within easy reach of Lerwick's shops, pubs, and harbor. **Pros:** comfortable beds; superb location; child-friendly. **Cons:** booked solid in the summer months. [$] *Rooms from: £80* ✉ *8 Clairmont Pl.* ☎ *01595/695705* 🌐 *www.alderlodge-guesthouse.com* 🛏 *11 rooms* 🍽 *Breakfast.*

$$ B&B/INN 🏨 **Kveldsro House Hotel.** If a fussy bed-and-breakfast doesn't suit you, try the plain but pleasing Kveldsro House, tucked away behind the town's main thoroughfare. **Pros:** minutes from the city center; cheery bar; excellent staff. **Cons:** generic hotel furniture; some walls a bit thin. [$] *Rooms from: £145* ✉ *Greenfield Pl., off Commerical St.* ☎ *01595/692195* 🌐 *www.shetlandhotels.com* 🛏 *17 rooms* 🍽 *Breakfast.*

SHOPPING

Anderson & Co. On Commercial Street, Anderson & Co. carries hand-knitted cardigans, jumpers, Shetland lace scarves, sheepskin slippers, and woven throws. ⊠ *60–62 Commercial St.* ☏ *01595/693714* ⊕ *www.shetlandknitwear.com.*

Ninian. The newest interpretations of traditional Fair Isle clothing, scarves, and throws as well as ceramics, gifts, and beautiful children's toys are found at Ninian. ⊠ *80 Commercial St.* ☏ *01595/696655* ⊕ *www.ninianshetland.co.uk.*

FodorsChoice ★ **Peerie Shop.** The Peerie (Shetland for small) Shop sells a colorful mix of knitwear, cards, ceramics, and interesting—and, yes, small—miscellanea. ⊠ *Esplanade* ☏ *01595/692816* ⊕ *www.peerieshop.co.uk.*

Shetland Times. The best bookshop within a radius of about 250 miles, the Shetland Times, the islands' newspaper and publisher, stocks a good selection of travel guides and local history titles. ⊠ *71–79 Commercial St.* ☏ *01595/695531* ⊕ *www.shetlandtimes.co.uk/shop.*

> **SHETLAND PONIES**
>
> The squat and shaggy Shetland pony has been a common sight for more than 12 centuries. Roaming wild over the hills, the pony evolved its long mane and dense winter coat. The animals stand between 28 and 42 inches tall, which made them ideal for working in cramped coal-mine tunnels in the 1850s, when child labor was restricted. They became a popular pet for the aristocracy in the late 19th century; many believe this helped save the breed. Today a studbook society protects the purity of the stock, and you'll see ponies at equine events and all over the island, chomping the grass.

THE SOUTH MAINLAND

14 to 25 miles south of Lerwick via A970.

The narrow 3- or 4-mile-wide stretch of land that reaches south from Lerwick to Sumburgh Head has a number of fascinating ancient sites (and an airport) as well as farmland, wild landscapes, and dramatic ocean views.

GETTING HERE AND AROUND

Arriving in Sumburgh by plane offers stunning views of Sumburgh Head and its golden sands. A fairly regular bus makes the hour-long trip between the airport and Lerwick, and it's also easy to drive here if you're based in Lerwick. You can rent a car from the airport or take a taxi. Jarlshof and Scatness are both within walking distance of the terminal.

ESSENTIALS

Visitor Information Sumburgh iCentre. ⊠ *Sumburgh Airport Terminal, A9070, Virkie* ☏ *01950/460905* ⊕ *www.shetland.org.*

EXPLORING
TOP ATTRACTIONS

FodorsChoice ★ **Mousa Broch.** Sandsayre Pier in Sandwick is the departure point for the passenger ferry to the tiny isle of Mousa, where you can see Mousa Broch, a fortified Iron Age stone tower rising about 40 feet high. The massive walls give a real sense of security, which must have been reassuring for islanders subject to attacks from ship-borne raiders. Exploring this beautifully preserved, curved-stone structure, standing on what feels like an untouched island, makes you feel as if you're back in 100 BC. From April to September, the ferry (£16 round-trip) departs for the island one or twice each afternoon. From May to July there are dusk boat trips (£25 round-trip) to catch the tiny storm petrels as they return from their day feeding at sea to their nests in the walls of the broch. The sight—and feel—of them swarming in the half-light is something you'll never forget. ⊠ *Sandsayre Pier, off A970, Sandwich ✛ 14 miles south of Lerwick* ☎ *07901/872339 ferry* ⊕ *www.mousa.co.uk.*

FAMILY **Shetland Crofthouse Museum.** Nine miles south of Sandwick this 19th-
Fodor's Choice century thatched house reveals the way of life of rural Shetlanders,
★ which the traditionally attired attendant will be delighted to discuss with you. The peat fire casts a glow on the box bed, the resting chair, and the wealth of domestic implements, including a hand mill for preparing meal and a straw "keshie" for carrying peat. One building made from an upturned boat was used for storing and drying fish and mutton: huts like this inspired the design of the new Scottish Parliament. ⊠ *East of A970, South Voe, Dunrossness* ☎ *01590/695057* ⊕ *www.shetland-museum.org.uk* ⊠ *Free (donations welcome)* ☽ *Closed Oct.–Apr.*

WORTH NOTING

FAMILY **Jarlshof.** In 1897, a huge storm blew away 4,000 years of sand to expose
Fodor's Choice the multilayered remains of Bronze Age, Iron Age, Pictish, and Viking
★ buildings; prehistoric wheelhouses; and earth houses that represented thousands of years of continuous settlement. It's a large and complex site, and you can roam—and photograph—the remains freely. The small visitor center is packed with details of the lives of former residents and illustrates Jarlshof's more recent history as a medieval farmstead and home of the 16th-century Earl of Orkney and Shetland, "cruel" Patrick Stewart, who enslaved the men of Scalloway to build Scalloway Castle. ⊠ *Sumburgh Head, off A970, Virkie* ☎ *01950/460112* ⊕ *www. historicenvironment.scot* ⊠ *£5.50.*

FAMILY **Old Scatness.** Plans are afoot to house Old Scatness under a huge protective dome, but if it's open during your trip, this ongoing excavation of an Iron Age village is a worthwhile stop. Enthusiastic and entertaining guides, most in costume, tell stories that breathe life into the stones and the middens, showing how its former residents made their clothes and cooked their food, including their staple dish: the ghastly seaweed porridge. It's open on Friday in season only. ⊠ *Off A970, Virkie* ☎ *01595/694688* ⊕ *www.shetland-heritage.co.uk/old-scatness* ⊠ *£6* ☽ *Closed Sept.–mid-May and Sat.–Thurs.*

Fodor's Choice **St. Ninian's Isle.** It was on St. Ninian's Isle that a schoolboy helping archae-
★ ologists excavate the ruins of a 12th-century church discovered the St. Ninian treasure, a collection of 28 silver objects dating from the 8th century. This Celtic silver is housed in the Museum of Scotland in Edinburgh (a point of controversy), but good replicas are in the Shetland Museum in Lerwick. Although you can't see the silver, walking over the causeway of golden sand (called a tombolo or *ayre*) that joins St. Ninian's Isle to the Mainland is an unforgettable experience. From Sumburgh, head

8 miles north on A970 and B9122, then turn left at Skelberry.

FAMILY Fodor's Choice ★ **Sumburgh Head Lighthouse and Visitor Centre.** Perhaps one of northern Europes's most stunning locations, this Robert Stevenson—grandfather of the writer Robert Louis—designed lighthouse, built in 1921, was the first lighthouse in Shetland. Sir Walter Scott was very taken with the location and based his novel *The Pirate*on the nearby landmarks of Jarlshof and Fitful Head. The stories of the Old Radar Hut—crucial during WWII—and the engine room with its deep booming foghorn are brought back to life here, while a Marine Life Centre has excellent displays on the birds, fish, and sea mammals found around the cliffs. If you walk round the dry-stone dikes, you will hear and probably see puffins, guillemots, and fulmars breeding, feeding, and fighting on the rocks, but if it's wet and wild, the circular café and Education Suite with its jaw-dropping panorama will provide enough drama. ✉ *Sumburgh Head, Sumburgh* ☎ *01950/461966* 🌐 *www.sumburghhead.com* 🎟 *£6* ⏲ *Closed Oct.–Mar.*

PUFFINS AND MORE

Every summer more than a million birds alight on the cliff faces in Shetland to nest, feeding on the coastal fish and sand eels. Bird-watchers can spot more than 20 species, from tiny storm petrels to gannets with 6-foot wingspans. Popular with visitors are the puffins, with their short necks, striped beaks, and orange feet. Look for them on the cliffs at Sumburgh Head near the lighthouse, 2 miles south of Sumburgh Airport. The visitor center has a wealth of information about nesting sites, as well as live puffin cams during breeding season.

WHERE TO STAY

$ B&B/INN FAMILY Fodor's Choice ★ 🏨 **Hayhoull B&B.** This lively bed-and-breakfast offers the chance to slip into the life of the buzzing Shetland community of Bigton. **Pros:** next to the bus stop for Lerwick; in friendly village next to the magical St. Ninian's Isle; children welcomed warmly. **Cons:** shared bathroom in two rooms; 4 miles to the nearest pub or restaurant. [$] *Rooms from: £80* ✉ *Off B9122, Bigton* ☎ *01950/422206* 🌐 *www.bedandbreakfast-shetland.com* 💳 *No credit cards* 🛏 *4 rooms* 🍴 *Breakfast.*

SHOPPING

Fodor's Choice ★ **Nielanell.** The designs here are rich in texture, color, and shape, but it's the philosophy behind the knitwear—she makes it for the day you feel your worst—that makes it so desirable. Most of the pieces are made to be worn in multiple ways, meaning you get three pieces for the price of one. ✉ *Hoswick* ☎ *01950/431413* 🌐 *www.nielanell.com.*

SCALLOWAY

6 miles west of Lerwick, 21 miles north of St. Ninian's Isle.

On the west coast of Mainland Island is Scalloway, which preceded Lerwick as the capital of the region. During World War II Scalloway was the port for the "Shetland Bus," a secret fleet of boats that carried British agents to Norway to perform acts of sabotage against the Germans, who were occupying the country. On the return trips, the boats would carry refugees back to Shetland. As you approach the town from the A970, look for the information board, which overlooks the settlement and its castle.

GETTING HERE AND AROUND

The town is 10 minutes by car from Lerwick, or you can get one of the fairly regular buses or even a taxi (£12).

EXPLORING

Scalloway Castle. This waterfront fortress was built in 1600 by Patrick Stewart, Earl of Orkney and Shetland. He was hanged in 1615 for his cruelty and misdeeds, and the castle was never used again. To enter, retrieve the key from the Scalloway Museum. You may explore these handsome ruins to your heart's content. ✉ *A970* ☎ *01856/841815* 🌐 *www.historicenvironment.scot* 🎫 *Free* 🕒 *Closed Oct.–mid-Apr.*

Scalloway Museum. This modern museum tells some fascinating stories about Scalloway and its well-traveled locals. There is a section dedicated to the exploits of the Shetland Bus, the WWII resistance movement that operated between Norway and Shetland, and cabinet upon cabinet of maritime artifacts and *proil* (sailors' booty) donated by locals. ✉ *Castle St.* ☎ *01595/880734* 🌐 *www.scallowaymuseum.org* 🎫 *£3* 🕒 *Closed Oct.–mid-Apr.*

WHERE TO EAT AND STAY

$ CAFÉ

🍴 **The Cornerstone.** This is the café handsome and historic Scalloway has been waiting for. The food—soups, quiche, and sandwiches by day or steaks and lasagna by night—isn't fancy, but it is made and served with great enthusiasm and generosity: you're unlikely to find a scone anywhere else as large as the ones here. **Known for:** mammoth scones; happy atmosphere. [$] *Average main: £12* ✉ *Burn Beach, Main St.* ☎ *01595/80346* 🌐 *www.thecornerstonebandb.com* 🕒 *No dinner Sun.–Thurs.*

$$ B&B/INN Fodor's Choice ★

🏨 **Scalloway Hotel.** Facing the harbor, this traditional stone lodging has fine views, especially at sunset. **Pros:** thoughtfully put together bedrooms; memorable meals from the restaurant. **Cons:** can get booked up in advance. [$] *Rooms from: £130* ✉ *Main St.* ☎ *01595/880444* 🌐 *www.scallowayhotel.com* 🛏 *4 rooms* 🍽 *Breakfast.*

WEISDALE

9 miles north of Lerwick.

This tiny place is less a village than a group of houses, but it does have a worthwhile gallery.

GETTING HERE AND AROUND

Take A971 from Lerwick. The No. 9 bus weekdays runs three times a day; the trip from Lerwick is 20 minutes.

EXPLORING

Bonhoga Gallery. Built in 1855 using stones from the Kergord estate's "cleared" (forcibly evicted) crofts, Weisdale Mill is now the Bonhoga Gallery, a contemporary art space showing quirky exhibitions by local, national, and international artists. Downstairs is a small but cake-laden café that looks over the Weisdale burn. An excellent shop sells artist-made housewares. ✉ *B9075* ☎ *01595/745750* 🌐 *www.shetlandarts.org.*

SHOPPING

Shetland Jewellery. This shop sells gold and silver Nordic- and Celtic-inspired jewelry, desk knives, and belt buckles made in the on-site workshop. ⊠ *Sound Side* ☎ *01595/830275* ⊕ *www.shetlandjewellery.co.uk.*

BRAE

15 miles north of Weisdale, 24 miles north of Lerwick.

A thriving community, Brae is where you can see the spoils of Shetland's oil money. The rugged moorland and tranquil *voes* (inlets) of Brae are the home of Busta House, one of the best hotels on the island.

GETTING HERE AND AROUND

There are buses from Lerwick to Brae, but the spread-out sights make it impossible to really see this area without a car. A970 is the main road, and B9078 will take you through Hillswick and to Eshaness.

EXPLORING

Eshaness and Ronas Hill. About 15 miles north of Brae are the rugged, forbidding cliffs around **Eshaness**; drive north and then turn left onto B9078. On the way, look for the defiant Drongs, striking sandstone stacks or pillars battered into shape by thousands of years of crashing seas. Then return to join the A970 at Hillswick, but before reaching Ura Firth, turn left toward the old crofting community of Heylor on Ronas Voe, beautifully documented by the pioneer filmmaker Jenny Gilbertson in the 1930s. Providing a front-on vista of rounded, red **Ronas Hill,** the highest hill in Shetland, Heylor's delightful sandy beach is known as the Blade. Beware: arctic terns—which Shetlanders call Tirricks—nest among the pebbles in May and June.

■ OFF THE BEATEN PATH

Mavis Grind. North of Brae the A970 meanders past Mavis Grind, a strip of land so narrow you can throw a stone—if you're strong—from the Atlantic, in one inlet, to the North Sea, in another. Keep an eye out for sea otters, which sometimes cross here.

■ OFF THE BEATEN PATH

Tangwick Haa Museum. After viewing the cliffs at Eshaness, call in at Tangwick Haa Museum, the 17th-century home of the Cheynes, now packed full with photographs, household items, and knitting, farming, and fishing equipment from the 18th to early 20th century. Upstairs is the Laird's Room—a traditional sitting room of the 19th century and a room of curiosities, including whale eardrums. Downstairs—next to the help-yourself café—there are rows of folders: ask one of the staff to let you hear what's in them and you will be rewarded with the soft, gentle voices of local elders telling you of life lived in Shetland. ⊠ *Off B9078, Tangwick* ☎ *01806/503389* ⊕ *www.tangwickhaa.org.uk* ⊠ *Free* ☉ *Closed. Oct.–Mar.*

WHERE TO EAT AND STAY

$ ✕**Braewick Café.** With a stunning position overlooking the Drongs

BRITISH (rocky columns standing in the sea), this eatery serves famously large portions popular with visitors and Shetlanders alike. Browse the local crafts in the shop while waiting for a crispy battered-fish supper, or just sit back on the sofas by the huge picture window and watch the dramatic sea and sky. **Known for:** supersized portions; lovely cakes;

wonderful ocean view. [$] *Average main: £10* ✉ *Off B9078, Eshaness* ☎ *01806/503345* 🌐 *www.eshaness.moonfruit.com* ⏲ *Closed Tues. and Wed. No dinner.*

$ SEAFOOD Fodor's Choice ★ 🍴 **Frankie's Fish & Chips.** Proudly claiming to be the northernmost fish-and-chips shop in Britain, this "chipper" is also the best of its kind on the islands. The combination of superfresh seafood—skate wings, squid, and crab legs—and light and crispy batter (including a gluten-free option) means Frankie's is everything a chip shop could be. **Known for:** Shetland mussels; skate wings and squid rings; its popularity (best to book). [$] *Average main: £11* ✉ *A970* ☎ *01806/522700* 🌐 *www.frankiesfishandchips.com.*

$$ HOTEL Fodor's Choice ★ 🏨 **Busta House.** Dating from the 16th century, Busta House—built by the well-heeled but ill-fated Gifford family—is one of the few grand houses of Shetland. **Pros:** truly haunting atmosphere; charming public rooms; lovely grounds. **Cons:** noisy plumbing; some rooms are a tight fit. [$] *Rooms from: £125* ✉ *Off A970* ☎ *01806/522506* 🌐 *www.bustahouse.com* 🛏 *22 rooms* 🍴 *Breakfast.*

YELL

11 miles northeast of Brae, 31 miles north of Lerwick.

A desolate-looking blanket bog cloaks two-thirds of the island of Yell, creating an atmospheric landscape to pass through on the way to Unst to the north.

GETTING HERE AND AROUND

Although you will see the odd walker or cyclist, a car is needed to explore the northern isles. To get to Yell, take A970 or B9076 and catch the ferry from Toft to Ulsta. On Yell, B9081 runs through Burravoe and up the east side and joins the A968, which leads to Gutcher and the ferry to Unst.

EXPLORING

Old Haa (*hall*) . The oldest building on the island, Burravoe's Old Haa is known for its crow-stepped gables (the stepped effect on the ends of the roofs), typical of an early-18th-century Shetland merchant's house. There's an earnest memorial to Bobby Tulloch, the great Shetland naturalist and champion of Shetland's bird population (1929–96), and the displays in the upstairs museum tell the story of the wrecking of the German ship, the *Bohus,* in 1924. A copy of the ship's figurehead is displayed outside the building. The Old Haa serves light meals with home-baked bannocks, cakes, and other goodies and also acts as a kind of unofficial information center. A crafts shop is on the premises, too. ✉ *Burravoe* ☎ *01957/702431* 🌐 *www.bobbytulloch.com* 🎫 *Free* ⏲ *Closed Oct.–Mar. and Mon.*

UNST

49 miles north of Lerwick.

Unst is the northernmost inhabited island in Scotland, a remote and special place, especially for nature lovers and those who want to experience a community on the edge of faraway. On a long summer evening, views north to Muckle Flugga, with only the ocean beyond, are incomparable. If you're a bird-watcher, head to the Hermaness and Keen of Hamar nature reserves.

GETTING HERE AND AROUND

A ferry (take the A968 at the village of Mid Yell to Gutcher) crosses the Bluemull Sound to Unst. A car is best for exploring, though there is limited bus service, including from Lerwick; taxis are an option.

EXPLORING

TOP ATTRACTIONS

Hermaness National Nature Reserve. A bleak moorland ending in rocky cliffs, the Hermaness National Nature Reserve is prime bird-watching territory. About half the world's population (6,000 pairs) of great skuas, called "bonxies" by locals, are found here. These sky pirates attack anything that strays near their nests, including humans, so keep to the paths. Thousands of other seabirds, including more than 50,000 puffins, nest on the cliffs, about an hour's walk from the reserve entrance. Gray seals haul out at the foot of the cliffs in fall, and, offshore, dolphins and occasionally whales (including orcas) can be seen on calm days.

A path meanders across moorland and climbs up a gentle hill, from which you can see, to the north, a series of tilting offshore rocks; the largest of these sea-battered protrusions is **Muckle Flugga,** meaning "big, steep-sided island," on which stands a lighthouse. The lighthouse was built by engineer Thomas Stevenson, whose son, the great Scottish writer Robert Louis Stevenson, used the outline of Unst for his map of Treasure Island. Muckle Flugga is the northernmost point in Scotland.

The visitor center has leaflets that outline a walk; mid-May to mid-July is the best time to visit. To get here from Haroldswick, follow the B9086 around the head of Burrafirth to the signposted car park. ⊠ *B9086, Burrafirth* ☎ *01957/693345* ⊕ *www.nnr-scotland.org.uk* ⊠ *Free* ☉ *Visitor center closed mid-Sept.–mid-Apr.*

Keen of Hamar Nature Reserve. The rare and unusual flora here includes Edmonston's Chickweed, hoary whitlow grass, and Norwegian sandwort, to name just a few. Near Baltasound, it's just off the A968, on the road past the famous **Unst Bus Shelter** (with its award-winning themed decor, the work of young locals). Please tread carefully to avoid squashing flowers or eggs and exercise caution on the cliff-top paths. ⊕ *Off A968* ☎ *01595/693345* ⊕ *www.snh.gov.uk.*

Unst Heritage Centre. The unique and colorful history of the people of Unst is told in this fascinating assemblage of artifacts, tools, photographs, and reconstructions, including a classroom and a *ben* or "good" end (sitting room) of a croft house. It will leave you with an enduring visual memory of the ways in which the locals learned, crofted, knitted, fished, and worshipped through the last two centuries. ⊠ *Haroldswick* ☎ *01957/711528* ⊕ *www.unstheritage.com* ⊠ *£3, includes Unst Boat Haven* ☉ *Closed Oct.–Apr.*

WORTH NOTING

Muness Castle. Scotland's northernmost castle was built in 1598 by Laurence Bruce of Cultmalindie, uncle of "cruel" Patrick Stewart. Despite being a ruin it is rather fetching, with circular corner towers and a scale-and-platt (that is, not circular but straight on) staircase. ✉ *B9084, Uyeasound* ⊕ *www.historicenvironment.scot* 🎫 *Free.*

Unst Boat Haven. Reflecting Shetland's intimacy with the sea, Unst Boat Haven displays a beautiful collection of traditional small fishing and sailing boats. ✉ *Beach Rd., Haroldswick* ☎ *01957/711528* ⊕ *www. unstheritage.com* 🎫 *£3, includes Unst Heritage Centre* ⊗ *Closed Oct.–Apr.*

WHERE TO EAT AND STAY

$
CAFÉ
FAMILY

✕ **Victoria's Vintage Tea Rooms.** Run by a Devon girl, who knows a thing or two about cream teas, this vintage-style café does a roaring trade right on the water at Haroldswick. The Shetland smoked salmon on Skibhoul (the local baker) bread is a sandwich worth getting excited about, as are the cakes, especially the Victoria Sponge and scones. **Known for:** seal and otter spotting; gluten-free options. 🟡 *Average main: £6* ✉ *Old Haroldswick Shop, Haroldswick* ☎ *01957/711885* ⊕ *victoriasvintagetearooms.co.uk* ⊗ *Closed Mon. No dinner.*

$
B&B/INN

🏨 **Gardiesfauld Hostel.** With options limited for on overnighter in Unst, this quiet and spacious youth hostel will appeal to travelers who want more than a quick day trip and take an interest in others who end up in the same remote location. **Pros:** perfect for travelers on a shoestring; quiet (especially outside school holidays); private rooms available. **Cons:** communal facilities; you can't guarantee silence. 🟡 *Rooms from: £32* ✉ *B9084, Uyeasound* ☎ *01957/755279* ⊕ *www.gardiesfauld.shetland. co.uk* 🚫 *No credit cards* ⊗ *Closed Oct.–Apr.* 🛏 *6 rooms* 🍽 *No meals.*

SHOPPING

Skibhoul Stores and Bakery. The bread from Skibhoul is so popular that large shipments of it head south to the rest of the Isles on Thursdays. It's also famous for the Oceanic sea-salt oatcakes and Balta biscuits. There's a small self-serve café so you can taste the wares. ✉ *Northside* ☎ *01957/711444.*

SPORTS

BICYCLING

Unst Cycles Hire. There are a few hilly bits but there are miles of road in Unst made for cycling. Bikes cost £10 per day or £15 for an electric bike. ✉ *Northbase Information Centre, Saxa Vord, Haroldswick* ☎ *01957/711393* ⊕ *www.unstcyclehire.co.uk.*

TRAVEL SMART
SCOTLAND

GETTING HERE AND AROUND

■ AIR TRAVEL

Scotland's main hubs are Glasgow, Prestwick (near Glasgow), Edinburgh, Inverness, and Aberdeen. Glasgow and Prestwick are the gateways to the west and southwest, Edinburgh the east and southeast, Aberdeen and Inverness the north. All these cities have excellent bus and train transportation services and well-maintained roads that link them with each other and other cities within Scotland. Taxis are also an efficient and reliable option, but they are three to four times the cost of going by public transport.

Traveling by air is straightforward in Scotland. Security is heavy but efficient. You can often breeze through check-in lines by using your airline's online check-in option or bag drop, but confirm this ahead of time.

Flying time to Glasgow and Aberdeen is 6½ hours from New York, 7½ hours from Chicago, 9½ hours from Dallas, 10 hours from Los Angeles, and 21½ hours from Sydney. Flying time to Edinburgh is 7 hours from New York, 8 hours from Chicago, 10 hours from Dallas, 10½ hours from Los Angeles, and 22 hours from Sydney. Not all airlines offer direct flights to Scotland; many go via London. For those flights allow an extra four to five hours of travel (two to three for the layover in London plus an additional hour or two for the duration of the flight).

Airline-Security Issues Transportation Security Administration. ⊕ www.tsa.gov.

AIRPORTS

The major international gateways to Scotland are Glasgow Airport (GLA), about 7 miles outside Glasgow, and Edinburgh Airport (EDI), 7 miles from the city. Both offer connections for dozens of European cities and regular flights to London's Gatwick (LGW) and Heathrow (LHR) airports. Aberdeen Airport (ABZ) has direct flights to most major European cities. Prestwick (PIK) has direct flights to some European cities at discounted rates. Inverness (INV) offers direct flights in and around the United Kingdom.

Airport tax is included in the price of your ticket. Generally the tax for economy tickets within the United Kingdom from European Union countries is £13. For all other flights it is £78. The standard rate for flights from the United Kingdom and European Union is £26; for all other destinations it's £146.

All Scottish airports offer typical modern amenities: restaurants, cafés, shopping, sandwich and salad bars, pubs, pharmacies, bookshops, and newsstands; some even have spas and hair salons. Glasgow and Edinburgh are the most interesting airports when it comes to a delayed flight. Good food and shopping options abound—try Discover Scotland, Scottish Fine Gifts, and Tartan Plus for Scottish-inspired goods.

There are plenty of hotels near all airports, and all airports also have Internet access.

Airport Information Aberdeen Airport. ☎ 0844/481–6666 ⊕ www.aberdeenairport. com. **Edinburgh Airport.** ☎ 0844/448–8833 ⊕ www.edinburghairport.com. **Glasgow Airport.** ☎ 0844/481–5555 ⊕ www. glasgowairport.com. **Glasgow Prestwick Airport.** ☎ 0871/223–0700 ⊕ www. glasgowprestwick.com. **Inverness Airport.** ☎ 01667/464000 ⊕ www.hial.co.uk/ inverness-airport.

GROUND TRANSPORTATION

The best way to get to and from the airport based on speed and convenience is by taxi. All airport taxi stands are just outside the airport's front doors and are well marked with clear signs. Most taxis have a set price when going to and from the airport to the city center but will turn on the meter at your request. Ask the driver to turn on the meter to confirm the flat-rate price.

If you're traveling with a large party, you can request a people carrier to transport everyone, luggage included. Luggage is included in the taxi fare; you should not be charged extra for it.

If you're traveling alone, a more economical transfer option is public transportation. Buses travel between city centers and Glasgow, Edinburgh, Aberdeen, and Inverness airports. Trams travel between Edinburgh Airport and the city center; Edinburgh Gateway station links the airport to the tram and rail network; trains go direct to Glasgow Prestwick Airport. All are fast, inexpensive, and reliable. *For more information and specific contacts, refer to the Orientation and Planning sections at the beginning of chapters.*

TRANSFERS BETWEEN AIRPORTS
Scottish airports are relatively close to one another and all are connected by a series of buses and trains. Flights between airports add hours to your journey and are very expensive (between £200 and £400). The best way to travel from one airport to another is by bus, train, car, or taxi. Normally you must take a combination of bus and train, which is easy and—if you travel light—quite enjoyable.

From Edinburgh Airport you can take the Citylink Air (£11.60) bus direct to Glasgow Airport in one hour. For those wanting to see Edinburgh and have time on their hands, take a tram (£5.50) or bus (£4.50) to the city center and then a train to Glasgow city center (£13.90) and a shuttle bus to Glasgow Airport (£7.50). This journey should take you less than two hours. Taxis are fast but costly. The price of a taxi from Edinburgh Airport to Glasgow Airport is around £90, a good choice if you're traveling with a few people. Renting a car would be a good choice if you want to get from Edinburgh to, say, Aberdeen Airport and you're traveling with a group of people. Otherwise, take a train from Edinburgh Gateway.

FLIGHTS
Scotland has a significant air network for a small country. British Airways (or British Airways Express) has flights from London's Heathrow Airport or from Glasgow, Edinburgh, Aberdeen, and Inverness to the farthest corners of the Scottish mainland and to the islands.

Among the low-cost carriers, Virgin has service from Heathrow; and easyJet flies from London Luton/Gatwick/Stansted to and between Glasgow, Edinburgh, Aberdeen, and Inverness, plus to and from Belfast. Flybe has services to Sumburgh (Shetland) and Kirkwall (Orkney) from Aberdeen, Inverness, Glasgow, and Edinburgh, where you can continue on to Bristol, Cardiff, Exeter, Manchester, Newquay, and Southampton. Flybe also runs the Dundee–London Stansted route.

Major Airline Contacts American Airlines. ☎ *800/433-7300 in U.S., 0844/369-9899 in U.K.* ⊕ *www.americanairlines.co.uk.* **British Airways.** ☎ *800/247-9297 in U.S., 0344/493-0787 in U.K.* ⊕ *www.britishairways. com.* **Delta Airlines.** ☎ *800/221-1212 in U.S., 0207/660-0767 in U.K.* ⊕ *www.delta.com.* **KLM.** ☎ *866/434-0320 in U.S., 020/7660-0293 in U.K.* ⊕ *www.klm.com.* **United Airlines.** ☎ *800/864-8331 in U.S., 0845/607-6760 in U.K.* ⊕ *www.united.com.* **Virgin Atlantic.** ☎ *800/862-8621 in U.S., 0344/209-7770 in U.K.* ⊕ *www.virgin-atlantic.com.*

From London to Edinburgh and Glasgow easyJet. ☎ *0330/365-5000* ⊕ *www.easyjet. com.* **Ryanair.** ☎ *0871/246-0000 in U.K.* ⊕ *www.ryanair.com.*

Within Scotland Flybe. ☎ *0371/700-2000* ⊕ *www.flybe.com.*

AIRLINE TICKETS
The least expensive airfares to Scotland are often priced for round-trip travel and must usually be purchased in advance. Airlines generally allow you to change your return date for a fee; most low-fare tickets, however, are nonrefundable.

If you intend to fly to Scotland from London, take advantage of the current fare wars on internal routes—notably among London's four airports and between Glasgow and Edinburgh. Among the cheapest fares are those from easyJet, which offers bargain fares from London Luton/Gatwick/Stansted (all with good rail links from central London) to Glasgow, Edinburgh, Aberdeen, and Inverness. However, British Airways now offers competitive fares on some flights.

▌ BIKE TRAVEL

Bicycling in Scotland is variable. The best months for cycling are May, June, and September, when the roads are often quieter and the weather is usually better. Because Scotland's main roads are continually being upgraded, bicyclists can easily reach the network of quieter rural roads in southern and much of eastern Scotland, especially Grampian. In a few areas of the Highlands, notably in northwestern Scotland, the rugged terrain and limited population have resulted in the lack of side roads, making it difficult—sometimes impossible—to plan a minor-road route in these areas.

Several agencies now promote routes for recreational cyclists. These routes are signposted, and agencies have produced maps or leaflets showing where they run. Perhaps best known is the Glasgow–Loch Lomond–Killin Cycleway. VisitScotland has advice on a site dedicated to cycling.

BIKING ORGANIZATIONS

The Cyclists' Touring Club publishes a members' magazine, route maps, and guides. Sustrans is a nonprofit organization dedicated to providing environmentally friendly routes for cyclists. Active Scotland, part of the national tourism agency, has a great list of bike routes ranked by area and difficulty.

TRANSPORTING BIKES

Although some rural bus services will transport cycles if space is available, don't count on getting your bike on a bus. Check well in advance with the appropriate bus company.

You can take bicycles on car and passenger ferries in Scotland, and it's usually not necessary to book in advance. Arrive early so that your bike can be loaded through the car entrance.

ScotRail strongly advises that you make a train reservation for you and your bike at least one month in advance. On several trains reservations are compulsory.

Bike Maps and Information ActiveScotland. ☎ 0131/473–3868 ⊕ active.visitscotland.com. **Cycling UK.** ☎ 01483/238301 ⊕ www.cyclinguk.org. **Sustrans.** ☎ 0131/346–1384 ⊕ www.sustrans.org.uk.

▌ BOAT AND FERRY TRAVEL

Because Scotland has so many islands, plus the great Firth of Clyde waterway, ferry services are of paramount importance. Most ferries transport vehicles as well as foot passengers, although a few smaller ones are for passengers only.

It's a good idea to make a reservation ahead of time, although reservations are not absolutely necessary. Most travelers show up on the day of departure and buy their tickets from the stations at the ports. Keep in mind that these are working ferries, not tourist boats. Although journeys are scenic, most people use these ferries as their daily means of public transportation to and from their hometowns.

The main operator is Caledonian MacBrayne, known generally as CalMac. Services extend from the Firth of Clyde in the south, where there's an extensive network, right up to the northwest of Scotland and all the Hebrides. CalMac offers 25 island-hopping itineraries, called Hopscotch, valid for 31 days, which can be combined for tailored exploration. Fares can range from £2 to £6 for a short trip to over £50 for a longer trip with several legs.

The Dunoon–Gourock route on the Clyde is served by Western Ferries (for cars) and Argyll Ferries (for passengers and cycles only).

Northlink Ferries operates a car ferry for Orkney between Scrabster, near Thurso, and Stromness, on the main island of Orkney; and between Aberdeen and Kirkwall, which is also on the mainland of Orkney. Northlink also runs an efficient ferry to Lerwick, Shetland, and Kirkwall, Orkney. The journey to Lerwick is overnight, but comfortable cabins are available. These ferries can be busy in summer, so book well in advance.

Cash and major credit cards are accepted for payment. *See the Orientation and Planning sections of each chapter for more details about ferry services.*

Information Argyll Ferries. ☎ *0800/066–5000* ⊕ *www.argyllferries.co.uk.* **Caledonian MacBrayne.** ☎ *0800/066–5000* ⊕ *www.calmac.co.uk.* **Northlink Ferries.** ☎ *0845/600–0449* ⊕ *www.northlinkferries.co.uk.* **Western Ferries.** ☎ *01369/704452* ⊕ *www.western-ferries.co.uk.*

▌ BUS TRAVEL

Long-distance buses usually provide the cheapest way to travel between England and Scotland; fares may be as little as a third of the rail fares for comparable trips and are cheaper if you buy in advance. However, the trip is not as comfortable as by train (no dining cart, smaller bathrooms, less spacious seats), and travel takes longer. Glasgow to London by nonstop bus takes 8 hours, 45 minutes; by train it takes about 5 hours, 30 minutes. Scotland's bus (short-haul) and coach (long-distance) network is extensive. Bus service is comprehensive in cities, less so in country districts. Express service links main cities and towns, connecting, for example, Glasgow and Edinburgh to Inverness, Aberdeen, Perth, Skye, Ayr, Dumfries, and Carlisle; or Inverness with Aberdeen, Wick, Thurso, and Fort William. Express service is very fast, and fares are reasonable. Scottish Citylink, National Express, and Megabus are among the main operators; there are about 20 in all. The Royal Mail Post Bus provides a valuable service—generally twice-daily—in the Highlands, Argyll, and Bute and the Western Isles. All buses are nonsmoking.

The London terminal is Victoria Coach station for National Express and Megabus.

DISCOUNTS AND DEALS

On Scottish Citylink, the Explorer Passes offer complete freedom of travel on all services throughout Scotland. Three permutations give 3 days of travel out of a 5-day period, 5 days of travel out of 10, and 8 days of travel out of 16. They're available from Scottish Citylink offices, and cost £49, £74, and £99 respectively.

National Express offers discounted seats on buses from London to more than 50 cities in the United Kingdom, including Glasgow and Aberdeen. Tickets range from £13 to £60, but only when purchased online. Megabus (order tickets online), a discount service, has similarly competitive prices between major cities throughout Scotland, including Aberdeen, Dundee, Glasgow, Inverness, and Perth.

Travelers ages 16 to 26 are eligible for 33.33% reductions with the Young Persons Coachcard (£10).

FARES AND SCHEDULES

Contact Traveline Scotland for information on all public transportation and timetables.

For town, suburban, or short-distance journeys, you buy your ticket on the bus, from a pay box, or from the driver. You need exact change. For longer journeys—for example, Glasgow–Inverness—it's usual (and a good idea; busy routes and times can book up) to reserve a seat online.

PAYING

Credit cards are accepted at most bus stations.

Bus Information Traveline Scotland. ☎ *0871/200–2233* ⊕ *www.travelinescotland.com.*

Bus Lines Megabus. ☎ *0900/160–0900* ⊕ *uk.megabus.com.* **National Express.** ☎ *0871/781–8181* ⊕ *www.nationalexpress.com.* **Royal Mail Post Bus.** ☎ *03457/740740* ⊕ *www.royalmail.com.* **Scottish Citylink.** ☎ *0871/266–3333* ⊕ *www.citylink.co.uk.*

CAR TRAVEL

If you plan to stick mostly to the cities, you will not need a car. All cities in Scotland are either so compact that most attractions are within easy walking distance of each other (Aberdeen, Dundee, Edinburgh, Inverness, and Stirling) or are accessible by an excellent local public transport system (Glasgow). And there is often good train or bus service from major cities to nearby day-trip destinations. Bus tours are a good option for day trips.

Once you leave Edinburgh, Glasgow, and the other major cities, a car will make journeys faster and much more enjoyable than trying to work out public-transportation connections to the farther-flung reaches of Scotland (though it is possible, if time-consuming, to see much of the country by public transportation). A car allows you to set your own pace and visit off-the-beaten-path towns and sights most easily.

In Scotland your own driver's license is acceptable. International driving permits (IDPs) are available from the American Automobile Association and, in the United Kingdom, from the Automobile Association and Royal Automobile Club. These international permits, valid only in conjunction with your regular driver's license, are universally recognized; having one may save you a problem with local authorities.

ELECTRIC VEHICLES

Renting an electric vehicle (EV) provides a clean and often affordable car rental option for urban touring and short journeys. A network of charging points in cities make it a viable option for small-group trips in and around Glasgow, Edinburgh, Aberdeen, Dundee, and Stirling especially. A good resource for checking charging-point availability and pricing is ⊕ *zap-map.com.*

GASOLINE

Expect to pay a lot more for gasoline, about £5.40 a gallon (£1.18 a liter) for unleaded. It's about 10p a liter higher in remote rural locations, even in the oil-producing region around Shetland. The British imperial gallon is about 20% more in volume than the U.S. gallon—approximately 4½ liters. Pumps dispense in liters, not gallons. Most gas stations are self-service and stock unleaded, superunleaded, and LRP (replacing four-star) plus diesel; all accept major credit cards.

PARKING

On-street parking is a bit of a lottery in Scotland. Depending on the location and time of day, the streets can be packed or empty of cars. In the cities you must pay for your on-street parking by getting a sticker from a parking machine; these machines are clearly marked with a large P. Make sure you have the exact change; the cost is around £3 for two hours, but can vary considerably from central to suburban zones, especially in Edinburgh and Glasgow. Put the parking sticker on the inside of your windshield. Parking lots are scattered throughout urban areas and tend to be more or less the same price as on-street parking.

The local penalty for illegally parked cars is generally £60 (£30 if paid within 14 days).

ROAD CONDITIONS

A good network of superhighways, known as motorways, and divided highways, known as dual carriageways, extends throughout Britain. In remote areas of Scotland where the motorway hasn't penetrated, travel is noticeably slower. Motorways shown with the prefix M are mainly two or three lanes in each direction, without any right-hand turns. These are the roads to use to cover long distances, though inevitably you'll see less of the countryside. Service areas are at most about an hour apart.

Dual carriageways, usually shown on a map as a thick red line (often with a black line in the center) and the prefix "a" followed by a number perhaps with a bracketed "t" (for example, "a304[t]"), are similar to motorways, except that right turns are sometimes permitted, and

FROM	TO	DRIVING TIME
Edinburgh	Glasgow	1 hour
Glasgow	Stirling	¼ hour
Stirling	Dundee	1¼ hours
Dundee	Aberdeen	1½ hours
Aberdeen	Inverness	2¾ hours
Inverness	Glasgow	3½ hours
Edinburgh	Inverness	3¼ hours
Glasgow	Dundee	1¾ hours

you'll find both traffic lights and traffic circles along the way. The vast network of other main roads, which typical maps show as either single red *A* roads, or narrower brown *B* roads, also numbered, are for the most part the old roads originally intended for horses and carriages. Travel along these roads is slower than on motorways, and passing is more difficult. On the other hand, you'll see much more of Scotland. The A9, Perth to Inverness, is a particularly dangerous road with the worst road accident record in Scotland because of the stopping and starting on the dual carriageway.

Minor roads (shown as yellow or white on most maps, unlettered and unnumbered) are the ancient lanes and byways of Britain, roads that are not only living history but a superb way of discovering hidden parts of Scotland. You have to drive slowly and carefully. On single-track (one-lane) roads, found in the north and west of Scotland, there's no room for two vehicles to pass, and you must use a passing place if you meet an oncoming car or tractor, or if a car behind wishes to overtake you. Never hold up traffic on single-track roads.

ROADSIDE EMERGENCIES
For aid if your car breaks down, contact the 24-hour rescue numbers of either the Automobile Association or the Royal Automobile Club. If you're a member of the AAA (American Automobile Association) or another association, check your membership details before you travel; reciprocal agreements may give you free roadside aid.

Emergency Contacts in the U.K. Automobile Association (AA). ☎ 0800/887766 ⊕ www.theaa.com. **Royal Automobile Club** (RAC). ☎ 0300/159–1111 ⊕ www.rac.co.uk.

Emergency Contacts in the U.S. American Automobile Association (AAA). ☎ 0800/028–9018 In U.K. (assistance via AA—affiliated with AAA) ⊕ exchange.aaa.com.

RULES OF THE ROAD
The most noticeable difference for most visitors is that when in Britain, you drive on the left and steer the car on the right. Give yourself time to adjust to driving on the left—especially if you pick up your car at the airport. One of the most complicated questions facing visitors to Britain is that of speed limits. In urban areas it's generally 20 mph or 30 mph, but it's 40 mph on some main roads, as indicated by circular red-rimmed signs. In rural areas the official limit is 60 mph on ordinary roads and 70 mph on divided highways and motorways. Traffic police can be hard on speeders, especially in urban areas. Driving while using a cell phone is illegal, and the use of seat belts is mandatory for passengers in front and back seats. Service stations and newsstands sell copies of the Highway Code (£2.50), which lists driving rules and has pictures of signs; or, you can download the information or get the mobile app at ⊕ www.highwaycodeuk. co.uk

Drunk-driving laws are strictly enforced and penalties are heavy. Be aware that the legal alcohol limit is lower than in the rest of the United Kingdom: just 50 mg in every 100 ml of blood. That equates to just under a pint of beer or glass of wine for an average male, and half a pint or a small glass of wine for a woman. To be safe, avoid any alcohol if you're driving.

CAR RENTAL
You can rent any type of car you desire; however, in Scotland cars tend to be on the smaller side. Many roads are narrow,

and a smaller car saves money on gas. Common models are the Renault Clio, Ford Focus, and Vauxhall Corsa. Four-wheel-drive vehicles aren't a necessity. Most cars are manual, not automatic, and come with air-conditioning, although you rarely need it in Scotland. If you want an automatic, reserve ahead. Green Motion rents electric, hybrid, and low–carbon dioxide cars with service pick-up points at Edinburgh and Glasgow airports.

When you're returning the car, allow an extra hour to drop it off and sort out any paperwork. If you're traveling to more than one country, make sure your rental contract permits you to take the car across borders and that your insurance policy covers you in every country you visit.

Rates in Glasgow begin at £26 a day and £130 a week for an economy car with a manual transmission and unlimited mileage. This does not include tax on car rentals, which is 20%. The busiest months are June through August, when rates may go up 30%. During this time, book at least two to four weeks in advance. Online booking is fine.

Companies frequently restrict rentals to people over age 23 and under age 75. If you are over 70, some companies require you to have your own insurance. If you are under 25, a surcharge of around £25 per day plus V.A.T. will apply.

Child car seats usually cost about £10–£25 extra; you must ask for a car seat when you book, at least 48 hours in advance. The same is true for GPS. Adding one extra driver is usually included in the original rental price.

Local Agencies Arnold Clark. ☎ 0141/237-4374 ⊕ www.arnoldclarkrental.com. **Green Motion.** ☎ 03338/884000 in U.K., 0207/186-4000 rest of the world ⊕ www.greenmotion. com.

Major Rental Agencies Avis. ☎ 0808/284-0014 ⊕ www.avis.co.uk. **Budget.** ☎ 0808/284-4444 ⊕ www.budget.co.uk. **Hertz.** ☎ 020/7026-0077 ⊕ www.hertz.co.uk.

National Car Rental. ☎ 0800/121-8303 ⊕ www.nationalcar.co.uk.

Wholesalers Auto Europe. ☎ 0800/358-1229 ⊕ www.auto-europe.co.uk. **Europe by Car.** ☎ 800/223-1516 in U.S. ⊕ www. ebctravel.com. **Eurovacations.** ☎ 877/471-3876 in U.S. ⊕ www.eurovacations.com. **Kemwel.** ☎ 877/820-0668 in U.S. ⊕ www. kemwel.com.

∎ TAXI TRAVEL

In Edinburgh, Glasgow, and the larger cities, black hackney taxis—similar to those in London—with their "taxi" sign illuminated can be hailed on the street, or booked by phone (expect to pay an extra 80p charge for this service in Edinburgh). If you call a private-hire taxi, expect a regular-looking car to pick you up. The only distinctions are that they have a taxi license and a meter stuck on the dashboard, along with an ID card for the driver. Private-hire taxis are cheaper than black hackney taxis and will pick you up only from a specific location, not off the street.

Scottish taxis are reliable, safe, and metered. In Edinburgh, meters begin at £2.10 weekdays and increase in 25p increments. Beyond the larger cities, most communities of any size have a taxi service; your hotel will be able to supply telephone numbers.

∎ TRAIN TRAVEL

Train service within Scotland is generally run by ScotRail, one of the most efficient of Britain's service providers. Trains are generally modern, clean, and comfortable. Long-distance services carry buffet and refreshment cars. Scotland's rail network extends all the way to Thurso and Wick, the most northerly stations in the British Isles. Lowland services, most of which originate in Glasgow or Edinburgh, are generally fast and reliable. A shuttle makes the 50-minute trip between Glasgow and Edinburgh every 15 minutes. It's a scenic trip with plenty of rolling fields, livestock, and traditional houses along the way. Rail service throughout the country, especially the Highlands, is limited on Sunday.

CLASSES

Most trains have first-class and standard-class coaches. First-class coaches are always less crowded; they have wider seats and are often cleaner and newer than standard-class cars, and they're a lot more expensive. However, on weekends you can often upgrade from standard to first class for a fee (often £10 to £25)—ask when you book.

FARES AND SCHEDULES

The best way to find out which train to take, which station to catch it at, and what times trains travel to your destination is to call National Rail Enquiries. It's a helpful, comprehensive service that covers all Britain's rail lines. National Rail will help you choose the best train to take, and then connects you with the ticket office for that train company so that you can buy tickets. You can also check schedules and purchase tickets on its website.

Train fares vary according to class of ticket purchased, time (off-peak travel will be much cheaper), and distance traveled. Before you buy your ticket, stop at the Information Office/Travel Centre and request the lowest fare to your destination and information about any special offers. There's sometimes little difference between the cost of a one-way and round-trip ticket, and returns are valid for one month. So if you're planning on departing from and returning to the same destination, buy a round-trip fare upon your departure, rather than purchasing two separate one-way tickets.

It's often much cheaper to buy a ticket in advance than on the day of your trip (except for commuter services); the closer to the date of travel, the more expensive the ticket will be. Try to purchase tickets at least eight weeks in advance during peak-season summer travel to save money and reserve good seats. You must stick to the train you have booked (penalties can be the full price), and you need to keep the seat reservation ticket, which is part of the valid ticket.

Check train websites, especially ScotRail, for deals. You can also check The Trainline, which sells discounted advance-purchase tickets from all train companies to all destinations in Britain.

Information National Rail Enquiries. ☎ 03457/484950 ⊕ www.nationalrail.co.uk. **ScotRail.** ☎ 0344/811–0141 ⊕ www.scotrail. co.uk. **The Trainline.** ☎ 0333/202–2222 ⊕ www.thetrainline.com.

PAYING

All major credit cards are accepted for train fares paid in person, online, and by phone.

RESERVATIONS

Reserving your ticket in advance is always recommended.

Tickets and rail passes do not guarantee seats on the trains. For that you need a seat reservation (essential for peak travel trains to and from Edinburgh during the summer festivals), which if made at the time of ticket purchase is usually included in the ticket price, or, if booked separately, must be paid for at a cost of £1 *per train* on your itinerary. You also need a reservation for the overnight sleeper trains.

TRAIN PASSES

Rail passes may save you money, especially if you're going to log a lot of miles. If you plan to travel by train in Scotland, consider purchasing a BritRail Pass, which also allows travel in England and Wales. There are Scotland-specific passes, too, for the Highlands, central region, and countrywide travel. All BritRail passes must be purchased in your home country; they're sold by travel agents as well as ACP, The Trainline, or Rail Europe. Rail passes do not guarantee seats on the trains, so be sure to reserve ahead. Remember that Eurail Passes aren't honored in Great Britain.

The cost of an unlimited BritRail adult pass for 4 days is $231/$349 (standard/first class); for 8 days, $335/$498; for 15 days, $498/735; for 22 days, $623/$934; and for a month, $735/$1,107.

Information ACP Rail International.
☎ 866/938–7245 ⊕ www.acprail.com. **BritRail Travel.** ⊕ www.britrail.com. **Rail Europe.** ⊕ www.raileurope.com.

FROM ENGLAND

There are two main rail routes to Scotland from the south of England. The first, the west-coast main line, runs from London Euston to Glasgow Central; it takes 5½ hours to make the 400-mile trip to central Scotland, and service is frequent and reliable. Useful for daytime travel to the Scottish Highlands is the direct train to Stirling and Aviemore, terminating at Inverness. For a restful route to the Scottish Highlands, take the overnight sleeper service, with sleeping carriages. It runs from London Euston, departing in late evening, to Perth, Stirling, Aviemore, and Inverness, where it arrives the following morning. The new *Caledonian Sleeper* operator as of 2015, Serco Abellio, has introduced some improvements to the long-established service. New trains, carriages, en suite berths, and sleeping pods are due in 2018.

The east-coast main line from London King's Cross to Edinburgh provides the quickest trip to the Scottish capital. Between 8 am and 6 pm there are usually trains every half hour to Edinburgh; three of them travel directly to Aberdeen. Virgin East Coast's limited-stop expresses like the *Flying Scotsman* make the 393-mile London-to-Edinburgh journey in about 4½ hours. Connecting services to most parts of Scotland—particularly the Western Highlands—are often better from Edinburgh than from Glasgow.

Trains from elsewhere in England are good: regular service connects Birmingham, Manchester, Liverpool, and Bristol with Glasgow and Edinburgh. From Harwich (the port of call for ships from Holland, Germany, and Denmark), you can travel to Glasgow via Manchester. But it's faster to change at Peterborough for the east-coast main line to Edinburgh.

SCENIC ROUTES

Although many routes in Scotland run through extremely attractive countryside, several stand out: from Glasgow to Oban via Loch Lomond; to Fort William and Mallaig via Rannoch (ferry connection to Skye); from Edinburgh to Inverness via the Forth Bridge and Perth; from Inverness to Kyle of Lochalsh and to Wick; and from Inverness to Aberdeen.

A private train, the *Royal Scotsman*, does all-inclusive scenic tours, with banquets en route. This is a luxury experience: you choose itineraries from two nights (£2,420) to seven nights (£9,200) per person.

Special Trains Caledonian Sleeper.
☎ 0330/060–0500, 141/555–0888
⊕ www.sleeper.scot. **The Royal Scotsman.**
☎ 0845/077–2222 in U.K., 800/524–2420 in U.S. ⊕ www.royalscotsman.com. **Virgin Trains.**
☎ 03457/225333 ⊕ www.virgintrainseast-coast.com.

ESSENTIALS

■ ACCOMMODATIONS

Your choices in Scotland range from small, local B&Bs to large, elegant hotels—some of the chain variety. Bed-and-breakfasts tend to be less expensive than large hotels, and are often different from those in the United States: many consist of spare rooms in someone's home, where breakfasts are cooked in the host's kitchen and served at the dining or kitchen table. Proprietors keep costs down, and guests get a more personal, if less private, Scottish touch. Recent economic stagnation and political uncertainty in the United Kingdom mean there are special deals if you look. For example, some lodgings offer discounted rates for stays of two nights or longer.

If you haven't booked ahead, you're not likely to be stranded. Even in the height of the season—July and August—hotel occupancy runs at about 80%. However, your choice of accommodations will be extremely limited if you show up somewhere during a festival or golf tournament. Your best bet will be to try for a room in a nearby village.

To secure your first choice, reserve in advance. One option is to reserve through local tourist information centers, making use of their "book-a-bed-ahead" services. Telephone bookings made from home should be confirmed by email or fax. Country hotels expect you to check in by about 6 pm.

Be sure you understand the hotel's cancellation policy. Some places allow you to cancel without any kind of penalty; others, particularly B&Bs, require you to cancel a week in advance or penalize you.

Smoking is banned in all indoor public spaces in Scotland, and this includes hotel rooms. Most hotels allow children under a certain age to stay in their parents' room at no extra charge, but others charge for them as extra adults; find out the cutoff age for discounts.

VisitScotland classifies and grades accommodations using a simple star system. The greater the number of stars, the greater the number of facilities and the more luxurious they are.

The lodgings we list are the cream of the crop in each price category. When pricing accommodations, always ask what's included. Many hotels and most guesthouses and B&Bs include a breakfast with the basic room rate. Meal-plan information appears at the end of a review. *Prices in the reviews are the lowest cost of a standard double room in high season, including 20% V.A.T. Hotel reviews have been shortened. For full reviews, visit Fodors.com*

APARTMENT AND HOUSE RENTALS

Rental houses and flats (apartments) are becoming more popular lodging choices for travelers visiting Scotland, particularly for those staying in one place for more than a few days. Some places may rent only by the week. Prices can be cheaper than a hotel (though perhaps not less than a bed-and-breakfast), and the space and comfort are much better than what you'd find in a typical hotel.

In the country your chances of finding a small house to rent are good; in the city you're more likely to find a flat (apartment) to let (rent). Either way, your best bet for finding these rentals is online. Individuals and large consortiums can own these properties, so it just depends on what you're looking for. Citybase Apartments is a handy resource for finding an apartment, from single studios to large apartments suitable for families and groups. Dreamhouse Apartments has swanky, serviced flats in Edinburgh, Glasgow, and Aberdeen. The National Trust for Scotland has many unique properties, from island cottages to castles, for rent. Knight Residence has 19 well-appointed, modern apartments in the heart of the

LOCAL DO'S AND TABOOS

GREETINGS

Although many Scots are fantastic talkers, they're less enthusiastic with greetings on the physical front. If you're in less familiar company, a handshake is more appreciated than a kiss or hug.

SIGHTSEEING

When you are visiting houses of worship, modest attire is appreciated, though you will see shorts and even bared midriffs. Photographs are welcome in churches, outside of services. Shorts and other close-fitting attire are allowed just about anywhere else at any time, weather permitting; these days locals tend not to cover up as much as they used to.

It's the same with food; Scots eat and drink just about anywhere, and much of the time they do it standing up or even walking.

ETIQUETTE

In Scotland it's rude to walk away from conversation, even if it's with someone you don't know. If you're at a pub, keep in mind that it's very important to buy a round of drinks if you're socializing with a group of people. You don't simply buy your own drink; you buy a drink for all of the people you're there with, and those people do the same. It can make for a very foggy evening and public drunkenness, especially on Friday and Saturday nights. Conversational topics that are considered taboo are money matters; the Scots are private about their finances.

Driving etiquette is carefully observed, too; be courteous and allow people to pass. Jaywalking isn't rude or illegal, but it's much safer to cross with the lights, especially if traffic is coming from a direction you might not be used to.

As for waiting in lines and moving through crowds, put your best foot forward. The Scots are very polite and you'll be noticed (and not in a good way) if you're not.

OUT ON THE TOWN

People may dress up for a special restaurant or for clubbing, but other people will be casual. Some restaurants and clubs frown on jeans and sneakers.

If you're visiting a family home, a simple bouquet of flowers is a welcome gift. If you're invited for a meal, bringing a bottle of wine is appropriate, as is some candy for the children. To thank a host for hospitality, either a phone call or thank-you card is always appreciated.

DOING BUSINESS

Punctuality is of prime importance, so call ahead if you anticipate a late arrival. Spouses do not generally attend business dinners, unless specifically invited. If you ask someone to dine, it's usually assumed that you'll pick up the tab. However, if you're the visitor, your host may insist on paying. Nonetheless, it's always polite to offer to pay.

LANGUAGE

The Scots language, which borrows from Scandinavian, Dutch, French, and Gaelic, survives in various forms, with each region having its own dialect. In the northeast they speak Doric, while the Shetland and Orkney "tongue" is influenced by the now-extinct Norn. The Gaelic language, the indigenous language of those from the Western Isles and Highlands, has been given a new lease on life. Many primary schools in the region are teaching a new generation of Gaelic speakers. The language has its own TV channel, BBC Alba, and is being promoted in a huge signage campaign. Otherwise, Scots speak English often with a strong accent (which may be hard for nonnative Brits and Americans to understand), but your ear will soon come to terms with it.

Old Town, Edinburgh; it has 16 similarly smart apartments in Inverness, many with spectacular terrace views.

International Agencies Citybase Apartments. ☎ *01524/544244* ⊕ *www.citybase-apartments.com.* **Dreamhouse Apartments.** ✉ *4 Woodside Pl., Glasgow* ☎ *0845/226–0232* ⊕ *www.dreamhouseapartments.com.* **Forgetaway.** ⊕ *www.forgetaway.com.* **Home Away.** ⊕ *www.homeaway.com.* **Knight Residence.** ✉ *12 Lauriston St., Edinburgh* ☎ *0800/304–7160* ⊕ *www.theknightresidence.co.uk.* **Villas & Apartments Abroad.** ☎ *212/213–6435* ⊕ *www.vaanyc.com.*

Local Contacts Embrace Scotland. ⊕ *www.embracescotland.co.uk.* **National Trust for Scotland.** ☎ *0131/458–0305* ⊕ *www.nts.org.uk/Holidays/Advanced-Search/.*

BED-AND-BREAKFASTS

Common throughout Scotland, B&Bs are a special British tradition and the backbone of budget travel. Prices average about £50 to £120 per night, depending on the region and the time of year. They're usually in a family home, occasionally don't have private bathrooms, and usually offer only breakfast. More upscale B&Bs, along the line of American B&Bs or small inns, can be found in Edinburgh and Glasgow especially, but in other parts of Scotland as well. Guesthouses are a slightly larger, somewhat more luxurious version. All provide a glimpse of everyday life. Note that local tourist offices can book a B&B for you; there may be a small charge for this service.

Reservation Services BedandBreakfast.com. ⊕ *www.bedandbreakfast.com.* **Sawdays.** ☎ *01172/047810* ⊕ *www.sawdays.co.uk.* **UK Bed and Breakfast Accommodation.** ⊕ *www.bedandbreakfasts.co.uk.*

FARMHOUSE AND CROFTING HOLIDAYS

A popular option for families with children is a farmhouse holiday, combining the freedom of B&B accommodations with the hospitality of Scottish family life. You'll need a car if you're staying deep in the country, though. Information is available from VisitBritain or VisitScotland, and from the Farm Stay UK.

Contacts Farm Stay UK. ☎ *024/7669–6909* ⊕ *www.farmstayuk.co.uk.*

HOME EXCHANGES

With a direct home exchange you stay in someone else's home while they stay in yours. Some outfits also deal with vacation homes, so you're not actually staying in someone's full-time residence, just their vacant weekend place. There can be yearly fees for exchange services of around $100 a year, so check.

Exchange Clubs HomeExchange.com. ☎ *800/877–8723 in U.S., 0203/608–9365 in U.K.* ⊕ *www.homeexchange.com.* **HomeLink International.** ⊕ *www.homelink.org.* **Intervac U.S.** ⊕ *www.intervac-homeexchange.com.*

HOTELS

Large hotels vary in style and price. Many lean toward Scottish themes when it comes to decoration, but you can expect the same quality and service from a chain hotel wherever you are in the world. Keep in mind that hotel rooms in Scotland are smaller than what you'd find in the United States. Today hotels of all sizes are trying to be greener, and many newer chains are striving for government environmental awards. Discounted rooms are another trend, as are discounts for room upgrades.

In the countryside some older hotels are former castles or converted country homes. These types of hotels are full of character and charm but can be very expensive, and they may not have elevators. Normally they have all the amenities, if not more, of their urban counterparts. Their locations may be so remote that you must eat on the premises, which may be costly.

Some small regional chains operate in Scotland that are not internationally known. Apex (in Edinburgh, Glasgow, Dundee, and London) is modish and has Scandinavian-inspired bedrooms; Malmaison (in Aberdeen, Dundee, Edinburgh, and Glasgow) is luxury on a budget; Hotel du Vin (Glasgow, St. Andrews, and Edinburgh), with its chic bistros, sumptuous bedding, and original art, may blow the budget.

Hotel Contacts Apex Hotels.
⊕ *www.apexhotels.co.uk.* **Hotel du Vin.**
⊕ *www.hotelduvin.com.* **Malmaison.**
⊕ *www.malmaison.com.*

▌COMMUNICATIONS

INTERNET
All newer laptops operate equally well on 110 and 220 volts and so require only an adapter. Never plug your computer into any socket without first asking about surge protection: although Scotland is computer-friendly, few hotels and B&Bs outside the major cities have built-in current stabilizers. It's worthwhile to purchase a surge protector in the United Kingdom that plugs into the socket.

All hotels and many B&Bs have facilities for computer users, such as dedicated computer rooms and wired or wireless connections for Internet access. Most cafés offer free Wi-Fi access.

PHONES
The good news is that you can now make a direct-dial telephone call from virtually any point on Earth. The bad news? You can't always do so cheaply. Calling from a hotel is almost always the most expensive option; hotels usually add huge surcharges to all calls, particularly international ones.

When you're calling anywhere in Great Britain from the United States, the country code is 44. When dialing a Scottish or British number from abroad, drop the initial 0 from the local area code. For instance, if you're calling Edinburgh Castle from New York City, dial 011 (the international code), 44 (the Great Britain country code), 131 (the Edinburgh city code without the initial 0), and then 225–9846 (the number proper).

CALLING WITHIN SCOTLAND
There are three types of public pay phones: those that accept only coins, those that accept only phone cards, and those that take British Telecom (BT) phone cards and credit cards. For coin-only phones, insert coins *before* dialing (minimum charge is 60p). Sometimes phones have a "press on answer" (POA) button, which you press when the caller answers.

Calls from residential phones are charged according to the time of day: evenings, nighttime, and weekend rates are cheaper. Daytime rates—weekdays 7 am–7 pm—are 4p per minute for a local call and 8p for a national call. A minimum fee of 60p (including a 40p connection charge) applies to calls from BT public pay phones, which will purchase two 10p units of time. Thereafter call time is purchased in 10p units. This excludes calls to free phone services. A daytime call to the United States will cost 46p a minute on a regular phone (evenings 7 pm–7 am, and weekends are a few pence cheaper), and 60p a minute on a pay phone.

To call a number with the same area code as the number from which you are dialing, omit the area-code digits when you dial. For long-distance calls within Britain, dial the area code (which usually begins with 01), followed by the telephone number. In provincial areas the dialing codes for nearby towns are often posted in phone booths.

To call the operator, dial 100; directory inquiries (information), 118500; international directory inquiries, 118505.

In Scotland, cell-phone numbers, the 0800 toll-free code, and local-rate 0345 numbers do not have a 1 after the initial 0, nor do many premium-rate numbers, for example 0891, and special-rate numbers, for example 08705.

Numbers that start with 0800, 0808, or national information numbers that start with 0345 and 0845 are free when called from a U.K. BT landline; other telephone-line providers charge other rates, and they cost anywhere from 20p to £1 a minute when called from a cellular phone. Additionally, 0870 numbers are *not* toll-free numbers; in fact, numbers beginning with 0871 or the 0900 prefix are premium-rate numbers, and it costs extra to call them. The amount varies and is usually relatively small when dialed from within the country but can be excessive when dialed from outside the United Kingdom. Many businesses, especially those offering low-cost services (such as Ryanair or Megabus) communicate with customers via their websites. If they do have a customer-service phone number, it's costly to use it. There are some handy cell phone Android and iPhone apps (including ⊕ *weq4u.co.uk*) that help you save money on premium-rate-number calls.

CALLING OUTSIDE SCOTLAND
The country code for the United States is 1.

To make international calls *from* Scotland, dial 00 for international access, then the country code, area code, and number. For the international operator, credit card, or collect calls, dial 155.

Access Codes AT&T Direct. ⊕ *www.att.com.*

CALLING CARDS
You can purchase phone cards for use on public phones from shops, post offices, and newsstands. They're ideal for longer calls and come in values of £5, £10 and £20. An indicator panel on the phone shows the number of units you've used; at the end of your call the card is returned. Where credit cards are taken, slide the card through, as indicated. Beware of buying cards that require you to dial a free phone number; some of these are not legitimate. It's better to get a BT, Post Office card.

MOBILE PHONES
If you have a multiband phone (some countries use different frequencies than what's used in the United States) and your service provider uses the world-standard GSM network (as do T-Mobile, Cingular, and Verizon), you can probably use your phone abroad. Roaming fees can be steep, however: 99¢ a minute is considered

reasonable. And overseas you normally pay the toll charges for incoming calls. It's almost always cheaper to send a text message than to make a call, since text messages have a very low set fee (often less than 5¢).

If you just want to make local calls, consider buying a new SIM card (note that your provider may have to unlock your phone for you to use a different SIM card) and a prepaid-service plan in the destination. You'll then have a local number and can make local calls at local rates.

Cell phones are getting less and less expensive to purchase. Rather than renting one, it may be cheaper to buy one to use while you're abroad. Rates run from as low as £20 a month for unlimited calls with a pay-as-you-go card.

Contacts Cellular Abroad. ☎ 800/287-5072 ⊕ *www.cellularabroad.com.* **Mobal.** ☎ 888/888-9162 ⊕ *www.mobalrental.com.*

▌CUSTOMS AND DUTIES

You're always allowed to bring goods of a certain value back home without having to pay any duty or import tax. But there's a limit on the amount of tobacco and liquor you can bring back duty-free, and some countries have separate limits for perfumes; for exact figures, check with your customs department. The values of so-called duty-free goods are included in these amounts. When you shop abroad, save all your receipts, as customs inspectors may ask to see them as well as the items you purchased. If the total value of your goods is more than the duty-free limit, you'll have to pay a tax (most often a flat percentage) on the value of everything beyond that limit.

Check ahead with the Department for Environment, Food and Rural Affairs if you want to bring a pet into Scotland.

Information in Scotland Department for Environment, Food and Rural Affairs. ☎ 03459/335577 ⊕ *www.defra.gov.uk.* **HM Revenue & Customs.** ⊕ *www.gov.uk.*

U.S. Information U.S. Customs and Border Protection. ⊕ *www.cbp.gov.*

▌EATING OUT

Today the traditional Scottish restaurant offers more than fish-and-chips, fried sausage, and black pudding. Instead you'll find the freshest of scallops, organic salmon, wild duck, and Aberdeen Angus beef, as well as locally grown vegetables and fruits. There's also a wide array of international restaurants: Chinese, French, Greek, Indian, Italian, Japanese, and Mexican (to name but a few) can be truly exceptional.

Places like Glasgow, Edinburgh, Dundee, and Aberdeen have sophisticated restaurants at various price levels; of these, the more notable tend to open only in the evening. But fabulous restaurants are popping up in the smaller villages as well. Dining in Scotland can be an experience for all the senses. These meals are rarely cheap, so don't forget your credit card.

Note that most pubs do not have a table service, so go to the bar and order your meal. You're not expected to tip the bartender, but you are expected to tip restaurant waitstaff by leaving 10% to 15% of the tab on the table.

There are a couple of vegetarian options on every menu, and most restaurants, particularly pubs that serve food, welcome families with young children. Smoking is banned from pubs, clubs, and restaurants throughout Britain.

The restaurants we review in this book are the cream of the crop in each price category. Properties are assigned price categories based on dinner prices. *Prices in the reviews are the average cost of a main course at dinner or, if dinner is not served, at lunch.*

DISCOUNTS AND DEALS

Many city restaurants have good pretheater meals from 5 to 7 pm. Lunch deals can also save you money; some main courses can be nearly half the price of dinner entrées. All supermarkets sell a large variety of high-quality sandwiches, wraps, and salads at reasonable prices. If the weather's dry, opt for a midday picnic.

MEALS AND MEALTIMES

To start the day with a full stomach, try a traditional Scottish breakfast of bacon and eggs served with sausage, fried mushrooms, and tomatoes, and usually fried bread or potato scones. Most places also serve kippers (smoked herring). All this is in addition to juice, porridge, cereal, toast, and other bread products.

"All-day" meal places are becoming prevalent. Lunch is usually served 12:30 to 2:30. A few places serve high tea—masses of cakes, bread and butter, and jam—around 2:30 to 4:30. Dinner is fairly early, around 5 to 8.

Familiar fast-food chains are often more expensive than home-cooked meals in local establishments, where large servings of British comfort food—fish-and-chips, stuffed baked potatoes, and sandwiches—are served. In upscale restaurants cutting costs can be as simple as requesting *tap* water; "water" means a bottle of mineral water that could cost up to £5.

Unless otherwise noted, the restaurants listed in this guide are open daily for lunch and dinner.

PAYING

Credit cards are widely accepted at most types of restaurants. Some restaurants exclude service charges from the printed menu (which the law obliges them to display outside), then add 10% to 15% to the check, or else stamp "service not included" along the bottom, in which case you should add the 10% to 15% yourself. Just don't pay twice for service—unscrupulous restaurateurs add a service charge but leave the total on the credit-card slip blank.

For guidelines on tipping, see Tipping below.

PUBS

A common misconception among visitors to Scotland is that pubs are cozy bars. But they are also gathering places, conversation zones, even restaurants. Pubs are, generally speaking, where people go to have a drink, meet their friends, and catch up on one another's lives. Traditionally, pubs are open until midnight, with last orders called about 20 minutes before closing time. In the bigger cities pubs can stay open until 1 am or later.

Some pubs are child-friendly, but others have restricted hours for children. If a pub serves food, it will generally allow children in during the day. Some are stricter than others, though, and will not admit anyone younger than 18. If in doubt, ask the bartender. Family-friendly pubs tend to be packed with kids, parents, and all of their accoutrements.

RESERVATIONS AND DRESS

It's a good idea to make a reservation if you can. For popular restaurants, book as far ahead as you can (often 30 days), and reconfirm as soon as you arrive. Large parties should always call ahead to check the reservations policy.

Online reservation services make it easy to book a table before you even leave home. Open Table has listings in many Scottish cities.

Contact OpenTable. ⊕ *www.opentable.co.uk.*

WINES, BEER, AND SPIRITS

Bars and pubs typically sell two kinds of beer: lager is light in color, very carbonated, and served cold, while ale is dark, less fizzy, and served just below room temperature. You may also come across a pub serving "real ales" or "craft beers," which are very flavorful beers from smaller breweries. Both traditional real ale and innovatively crafted brews have a fervent following; check out the Campaign for Real Ale's website, ⊕ *www.camra.org.uk.*

You can order Scotland's most famous beverage—whisky (most definitely spelled without an *e*)—at any local pub. All pubs serve single-malt and blended whiskies. It's also possible to tour numerous distilleries, where you can sample a dram and purchase a bottle. Most distilleries are concentrated in Speyside and Islay, but there are notable ones on Orkney and Skye. In recent years a new breed of craft gin producers have opened stills, many producing small batches of botanically infused tipples and offering tours, tastings, and lessons.

The legal drinking age in Scotland is 18.

■ ECOTOURISM

Ecotourism is an emerging trend in the United Kingdom. The Shetland Environmental Agency Ltd. runs the Green Tourism Business Scheme (GTBS), a program that evaluates sites and lodgings in England, Scotland, and Wales and gives them a gold, silver, or bronze rating according to their sustainability. You can find a list of green hotels, B&Bs, apartments, and other properties on the GTBS website. Also check out the VisitBritain and VisitScotland websites, which have information and tips about green travel in Britain.

Contact Green Tourism Business Scheme. ☎ *01738/632162* ⊕ *www.green-business.co.uk.*

■ ELECTRICITY

The electrical current in Scotland, as in the rest of Great Britain, is 220–240 volts (in line with the rest of Europe), 50 cycles alternating current (AC); wall outlets take three-pin plugs, and shaver sockets take two round, oversize prongs.

Consider making a small investment in a universal adapter, which has several types of plugs in one lightweight, compact unit. Most laptops and mobile-phone chargers are dual voltage (i.e., they operate equally well on 110 and 220 volts), so require only an adapter. These days the same is true of small appliances such as hair dryers. Don't use 110-volt outlets marked "for shavers only" for high-wattage appliances such as hair dryers.

▌EMERGENCIES

If you need to report an emergency, dial 999 for police, fire, or ambulance. Be prepared to give the telephone number you're calling from. You can get 24-hour medical treatment at British hospitals, but as in U.S. hospitals you should expect to wait for treatment. Treatment from the National Health Service is free to British citizens; as a foreigner, you will be billed after the fact for your care. (Prices are nowhere near what they are in the United States.)

General Emergency Contact Ambulance, fire, police. ☎ *999.*

U.S. Embassies American Consulate General. ✉ *3 Regent Terr., Calton* ☎ *0131/556–8315* ⊕ *uk.usembassy.gov/ embassy-consulates/edinburgh/.* **U.S. Embassy.** ✉ *24 Grosvenor Sq., London* ☎ *020/7499–9000* ⊕ *uk.usembassy.gov.*

▌HEALTH

SPECIFIC ISSUES IN SCOTLAND

If you take prescription drugs, keep a supply in your carry-on luggage and make a list of all your prescriptions to keep on file at home while you are abroad. You will not be able to renew a U.S. prescription at a pharmacy in Britain. Prescriptions are accepted only if issued by a U.K.-registered physician.

If you're traveling in the Highlands and islands in summer, pack some midge repellent and antihistamine cream to reduce swelling: the Highland midge is a force to be reckoned with. Check ⊕ *www.smidgeup.com/midge-forecast/* for updates on these biting pests.

OVER-THE-COUNTER REMEDIES

Over-the-counter medications in Scotland are similar to those in the United States, with a few significant differences. Medications are sold in boxes rather than bottles, and are sold in very small amounts—usually no more than 12 pills per package. There are also fewer brands than you're likely to be used to—you can, for example, find

aspirin, but usually only one kind in a store. You can buy generic ibuprofen or a popular European brand of ibuprofen, Nurofen, which is sold everywhere. Tylenol is not sold in the United Kingdom, but its main ingredient, acetaminophen, is—although, confusingly, it's called paracetamol.

Pharmacies are sometimes referred to as chemists. The biggest drugstore chain in the country is Boots, which has outlets in all but the smallest towns. If you're in a rural area, look for shops marked with a sign of a green cross.

Supermarkets and newsagents all usually have a small supply of cold and headache medicines, often behind the cash register. As in the United States, large supermarkets will have a bigger supply.

MEDICAL INSURANCE AND ASSISTANCE

Consider buying trip insurance with medical-only coverage. Neither Medicare nor some private insurers cover medical expenses anywhere outside of the United States. Medical-only policies typically reimburse you for medical care (excluding that related to preexisting conditions) and hospitalization abroad, and provide for evacuation. You still have to pay the bills and await reimbursement from the insurer, though.

Another option is to sign up with a medical-evacuation assistance company. A membership in one of these companies gets you doctor referrals, emergency evacuation or repatriation, 24-hour hotlines for medical consultation, and other assistance. International SOS Assistance Emergency and AirMed International provide evacuation services and medical referrals. MedjetAssist offers medical evacuation.

Medical Assistance Companies AirMed International. ⊕ *www.airmed.com.* **International SOS.** ⊕ *www.internationalsos.com.* **MedjetAssist.** ⊕ *www.medjetassist.com.*

Medical-Only Insurers International Medical Group. ⊕ *www.imglobal.com.* **Wallach & Company.** ☎ *800/237–6615, 540/687–3166* ⊕ *www.wallach.com.*

SHOTS AND MEDICATIONS

No particular shots are necessary for visiting Scotland from the United States.

Health Warnings National Centers for Disease Control & Prevention (*CDC*). ☎ *800/232–4636 international travelers' health line* ⊕ *wwwnc.cdc.gov/travel.* **World Health Organization** (*WHO*). ⊕ *www.who.int.*

■ HOURS OF OPERATION

Banks are open weekdays 9 to 5. Some banks have extended hours on Thursday evening, and a few are open on Saturday morning. The major airports operate 24-hour banking services all week.

Service stations are at regular intervals on motorways and are usually open 24 hours a day, though stations elsewhere are open 7 am to 9 pm; in rural areas many close at 6 pm and on Sunday.

Pharmacies are usually open Monday through Saturday from 9 to 5 or 5:30. At other times, most larger communities will have a supermarket with extended hours that has a pharmacy on the premises, or a rotation system for pharmacists on call (check any pharmacy window for the number to call). In rural areas doctors often dispense medicines themselves. In an emergency the police should be able to locate a pharmacist.

Most museums in cities and larger towns are open daily, although some may be closed on Sunday and Monday. In smaller villages museums are often open when there are visitors around—even late on summer evenings—but closed in poor weather, when visitors are unlikely; there's often a contact phone number on the door.

Usual business hours are Monday through Saturday 9 to 5 or 5:30. In small villages many shops close for lunch. Department stores in large cities and many supermarkets even in smaller towns stay open for late-night shopping (usually until 7:30 or 8) one or more days a week. Apart from some newsstands and small food stores, many shops close Sunday except in larger towns and cities, where main shopping malls remain open. Big supermarkets like Asda and Tesco are open around the clock.

HOLIDAYS

The following days are public holidays in Scotland; note that the dates for England and Wales are slightly different. Ne'er Day and a day to recover (January 1–2), Good Friday, May Day (first Monday in May), Spring Bank Holiday (last Monday in May), Summer Bank Holiday (first Monday in August), St. Andrews Day (November 30; for Scots government but optional for businesses), and Christmas (December 25–26).

■ MAIL

Stamps may be bought from post offices (open weekdays 9 to 5:30, Saturday 9 to noon), from stamp machines outside post offices, and from newsstands. Mailboxes—known as post- or letter boxes—are painted bright red; large tubular ones are set on the edge of sidewalks, and smaller boxes are set into post-office walls. Allow at least four days for a letter or postcard to reach the United States by airmail. Surface mail service can take up to four or five weeks.

Airmail letters and postcards to the United States cost £1.17 (under 10 grams) or £1.40 (under 20 grams). Within the United Kingdom first-class letters cost 65p, second-class letters and postcards 56p. The Royal Mail website is ⊕ *www. royalmail.com.*

If you're uncertain where you'll be staying, you can arrange to have your mail sent to the nearest American Express. The service is free to cardholders; all others pay a small fee. You can also collect letters at any post office by addressing them to *poste restante* at the post office you nominate. In Edinburgh a convenient central office is St. James Centre Post Office, St. James Centre, Edinburgh, EH1 3SR, Scotland.

SHIPPING PACKAGES

Most department stores and retail outlets can arrange to ship your goods home. You should check your insurance for coverage of possible damage. If you want to ship goods yourself, use one of the overnight postal services, such as Federal Express, DHL, or TNT.

To find the nearest branch providing overnight mail services, contact the following agencies.

Express Services DHL. ☎ *0844/248–0844* ⊕ *www.dhl.co.uk.* **FedEx.** ☎ *03456/070809* ⊕ *www.fedex.com.* **TNT.** ☎ *0800/100600* ⊕ *www.tnt.com.*

∎ MONEY

Prices can seem high in Scotland, though this has improved because of the economic downturn. However, travelers do get some breaks: national museums are free, and staying in a B&B or renting a city apartment brings down lodging costs.

Prices throughout this guide are given for adults. Substantially reduced fees are almost always available for children, students, and senior citizens.

∎**TIP→** Banks never have every foreign currency on hand, and it may take as long as a week to order. If you're planning to exchange funds before leaving home, don't wait until the last minute.

ATMS AND BANKS

ATMs are available throughout Scotland at banks and numerous other locations such as railway stations, gas stations, and department stores. Three banks with many branches are Lloyds, Halifax, and the Royal Bank of Scotland.

Your own bank will probably charge a fee for using ATMs abroad; the foreign bank you use may also charge a fee. Nevertheless, you'll usually get a better rate of exchange at an ATM than you will at a currency-exchange office or even when changing money in a bank. And extracting funds as you need them is a

safer option than carrying around a large amount of cash.

Avoid exorbitant **Dynamic Currency Conversion** fees by asking to be charged in local currency, i.e., in GBP. Do not accept the enticing ATM screen option to "Convert into your home currency," which will incur extra hidden costs.

∎**TIP→ PINs with more than four digits are not recognized at ATMs. If yours has five or more, remember to change it before you leave.**

ATM Locations MasterCard. ☎ *0800/964767* ⊕ *www.mastercard.com.* **Visa Plus.** ☎ *0800/891725* ⊕ *www.visadps.com.*

CREDIT CARDS

Credit cards are accepted almost everywhere and for everything (except for bus and taxi fares), as are debit cards. Most cards issued in Europe are now chip-and-PIN credit cards that store user information on a computer chip embedded in the card. In the United States, all credit cards were required to switch to "chip-and-signature" cards in 2015. While European cardholders are expected to know and use their PIN number for all transactions rather than signing a charge slip, U.S. chip-and-signature cards usually still require users to sign the charge slip. (Very few U.S. issuers offer a PIN along with their cards, except for cash withdrawals at an ATM, though this is expected to change in the future.) The good news: unlike the old magnetic-strip cards that gave American travelers in Europe trouble at times, the new chip-and-signature cards are accepted at many more locations, including in many cases at machines that sell train tickets, machines that process automated motorway tolls at unmanned booths, and automated gas stations—even without a signature or PIN. The bad news: not all European locations will accept the chip-and-signature cards, and you won't know until you try, so it's a good idea to carry enough cash to cover small purchases. The use of contactless cards, devices, and phone apps has accelerated in the United Kingdom in recent years: a transaction limit of £30 is widespread unless more secure biometric technology is involved.

Visa and MasterCard are more widely accepted than American Express; it is a good idea to travel with a picture ID in case you're asked for it.

CURRENCY AND EXCHANGE

Britain's currency is the pound sterling, which is divided into 100 pence (100p). Bills (called notes) are issued in the values of £50, £20, £10, and £5. Coins are issued in the values of £2, £1, 50p, 20p, 10p, 5p, 2p, and 1p. Scottish coins are the same as English ones, but have a thistle on them. Scottish notes have the same face values as English notes, and English notes are interchangeable with them in Scotland.

At this writing, the exchange rate was U.S. $1.30 to the pound.

All the leading online search engines do currency conversions. XE.com is another good currency conversion website with some handy tables and conversion apps.

Conversion Sites XE.com. ⊕ *www.xe.com.*

▮ PACKING

Travel light. Porters are more or less extinct these days (and very expensive where you can find them). Also, if you're traveling around the country by car, train, or bus, large, heavy luggage is more of a burden than anything else. Save a little packing space for things you might buy while traveling.

In Scotland casual clothes are the norm, and very few hotels or restaurants insist on jackets and ties for men in the evening. It is, however, handy to have something semi-dressy for going out to dinner or the theater. For summer, lightweight clothing is usually adequate, except in the evening, when you'll need a jacket or sweater. A waterproof coat or parka and an umbrella are essential at any time of year. You can't go wrong with comfortable walking shoes, especially when you're climbing

Edinburgh's steep urban hills or visiting Glasgow's massive museums. Drip-dry and wrinkle-resistant fabrics are a good bet because only the most prestigious hotels have speedy laundering or dry-cleaning service. Bring insect repellent if you plan to hike.

Some visitors to Scotland appear to think it necessary to adopt Scottish dress. It's not unless you've been invited to a wedding, and even then it's optional. Scots themselves do not wear tartan ties or Balmoral "bunnets" (caps), and only an enthusiastic minority prefers the kilt for everyday wear.

▮ PASSPORTS AND VISAS

U.S. citizens need only a valid passport to enter Great Britain for stays of up to six months. Travelers should be prepared to show sufficient funds to support and accommodate themselves while in Britain (credit cards will usually suffice for this) and to show a return or onward ticket. If you're within six months of your passport's expiration date, renew it before you leave—nearly extinct passports are not strictly banned, but they make immigration officials anxious, and may cause you problems. Health certificates are not required for travel in Scotland.

If only one parent is traveling with a child under 17 and his or her last name differs from the child's, then he or she will need a signed and notarized letter from the parent with the same last name as the child authorizing permission to travel. Airlines, ferries, and trains have different policies for children traveling alone, so if your child must travel alone, make sure to check with the carrier prior to purchasing your child's ticket.

U.S. Passport Information U.S. Department of State. ☎ *877/487–2778* ⊕ *www.travel.state. gov/passport.*

▌ RESTROOMS

Most cities, towns, and villages have public restrooms, indicated by signposts to the "WC," "toilets," or "public conveniences." They vary hugely in cleanliness. You'll often have to pay a small amount (usually 30p) to enter; a request for payment usually indicates a high standard of cleanliness. Gas stations, called petrol stations, usually have restrooms (to which the above comments also apply). In towns and cities, department stores, hotels, restaurants, and pubs are usually your best bets for reasonable standards of hygiene.

▌ SAFETY

Overall, Scotland is a very safe country to travel in, but be a cautious traveler and keep your cash, passport, credit cards, and tickets close to you or in a hotel safe. Don't agree to carry anything for strangers. It's a good idea to distribute your cash, credit cards, IDs, and other valuables between a deep front pocket, an inside jacket or vest pocket, and a hidden money pouch. Don't reach for the money pouch once you're in public. Use common sense as your guide.

**General Information and Warnings
U.K. Foreign & Commonwealth Office.**
⊕ *www.gov.uk/government/organisations/
foreign-commonwealth-office.* **U.S. Department of State Travel Information.** ⊕ *www.
travel.state.gov.*

▌ SHOPPING

Tartans, tweeds, and woolens may be a Scottish cliché, but nevertheless the selection and quality of these goods make them a must-have for many visitors, whether a made-to-measure traditional kilt outfit or a designer sweater from Skye. Particular bargains can be found in Scottish cashmere sweaters; look for Johnstons of Elgin. Glasgow is great for designer wear, although prices may seem high.

Food items are another popular purchase: whether shortbread, smoked salmon, boiled sweets, *tablet* (a type of hard fudge), marmalade and raspberry jams, Dundee cake, or black bun, it's far too easy to eat your way around Scotland.

Unique jewelry is available all over Scotland, but especially in some of the remote regions where get-away-from-it-all craftspeople have set up shop amid the idyllic scenery.

Scottish antique pottery and table silver make unusual, if sometimes pricey, souvenirs: a Wemyss-ware pig for the mantelpiece, perhaps, or Edinburgh silver candelabra for the dining table. Antique pebble jewelry is a unique style of jewelry popular in Scotland; several specialized antique jewelry shops can be found in Edinburgh and Glasgow. Antiques shops and one- or two-day antiques fairs held in hotels abound all over Scotland. In general, goods are reasonably priced. Most dealers will drop the price a little if asked "What's your best price?"

▌ SIGHTSEEING PASSES

Discounted sightseeing passes are a great way to save money on visits to castles, gardens, and historic houses. Just check what the pass offers against your itinerary to be sure it's worthwhile.

The Explorer Pass, available from any staffed Historic Scotland (HS) property and from many tourist information centers, allows visits to HS properties for 3 days in a 5-day period (£31) or 7 days in a 14-day period (£42). The Discover Scotland pass is available for 3 days (£27), 7 days (£32), or 14 days (£37) and allows access to all National Trust for Scotland properties. It's available to overseas visitors only and can be purchased online and by phone, or at properties and some of the main tourist information centers.

Discount Passes Historic Scotland.
☏ *0131/668–8600* ⊕ *www.historicenvironment.scot.* **National Trust for Scotland.**
☏ *0131/458–0303* ⊕ *www.nts.org.uk.*

▮ TAXES

An airport departure tax of £78 (£13 for within United Kingdom and EU countries) per person is included in the price of your ticket. The Scottish Government is planning to reduce APD (air passenger duty) by 50%.

The British sales tax, V.A.T. (value-added tax), is 20%. It's almost always included in quoted prices in shops, hotels, and restaurants. The most common exception is at high-end hotels, where prices often exclude V.A.T. Further details on how to get a V.A.T. refund and a list of stores offering tax-free shopping are available from VisitBritain.

When making a purchase, ask for a V.A.T.-refund form and find out whether the merchant gives refunds—not all stores do, nor are they required to. Have the form stamped by customs officials when you leave the country or, if you're visiting several European Union countries, when you leave the EU. After you're through passport control, take the form to a refund-service counter for an on-the-spot refund or mail it to the address on the form after you arrive home.

▮ TIME

Great Britain sets its clocks by Greenwich Mean Time, five hours ahead of the U.S. East Coast. British summer time (GMT plus one hour) requires an additional adjustment from about the end of March to the end of October. Timeanddate.com can help you figure out the correct time anywhere.

Time Zones Timeanddate.com. ⊕ *www. timeanddate.com/worldclock.*

▮ TIPPING

Tipping is done in Scotland as in the United States, but at a lower level. Some restaurants include a service charge on the bill; if not, add about 10% to 15%. Taxi drivers, hairdressers, and barbers should also get 10% to 15%.

TIPPING GUIDELINES FOR SCOTLAND	
Bartender	£1–£5 depending on the size of the round (in the more modern bars). It's common in traditional pubs to buy the bartender a drink as a tip
Bellhop	£1–£3 per bag
Hotel Concierge	£10 or more, if he or she performs a service for you
Hotel Doorman	£2–£5 if he helps you get a cab
Hotel Maid	£2–£3 a day (either daily or at the end of your stay, in cash)
Hotel Room-Service Waiter	£1–£2 per delivery, even if a service charge has been added
Porter at Airport or Train Station	£1 per bag
Skycap at Airport	£1–£2 per bag checked
Taxi Driver	10%–15%, but round up the fare to the next pound amount
Tour Guide	10% of the cost of the tour, but optional
Valet Parking Attendant	£2–£3, but only when you get your car
Waiter	10%–15%, with 15% being the norm at high-end restaurants; nothing additional if a service charge is added to the bill
Other	Restroom attendants in more expensive restaurants expect some small change or £1. Tip coat-check personnel at least £1–£2 per item checked unless there's a fee.

▮ TOURS

GENERAL-INTEREST TOURS

Many companies offer fully guided tours in Scotland, from basic to luxury. Most of these are full packages including hotels, all food, and transportation costs in one flat fee. Because each tour company has different specialties, do a bit of research—either on your own or through a travel agent—before booking. You'll want to know about the hotels you'll be staying in, how big your group is likely to be, precisely how your days will be structured, and who the other people are likely to be.

CIE Tours. It offers all-inclusive tours of Scotland with various themes, from distillery tours to cruises to Home of Golf and St. Andrews packages. ☎ *0800/680-0611* ⊕ *www.cietours.com* ✉ *From £589 for a 5-day Taste of Scotland tour.*

Globus. Covering Scotland and Great Britain, Globus offers many packages including a 7-day Bonnie Scotland tour from Glasgow to Edinburgh, and a 14-day one that also delves into the Highlands and islands. ☎ *866/755-8581* ⊕ *www.globus-journeys.com* ✉ *From $1,749, excluding airfare, for 7-day Bonnie Scotland.*

Heart of Scotland Tours. Offered here are small-group (16 maximum) minibus tours that aim to take you off the beaten track. ☎ *0131/228-2888* ⊕ *www.heartofscotlandtours.co.uk* ✉ *From £44 for a Best of Scotland in a Day excursion.*

Rabbie's Trail Burners. These minibus guided tours include handy day trips for small groups (16 maximum) and depart from Edinburgh and Glasgow. The company has won numerous awards including the Scottish Thistle award for sustainable tourism. ☎ *0131/226-3133* ⊕ *www.rabbies.com* ✉ *From £28 for day trips (Rosslyn Chapel & Scots Borders); 2-day Loch Ness & Inverness trip starts at £73.*

SPECIAL-INTEREST TOURS

You can find tours for many special interests from whisky and vegetarian-friendly to cultural, historic, and wildlife-themed packages.

Celtic Dream Tours. This outfit specializes in extended Celtic-inspired luxury excursions and custom tours, as well as vegetarian-/vegan-friendly and Burns literary adventures. ☎ *813/317-6039* ⊕ *www.celtic-dreamtours.com* ✉ *From $3,395 double*

occupancy for 12-night Scotland's Villages, Beaches & Less Traveled Roads tour.

The Wayfarers. Enjoy walking tours through the countryside and scenic towns, exploring natural and historic sights. ☎ *800/249-4620* ⊕ *www.thewayfarers.com* ✉ *From $4,395 per person (double occupancy) for The Highlands 6-night tour.*

GOLF TOURS

Scotland has fabulous golf courses; a tour can help enthusiasts make the most of their time. VisitScotland has a dedicated golf website with a list of tour companies.

Golf Scotland. This company has provided luxury golf tours, including tournament specials and the Gleneagles Experience tour, since 1988. ☎ *866/875-4653* ⊕ *www.golfscotland.com* ✉ *From $1,145 per person for the Gleneagles Experience.*

Scotland for Golf. Established by St. Andrews pros in 1999, this is the company to consider for those seeking to tour Fife's finest fairways, including the Old Course. ☎ *01334/611466* ⊕ *www.scotlandforgolf.co.uk* ✉ *From $500 per person for His & Her 1-night break playing on the Old Course.*

PRIVATE GUIDES

Scottish Tourist Guides Association. The association has members throughout Scotland who are fully qualified professional guides able to conduct walking tours in the major cities, half- or full-day tours or extended tours throughout Scotland, driving tours, and special study tours. Fees are negotiable. ☎ *01786/447784* ⊕ *www.stga.co.uk.*

❚ TRIP INSURANCE

Comprehensive trip insurance is valuable if you're booking a very expensive or complicated trip (particularly to an isolated region) or if you're booking far in advance. Comprehensive policies typically cover trip cancellation and interruption, letting you cancel or cut your trip short because of illness, or, in some cases, acts of terrorism in your destination. Such policies might also cover evacuation and medical care. (For trips abroad you should have at least medical-only coverage. *See Medical Insurance and Assistance under Health.*) Some also cover trip delays because of bad weather or mechanical problems and lost or delayed luggage.

Another type of coverage to consider is financial default—that is, when your trip is disrupted because a tour operator, airline, or cruise line goes out of business. Generally you must buy this when you book your trip or shortly thereafter, and it's available to you only if your operator isn't on a list of excluded companies.

Always read the fine print of your policy to make sure that you're covered for the risks that most concern you. Compare several policies to be sure you're getting the best price and range of coverage available.

Comprehensive Insurers Allianz. ☎ 866/884–3556 ⊕ www.allianztravelinsurance.com. **CSA Travel Protection.** ☎ 800/348–9505 ⊕ www.csatravelprotection.com. **Travel Guard.** ☎ 800/826–4919 ⊕ www.travelguard.com. **Travel Insured International.** ☎ 800/243–3174 ⊕ www.travelinsured.com. **Travelex Insurance.** ☎ 888/228–9792 ⊕ www.travelexinsurance.com.

Insurance Comparison Information InsureMyTrip.com. ☎ 1-401/773–9300 ⊕ www.insuremytrip.com. **Squaremouth.com.** ☎ 800/240–0369 ⊕ www.squaremouth.com.

❚ VISITOR INFORMATION

See the Orientation and Planning section at the start of each chapter for regional tourist information offices; look for Essentials sections in towns for local offices.

Contacts in Britain VisitScotland. ✉ *Princes Mall, 3 Princes St., Edinburgh* ☎ *0131/473–3868* ⊕ *www.visitscotland.com.*

ONLINE RESOURCES

VisitScotland is Scotland's official website and includes a number of special-interest sites on topics from golf to genealogy. VisitBritain, Great Britain's official site, has ample information on Scotland's sights, accommodations, and more.

Historic Scotland cares (which is being renamed Historic Environment Scotland) for the more than 300 historic properties described on its site. The National Trust for Scotland has information about stately homes, gardens, and castles. Both offer sightseeing passes *(see Sightseeing Passes above).*

All About Scotland VisitBritain. ⊕ *www.visitbritain.com.*

Historic Sites Historic Scotland. ⊕ *www.historicenvironment.scot.* **National Trust for Scotland.** ⊕ *www.nts.org.uk.*

INDEX

PHOTO CREDITS

NOTES

Fodor's ESSENTIAL SCOTLAND

Editorial: Douglas Stallings, *Editorial Director*; Margaret Kelly, *Senior Editor*; Alexis Kelly, Jacinta O'Halloran, and Amanda Sadlowski, *Editors*; Teddy Minford, *Content Editor*; Rachael Roth, *Content Manager*

Design: Tina Malaney, *Design and Production Director;* Jessica Gonzalez, *Production Designer*

Photography: Jennifer Arnow, *Senior Photo Editor*

Maps: Rebecca Baer, *Senior Map Editor*; Maps_IllustrationsMaps_Illustrationser DePrima, *Editorial Production Manager*; Carrie Parker, *Senior Production Editor*;

Elyse Rozelle, *Production Editor*; David Satz, *Director of Content Production*

Business & Operations: Chuck Hoover, *Chief Marketing Officer*; Joy Lai, *Vice President and General Manager*; Stephen Horowitz, *Director of Business Development and Revenue Operations;* Tara McCrillis, *Director of Publishing Operations;* Eliza D. Aceves, *Content Operations Manager and Srategist*

Public Relations and Marketing: Joe Ewaskiw, *Manager;* Esther Su, *Marketing Manager*

Writers: Nick Bruno, Robin Gauldie, Michael Gonzalez, Shona Main, Eilidh McCabe, Joseph Reaney

Editors: Salwa Jabado (lead editor), Linda Cabasin, Denise Leto

Production Editor: Jennifer DePrima

Production Design: Liliana Guia

Copyright © 2018 by Fodor's Travel, a division of Internet Brands, Inc.

Fodor's is a registered trademark of Internet Brands, Inc. All rights reserved. Published in the United States by Fodor's Travel, a division of Internet Brands, Inc. No maps, illustrations, or other portions of this book may be reproduced in any form without written permission from the publisher.

1st Edition

ISBN 978-1-64097-012-0

ISSN 2574–0636

All details in this book are based on information supplied to us at press time. Always confirm information when it matters, especially if you're making a detour to visit a specific place. Fodor's expressly disclaims any liability, loss, or risk, personal or otherwise, that is incurred as a consequence of the use of any of the contents of this book.

SPECIAL SALES

This book is available at special discounts for bulk purchases for sales promotions or premiums. For more information, e-mail SpecialMarkets@fodors.com

PRINTED IN THE UNITED STATES OF AMERICA

10 9 8 7 6 5 4 3 2 1

ABOUT OUR WRITERS

 Based in Dundee, **Nick Bruno** is a travel writer, journalist, and a Fodor's contributor for over a decade. He has authored many books and features about both Italy and Scotland, and also works for the BBC. An interest in history has led to a project researching the lives of Italians—including his paternal family—before, during, and after Il Ventennio Fascista. For this edition, he updated Experience Scotland, Fife and Angus, Orkney and Shetland Islands, and Travel Smart Scotland.

 Robin Gauldie was born in Dundee and read history at Edinburgh University before training as journalist on local newspapers in Tayside. Since 1990 he has been a freelance journalist specializing in travel and the tourism industry, and is the author of more than 30 travel guidebooks to destinations in Europe, Asia, Africa, and South America. When not traveling he divides his time between his home in Edinburgh's New Town and a village house in Languedoc, southern France. Robin updated Aberdeen and the Northeast and Argyll and the Isles.

 Mike Gonzalez is emeritus professor of Latin American Studies at Glasgow University and also writes regularly for the *Herald* and other publications on politics and culture. Mike's assignment for Fodor's was the Glasgow, the Borders and the Southwest, and the Central Highlands. His travels took him to places familiar and less familiar, and included exploring a tiny island on Islay whose houses were once an imperial center and walking in a hidden sculpture park in the hills near Dumfries.

 Shona Main grew up in Shetland; after moving to the mainland, she spent some informative years working on magazines for teenagers. She had a brief career in law and politics before she returned to writing. Now living in Dundee, Shona is working on her first novel, which is inspired by the island she grew up on, and has also moved into filmmaking. Her debut documentary, *Clavel,* follows a Shetland crofter through the seasons. She updated the Orkney and Shetland islands for this edition.

 Eilidh McCabe is an editor at travel writing agency World Words and is the short fiction editor of the *Glasgow Review of Books*. Having lived in Shanghai, Berlin, and London, she has spent the past few years falling back in love with her hometown of Glasgow. She updated the Inverness and Around the Great Glen chapter for this edition.

 Joseph Reaney is an experienced travel writer and editor based part-time in Scotland and part-time in the Czech Republic—and regularly writes about both. He contributes to *National Geographic, Forbes Travel Guide*, and *USA Today*, among others, and runs his own travel content writing agency, World Words. When he has the time, he also writes and directs short films and comedy sketches. He updated two chapters for this edition: Edinburgh and the Lothians, and The Northern Highlands and the Western Isles.